S0-AQL-188

The EXPLORATION
of AUSTRALIA

Dear Willie,

We wish you a very happy Xmas and a happier New Year (1988).

With love.

From,

Alfy & Avril.

ACKNOWLEDGMENTS

Many individuals and organisations assisted in the
preparation of this book. The author and editors are
responsible for the interpretation and opinions expressed in
the text, but wish to acknowledge particularly the advice
given on specialised aspects by Brigadier (retired) Lawrence
FitzGerald, OBE, who for many years was in command of
the Australian Army Survey Corps; Captain J.J. Doyle,
Royal Australian Navy Hydrographic Office; George
Benwell, Department of Surveying, University of
Melbourne; Edgar Beale, author of several notable works on
Australian explorers; Ken Wise, Department of Resources
and Energy, Canberra; Dr Ken McCracken, CSIRO Office
of Space Science, Canberra; C. Weenstra, national mapping,
Department of Resources and Energy; R.S. Goleby, space
projects branch, Department of Science, Canberra.

Cover photograph by Edward Stokes; painting by Nicholas
Chevalier. Page six illustration from Leichhardt's journals

Historic picture research by Debby Cramer
Author's manuscript typed by Sarah Cannon

Edited and designed by Reader's Digest Services Pty Ltd

Editor	Margaret Fraser
Designer	Denese Cunningham
Research editor	Vere Dodds
Editorial assistants	Monica Chaplain, Kristina Resanceff, Karen Wain
Art assistants	Helen Briggs, Caroline Goldsmith, Wayne Riley
Project coordinator	Robyn Hudson
Production controller	Judith Clegg

First edition
Published by Reader's Digest Services Pty Ltd
(Inc. in NSW)
26-32 Waterloo Street, Surry Hills, NSW 2010

© 1987 Reader's Digest Services Pty Ltd
© 1987 Reader's Digest Association Far East Limited
Philippines copyright 1987 Reader's Digest Association
Far East Limited

National Library of Australia cataloguing-in-publication
data:
Cannon, Michael 1929 –
    The exploration of Australia.

    Includes index.
    ISBN 0 86438 036 4.

    1. Australia – Discovery and exploration. 2. Australia –
    Exploring expeditions. I. Reader's Digest Services.
    II. Title.

919.4'04

The EXPLORATION of AUSTRALIA

Michael Cannon

READER'S DIGEST SYDNEY

Contents

CHAPTER FIVE The conquest of Queensland

CHAPTER SIX The lure of the unknown west and centre

CHAPTER SEVEN Courageous invaders of the hostile deserts

CHAPTER EIGHT The age of scientific expeditions

CHAPTER NINE New technology revolutionises exploration

A dream that came true

The story of Australia's discovery and exploration reads like a romantic epic. It begins in ancient times when geographers invented a massive southern continent, reasoning that one must exist, or the world would tip over. Then Marco Polo, returning from China, spread rumours of a distant land filled with 'plentye of gold'.

Portuguese and Spanish navigators possibly discovered the real Australia and sailed away again. The Dutch certainly found and mapped much of the western and northern coastline during the seventeenth century — but they decided not to colonise such a desolate-looking land.

By the middle of the eighteenth century, the Great South Land was still more dream than reality. French and British interest flickered into life at almost the same period, but the British moved more decisively. Secretive officials of the Admiralty sent James Cook to report on unknown regions of the Pacific Ocean. Cook's discovery of Australia's eastern coastline provided an almost complete picture of the continent's true shape and position. His reports on its fertility had a deep impact on British strategic thinking.

Explorers become national heroes
The next step, colonisation by military force and convict labouring gangs, followed within a few years. European technology was advanced just enough to transport these settlers to the furthest end of the globe, and keep them alive while they struggled to become self-sufficient in an environment that must have seemed nearly as alien as settlement on the moon would to us today.

Almost completely overlooked was Australia's previous discovery by tribes of wandering Aboriginals. These pioneers had successfully settled the land by learning to live in harmony with natural cycles, rather than by the application of technology.

Later arrivals from civilisations that had harnessed the wind to drive their ships, used magnetic fields and star patterns for navigation, and could manipulate chemicals and metals to produce deadly explosive devices, regarded the native inhabitants of Australia as simple primitives. Few took the trouble to learn from them the ways of best coping with such an alien and harsh place.

After difficult beginnings, settlements round Sydney and Hobart began to prosper. Whale-oil and wool were in demand on European markets. Concentration soon turned to breaking out of the coastal fringes.

The hectic period from the conquest of the Blue Mountains in 1813 to the gold rushes of the eighteen-fifties is brimful with stories of dauntless adventure, closely paralleling the push westwards into the American continent. Enterprising colonists led their long-suffering convict parties over unexplored mountain, river and plain to find vast areas suitable for grazing. Expedition leaders became national heroes, even if the prime motive was overwhelmingly economic. At first, British strategists intended occupying only the eastern half of Australia. But after the Napoleonic Wars, a bolder ambition began to seem both practical and possible. Why not take over the whole huge continent?

Peacetime spared the resources needed to complete surveys of the coastline and surrounding oceans so valiantly commenced by Matthew Flinders. Forts could be built to defend lonely stretches of the north. Even more important, new settlements could be authorised. As the ports at Perth, Adelaide, Melbourne and Brisbane developed, they formed bases for new pushes by explorers, surveyors and pastoralists into the hinterlands. Exciting discoveries were regular events and dark unknown areas of the map were gradually rolled back.

Many pastoralists were content to follow the leapfrogging technique of driving their flocks just beyond the furthest station into fresh grasslands and squatting there. The great explorers whose stories are told in this book were made differently. Sometimes their minds were seized with imperialist visions of occupying the whole continent and with promoting their own careers in the process. Charles Sturt, for instance, admitted his personal ambition, but also claimed 'an earnest desire to promote the public good'. In the context of the times, that meant discovering more and more agricultural land, which would lead to new farms and towns, all filling up with ambitious Anglo-Saxons.

The attraction of the unknown
Curiosity was another powerful motive for exploration. The born farmer settled down on suitable land and rarely left it. The more restless and adventurous character wanted to know what was over the next hill; what lay east, north, south and west of him. The explorer, particularly in the Australian outback, was an incurable optimist, convinced that if he kept on travelling, there would be greener fields, better soil, larger rivers — even a delightful inland ocean — somewhere over the horizon. The dream that might become reality was the great lure.

Such illusions and delusions, mingled with occasional truth, irresistibly drew the true explorer onwards. After most of Australia's fertile areas had been discovered, and the gold rushes had brought large new populations to the south-east, it might have been thought that the remainder of the land could be conquered piecemeal by the slow advance of pastoralists. Not so. Explorers turned their attention to penetrating desert areas that had brought legendary figures like Sturt, Eyre and Leichhardt to their knees.

In that extraordinary era of the eighteen-sixties and seventies, Stuart and Burke battled to be first across central Australia from south to north, while numerous others tried to cross the central deserts on an east-west line. Seemingly the only practical benefits were to establish routes for overland telegraphs, and to show men where they should *not* settle.

Yet explorers kept on throwing themselves against the desert regions. Some other factor was at work — a longing for the raw simplicities of nature, perhaps, coupled with revulsion for the man-made creations in their new cities.

Out in the desert, an explorer had to depend on his own forethought and decisions, his ability to outface disaster and chance.

Ernest Giles, the most sensitive of desert adventurers, believed that 'An explorer is an explorer from love'. His repeated plunges into the worst deserts showed how much he enjoyed the heightened intensity that comes from fighting for survival against all odds in conditions where no help can come from outside. It was the ultimate test of self-reliance, ending often enough in death.

Ironically, the determined efforts of all such adventurers built a spiritual base uniting the nation. By the end of the nineteenth century, explorers were regarded as Australian heroes rather than men from any one colony. They had joined isolated settlements, filled in spaces on the map and changed Australia to a continent flaunting its slogan of 'One People, One Flag, One Destiny'.

Even some personal characteristics of explorers seemed to seep into the new national consciousness: a willingness to take risks, an ability to roll with natural blows and accept suffering without complaint, a certain callousness towards other races, and wry humour in the face of disaster. These are universal human attributes, but they seemed to become pronounced in outback Australia, particularly after being called on to the full during the worst days of the First World War.

Exploration during the twentieth century took advantage of refinement in transport, navigation and mapping techniques, until no part of the continent and its seas was left uncharted. Some areas of Australia remain a challenge to adventurous travellers, no matter how well equipped they may be, and can still deal savage blows to the unwary.

The exploration story is not yet over, not as long as the Australian character is still attracted to the unknown. This passion may explain why a nation with a small population devotes resources to continue exploring — in space. Our land frontiers may have largely disappeared, but skywards, among Giles's 'glittering bands of brilliant stars shining in the azure vault of heaven', lies the greatest frontier. It seems likely that amazing travellers' tales are still to come.

MICHAEL CANNON

Sea explorers finally discover Australia's true shape and position

Before British settlement in 1788, Australia's coastline was known only in parts, even though long stretches of the east and west coasts had been mapped. In 1799, Bass proved Tasmania to be an island; in 1803, Flinders reported after sailing round the mainland that east and west coasts were both part of the one island-continent

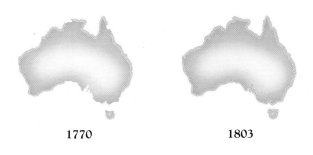

1770   **1803**

Land explorers penetrate every corner of the continent

The pattern of exploration that emerges is one of steady expansion inwards from the coastal settlements. For the first fifty years, the push was concentrated in the south-east and Tasmania.

After most of the fertile regions had been explored, attention turned to the centre. As late as the 1870s, explorers still hoped to find an inland pastoral paradise tucked amid the deserts

1813   **1830**   **1842**

1848   **1862**   **1875**

Detail from Interior of an art gallery, *seventeenth century Flemish school*

CHAPTER ONE

Who really discovered the Great South Land?

How Aboriginals came to be Australia's first settlers

To most of us it may come as a surprise to learn that Aboriginals were the original explorers of Australia. We have been so accustomed to thinking of Portuguese, Dutch or British sea captains as first discoverers that we forget the dark-skinned race which came here in the Dreamtime and began the long process of populating the empty continent. Many an epic of courage and endurance, equal to anything you will read in this book, must have been performed, but we know nothing about them. No written or pictorial records survive to tell the story of the black mariners and overland venturers who first made Australia home.

If we go far enough back, we find that Australia was once almost joined to Asia by a land bridge. Over that bridge travelled the Aboriginals' ancestors, probably by paddling in flimsy craft across short intervening waterways. One way or another they became the first known discoverers, the first explorers and the first settlers of what we call Australia.

Scientists have not yet been able to establish exactly the dates of these events. Some researchers think that a sudden increase in destructive bushfires

A casual prowess *at hunting turtles from sturdy dug-out canoes won these northern Aboriginals a somewhat grudging admiration from artist Thomas Baines and his companions*

one hundred and thirty thousand years ago shows that Aboriginals had already populated the country. But the consensus among archaeologists who have analysed human remains is that Aboriginal occupation of Australia dates back some forty to fifty thousand years.

What is certain is that for most of the period, Papua New Guinea, the mainland and Tasmania were all part of the same land mass. This is because ocean levels all over the world were much lower than today. During the last ice age, huge quantities of sea water were frozen solid round swollen polar caps, with ice sheets extending much further into today's temperate zones. Sea levels were as much as one hundred and eighy metres below the

Even in flimsy bark canoes, *the Aboriginals displayed the skills necessary to have survived sea voyages and reach Australia's mainland*

present coastlines. Wherever you find shallow water round a continent today, you can be sure that the area once stood well above the waves.

Skilled boat-builders
Even so, short distances between Asia and Australia were still covered by the sea. It was essential for the first Aboriginal explorers migrating southwards to learn to build and sail small vessels.

Early artists *appreciated Aboriginal insights into the strange landscape. Augustus Earle gave his Aboriginal guide pride of place in his 1830 canvas of a Blue Mountains waterfall*

A good deal of evidence survives to show that Aboriginals were skilled boat-builders. Some of the early European explorers described rafts and canoes that were quite capable of sailing from island to island. One painting by Thomas Baines shows a north Australian native standing in a canoe to spear a turtle in choppy seas. Phillip Parker King, RN, sketched natives paddling on a raft made of logs tied together with vines. He described another raft he saw in 1838 that was over five metres long, with roots forming bulwarks at stem and stern, while a platform of small poles covered with grass 'gave a sufficient flooring to this rude specimen of a raft.'

Although these examples are comparatively recent, there is little doubt that Aboriginals developed the technology to island-hop to the new land. The main stream probably came through Java, which forty thousand years ago was joined to today's Asian mainland. At the eastern end of Java, the emigrants would take to boats or rafts to cross short distances between islands as far as Timor,

WHITE INTRUDERS GET A MIXED RECEPTION

Botanists on board James Cook's *Endeavour* gave the first known descriptions of east coast Aboriginals.

Like all early white observers, they were puzzled by the Aboriginals' alternating shyness, fear, aggression and friendliness. European habits of thought could not cope with what seemed unpredictable reactions.

On 28 April 1770, Sydney Parkinson sketched two Aboriginals who tried to prevent Cook's landing at Botany Bay. 'Their countenance bespoke displeasure', he wrote. 'They threatened us, and discovered hostile intentions, often crying to us, warra warra wai'. But the blacks were forced to retreat before the unprecedented power of the white man's musket.

Aboriginals further north were often just as warlike. Yet on 17 July 1770, when the *Endeavour* was careened near today's Cooktown, Joseph Banks and Daniel Solander met several natives in a canoe who 'came to us without any signs of fear'. One gave an exhibition of spear-throwing 'with a degree of swiftness and steadyness that realy surprizd me', wrote Banks. 'They venturd on board the ship and soon became our very good friends', trading many weapons which the botanist took back to England with his collections.

Cook himself summarised the conditions of the Aboriginals in an almost envious way. 'They may appear to some to be the most wretched people upon Earth',

Sydney Parkinson *displayed the idealism of the explorer-artists when he gave these 'Two Natives of New Holland' a Grecian nobility*

he wrote, 'but in reality they are far more happier than we Europeans; being wholly unacquainted not only with the superfluous but the necessary Conveniences so much sought after in Europe, they are happy in not knowing the use of them'.

Most explorers and settlers were not able to share his favourable impression.

from which it was then only a few kilometres across water to the enlarged ancient continent of New Guinea-Australia. Other emigrants perhaps followed a more northerly route from the Celebes to New Guinea, then across the dry land of what is now Torres Strait.

Between eighteen and ten thousand years ago, the last Ice Age slowly came to an end. Frozen waters began to melt, with the result that sea levels steadily rose. Coastal settlements all over the world were inundated; tribes were forced to move inland or across the seas to higher points. The shape of continents as we know them today began to emerge. And Australia, with its people, wildlife and flora, was cut off from any easy connection with its Asian ancestry.

During a time of vast climatic changes, the Aboriginals were left alone to make the best they could of their adopted homeland. They evolved systems of living in tune with natural forces, managing to thrive under pressures we can now only dimly comprehend.

Thousands of years passed as tribal lore expanded. Those Aboriginal explorers who had ventured as far south as Tasmania were finally cut off by the flooding of Bass Strait and evolved somewhat differently. But Aboriginals everywhere could still be recognised as branches of the original race of explorers.

Much more damaging than the slow rising of the oceans was the upsurge of an adventurous, aggressive and exploitative group of white seekers after rich new lands to renew the fortunes of Europe.

New invaders upset the balance
During those thousands of years when Aboriginals had been adapting themselves to live in harmony with natural forces, the fair-skinned race had been learning how to utilise, expand and deflect the same forces. The ships in which they mastered the wide oceans, the cannons they fired, the very art of preserving food for long voyages, were so far removed from anything the Aboriginals had ever visualised, that the white men sometimes seemed like fearful apparitions from another world.

To explorers who had inherited the civilisations of the Middle East, Greece, Rome and the Renaissance, the Aboriginals at first appeared almost beneath contempt. The earliest known description of them was given by Jan Carstensz, a Dutch navigator whose yacht accompanied the vessel *Arnhem* to Arnhem Land in 1623. Cartensz wrote:

The natives are in general utter barbarians, all resembling each other in shape and features, coal-black, and with twisted nets wound round their heads and necks for keeping their food in; so far as we could make out, they chiefly live on certain ill-smelling roots which they dig out of the earth…it may safely be concluded that they are poor and abject wretches, caring mainly for bits of iron and strings of beads.

This cruel judgement set the tone for most European reactions to Aboriginals. Since the dark-skinned inhabitants were widely regarded as being little removed from animals, they could often be exploited or massacred with as little compunction as a bullock to slaughter.

Aboriginals fought back *against the white usurpers, but the odds were against them as this confrontation on the Murray shows*

In turn, many Aboriginal tribes overcame their initial fears, and fought back as best they could against the novel weapons of the strange white beings who were tramping without permission through traditional tribal lands.

Fortunately a number of white explorers were well-educated and kind-hearted. They did their best to understand Aboriginal ways of life, and to pacify the tribes when disputes arose. Charles Sturt and E. J. Eyre were notably successful in avoiding confrontations. Ludwig Leichhardt, faced with an angry and fearful tribe, cut the shining brass buttons from his coat and laid them on a newspaper. The Aboriginals 'passed them from one to the other with gestures of surprise and admiration'. After a few minutes 'they seemed to throw off all fear and crowded around', feeling Leichhardt's clothing 'as if wondering at the kind of animal which produced such a skin — and every now and then bursting out into loud shouts of laughter.'

An inevitable ending
But the coming of even the most diplomatic white explorers virtually meant the end, within only a few decades, of Aboriginal tribal systems that had taken thousands of years to evolve. Today that ending seems inevitable, for if British explorers had not seized the continent, some other colonising power would soon have done so. Had it not been for a series of historical accidents, modern Australia might just as easily have been settled by the Dutch, French, Portuguese, Germans or Japanese.

In any of these events, the Aboriginal race would still have been shattered. All we can do, as we marvel at the achievements of European explorers in Australia, is to remember that they were not the first to discover and settle these lands. □

Aboriginal 'invaders' take up their land

Thousands of years before the European invasion, Aboriginal 'invaders' had flowed down from the direct north to populate every part of Australia

JAVA

PAPUA NEW GUINEA

suggested routes of colonisation
suggested routes of entry
land above sea level during the last ice age, some 53 000 years ago

William Cawthorne, *artist and schoolteacher, recorded how Aboriginals used teamwork to increase the tribe's catch*

More than mere baggage carriers or guides, *Aboriginals helped both explorers and settlers survive by showing them the secrets of bush food and by finding water*

Aboriginal knowledge helped white explorers

Europeans who were observant enough to appreciate the Aboriginals' highly detailed knowledge of the continent and its resources benefited from their guidance.

When Governor Arthur Phillip inaugurated modern inland exploration, he was assisted by two Manly Aboriginals, Bennelong and Colebe. They acted as guides and translators.

Bungaree, from Broken Bay, accompanied Matthew Flinders on the *Investigator*'s great voyage of 1801-1802. He was undoubtedly the first Aboriginal to circumnavigate the continent. Bungaree's presence helped to allay the fears of tribesmen who had never before seen Europeans.

Wylie, of the King George Sound tribe, accompanied E. J. Eyre across the Great Australian Bight in 1841, saving the explorer's life on several occasions.

Brave companions, trusted guides

Four years later Ludwig Leichhardt praised 'the wonderful quickness and accuracy' with which his guides recognised localities: *The impressions on their retina seem to be naturally more intense than on that of the European; and their recollections are remarkably exact, even to the most minute details. Trees peculiarly formed or grouped, broken branches, slight elevations of the ground — in fact, a hundred things, which we should remark only when paying great attention to a place — seem to form a kind of Daguerreotype impression on their minds . . .*

Yuranigh, of the Molong tribe, guided Thomas Mitchell through central Queensland in 1846. He was described by the surveyor as his 'guide, companion, counsellor and friend'. Two years later Jackey Jackey, of the Muswellbrook tribe, bravely attempted to save Edmund Kennedy from attacks by Queensland Aboriginals.

White explorers were also greatly helped by Aboriginal knowledge of waterholes and natural foods. Alexander Mollison, a pioneer squatter traversing unknown parts of Victoria in 1836, supplemented his men's rations with a type of yam which the natives called 'murnong'. 'When roasted in the ashes', wrote Mollison, 'it is palatable and no doubt, wholesome and nutritious'.

E. P. S. Sturt, brother of the famous explorer, described how other Aboriginals managed to catch 'vast numbers of ducks' without modern aids, by extending a flaxen net between trees at the end of a long lagoon. As the ducks flew by, they threw boomerangs 'whizzing over the heads of the birds', forcing many into the net.

Charles Browning Hall, a squatter who discovered Hall's Gap in the Grampians, found native fish weirs in many local streams; and long slender sticks like fishing rods, fitted with woven grass nooses in which birds could be caught. In Queensland, Captain John Mackay reported the use of barbed fish-bone spear heads, with which natives were able to spear dugong, turtle, and large fish.

Aboriginals learned secrets of desert survival long before white men came. E. J. Eyre gave an 'almost unlimited catalogue of edible articles used', including fish, frogs, lizards, rodents, berries, roots, leaves, ants and fungi. Except in extreme conditions, the Aboriginal could always manage to exist. 'It rarely happens', wrote Eyre, 'that any season of the year, or any description of country does not yield him both animal and vegetable food'.

White men who borrowed this knowledge usually survived: those who ignored it were often defeated in their attempts to penetrate the secrets of the huge continent.

Waddies *were used to knock parrots out of trees to provide fresh meat for the tribe*

Technology *of spears and woomeras brought the emu within reach of Aboriginal hunters. Samuel Thomas Gill, who specialised in 'correct resemblance', recorded their techniques*

Ptolemy, the Greek astronomer, *was the inspiration for this map printed in 1486. His view of a world balanced by a vast southern continent influenced later theories*

Australia must be there...

*T*he story of early visits to Australia by non-Aboriginal people consists of riddles concealed within mysteries. Tantalising clues abound, but no certainty seems possible unless science finds ways of uncovering new evidence.

We know that ancient Greek thinkers believed a vast continent must exist in the south, to balance the familiar continents of the northern hemisphere. Otherwise, they argued, the earth would simply tip over and fall into the void. Some early maps bore the legend:

The fourth continent [Australia] is unknown to us and is uninhabitable because of the heat of the sun. There sciapodes are alleged to live, one-legged beings of incredible speed . . . called sciapodes because in the heat they lie on their backs in the shade of their own enormous foot.

It is tempting to suppose that this was a description of kangaroos, perhaps brought back by Phoenician or Egyptian sailors, then wildly exaggerated, before finding its way on to ancient maps. But no proof exists.

Marco Polo's theory

The Chinese seem to have a better claim to being the first non-Aboriginal discoverers of Australia. Chinese seamen and merchants were constant visitors to the east coast of Africa from at least 860 AD onwards. The great ocean-going junks of the Ming dynasty's navy — far larger than any European ships of the time — also explored most of the Indonesian archipelago, and might easily have touched on the Australian continent. An ancient Chinese soapstone carving and fragments of Ming porcelain have been found in northern Australia.

Certainly the Chinese would have heard of the southern continent from their friends, the trepang-fishers of Macassar in the Celebes. Every year from

about the eleventh century the Macassarese sailed to Australian waters to catch trepang (also known as a sea-slug, *bêche-de-mer*, or sea cucumber). After being dried in the sun, the slug was greatly prized by the Chinese who used it to make rich soups.

To process their catches, the Macassarese established temporary settlements at several points in northern Australia. These fishermen too can be regarded as early discoverers, although they did not attempt to penetrate inland.

Stories seeming to verify the existence of the fabled southern land began to circulate in Europe after the remarkable travels of Marco Polo. Polo, son of a Venetian merchant, took the overland caravan route to China with his father and uncle in 1271. He became a favourite of the Emperor Kublai Khan, but after the khan's death took the sea route home in 1292 via Malaysia and Sumatra.

Marco Polo did not see Australia, but described in his memoirs a 'great and rich' country about three hundred kilometres south of Java. 'There is found great plentye of gold, and a great number of the small white shells of the sea', wrote Polo. 'Into this Ilande there commeth very fewe Strangers, for that it standeth out of the way'.

Marco Polo was writing entirely from hearsay, and his distances and directions were inaccurate. Even so, his book was taken as confirmation that extraordinary discoveries were still waiting to be made in the antipodes. On the eve of Europe's era of expansion and colonisation, the story of his travels had an explosive effect that proved irresistible.□

A Chinese soapstone carving, *dating from the early 1400s, found in Darwin in 1879, and* below, *Aboriginal artwork showing Malay trepang fishers, hint at early visitors*

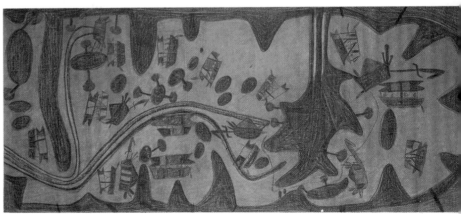

How navigators found their way across trackless oceans

Portuguese and Spanish navigators were the thrusting prow of Europe's maritime invasion of unknown worlds after the thirteenth century. But even the best seamen of those times had to develop scientific techniques to ensure successful voyages. When ships are close to known land, navigation problems are minor. With simple observations and rough maps, seamen can find their way from one landmark to another. But when they sail into the trackless ocean, new techniques are needed to find their position, destination and way back.

The magnetic compass — here a 1750 wooden bowl compass from England, above, and a 1720 Dutch model — had kept ships on course from the fifteenth century

As far as we know, Viking and Arab seamen were the first to solve these difficulties. The Vikings developed an elementary form of compass called a sun shadow-board, based on the fact that their coastline ran roughly north and south. They floated a wooden disc fitted with a central pin in a tub of water. When the sun reached its highest point, they marked the radius that the tip of the pin's shadow reached on the disc.

On the return journey, the Vikings sailed north or south until the shadow reached the same distance from the pin's

A sailor with a sounding lead, from a 1620 Dutch work on seamanship. Gradually, distance, time, depth, direction and place were falling subject to measurement of an accuracy which made possible systematic explorations

centre. Then they simply sailed east again towards the rising sun to reach their own coastline.

More accurate methods of calculating a ship's position were developed by the Arabs. They relied on the fact that stars (including the sun) appear to sink in the northern sky as a ship sails southwards. The degree to which they 'sink' is mathematically precise.

To measure these angles (called the Altura), Arab seamen invented an instrument known as the Al-Kemal, or guiding line. This was a horn rectangle or cross-staff with a knotted cord fastened to the centre. The user held the instrument at arm's length and aligned its base with the horizon. He then moved the device towards himself until the North Star was aligned with the top. The knotted cord meanwhile was stretched to the tip of his nose and a reading taken.

The number of knots counted indicated roughly the latitude at which the navigator stood. Once the correct latitude was reached, it was simply a matter of turning the ship east or west and sailing on until the familiar landmarks of the known coastline appeared.

Improvements to the compass

These rough and ready methods were vastly improved when the first magnetic compasses came into use. Their origin is uncertain, but they are generally thought to have been introduced into Europe from the sophisticated culture of China in the twelfth or thirteenth century.

In its simplest form, the compass consisted of a splinter of magnetic lodestone, attached to a straw, cork, or piece of light wood. When floated in a bowl of water, the lodestone always pointed to the magnetic pole. Even if the sun and stars could not be seen, navigators could now be sure of the general direction in which they were heading when they set sail on the open seas.

By the fifteenth century the compass had been vastly improved. The magnetised needle was pivoted on a pin, swinging above a wind-rose marked with thirty-two directional points. All this was enclosed in a weatherproof brass

The backstaff, an advance on the ancient astrolabe, helped the navigator fix latitude by enabling him to measure the sun's altitude without blinding himself. The scene was being set for more, recordable discoveries

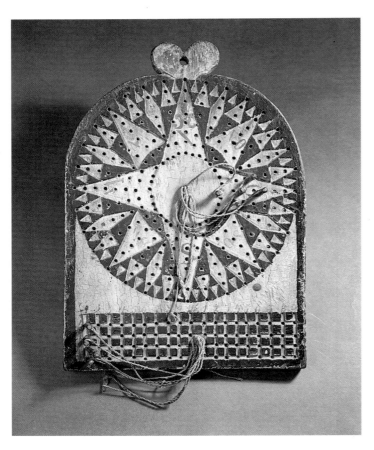

The traverse board, left, *was used until the end of the nineteenth century to keep track of a ship's course. The navigator pegged the appropriate compass point every half hour by the hour glass. Markers on this board show progress to the east*

Every 15 minutes *it was the duty of the ship's boy to turn the sand glass; right, a sixteenth century model, 12cm high. Each half hour he rang the bell which alerted the navigator to peg the traverse board and record the ship's course*

bowl, suspended on gimbals which kept the compass level in any storm.

The next major problem faced by early navigators was to estimate distance. On solid land this was easy enough, using various devices such as counting the number of revolutions made by a cart wheel of known circumference. But how could it be done on the open sea?

The first solution was called dead reckoning. In this method, a log of wood attached to a cord was thrown from the ship's bow. The number of seconds it took to reach the stern was counted. Since the ship's length was known, its speed through the water could then be calculated. Further calculations each day gave a rough idea of how much distance had been covered in a particular direction. This enabled the navigator to fix his approximate position on the chart.

Later the technique was improved by playing out a line with knots tied at regular intervals. This was the origin of the term knots, still used for measuring the speed of ships today.

The Portuguese traverse board

So far so good. If sailing ships always travelled in calm seas following a straight line to their objective, navigation would have been fairly simple. But such conditions rarely occurred. The typical sailing voyage followed a zigzag course, with the ship constantly tacking, running or veering in accordance with changing

winds and currents. These all had to be reconciled with the navigator's desired course, leaving room for error.

To overcome these variables, the Portuguese developed the traverse board. It consisted of a wooden wind-rose, with holes drilled along each point of the compass. Every half-hour's run was timed by the ship's boy who watched a sand-glass and sounded the bell: eight bells to each four-hourly watch or shift.

Making lines for others to follow

As soon as he heard the bell, the helmsman placed a wooden peg in the correct compass point. Once a day the navigator tallied the pegs and calculated how far the ship had travelled and in which directions. By amalgamating all his information, the navigator could then draw a straight line on his map, instead of showing all the ship's manoeuvres.

Later voyagers using the same map could then make their own manoeuvres according to weather conditions, yet arrive at the same destination.

Meanwhile, an ancient Babylonian device known as the astrolabe was brought to Europe and improved. This instrument had a pointer fixed to the centre of a large circular scale. When the navigator sighted along the pointer at sun or stars, their angle above the horizon could be estimated and the ship's latitude calculated from astronomical tables.

A further improvement called the

backstaff enabled the sun's altitude to be measured without blinding the observer. The quadrant included a plumb-line for calculating latitude when sun or stars were visible but the horizon was obscured for any reason.

These developments evolved into the modern sextant and octant, first constructed by the English astronomer John Hadley in the early eighteenth century. They enabled far more precise readings of sun and stars to be made, both at sea and on land and proved a major advance.

By the seventeen-sixties, when James Cook's first great voyage was being planned, a ship's latitude could be fixed with fair accuracy. But the establishment of longitude — and hence the ship's exact position on the globe — was a much more difficult problem.

'Longitude' Harrison's chronometer

On a long voyage, the old method of dead reckoning became hopelessly incorrect. Even a superb navigator like Cook was eight hundred kilometres out in his reckoning when he reached Africa's Cape of Good Hope. Since sailing distances were usually over-estimated, most old maps showed the continents as being much wider than their real shape.

Without precise maps or radio signals, longitude could be discovered only by comparing ship's time with Greenwich mean time. It was theoretically possible for a navigator to discover Greenwich time through a series of astronomical observations, and application of highly sophisticated mathematics. Publication of the *Nautical Almanac* in the seventeen-sixties simplified this process, helping Cook to make the first reasonably accurate charts of points visited.

The keeping of correct ship's time remained a problem until the acceptance of John Harrison's chronometer. Harrison was born in Yorkshire in 1693, son of a humble carpenter. When he was seventeen years old, the British Parliament offered a reward of £20,000 for an accurate means of establishing longitude.

Sydney gets it own time

Harrison worked on the problems for the next fifty years, winning the nickname of 'Longitude' Harrison. Finally he solved the puzzle of differing expansion rates of metals used in clocks, and designed a remarkably accurate timepiece. Cook took it on his second voyage, acclaiming it in his journal as 'our faithfull guide through all vicissitudes'.

Establishing precise longitudes remained difficult in Australia for some years. Even the best chronometers made in England gained or lost a little time during the long voyage across the world.

The problem was solved by the calculation of Sydney mean time to replace Greenwich time in southern areas. A timber observatory was built on Dawes

Point in 1788 and fitted with a transit telescope provided from Greenwich by the Astronomer Royal.

By averaging multiple observations Matthew Flinders was able to determine the longitude of Dawes Point within a maximum error of two minutes and rate his chronometers accordingly.

Later a new observatory was built on Flagstaff Hill, where accurate Sydney time was signalled to ships in the harbour by dropping a time ball raised in a tower. Every navigator could calculate his precise position anywhere in Australian waters — provided of course his timekeepers remained accurate.

Well-equipped land explorers also took chronometers to assist in making accurate maps of their journeys.

Overcoming magnetic variations

The final navigational problem of sailing-ship days was that of magnetic variation (declination) which affected compass readings. Differences between magnetic north and true north became glaringly apparent when long voyages and accompanying maps were made.

Navigators found these differences could be resolved by making calculations from accurate astronomical tables.

The presence of iron, even in wooden ships, also caused compass deviation. Matthew Flinders conducted many experiments while sailing off the coast in HMS

A 1769 replica of the marine timekeeper which was John Harrison's life work. He solved the problem of measuring time and place at sea

Investigator in 1802 and produced a new series of mathematical calculations which overcame the problem.

All these efforts, extending over thousands of years, allowed navigators to guide their ships across the oceans towards destinations they had never seen except on charts and to leave 'tracks' for others to follow. □

INSTRUMENTS USED BY MARINERS TO SHOOT THE SUN

When an officer stands on a ship's bridge and 'shoots the sun', he measures the angle between the horizon and the sun with a sextant. Developed from the octant (a graduated arc of one-eighth of a circle), the sextant (one-sixth, or sixty degrees) is basically a telescope mounted on a frame, with two mirrors, one of them rotatable.

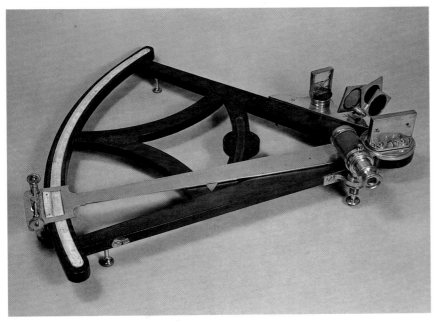

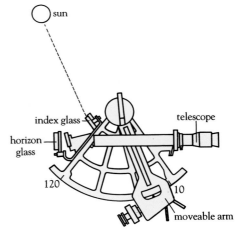

By the middle of the eighteenth century, the sextant had taken the place of the backstaff and quadrant to measure latitude. A sextant similar to the one pictured here, from London's National Maritime Museum, was among the armory of instruments used by Captain Cook to chart a third of the world

Clues that point to Spanish and Portuguese discovery

In medieval times European civilisation ended at Cape St Vincent, a south-western promontory of Portugal, where the long Atlantic rollers brought dreams of strange adventures. Here, nearly six hundred years ago, young Prince Henry of Portugal stood staring into the unknown. Wise men of the early fifteenth century told him that the world ended not far beyond the horizon: that the oceans crashed over the edge like a huge waterfall.

Was it so? Henry, a commonsense man in a world plagued by religious dogma, doubted it. Logic told him that the known parts of the African land mass extended even further south. Thus it might be possible to find a sea route round the continent to the rich lands described by Marco Polo. The prince's lifelong support for that radical idea won him the title of Henry the Navigator — even though he never went on any voyage of discovery.

In 1434, Henry instructed one of his best captains, Gil Eannes, to attempt penetration of the ocean southwards of the known Canary Islands. Eannes succeeded in passing the dreaded reefs of Cape Bojador off the African coast, where sandstorms blotting out the sun had given earlier mariners hellish visions of a 'Sea of Darkness'.

Henry's logic proved correct. One expedition after another crept past previous landmarks to map most of the African coast. By 1497 King Manuel I was able to despatch Vasco da Gama with a trading fleet, confident that he would reach India. Da Gama's success broke the Arab grip on the profitable trade in spices, oils, silks, gold and jewels. Henceforth, trading with 'the far East' would be practically monopolised by European maritime interests.

Spanish power consolidates

Meanwhile, Portugal's Spanish neighbours consolidated the power of their monarchies by driving the Moors out of Spain. King Ferdinand of Aragon and Queen Isabella of Castile, who united their dynasties by marrying in 1469, began to look to the building of a Spanish empire abroad.

Isabella in particular listened to the wild theories of the Genoese mariner Christopher Colombus, who claimed that by sailing west (instead of south and east like the Portuguese), ships would find a shorter route to Marco Polo's fabulous lands. In his famous voyage of 1492 Colombus discovered the Americas — although until his dying day he insisted it was part of Asia.

The scene appeared to be set for a lengthy conflict between Spain and

PRINCE HENRY THE NAVIGATOR
FROM A PORTUGUESE MANUSCRIPT

Portugal over colonial territories. In a breathtaking act of diplomacy, Pope Alexander VI averted war by submitting to division of the new world between the two nations. Under the Treaty of Tordesillas in 1494, an imaginary line was drawn through the Atlantic Ocean three hundred and seventy leagues (about eighteen hundred kilometres) west of the Cape Verde Islands. All territories to the east of the line were subject to Portuguese exploitation; all territories to the west, including most of the Americas, were subject to the Spanish.

The significance of this for European discovery of Australia was that the Portuguese would approach the mystery continent from the west; while the Spanish would approach it from the eastern Pacific.

Activity in the South Pacific

In 1516, only twenty-four years after Columbus discovered America, the Portuguese settled in Timor. This brought them within less than five hundred kilometres of the Australian coast.

Five years later the great Portuguese navigator Ferdinand Magellan, spurned by his own king, sailed a Spanish fleet into the Pacific through the straits that bear his name north of Cape Horn. Magellan was killed in the Philippines, but one of his ships survived to complete the circumnavigation of the world. Spanish ambitions in the South Pacific began to increase.

The question that comes down to us today is whether Portuguese or Spanish navigators ever reached the Australian mainland. It seems scarcely credible that two vigorous maritime nations with vital interests in the Pacific should not attempt to locate the missing continent, nor leave traces of their movements on land once they found it.

Fairly substantial evidence exists that a Portuguese fleet of three caravels, led by Captain Cristovao de Mendonca, touched on the Australian coast at several points in the early fifteen-twenties. Although no logs or journals of Mendonca's voyage survive, he possibly sailed past Papua New Guinea before turning south to continue down the east coast of Australia. If this is ever proven, it means that Mendonca may have discovered the fertile east coast nearly two and a half centuries before James Cook.

The Mahogany Ship mystery
Evidence of Portuguese or even Spanish exploration was provided by the sighting of a wrecked ship in sandhills near

The Straits of Magellan, forbidding second gateway to the Pacific, opened by Magellan and del Cano with their immortal voyage past South America just north of the Horn in 1519-21

Warrnambool, Victoria, by sealers in 1836. The wreck was inspected many times by reliable witnesses during the nineteenth century. All agreed that it was built of tough red wood like the mahogany used in some early vessels. Her construction was on lines quite unfamiliar to British mariners of the day.

A local resident, J. F. Archibald (later proprietor of the *Bulletin*) took a piece of timber from what became known as the Mahogany Ship. Recently this was analysed by the radiocarbon method and

FERDINAND MAGELLAN
PORTUGUESE NAVIGATOR

dated to between 1660 and 1710. This was too late for Mendonca, but well within the range of Spanish exploration.

Unfortunately the wreckage of the Mahogany Ship disappeared by 1890. Some researchers think it is buried beneath drifting sand: the search for it continues to this day.

Perhaps the most controversial evidence in support of Portuguese discovery of Australia comes from the so-called Dieppe maps, which are claimed to depict the continent and nearby islands. Australia is said to be the large land mass named Java la Grande.

Apparently based on originals stolen from the Portuguese, the maps were prepared by the renowned French school of cartographers in Dieppe between 1536 and 1550, and presented to the Dauphin, later King Henry II of France.

One cartographer, a Scot named John Rose, alias Jean Rotz, was induced into the service of the English king, Henry VIII. Rose copied a Dieppe map and presented it to his new master in 1542. From there the map found its way into the hands of Joseph Banks, the English botanist. Banks may have shown it to his friend James Cook, but there is no evidence that either man recognised Java la Grande as Australia.

At first sight, the versions of the Dieppe maps held in England look nothing like Australia. However, some researchers claim that when redrawn on Mercator's projection, and corrected for supposed magnetic errors, a distinct similarity emerges. Lawrence FitzGerald, an Australian cartographer, has matched sections of the Dieppe maps with modern maps of the Australian coastline and offshore islands; they coincide strikingly. Other historians have attacked the whole idea: the debate seems likely to continue for many years.

Spain keeps its discoveries secret

The Spanish meanwhile had subdued much of the American continent, and become active in the South Pacific. During the 1590s they reached the Marquesas, the Solomon Islands and the Philippines.

In 1605, a skilled Portuguese-born navigator named Pedro de Quiros was employed by the Spanish to search for the legendary south land. Setting out from Lima in Peru, Quiros sailed practically due west until he reached Vanuatu in May 1606. He mistakenly thought that these islands were outlying promontories of a much larger land mass. He named it *Tierra Austrialia del Espiritu Santo*, in

honour of the royal house of Austria which was allied with the Spanish monarchy.

Quiros's report to King Phillip III of Spain, entitled *Terra Australis Incognita*, was published in Seville in 1610. Seven years later it was translated and republished in London, becoming the first book printed in English on the 'discovery' of Australia. The translation read in part:

This vnknown Countrey is the fifth part of the Terreftriall Globe, and extendeth it

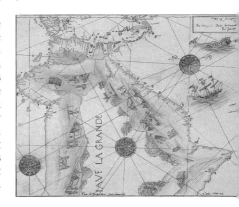

Portuguese maps *may have been copied by French cartographers in the sixteenth century. This facsimile of part of one Dieppe map shows a land mass named Java La Grande and which possibly is Australia, charted by Portuguese*

Spanish and Portuguese sailors penetrate the Pacific

Spain searched the Pacific for the southern continent from bases in South America, but south-east trades usually pushed ships towards the equator. Charts and discoveries made by Magellan, Quiros and Torres were kept secret

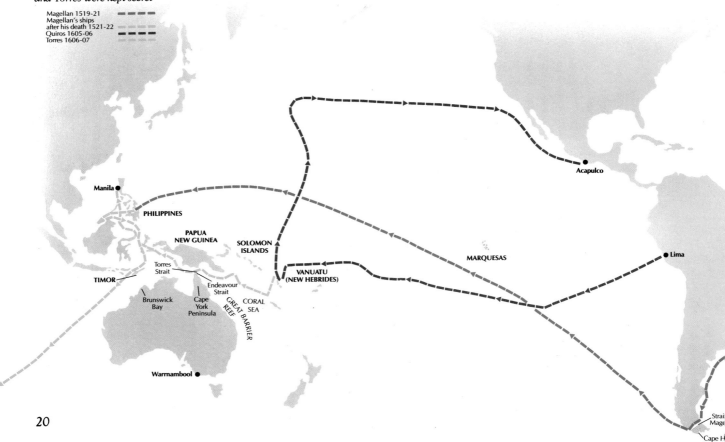

Magellan 1519-21
Magellan's ships after his death 1521-22
Quiros 1605-06
Torres 1606-07

Acapulco

Manila ●

PHILIPPINES

PAPUA NEW GUINEA

SOLOMON ISLANDS

Torres Strait

TIMOR

Endeavour Strait

Brunswick Bay

Cape York Peninsula

GREAT BARRIER REEF

CORAL SEA

VANUATU (NEW HEBRIDES)

MARQUESAS

Lima ●

Warrnambool ●

Strait Mage

Cape H

STRANGE ART MAY DEPICT FIRST WHITE EXPLORERS

In 1838 the English traveller George Grey believed himself to be the first white man to explore the area inland from Brunswick Bay, in north-western Australia.

To Grey's astonishment, while investigating caves near the Glenelg River in today's Kunmunya Aboriginal Reserve, he saw 'a most extraordinary large figure peering down on me'. The apparition was a drawing at the entrance to a cave, which itself contained 'many remarkable paintings'. One gigantic white head 'was encircled by bright red rays'. Other figures were draped in long garments such as priests might wear, and had haloes, or possibly helmets, over their heads.

Further on, Grey found a European head, sixty centimetres long and distinctly non-Aboriginal, carved into a large sandstone rock. A fair amount of weathering had occurred. Three days later he found more paintings in the unique series.

Suggestions have since been made that the figures were of visitors from outer space, the 'haloes' being space helmets and the garments space suits.

It seems more likely that Portuguese or Spanish mariners and priests visited the area at some unknown time after white settlement of the south-east-Asian islands known as the East Indies, and were depicted in the cave by Aboriginal artists.

'...**looking over some bushes,** *at the sandstone rocks which were above us, I suddenly saw from one of them, a most extraordinary large figure*'

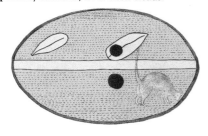

Grey wrote: *'I thought of the curious paintings we had this day seen, — of the timid character of the natives, — and wondered how long these things were to be'*

felfe to fuch length, that in probabilitie it is twice greater in Kingdoms and Seignories, then all that which at this day doth acknowledge fubiection and obedience vnto your Maieftie . . . to all the Titles which you alreadie doe pofeffe, you may adjoyne this which I reprefent, and that the name TERRA AVSTRALIS INCOGNITA *may be blazoned and fpread ouer the face of the whole world.*

In June 1606 a storm separated the three ships of Quiros's fleet. The navigator of the *Almiranta,* Luis Vaez de Torres, decided to press on in a general westerly direction. He sailed safely through the Coral Sea off Queensland's coast, avoiding the perils of the Great Barrier Reef, and arrived off the south-eastern tip of Papua New Guinea.

Most historians believe that Torres then hugged the southern coastline of Papua New Guinea to avoid the dangers of Torres Strait. However, in 1976 an experienced modern navigator, Brett Hilder, retraced Torres's route to show that he probably found his way through Endeavour Strait off Cape York Peninsula. If this was so, Torres could have sighted that part of the Australian mainland long before any other European, but may not have recognised it as such.

Torres finally arrived in Manila in May 1607, and sent home a despatch reporting his discoveries. The Spanish authorities, fearing Dutch and British interest in the area, suppressed the news. Not until the British occupation of Manila one hundred and fifty-five years later did a version of Torres' report come to light. An employee of the British East India Company, Alexander Dalrymple, recognised its importance, and sent a copy to London.

Thus when Cook and Banks sailed in 1770, they may already have suspected that New Guinea was a separate island, and that a passage lay somewhere through Torres Strait. It takes nothing from Cook's stature to acknowledge his debt to those who preceded him.□

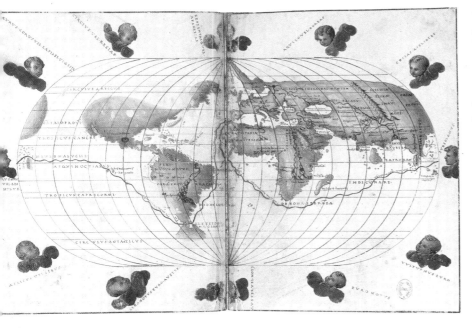

A Portuguese, Magellan, *headed a Spanish expedition that first circumnavigated the world. This 1536 map showing his route is Italian-made. It shows that, though knowledge of geography had come a long way, North and South America are still not clearly defined, while Australia is not shown at all*

New ships designed for world voyages

Carvel construction — planks laid edge-to-edge — gave a stronger, smooth-sided hull. Wooden wedges were driven in between planks at intervals

Clinker-built hulls had a ridged appearance, caused by overlapping planks attached to a rib or frame by clenched nails or rivets

Before Australia could be discovered by Europeans, new types of vessels, which could sail vast distances carrying substantial cargo and provisions and return safely to their homeland, had to be developed.

Viking longships were capable of remarkable voyages, but suffered disadvantages. They were open to the weather, could not carry much food or cargo and were rigged with only one sail to run before a following wind. In unfavourable weather the crew had to row.

Other shipwrights of northern Europe built boats with protective decking, and invented the centre stern rudder for easier steering. However, their dumpy-looking square-rigged vessels were designed mainly for coastal trading or fishing.

Ship builders in the great age of Portuguese expansion drew on this technology, but relied more on the example set by the Arab dhows and baghlas then trading in the Mediterranean.

Instead of the clinker-built (overlapping planks) construction typical of northern vessels, the Portuguese used carvel (flush planking) sides that presented a slimmer and smoother surface to the water. Hence the name caravel.

Fast, manoeuvrable vessels

In place of the great rectangular sails of northern vessels, the Portuguese adopted Arabian triangular lateen sails, which could veer around the two main masts according to wind direction and chosen route.

The result of these innovations was a vessel much faster and more manoeuvrable than anything seen before. The caravel could sail confidently into contrary winds, and by a series of tacks, or zig-zag sailing, usually reach any desired destination well before the square-rigger had completed its clumsy manoeuvres. The caravel's shallow draught also made it suitable for exploring in shoal waters.

Later caravels were fitted with a third mast carrying a square-rigged sail to take advantage of following winds, and a high poop deck to prevent the vessel being pooped, or swamped by following seas.

Once the most intensive phase of exploration was over, both Portuguese and Spanish traders built much larger ships called carracks and galleons that were capable of carrying huge amounts of cargo. These returned to large square-rigged sails, enabling them to make good time before favourable tradewinds. One or two lateen sails were retained, to assist flukey winds to fill the main sails. The jib on modern yachts is a direct descendant of these developments.

From the 1400s two great European ship-building traditions began to merge — the smooth hulls and triangular sails of the south and the clinker-built square-riggers of the north

By 1540, as this contemporary painting shows, the Portuguese were sailing tall cargo ships called carracks, carvel-built, three-masted vessels with both lateen and square sails

The caravel started out as a fishing boat but added a square sail and took to the open seas, proving that ships could sail far into the Atlantic and still return. Bartholomew Diaz rounded the Cape of Good Hope in 1488 in the swift, low-hulled caravel seen here

The square sail — actually more a rectangle, often with head and foot longer than the sides — was combined with smaller lateen, or triangular sails set at a 45-degree angle from the mast to take advantage of flukey winds

Dutch merchantmen reverted to square rigging to give speed before the trade winds. But a lack of manpower also meant that they were kept simple for easy handling. A rather bulbous and relatively flat-bottomed vessel, typified in this painting by Verbeek, was seen as the superior trader of the seventeenth century Dutch empire

The Dutch fix Australia's true position on a shrinking globe

Holland's *increasingly powerful merchant fleet extended the limits of the known world in a voracious quest for profits in the form of gold, spices and souls for Protestantism*

When Dutch explorer Dirk Hartog *made landfall at Cape Inscription, WA, in 1616, he nailed a pewter plate to a post proclaiming that: 'On 25th October arrived here the ship Endraght of Amsterdam; the first merchant Gilles Mibais of Luyek; Captain Dirk Hartog, of Amsterdam, the 27th ditto set sail for Batavia …'*

While Portugal and Spain wallowed in the riches flowing from their world empires, a vigorous young maritime nation was rising on their back doorstep. During the fifteen-seventies, Protestant Holland fought its way clear of Spanish domination and began the task of building its own empire. The new republic was about to enter its age of glory.

Dutch captains, navigators, shipbuilders and map-makers soon surpassed those of older nations. By the early seventeenth century, Amsterdam and its Dutch East India Company had become the world's leading traders. But they were traders with a difference. Rigorous scientific methods ensured that each generation of navigators built and improved on the tested methods of its predecessors.

Dutch merchants rapidly established themselves throughout the East Indies, the name for that close-linked chain of lands stretching from the Andaman Islands north of the equator, through today's Malaysia and Indonesia, from the Celebes through to western Papua New Guinea. The Dutch took over much of the trade in spices, tea, gold and Chinese porcelain. Year after year their capacious ships known as East Indiamen took back to Europe the wealth that supported a burgeoning civilisation.

During this expansionary phase, the Dutch became curious about the great continent, which they knew lay somewhere to the south-east of their East Indies island possessions.

In 1605 Willem Jansz, skipper of the three-masted pinnace *Duyfken* (Little Dove), was sent on an expedition 'to discover the great land of Nova Guinea

made an ingenious suggestion that resulted in the discovery of practically the whole coastline of Western Australia.

Previously the Dutch had followed the old Portuguese sea routes along the coast of Africa, past Mauritius, and on to Sri Lanka or the East Indies. In 1610 Brouwer suggested that ships should sail far south to the Roaring Forties, bowl along before the westerly winds, which prevail at forty degrees south, and turn north when they reached the longitude of the East Indies. Then the prevailing south-east trade winds would take them safely to their destination.

Brouwer himself pioneered this route in 1611, cutting several months off the usual sailing time from Holland. That meant extra profits for the company and less chance of scurvy for its seamen.

Pioneers of the Roaring Forties route

As we saw earlier, it was very difficult for navigators of that era to calculate their longitude accurately. Inevitably some ships sailed too far along the Roaring Forties before turning north. Several simply crashed into the reefs or coastline of Western Australia. Others had narrow escapes and were able to record the information on charts, which rapidly grew into a reasonably accurate outline of the western half of Australia.

The first Dutch ship to sight the west coast was the *Eendracht*, captained by Dirk Hartog. On 25 October 1616, Hartog entered Shark Bay, site of Carnarvon and the NASA space tracking station. He landed at Cape Inscription, the northern point of Dirk Hartog Island, and there fixed on a post a pewter plate inscribed with a memorial of his discovery. He named the mainland Eendrachtsland. The pewter plate was removed in 1697 by Willem de Vlamingh and lost until 1902: it is now kept in the Rijksmuseum in Amsterdam.

Other Dutch sightings of Australia followed rapidly. On 11 May 1618, Haevick Claesz in the *Zeewolf* made landfall in the vicinity of today's Onslow, north-west of Exmouth Gulf. 'On our chart it is nothing but open sea', Claesz remarked. Two months later Leenaert Jacobsz in the *Mauritius* sighted land at about the latitude of Northwest Cape. On a nearby island he found human footprints: the new land was inhabited.

The following year Dutch seamen discovered the southern part of Western Australia. Frederik de Houtman, a forty-eight-year-old pioneer of Dutch settlement in the East Indies, sailed in the *Dordrecht*. On 19 July 1619, he made landfall at thirty-two degrees, twenty minutes south — just south of today's Perth. 'It seems to be fine country', Houtman reported. He named it Dedelsland after his associate Jacob Dedel, councillor of the East Indies. A landing was attempted, but the large ship could not be brought safely close to shore.

Houtman followed the coastline northwards, then put out to sea, just managing to escape being wrecked on the extensive coral shoals of Houtman

and other east and south lands'. Jansz sighted the coast of Papua New Guinea probably in February 1606, then was forced southwards by shoal water into the Gulf of Carpentaria (named after Pieter de Carpentier, Governor-General of the Dutch East Indies).

First European sighting of the mainland

In March 1606, Jansz made the first positively known sighting by a European of the Australian mainland — at the mouth of the Pennefather River on the Gulf's eastern coast. He took the ship's boat a few kilometres upstream and came across a party of Aboriginals. This first known encounter between white and black could be read as a bad omen for the future, for one of the *Duyfken*'s crew was speared to death.

Jansz continued sailing south along the coast. He passed today's Duyfken Point, near Weipa, and mapped as far as Cape Keer-weer (Turnabout) at nearly fourteen degrees south, before turning north toward his home base in Java.

Four years after Jansz's pioneering voyage, Dutch mariner Hendrik Brouwer

Roaring Forties carry the Dutch onto the coast of Western Australia

Although keen to reach the wealth of the East Indies, the Dutch tiptoed across the Indian Ocean via Mauritius until a lateral thinker called Brouwer changed the course of history. He *suggested using the Roaring Forties to speed ships across the southern ocean before turning north. The new route meant the Dutch literally began to bump into Australia from 1611 onwards*

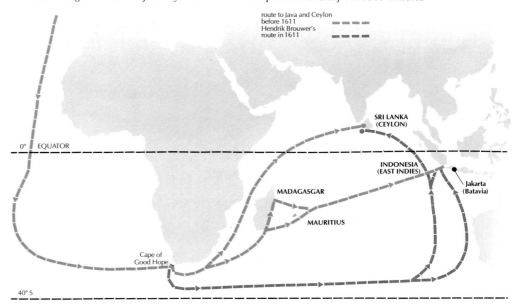

Abrolhos (Portuguese for 'Look out!'). He carefully charted their position as a warning to other navigators. This did not prevent the *Batavia* from being wrecked there ten years later in 1629. In the aftermath of the wreck, a depraved section of survivors mutinied and massacred one hundred and twenty-five men and women passengers. Thirteen of the ringleaders were later captured and hanged.

In 1622 the *Leeuwin*, sailing far to the south, discovered the headland still known as Cape Leeuwin. As navigation became more accurate, the Cape was commonly used as the desired landfall for sailing ships approaching Australia from the south-west.

Australia's true shape becomes clearer

The Dutch East India Company now decided to pursue Willem Jansz's 1606 exploration of northern Australian waters. News of the Spanish discovery of Torres Strait only three months after Jansz's voyage had been suppressed, and was completely unknown to Dutch authorities. They believed that Papua New Guinea and Australia formed a continuous land mass, and they set about investigating its coastline, shoal waters and possibilities for trade.

In 1623 Jan Carstensz led a mission consisting of two yachts, the *Pera* and *Arnhem*, commanded by Willem van Colster, to take up where Jansz had left off. Carstensz approached what we now know is Torres Strait, but found the water

FREDERIK DE HOUTMAN
DUTCH EXPLORER

so turbid and shoals so numerous, that he believed it could be only a shallow bay leading to a 'Dry Bight'. Carstensz reported 'an empty and drowned land, full of underwood and warped trees.'

Sailing round the Gulf coast, Carstensz's men seized an Aboriginal to take back to Djakarta, then known as Batavia, for questioning. They seemed surprised that two hundred tribesmen

should attack them and force them to retreat to their boats.

After discovering and naming the Staaten river on Cape York Peninsula, Carstensz erected a wooden board with an inscription to mark their arrival. He retraced the same route home in order to check his observations, but could bring no good news. To him Australia seemed 'the driest, poorest area to be found in the world . . . we could not find one fruitful tree nor anything that could be of use to mankind'.

Nevertheless, accidental discoveries continued. Late in 1626 a Dutch ship called the *Gulden Zeepaard*, bound for Djakarta, was separated from a convoy during a storm. Fierce westerlies drove the ship in a new direction, along the unknown southern coast of Australia.

Pieter Nuyts, a high company official, appears to have taken command. Even while the ship ran before the gale, he caused the new land to be charted as carefully as possible. In this way an important fifteen hundred extra kilometres of coastline was added to Dutch maps, and the true shape of Australia became increasingly apparent.

The *Gulden Zeepaard* (Golden Seahorse) penetrated as far as the Nuyts

Not all the Dutch discoveries *were of strange lands. Vlamingh, whose ships are seen here at anchor in the Swan River in 1697, was the first to see black swans, thought to be a zoological impossibility. He took two back to Batavia*

This state-of-the-art French map, *based on the discoveries of the Dutch, but still leaving the east coast to the imagination, was the starting-off point for James Cook when he attempted to complete the cartographic picture of the mysterious continent a century later*

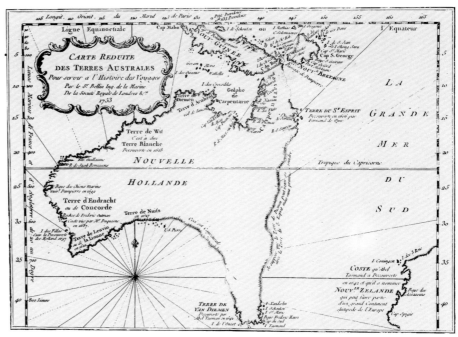

Archipelago, south-west of today's town of Ceduna, before retracing its route and arriving in Djakarta in April 1627.

The following year the ship *Vianen* under Frederikszoon de Witt, attempting to catch a homeward-bound convoy by following a new route, ran aground on 'the South Land beyond Java' — somewhere between today's Onslow and Exmouth. Only by jettisoning twenty tonnes of pepper and copper could the skipper manage to refloat. For many years the area was known as De Witt's Land.

Dutch interest in Australia revived after the government appointed forty-three-year-old Anthony Van Diemen Governor-General of the East Indies. Van Diemen had an extraordinary career: he went bankrupt as a young merchant, was forced to enlist as a marine, and accompanied the *Mauritius* on its visit to Australia in 1618. Thereafter the dream of adding the unknown continent to the Dutch empire was always with him.

Tasman discovers Van Diemen's Land
Immediately after his meteoric rise to the top position in the East Indies in 1636, Van Diemen sent Gerrit Pool and Pieter Pietersz in the yachts *Klein Amsterdam*

and *Wezel* to carry on the exploration of northern Australia. The expedition was a failure, although the name Van Diemen Gulf, south of the Cobourg Peninsula, remains on the map today.

Nothing daunted, Anthony Van Diemen began planning the most ambitious voyage of discovery ever mounted in the East Indies. In 1642 he commissioned Abel Jansz Tasman, an adventurous thirty-nine-year-old skipper who had risen from the rank of common seaman, to take two ships as far south and

east as possible. This would show whether Australia was really connected to Antarctica, as shown in ancient maps.

Commercial benefits remained paramount. Van Diemen argued that because of its latitude, the south land must contain 'many excellent and fertile regions' — perhaps even 'rich mines of precious and other metals'. The Governor-General therefore instructed the reliable Tasman that if he encountered an unknown civilisation, he should 'parley with its rulers and subjects, letting

Dutch navigators begin to give Australia a recognisable shape

First by accident, and then increasingly by design, the Dutch voyagers touched upon more and more extremities of a land that almost seemed to shrug them off. Their focus was the riches of Indonesia

and the country they now saw taking shape was a disappointment. It was Van Diemen who revived the dream of new sources of wealth to be found to the south and inspired fresh hopes of discoveries

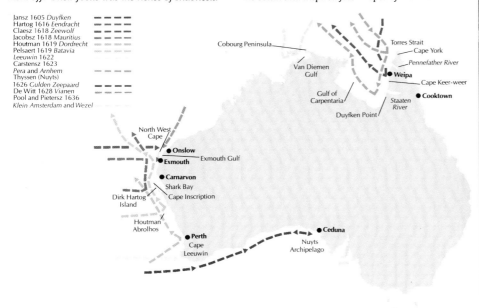

Jansz 1605 *Duyfken*
Hartog 1616 *Eendracht*
Claesz 1618 *Zeewolf*
Jacobsz 1618 *Mauritius*
Houtman 1619 *Dordrecht*
Pelsaert 1619 *Batavia*
Leeuwin 1622
Carstensz 1623
Pera and *Arnhem*
Thyssen (Nuyts)
1626 *Gulden Zeepaard*
De Witt 1628 *Vianen*
Pool and Pietersz 1636
Klein Amsterdam and *Wezel*

0   800 km

ANTHONY VAN DIEMEN
EAST INDIA COMPANY CHIEF

them know that you have landed there for the sake of commerce'.

Tasman sailed from Djakarta on 14 August 1642, in command of the ship *Heemskerck* and the flute (a warship stripped of most of its arms and used as a transport vessel) *Zeehaen*. Enough provisions were carried to last twelve months — although everyone knew that unless fresh food were found along the way, they would eventually suffer the too familiar agonies of scurvy.

Tasman first sailed for Mauritius to top up their provisions, then headed south. By early October the ships had reached the Roaring Forties. They continued south-easterly, to reach nearly fifty degrees south, the freezing latitude of Kerguelen Island.

Huge seas and fierce winds forced Tasman to change his course to north-easterly. Had it not been for this circumstance, he would have missed Australia completely. As it was, his ships were blown towards the southern tip of the island now known as Tasmania.

On 22 November 1642, in latitude forty-two degrees, fifty minutes, Tasman noted that the compass needle was fluctuating 'very suddenly'. 'It may be that there are lodestones hereabouts', he wrote. Two days later he sighted 'high

mountains to the ESE'. These were probably Mount Heemskirk and Mount Zeehan on Tasmania's west coast, named by Matthew Flinders in honour of his Dutch predecessors.

Tasman wrote proudly in his journal: 'As this land has not before been known to any European, we called it *Antony Van Diemen's Land*, in honour of our High

Between Dirk Hartog's landing *on the island that bears his name in Shark Bay and William Dampier's 70 years later, much of Australia's western and southern coast was charted*

Magistrate the Governor-General, who sent us out to make discoveries'.

Despite 'foggy rainy weather', and natural caution when sailing off a lee

Abel Tasman finds Van Diemen's Land, but misses the continent close by it

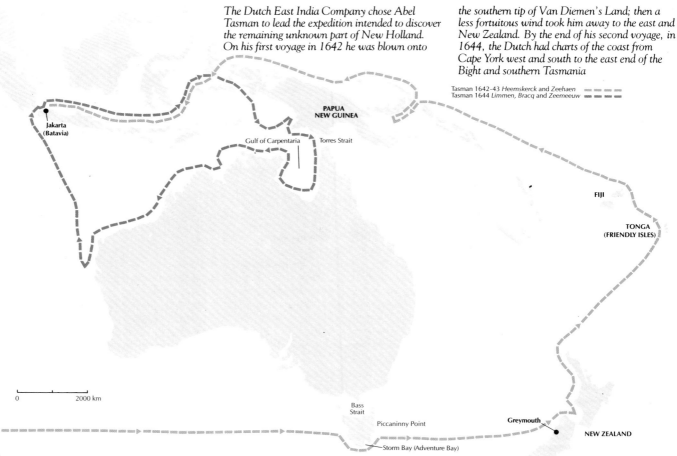

The Dutch East India Company chose Abel Tasman to lead the expedition intended to discover the remaining unknown part of New Holland. On his first voyage in 1642 he was blown onto the southern tip of Van Diemen's Land; then a less fortuitous wind took him away to the east and New Zealand. By the end of his second voyage, in 1644, the Dutch had charts of the coast from Cape York west and south to the east end of the Bight and southern Tasmania

Tasman 1642-43 *Heemskerck and Zeehaen* == == ==
Tasman 1644 *Limmen, Bracq and Zeemeeuw* ■■ ■■ ■■

Jakarta (Batavia)

Gulf of Carpentaria

PAPUA NEW GUINEA

Torres Strait

FIJI

TONGA (FRIENDLY ISLES)

0   2000 km

Bass Strait

Piccaninny Point

Greymouth

NEW ZEALAND

Storm Bay (Adventure Bay)

shore, many parts of southern Tasmania were sighted and charted during the next twelve days.

On 29 November a renewal of fierce squalls forced the ships to seek shelter in what Tasman named Stoorm Bay (renamed Adventure Bay by Tobias Furneaux in 1773, it is south of today's Storm Bay).

On 2 and 3 December, some of the crew were able to row ashore and gather green plants, including sea parsley (also known as wild celery, *Apium prostratum*), to fight off scurvy. The seamen 'heard human voices, and a sound like that of a trumpet or little gong not far off, but they could see nobody'. Steps cut into a tree were over seven metres apart, leading the white men to fear that 'the people here must be very tall'. Marks in the ground resembled those of 'the claws of a tiger'.

The Dutch take possession

In a small bay, probably today's Frederick Henry Bay, the ship's carpenter swam through the surf, set up a post on shore, 'and left the Prince's [Stadtholder's] flag flying upon it'. In this way the Dutch took possession of what they called Van Diemen's Land. On the map completed after his return to Djakarta, Tasman enthused:

It is impossible to conceive a Country that promises fairer from its Situation than this of Terra Australis; no longer incognita, as this Map demonstrates, but the Southern Continent Discovered. It lies Precisely in the richest Climates of the World . . . Whoever perfectly discovers and settles it will become infallibly possessed of Territories as Rich, as fruitful, & as capable of Improvement, as any that have been hitherto found out, either in the East Indies, or the West.

But for reasons we will never know (probably simply unfavourable winds), Tasman did not try to circumnavigate Tasmania and so perhaps catch sight of the south-eastern mainland of Australia. In his journal for 5 December 1642, Tasman merely wrote: 'We assembled the Council, and resolved to keep our course eastward'. This was at latitude forty-one degrees, thirty-four minutes south, slightly to the north of what is now called Piccaninny Point.

The great discoveries of Bass Strait and Australia's fertile east coast were to be left after all to British navigators. On such chance decisions the fate of nations and empires turn — for if Tasman had continued northwards, he might well have persuaded the authorities to make eastern Australia into yet another outpost of the Dutch empire.

Sailing eastward along forty-two degrees, ten minutes south, Tasman discovered New Zealand on 13 December 1642. He described the sighting, north of

today's Greymouth, as 'large high land' with mountain tops covered in 'dark clouds', while further north 'the land was barren'. As with Tasmania, Tasman did not attempt to circumnavigate his discovery. He simply assumed that both

lands were part of larger continents.

Tasman continued north-east to discover Tonga and some of the Fiji Islands. Returning towards Australia, he sighted the entrance to Torres Strait but merely charted it as a bay, coasting round northern Papua New Guinea to return safely to his Djakarta headquarters.

In 1644 Tasman was commissioned to attempt to find a passage between Australia and Papua New Guinea, which some cartographers persisted in believing must exist. He failed, but on the return journey mapped quite accurately a large section of the Gulf of Carpentaria and Australia's north-western coastline.

Unfortunately for the Dutch, none of Tasman's arduous labours revealed lands rich in jewels, gold, silks or spices for which their merchants hungered. The directors of the East India Company wrote in their secret reports: 'It were to be wished that the said land [New Holland: Australia] continued still unknown and never explored, so as not to tell foreigners the way to the Company's overthrow.' And in 1645 Tasman's greatest supporter, Governor-General Van Diemen, died. Tasman eventually settled in Batavia and died there, a rich landowner, in 1659. Dutch expansion slowed down, and Australia was left in its ancient peace for more than another century.□

'Uncommonly large profit' was the aim of the Dutch when they sent Abel Tasman, a seasoned seaman but little more, on his voyage south. He reported only a 'rich clime', and his masters lost interest in further exploration

LEMUEL GULLIVER TRAVELS TO AUSTRALIA

The brilliant British satirist Jonathan Swift was inspired by the Dutch discoveries of Australia's south coast to write his classic work *Gulliver's Travels*.

His hero, Lemuel Gulliver, was said to have sailed from Britain in the *Antelope*. Gulliver claimed: 'In our Passage . . . to the *East-Indies*, we were driven by a violent Storm to the Northward of *Van Diemen's Land*. By an Observation, we found ourselves in the Latitude of 30 Degrees 2 Minutes South'.

This could place Gulliver somewhere in the Great Australian Bight. When he awoke after his ship was wrecked, he found himself tied down by tiny humans several centimetres tall. Many adventures followed in the land of Lilliput.

During another of his voyages, Gulliver's seamen mutinied and set him ashore on an island of the Nuyts Archipelago. Here he was saved by horse-like creatures called Houyhnhnms.

Gulliver's Travels is one of the greatest works of satire in the English language, but ironically, is usually read in the bowdlerized children's version.

Chart *from an early edition of Gulliver's Travels: the most outlandish region Swift could think of*

Swift *saw Lilliput in the Bight*

Dutch maps replace guesswork

As part of their rational, scientific approach to world exploration, Dutch cartographers in the late sixteenth century began to replace medieval fantasies on their maps with actual observations.

During the fifteen-sixties, the great Flemish cartographer Gerardus Mercator invented a method of depicting the globe on a flat sheet of paper. Latitudes and longitudes were drawn at right angles instead of curves. Although useless near the poles, Mercator's maps enabled ships sailing in the most-used middle latitudes to plot a straight-line course and preserve direction much more accurately.

A flourishing school of map-makers and printers grew up in Holland to keep pace with the rapid expansion of the Dutch empire. Ships' navigators were instructed to report their observations fully and promptly for inclusion in constantly revised maps.

Navigation was greatly assisted by the invention of the telescope in 1608 by Dutch optician Hans Lippershey. His basic idea was later improved by the Italian physicist Galilei Galileo and the English mathematician Isaac Newton. With good telescopes, mariners could communicate more easily with other ships at sea by reading their signals at a distance. They could spot the rippling water or waves that signalled danger. And eventually, they could make the astronomical observations on which fully accurate navigation far from land depended.

Superstitious beliefs continued to show up on maps for some time. Gerard de Jode's map of Papua New Guinea, published in Antwerp in 1593, depicted a large shapeless continent to the south, infested with lions and griffins.

Even a century later, Justus Danckerts's map showed the east coast of 'Hollandia Nova' as being populated by wealthy merchants with caravans of elephants. But the imagined land mass reaching to the south pole had been abandoned. In its place was a reasonably accurate outline of much of Australia and Papua New Guinea.

Completion of the true representation of most of Australia had to wait a further century until James Cook's voyage from 1768 to 1771.

Under the increasingly skilled hands *of the Dutch map-makers, the South Land — Hollandia Nova — began to take shape, but Justus Danckerts had to leave the south and east to the imagination that made cartography an art*

GERARDUS MERCATOR
FLEMISH CARTOGRAPHER

By the end of the sixteenth century *the Dutch passion for scientific exploration and for documentation was in full flower. Map-making, especially the production of magnificent multi-volumed atlases, and the new aids that made advances in navigation possible, had become an important branch of Dutch baroque art. In this art gallery scene painted in the early seventeenth century, a globe, compass, astrolabe and atlas take their place among the sumptuous artworks covering the walls. Obviously, such objects were revered and admired in their own right*

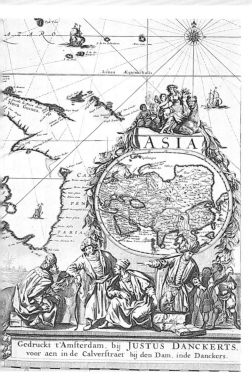

One of Holland's thriving sixteenth century map-printing houses — maps were printed directly from line engravings or etchings in copper plates until 1850, and coloured by hand until much later

Gerard de Jode's 1593 map of New Guinea has a stalwart little group of islands perched precariously above a mythical land. The inscription says it is uncertain whether New Guinea is an island or part of Terra Australis

Abel Tasman's voyages left leading Amsterdam publisher Hugo Allardt with enough information to produce the then definitive shape of the South Land without sacrificing the valued artistic embellishments

Britain decides to investigate the unwanted, unknown land

To understand the chances and coincidences that led to Britain's becoming the European coloniser of Australia, it is necessary to go back four centuries from today.

In 1588 Phillip II of Spain, then at the height of his arrogant power, decided to send an 'Invincible Armada' of warships to bring the intransigent Protestant English government of Queen Elizabeth I to its knees. Apart from religious fury, Phillip had been provoked beyond endurance by the piratical raids of English seamen like Francis Drake, who plundered Spanish treasure ships at will.

But the Spanish Armada was an appalling failure. Torn to pieces by continuous storms, and harried by small British ships snapping at its heels, ragged remnants of the Spanish fleet crept back to face Phillip's wrath.

The crumbling of Spanish power was of greatest immediate benefit to Dutch empire-builders. Britain itself descended in 1642 into the chaos of civil war, ending with the triumph of Puritan forces under Oliver Cromwell and execution of King Charles I. Restoration of Charles II

in 1660 and the succession of James II in 1685 led to renewed periods of turmoil. When James tried to reintroduce Roman Catholicism, he was deposed in another revolution in 1688.

British parliamentary leaders asked William, Stadtholder of Holland, and his wife Mary, daughter of James II, to become joint monarchs: he was proclaimed King William III in February 1689. A Bill of Rights was enacted, and a long period of constitutional government began, under which British trade and empire-building flourished.

Dampier visits western Australia

With rapidly developing maritime strength, Britain began to take over from declining Spanish and Portuguese imperialists. Francis Drake had already been knighted in 1580 by Elizabeth I for performing the first British circumnavigation of the globe, during which he

SIR FRANCIS DRAKE
NAVAL ADVENTURER

passed quite close to Australia's north through the East Indies.

The British East India Company was formed twenty years later to trade with the East Indies and China. In 1622 one of its ships, the *Tryal*, became the first British vessel wrecked in Australian waters. (The wreck was found by skindivers near the Monte Bello Islands off the north-west coast in 1969.)

The British Empire began to develop apace. During the sixteen-fifties and

---

A CANNON IS SALVAGED FROM THE SHIP *TRYAL*

Just six years after Dutchman Dirk Hartog made the first European landfall in Western Australia, that same uncharted coast was to claim its first English victim. *Tryal*, nine months out from Plymouth under the command of John Brooke, was carrying silver for the king of Siam.

A submerged coral reef, unsuspected by

The wreck site of the Tryal was discovered in 1969, but only anchors and several worn cannons were found. Then in 1985, a well-preserved cannon was found embedded in the ocean floor and was excavated by a team from the Western Australian Maritime Museum

these Atlantic sailors who were relaxing in the calm conditions after a stormy southern voyage, snared the ship silently in deep water twenty-four kilometres off the coast. As the ship broke up, two boats, one led by Brooke, the other by mate Thomas Bright, set out for Batavia. The Governor-General was to report to Holland 'The 46 persons put off from her (the *Tryal*) in the utmost disorder, leaving 97 persons whose fate is known to God alone'

Covered in a crust of marine particles, the cannon was brought to Fremantle and cleaned before conservation treatment began

'The sea-fish that we saw here are chiefly sharks... I therefore give it the name Shark's Bay' wrote Englishman William Dampier in 1688

sixteen-sixties, Britain and Holland fought intermittent battles for colonial supremacy. The Royal Navy won practical command of the oceans: Holland was forced to give up its colony of New York to the English. Britain also captured Jamaica from the Spanish, and began trading widely in its tropical produce.

In 1688 William Dampier, thirty-six-year-old son of a Somerset farmer, became the first Englishman to set foot on Australian soil. Dampier followed in Francis Drake's tradition of combining trade with outright piracy. When he landed at King Sound near Buccaneer Archipelago on Australia's north-west coast, he didn't rate the new continent very highly:

The Land is of dry sandy soil, destitute of Water, except you make Wells, he wrote. There was pretty long Grass growing under the Trees; but it was very thin. We saw no Trees that bore Fruit or Berries. We saw no sort of Animal, nor any track of Beast, but once; and that seemed to be the tread of a Beast as big as a great Mastiff-Dog. Here are a few small Land-birds, but none bigger than a Blackbird: and but a few Sea-fowls.

Dampier viewed the north-western Aboriginals with contempt as 'the miserablest People in the world . . . They have great Bottle Noses, pretty full Lips, and wide Mouths. The two Fore-teeth of their Upper jaw are wanting in all of them, Men and Women, Old and Young, whether they draw them out, I know not: Neither have they any Beards'.

The British Admiralty was more interested in Australia's strategic possibilities. In 1699 it commissioned Dampier to return in HMS *Roebuck* to chart the north-west coast and surrounding waters. The ex-pirate named Shark Bay, then coasted north-east as far as Roebuck Bay, failed to find fresh water and left the area in disgust.

Sailing north of Papua New Guinea, Dampier discovered New Britain, largest island of the Bismarck Archipelago. He

WILLIAM DAMPIER
PAINTING BY WILLIAM DOBSON

Western Australia fails to keep its first British visitors

Dampier, a vagabond with a passion for natural history and a talent for popular writing, glanced off several points on the West Australian coast looking for fresh water. He found nothing but sand, flies, animal tracks and 'wild natives'

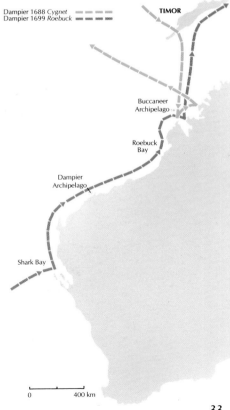

Dampier 1688 *Cygnet*
Dampier 1699 *Roebuck*

TIMOR

Buccaneer Archipelago

Roebuck Bay

Dampier Archipelago

Shark Bay

0   400 km

had hoped to sail south to discover the extent of the Australian mainland, but the leaky condition of his ship forced him to return home. Once again, Australia was not yet to be colonised by Europeans.

Scientists and the Navy show interest
The Admiralty turned its attention to other regions, where the British Empire continued to grow in strength.

After the War of Spanish Succession ended in 1714, Spain was forced to yield Gibraltar to Britain, and France was forced to give up parts of Canada. The Seven Years War ended in 1763 with Spain ceding Florida to Britain, and France surrendering its possessions in India. Meanwhile the British East India Company under Robert Clive had seized the territory of Bengal.

Within just half a century, the foundations had been laid for the greatest maritime empire the world has ever seen. Only a seemingly trivial rebellion, which began among the American colonists in 1775, marred the triumphal scene.

When the British seized Manila in 1762, an employee of the East India Company, a twenty-five-year-old Scot named Alexander Dalrymple, discovered Luis de Torres's long-suppressed *Account* of his voyage between Papua New Guinea and Australia. Two years later he published a book entitled *An account of the Discoveries made in the South Pacifick.* This inspired British scientific and naval circles to try and discover the secrets of the almost unknown southern ocean.

The Royal Society in London had already begun planning a voyage to the South Seas. Its object was to record the transit of Venus between earth and sun on 3 June 1769 — an event which would not recur for one hundred and five years. Accurate timing and measurement in clear skies would help establish the earth's precise distance from the sun and aid navigational science in many ways.

As the expedition was being planned, Captain Samuel Wallis returned home in HMS *Dolphin* with significant news. Nowhere in the south-eastern Pacific had he found Dalrymple's great continent. But he had discovered several islands including Tahiti, which was chosen as the site

for an observatory for making the necessary astronomical observations.

At first the scientists were inclined to appoint Dalrymple to lead the expedition. But the Royal Society could not find sufficient funds for a ship and appealed to the Navy to help. For reasons of their own, the Admiralty Lords agreed, provided the vessel remained under their command. The argumentative Dalrymple refused to take second place: he dropped out of the expedition and out of history.

Cook opens his secret instructions
Casting around for a suitable commander, the Admiralty hit upon an outstanding forty-year-old ship's master named James Cook. Son of a Scottish labourer and his Yorkshire-born wife, Cook had served as a merchant seaman before joining the Royal Navy, where he educated himself in the complex mathematics of marine navigation. Cook would never have won a spelling contest, but he appears to have had a natural genius for rapid calculation.

During the war against France in the

Tahiti was the site selected by the Royal Society for observing the 1769 transit of Venus. James Cook's first task was to oversee the construction of Venus Fort and ensure all was ready for the scientific program. But he was also under secret orders from the Navy . . .

seventeen-fifties, Cook distinguished himself during the capture of key possessions in Canada. His charts of the St Lawrence River, Nova Scotia and Newfoundland brought his navigational skills to Admiralty attention. Here was a man who could chart remote coastlines, obey orders, keep secrets and not attract too much attention to the Admiralty's strategic intentions. On 25 May 1768, Cook was promoted to lieutenant, and given command of a slow but solid three hundred and sixty-eight tonne, twenty-two gun converted collier renamed *The Endeavour Bark.* The ship's total complement of ninety-four included a wealthy and influential young botanist, Joseph Banks, with his eight assistants.

The *Endeavour* sailed from Plymouth on 26 August 1768. As far as the world

Dampier's drawings and vivid descriptions of discoveries on his voyages increased British popular and scientific interest in the region

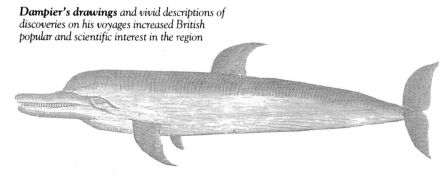

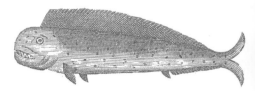

Dampier distinguished 'a dolphin as it is usually called by our seamen', above, caught in the open sea from a dolphin taken near the Australian coast 'called by our seamen a porpoise' in A Voyage to New Holland, *his book about his 1699 visit*

knew, this was purely a scientific expedition. In the normal course of events, it could have been viewed as a minor part of the technological explosion which during the same decade was leading James Hargreaves and Richard Arkwright to invent the first successful spinning machines, and James Watt to develop a practical steam engine.

In the expansion of British influence, the voyage of the *Endeavour* had results equally as important. Rounding Cape Horn and sailing through the empty stretches of the Pacific, the ship arrived at Tahiti, where its astronomers carried out their abstruse calculations and observed the transit as planned. By August 1769 all were ready to sail on — where?

This was the moment at which Lieutenant Cook had been instructed to open his second and highly secret orders. We have to guess at the excitement with which this normally reserved officer broke the seal and read the new commands from their Lordships. Here are the key extracts:

Whereas there is reason to imagine that a Continent or Land of great extent may be found . . . you are to proceed to the southward in order to make discovery of the

JAMES COOK
NAVAL COMMANDER

Continent above-mentioned until you arrive in the Latitude of 40°, unless you sooner fall in with it . . . You are also to carefully to observe the Nature of the Soil, and the Products thereof; the Beasts and Fowls that inhabit or frequent it, the fishes that are to be

found in the Rivers or upon the Coast and in what Plenty; and in case you find any Mines, Minerals or valuable stones you are to bring home Specimens of each, as also such Specimens of the Seeds of the Trees, Fruits and Grains as you may be able to collect . . . You are likewise to observe the Genius, Temper, Disposition and Number of the Natives, if there be any, and endeavour by all proper means to cultivate a Friendship and Alliance with them, making them presents of such Trifles as they may Value, inviting them to Traffick, and Shewing them every kind of Civility . . .

'Possession in the name of the King'
You are also with the consent of the Natives to take possession of the Convenient Situations in the Country in the Name of the King of Great Britain; or, if you find the Country uninhabited take Possession for His Majesty by setting up Proper Marks and Inscriptions, as first discoverers and possessors.

There was the task which would make a relatively unknown junior officer, born of humble parents, famous for ever in the annals of discovery. The turning point for the lost Australian continent had come at last.□

British sailors circle the globe and master the oceans before giving Australia serious attention

Despite Sir Francis Drake's circumnavigation of the globe in 1579, British exploration of the Pacific was slow to get under way. John Byron crossed the Pacific to reach China. Samuel Wallis
and Phillip Carteret took their different routes westward. For 70 years after Dampier's dismissal of the west coast no voyages disturbed Australia — until James Cook landed at Botany Bay

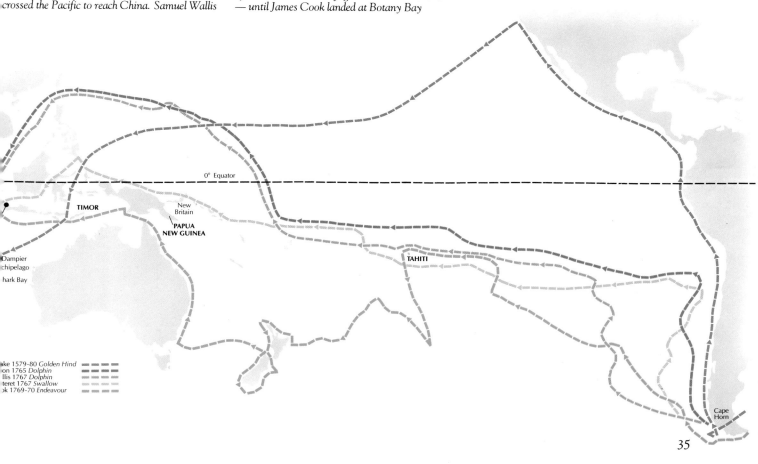

Vlamingh *sailed along the coast near the Gascoyne River mouth in February 1697. Although the expedition spent two months between Perth and North West Cape, Dutch authorities lost interest after its reports*

Yampi Sound, *north of King Sound, was named by J. L. Stokes on the Beagle in 1838 after the local Aboriginal word for fresh water. The shortage of water deterred many early callers*

The coast rejected by Dutch and British sailors after trade

Long before Australia's true nature was discovered and its outline charted, Europeans had great expectations of the riches and splendid civilisations that would be found in the southern continent. As Dutch and British sailors began to reach the Indian Ocean shores in the seventeenth century, disappointing reports were sent back to Europe. Vlamingh was unimpressed; Dampier was vehemently critical of the barren, wild and waterless shoreline.

Since the earliest landfalls occurred on the barest parts of Western Australia's coast, it is not surprising that first impressions were unfavourable. The state has a coastline some 12 500 kilometres long. Capes break the monotony between Wyndham and Broome, and between Port Hedland and Shark Bay, but most of the coast is featureless. Today, it still seems rugged and uninviting. A maze of reefs, shoals, islands and mudflats separates the mainland from the Indian Ocean. There is not much vegetation because of the high temperatures, drying offshore winds and extreme tides. The combination of inhospitable landscape, unfriendly inhabitants, lack of water and edible plants postponed settlement for at least a century.

Harsh rocky shores in King Sound. Its extreme tidal range and its many shoals and reefs made the sound dangerous for sailing ships even after it was charted by P. P. King

James Cook discovers and claims the east coast

Leaving the sensual delights of the Society Islands on 9 August 1769, HMS Endeavour sailed south to make another search for the imagined continent filling the seas between South America and New Zealand. Gales and squalls pursued her.

After several weeks Cook gave up the hopeless task, and headed west along latitude thirty-nine degrees south. Here, as he fully expected from his studies of Tasman's maps stolen from the Dutch, he discovered the east coast of New Zealand. At first, wrote Joseph Banks, 'all hands seem to agree that this is certainly the continent we are in search of'.

From 7 October 1769 to 26 March 1770, the *Endeavour* circumnavigated the north and south islands, proving beyond doubt that they were not connected to the Dutch discoveries in New Holland. Cook was particularly impressed by the possibilities of the north island for settlement 'by an industrious people'.

After a conference with his officers, Cook decided 'to steer to the Westward until we fall in with the E. coast of New Holland'. Sailing along latitude thirty-eight degrees south, at dawn on 19 April 1770 (All dates are in ship's time, as recorded in Cook's journal. Ship's time ran from noon to noon, and is one day less than modern dating, because it does not take into reckoning the International Date Line running through the Pacific Ocean) Lieutenant Zachary Hicks, officer of the watch, sighted land and immediately woke his commander. Cook named the low sandhills Point Hicks, without knowing whether what they saw was an island or part of a continent.

Cook noted in his journal that 'by our Longitude compared with that of Tasman's, the body of Van Diemen's Land ought to have bore due south from us'. However, he added, several indications 'makes me Doubtfull whether they are one land or no'. He already suspected the existence of Bass Strait separating Tasmania and the mainland.

An astonishing feat of navigation

The explorer had a crucial decision to make. If he continued on a westerly course, he might prove the existence of a strait, and finally join up with earlier Dutch discoveries in the Great Australian Bight. As we now know, that would have proved Tasmania an island, and probably led to the immediate discovery of Victoria and South Australia. These areas might then have become the sites for the first convict settlements in Australia, instead of Sydney.

But the tail-end of a severe gale was still blowing out of Bass Strait on to the little vessel. To beat against it would be exhausting work for men who had already been too long at sea. And there seemed little glory in merely making an apparent confirmation of old Dutch discoveries.

In the end, Cook made the logical decision — to fly before the favourable wind up the unknown east coast. 'We got Topgallant Yards aCross, made all sail', he wrote, 'and bore away along shore NE for the Eastermost land we had in sight'.

Next day, 20 April 1770, Cook sighted Gabo Island and Cape Howe (named after Admiralty Lord Richard Howe). The explorers now had their first clear sight of the continent. Cook wrote: *The weather being clear gave us an oppertunity to View the Country which had a very agreeable and promising Aspect, the land is of Moderate height diversified with hills, ridges, planes and Vallies with some few small lawns, but for the most part the whole was cover'd with wood, the hills and ridges rise with a gentle slope, they are not high neither are there many of them.*

Captain James Cook — 'plain both in address and appearance' wrote David Samell, surgeon in the Discovery. He declared this portrait, after Nathaniel Dance, an 'excellent likeness'

By 21 April the *Endeavour* reached Cape Dromedary, north of today's Bermagui. Cook named the 806-metre hill behind it Mount Dromedary 'on account of its figure'. 'We saw the smook of fire in several places a certain sign that the Country is inhabited', he wrote.

The latitude given in Cook's journal was practically the same as today's reckoning. His longitude (reckoned west from Greenwich because of the direction from which he had come) was only a fraction of one degree different to modern calculation — an astonishing feat of navigation considering the distance he had traversed, and the difficulties of taking lunar observations at sea.

Later the same day, the ship flew past Bateman's Bay, which Cook named after Nathaniel Bateman, captain of HMS *Northumberland* on which Cook had been master. 'It is the only likely anchoring place I have yet seen upon the coast', wrote Cook.

Sailing past today's Ulladulla, on 22 April Cook sighted 'a remarkable peaked hill laying inland' and named it the Pigeon House. Other 'pretty high Mountains' in the neighbourhood were covered with trees which 'hath all the appearance of being stout and lofty'.

A few kilometres further north, round today's Wreck Bay, Cook named Cape St George (today St George's Head). Running northwards before a fresh southwesterly on 25 April, Cook spotted a sheltered bay (Jervis Bay) but decided not 'to loose time in beating up to it'.

On 26 April, in latitude thirty-four degrees, ten minutes, Cook sighted 'some white cliffs which rise perpendicularly from the sea to a moderate height'. These were probably the cliffs at Stanwell Park or Garie Beach in Royal National Park.

Cook sails into Botany Bay

Flukey winds and a strong southerly current now pushed the *Endeavour* southwards. On 27 April she was back to latitude thirty-four degrees, twenty-one minutes, slightly to the north of what Cook named Red Point: 'some part of the land about it appeared of that colour'. Possibly it was the red promontory now known as Flagstaff Point, behind which today's Wollongong stands.

Driven still further south, on 28 April Cook attempted to land in the ship's yawl, either near today's Tom Thumb Lagoon (now part of Port Kembla) or Lake Illawarra. He caught a distant view of several natives and canoes on shore, but found that 'we no where could effect a landing by reason of the great surff which beat every where upon the shore'.

Favourable winds now took the *Endeavour* rapidly northwards again. On 29 April 1770 came a great day in the exploration of Australia, when Cook landed at 'a Bay which appeard to be tollerably well shelterd from all winds'. First he called it Stingray Harbour because of the large numbers of these fish sighted. Later he changed the name to Botany Bay, after the wealth of unique plants found by his botanists on its shores, including several varieties of banksia named after Joseph Banks.

Entering the bay, Cook named its south head Cape Solander and its north head Cape Banks after two of the scientists on board. His exact landing place was at Kurnell (after the Aboriginal name Kundel). Two natives threw spears at the interlopers, but disappeared when Cook fired a musket loaded with small shot. He then allowed the cabin boy Isaac Smith, later an admiral, to jump ashore first.

Finding only 'a few Small hutts' but not much fresh water, Cook and his men rowed across to the opposite headland, site of today's La Perouse. Here was found

New South Wales, as Cook called it, becomes a British possession

In the early light of dawn Lieutenant Zachary Hicks aboard the Endeavour spotted land extending from NE to West'. Cook bore northward, setting foot on Australian soil for the first time at Botany Bay before continuing on to chart the coast, leaving on the map such names as Port Stephens, Cape Hawke, Keppel Bay to honour well known Englishmen, descriptive names like Point Upright, Glass House, Sandy Cape, or names that reflected the circumstance of the day, like Cape Tribulation, Weary Bay, Thirsty Sound, and Providential Channel

sufficient water and wood to replenish the ship's supplies. But upon each attempt to communicate with the Aboriginals, 'neither words nor actions could prevail upon them to come near us'.

Cook instructed that the Union Flag be hoisted on shore every day to denote British occupation. The ship's name and date were carved into a tree.

For several days Cook and his men explored Botany Bay and surrounding country. They found areas of good soil, so lightly timbered that a 'great part of it might be cultivated without being oblig'd to cut down a single tree'. Sydney Parkinson noted that there were 'two sorts of parroquets, and a beautiful loriquet: we shot a few of them, which we made into a pie, and they ate very well'.

After harvesting a mound of dry grass to feed the sheep and pigs on board, Cook sailed away from Botany Bay on 6 May 1770, never to return.

British names go on the maps
At noon on 6 May the *Endeavour* passed the entrance to Port Jackson, which was named after George Jackson, naval judge-advocate. Cook recommended it as a safe anchorage, but did not change course to investigate further. On the following day he sighted the hills above Narrabeen Lagoon, and later in latitude thirty-three degrees, thirty-three minutes 'some pritty high land which projected out in three bluff points' — somewhere near the entrance to Broken Bay.

Northerly winds slowed the ship's progress for some time. On 10 May Cook sighted a 'round rock or Island laying close under the land'. This was Nobby's Head at the still hazardous entrance to Newcastle harbour, which Cook did not attempt to enter.

Smoky Cape on the north coast of NSW — Cook so named it for the 'great quantity of smook' that shrouded it when he sailed past

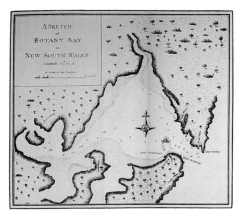

Cook first named Botany Bay Sting-Rays Harbour, but changed to the final version because of the exciting quantity of new plants found

The next important landfall came at latitude thirty-two degrees, forty minutes. Late on 11 May Cook climbed to the masthead, to sight an inlet which appeared 'shelterd from all winds'. He named it Port Stephens after Sir Philip Stephens, Secretary to the Admiralty.

Running well now before a southerly breeze, Cook sighted and named Cape Hawke near today's Forster. On 13 May he reached a headland on which fires 'caused a great quantity of smook'. Cook named it 'Smooky Cape' — that is, Smoky Cape in what is today's Hat Head National Park.

By 15 May the *Endeavour* was coasting opposite another headland which Cook named Cape Byron (Byron Bay) after Commodore John Byron, who circumnavigated the world in 1764 to 1766 in HMS *Dolphin*.

The following day Cook arrived off Fingal Head, near today's border between New South Wales and Queensland. He named Mount Warning, now the site of a national park, and sighted the north head of the Tweed River (Tweed Heads). At sunset, wrote Cook, 'we discoverd breakers on our larboord bow' — these

rolled towards today's North Stradbroke Island. Cook named the island's northern shore Morton Bay after James Douglas, fourteenth Earl of Morton, president of the Royal Society. Later an *e* was added by mistake, and the name transferred to today's large Moreton Bay, into which the Brisbane river flows.

With the wind still favourable, Cook continued running north, observing the Glass House Mountains on 17 May and describing Noosa Head. The following day he named Double Island Point and Wide Bay, commenting that 'the land here abouts appears more barren than any

we have yet seen on this coast'. On 20 May he sailed along the Seventy-Five Mile Beach of Fraser Island.

On a 'black bluf' northerly point at latitude twenty-five degrees south, Cook saw a number of Aboriginals gathered, and named it Indian Head.

Continuing north to avoid extensive sandy shoals, Cook noticed continual flights of brown boobies heading only to the south-south-east, leading him to believe 'there was a Lagoon, River or Inlet of shallow water to the southward'.

He turned the *Endeavour*'s head to the west, and thus succeeded on 21 May in

discovering a huge bay concealed behind Fraser Island. This he named Hervey Bay after Captain (later Admiral) Augustus John Hervey, third Earl of Bristol. Cook did not sight the Mary River which flows into the bay, but noted that the land was 'thickly cloathed with wood'.

Two days later an extraordinary event occurred. Cook's clerk Richard Orton had been drinking heavily in the evening. Wrote Cook: 'some Malicious person or persons in the Ship took the advantage of his being drunk and cut off all the cloaths from off his back, not being satisfied with this they some time after

Australian artist Emanuel Phillips Fox depicted a heroic, well-dressed first landing by Cook and botanist Joseph Banks at Botany Bay in this 1902 painting, executed in London. After an initial bout of spear-throwing, Cook could not persuade the Aboriginals to communicate

went into his Cabbin and cut off a part of both his Ears as he lay asleep in his bed'.

An infuriated Cook failed to discover the culprits, although suspicion fell on two midshipmen, James Magra (Matra) and Patrick Saunders. The most likely motive for the assault was that Orton's ears had picked up damaging tales which he had conveyed to Cook.

Cape Hillsborough, near today's Mackay, was one of the points Cook saw as the Endeavour slipped into the inner passage of the Great Barrier Reef. The cape, seen here looking east from Casuarina Beach, forms part of a national park

On 23 May Cook landed on the south shore of Bustard Bay, in latitude twenty-four degrees, ten minutes, where a small stream of fresh water enters the sea. His men shot a bustard or plains turkey: 'as it weigh'd 15 pounds our Dinner was not only good but plentyfull', Joseph Banks wrote with satisfaction.

During the night of 24 May the *Endeavour* ran past Port Curtis, entry to today's Gladstone. On the morning of 25 May, Cook sighted the north-eastern point of Curtis Island, naming it Cape Capricorn on the assumption it was part of the mainland. Matthew Flinders corrected this error in 1802.

The following day Cook sighted the Keppel Isles, naming them after Rear-Admiral Augustus Keppel. The *Endeavour* sailed between the islands and the mainland, where Yeppoon is now located. 'We saw smooks a good way inland', wrote Cook, 'which makes me think there must be a River Lagoon or Inlet into the Country'. He was right: the Fitzroy River runs into Keppel Bay.

One degree further to the north, Cook passed Flat Island and Peak Island on 28 May and named Cape Manifold. Sailing north-westerly to follow the coastline, Cook discovered Townshend Island, later named by Flinders after 'Spanish Charles' Townshend, Admiralty Lord.

Although he had no way of knowing it, Cook was now beginning to enter the confusing inner passage of the Great Barrier Reef. In difficulties with rapidly shoaling waters of the Northumberland Islands (named after the Duke of Northumberland, prominent member of the Royal Society), Cook assigned the ship's boats to find a suitable channel, while he landed on the mainland of Broad Sound to search for fresh water. Not a drop could be found in the 'hard redish Clay'.

Banks had better fortune, discovering 'millions of butterflies', new plants and ants, and the 'very singular Phaenomenon' of a fish that travelled over dry land, now commonly called the mud-skipper.

Serene sailing in the Whitsundays
Putting well out to sea to avoid shoal water during 'hazy, rainy weather', the *Endeavour* passed the Bedwell Islands on 1 June 1770. Cook sighted and named Cape Palmerston after the second Viscount Palmerston, Admiralty Lord. A fresh southerly breeze and open water took the ship rapidly past the site of today's Mackay to Cape Hillsborough, which Cook named after the Secretary of State for the Colonies.

On 3 June — Whitsunday — Cook sighted the entrance to the beautiful Whitsunday Passage. He named the westerly point Cape Conway after General Henry Conway of the British Army. 'The whole passage is one continued safe harbour', wrote Cook. The land was 'tolerable high and distinguished by hills and Vallies which are diversified with woods and Lawns that look'd green and pleasant'.

Cook named the outer islands Cumberland Islands in honour of the Duke of Cumberland, a younger brother of George III; and Cape Gloucester (Gloucester Island) after the Duke of Gloucester, another younger brother. Cape Edgecumbe on the mainland he named after the first Earl of Mount Edgecumbe.

By 5 June the *Endeavour* was coasting in 'serene weather' off Cape Upstart, so named by Cook because it 'riseth up singley'. He noted nearly nine degrees of compass variation, 'owing to Iron ore or other Magnetical matter in the earth'.

On 6 June Cook charted Cleveland Bay, on which today's Townsville stands, naming it after John Cleveland, former Admiralty Secretary. Off shore Cook named the 'ruged, rocky and barrenest' Magnetic Island, because 'the Compass would not travis well when near it'.

Still sailing easily to the north, on 7 June Cook named the Palm Islands, today the site of a government Aboriginal settlement. Lieutenant Hicks landed on one island to gather coconuts, but found the trees were only cabbage palms.

Later that day Hinchinbrook Island was discovered, although Cook thought it was part of the mainland. To its north he named Rockingham Bay after the Marquis of Rockingham, former Prime Min-

The beauties of the Whitsunday Passage did not mean Cook, now sailing well within the waters of the Great Barrier Reef, could relax. Both the reef and the islands lying off the main coastline were navigated with great caution

When small ships conquered vast unknown oceans

By the time of James Cook's voyages of the seventeen-seventies, exploring ships had been developed to a new peak of efficiency, an impressive achievement, considering they weighed only a few hundred tonnes.

The helmsman, instead of being located in semi-darkness below deck next to the rudder, now steered from the open deck. The wheel was connected to the rudder by a complex system of ropes and pulleys, giving much improved control against contrary winds and strong tides.

After 1750 the keels of British ships were sheathed in copper for greater protection against worms and rot. Stone ballast in the capacious spreading holds was replaced with more compact iron or lead.

Scores of heavy water casks were carried. The contents eventually went putrid, forcing the captain to aim constantly at finding watering places. Quantities of firewood and coal were also needed on board to provide one hot meal a day from the ship's galley — itself a dangerous innovation in wooden vessels. Remaining meals were based on salted meat, cheese and 'biscuit' or hard baked dough which soon became infested with weevils.

Officers enjoyed reasonably spacious quarters at the rear of the ship, where they controlled the helm in case of mutiny. Here they could lay out their maps and instruments, and enjoy some kind of social life in calm weather.

The crew were still crowded between decks 'before the mast', but at least by Cook's time their quarters were ventilated by portholes and occasional fumigation.

Having been a common seaman himself, Cook took great care with his men's health. By observation rather than scientific training, he knew that lack of fruit and vegetables containing vitamin C eventually caused the dreadful disease of scurvy, when men's gums went black, their teeth fell out and their swollen joints could not support the weight of their bodies.

Officers managed to combat the disease by taking private stores of dried fruit and orange juice preserved by mixing it with brandy.

As long as supplies lasted, Cook insisted that every seaman should eat sauerkraut (pickled cabbage) on alternate days. If any man showed signs of scurvy, he was immediately dosed with malt.

By the time the *Endeavour* reached the Australian coast, these items were almost exhausted. The botanists identified several mainland plants they thought could be cooked and eaten. Joseph Banks listed them; 'as I believe', he wrote, 'some of them were never eat by Europeans before'. They included palm-tree cabbage, figs, Indian kale, purslane, 'a Kind of Beans, very bad, a kind of Parsley and a plant something resembling spinage', and Burdekin plums.

By the use of these foods Cook lost not a single man from scurvy, although many died from other diseases unrelated to the voyage, such as tuberculosis. And one seaman died after helping himself to the rum.

Provisions *ordered for the voyage by Cook and recorded in the Victualling Board's minutes for June 15, 1768:*

Bread in Bags 21,226 pounds
Ditto in Butts, 13,440 pounds
Flour for Bread in Barrells 9,000 pounds
Beer, in Puncheons 1,200 gallons
Spirits 1,600 gallons
Beef 4,000 pieces
Flour in lieu of ditto in half barrells, 1400 pounds
Suet 800 pounds
Raisins 2500 pounds
Pease in Butts 187 Bushells
Oatmeal 10 ditto
Wheat 120 Bushells
Oil 120 gallons
Sugar 1500 pounds
Vinegar 500 gallons
Sour Krout 7860 pounds
Malt in Hogsheads 40 Bushells
Salt 20 ditto
Pork 6,000 pieces
Mustard seed 160 pounds

It was an impressive feat *of organisation to cram onto the Endeavour many casks of provisions, cables, anchors, eight tonnes of iron ballast, six carriage guns, eight swivel guns, a long boat, pinnace and yawl (carried stacked on the top deck). In July Cook was informed he would be taking Joseph Banks, Daniel Solander and astronomer Charles Green with him as scientific observers, plus their personal servants. Already, at Deptford, shipwrights had adapted the collier's hull, masts and yards for 'foreign service', adding storerooms, more deck space and cabins: when Endeavour moved to Plymouth, shipwrights and joiners came on board again to refit the cabins for the extra gentlemen and to make a platform over the tiller which swung in a wide arc across the quarterdeck and would have made walking in the area hazardous for the non-sailor guests. Then, only eleven days before sailing, Cook was notified that the ship's company was to be increased from 70 to 85 men, including a party of 12 marines.*

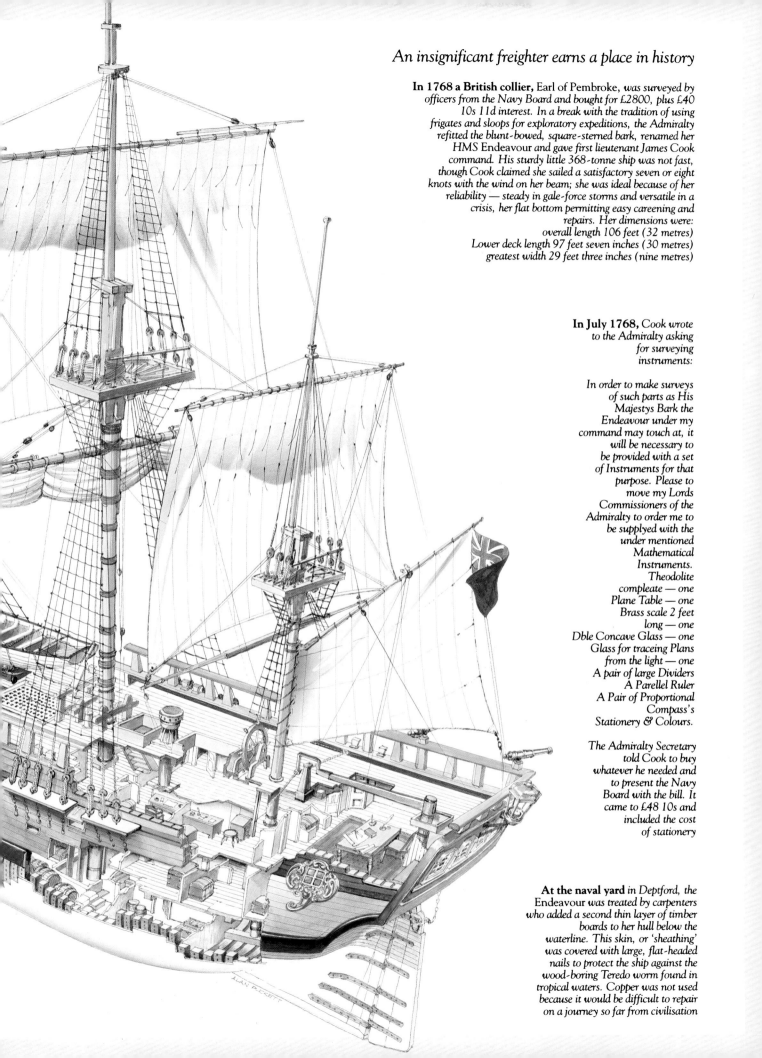

An insignificant freighter earns a place in history

In 1768 a British collier, Earl of Pembroke, was surveyed by officers from the Navy Board and bought for £2800, plus £40 10s 11d interest. In a break with the tradition of using frigates and sloops for exploratory expeditions, the Admiralty refitted the blunt-bowed, square-sterned bark, renamed her HMS Endeavour and gave first lieutenant James Cook command. His sturdy little 368-tonne ship was not fast, though Cook claimed she sailed a satisfactory seven or eight knots with the wind on her beam; she was ideal because of her reliability — steady in gale-force storms and versatile in a crisis, her flat bottom permitting easy careening and repairs. Her dimensions were:
overall length 106 feet (32 metres)
Lower deck length 97 feet seven inches (30 metres)
greatest width 29 feet three inches (nine metres)

In July 1768, Cook wrote to the Admiralty asking for surveying instruments:

In order to make surveys of such parts as His Majestys Bark the Endeavour under my command may touch at, it will be necessary to be provided with a set of Instruments for that purpose. Please to move my Lords Commissioners of the Admiralty to order me to be supplyed with the under mentioned Mathematical Instruments.
Theodolite compleate — one
Plane Table — one
Brass scale 2 feet long — one
Dble Concave Glass — one
Glass for traceing Plans from the light — one
A pair of large Dividers
A Parellel Ruler
A Pair of Proportional Compass's
Stationery & Colours.

The Admiralty Secretary told Cook to buy whatever he needed and to present the Navy Board with the bill. It came to £48 10s and included the cost of stationery

At the naval yard in Deptford, the Endeavour was treated by carpenters who added a second thin layer of timber boards to her hull below the waterline. This skin, or 'sheathing' was covered with large, flat-headed nails to protect the ship against the wood-boring Teredo worm found in tropical waters. Copper was not used because it would be difficult to repair on a journey so far from civilisation

ister. Cape Sandwich was named after the Earl of Sandwich, Postmaster-General, who once spent twenty-four hours at the gambling table without food other than beef sandwiches, and hence had the delicacy named after him.

North of Rockingham Bay Cook charted the Family Islands, then Dunk Island, named after George Dunk, Earl of Halifax. Here many years later E. J. Banfield wrote his classic work *Confessions of a Beachcomber*.

The *Endeavour's* troubles begin
Following another good run north, on 9 June Cook named the Frankland Islands after Admiral Sir Thomas Frankland. Fitzroy Island and Cape Grafton were named after Augustus Fitzroy, third Duke of Grafton.

Hauling round Cape Grafton, Cook discovered Mission Bay, but missed Trinity Bay on which Cairns is located. Green Island and Snapper Island were discovered to the north-west, but the Barrier Reef was now closing in upon an unsuspecting Cook. At latitude sixteen degrees, sixteen minutes, he later named a small point Cape Tribulation, 'because here begun all our troubles'.

On the clear moonlit night of 11 June 1770, the *Endeavour* was sailing close to the wind north of Pickersgill Reef, in seventeen fathoms of high tide. Suddenly, before the leadsman could even make another cast, wrote Cook, 'the Ship Struck and stuck fast' upon a submerged coral reef.

Cook ran instantly from his cabin 'upon deck in his drawers', ordered all sails to be taken in, hoisted out the ship's boats, and sounded all round the hull. The vessel was impaled 'quite fast' on the jagged coral of what was later called Endeavour Reef. Every effort to kedge her off with anchors and boats failed.

A turn at the pumps for everyone
The only solution was to lighten the ship and wait for the next high tide. Fortunately she was taking in little water: it was later found that a large piece of coral blocked much of the gaping hole in her bottom. Six heavy guns, ballast, water casks and oil jars were heaved over the side. The first high tide failed to float the ship but forced in more water, so that every man from Cook downwards had to take a turn at the pumps.

With the next high tide Cook 'resolved to resk all and heave her off' into deep water, then run for the mainland before she sank. This effort succeeded. With more than a metre of water in the hold and men sweating over the pumps, the *Endeavour* wallowed her way towards Weary Bay.

The seamen managed to fother a sail

covered with oakum and dung over the ship's bottom: this was sucked into the hole and reduced the leak so much that Cook decided to run for a better harbour where the ship could be repaired.

In this way the explorers discovered Cook Harbour where Cooktown now stands. On 18 June they warped the *Endeavour* into the bay and moored by 'a Steep beach on the south side'. While camp was being established, Cook climbed the highest hill and observed the Endeavour river, but thought the country gave 'a very indifferent prospect'.

To careen the ship, its hold was emptied and its bow hauled on shore at high tide. Low tide showed a remarkable sight — a hole punched neatly through four planks as though done with carpenter's tools.

By 26 June the ship had been repaired, but attempts to float her off by lashing empty water casks to the bows failed. While waiting for the next spring tide, parties explored a few kilometres inland, gathered wild yams, observed fruit bats 'as black as the Devil', and took many astronomical observations.

Early in July the men managed to heave the ship off shore. Eight tonnes of water were taken aboard, along with large supplies of turtle caught with boat hooks. 'The meanest person in the Ship had an equal share with my self or any one on board', wrote Cook in his log.

'The best greens we found here was the Tarra (a type of yam, now called taro) or Coco Tops which grows in most Boggy Places; these eat as well as, or better than, Spinnage', wrote Cook during his six week Endeavour Bay sojourn

Cape Tribulation, so named 'because here began all our troubles'. Cook went ashore on 10 June in search of water in the adjacent bay, which he called Trinity Bay, the site of Cairns

46

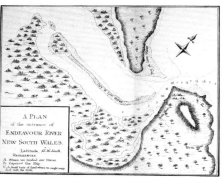

'At 1 pm the ship floated *and we warped her into the harbour and moor'd her along side of a Steep beach on the south side', Cook wrote. 'In the AM made a stage from the Ship to the shore — erected two tents one for the Sick and the other for the Stores and Provisions'. The illustration is from John Hawkesworth's* Voyages, *1773; the map of the entrance to the river is by Cook*

With the **Endeavour** *refloated and the hole in its side caused by running aground on coral temporarily stopped, Cook sought a suitable harbour for beaching the ship. He found it at what he called Endeavour River, site of present-day Cooktown. The repairs, then poor weather, were to keep him here over a month*

After the ship was laid upon its other side so that repairs could be completed, several Aboriginals who had previously fled from the white men's approaches came alongside in a canoe and accepted gifts. 'Their features were far from being disagreeable', wrote Cook, 'the Voices were soft and tunable'. He was rather shocked to find that even the women were totally naked. But after the Aboriginals were refused a share of turtle meat, they went on shore and set fire to grass all round the seamen's camp. Fortunately only a sow with a litter of young pigs was scorched. One piglet was converted into instant roast pork.

A narrow escape from destruction
By 4 August the *Endeavour* was again seaworthy, taking in only about two centimetres of water an hour. Cook sailed cautiously through shoal waters north of Cooktown to discover Cape Bedford, which he named after the fourth Duke of Bedford, former Admiralty Lord. To seaward Cook could perceive 'nothing but breakers all the way'. He added, 'I was quite at a loss which way to steer'.

Increasing gales added to the danger. Yet by 12 August Cook had managed to work his way past Cape Flattery, to land on Lizard Island (today a national park, but almost bereft of lizards). Here, many kilometres from the mainland, Cook was surprised to find native huts which could have been built only by Aboriginals arriving in canoes.

North-east of Lizard Island Cook discovered on 14 August a wide break in the

Barrier Reef, later named Cook's Passage and used by north-south shipping for many years to come.

The *Endeavour* had now sailed more than sixteen hundred kilometres with men heaving the lead day and night — 'a circumstance', wrote Cook, 'that I dare say never happen'd to any ship before and yet here it was absolutely necessary'. Thankfully Cook abandoned the maze of shoals near the mainland and headed out to open sea. Many essential provisions were running short, and soon the prevailing winds would change from south-east to north-west.

Cook's remaining aim was to establish whether a strait really existed between Australia and Papua New Guinea. Running before the fresh south-easterly trade wind, on 15 August he turned due west and sailed along latitude thirteen degrees, two minutes.

The following day Cook again sighted the Barrier Reef. Early next morning 'the roaring of the Surf was plainly heard'. The ship was about ninety metres from an almost perpendicular 'wall of Coral Rock'. Destruction, wrote Cook, was only 'the breadth of one wave' away.

All available men jumped to the boats and rowed furiously to tow the *Endeavour* back into the ocean. 'In this truly terrible situation not one man ceased to do his utmost', wrote Cook. Then 'a small air of wind sprung up', and aided by an ebb tide racing through a narrow opening in the reef, the ship reached open sea again.

On 17 August Lieutenant Hicks in a small boat discovered a wider opening which Cook determined to penetrate, lest he miss a strait south of Papua New Guinea. The *Endeavour* 'was hurried through in a short time by a rappid tide like a Mill race'. Cook named the entrance Providential Channel.

Despite the renewal of shoal water,

At Cape York, Cook was to write: 'The Eastern Coast from the Latitude of 38 degrees South down to this place I am confident was never seen or visited by any European before us'. He claimed the whole coast for George III before sailing away

Cook 'came to a fix'd resolution' to keep close to the mainland until he reached its end. Night and day now, he sent 'two boats ahead to derict us' through the 'very erregular' depths. Many more islands, capes and bays on that remote and difficult coast were sighted and named after British notables.

By 21 August the *Endeavour* had worked its way to the tip of Cape York Peninsula, which Cook named in honour of the Duke of York.

Australia's east coast is claimed

On the following day he landed on Possession Island, just to the west of Cape York. 'We were in great hopes that we had at last found a Passage into the Indian Seas', wrote Cook. And so it proved. He had solved the problem that had baffled the best Dutch navigators approaching Torres Strait from the opposite direction.

'I now once more hoisted English Coulers', wrote Cook, 'and in the Name of His Majesty King George the Third took possession of the whole Eastern Coast . . . down to this place by the name of "New South Wales"...'

On 23 August Cook sailed through Endeavour Strait into open sea, giving thanks that 'the dangers and fatigues of the Voyage was drawing near an end'. Finally in his journal Cook became enthusiastic about the possibilities of the new land, writing:

This Eastern side is not that barren and Miserable Country that Dampier and others have described the Western side to be. We are to Consider that we see this Country in the pure state of Nature the Industry of man has had nothing to do with any part of it and yet we find all such things as nature hath bestowed upon it in a flourishing state. In this Extensive Country it can never be doubted but what most sorts of Grain, Fruits, Roots, etc of every kind would flourish here were they once brought hither, planted and cultivated by the hand of Industry.

After the *Endeavour*'s return to Eng-

ONE OF THE WORLD'S NATURAL MIRACLES

The Great Barrier Reef, discovered accidentally by James Cook in 1770, is by far the world's largest coral formation. It extends about twenty-three hundred kilometres from the Bunker Islands in latitude twenty-four degrees south nearly to the mouth of Papua New Guinea's Fly River at eight degrees south.

Most scientists accept Charles Darwin's theory that the outer edge of the continental shelf has been subsiding for a long period. Billions of tiny coral polyps have grown to maturity in the warm water then died, their upward growth matching the rate of subsidence. Their remains form rock-hard reefs, islands, lagoons and cays of extraordinary beauty, teeming with colourful fish, molluscs, turtles, oysters and nesting birds.

The southern section of the reef is far out to sea, but towards the north it closes up to the coast like a funnel. The outer reef is close to the edge of the continental shelf and is exposed to huge Pacific breakers. Giant clams (*Tridacna gigas*), the world's largest shellfish, weighing more than one hundred kilos, are found on loose sandy parts in northern waters.

Several islands and inlets of the Barrier Reef area have become popular tourist resorts in recent years, attracting many overseas visitors to the area where Cook and his men once battled to understand the nature of this remarkable coastline.

The Great Barrier Reef —one of the wonders of the world, but a trial for Captain Cook as he strove first to escape its tricky shoals, then to get back into calm waters

land on 13 July 1771, attempts were made to suppress the full extent of Cook's discoveries. The whole crew was instructed 'not to divulge where they had been'. According to the London *Evening Post*, 'the Admiralty seized all the officers' papers', including Cook's own journals. A rewritten account was published and pirated, but not until 1893 was the Admiralty Hydrographer permitted to publish the full story. The secret instructions to Cook to claim the continent for Britain remained unknown until 1923.

Cook himself remained dissatisfied because he had not discovered another continent east of Australia, in the place so confidently predicted by the armchair geographers. In 1772 the Admiralty promoted him commander and sent him on a further search in latitudes fifty degrees to seventy degrees south, near the Antarctic continent.

Because of Cook's narrow escapes on the Barrier Reef during the first voyage, two ships, the *Resolution* and *Adventure*, were provided. For the first time Cook used John Harrison's perfected chronometer, enabling him to establish longitudes almost exactly.

On 17 January 1773, the *Resolution* became the first ship ever to cross the Antarctic Circle, in latitude sixty-seven degrees south, where pack ice prevented further penetration. The sails were frozen stiff. They were 'like board of plates or metal', wrote Cook.

The following month severe gales and fog separated the two vessels. Commander Tobias Furneaux in the *Adventure* headed for Van Diemen's Land to replenish his water supplies. Following a series of navigational errors, Furneaux gave his decided opinion 'that there is no straits between New Holland and Van Diemen's Land, but a very deep bay'. Cook was prepared to take his word for it.

After exploring many Pacific islands, among them New Caledonia and Norfolk Island, Cook returned home in 1776 to be promoted to post-captain and acclaimed as Britain's foremost explorer.

Soon he was off again, on a third Pacific voyage in the *Discovery*. He landed in Hawaii in January 1779 and at first was greeted almost as a god. When he returned on 14 February, his ship damaged after a gale, the natives realised he was no god. Some stole the ship's

Cook's third, and last, voyage *saw extra hands kept to a minimum — but a professional draughtsman was considered essential, his brief to be both faithful and entertaining. Thus it fell to John Webber to record Cook's death when previously-friendly natives, perhaps through a misunderstanding, became hostile. On 21 February the British ships lowered their flags, their guns were fired, and Cook was buried at sea*

cutter. Cook stormed ashore with a party of marines, was met by a war party and stabbed to death. His butchered remains were buried at sea by the survivors.

King George III is said to have wept when he heard the news. That same year, Joseph Banks gave evidence to a House of Commons committee that Cook's discovery of the Australian east coast could be put to use as a convict settlement.

The grass, he recalled, was 'long and luxuriant'; there was 'abundance of Timber and Fuel'; the country was 'well supplied with Water'; and altogether it could 'support a very large Number of People'.

After the surprises of the American Revolution, Banks's words were recalled, and modern Australia was born.□

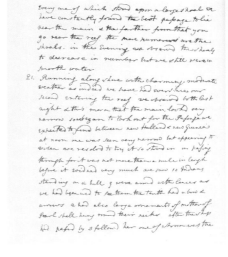

The young Joseph Banks, *painted here by Sir Joshua Reynolds, was already a wealthy and well-known botanist when he set sail with Cook in the Endeavour, complete with a personal staff of four naturalists and artists, and four servants, to collect and classify the plants of the new world. He recorded his enthusiastic impressions of the plants, animals and Aboriginal customs in his Endeavour journal, a page of which is shown above. Back in England, he set five artists to complete the plant illustrations*

Hibbertia banksii *was one of the many local flowers to be recorded by Joseph Banks and later named after him*

SYDNEY PARKINSON
ARTIST AND AUTHOR

Australia's botanical wonders are revealed to the world

The scientists who accompanied Cook soon realised that the isolated continent of Australia held a wealth of living wonders seen nowhere else in the world.

The young botanist Joseph Banks, with Swedish-born Daniel Solander as his main assistant, began collecting Australian plants at Botany Bay. Altogether they identified more than thirty-six hundred plant species and took back thirty thousand specimens — nearly one-third of them Australian varieties new to science.

Many plants were dried on the *Endeavour's* deck, then pressed between the leaves of special albums for preservation.

Others were kept fresh between damp cloths, and passed on to the expedition's artist, Sydney Parkinson, for reproduction as drawings and watercolours. Parkinson completed nearly one thousand exquisite sketches before dying of dysentery in Djakarta.

On his return to England, Banks transferred to his London house the vast collections of drawings, notes, plants, seeds, mounted insects, stuffed birds and even a kangaroo skull.

He engaged five artists to complete Parkinson's work, but the vast enterprise of engraving and publishing his paintings could not be completed until the nineteen-eighties.

Even so, the curious productions of the distant south land intrigued educated Englishmen and kept interest alive in its possibilities. Scientists longed to know more.

Hibiscus meraukensis, *from the Florilegium.*
The hibiscus, of which some 40 species are native,
were among the blooms to delight Banks

Banksia serrata, *or red honeysuckle, so called*
because its flower-spikes hold so much nectar,
was used by Aboriginals to make a sweet drink

DR DANIEL CARL SOLANDER
SWEDISH NATURALIST

Banks *never completed*
the publication of his 743
flower paintings, but in
1984 the British Museum
and Alecto Historical
Editions produced the first
limited edition volume in a
project to publish all 738 of
the surviving plates from
Banks's Florilegium. The
copper plates first had to be
painstakingly cleaned and
burnished, then chrome-
hardened to protect them
while printing. A
seventeenth century
technique was revived to
colour each plate before
printing on a hand press.
Here an artist in London's
Egerton-Williams studios
works at hand-colouring a
plate. The whole series was
to be completed by 1988

Sydney Cove, by Edward Dayes, 1804

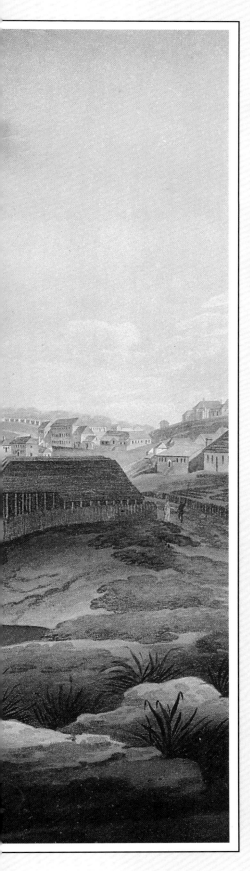

CHAPTER TWO

Survival and the search for prosperity

Convicts and their guards are trapped in a natural prison

*T*he year was 1787. In Philadelphia, the newly-independent United States of America proudly finalised a Constitution that appeared to guarantee the democratic rights of every citizen. Thousands of kilometres away, in a Britain still ruled by aristocrats, the very reverse was happening. After losing their American colonies through arrogance and stupidity, British rulers now planned to ship their surplus convict population to the farthest part of the world. Those expelled were to colonise the eastern coast of the strange southern continent claimed for Britain by Captain James Cook of the Royal Navy, less than twenty years before.

So the famous First Fleet set sail from Portsmouth. Into its eleven tiny vessels were crammed Governor Arthur Phillip, RN; his staff of nine officers; 443 seamen; 211 marines; 27 wives; 659 male and female convicts; 32 assorted children; and food, tools and animals for their maintenance. These were to be the founders of European civilisation in Australia.

After an eight-months' voyage, the fleet anchored in Cook's Botany Bay. Phillip quickly decided to abandon this swampy area. He sailed up the coast and through Sydney Heads to discover what he jubilantly called 'the finest harbour in the world'. On 26 January 1788, some officers and convicts landed at the Tank stream, and began cutting down scrub for firewood. Tents, huts, roads, even a primitive government house, soon sprang up. Years of semistarvation followed while men scratched at the unfamiliar soil, grew meagre crops, and gazed desperately out to sea for supply ships to arrive.

At first it was not obvious to the colonists that they had trapped themselves in a large natural prison. There

seemed enough space for them to spread out along the waterways and across the plain south of Sydney.

Five weeks after arrival, Governor Phillip set out again through the Heads in a longboat to examine Broken Bay, some twenty kilometres north. On his right-hand side he discovered 'a very extensive branch' of river and swamp now called Brisbane Water, location of today's Woy Woy and Gosford. To the westward Phillip discovered the mouth of the Hawkesbury river, 'affording shelter for any number of ships'. He named it after Lord Hawkesbury, President of Trade and Plantations in London. To the south around the headland now called Barrenjoey and Palm Beach, Phillip found 'the finest piece of water I ever saw'. He named it Pitt Water, after British Prime Minister William Pitt. But its rocky heights seemed 'accessible to birds only'.

In April 1788, Phillip explored part of Middle Harbour, landing first at Shell Cove near today's Spit Bridge. Investigating a run of fresh water, he took a

Arthur Phillip *was Australia's first great British land explorer. This portrait of him in naval dress was painted by Francis Wheatley in 1786, a year before the First Fleet sailed for Botany Bay*

small party of officers and marines northwards and discovered Lake Narrabeen — 'tho' not without great labour,' he wrote wryly, 'for it is surrounded with a bog and large marsh in which we were frequently up to the middle'.

The need to find more farmlands

Those areas, now so heavily populated, did not seem to give the easy access, ample water and good soil for which Phillip was searching. But at one point of his expeditions he had seen 'a very fine view of the mountains inland'. The northernmost he named Carmarthen Hills, after the Marquess of Carmarthen, Foreign Secretary. A rise to the south he

In January 1788, *the First Fleet entered Port Jackson after rejecting Botany Bay. Immediately the huge task of settling the strange new land was begun. The first challenge was to find fertile land for growing crops and grazing stock brought from the Cape of Good Hope and Rio de Janeiro*

called Richmond Hill, after the Duke of Richmond. The southernmost mountain in sight he called Landsdowne Hills, after the Marquis of Lansdowne. 'From the rising of these mountains I did not doubt but that a large river would be found,' Phillip wrote.

On 22 April 1788, Phillip set out with eleven men and six days' food. They travelled as far as they could by boat up Sydney Harbour, thus tracing the Parramatta river twenty-four kilometres to its navigable head. Six months later the settlement of Rose Hill, afterwards renamed Parramatta, was established there.

Sydney's puzzling river system

For four days Phillip and his men trekked westward through mostly level, fertile, 'pleasing and picturesque' country towards the Carmarthen Hills — which were of course part of the haze-tinted Blue Mountains. After forty-eight kilometres their food ran short and deep ravines began to impede their progress. Phillip regretfully retraced his route to Sydney, promising that the new country he had discovered 'shall be settled and cultivated early in the spring'.

But where was the great river or rivers which Phillip felt sure must fall out of the Blue Mountains? On 28 June 1789 the indefatigable head of government decided to trace his Hawkesbury river as far upstream as possible. As his men rowed on, the high rocky country gave way to timber and rich soil which seemed good for farming. Phillip's party followed the tortuous course of the Hawkesbury to a rise which they climbed and recognised as Richmond Hill first seen back in April the year before. They came to the junction of another stream later known as the

Grose river. Halted by rocky falls, they could proceed no further, and returned the way they had come.

Meanwhile, on 26 June 1789, Watkin Tench, a vigorous thirty-one-year-old captain of marines, led an expedition westerly from the site of Parramatta. After a march of less than two days, they found themselves 'on the banks of a river, nearly as broad as the Thames at Putney, and apparently of great depth'. The soil needed only clearing of trees to be suitable for agriculture.

When Phillip returned from his boat trip along the Hawkesbury, he named

This watercolour view of the Hawkesbury's entrance was painted by William Bradley, the Sirius officer who surveyed Broken Bay

Tench's river the Nepean, after Evan Nepean, Under-Secretary of the Home Department in London. A puzzle remained: the Nepean seemed to flow towards the Grose and Hawkesbury rivers, but did they all form part of one great river system surrounding Sydney?

Phillip made a final attempt to discover the truth. On 11 April 1791, he formed a strong party of twenty-one men, including two Aboriginal guides —

Parramatta in 1791, when it was known as Rose Hill, was already a small farming community

Even today, seen from Emu Plains, the mountains west of Sydney present a wall-like face to the traveller. So many gorges are dead ends; every ridge seems to fall away in sheer cliffs. It was to take many efforts and twenty-five years before any kind of route was found

HOW ROUTES WERE MEASURED AND RECORDED

Early explorers had to record their movements so they could find their way home and guide other explorers and future settlers eager to find new land.

Watkin Tench described how he and William Dawes kept track: *Our method ... was to steer by compass, noting the different courses as we proceeded; and counting the number of paces, of which two thousand two hundred, on good ground, were allowed to be a mile. At night we halted, all these courses were separately cast up, and worked by a traverse table, in the manner a ship's reckoning is kept; so that ... we always knew exactly where we were, and how far from home: an unspeakable advantage in a new country, where one hill, and one tree, is so like another that fatal wanderings would ensue without it.*

Gentleman's Halt, *where Phillip was forced to turn back during his 1789 attempt to trace the Hawkesbury river all the way upstream*

the first of many occasions on which Australian natives would be used to find a route and interpret the dialects of other tribes. Every man except the Governor carried a knapsack weighed down with ten days' provisions, water canteen, gun, blanket, kettle and hatchet.

Travelling north-westerly from Parramatta, Phillip's party soon reached the Hawkesbury. Attempting to march upstream towards Richmond Hill, they were stopped by the swiftly flowing South creek. They could neither ford it nor fell a tree across to make a bridge. Their Aboriginal guides delightedly mimicked the men's sufferings as they were stung by nettles along the river bank or were 'shaken nigh to death' by falls. Phillip, already ailing, and fated soon to leave Australia forever for health reasons, sadly ordered a return to Parramatta.

In May 1791, the two marine officers

Watkin Tench and William Dawes at last solved the puzzle of the rivers. By following a slightly different overland course, they reached the western side of South creek. From there they found it easy to get to Richmond Hill. 'This excursion completely settled the long contested point about the Hawkesbury and Nepean,' Tench enthused in his journal. 'We found them to be *one river*'.

Crossing in a borrowed native canoe, the men penetrated a few kilometres further towards the Blue Mountains, as far as Knight Hill, 'until we were stopped by a mountainous country'. But at least the routes of the main rivers were now known, and a new phase of exploration could begin amid optimism. □

WATKIN TENCH,
DISCOVERER OF THE NEPEAN RIVER

The first forays spread out from a land-hungry Sydney

It took three years to trace the whole Hawkesbury-Nepean river system and to settle its fertile plains. But explorers searched in vain for routes to the continent's vast interior and most colonists continued to be confined within the Sydney basin

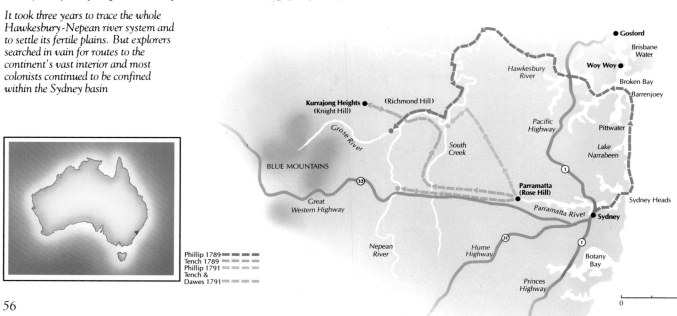

Phillip 1789
Tench 1789
Phillip 1791
Tench & Dawes 1791

Explorers come face to face with unique wildlife

Australia was isolated by sea for so long — probably several million years — that animals seen nowhere else in the world had time to evolve. Ignorant of evolutionary theory, European explorers were frequently astonished by what they observed in the new land. Each new discovery caused excitement.

Kangaroos were first described by Francisco Pelsaert, captain of the Dutch ship *Batavia* which ran onto a coral reef off Western Australia in 1629. Landing near today's Geraldton, Pelsaert saw 'creatures of miraculous form' which ran 'on the flat of the joint of the leg' and suckled their young in a pouch under the belly.

The platypus was first seen by white men in the Hawkesbury river in 1797. Colonel David Collins was so astounded by its rubbery bill and membraned feet that he named it *Ornithorhynchus paradoxus*. Some zoologists viewing specimens sent in spirits to London thought they were fakes put together from other animals. Charles Darwin saw a live platypus during his visit in 1836, describing it as 'a most extraordinary animal', a sort of combination fish, bird and mammal.

Emus, among the largest living birds but flightless, were shot for food from the earliest days of white settlement. They were called 'the Australian ostrich'. Live specimens sent back to England for naturalists to study usually died or managed to escape.

A Tasmanian *ringtail possum was given this stretched-out body by artist John Webber, a member of Cook's 1777 expedition*

Possums were first described by naturalists accompanying Captain Cook in 1770. They called them by the American Indian name 'opossum', but Australian possums belong to a different natural order. Arthur Phillip's *Voyage to Botany Bay* showed the rare black spotted possum, 'resembling a polecat, having the back spotted with white'.

The wombat, a powerful burrowing marsupial, was first brought to Governor John Hunter in 1797 on a ship which rescued some survivors of the wrecked *Sydney Cove*. Matthew Flinders caught and helped to eat a wombat on Clarke Island off Tasmania in 1798. 'Its flesh resembles lean mutton in taste, and to us was acceptable food', he reported laconically. The naturalist George Caley tried to send a live 'whombat' to England in 1805, but it managed to slip its collar and escape at Parramatta.

Emus *were hunted as food, and explorers often referred with awe to the bird's speed and power*

The platypus *confounded all the naturalists back in London. This watercolour was made in 1810 by J.W. Lewin*

Kangaroos *amazed and bewildered early observers, who often portrayed them in bizarre or unrealistic poses and shapes*

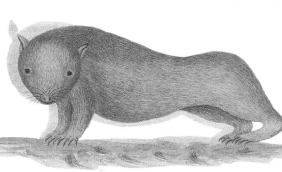

Wombats *were seen to be a southern hemisphere version of the badger, only more friendly and docile in manner*

Forlorn attempts fail to crack the Blue Mountains barrier

Curved in a semicircle behind the Nepean-Hawkesbury river system, the Blue Mountains practically enclose the Sydney area from Broken Bay in the north to Bulli in the south. Although less than fifteen hundred metres high, their sheer walls and precipitous gorges formed an apparently impassable barrier to early explorers.
William Dawes, the steadfast lieutenant of marines, made the first serious attempt to break through the misty blue range that threatened to constrict Sydney's expansion.

In December 1789, just a few months after French revolutionists stormed the Bastille in a European world as remote as another planet from Australian concerns, Dawes and two companions crossed the Nepean river near today's Penrith, less than sixty kilometres west of Sydney.

The men traversed Emu Plains and reached a rise which they called Mount Twiss, after Captain Twiss of the Royal Engineers. This point, shown clearly on Dawes's map of 1791, appears to be just beyond today's Linden railway station. But, as Governor Phillip reported to London, the adventurers 'met with such a constant succession of deep ravines, the sides of which were frequently inaccessible, that they returned, not having been able to proceed more than fifteen miles in five days'.

In August 1790 Dawes, accompanied by his friends Watkin Tench and a sea captain named Hill, decided to tackle the mountains in a west-south-west route from Parramatta. They became tangled in the gorges of the Warragamba and Wollondilly rivers (now a large reservoir) and could make little headway.

William Paterson, a twenty-eight-year-old captain in the New South Wales Corps, and already noted for his explorations in South Africa, was next to try his hand. Paterson's method was to send boats via the Hawkesbury river to Richmond Hill. His party embarked and rowed westward up the Grose river in September 1793. Within the first sixteen kilometres they encountered five waterfalls, leading to such difficulties in portaging the boats that they returned, 'leaving the western mountains to be the object of discovery at some future day'.

Defeated by 'impassable chasms'
The following year, Henry Hacking, quartermaster of the *Sirius* in the First Fleet, and now about forty-four years of age, set off past Emu Plains towards the present site of Springwood. He claimed to have penetrated about thirty-five kilometres over ridges of high rocks, but gave few other details. Faced with 'impassable

Parramatta was an administrative and farming centre until the Blue Mountains were crossed. After 1813, as more farmland became available, its prominence began to fade and it was overshadowed by the busy port of Sydney

barriers' in every direction, he too was forced to admit defeat.

In November 1795, Hacking led a party to the Cow Pastures, near today's Camden, where a few cows and bulls which had escaped from First Fleet guards were grazing. To the government's delight the herd had increased to about sixty animals — a welcome addition to Sydney's food supplies. In 1796 Port Hacking, just south of Botany Bay, was

named after the explorer. Some years later, Hacking turned to thieving, was transported to Van Diemen's Land, reprieved and became a government pilot in Hobart.

George Bass, an enterprising twenty-five-year-old naval surgeon who had just discovered Port Hacking in the tiny boat *Tom Thumb*, was next to tackle the Blue Mountains. In June 1796, he and two companions set off to explore the wild country between the Grose and Warragamba rivers. Although well equipped with scaling-irons, hooks and long ropes, the 'impassable chasms' defeated them. Bass reported fifteen days of 'unparalleled fatigue and danger'. From one peak he could see further to the west 'a second chain of mountains much higher' than any he had passed.

Bass did not give up easily. Later the same year, he decided to see what lay between the Cow Pastures and the ocean. Was it possible perhaps to escape the Blue Mountains vice in a southerly or easterly direction, and ultimately work back around its foothills?

With Bass was James Williamson, a book-keeper and acting commissary, later dismissed for defrauding the government. They set off from Mount Hunter, past today's Camden, and trekked with ease through the Cow Pastures. But further eastwards they had to work through increasingly mountainous and barren land, roughly where Woronora Reservoir is now located. Finally they emerged at the sea a few kilometres south of Port Hacking. Part of their route is still preserved because it lies inside Australia's

Many artists were to find the defeating chasms a source of inspiration. This Conrad Martens pencil sketch shows the Grose Valley from Bowen Mountain as it looked in 1876

WILLIAM PATERSON, EXPLORER, SOLDIER AND LIEUTENANT-GOVERNOR

first national park, declared in 1879, and called the Royal National Park. To Bass and Williamson, this route too seemed closed as an escape from Sydney.

Bass's idea of a southern outlet was dramatically reinforced within a few months, when survivors of a remote shipwreck were found staggering about on the sands of Port Hacking. To the amazement of Governor John Hunter, the men said they had walked overland, several hundred kilometres up the east coast from Cape Everard, after their vessel *Sydney*

Cove ran aground on 8 February 1797.

Seventeen survivors spent six weeks beating through scrub and living off the land. Only three remained alive, but they showed that an overland route from Sydney was possible. Today we call it the Princes Highway.

Barrallier faces an appalling scene
Francis Louis Barrallier, twenty-nine-year-old son of a French naval surveyor, made his bid for fame in attempting a Blue Mountains crossing in 1802. Governor Philip Gidley King had appointed him to superintend Sydney's defences against any invasion attempt by his French countrymen. Finally King gave way to Barrallier's pleas to be allowed his turn at solving the mountains puzzle.

Barrallier made a preliminary journey south-west from Parramatta, past the present sites of Camden and Picton. Turning north-westerly and following high ground, he reached a ridge overlooking what he named the Nattai river. Here he formed an advance depot and built huts containing reserve supplies.

Geographers differ on the precise points reached by Barrallier during his main expedition in November 1802. Some have him following the Nattai river to its junction with the Wollondilly river. Others have him further north on the Tonalli river (Tinkettle creek), and

A series of dead ends in mountain gorges

Many capable and determined men set out to cross the mountains, only to return to Sydney defeated by the rugged canyons and rocks walls. The harshness of the terrain led Caley to call it the Devil's Wilderness. And still today, there are few easy routes through the ranges

Bass 1796
Bass & Williamson 1796
Barrallier 1802
Caley 1804

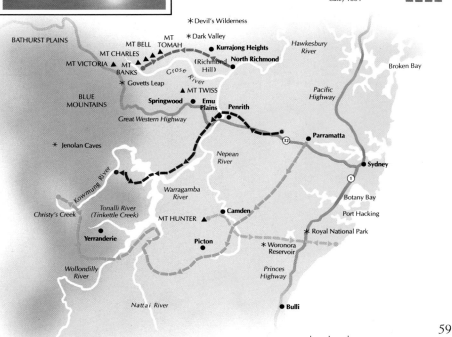

0   40 km

then passing near today's Yerranderie to Christy's creek in precipitous country. The once confident Barrallier was baffled by 'immense overhanging rocks, which seemed to be attached to nothing, offering an appalling scene'. One hill 'appeared to me so steep, nearly perpendicular, that my courage failed me when thinking of undertaking its ascension'.

Whatever the truth of his precise whereabouts, Barrallier found himself in an impossible situation. 'I was mortified to find myself on the summit of a perpendicular mountain from whence I saw a continued chain of mountains bounding the horizon', he wrote. Without knowing it, the explorers were only about twenty-five kilometres south of Jenolan Caves.

Facing an unclimbable waterfall, his supplies nearly exhausted, and 'unable to procure any beasts for the subsistence of my troops, except some snakes, which it was repugnant to eat' Barrallier was forced to order a retreat.

'The result of his journey is that this formidable barrier is impassable for man', Governor King reported to London.

An eccentric naturalist named George Caley disagreed. Caley was the bright son of a Yorkshire horse-dealer, and taught himself the elements of botany. In 1798, Sir Joseph Banks agreed to pay him fifteen shillings a week to investigate Australian flora and fauna.

In 1802, the thirty-two-year-old Caley scoffed at the general opinion of Sydney that the Blue Mountains would never be conquered. Having explored the foothills on botanical expeditions, Caley wrote to Banks that 'a party conducted under an intelligent and frugal person, provided the weather happens favourable, might gain the object'. Caley watched Barrallier's expedition leave, and felt it would fail because the Frenchman took slow bullocks instead of fast horses.

In November 1804, Caley had the chance to put his theories into practice. Leaving North Richmond, he went roughly north-west past today's Kurrajong Heights, then south-west past Dark Valley into a gloomy area cut by the northern branch of the Grose river. On 7 November, Caley confided to his journal that 'the dreary appearance, abruptness, intricate and dangerous route we experienced at this place, induced me to call it the Devil's Wilderness'.

Caley's rough experiences

Further westward and then southward the party pressed, past Mount Tomah, Mount Bell, Mount Charles and finally to Mount Banks, emerging nearly opposite Govett's Leap.

'Every day sweat poured down in torrents,' wrote Caley, 'and our cloaths were commonly as wet as if they had been dipped in water.' Their water supply ran low, and rivers were completely inaccessible from the heights they trod. As a substitute, the men chewed green acidic fruit from native currant bushes.

Caley had provided solid cakes of 'portable soup' for his party. Broken down with the tiny amounts of water in which their salt pork was boiled, and with birds added when they were able to shoot any, the soup helped to save their lives.

At Mount Banks, Caley was less than ten kilometres in a direct line from Mount Victoria. Had he been able to climb that peak, he would have seen the wide Bathurst Plains, lying invitingly to the westward. But all his luck and most of his rations had run out. When the men got back to the nearest farm, they had only two and a half kilos of food left.

After hearing Caley's very rough experiences, Governor King concluded in his report that 'the extension of agriculture beyond the first range of mountains' was a chimerical idea that must be given up. It seemed the end of all exploration of the implacable Blue Mountain ranges.□

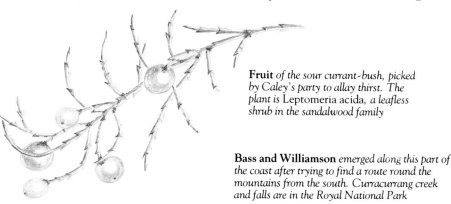

Fruit of the sour currant-bush, picked by Caley's party to allay thirst. The plant is Leptomeria acida, a leafless shrub in the sandalwood family

Bass and Williamson emerged along this part of the coast after trying to find a route round the mountains from the south. Curracurrang creek and falls are in the Royal National Park

Convicts take on the challenge of exploration

Transported convicts played an important role in opening up different parts of unknown Australia. In January 1798, governor John Hunter reported that Irish convicts around Sydney had become convinced 'there was a colony of white people at no very great distance in the back country — 150 or 200 miles — where there was abundance of every sort of provision without the necessity of so much labour'.

To break them of this fantasy, Hunter allowed several convicts to explore, under guard, south-west of Sydney. West of the Nepean river they sighted many 'whombatts', 'cullawines' (koala bears), and 'emews', but could not catch them. For two days they had nothing to eat except 'one rat about the size of a small kitten'.

After penetrating past today's Berrima, the novice explorers became totally disillusioned. Starving they trekked back to gaol.

Two months later, Hunter organised a better equipped party. This time the guide was a 'wild white man' named John Wilson, a Lancashire thief who reached Australia with the First Fleet and later lived in the bush with Aboriginals. Henry Hacking, quartermaster of the *Sirius*, accompanied him.

Hunter also sent his nineteen-year-old servant John Price, instructing him to keep a journal. The explorers left Prospect Hill on 9 March 1798. Ten days later they had crossed the Wingecarribee river. Wrote Price, 'we counted our biscuits and found we had thirty apiece; we allotted that two biscuits should be our day's allowance'. Fortunately John Wilson 'saw a large green, yellow and black snake; he directly ran and caught it by the head, which made us an excellent dinner'.

That day the men passed through 'a most beautiful country', west of today's Sutton

Convicts *usually got the job of pushing a measuring wheel, or perambulator, to estimate distances*

Forest, 'fine large meadows and ponds of water in them'.

By 23 March they were able to climb Mount Towrang, nine and a half kilometres east of today's Goulburn, but concluded that ahead lay only 'scrubby, hilly country'. Had they persevered just one more day, they would have discovered the extensive Goulburn Plains, and the whole history of New South Wales would have changed. But, wrote Price, 'we concluded to return back, for fear that we should not have biscuits enough to bring us back'. Wilson promptly returned to living in the wilds. He was killed the following year by an Aboriginal in a dispute over a native woman. After Price's adverse report, the south-westerly route was practically ignored

The view from Mount Towrang *once made Wilson, Hacking and Price turn back to Sydney. Today it would delight any traveller.*

for twenty years. It was left to another ex-convict named James Meehan to discover the rich sheep-grazing Goulburn Plains.

Meehan was a young Irishman, transported for his part in the great Irish uprising of 1798. Assigned to the Survey Department, Meehan became so adept at measuring land grants that he was pardoned and appointed Deputy Surveyor-General.

Goulburn Plains discovered

In 1818 Governor Lachlan Macquarie decided to seek a land route from Sutton Forest to Jervis Bay. This excellent harbour south of Sydney had been discovered from the sea in 1791 by Lieutenant James Bowen, a naval agent aboard the convict ship *Atlantic*, and named after Admiral Sir John Jervis, RN.

Macquarie arranged for Meehan to be accompanied by two prominent pastoralist-explorers Charles Throsby and Hamilton Hume. Both were anxious to find an outlet for their produce through Jervis Bay.

On 3 March 1818, the party set out from the Liverpool district. Distances were measured by a convict pushing a 'perambulator' or measuring wheel. By 25 March they could see the deep gorges of the Shoalhaven river where it runs eastward to the coast.

The land appeared so 'broken and irregular' that they decided to split into two parties. Charles Throsby led his men in a southerly direction, and managed to ford the Shoalhaven west of today's Nowra, to arrive safely at Jervis Bay on 3 April 1818.

Meehan's party followed the Shoalhaven gorge upstream, hoping to find its headwaters, skirt around them, and thus reach Jervis Bay from a southerly direction. Meehan failed, the lie of the country forcing him even further to the south-west. So, without meaning to, on 4 April 1818 Meehan discovered south of today's Goulburn a large lake covered with innumerable ducks and water fowl. He named it Lake Bathurst.

The following day Meehan turned again for home in a southerly direction. Again by accident, he discovered the vast extent of the Goulburn Plains. The surveyor described them as 'beautiful ... surrounded by a chain of grassy forest hills'. He named the area after Henry Goulburn, Colonial Under-Secretary.

Other ex-convicts such as Joseph Wild and John Warby played an important role in exploration, as later pages show.

Opportunities for a new breed of explorer

Convict initiative, ambition and labour were largely responsible for finding useful land in the fertile Shoalhaven and Southern Tablelands districts of New South Wales. Some convicts won freedom by their endeavours

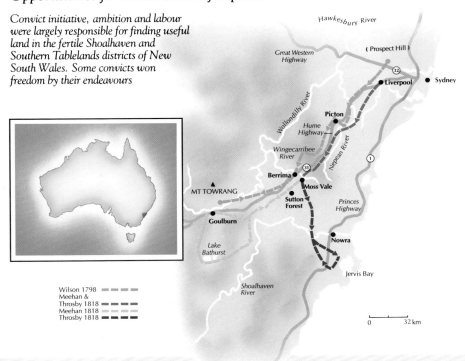

Wilson 1798
Meehan & Throsby 1818
Meehan 1818
Throsby 1818

0   32 km

Cliffs and ridges that were to disappoint and defeat so many

The Blue Mountains are not mountains at all, but a plateau deeply dissected by rivers — in particular, the Coxs, Nepean and Grose. Giant cliffs extend for more than one hundred kilometres along the river valleys. Although none of the cliff faces is higher than two hundred and fifty metres, the valley floors are often six or seven hundred metres below. More than one hundred million years ago, most of the eastern New South Wales basin, which had been under the sea, began to be thrust upward. The underlying sandstone was exposed and eastward-flowing rivers gradually cut deep chasms through the soft sedimentary stone. The sandstone also is cut through by vertical joints, which eventually break off leaving high sheer cliffs. Valleys are wider on the western side of the plateau, and become narrow further east where the rivers are still working their way through the sandstone layers. Even today, these cliffs and gorges trap unwary or inexperienced walkers.

Sharp-ridged plateaus and sheer-walled valleys are still an awesome sight

Kanangra Walls, *left, in the heart of the Kanangra Boyd National Park, provides one of the most spectacular views in the Blue Mountains region, as well as being a text-book example of the difficulties that faced explorers. Sheer cliffs, below, up to 300 metres high, line the valleys; fallen rocks lie in river beds*

New tactics and a little luck open a way west

In 1812, most of Napoleon's 600,000 invading French troops were dying in the deep snows of a severe Russian winter. At the same time, pastoralists around Sydney gazed at the burnt grass and dusty soil of the parched Australian summer of 1812-1813. It was essential, they decided, to find wider grazing areas and more water for their fast-growing herds.

Nearly a quarter-century had passed since the landing of the first white settlers at Sydney Cove, but still the conundrum of the Blue Mountains had not been solved. Three friends got together to discuss a new approach. Their leader was Gregory Blaxland, thirty-five-year-old descendant of a prosperous Kent family, who had been granted nearly two thousand hectares near Sydney to graze his cattle. The second man was William Lawson, four years older than Blaxland, trained as a surveyor and soldier, and holder of nearly four hundred hectares near Prospect. The third friend was William Charles Wentworth, much younger at twenty-three, holder of seven hundred hectares on the Nepean river, and ablaze with enthusiasm for the colony's future.

The three men decided that previous explorers had gone astray by trying to follow the rivers, entangling themselves in impassable gorges. Instead, they would follow the mountain ridges. Quite by chance, they selected the main Blue Mountains ridge — one of the few continuous routes by which a crossing is possible from east to west.

Forming a small party, with four convict servants and four horses to carry their gear, the men set off from Emu Island near today's Penrith on 11 May 1813. During the first few days their theory seemed unworkable. Every ridge they explored 'proved to terminate in a deep rocky precipice', wrote Blaxland. They had to cut their way with axes through about thirteen kilometres of 'thick brush-wood' south of Grose Head, where Springwood railway station is now located. Water had to be carried up steep one hundred and eighty metre inclines from the Grose river.

On 19 May 1813, the explorers began to ascend the second ridge of the mountains. They discovered a pyramid of stones, which they thought might have been left by George Bass to mark the furthest point he had reached in 1796.

By 22 May, the party had battled through to the highest ridge south of Mount Banks, from where they could take a bearing back to Prospect Hill. But to the west they found their progress

In 1815, *just after the mountains trail was blazed, Macquarie followed it taking Lewin who painted the party camped at Springwood*

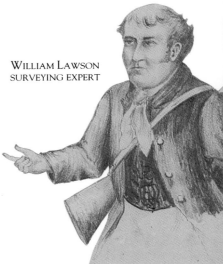

WILLIAM LAWSON
SURVEYING EXPERT

GREGORY BLAXLAND
MERCHANT

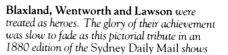

John Lewin, *artist and engraver, painted this watercolour of Emu ford on the Nepean a short distance from where Blaxland, Wentworth and Lawson set out to cross the mountains*

Blaxland, Wentworth and Lawson *were treated as heroes. The glory of their achievement was slow to fade as this pictorial tribute in an 1880 edition of the* Sydney Daily Mail *shows*

WILLIAM CHARLES WENTWORTH
STATESMAN

stopped by an impassable barrier of rock, which appeared to divide the interior from the coast as with a stone wall'. Attempts to climb around this one hundred and twenty metre monolith 'were baffled in every instance'.

The men retraced their steps northward and then westward, towards what is now known as Wentworth Falls. Again they were able to follow the ridges, but only by forcing their way through growth full of small thorns'. On 24 May they passed the site of today's Leura railway station, on 25 May today's Katoomba, and on 27 May Blackheath.

On 28 May 1813, they clambered up Mount York. Here, to their great satisfac-tion, wrote Blaxland, 'they discovered what they had supposed to be sandy barren land below the mountain was forest land, covered with good grass'. Later that day they 'contrived to get their horses down the mountain by cutting a small trench with a hoe'.

After resting, on 1 June 1813 the party crossed open meadows along today's river Lett, 'covered with high good grass'. Gratefully they sucked the sweetness from honeysuckle trees all around.

A little further ahead they could see a high hill, 'in the shape of a sugar loaf', later to be called Mount Blaxland. In the afternoon they climbed it, and from the summit 'descried all around, forest or grassland, sufficient in extent, in their opinion, to support the stock of the colony for the next thirty years'.

The Blue Mountains had at last been almost conquered. A way inland was open to settlers.

A few months after the three explorers returned in triumph, Governor Lachlan Macquarie instructed George William Evans to plan a road across the mountains and if possible penetrate beyond Mount Blaxland.

Evans, an almost self-educated surveyor born in London in 1780, was already noted for his explorations around Sydney. In 1804 he discovered the Warragamba river and traced it upstream to today's Warragamba Dam. Eight years later Evans landed a small party from the sea at Jervis Bay, surveying the first practical route northwards along the coast to today's Wollongong and Appin. At the end of this arduous trek he apologised in his report for not being able to measure the entire distance: 'not any of us having eat any thing for three days we were very weak'.

Evans surveys a road to the west
This courageous civil servant set off in the footsteps of Blaxland, Lawson and Wentworth on 19 November 1813. He decided to push ahead as quickly as possible while the horses were still fresh, leaving the measurement of exact distances for the return journey. Despite constant rain Evans reached the previous explorers' finishing point within a week, stopping at 'a very handsome mount, which I take the liberty to call Mount Blaxland', he wrote.

HOW EVANS CROSSED THE MACQUARIE RIVER

On 8 December 1813, surveyor George Evans was halted by the wide expanse of the Macquarie river near Bathurst. 'I made up my mind to contrive a bridge,' he reported.

His men began: *by driving two forked logs into the Mud as far in the water as we dare venture, and by laying a piece of wood in the Forks, form a Gallows, a party swam across and did the same on the other side; we then fell trees as large as all six of us could carry, and rolled them down the bank; as soon as one end was carried into the water the stream sent it round, and the ropes secured around the end prevented it being carried too far; we lifted two of these up, which reached from one Gallows to the other, and two from each bank to a Gallows, over which we passed our necessaries; and swam the Horses, first conveying to the other side a Rope that held them, otherwise the force of the water would have carried them a great distance as it did the men who swam across.*

The following day, 27 November, a shock lay in store. It became obvious to Evans that the main dividing range had still to be crossed. The mountains ahead were 'so very steep' that the store cattle had to be left behind on the plateau. Two days later Evans and his men found themselves 'completely entangled among the hills'. But by 1 December, Evans was clear of the worst obstacles. He named a 'remarkable' mount to the north after himself. Here he was able to see 'at least fifty miles west' towards 'a great extent of grazing land'. His spirits continued to rise. Next day he discovered a fine waterway which he named the Fish river: 'if we want a fish it is caught immediately; they seem to bite at any time'.

Cox builds the Great Western Highway

On 6 December 1813, Evans arrived at extensive plains where 'the soil is exceeding rich and produces the finest grass intermixed with variety of herbs'. At a loss for language to describe the area fully, he named it Macquarie Plains after his patron, and the main stream Macquarie river. There, on 9 December, Evans camped on the site of Bathurst.

The party ventured some distance further along the Macquarie river, nearly to its junction with the Turon river. On 16 December, being nearly one hundred and sixty measured kilometres from Mount Blaxland, his horses and men practically worn out, Evans decided to turn for home. As promised, when they retired through the Blue Mountains, they measured every metre of the way by surveying-chains. At one stage they barely escaped a great bushfire raging 'with violence through thick underwood'. Evans blithely commented that the burning made chain-measuring easier.

Back at Emu Plains by 8 January 1814, Evans reported to Macquarie that a dozen men 'might clear a good road in three months for a cart to travel over the mountains'. The delighted Governor commissioned William Cox, a fifty-year-old Hawkesbury landowner and magistrate, to make him such a road.

Cox chose thirty strong convicts: in six months they built the original Great Western Highway, one hundred and sixty-one kilometres and twelve bridges through rugged country to Bathurst. Macquarie reported that their 'incredible labour and perseverance' did them 'infinite honour', and granted them all free pardons.

Pastoralists and their flocks swarmed over the new road and fanned out across the plains around Bathurst. 'The handsomest country I ever saw,' Evans had written, and the newly-prosperous graziers agreed heartily.

In May 1815 Macquarie sent George Evans on another expedition south-west of Bathurst, 'in the hope of falling in with

Mount York looking west from where Blaxland, Wentworth and Lawson crossed the mountains. Their hopes for the 'forest land covered with good grass' have long since been fulfilled

Augustus Earle *painted the view from Mount York to the Bathurst Plains in 1827. Convicts breaking stones are transforming Cox's track into a primitive highway*

the Macquarie river in that direction'.

Evans passed over much "handsome and fine country' near today's Blayney and Cowra. On 23 May he discovered the Abercrombie river, but decided to retrace his steps north-west so that he passed Mount Macquarie.

This brought him to the gorge of the Belubula river, forcing him to turn south-west. In this way Evans discovered, on 27 May 1815, the upper reaches of the Lachlan river, where the soil was rich and water so plentiful that he thought it could become 'a second Hawkesbury'.

Stunned to find the Lachlan flowing towards the inland instead of to the sea, Evans traced it a few kilometres north-west to its junction with Mandagery creek. Into a large red gum he carved 'Evans 1st June 1815'. Now shortage of food forced him to retrace his steps. On the way back he saw distant mountains covered with snow, providing a new puzzle for future explorers.

Poor Evans! When news of his tremendous discoveries of 1813-1815 was sent back to London, Earl Bathurst, a fifty-four-year-old extreme Tory who was Secretary for the Colonies, replied that Evans 'does not appear from the style of his journal to be qualified by his education for the task of giving information respecting this new country'.

Macquarie, himself the offspring of illiterate tenant farmers, was thus prohibited from giving the heroic explorer command of the next vital expeditions, intended to trace the full courses of the Lachlan and Macquarie rivers and to find perhaps an inland sea. The Governor replied to Earl Bathurst that it was simply 'an Act of Justice' to allow Evans as original discoverer to accompany the expeditions, and appointed him second-in-command under John Oxley.□

The Blue Mountains road *painted by Augustus Earle. This London-born artist, who had studied at the Royal Academy, published his* Views in Australia *in 1826 and* Views in New South Wales and Van Diemen's Land — Australian Scrapbook *in 1830. The National Library in Canberra holds 126 of his watercolour drawings. Earle died in London in 1838*

For many years *after 1813, work gangs of chained convicts breaking rocks and building bridges along the western road were a familiar sight to travellers. This 1832 naive painting shows the section of road at Mt. Victoria, then known as Major Mitchell Pass, before it drops to the plains*

Conquerors of the mountains

It was either Blaxland or Lawson who suggested climbing and following the ridges instead of walking up the valleys. There are still only two main routes through the mountains from Sydney

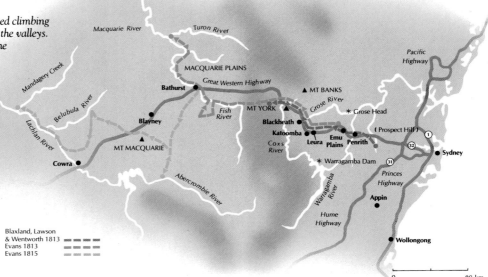

Blaxland, Lawson & Wentworth 1813
Evans 1813
Evans 1815

0   80 km

Macquarie's party *travelled along Evans's road across the Blue Mountains, passing through the Sidmouth Valley, right, and crossing a bridge over the Campbell river, above, just five kilometres above its junction with the Fish river. Lewin recorded the vice-regal expedition*

An enthusiastic and energetic Governor makes his own journeys of exploration

Lachlan Macquarie, Australia's most popular early Governor, could not expose himself to the life-and-death risks run by his pioneer surveyors. But he always took keen interest in their discoveries.

During his reign from 1810 to 1821, Macquarie travelled extensively over the new areas opened up and even did a little harmless exploration of his own.

The Governor left on his first tour through the Bankstown district on 6 November 1810, naming the towns of Windsor, Richmond, Liverpool, Castlereagh, Pitt-town and Wilberforce.

On 22 November Macquarie decided to explore the country around the presumed head of the Georges river, west of today's Bankstown airport. His guide was John Warby, a thirty-six-year-old transported convict who became a stockman and sired fourteen children after his release and marriage to another ex-convict, Sarah Bentley.

Macquarie, Warby and their party rode through 'very fine rich land' alternating with rocky gullies to find 'the main and principal branch of George's river, which it would appear, comes from a more westerly point than has hitherto been supposed'. The Governor decided to open the district to smallholders under the name *Airds*, after his wife's family estate.

On 29 November 1810, Macquarie explored the Warragamba river discovered by George Evans six years earlier.

With a small party including his wife, the Governor was rowed in leisurely manner up the Nepean to its confluence with the new stream. 'We halted at a beautiful romantic spot on the right bank', wrote Macquarie, 'in order to take our breakfast'.

Further up the Warragamba they were stopped by a waterfall. Nevertheless, reported Macquarie proudly, 'we had explored two miles higher up than Mr Evans or any other person had ever before attempted to do'. There spoke the spirit of the true discoverer.

Macquarie was enthralled by the results of George Evans's explorations beyond the Blue Mountains in 1813.

By 1815, when the convict-built road was complete, Macquarie decided to see the vast new district for himself. Riding comfortably by carriage with his wife, the Governor named many points such as Cox's Pass along the way. They arrived in Bathurst in eleven days, where the Union Jack was hoisted and the town named on 7 May 1815. During the next week Macquarie, showing his usual keenness, investigated the surrounding district in every direction, naming Winborndale and other localities.

Vice-regal processions through the colonies
Macquarie also paid visits to Van Diemen's Land, Newcastle, Goulburn, Port Macquarie and the Illawarra district, naming hundreds of today's localities. By the time he resigned his governorship — sick at heart from Commissioner Bigge's niggling criticisms — the colonies were resounding with his enthusiasm for new discoveries and development. He sailed for England in February 1822 and was dead by July 1, 1824. News of his death sent the settlers into deep mourning. 'Macquarie was a prince of men, Australia's pride and joy!' wrote the ex-convict poet Michael Robinson, echoing the feeling in all hearts.

ELIZABETH MACQUARIE
PAINTING BY RICHARD READ

LACHLAN MACQUARIE
PAINTING BY RICHARD READ

Oxley searches for a non-existent inland ocean

JOHN OXLEY, NAVAL OFFICER,
SURVEYOR, EXPLORER

Governor Macquarie and his surveyors found themselves totally unable to visualise the courses of the inland rivers of New South Wales. Flowing north-west from Bathurst was the noble, apparently endless Macquarie river. Did its waters curve round and join the newly-discovered Lachlan river, which seemed to flow in the same general direction? Did they make together a mighty watercourse — another Nile — which perhaps lapped finally into some breathtaking inland sea? The prospect of marvellous discoveries seized men's minds with visions of a vast fertile continent, seat of a new empire far richer than Britain.

Macquarie appointed John Oxley, his thirty-two-year-old Surveyor-General, to lead the critical new expedition of discovery. Oxley, born in Yorkshire, had trained in the Royal Navy, and carried out coastal survey work in Western Port and Van Diemen's Land.

On 24 March 1817, the Governor instructed Oxley to trace the course of Evans's Lachlan river. By 25 April, the party had set up a depot at the junction of the Belubula and Lachlan rivers. Showing considerable foresight, they carried portable boats on the backs of pack-horses. After erecting the boats, they were able to cram in them most of the thirteen men and supplies. Other men followed the river bank as closely as possible leading the horses.

'Condemned to perpetual desolation'

After three days, this curious cavalcade had covered over fourteen kilometres. In nearby low hills, the explorers found specimens of quartz and iron ore, but could not know that fifty-four years later, there would be some 25 000 people grubbing for gold in this district.

On 5 May the party floated past today's town of Forbes, ascending the Jemalong Range to view the countryside. 'It is impossible to fancy a worse country,' Oxley wrote scornfully, 'intersected by swamps and small lagoons in every direction; the soil a poor clay, and covered with stunted useless timber'.

But, he added, 'if the country itself is poor, the river is rich in the most excellent fish'. One of his men caught for dinner a speckled cod weighing thirty-one kilos, and measuring one hundred and six centimetres.

By 9 May the explorers reached a huge marshy plain, which Oxley named Field's Plains in a wry tribute to Judge Barron Field of the Supreme Court. The Lachlan river here became 'separated into

branches, and lost among the immense marshes of this desolate and barren country', Oxley wrote. Today the town of Condobolin sits on the north side of these extensive waterways, but the countryside is no longer barren. The river has been dammed and many of the swamps drained to make highly productive land.

Unwilling to trust his horses to the endless swamps, Oxley left the Lachlan on 14 May 1817 and headed in a south-westerly direction. This took his party over a practically waterless route, where only 'the contents of small muddy holes' saved them. After a thirty-six-hour waterless stage they reached the base of the Cocoparra Range on 1 June, and found a little water in the rocky holes. They optimistically planted peach, apricot and quince seeds, but Oxley doubted that 'these desolate plains' would 'be ever again visited by civilised man'.

A large and tasty Murray cod Maccullochella peeli, *gave Oxley's party a fine meal. The fish were once plentiful in the rivers of the Murray system*

Oxley decided it would be 'highly imprudent to continue longer' to the south-west. At this stage he was only a few kilometres from today's Griffith and the Mirrool creek. He turned north-westerly, setting a course the road and railway now closely follow. This unwittingly brought the party back on 23 June to the boggy banks of the Lachlan river, near today's town of Hillston.

'Our astonishment was extreme', wrote Oxley. 'Every thing seems to run counter to the ordinary course of nature in other countries'.

Again travelling downstream, Oxley described on 30 June 'immense plains extending to the westward as far as the eye could reach'. He thought they were unsuitable for agriculture, not knowing that later generations would find them

No longer 'desolate plains', *the Murrumbidgee irrigation area has been transformed from barren desert into one of the most highly developed farming areas in the country and the town of Griffith is its thriving centre*

excellent for fine wool production.

Not a semblance of a hill could be seen, no natives, animals or birds. The explorers seemed to be the sole living creatures. Oxley reflected in his journal: 'Nothing can be more melancholy and irksome than travelling over wilds, which nature seems to have condemned to perpetual loneliness and desolation.' Again on 5 July 1817: this country must 'remain forever uninhabitable, and useless for all the purposes of civilised man.'

On 7 July the explorers made camp at the site of Booligal. Fourteen kilometres further on, the Lachlan deteriorated into a series of muddy waterholes. What was

Macquarie Marshes, near Warren, where Oxley began to realise there was no inland sea, only the wetlands formed by the Macquarie river

the point of continuing? Obviously most of the Lachlan's water dissipated itself in the marshes already passed.

Wrote the disappointed explorer: 'This originally unlooked for and truly singular termination of a river, which we had anxiously hoped and reasonably expected would have led to a far different conclusion, filled us with the most painful sensations'.

Oxley and Evans push back the frontier

Their strenuous expeditions opened up grazing land in north-west New South Wales and encouraged the spread of settlement along the coast north of Newcastle and Port Stephens. By the end of 1818, reports of their discoveries were circulating among land-hungry squatters

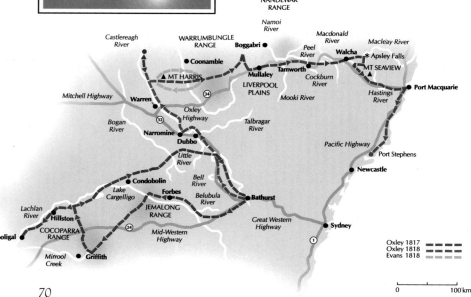

Oxley 1817
Oxley 1818
Evans 1818

0   100 km

THE GREAT ILLUSION OF AN INLAND SEA

The legend of an inland sea plagued Australian explorers for years. In 1798 Sir Joseph Banks wrote: 'It is impossible to conceive that such a body of land, as large as all Europe, does not produce vast rivers, capable of being navigated into the heart of the interior'.

In his book *Voyage to Terra Australis*, Matthew Flinders speculated that Australia 'might be composed of two or more islands' split by a sea channel. Alternatively, if the coastline was continuous, the interior of the continent might be 'principally occupied by a mediterranean sea'.

When John Oxley failed to follow the Macquarie river to that supposed inland sea in 1818, he still could not abandon the illusion. The river, he wrote, 'presented too important a body of water' simply to vanish without emerging into some wonderful 'ultimate termination'. Many would risk their lives chasing the same idea.

On 9 July Oxley decided to return, following the river as far as possible. This led to the discovery of Lake Cargelligo, which now boasts a town and airfield. By 3 August Oxley was satisfied that the course of the Lachlan was sufficiently known. His men built a raft to take across their few remaining provisions, and set off on a direct landward course for home. The result was the discovery of the Bogan river on 13 August, Little river on 16 August, and Bell river on 18 August.

In nineteen arduous weeks Oxley's party had covered more than eleven hundred kilometres, recording the nature of much of western New South Wales.

Invaluable new discoveries

Governor Macquarie sent a report to Earl Bathurst on 5 September 1817 telling of his 'great disappointment and mortification' at the failure of his hopes for the Lachlan. But he felt that greater prospects lay ahead in the upper reaches of the Macquarie river. That was to be the scene of the next adventure for Oxley and Evans.

Oxley left Bathurst on 28 May 1818, some of his party travelling by land and the remainder floating north and north-west along the river. On 11 June they passed the site of today's Dubbo, and discovered the junction of the Erskine

The expedition's view *of the Warrumbungle Range, then called Arbuthnot's Range, appears in Oxley's journals published in 1820*

river (since renamed the Talbragar).

Soon they reached what is now Narromine. Oxley was perturbed to see that the once-noble river now tended to become 'contracted into narrow rocky channels'. Approaching today's town of Warren, it became obvious that the river when flooded must overflow its low banks and inundate the surrounding countryside.

About forty-eight kilometres past Warren, on 27 June 1818 Oxley spied a hill near the river bank, naming it Mount Harris. Climbing it, to the east he saw suddenly rising from the plain 'a most stupendous range of mountains, lifting their blue heads above the horizon'. Oxley named it Arbuthnot's Range, but today it is called Warrumbungle.

Oxley pressed on northwards along the increasingly marshy and diffused Macquarie river, still 'sanguine in my expectations of soon entering the long sought for Australian sea'. Finally, on 30 June, he had to admit defeat. 'We perceived that the waters which had overflowed the banks were spreading over the plains,' Oxley wrote. 'The safety of the whole party was now at stake.'

An immediate retreat was ordered for most of the group. Oxley himself continued in one boat with four volunteer oarsmen, expressing his 'ardent desire' to 'throw some light on the obscurity in which the interior of this vast country is still involved'. But on 3 July, about ninety-six kilometres from Mount Harris, the explorers found that all land-

Beyond the Warrumbungles *lie the Liverpool Plains, a sight that cheered the weary party after country that 'baffled all description'*

marks and trees had vanished. They were lost in an endless swamp, surrounded by rustling high reeds. It took them four days to row back against the current to rejoin the main party.

Oxley decided that the most valuable thing he could do with his remaining time and provisions was to head east across the unknown country of the Warrumbungles towards the coast.

His decision led to invaluable new discoveries. On 12 July 1818 his second-in-command George Evans discovered the Castlereagh river just south of today's Coonamble, naming it after Lord Castlereagh, Secretary for the Colonies. To Oxley it was further proof of an inland sea: 'The circumstances of the river and other large bodies of water crossed by Mr Evans all flowing to the north, seems to bear out the conclusion that these waters have but one common reservoir'.

Following a different route to the Warrumbungles, the party 'struggled for nine miles through a line of country that baffles all description: we were literally up to the middle in water the whole way'.

For ten rain-soaked days, Oxley headed north-east towards today's Narrabri and the Nandewar Range. The men found themselves trapped in thick forests of ironbark trees, with dangerous quicksands in every direction. On 20 August, exhausted by the effort of getting through the bogs, they turned back to today's Rocky Glen and their former easterly route.

Apsley Falls, *east of Walcha, in the Apsley Gorge National Park. They are as spectacular today, left, as when George Evans sketched them, below. This illustration also comes from Oxley's Journals describing his two expeditions into the interior of New South Wales*

On 26 August 1818, past today's Mullaley, the explorers climbed a low rise and saw to their delight 'hills, dales, and plains of the richest description'. Here at last was some recompense for their efforts. They had discovered the fertile Liverpool Plains, naming them after Lord Liverpool, British Prime Minister. The following day, in high spirits, they crossed the Mooki river, which further north becomes the Namoi.

By 2 September the party reached the present site of Tamworth on the Peel river, naming it after another Prime Minister, Robert Peel. 'It would be impossible to find a finer or more luxuriant country than it waters', wrote Oxley. 'No place in the world can afford more advantages to the industrious settler'.

A few days later the Cockburn and Macdonald rivers were discovered as the explorers pressed eastwards.

Their first glimpse of the ocean
Now they came to more difficult country. On 11 September 1818, their triumphal march was halted by the deep canyons of the Apsley river near today's Walcha. After four days of searching for a crossing place, Oxley discovered the Apsley Falls, named after another Colonial Secretary of State. 'We were lost in astonishment at the site of this wonderful natural sublimity, which is perhaps scarcely to be

exceeded in any part of the Eastern World', wrote Oxley. His men were able to cross in calmer water upstream.

Struggling on through precipitous ranges, the party reached Mount Seaview on 23 September and won their first glimpse of the ocean. 'Bilboa's ecstasy at the first sight of the South Sea could not have been greater than ours', wrote a relieved Oxley.

The country ahead of them was broken into 'considerable forest hills and pleasing valleys'. They sighted a stream which they called the Hastings river after the Governor-General of India. Marching cheerfully through great stands of cedar, the travellers met two Aboriginals and exchanged a tomahawk for a bark canoe to ferry across their provisions.

On 8 October 1818, with 'great joy and satisfaction', the weary men arrived at a fine harbour and river estuary which they named Port Macquarie. Their discoveries would, thought Oxley, 'throw open the whole interior to the Macquarie river, for the benefit of British settlers'.

From the beach the party followed the coast southwards, building boats to cross large waterways, and arriving safely at Newcastle on 5 November 1818 with many vital discoveries to report. Even if the far inland remained an enigma, the north coast of New South Wales was ripe for settlement.□

New Town, Hobart, by Louis de Sainson, 1827-28

CHAPTER THREE

Daring expeditions claim an entire continent

Bounty mutineers unwittingly launch Bligh on one of the outstanding feats of naval history

WILLIAM BLIGH
GOVERNOR OF NEW SOUTH WALES
1806-1809

Forty-one days adrift on unknown seas

While the Napoleonic wars tore Europe to pieces, and men threw themselves against the forbidding mountain barriers around Sydney, other explorers set out in tiny ships to determine the destiny of the Australian continent.

Norfolk Island, a thirty-five hundred hectare blob lying in the Tasman Sea about fifteen hundred kilometres north-east of Sydney, had been discovered by James Cook in 1774. A small party under Lieutenant Philip Gidley King occupied the island only a few weeks after the first British settlement of Sydney in 1788. The infant penal colony optimistically planned to exploit Norfolk's tall pine trees for ships' masts and to grow flax for sailcloth.

On the way back to Sydney in HMS *Supply*, Lieutenant Henry Lidgbird Ball discovered Lord Howe Island, naming it after the first lord of the Admiralty. 'It abounds in turtles,' Ball reported. When he returned to harvest the lumbering reptiles to feed the starving residents of Sydney, he found that the turtles had disappeared. Food had to be sought from Java instead.

Meanwhile, another Royal Navy officer, thirty-five-year-old William Bligh, was doggedly charting part of the north-east coast of Australia from an open launch crammed with dying men.

The courageous, irascible officer, 'Bully' Bligh, had been thrown off his own frigate near Tahiti on 28 April 1789. Most of his men, led by twenty-six-year-old acting-lieutenant Fletcher Christian, seized HMS *Bounty* so they could sail back to the delights of Tahiti. Later, some of the mutineers took their native wives to Pitcairn Island, remaining undiscovered for nearly twenty years.

Bligh and eighteen men who refused to join the mutineers were allowed to collect a small set of sails, cordage, 68 kilos of bread, a 127-litre cask of water, rum and wine, a quadrant and compass.

Cast adrift in their small boat, all agreed to live on 'one 25th of a pound of bread for breakfast, and the same quantity for dinner', with a cupful of water daily.

They made for nearby Tofoa but the inhabitants were hostile and one man was killed in the fight to escape.

Commander Bligh decided to rely on his memory of Cook's maps, and steered towards the nearest known settlement on Timor, nearly six thousand kilometres away. A month later, when their food was nearly gone, the starving men managed to catch by hand a couple of birds known as noddies and boobies. 'The body, with the entrails, beak, and feet,' wrote Bligh, 'I divided into 18 shares …we made a good supper.'

Bligh turns disaster into achievement
Next day, to their delight, they saw trees and driftwood floating in the water, and realised they were near the Great Barrier Reef. Steering north-west, and continuing his careful charting under appalling conditions, Bligh discovered a break in the surf-swept reef on 29 May.

Thankfully the castaways sailed into

Bligh's extraordinary navigational skills demonstrated on an epic voyage

Relying on memory and training, William Bligh steered an open boat six thousand kilometres through a maze of reefs and islands, charting part of the north Australian coast as he went

THE DOOMED VOYAGE OF HMS *PANDORA*

***An engraving of the wreck** based on a sketch by* Bounty *mutineer Peter Heywood*

When William Bligh returned to England, the Admiralty lost no time in sending HMS *Pandora* under Captain Edward Edwards to find and arrest the *Bounty's* reckless mutineers.

Edwards discovered fourteen sailors still lingering on Tahiti. He confined them in a tiny wooden cell on the quarterdeck, jocularly referred to as 'Pandora's Box'. The prisoners were treated with extreme brutality by the crew.

But on 28 August 1791, when trying to find a passage home through uncharted sections of Torres Strait, the *Pandora* struck a reef and sank several hours later.

The surviving crew and prisoners now had to duplicate Bligh's feat of reaching Timor in small boats. They found watering places on the Australian coast, were attacked by Aboriginals, and discovered new channels and anchorages.

The men protected themselves from the blazing sun with wet shirts, but, recorded Captain Edwards laconically, 'those who drank their own urine died in the sequel of the voyage.'

Three of the *Bounty* mutineers who reached England alive after all these adventures were hanged. William Bligh was appointed Governor of New South Wales.

---

he calm water beyond. They threw hemselves ashore on Restoration Island, gathered fresh oysters for dinner, drank heir fill from a stream, and ate wild erries. The result was racking diarrhoea, most of us having had no evacuation by tool since we left the ship'. But soon, wrote Bligh, 'all our past hardships eemed to be forgotten.'

The following day, this determined commander ordered more oysters and lams to be gathered, and water vessels lled. With new vigour the crew sailed heir boat further up the Queensland oast, catching dog-fish and gathering water from rock pools on islands as they assed. On 31 May Bligh named Sunday sland. Here they stopped at night to atch more noddies. When one man lumsily disturbed the nesting birds, wrote Bligh, 'I was so much rovoked...that I gave this offender a ood beating.'

On 2 June 1789, the voyagers arrived at Turtle Island, named by Bligh after the large number of turtle shells and bones lying around. Next day they sailed past the Bay of Islands after clearing the tip of Cape York Peninsula, and turned into the perilous Prince of Wales Channel for the long run to Timor.

This extraordinary voyage now seemed to Bligh almost like a pleasure cruise. 'For my own part, incredible as it may appear,' he wrote, 'I felt neither extreme hunger nor thirst. My allowance contented me, knowing that I could have no more.'

On 5 June Bligh caught another booby in his hand. 'The blood was divided among three of the men who were weakest,' he wrote. Two days later, when two of the men 'appeared to be giving way very fast,' he carefully fed them a teaspoon or two of wine. Next day a seaman caught a dolphin, and all gorged themselves on its raw flesh.

Survival and court martial
By 10 June many of the men exhibited 'extreme weakness, swelled legs, hollow and ghastly countenances' and other signs of 'approaching dissolution.' But two days later, 'with an excess of joy,' the castaways sighted Timor. 'Our bodies were nothing but skin and bones,' wrote

Bligh, 'our limbs were full of sores, and we were clothed in rags.' Some of the men subsequently died, but most survived to serve again in the Royal Navy.

To everyone, including the Dutch Governor, William Van Elte, it seemed 'scarce credible' that in an open boat, with practically no facilities, the seamen had reached Timor in forty-one days from their casting-off spot at Tofoa. Not only that, Bligh had carefully kept a log of observations, calculated distances travelled and charted much of Queensland's north-eastern coastline. He did not pretend to have supplanted Cook's charts, but wrote humbly that perhaps 'more advantage may be derived from the possession of both our charts, than from either of them singly.'

On his return to London, Bligh was honourably acquitted by a court martial. He was promoted to captain, and sent in HMS *Providence* in a fresh attempt to transplant bread-fruit from Tahiti to the West Indies.

En route, Bligh landed in February 1792 at Adventure Bay and Storm Bay in Van Diemen's Land, discovering the strait now known as D'Entrecasteaux Channel. On shore he placed Mount Wellington on the map, described an echidna, and roasted and ate a wombat ('found of a delicate flavour'). □

***Adventure Bay, Tasmania,** painted by George Tobin, an officer on the* Providence. *Many expeditions called at the bay before Bass Strait was discovered in 1798. Timor's governor and residents,* right, *give a warm welcome to a triumphant Bligh and his sailors*

Convicts on the run discover Newcastle and Port Stephens

In 1791, while Captain Edwards in HMS Pandora was tracking down the Bounty mutineers, convict fishermen in Sydney planned a daring escape by small boat to Asia. Prime movers in the plot were William Bryant, a transported smuggler, and his Cornish wife Mary, sentenced to seven years for stealing a cloak. They had two children: a three-year-old girl and a baby boy, and claimed they fled from Sydney to avoid starvation.

The couple enlisted seven more convicts. From a visiting Dutch ship they obtained a rough chart of the known coastline, a compass, quadrant, bags of flour and rice, a kilo or two of salt pork, soap, and thirty-six litres of water. On 28 March 1791, the group slipped through the Heads in their six-oared fishing ketch.

James Martin, one of the escapees, later deposed: *After two days sail reach a little creek about 2 Degrees to they northward of Port Jackson — there found a quantity of fine burning coal — there remained 2 nights and one day and found a varse quantity of cabage tree which we cut down and procured they cabage.* The party was at today's Newcastle, industrial centre and outlet of the Hunter river.

Martin's deposition continued: *After 2 days sail we made a very fine harbour, seeming to run up they country for many miles and quite commodious for they anchorage of shipping — Here we found aplenty of fresh water.* This was Port Stephens, a large estuary sighted but not entered by Captain Cook twenty years earlier.

Many death-defying adventures followed as the reckless escapees worked their long, slow way up the Queensland coast. On one occasion their lives were saved when they found 'a great Quantity of very fine Large Turtles' which provided 'a Noble Meal'.

Caulking their leaky boat with soap, they passed safely through the Bay of Islands. Chased from the shores of the Gulf of Carpentaria by angry natives, they were forced to follow Bligh's route to Timor. Here they passed as survivors of a wrecked brig and were warmly welcomed by the Dutch Governor.

Then Captain Edwards and survivors from the wrecked HMS *Pandora* scrambled ashore at Timor. The real story soon came out. William Bryant, his two small children and three other convicts died in captivity on the passage back to England. The remainder were imprisoned for a time, then freed after applications by James Boswell, noted civil servant and biographer of Samuel Johnson.

Mary Bryant, who had lost her whole family, retired to her native village in Cornwall on a £10 annual pension paid by Boswell 'as long as she behaved well. Of her amazing adventures in Australia, she scarcely ever spoke again.

For several years the Sydney authorities did little about the discovery of Newcastle and Port Stephens. In 1795 Lieutenant-Governor William Paterson sent surveyor Charles Grimes to examine Port Stephens. Grimes reported extensive mangrove swamps and shoal waters, although he was pleased to find 'oysters growing as far up the rivers as we could go.' Paterson concluded that there was no reason ever to visit the inlet again.

Convicts were again responsible for the next major exploration northwards. On 5 September 1797, a determined gang of Irishmen seized the schooner *Cumberland*, 'our largest and best boat', Governor Hunter complained bitterly.

The forces of vengeance were compelled to follow in two row-boats. One, under twenty-eight-year-old Lieutenant John Shortland, paddled more than sixty-six kilometres northward, past Nobby's Head and into a fine river which Shortland named the Hunter. He brought back specimens from the 'considerable quantity of coal discovered'. This led directly to Australia's first-ever overseas export — a shipment of coal to Bengal in 1799. In later years the combination of coal and steelworks enabled Newcastle to grow into the second-largest city in New South Wales.

Newcastle in 1812 was still a penal settlement and remained so until 1820. Convicts worked as miners, timber-cutters and lime burners

The tiny **Tom Thumb**, almost lost in the swell caused by a stiff southerly, makes a run north for Sydney. Flinders is on the tiller, Bass holds the sheets and Martin is bailing. Queensland artist Hugh Sawrey was born in 1923 and is best known for his paintings of outback scenes

Bass and Flinders challenge the oceans in tiny boats

The Royal Navy thrived on daring young men with a longing for far places and high adventure. One of its eager recruits was George Bass, son of a poor Lincolnshire tenant farmer. Another was Matthew Flinders, son of a surgeon in the same district.
Desire to voyage into the unknown brought these two together in epic achievements of Australian discovery. The same longings, followed too far, led to the total disappearance of Bass and the incarceration of Flinders in a French prison for the best years of his life.

George Bass was a twenty-three-year-old junior naval surgeon in 1794 when he applied for a place in HMS *Reliance*, bound for Sydney. Matthew Flinders was a twenty-year-old master's mate in the same ship. With their common interest in navigation techniques, the two became close friends.

Arriving in Sydney in September 1795, the young men fitted mast and sails into a two and a half metre row-boat they called *Tom Thumb*. On holidays they ventured out from Sydney Harbour into the ocean, south past the bays of Bondi and Coogee, and into Botany Bay and Georges river. These they charted with great accuracy, impelling Governor Hunter to establish a settlement at Bankstown.

Hunter encouraged the adventurers to continue their unpaid work. They were given the use of a slightly larger boat, also christened *Tom Thumb*.

On 24 March 1796, Bass, Flinders and a ship's boy named William Martin, set out with ten days' bread, meat and a few watermelons. They were searching for a river thought to emerge somewhere south of Botany Bay. On the second day out, venturing too close to shore, *Tom Thumb* was lifted by a huge wave and smashed onto the sand. Guns, food, instruments and clothing were soaked.

With difficulty the three re-launched the boat, sailed on and spent the following night tossing at sea south-east of today's Port Kembla. Next morning two Aboriginals on shore showed them a small stream running out of Lake Illawarra. This was a useful place to replenish their water and dry out their belongings, but was scarcely the large river they were hoping to find. Their hopes as well as their luck were beginning to run out.

More than half their provisions were now gone. On the fifth day they turned back from what is now called Bass Point, just below Shellharbour, and began to row hard for Sydney. During the night a southerly gale sprang up. They were forced to run before the wind in total darkness, skirting a dangerous coast. For many hours Bass kept a firm grip on the sail sheet, drawing it tighter when he sensed a heavier than usual following sea. Flinders steered as best he could with a trailing oar: 'A moment's inattention would have sent us to the bottom,' he later wrote. The boy William Martin bailed for his life.

At storm-wracked dawn they came to an inlet, dashing in behind its point to shelter from the gale. Where they anchored was promptly named Providential Cove. Today it is a popular picnic spot in the Royal National Park known as Wattamolla. Next morning they discovered the entrance to the great waterway of Port Hacking. By 2 April 1796, they were able to sail their battered craft to the safety of Sydney and report their few discoveries.

Routine naval tasks occupied Bass and Flinders for several months. Then the arrival of survivors of the *Sydney Cove* made men wonder if, after all, an undiscovered strait might exist between the mainland and Tasmania.

On sighting Point Hicks, James Cook had written: 'I cannot determine whether

MATTHEW FLINDERS
MINIATURE BY WETHERILL

GEORGE BASS
BY AD COLQUHOUN

it joins Van Diemen's Land or not.' Captain Furneaux had pronounced bluffly, 'There is no strait.' John Hunter in the *Sirius* wrote: 'There is in that space either a deep gulf or a strait.' But no one knew for sure. Now the young surgeon George Bass would find out.

Bass persuaded Hunter to allow him the use of a whaleboat and six naval volunteers to investigate the south-eastern coastline. The boat, built in Sydney of banksia wood, lined with cedar, was eight and a half metres long, with a curved keel and pointed fore and aft. Such boats had been found suitable for many kinds of difficult work.

He discovers Western Port

Carrying six weeks' provisions, the party left Sydney on 3 December 1797. At first they had to shelter from a gale in their former haven at Port Hacking. By 7 December they arrived at an inlet and river which Bass named the Shoalhaven. He praised the countryside as 'rich and good.'

On 19 December Bass discovered Twofold Bay, soon to become an important whaling port. As the wind turned north-easterly, he did not stay to examine it closely, but pushed on rapidly round Cape Howe. Now the whaleboat was entering regions never before sighted by British seamen.

By 2 January 1798, Bass and his men were skimming along the Ninety Mile Beach. Ahead they could see the 'high, hummocky' hills of Wilson's Promon-

Wattamolla, where Flinders, Bass and the boy Martin took shelter in March 1796. Today, the bay is a popular refuge from Sydney's bustle

tory, named after a London merchant. Just as complete triumph was in sight, the weather broke. Foul winds forced Bass to veer south towards Van Diemen's Land. The planks started grinding, and 'water was observed to gush in through the boat's side pretty plentifully.' Desperately tacking back towards the mainland, Bass succeeded in reaching the Promontory's western side. 'We had a bad night of it,' he recorded laconically.

Continuing north-west along the Victorian coast on the morning of 5 January 1798, Bass made a discovery which was to change history. 'Seeing a

large break in the land,' he wrote, 'we stood in for it and found a strong outset of tide.' This was Western Port, described by Bass as 'a very extensive harbour', and named 'from its relative situation to every other known harbour on the coast.' Western Port later became the base for attempts to settle the southern coast.

After twelve days' exploration of the area, with provisions running low, Bass 'very reluctantly' set off on the return voyage. During a further week of rough weather, the men succeeded in landing on Wilson's Promontory. At a beach still known as Sealers' Cove, they killed seals and dried their flesh to chew while rowing. Meanwhile Bass explored the peninsula, viewing from its rocky heights much of Gippsland, which would not be settled for another forty years.

Six fatiguing weeks of sailing and rowing were necessary to take the explorers home. On Sunday 25 February 1798, with a final great effort, the men 'got upon the oars and rowed up to Port Jackson' by ten o'clock at night.

In his final report to the Governor, Bass reaffirmed his belief in the existence of a southern strait, even though he had not penetrated its full extent. Bass wrote: *Whenever it shall be decided that the opening between this and Van Diemen's Land is a strait, this rapidity of tide, and that long S.W. swell that seems to be continually rolling in upon the coast to the westward, will then be accounted for.*

All that was needed now to prove Bass's theory beyond doubt was a circum-

---

GEORGE VANCOUVER MISSES A GREAT OPPORTUNITY

Simple bad luck prevented Captain George Vancouver, RN, from discovering the ocean strait between the Australian mainland and Tasmania several years before George Bass.

In 1791 the Admiralty sent the thirty-four-year-old captain, a seasoned veteran of Cook's and other voyages, to explore the southern coastline of Australia. 'In the present age,' thought Vancouver, 'it appears a real blot in geography.'

Sailing in the new sloop HMS *Discovery*, Vancouver made landfall at Cape Leeuwin on the south-western tip of Western Australia on 26 September 1791. Continuing to travel south-east he named Chatham Island and Cape Howe.

Two days later Vancouver discovered 'one very excellent port, which I have honoured with the name of King George the Third's Sound.' He thought that from its safety, fertility and availability of oysters, 'it may be worthy some further attention.' Today, as King George Sound, it is the harbour for Albany.

Vancouver examined another four hundred and eighty kilometres of coastline, 'in

which space we saw no other haven or place of security for shipping.' Persistent easterly winds then forced him to tack south-easterly, so that he followed the usual route round Tasmania instead of discovering Bass Strait and Victoria.

An Italian map of 1798 shows an uncertainty about Australia's south-east corner that Bass and Flinders would soon dispel

George Vancouver charted much of the coast north of San Francisco and established that there was no link between the Pacific and Hudson Bay. Canada's city and island of Vancouver are named after him

navigation of Van Diemen's Land. Governor Hunter was still a little cautious. On 3 September 1798, he reported to London that there was 'probably a safe and navigable passage'.

As soon as Flinders returned from a mission to Norfolk Island, the Governor commissioned him to take a leaky twenty-five-tonne sloop *Norfolk*, built of Norfolk Island pine, on the new voyage of discovery. With Bass as his second-in-command, an eight-man crew and provisions for three months, Flinders sailed through Sydney Heads at dawn on 7 October 1798. Two days later he closely examined Twofold Bay, stressing its importance as the only known place of shelter for large vessels on the eastern coastline south of Jervis Bay. Whalers, he correctly predicted, 'might find some right fish here.'

By 17 October the *Norfolk* reached the Kent Islands, and by 18 October the Furneaux group. Gales prevented Flinders from sailing west: he used these days to chart islands off the north-east tip of Van Diemen's Land. One of them is now called Flinders Island.

By the end of October the weather abated. Flinders was now able to begin a close examination of Van Diemen's Land itself. On 3 November 1798, he saw the first cliffs rising from its low shoreline.

Mount Rugby near Port Davey *on Tasmania's west coast impressed Flinders with its grandeur, though he thought it inhospitable. Other places he passed seemed to be well suited for settlement and governors encouraged settlers to follow him*

Bass and Flinders prove that Tasmania is an island

Tasmania's relationship to the mainland had long been a puzzle. Bass's voyage to Wilson's Promontory in 1798 convinced him that there was a strait. In 1798-99, he and Flinders circumnavigated the island in the Norfolk and their reports prompted action by the Admiralty

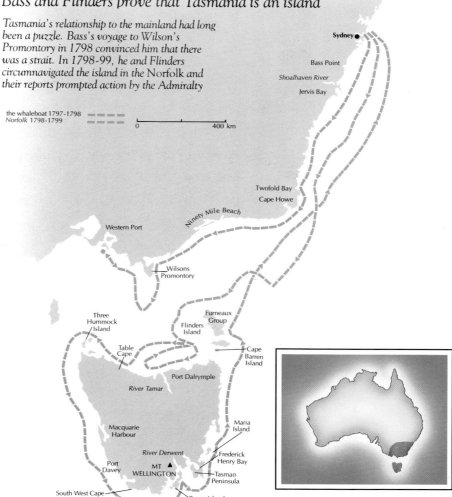

Flinders's sextant. *After serving the master navigator well, like him it had to survive shipwreck and gaol on the way home to England*

The *Norfolk* entered 'a large basin or bay', later named Port Dalrymple after Admiralty hydrographer Alexander Dalrymple. Four black swans caught in the estuary that evening 'afforded us much joy,' wrote Flinders. 'As one swan will serve three or four people for a day, they constituted the greatest part of our food.'

Picking their way through frequent shoals, the men sailed up the estuary to discover a river which 'opened out to a large piece of water like a sea'. This was later named the Tamar river, after the English stream dividing Cornwall and Devon. Transferring to a small boat, Flinders and Bass penetrated to within a few kilometres of today's Launceston.

Only too soon it was time to resume their coastal run. But from 20 November new westerly gales forced them to run back to the Furneaux Islands. Not until 3 December did the wind change to north-easterly. This enabled *Norfolk* to run steadily westwards along the northern coast of Van Diemen's Land. Near today's town of Wynyard, Flinders named Table Cape. By 9 December he arrived at Three Hummock Island, off the extreme north-western tip of the main island.

At last able to turn due south into the open ocean, Flinders wrote that all indications 'did now completely satisfy us that a very wide strait did really exist between Van Diemen's Land and New South Wales, and also now that we had certainly passed it.'

The run down the dangerous west coast took only four days. Stiff westerlies forced Flinders to keep *Norfolk* a safe distance from the rocky shores, but he was still able to carry out a running survey. Hazy weather prevented Flinders from sighting the entrance to today's Macquarie Harbour as he ran past it on 11 December. The following day he observed two round hills later named Point St Vincent, with 'the appearance of a considerable opening', which became Port Davey. But the mountains round it seemed both stupendous and barren. 'The eye ranges over these peaks,' wrote Flinders, 'with astonishment and horror.'

By 13 December 1798, the *Norfolk* had weathered South West Cape and was able to confirm bearings well charted by navigators from Tasman onwards. Westerly squalls drove the little vessel past Adventure Bay at Bruny Island and into Frederick Henry Bay.

On 24 December Flinders was able to beat back to the Derwent river, anchoring in Risdon Cove. 'Very beautiful country, with a rich luxuriant soil,' he noted. On Christmas Day, Bass climbed Mount Wellington, overlooking today's Hobart. He found the mountain 'covered with large timber, to its very top.'

Setting sail again on New Year's Day 1799, the explorers rapidly rounded the Tasman Peninsula and sailed past Oyster Bay at Maria Island. On 7 January they were back at Cape Barren Island, completing their circumnavigation. Five days later they laid the sloop alongside HMS *Reliance* in Sydney Harbour, reporting happily to John Hunter, who promptly named the new shipping lane 'Bass's Strait'.

The results for Australia were important. As Flinders pointed out in his report the passage from Britain to Sydney would be shortened by at least a week: 'the expense — the wear and tear of a ship — for even one week is an object to most owners, more especially if freighted with convicts'.

Even more significant consequences followed. When Flinders's charts were published in London in June 1800, naval strategists realised that vast possibilities lay in the unexplored southern land masses of Australia. Was revolutionary France to be allowed a foothold in this new world? On the whole, the Lords of the Admiralty thought not. □

FLINDERS FILLS IN GAPS IN THE EAST COAST

After returning from Van Diemen's Land, Matthew Flinders spent several weeks filling in gaps in Cook's charts, where the great discoverer had run at night along the northern New South Wales and southern Queensland coasts.

On 11 July 1799, with the *Norfolk* leaking badly from a sprung plank, Flinders put into a likely opening and discovered Shoal Bay, where the Clarence river enters the sea. On shore he found native huts of 'superior' construction, with framework of woven vines and weatherproof bark covering.

Further north, Flinders examined most of Moreton Bay and charted its islands. 'Their appearance very pretty,' he noted. He missed the mouth of the Brisbane river, but to the north found Pumicestone Channel, which separates Bribie Island from the mainland.

Here three of his seamen made a grotesque attempt to entertain Aboriginals by dancing Scottish reels. Without music, wrote Flinders, their performance was viewed by the natives 'without much amusement or curiosity.'

On 3 August Flinders passed Fraser Island with its unique mineral sandhills. He sailed round it and charted Hervey Bay. All the time, he was using the tallest of the remarkable Glass House Mountains as a check on his bearings. On his return to Sydney, Flinders presented charts which served mariners for many years.

Queensland's Glass House Mountains *seen from Redcliffe Peninsula. Cook and*

Flinders used these striking mountains to check bearings when charting Moreton Bay

With just one decrepit ship at his command, Flinders sails round Australia

While First Consul Napoleon Bonaparte was confirming himself as virtual dictator of France, Matthew Flinders was sailing back to England to publish his first work, Observations on the Coasts of Van Diemen's Land.
Although preoccupied with war preparations, the Admiralty agreed with Sir Joseph Banks that the brilliant young navigator, worthy successor to James Cook, should attempt to chart the entire thirty-three thousand kilometre coastline of Australia. Circumnavigation would help to place the continent firmly in British hands. It would not only solve many geographical mysteries, it would also stimulate commerce and settlement.

But the best the Admiralty could provide for this immense task was a decaying three hundred and thirty-four tonne sloop, HMS *Xenophon*. The vessel was not good enough to fight the French, but was allowed to sail to the other side of the world to chart dangerous waters washing unknown coasts. Her rotting timbers concealed by copper sheathing, she was handed over to the eager explorer and renamed HMS *Investigator*.

Promoted to commander, Flinders set sail in July 1801, accompanied by artists, naturalists and astronomers. His first task was to explore the almost unknown south coast of Australia, which was 'yet to be examined for harbours', and might even yield entry to an unknown sea.

The *Investigator* made landfall at Cape Leeuwin on 6 December 1801. From there on, perfecting the techniques he had learned in the *Norfolk*, Flinders kept his ship so close to the shore that all entrances and breaking or rippling water could be recognised. At night, or when the weather was too rough, *Investigator* hauled away from the coast, then sailed close in again to the same point. This tedious method was the only way in which accurate charts could be made from the decks of sailing ships.

The Bight's impenetrable cliffs

At twilight on 8 December, Flinders used George Vancouver's chart of 1791 to guide the *Investigator* safely into King George's Sound. For three weeks his men explored the area thoroughly, finding wood, water, oysters and seals which could be killed for their oil.

The naturalists 'ranged the country in all directions'. The local Aboriginals seemed friendly enough. To entertain them, marines paraded on shore. 'When they saw these beautiful red-and-white men, with their bright muskets, drawn up in a line,' wrote Flinders, 'they absolutely screamed with delight.'

By 9 January 1802, the *Investigator*

reached the Recherche Archipelago, discovered by the Dutch but named by French captain Bruni d'Entrecasteaux in 1792. This extensive group of small islands, now a permanent wildlife sanctuary, stretches about one hundred and ninety kilometres east from Esperance.

Off one island the seamen caught a huge shark, measuring some two hundred and fifty centimetres round its middle. When its stomach was opened for inspection, its stench 'became intolerable,' wrote Flinders. Inside was 'a tolerably large seal, bitten in two.'

The untouched country of the main-

The blank *that existed on Australian maps when Flinders undertook his voyage in the* Investigator. *He hoped to find an opening to the interior from the southern coast*

land, covered with small shrubs, 'yielded a delightful harvest to the botanists', but it seemed useless for agriculture.

On 26 January Flinders crossed the 129th degree of longitude which today marks the border of Western Australia and South Australia. Now in uncharted shallows, he was stunned to discover hundreds of kilometres of huge limestone

Flinders was accompanied *by those he called 'the scientific gentlemen' – botanists and naturalists. It was as well that natural history*

painter Ferdinand Bauer recorded these specimens. The originals were ruined when the ship taking them back to England ran aground

back alive for the naturalists to examine.

Late the same afternoon Thistle took seven men in the ship's cutter to search the mainland for fresh water. By nightfall they had not returned. Next day searchers found the boat stove in and floating upside down. Apparently it had been dashed against the rocks, and all men aboard — most of them non-swimmers — drowned. Flinders, much saddened by this event, named the southern extremity of the mainland Cape Catastrophe but today it is known as West Point.

After vainly searching for survivors for several days, on 24 February 1802 several junior officers discovered Port Lincoln, named by Flinders 'in honour of my native province'. Some settlers later thought it should become the capital of South Australia, but shortage of fresh water limited its possibilities. Even the *Investigator*'s men had to sink wells to find supplies of discoloured water. Ten days were spent obtaining sixty tonnes of water to fill the ship's casks.

Flinders fails to find a waterway

Continuing towards the head of Spencer Gulf, on 6 March 1802 the explorers passed the Sir Joseph Banks Group of islands. Three days later they arrived at today's Port Whyalla. Rounding Point Lowly, they entered increasingly difficult shoal waters and mangrove swamps.

Flinders was now losing hope of discovering a great waterway penetrating the

---

cliffs thrust from the sea-bed by ancient convulsions, and reaching forty to ninety metres above today's sea level.

These barren cliffs form the southern rampart of the Nullarbor Plain, but Flinders wondered wistfully if they 'may even be a narrow barrier between an interior and exterior sea.' He continued to search for just a single break in that desolate cliff line through which he might enter and discover the truth about the mysterious country behind.

A total blank on the maps

On 28 January Flinders anchored in Fowlers Bay, 'a well sheltered cove affording wood and water,' naming it after his first lieutenant Robert Fowler. Fowlers Bay was to become a whaling centre and a supply depot for Edward John Eyre's exploration of the Nullarbor many years later.

Flinders spent several days charting islands in the Nuyts Archipelago and the mainland bays where today's towns of Ceduna and Smoky Bay stand.

On 9 February 1802, the *Investigator* left Streaky Bay to follow a part of the southern coast that was a total blank on any known map. Flinders named Cape Radstock after Admiral Lord Radstock, then penetrated by ship's boat through a narrow entrance into Venus Bay.

Four days later Flinders encountered a new cluster of offshore islands which he named the Investigator Group. The largest, Flinders Island, alone gave good anchorage. There Flinders shot five small kangaroos, 'not bigger than a cat', for fresh meat and zoological study.

On 20 February Flinders observed the opening of a large gulf, over six kilometres wide. The first steady ebb tide

seen on that coast rippled past the ship. Every man's heart leaped: 'Large rivers, deep inlets, inland seas, and passages into the Gulph of Carpentaria, were terms frequently used in our conversations of this evening,' wrote Flinders. They had discovered Spencer Gulf, named after the president of the Board of Admiralty. Ships now sail up the gulf to Whyalla.

Early next morning Flinders landed on an island at the entrance, naming it Thistle Island after John Thistle, ship's master, who had accompanied Bass and Flinders on their Tasmanian voyage. They found an unusual large speckled snake: Thistle carefully sewed up its mouth with twine and took the reptile

---

DISCOVERING NEW WORLDS FOR SCIENCE

A remarkably strong team of scientists and artists accompanied Matthew Flinders on his pioneer circumnavigation of Australia in 1801-2.

Leader of the botanical group was twenty-eight-year-old Robert Brown, a surgeon's mate whose hobby was natural history. Brown's collection in Australia of hundreds of plant specimens previously unknown to science soon made him world-famous.

His botanical artist on the *Investigator* was a forty-year-old Austrian, Ferdinand Lukas Bauer. In an age when photography was unknown, Bauer's exquisitely detailed drawings revealed Australian plants to the scientific world.

The *Investigator*'s landscape artist, William Westall, was only twenty years old. Much of his best work was lost when the *Porpoise* was wrecked on the return voyage to England.

Also on the pioneer *Investigator* voyage

WILLIAM WESTALL
PAINTED BY HIS SON ROBERT

were the astronomer John Crosley, mineralogist John Allen, and Kew gardener Peter Good. The cabin boy, fifteen-year-old John Franklin, later became a famous Arctic explorer and governor of Tasmania.

continent from the south. Even in small boats it was impossible to proceed further than where Port Augusta is today. The chagrined commander wrote: 'It seemed remarkable, and was very mortifying, to find the water at the head of the gulph as salt nearly as at the ship', in other words, no large freshwater river.

Sailing out of this disappointing gulf, on 22 March 1802 Flinders discovered a large island, about one hundred and forty-four kilometres long and forty-eight kilometres wide, on which kangaroos abounded. Flinders himself killed ten with 'a double-barrelled gun, fitted with a bayonet', and his companions killed many more with small-shot and sticks. Officers and men gorged themselves on kangaroo steaks 'by day and by night', while the heads, forequarters and tails were boiled down into soup.

His meeting with French explorers

After two days the men returned through Investigator Strait to exploration of the mainland. Flinders soon realised they had rounded a peninsula, which he named Yorke Peninsula after Charles Philip Yorke, First Lord of the Admiralty. The new gulf was named St Vincent. Naming the 726-metre Mount Lofty and using it as his main reference point, Flinders carefully charted the gulf, but missed the Port river on which Port Adelaide is now located.

On 7 April 1802, Flinders sailed round Cape Jervis and through Backstairs Passage into a sheltered bay, today the holiday resort of Victor Harbor. The lookout reported a white rock ahead: to Flinders's astonishment it proved to be a ship flying French colours. 'We cleared

for action, in case of being attacked,' he wrote. But flags of truce were hoisted, and Flinders was able to board Nicolas Baudin's vessel *Le Géographe*, which had been exploring Van Diemen's Land and Bass Strait.

Flinders named the location of this historic meeting Encounter Bay. Later he was surprised and angered to see on French charts that points discovered by British and even Dutch seamen had been given French names.

At the eastern end of Encounter Bay, Flinders noted the low, sandy coast, but failed to see the entrance to Lake Alexandrina and thus to the Murray river.

By 20 April 1802, Flinders had rounded Cape Nelson, near today's Portland, and Lady Julia Percy Island, near Port Fairy, but the weather was so squally that little of that fertile shore could be seen.

Entering Bass Strait, Flinders kept a sharp lookout for King Island, which had been named in January 1801 by John Black, commander of the brig *Harbinger*. Flinders carefully charted its dangers, and landed his naturalists to pick up samples of plant and animal life.

On 26 April the weather was calm enough for the *Investigator* to approach today's Point Lonsdale, at the difficult entrance to Port Phillip Bay. Not knowing that John Murray had discovered Port Phillip only two months earlier in the *Lady Nelson*, Flinders decided to dare the 'strong ripplings like breakers' which formed the notorious Rip guarding the entrance. He had 'every man ready for tacking at a moment's warning'. But the strong tide carried the *Investigator* safely through into an 'extensive harbour'.

'It was almost incredible,' wrote Flinders, 'that such a vast piece of water should not have a larger outlet.' He carried out extensive surveys, particularly from the height of Arthur's Seat, from where Bass's Western Port Bay could be seen. Flinders also explored Corio Bay, landing on a point he named Indented Head, where the colony's first sheep were later to be brought ashore and taken through today's Geelong. Climbing the 335-metre Station Peak (now Flinders Peak) in the You Yangs, he praised the surrounding grassland but failed to discern any of its watercourses.

By 3 May 1802, his provisions were running short. Flinders decided to make a quick run along the known coastline to Sydney, where he arrived without incident on 9 May.

By 22 July 1802, the *Investigator* had been refitted, and 13,600 kilos of biscuit (a mix of flour and water, often called hard tack), 3600 kilos of flour, and 6820 litres of rum taken aboard. Flinders was ready to survey the coast of Queensland and Torres Strait. Only Cook's and Bligh's running surveys of these areas were available to mariners. The British East India Company in particular wanted better charts so that its ships bound for India and China could sail safely to Sydney. And as a bonus, the entrance to an inland sea might be found at last somewhere along the shores of Carpentaria.

Hazards of the Barrier Reef

The *Lady Nelson* with its sliding keels was ordered to accompany Flinders, for it was supposed to be able to sail up any river more than one hundred and eighty centimetres deep.

On 8 August 1802, Flinders discovered an excellent new harbour which he named Port Curtis, after Admiral Sir Roger Curtis, commander-in-chief at the Cape of Good Hope. Today it is the site of Gladstone. Unfortunately, John Murray ran the *Lady Nelson* onto a reef, and its main sliding keel was destroyed.

On 21 August, sailing north of today's Yeppoon, Flinders discovered Port Bowen. He named it after Captain James Bowen, RN, but today it is called Port Clinton. Here Flinders found plenty of fresh water, fish, and pine logs to replenish his supplies, and allowed his scientific gentlemen to go botanising in 'romantic' hills to the north.

A month later, sailing off today's Mackay on 22 September, Flinders was faced with a new difficulty. His younger

Encounter Bay *supported two whaling stations by the time George French Angas painted this scene in 1847. Whalers and sealers were often the first Europeans to inhabit this coast*

brother Samuel had been taken on board the *Investigator* as second lieutenant. Samuel had been so intent on calculating the distances of sun and moon that he had forgotten to wind up the ship's timekeepers. As Matthew Flinders explained: 'To go away for Torres Strait and the Gulph of Carpentaria without good rates, was to cripple the accuracy of all our longitudes.' With great difficulty, the commander averaged previous days' readings and reset the time-keepers by calculation. But from here on his charts were not as reliable.

Throughout October 1802 Flinders threaded his way through the Great Barrier Reef. He found it 'glowing under water with vivid tints of every shade between green, purple, brown, and white; equalling in beauty and excelling in grandeur' the most brilliant flowers. But most of the apparent gaps in the reef were 'choked up with small reefs', where 'the tide runs with extraordinary violence'. For a sailing ship, thought Flinders, 'no situation can be more dangerous.'

Eventually he was able to find one escape route north-east of Townsville through the spectacular but dangerous area. Today it is known as Flinders Passage. However, warned Flinders, if any captain 'do not feel his nerves strong

enough to thread the needle', he would 'strongly recommend' him not to approach the area.

The little *Lady Nelson* lost part of her rear keel and most of her anchors in battling the reef, and now 'sailed so ill', that Flinders sent her back to Sydney.

By early November 1802 Flinders had rounded Cape York and sailed into the Gulf of Carpentaria between Wednesday Island and Prince of Wales Islands.

Following old Dutch charts of the Gulf, he found the shallow Van Diemen Inlet, but warned that 'no navigator would now think of attempting to enter it with a ship.' In fact, all hopes of a waterway from the Gulf to an inland sea must be abandoned.

'The increasing shallowness of the water,' wrote Flinders, 'disappoint the hopes of a strait or passage leading out at some other part of Terra Australis.'

Last days of the *Investigator*
By late November the *Investigator* was leaking so badly — taking in twenty-five centimetres of water an hour even in calm weather — that Flinders felt it essential to careen her at Sweers Island (now an Aboriginal reserve). The master's report was terrifying. Of ten timbers on one side, five were 'entirely rotten'.

The anchor bolts had started. The beam ends were 'universally in a decaying state'. John Aken, master, thought the ship might stay afloat for six months in calm weather, but would founder in any gale or on any shoal.

Flinders was thrown into despair. ' had ever endeavored to follow the land so closely,' he wrote, 'that the washing of the surf upon it should be visible.' But this was the very thing that would invite disaster. With heavy heart, the navigator ordered temporary repairs. He decided to complete the examination of the Gulf, then run westward to safety.

On 3 December the patched-up vessel discovered the Bountiful Islands, so called because the crew killed forty-six massive green turtles, averaging one hundred and thirty-six kilos each, and took the meat on board for the homeward trip. One huge turtle contained nearly two thousand eggs.

Heading westwards, Flinders circumnavigated Groote Eylandt. But on Morgan Island near by, a marine named Thomas Morgan dropped dead of sunstroke; and the master's mate, named Whitewood, was speared after making a friendly approach to Aboriginals.

On 16 February 1803, discovering a large opening west of Gove Peninsula,

Matthew Flinders reveals the true shape of the continent

The voyage of the Investigator *completed the map of the coastline. This knowledge encouraged Britain to claim the whole country and ended all conjecture that a strait from the Gulf of Carpentaria to Spencers Gulf separated the east and west of Australia*

TIMOR

Melville Bay
Wednesday Island
Flinders Passage
Prince of Wales Island
Gove Peninsula
Torres Strait

Morgan Island
Groote Eylandt
Gulf of Carpentaria
Cape York Peninsula

Bountiful Islands

Sweers Island
Van Diemen Inlet

GREAT BARRIER REEF

Townsville

Mackay

Port Clinton
Yeppoon

Gladstone (Port Curtis)

Brisbane

NULLARBOR PLAIN

Fowlers Bay
Ceduna
Port Augusta
Streaky Bay
Spencer Gulf
Nuyts Archipelago
Yorke Peninsula
Whyalla
St Vincent Gulf
Cape Radstock
MT LOFTY
Investigator Group
Esperance
Cape Leeuwin
King George Sound
Port Lincoln
West Point
Adelaide
Victor Harbor
Recherche Archipelago
Investigator Strait
Lake Alexandrina
Cape Jervis
Cape Nelson
Encounter Bay
Geelong
FLINDERS PEAK
Point Lonsdale
Arthurs Seat
Sydney

0   300 km

Investigator December 1801-June 1803
Porpoise 1803

Port Fairy
King Island
Bass Strait

86

Flinders named it Melville Bay after Viscount Melville, Admiralty Lord. 'It is the best harbour we found in the Gulph,' wrote Flinders. 'Four or five sail might swing there in perfect security.'

Two days later the *Investigator* came across part of a large fleet of sixty Malayan proas carrying one thousand men sent by the Rajah of Boni to gather the delicacy known as trepang, bêche-de-mer, or sea cucumber. After drying and smoking, huge quantities were sold to Chinese traders who met the Malayans at Timor. Flinders was surprised to find that the proas had no charts — their sailors steered across open water with the aid of a small compass until they sighted land.

In March 1803 Flinders ran for Timor, taking on supplies — and the germs of a dysenteric disease that disabled most of his officers and crew during the long voyage via western and southern Australia to Sydney. Seven men died on the nightmare trip before the *Investigator* dropped anchor on 9 June 1803. The crew was rushed into hospital where, by the Governor's order, they were given the best food and a half-litre of port wine each per day to help them recover.

Six years in a French prison

The poor old *Investigator* was eventually sent back to England and broken up.

Despite his valuable charts and hundreds of specimens obtained in the north — not to mention his achieving the first

Wreck Reef *by William Westall. He and eighty men from the* Porpoise *and* Cato *sheltered here while Flinders took an open boat and thirteen men over 1000 kilometres to Sydney for help*

known circumnavigation of the continent — Flinders felt he had not fulfilled his original instructions.

In July 1803 he arranged a passage back to England to beg for another ship. A green-house was built on the quarter-deck of HMS *Porpoise* then in Sydney, and all the *Investigator*'s botanical specimens loaded aboard. The proposed route was through Torres Strait, where Flinders would lay down on his charts 'as many more of its dangers as circumstances would admit.'

But on 17 August the *Porpoise* ran aground on Wreck Reef, a coral outcrop about eleven hundred and eighty kilometres north-north-east of Sydney. Flinders navigated her cutter with a few men back to Sydney and led rescue ships to pick up survivors from the reef.

Flinders sailed with his precious charts in the twenty-nine tonne schooner *Cumberland*. This too leaked badly, and on 17 December 1803, Flinders was forced to sail into Mauritius for repairs. He was unaware that war had broken out again between Britain and France.

General De Caen, Governor of Mauritius, took malicious pleasure in accusing Flinders of spying and detained him for more than six dreary and frustrating years. During this time the first volumes of Baudin's expedition to Australia were published, falsely claiming for France many areas that Flinders had first seen and charted. □

THE TRAGIC FATE OF BASS AND FLINDERS

Flinders's *health and hopes were shattered by his enforced stay on French Mauritius*

Australia's great marine explorers, George Bass and Matthew Flinders, ended their brief lives tragically.

George Bass decided to leave the Navy and make his fortune as a South Pacific trader. On 5 February 1803, he sailed his brig *Venus* out of Sydney and was never heard of again.

Matthew Flinders was thirty-six when he was released from French captivity, but looked twice his age. From 1810 to 1814, he prepared his great work *A Voyage to Terra Australis* for publication.

On 18 July 1814, the first copy was rushed to his tiny house in London and placed in his hands. But the explorer was already unconscious and died next day, not knowing that many of his maps would guide Australian shipping through the nation's period of greatest development.

Sliding keels are invented and the Victorian coast yields its secrets

While fighting the American War of Independence, His Grace the Duke of Northumberland remarked one day to Captain John Schanck, RN, that 'if cutters were built much flatter', with deeper keels, they would sail faster and closer to the wind, thus confounding Yankee seamen.

Schanck agreed. He suggested that 'if this deep keel was made moveable, and screwed upwards into a trunk or well, formed within the vessel', such a boat could enter very shallow waters for close exploration. In 1774 Schanck built the first model in Boston, following it with others in England commissioned by the Royal Navy.

The sixty-tonne *Lady Nelson*, constructed in 1799 especially for Australian exploration, showed further improvements. It had three separate sliding centreboards, enabling her to cope with many different conditions in unknown waters. Lieutenant James Grant, a twenty-eight-year-old Scot who assisted Schanck's experiments, was given command.

A western approach to Bass Strait

With fifteen men and provisions for nine months, the *Lady Nelson* left England in March 1800. Delayed at the Cape of Good Hope, Grant received there a copy of Matthew Flinders's first chart of Bass Strait, with instructions to explore it again from west to east. Grant was told that he should enter any large rivers, and 'take possession in His Majesty's name, with the consent of the inhabitants, if any.' If uninhabited, he should erect 'some proper description as first discoverer and possessor.' He should also plant fruit trees and vegetables, and collect samples of useful 'plants, shrubs, and grasses.' Obviously, permanent settlement was intended.

Grant reached the unexplored section of the coastline on 3 December 1800, naming Cape Northumberland after the Duke who was British commander-in-chief. Beyond it Grant could see Mount Gambier, which he named after Admiral James Gambier.

The following day Grant named Cape Bridgewater after another Duke, and Cape Nelson after the famous warship, but could not find a safe place to land.

On 7 December Grant rounded the Lawrence Rocks to discover Portland Bay, naming it after the Duke of Portland. The land he found 'truly picturesque and beautiful', but again the heavy surf and onshore winds prevented him from landing. Sailing further east, that same day Grant named Cape Otway after Captain William Otway, RN.

On 8 December Grant missed his chance of discovering Port Phillip Bay. He could see an opening in the coastline, and named it Governor King's Bay, with an eastern extremity which he named Cape Schanck after the designer of *Lady Nelson*. 'I had my doubts

The sliding keel was a boon to coastal exploration. It made ships more manoeuvrable without sacrificing size. Long expeditions required ships large enough to take the necessary men and provisions. Now larger ships could work close to shore and enter unknown bays and rivers with less risk of running aground

whether this land should not have been followed,' Grant wrote. But a favourable wind and shortage of provisions made him decide to run for Sydney along the remaining coastline already charted by Flinders.

In March 1801 Governor King sent the *Lady Nelson* back to survey the main bays on the Victorian coastline. He firmly instructed Grant: 'You will persevere in exploring them on all sides.'

On 21 March Grant sailed into Western Port, naming Seal Island at the entrance for its thousands of large seals. Two days later he anchored off Churchill Island, today a national park. There he built a blockhouse — the first European structure on Victorian soil — and began a small farm. 'I sowed in it wheat, seeds of different sorts, planted onions and potatoes, with cucumber, pumpkin, and melon seeds,' Grant reported.

By the end of April, Grant's officers had completed the survey of Western Port and one hundred and twelve kilometres of the coast towards Wilson's Promontory. Severe westerly gales forced the *Lady Nelson* back to

Sydney again. Grant had been very successful, but Governor King felt there was still much to be discovered in the south. He allowed Grant to return to naval service in Britain, and in November 1801 appointed twenty-six-year-old acting-lieutenant John Murray to command *Lady Nelson*.

Murray returned to Churchill Island early

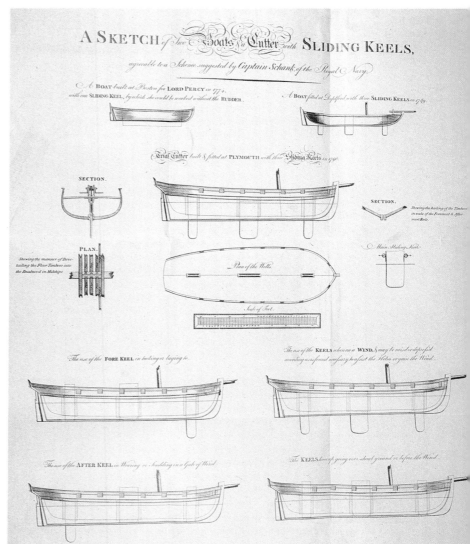

A SKETCH of two Boats of a Cutter with SLIDING KEELS, agreeable to a Scheme suggested by Captain Schank of the Royal Navy.

The Lady Nelson *entered this picturesque bay between Portsea and Sorrento, only after Murray had made certain his ship could pass safely through the Rip. His caution was justified — many ships later ran foul of the Rip guarding the entrance to Port Phillip Bay*

in December. He found Grant's wheat 'in full vigour, 6 ft high and almost ripe...the straw being very near as large as young sugar cane.' On the mainland near by, Murray found a fresh spring that was 'equal to the watering of a line of battleships.'

After Christmas a boat party led by first mate, William Bowen, encountered Aboriginals on shore. They insisted that the seamen remove their clothes before negotiating. 'All our people got out of the boat stark naked as was desired,' Bowen reported. The natives expressed 'a good deal of wonder' at the colour of his skin: made 'significant signs that he must have washed himself very hard.' In good humour, gifts were exchanged.

On 4 January 1802, Murray sailed the *Lady Nelson* to the perilous entrance to Port Phillip. Climbing to the masthead, he observed, so he thought, that a reef 'did nearly stretch across the whole way, but inside saw a fine sheet of smooth water of great extent.' But with the wind blowing dead on to a lee shore, he decided to play safe. He sailed off to complete the charting of King Island.

Early in February, Murray sent William Bowen in the ship's launch to test the entrance to Port Phillip. The launch safely floated through the Rip, and spent two days investigating the huge, almost landlocked harbour, where no British seamen had ever been before.

By 14 February 1802, the winds were favourable for Murray to work *Lady Nelson* through the strong outflowing tides and rippling water of the entrance. He anchored between today's seaside resorts of Portsea and Sorrento. A prominent peak nearby was named Arthur's Seat, after its similarity to a mountain near Edinburgh where Murray was born. Near by, he thought, 'the hills and valleys rise and fall with inexpressible elegance.' Everywhere the soil seemed good and water sufficient.

The Admiralty shows its gratitude

Murray spent a month in leisurely examination of Port Phillip. He missed the entrances to the Yarra river and smaller streams, but on 21 February discovered Corio Bay, site of Geelong. On 5 March he found the deep South Channel, which would allow ships of any size to enter Melbourne's ports.

Returning to Sydney with all this good news, Murray confidently expected to be made full lieutenant. Governor King supported his application. But some desk-bound Admiralty clerk revealed that Murray had not served the full six years required by regulation when he passed his examination as lieutenant at the Cape of Good Hope.

For this 'imposition attempted', the Admiralty refused Murray a commission, 'nor will they allow him to pass for an officer at any future period.' This was the reward for discovering a harbour second only to Port Jackson, one that would become the site of two great cities, Melbourne and Geelong.

After being sent back to England in disgrace, Murray dropped out of sight: no one seems to know when or how he died.

To complete the survey of Port Phillip, Governor King sent Charles Grimes, thirty-one-year-old English-born superintendent of public works at the Hawkesbury river.

Grimes arrived on 20 January 1803 in the schooner *Cumberland*. He reported adversely on the Mornington Peninsula for its sandy soil and lack of water.

On 2 February, at the head of Port Phillip, Grimes discovered the Yarra river. His men rowed up it as far as today's Dight's Falls. A few days later, down the western side of the bay, he sketched the outlets of the Werribee and Little rivers.

Grimes's report to King was so equivocal that the Governor could no longer recommend a settlement at Port Phillip. But it was too late. An expedition of several hundred convicts and marines under Lieutenant-Colonel David Collins had already left England. They would settle at Sorrento briefly before moving on to Van Diemen's Land — leaving the Port Phillip district to be discovered again in the eighteen-thirties.

Unflattering reports delay Melbourne's start

Murray discovered and surveyed Port Phillip Bay one month before Flinders arrived there in 1802. Both were impressed by the bay and its environs. Later negative reports meant that planned settlement of the area was delayed until the 1830s

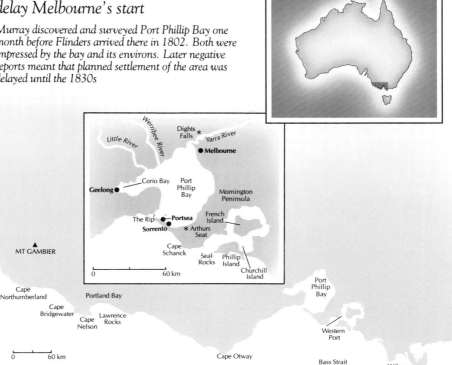

French explorers nibble at the continent's edges

After the great Dutch and British navigators established the true shape of Australia, French explorers backed by their government began to display a suspiciously keen interest in the remote but exciting new continent.

They even claimed prior discovery of Western Australia because of a controversial voyage by Paulmier de Gonneville in 1503-4. Gonneville reported he had discovered a southern land where the natives thought the Frenchmen had arrived straight from heaven. But all available evidence shows that Gonneville's ship was blown onto the coast of South America.

In the lull after discoveries by the Dutch and William Dampier, a French intellectual named Charles de Brosses published in 1756 a work entitled *History of Navigation to the Southern Lands*. He sent a copy to Louis XV, attempting to persuade him to authorise a convict colony 'in a region I have called Australasia.'

The appearance of this book must be regarded as one of the pivotal events in our history. If the king had accepted the suggestion, mass resettlement of the urban poor might have prevented the French Revolution thirty years later. Napoleon would probably have remained a discontented junior officer. Australia would have been at least partly French instead of entirely British.

These dramatic possibilities were not to become reality. Louis XV was more interested in his mistresses, the Marquise de Pompadour and Madame Du Barry, and in the excitement of local wars. He could not be concerned with the awful poverty and increasing restlessness of the lower classes in his own country.

Only a few geographical expeditions were authorised during the Royalist period.

In 1768 Louis de Bougainville, sailing from South America in search of the mysterious east Australian coast, sighted what was probably the outer edge of the Great Barrier Reef. Should he turn south into colder regions or north into the tropics? Like others before him, Bougainville made the wrong decision. He too turned north towards New Guinea, and the Australian coast best suited to colonisation was left untouched

La Pérouse and Louis XVI *discuss hopes for the Pacific that were never to be realised. La Pérouse vanished in 1788 and the French Revolution was to overturn the government at a time when Britain was already settling its newest colony. Above,* Le Géographe *and* Le Naturaliste, *the ships given to Nicolas Baudin in 1801 for his expedition to map as much as he could of Australia and to spy on Britain's activities*

until Cook's discovery two years later.

In 1772, Francois de St Allouarn came at Australia from the other direction, well known to Dutch seamen and to William Dampier. He landed on an island in Shark Bay, raised a flag and took possession of Western Australia in the name of King Louis XVI. The gesture was a vain one, for the French court was in too much turmoil to follow the acquisition with a permanent settlement.

In 1785 came the final pre-revolutionary French expedition. The implications of Cook's discoveries had at last galvanised the French into fullscale exploration. As the British debated the best method of exploiting Australia's east coast, Louis XVI quietly sent the Comte de la Pérouse with two ships to survey likely spots for French settlement. Aboard were copper plates engraved with the royal arms, to be used as permanent notification of French ownership.

Another of the curious accidents of Australian history now occurred. La Pérouse took nearly eighteen months to find his way via South America to Cook's landfall at Botany Bay. He was delayed by the royal instructions to make a thorough report on the Pacific area, and by a massacre of his men in Samoa. When he arrived at Botany Bay on 24 January 1788, the first convict fleet from Britain was already there. It had arrived just six days earlier!

Baudin seeks refuge in Sydney

After a short stay, La Pérouse sailed away into oblivion. His ships were wrecked on a small island near Vanuatu. There were no survivors, and relics were not found until nearly forty years later. An unsuccessful search expedition under Rear-Admiral Bruni d'Entrecasteaux in 1792 took the opportunity of carefully charting

the southern coast of Van Diemen's Land, still assuming it formed part of the main land mass.

Meanwhile the French Revolution had swept away the Bourbon monarchy. Ten years later Napoleon Bonaparte in turn overthrew the elected Directory to become First Consul, and turned his eyes enviously to Britain's growing empire. In 1800 he dispatched two ships under Nicolas Baudin, allegedly to complete the mapping of Australia, but also to survey British strength in the area.

By 1802 Baudin's crew had fallen prey to scurvy, long abolished from the British Navy. Of one hundred and seventy Frenchmen, only twelve could still stand upright. The sick lay like dead men with shrivelled lips, ulcerated mouths and black tumours erupting on their bodies.

Baudin abandoned his mapping of the coast and fled for the refuge of Sydney Cove. Some of his men died, but on Governor King's orders the remainder were nursed back to health. This did not prevent one officer from urging the military commander on the French island of Mauritius to attack Sydney as quickly as possible. 'Today we could destroy it easily,' he wrote. 'We shall not be able to do so in twenty-five years time.'

When the French departed to continue charting Bass Strait, Governor King sent the schooner *Cumberland* under Lieutenant Charles Robbins to follow them and raise the British flag over the French camp on King Island. Baudin wrote sardonically to King:

That childish ceremony was ridiculous... I

have no knowledge of the claims which the French Government may have upon Van Diemen's Land, nor of its designs for the future; but I think that its title will not be any better grounded than yours... Everyone knows that Tasman and his heirs did not bequeath it by will to you...

Fears of a French invasion

British colonists took the matter more seriously. In May 1803 Governor King sent Lieutenant John Bowen to occupy Van Diemen's Land, warning him:

In case any French ships, or ships of any other nation, should attempt to form an establishment anywhere in the neighbourhood of where you are settled, you will inform the Commanding Officer of His Majesty's right to the whole of Van Diemen's Land, founded on such claims as you do not doubt His Majesty will assert. If they persevere after this, you will endeavour to prevent them carrying their intention into effect, but without any act of hostility if it can be avoided; nor will you on any account suffer His Majesty's flag to be insulted.

The British Government had similar thoughts and on almost the same day, had decided to colonise Port Phillip. Here, thought the London authorities, the establishment of a French base 'might, in the event of hostilities, greatly interrupt the communication with Port Jackson, and materially endanger the tranquillity and security of our pos-

King George Sound in Western Australia, painted by Louis Auguste de Sainson, draughtsman on Dumont d'Urville's 1826 voyage

sessions there.' These precautions were wise. In November 1803 news was received in Sydney that war had again broken out between Britain and France. Governor King immediately issued a General Order inviting the free inhabitants of Sydney to enrol for training in the use of cannon and warning foreigners not to leave their ships without permission from the authorities.

Sydney's harbour defences at this time could scarcely be called massive. Governor Phillip had set up eight ship's guns behind a pile of rocks on Dawes Point. Governor Hunter placed a few large guns at the eastern end of Sydney Cove and on Garden Island. 'Those of a smaller size I have removed to the most commanding eminences which cover the town of Sydney,' he reported in 1800. The following year Governor King rebuilt the western battery, which he claimed 'is now capable of annoying any vessel with effect.' Further guns were placed at South Head to command the entrance to the harbour. But in 1804, an officer reported that there was 'not one artilleryman in the whole colony; and when the guns were to be loaded, even for a salute upon a holiday, the master shipwright was the person selected for that service.' The brass field pieces frequently refused to explode; while the guns near the harbour entrance had become 'nearly burried in the sand.'

Fortunately for the British, French sea power was virtually destroyed by Nelson at the battle of Trafalgar in 1805. Napoleon sent several thousand troops to Mauritius, as the springboard for an attack on Sydney, but sufficient ships were never available to transport an expeditionary force.

Meanwhile, the alleged results of Baudin's expedition were published in Paris in 1808. Accompanying maps depicted the whole of southern Australia as *Terre Napoleon*, and French names were attached to prominent landmarks.

Matthew Flinders, at this time imprisoned by the French on Mauritius, complained bitterly. In February 1809 he wrote to Sir Joseph Banks:

This is an injustice to our nation in general, and to Lieutenant Grant and to me in particular, for the greater part of that coast was discovered by us... Even my discovery of the north coast of Van Diemen's Land in 1798 is represented in that letter to be a new discovery of the Géographe.

In 1812 war broke out between Britain and America. A strange character named Jorgen Jorgensen, for some years employed as a British spy, advised Earl Bathurst in 1813 that the French and Americans had concocted a plot to invade Australia. Four French frigates under Baudin's former officers were to meet American ships near the Falkland Islands, sail to Broken Bay, and there disembark hundreds of soldiers, horses and field guns. Their strategy was to proceed up the Hawkesbury river, release and arm any willing convicts, and conquer Parramatta before attacking Sydney from the landward side.

Governor Macquarie immediately requested more artillery and extra rifles to arm trustworthy settlers as a militia force. But Napoleon was defeated at Waterloo in 1815 and nothing more was heard of the rumoured invasion plan.

Keen interest in Western Australia

British settlers in Australia were not yet quite free of French designs. Napoleon's claims lapsed with his defeat and exile. But even the restored monarchy had territorial ambitions.

In 1822, Captain Louis Duperrey was ordered to report on the land claimed fifty years earlier by St Allouarn in Western Australia, as a possible site for a penal colony. He was unable to follow these instructions, but his navigator, Jules de Blosseville, recommended the south-west coast instead.

This opinion was supported by Dumont d'Urville, one of Duperrey's officers, who in 1826 visited the site of Albany and remarked: 'I cannot understand why the British have not already occupied such a fine place.'

Both expeditions sailed through Bass Strait and along the New South Wales coast, taking keen interest in the empty lands from Port Phillip to Twofold Bay.

In some consternation, Earl Bathurst wrote from London to Governor Darling:

The sailing of Two French Ships on a Voyage of discovery has led to the consideration how far our distant possessions in the Australian Seas may be prejudiced by any designs which the French may entertain of establishing themselves in that quarter... So advantageous a point as Western Port would not be neglected by them... Your attention is earnestly directed to the formation of a Colony at that place...

Earl Bathurst also instructed formation of settlements at Fremantle and Albany, and occupation of Dampier's Shark Bay in Western Australia.

At all points the French were locked out of Australia. Had they persevered, Britain no doubt would have used force to evict them. What the French did achieve was the concentration of British strategists upon the development and defence of the continent. All our subsequent history flows from their decision to claim the entire continent for Britain. □

French flirtations with Australia's exploration

Baudin's expedition was a scientific success, but did little to further French claims in Australia as the government did not heed his final recommendations. From the beginning, the French failed to develop a consistent and determined policy to colonise Australia

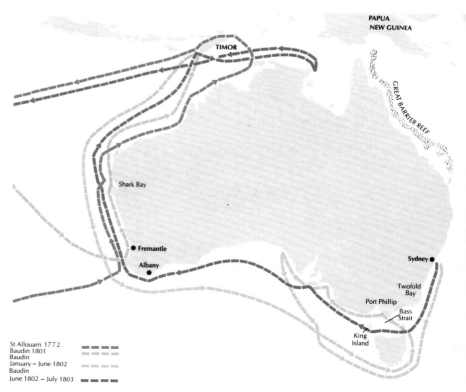

St Allouarn 1772
Baudin 1801
Baudin
January – June 1802
Baudin
June 1802 – July 1803

Adventures and surprises in Van Diemen's Land

Ever since Abel Tasman's great voyage of 1642, the southern tip of Van Diemen's Land had been included in maps of 'New Holland'. (The name Tasmania, although widely used from the eighteen-twenties, did not become official until 1856.) But Europeans had never attempted to explore the land in detail. Its mountains, rivers, pastures and mineral wealth were still practically unknown at the beginning of the nineteenth century.

In 1793 the directors of the British East India Company decided to seek profitable lands south of the equator. They sent two small ships, the *Duke of Clarence* and *Duchess of Bengal*, from Calcutta commanded by John Hayes, a twenty-five-year-old naval lieutenant who had proved his courage in Britain's wars against Indian princes.

Hayes was originally commissioned to investigate the potential wealth of New Guinea. Adverse easterly winds prevented him from sailing through Torres Strait: instead he headed south along the coast of Western Australia and south-east towards Tasmania.

During April 1793, storms prevented Hayes from anchoring in Bligh's Adventure Bay. Sailing on, he entered a beautiful river which he named the Derwent, after the stream near his birthplace in Cumberland, England. Today the deep natural harbour is the setting for Hobart.

Sailing further upstream, Hayes discovered the fertile Risdon Cove, which he named after William Risdon, second officer of the *Duke of Clarence*. Ten years later this became the site of the first British settlement.

Once Bass and Flinders had established that Tasmania was an island, the British determined that it should not fall into French hands. In March 1803 Governor King summoned twenty-three-year-old Lieutenant John Bowen, RN, to his office. In Bowen's words, the Governor proposed 'a service of much importance to the mother country'. He had 'long intended to form a settlement on Van Diemen's Land, to counteract any of the supposed intentions of the French.'

Bowen sailed in the *Lady Nelson*, with the whaler *Albion* as tender, carrying forty-nine pioneer settlers, including twenty-one male and three female convicts. In September 1803 they landed at Risdon Cove and established the first white settlement in Tasmania. Early in 1804 David Collins decided to abandon the sandy, almost waterless fortress he had established on the mainland inside Port Phillip Bay. Two of his soldiers expressed 'dissatisfaction at daily drill' ordered in the intense heat. One was punished with five hundred lashes and the other with seven hundred. Mutiny seemed likely: Collins decided to ship the entire settlement to the Derwent river where reinforcements were available.

The first important discoveries

Collins took command at the Derwent on 16 February 1804. On the advice of surveyor George Harris, he established a new settlement downstream at the site of today's Hobart, naming it Sullivan Cove after John Sullivan, Under-Secretary of

The settlement at Port Dalrymple *began in 1804 under the administration of Lieutenant-Colonel Paterson. Its isolation was broken by discovery of an overland route to Hobart*

the Colonial Office. Slowly, with many difficulties reminiscent of early Sydney, a permanent base was established from which exploration of the island's interior could begin.

The botanist Robert Brown made the first important discoveries. Quitting the unhappy, half-starved settlement early in 1804, he trekked about eight kilometres along the Derwent and its tributaries. Although disappointed in the number of unique botanical species found, he was able to send back to Sir Joseph Banks more than seven hundred 'very interesting plants' for the Royal Gardens at Kew. Banks wrote that these constituted 'a large portion of the newest ornaments' of that unparalleled collection.

While soldiers and convicts at Hobart grumbled and wondered where their next meal would come from, Brown climbed Mount Wellington ten times and 'found it uncommonly productive' of new specimens. From the summit he sighted the Huon river, named after its maritime discoverer, Captain Huon de Kermadec of the d'Entrecasteaux expedition. Brown, after battling through dense undergrowth, became the first white man to reach it overland in May 1804.

The same year, other settlers began exploiting Matthew Flinders's discovery of the Tamar in northern Tasmania.

In January 1804 William Collins, forty-four-year-old former naval officer and free settler, recommended the colonisation of Port Dalrymple at the mouth of the Tamar. Governor King agreed that such a settlement would help to protect Bass Strait against foreign incursions. In October 1804 he sent Lieutenant-

HOW FEMALE ABORIGINALS CAUGHT SEALS

On his boat trip round Tasmania in 1815-16, James Kelly described how native women on Bass Strait islands clubbed seals for their skins, worth £1 each in Hobart.

They went to the water's edge, wrote Kelly, *and wet themselves all over their heads and bodies, which operation they said would keep the seals from smelling them…*

The women all walked into the water in couples, and swam to three rocks about fifty yards from the shore. Two women went to each rock with their clubs in hand, crept closely up to a seal each, and lay down with their clubs alongside. Some of the seals lifted their heads up to inspect their new visitors and smell them. The seals scratched themselves and lay down again. The women went through the same motions as the seal, holding up their left elbow and scratching themselves

Fur seals *prefer rocky inaccessible places*

with their left hand… After they had lain upon the rocks for nearly an hour, the sea occasionally washing over them (as they were quite naked, we could not tell the meaning of their remaining so long), all of a sudden the women rose up on their seats, their clubs lifted at arm's length, each struck a seal on the nose and killed him; in an instant they all jumped up as if by magic and killed one more each. After giving the seals several blows on the head, and securing them, they commenced laughing aloud and began dancing.

Colonel William Paterson in the armed cutter HMS *Integrity*, with thirty-four soldiers and seventy-five convicts to establish the new outpost.

Paterson's main tasks were to prevent 'foreigners of any nation from building any habitation on any part of the coasts', and to observe where British settlers 'can be advantageously placed.'

These instructions were the motive for initial exploration of the northern part of the island. The first camp was set up at York Cove, but one year later settlement shifted to the site of Launceston. In December 1804 Paterson sent to King a full survey of the Tamar and adjoining rich pasture lands. He discovered its spectacular main tributaries, naming

them the North and South Esk rivers. Another party travelled west to explore the Asbestos Range, now a national park.

Linking north and south

The problem now was that there were two British settlements in Tasmania, but they could communicate only by the arduous east or west coast sea routes. Was it possible to establish an overland track and discover what lay in the centre of the mountainous island?

In February 1807 the commandant at Port Dalrymple sent twenty-one-year-old Lieutenant Thomas Laycock with four other members of the New South Wales Corps to make the crossing. Relying mainly on compass bearings, the soldiers made 'a very fatiguing journey' along Lake river, past lakes Crescent and Sorell, and along the river Clyde to the Derwent. Totally exhausted, they were found at the junction of the Jordan and Derwent rivers by a party led by Judge-Advocate Samuel Bate.

After Laycock and his men recovered, they were 'liberally supplied' for a return journey. This time they followed an easier course slightly to the east, over 'a fine level country' close to the route of today's Midland Highway. On 20 February 1807, Laycock again ascended the mountains to reach Lake river, discovered deposits of 'very fine limestone suitable for building, and returned to Launceston along the South Esk river.

This notable expedition paved the way for a proper survey of Tasmania's inland regions. In October 1807 surveyor Charles Grimes mapped the lands around Port Dalrymple and traced the easiest route for the Midland Highway, which still joins Tasmania's two largest cities. The way had been opened for free settlers to expand right across the island. □

In 1807, a route is found through the centre of the island

The opening of an overland route between the northern and southern settlements was a major achievement in the arduous task of opening up Tasmania's rugged interior. Continuous privation and exhaustion like that experienced by this first successful exploring party were to become familiar features of the island's history

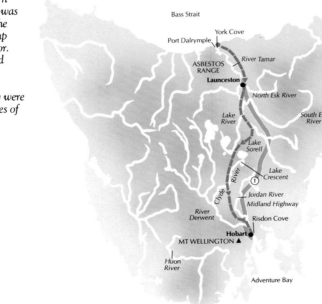

Bass Strait
York Cove
Port Dalrymple
River Tamar
ASBESTOS RANGE
Launceston
North Esk River
Lake River
South Esk River
Lake Sorell
Lake Crescent
Clyde River
Jordan River
Midland Highway
River Derwent
Risdon Cove
Hobart
MT WELLINGTON ▲
Huon River
Adventure Bay

0   80 km

Laycock 1807 ▬ ▬ ▬

Epic voyages reveal Tasmania's coastline

A painting by William Duke, c1849, *shows whaling off Tasmania. Whaling was Australia's first primary industry and main export*

Before 1820, the first white Australian-born seamen were beginning to continue the work of British mariners who had charted so much of the coast.

Prominent among the local 'cornstalks' was James Kelly, born in Parramatta in 1791, son of a cook and an Irishwoman transported from Dublin. Even before he was twelve, the boy began to learn the rough life of a sealer and sandalwood trader. But he was a survivor.

In 1812, Kelly was engaged by the pioneer of Tasmanian whaling, Dr Thomas William Birch of Hobart, to command his tiny fleet. Three years later Kelly embarked in a whaleboat named *Elizabeth* with four strong oarsmen, intending to explore the commercial possibilities of the Tasmanian coastline. Dr Birch apparently accompanied them part of the way, remaining further offshore in the schooner *Henrietta Packet*.

The boats sailed south-westerly on 12 December 1815. Five days later *Elizabeth* entered 'a large inlet' on the west coast, which was named Port Davey after Thomas Davey, Lieutenant-Governor. For several days Kelly's men cleared ground, planted seeds at Garden Point and roughly charted the harbour.

Arriving at the Wanderer river on 25 December, they celebrated Christmas Day by roasting two black swans, stewing up a sea pie (meat and vegetables boiled together and covered with a paste of flour and water), throwing a glass of brandy into the surf and giving 'three hearty cheers.'

Kelly's strenuous voyage

Three days later, Kelly's whaleboat discovered Macquarie Harbour, sailing through the dangerous entrance known as Hell's Gate, into Kelly Channel. From the strong current, Kelly correctly deduced that 'there must be a large river in the southeast direction.' He named it after James Gordon, magistrate at Pitt Water near Sorell. Kelly returned often to harvest Huon pine.

On 1 January 1816, Kelly discovered the Pieman river which flows into Hardwicke Bay, but nearly lost his boat in heavy surf. During a gale next day the *Elizabeth* was 'pooped by a heavy sea that filled her to the thwarts', and was saved only by desperate baling. Most of the food was ruined, and daily rations were cut severely.

On 4 January the party landed on Hunter Island, off Tasmania's north-east tip, but they were stoned by a large group of Aboriginals. Kelly drew a pair of duelling pistols and fired into them, enabling his party to escape. By 9 January they arrived safely at Port Dalrymple where they were at first mistaken for bushrangers and arrested.

Quickly released and rewarded with ample food, liquor and new clothes, Kelly's men sailed on down the better-known east coast-

Whalers chart many of the bays and harbours round the coast

Kelly and Hobbs battled dangerous swells and unpredictable currents, discovering valuable riverlands and harbours along Tasmania's coast

line to arrive at Hobart on 30 January 1816. Lieutenant-Governor Davey rewarded Kelly for the strenuous voyage with a land grant on Bruny Island. Kelly built a house on the bank of the Hobart Town rivulet, and was later appointed harbour master.

The offshore search for land to settle

Kelly's voyage was repeated in 1824, when Lieutenant-Governor William Sorell sought more detailed information on remote harbours and their hinterlands.

For the task he commissioned thirty-two-year-old James Hobbs, an ex-naval settler who had first arrived in Tasmania with the deposed Governor Bligh.

With two open boats manned by twelve convicts, Hobbs arrived at Port Esperance off D'Entrecasteaux Channel on 7 February 1824. He praised it as 'an excellent harbour', its hills covered with 'the finest stringy-bark trees I ever saw.'

At stormy South Cape Bay, Hobbs attempted to penetrate inland by wading knee-deep up the South Cape rivulet, surrounded by impenetrable scrub. After only five kilometres his totally exhausted men were forced to return.

Hobbs described most of the south-west coast as 'totally unfit for any purpose useful to civilised man.' His pessimism was intensified when fierce gales smashed the keel of his large boat and nearly swamped the other.

After repairs at Port Davey and Macquarie Harbour, Hobbs made further inland expeditions. Again he reported that the western lands in most parts were 'totally useless' except for growing timber.

On 20 June 1824, Hobbs arrived at Cape Portland on the island's north-eastern tip. He examined the Ringarooma river, describing it as 'one of the finest fresh-water rivers I ever saw in this part of the country.' It was surrounded by 'exceedingly fine land' growing 'the greatest abundance of the best grass'. Here the town of Gladstone would rise.

A fortnight later, Hobbs gave a moderately encouraging report of the George river, where St Helens now stands. Shipping could safely shelter near by, although Hobbs could not see 'any vast extent of good land'.

After their five months' voyage, Hobbs and his men returned without injury to Hobart. His information enabled survey maps to be improved and settlement to extend.

Captain Kelly's house *on the Hobart Town rivulet. Never far from the sea, Kelly became harbourmaster and later owned a whaling fleet*

British investors take the best of northern Tasmania

*I*n the remoulding of the world that followed the Napoleonic wars, South American nations threw off the Spanish yoke. US President James Monroe warned European nations never to interfere in his hemisphere. In victorious Britain, the Industrial Revolution gathered pace. The first steam railway opened to the public in 1825. Large numbers of rural poor were forced into steam-powered factories, or into criminal behaviour which often earned them transportation to Britain's new empire in the Pacific. And the wide lands of Australia began to be regarded as the source of fine wool that would maintain Britain's manufacturing pre-eminence on world textile markets. How simple it all seemed!

Convict Jorgen Jorgensen *earned his freedom by exploring for the Van Diemen's Land Company. His self-portrait is oddly modern*

Ruins at Circular Head *are of convict barracks built in 1826. They were among the first buildings erected in northern Tasmania; the Land Company built a town at nearby Stanley for free settlers. Today it is listed on the National Estate*

In line with imperial policy, a new syndicate with eighteen directors, known as the Van Diemen's Land Company, was enthusiastically supported in London in 1825. The government offered the company over one hundred thousand hectares of grazing land in uncharted north-west Tasmania for a total price of only $925, payable in five years. Colonial Secretary Lord Bathurst instructed the directors to select an area 'beyond the ramparts of the known lands'. In this commercially practical mood the next phase of Tasmanian exploration began.

The company wisely appointed as its Tasmanian manager Edward Curr, an enterprising twenty-seven-year-old Hobart merchant. In 1826 Curr sent surveyor Joseph Fossey and agricultural expert Alexander Goldie to pick out the best areas of north-west Tasmania. They landed in a whaleboat at Circular Head, and during August discovered sections of the Duck river. The following month they explored the inland from Rocky Cape, discovering Detention river. All told, the two men located more than twenty-eight thousand hectares of good grazing land between Circular Head and Cape Grim, although it was broken up by unusable forest and mountain areas.

After bitter debate, Lieutenant-Governor George Arthur permitted company officials to select strips of the best land instead of taking one huge tract. Arthur complained to London that 'scarcely less than one-fourth of the whole island' would satisfy the company, but his protests were in vain.

Edward Curr immediately organised a new round of explorations designed to pick the eyes out of northern Tasmania west of the Tamar. In February 1827 he sent Henry Hellyer, a thirty-seven-year-old surveyor, on the first land expedition south-east of Circular Head, through some of Tasmania's wildest areas.

Crossing the Cam river, on 14 February 1827, Hellyer discovered and climbed St Valentine's Peak. From the top he could see two extensive tracts of apparently fine country, 'gently rising, dry, grassy hills resembling English enclosures in many respects, being bounded by brooks between each, with belts of beautiful shrubs in every vale.' Land along the Leven river he described as 'having very much the appearance of a nobleman's domain.' Hellyer named the smaller northerly tract Hampshire Hills after his native county.

Two days later the surveyor crossed a 'noble river' later named the Hellyer; and on 19 February 1827, came to an even larger and more violent stream which he named the Arthur. With great difficulty he crossed and recrossed, fighting his way through almost impenetrable country, living on half a litre of mixed flour and water per day. Hellyer emerged in sight of Circular Head a fortnight later, emaciated and ragged, but triumphant.

Hellyer's Arthur River, which he had to cross many times, is typical of the often treacherous rivers that confronted explorers

Highfield was built in the 1830s and designed by Henry Hellyer. This picturesque estate in Stanley was the Land Company's headquarters until the 1920s

A land company pays explorers to find pastures

The Van Diemen's Land Company was the first large-scale agricultural venture in Tasmania. It was founded at a time when monopolistic, privileged land companies were fading out, but it was responsible for opening up much of north-west Tasmania

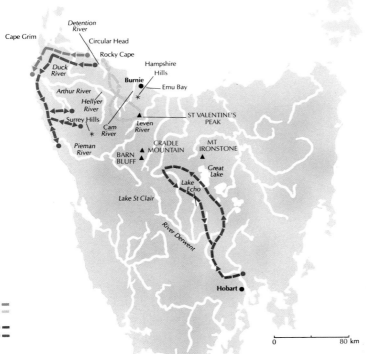

Goldie 1826
Hellyer 1827 and after
Jorgensen 1826
Jorgensen 1827

Hellyer continued his mountain explorations for several years, discovering Cradle Mountain and Barn Bluff among other landmarks. But, always reserved and rather sensitive, he could not tolerate criticism of the value of some of his discoveries. In 1832 he lapsed into deep depression and committed suicide.

Still no overland route

During the late eighteen-twenties the Van Diemen's Land Company employed an even more peculiar character named Jorgen Jorgensen. Born in Denmark in 1780, Jorgensen joined the Royal Navy under the name John Johnson and served on HMS *Lady Nelson*. He was present at the first settlement on the Derwent river and claimed to have harpooned the first whale in its waters.

Jorgensen's subsequent adventures included leading a revolution in Iceland and operating as a British spy in Europe during Napoleon's last days in power. Back in London he descended into petty crime, was transported to Tasmania and assigned to the Van Diemen's Land Company in 1826.

Jorgensen was first given the impossible task of finding a direct overland route from Hobart to Circular Head in the north-west. He seems to have pen-

etrated about half the distance, beyond Great Lake (discovered in 1817 by John Beamont) to Ironstone Mount. Here he was halted by 'a frightful chasm many miles in width.'

'The snow was falling in a dense shower,' he reported. 'Our clothes were torn to tatters; we were distressed for fuel...the weather was so foggy that we could see only a short distance before us.'

The men were forced to return to Hobart, probably via Lake Echo, although Jorgensen claimed to have discovered Lake St Clair, source of the Derwent, along with 'a considerable extent of fine open country, of itself sufficiently large to comprise the quantity of good land which the Company was to receive.' Jorgensen received £8 for his discoveries, from which the cost of his ruined boots was deducted.

In 1827 Jorgensen was instructed to try again for an overland mountain route to Hobart, but this time to start from the Pieman river on the west coast. His party landed in a bay a few kilometres north of the Pieman, ascended about twenty-eight kilometres through drenching rain into mountainous country, then simply gave up and returned to the coast. They trekked north and west along the coastline to Circular Head, using a route already well known. For his efforts Jorgensen was granted a conditional pardon and employed as a constable in charge of other convicts.

The Van Diemen's Land Company was finally authorised to acquire one hundred and sixty-two thousand hectares, mainly at Cape Grim and southwards from Emu Bay, near today's Burnie. But high expenses and severe stock losses forced the company to abandon large-scale grazing. A tenant-farming scheme which began in 1840, and timber exporting in the eighteen-eighties, ensured the company's survival for many years. □

Solving the intricate puzzle of Tasmania's river systems

Throughout the eighteen-twenties, the exact location of many lakes and rivers in Tasmania's western wilderness continued to baffle settlers and surveyors. So mountainous was the terrain, and so unpredictable the courses of its foaming rivers, the whole area from Cradle Mountain south to Lake Pedder was wrapped in mystery and surmise.

When twenty-three-year-old Welsh-born army officer Edward Dumaresq was appointed surveyor-general in 1825, he could achieve little beyond the measurement and valuation of easily accessible easterly lands subdivided for farming. The western wilderness remained practically untouched.

This did not at all suit George Frankland, an eager twenty-eight-year-old professional surveyor who replaced Dumaresq as surveyor-general in 1828. Instructed by Lieutenant-Governor Arthur to begin a trigonometrical survey of the island, Frankland took this to mean the entire island. Like true explorers everywhere, he delighted in being the first to unravel mysteries.

With his teams of hardbitten convicts working as explorer-labourers, Frankland proceeded into the mountains in 1829. He had up to four hectares cleared on the top of each peak, and there erected tall trigonometrical stations with sloping timber sides, which could be seen from other peaks all round. Frankland's closely measured base lines averaged six kilometres. By means of triangulation, using carefully observed angles to neighbouring peaks, Frankland was able to plot the first true maps of even the wildest areas. The same method was used to correct 'gross inaccuracies' in earlier farmland surveys, where the borders of almost every land grant could not be reconciled with its neighbours.

Soon it was discovered that latitudes and longitudes given by explorers such as Jorgen Jorgensen were inaccurate by many kilometres, and may even have been falsified. The official maps of earlier surveyor Thomas Scott were similarly inaccurate and had to be thrown out.

Another government surveyor, William Stanley Sharland, discovered the Nive river but thought it was the Derwent; and crossed the Franklin river but thought it was the King. Frankland impatiently dismissed Sharland from the survey department.

Despite constant criticism of his slow progress, Frankland doggedly continued to correct the old maps. Surveying, he wrote, 'has a twofold nature: first, to represent the country as it is; secondly, to mark out certain extents on the surface, varying in shape and size in every imaginable contingency of ground. The tediousness of the process, and the arduous nature of the service, can only be justly appreciated by those who have attempted it themselves.'

Frankland provides correct maps of the western wilderness

Surveyor-General George Frankland found the sources of the Derwent, Huon and Nive rivers, ending confusion over their courses and their naming. For eight years he travelled almost unceasingly and the hardship he experienced probably caused his early death from influenza when he was 38

Early in February 1835, Frankland resolved to solve the puzzle of the mountain river systems — in particular, the true source and course of the Derwent river. 'The general impression existing at the period of my departure,' he wrote, 'was that the Nive was in fact no other than the Derwent itself.'

On 9 February 1835, Frankland left Marlborough, an outlying station on the Nive, and travelled westward over boggy marshes. The next day he discovered and named the Humboldt river. On the following 'we suddenly found ourselves on the edge of a beautiful Lake in the heart of Scenery of the most picturesque Character.' This was Lake St Clair, whose shores had never before been trodden by Europeans. Although compil-

ng an official report, Frankland wrote, 'I feel it difficult to avoid expressing the impressions of delight which were inspired by the first discovering of such a romantic Country.'

Very soon the explorers' progress was arrested by a large river falling out of the lake, and being to all appearance the Derwent.' A few hundred metres downstream they found a large tree lying across the foaming river and crossed over.

On 12 February 1835, Frankland climbed 1426-metre Mount Olympus on the western shore, naming it for the 'stupendous groups of columns hanging over our heads in the most imposing manner.' From this peak he could see to the north-east dozens of smaller lakes — today's Central Plateau conservation

area. To the west he sighted the peak of Frenchman's Cap towards Macquarie Harbour. To the south-east, 'the eye ranged over extensive plains watered by the Derwent.' The view all round, wrote Frankland, 'was beyond all description.'

Success beyond expectations
On 14 February Frankland sent two of his men to follow the Derwent's east bank. Frankland continued along the west bank, discovering Mount King William I looming over Lake King William. He then followed 'a very fine river', naming it the Guelph, until it brought him to the Guelph Basin and its junction with the Derwent. On the opposite bank his men had discovered the junction with the river Nive.

The lower reaches of the Huon provided settlers with farming lands and today this is where most of Tasmania's apples are grown. The river was first sighted in 1792, but its upper reaches are especially rugged and were not much penetrated before Frankland's 1835 expedition. Parts are still unexplored more than a century later

On 18 February Frankland left the Derwent and struck away to the north-east, which brought him back to the Nive and 'the most beautiful marsh imaginable, filled with wild Cattle'. There he heard in the plangent air the distinct notes of a bugle and followed the sound to a property, Morley's Station.

After resting his men, Frankland now set out to find the upper reaches of the Huon river. Each man carried thirty-six

Rugged mountains in South West National Park made exploration slow. Frequent heavy rains created a confusing array of small streams

kilos of food for the trek south through unknown country.

On 1 March 1835, they forded the Derwent again, where 'some caution was requisite to avoid being swept away by the torrent.' Enveloped in dense forests through which the daylight rarely penetrated, lashed by 'snow, sleet and wind', they arrived three days later at Wylds Craig. From this peak, wrote Frankland, 'the whole Country lies stretched at your feet.' To the south-west they could see the Gordon river, flowing into Lake Gordon before finally emptying itself into Macquarie Harbour, where James Kelly had seen its outlet on his 1815 whaleboat voyage.

Frankland realised that he must now obey an urgent summons from the Lieutenant-Governor to attend to his 'proper duties' in Hobart. Reluctantly he handed command of the expedition to surveyor John Helder Wedge.

Wedge thus had the honour on 11 March of exploring Lake Pedder, named after Sir John Lewes Pedder, first chief justice of Tasmania. He traced the Huon river to a point near today's Huonville, meeting there on 20 March a boat carrying fresh supplies. On the following day Wedge reached Hobart 'by the bridle road cut through the forests'.

Frankland summed up his own achievement: 'Thus in the course of two months I had the satisfaction of succeeding beyond my expectations in gaining a knowledge of the sources of the Derwent, the Huon, and the Nive, and of their principal tributaries, together with the countries on their banks.' He thought that 'Every encouragement should be given to Settlers to form Establishments in the new Country.'

Frankland was now able to complete most of his new map of Tasmania, which in 1836 replaced the misleading maps previously used. Robert Hay, Colonial Under-Secretary in London, called it 'by far the most valuable contribution that has been received from any of the Colonies during my time.' But within two years Frankland, racked by a virulent strain of influenza and worn out by his exertions, was dead. He was thirty-eight. □

Lake Pedder was discovered by Wedge in 1835 as he travelled south from Frenchman's Cap. Today he would not recognise the area. The Serpentine River was dammed in the 1970s, causing the lake to engulf part of the Huon

Land explorers borrow seamen's techniques

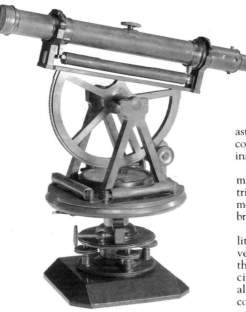

Sir Thomas Mitchell, *had the decided advantage over other explorers in that he carefully laid down the main features of the landscape by the method of triangulation. He was said to 'leave no elevation unclimbed' to seek connecting points, carrying his own sophisticated theodolite (pictured)*

Explorers and surveyors on Australia's unknown land surfaces used some of the navigational devices developed by mariners.

Establishing direction is much simpler on land than at sea. Fixed landmarks can be noted on maps, and land surfaces remain static unlike tossing ocean waves.

Compasses were used by all explorers to determine roughly their direction of travel. Magnetic deviations sometimes led them astray. When Thomas Learmonth climbed Mount Elephant in Victoria's Western District in the eighteen-thirties, he found its ironstone exerted such a pull on the needle that he had to stand on his companions' shoulders to get more accurate readings.

Some of the best explorers were former

The circumferentor, *of which this is a more advanced type, was effectively the poor man's theodolite. Surveyors observed their compass bearings through eyeholes in its vertical arms*

The transit theodolite – *basically a telescope sight and a spirit-level mounted on a tripod. It measured vertical and horizontal angles*

mariners who were familiar with use of the sextant to establish exact latitudes reached.

In ravines or dense bush where the horizon could not be seen, they often used a device called an artificial horizon. This was a plate or trough containing mercury, which formed its own level and reflected the sun, so that readings could be taken of elevation. John Oxley complained in 1817 that his artificial horizon was 'so shaken by the horse forcing his way through the scrubs' that most of the mercury was lost. Faced with the same problem, another explorer used treacle instead of mercury.

Theodolites, most useful tools of all

The surveyors' most useful tool was the transit theodolite. This instrument was suggested by English mathematician Leonard Digges in 1571, but in its simplest form was first built by Jonathan Sisson early in the eighteenth century.

The device consisted of a powerful telescope mounted to revolve in both vertical and horizontal planes. Microscopes fixed over vernier scales allowed reading of bearings to be taken extremely accurately. Both

astronomical and geographical observations could now be made in the field with the one instrument.

The theodolite also enabled fairly accurate maps of large areas to be made by means of triangulation. Settlers' blocks could then be measured, borders fixed and lines of roads and bridges laid down.

A more elementary version of the theodolite was used by some early Australian surveyors. A circumferentor was equivalent to the mariner's wind-rose. It consisted of a circular brass plate, engraved with bearings for all three hundred and sixty degrees of the compass.

The surveyor set up his circumferentor on a rise, aligned its north mark with compass readings, then sighted across its face to obtain bearings for all fixed landmarks in sight. This was a fairly rough technique, but it made possible such achievements as the original survey of Melbourne.

Measuring height in a billy of hot water

To calculate height of rising land above sea level, nineteenth-century surveyors often carried an upright mercury barometer fitted with an altitude scale. Corrections had to be made for air temperature and capillary changes in the mercury. Failing a barometer, height could be roughly calculated by measuring the temperature at which a billy of water boiled on the camp-fire.

Surveyors wishing to measure long distances arranged for one of their men to push a 'perambulator' or measuring wheel, noting the number of revolutions per stage.

Accurate measurement of shorter distances was carried out by laying down Gunter chains, consisting of one hundred metal links measuring exactly sixty-six feet, approximately two hundred centimetres. (One chain is the length of a cricket pitch.)

The Fuller calculator *had the same functions as a slide-rule, enabling quick and accurate calculations to be made in the field. Its rotating and sliding cylinders were equivalent to a slide-rule 13 metres long. Mechanical calculators superseded it only in the 1930s*

An 1864 chronometer *in its carrying case. It gave accurate time regardless of temperature or pressure to allow calculation of longitude*

Tasmania's green wilderness: still a challenge to adventurers and explorers

It is only two hundred and ninety-six kilometres from north to south, three hundred and fifteen kilometres east to west, but this magnificent island-state contains remote corners still not fully mapped. Tasmania is the world's most mountainous island and its exploration was fearsomely difficult and slow. Sudden changes of weather bring poor visibility, freezing temperatures and seemingly endless downpours of rain that can turn a day's trek into a week of enforced isolation.

Their inaccessibility and ruggedness may have made Tasmania's mountain areas a 'green hell' for early explorers, but ensured the survival of a spectacularly beautiful remnant of the world's great temperate forests

Cradle Mountain, *at the northern end of Cradle Mountain Lake St Clair National Park, is today easily accessible*

Dense eucalypt forest *in the Asbestos Range seems almost impenetrable*

Mount Olympus *in the central western highlands was named by George Frankland, the Surveyor-General, in 1835. Bounded by sheer cliffs, it towers above the central plateau lakes.*

The Gordon River *is almost dwarfed by great chasms as it weaves through the wilderness for some 200 kilometres. Few people have seen its full beauty*

Chilling rains *are frequent in the steeply winding gorge of the Hellyer River,* above. *Flood-worn boulders,* left, *frame its banks*

Lake St Clair *lies in a long trough between Mount Olympus and the Traveller Range. It has densely forested shores, and nearby spectacular peaks delight today's travellers*

Frenchmans Cap *in the Deception Range is 1443 metres high. It may have been seen and named by Vancouver as he sailed up the west coast in 1791*

George Robinson's amazing walk round Tasmania

Robinson, the Aboriginals' champion, in a painting, The Conciliation, by Benjamin Duterrau. Robinson walked hundreds of kilometres to meet and help Aboriginals

*T*he educated ruling class in the island colony did not quite know what to make of him. George Augustus Robinson, born in London in 1788, was merely a self-educated carpenter and builder in Hobart Town. But he was also deeply religious, and arising from his faith was the belief that 'conciliation' instead of persecution of Tasmania's remaining Aboriginals could lead to social harmony. His doomed mission took him round the island.

In 1829 Robinson persuaded Lieutenant-Governor George Arthur to allow him to care for the Aboriginals of Bruny Island, south of Hobart. Soon he evolved the idea that he should travel throughout Tasmania to tell Aboriginals that a humane government would resettle, feed, civilise and christianise them.

With scarcely anything but his clothes and a small bag of wheatmeal, the forty-two-year-old missionary set off from Recherche Bay on 3 February 1830, accompanied by several Aboriginals he had befriended. They would teach him how to live off the land and would interpret his message to strange tribes.

During the next four years the little group walked round practically the whole perimeter of Tasmania, besides undertaking several arduous journeys inland. 'The idea had been ridiculed as visionary,' Robinson noted in his journal. Master mariners who knew the island stated firmly that 'it would be impossible to travel along the coast.'

At first Robinson wondered if they were right. En route to Port Davey the party pulled themselves through swamps 'half way up our legs in mud', and crawled through dense forests 'on knees and hands'. At night, heavy rain chilled them to the bone. By day Robinson learned to live on bulbous *tara* or bracken roots, oysters from the rocks, and a little ground wheat. For three days he was very ill with 'violent pain in the bowels'. But by 13 March 1830, he was able to climb high ridges which he named Arthur's Range, and view 'mountains rising upon mountains to a great altitude'.

There were no tribal Aboriginals at those heights waiting to be christianised. Robinson returned to the coast, slipping along narrow native tracks, trekking northwards along high rocky cliffs where the sea broke 'with such force that I frequently felt the spray.'

By 20 April, 'having been twenty days without animal food', Robinson reached Macquarie Harbour. He encountered sev-

GEORGE ROBINSON
PROTECTOR OF ABORIGINES

eral parties of natives, but most hid themselves and refused to accompany the missionary who had come so far to save them from extinction. 'This was the first time that ever white man had visited their territory for the avowed purpose of doing them good,' he wrote.

After a few days' rest, the northwards odyssey continued. To cross large raging rivers, the ex-carpenter showed his companions how to make rafts by lashing trees and driftwood together. The remaining wheatmeal became mixed with sand on these crossings, but on 13 May their dog caught a kangaroo 'which we roasted and ate heartily of', probably saving their lives. After fording several more rivers, the party arrived safely at the Van Diemen's Land Company settlement at Cape Grim on 14 June.

Shocking stories of atrocities

Now began the lengthy but easier trip along Tasmania's north coast to Launceston. Short of food again by 25 July, Robinson learned to eat the soft, white bases of native grass trees. The Aboriginals took stones, beat the core of young plants, and stripped off the outer leaves. 'I ate some and found it very nutritious,' wrote Robinson, 'in taste like a roasted chestnut.'

During August snow began to fall: 'It was exceeding heavy travelling and we were continually wet,' wrote Robinson. But at night, under a blanket rigged as a tent, 'I slept as soundly and felt as happy as I could wish.'

At the small European settlements of Emu Bay and Port Sorell, Robinson heard shocking stories of atrocities committed on the Aboriginals by convict servants of the Van Diemen's Land Company. Now he understood why blacks were so scarce on the coastline. 'The only difficulty I have is to approach the natives,' he wrote. 'In every case they have fled.'

Early in October 1830 Robinson passed through George Town and Launceston, but found the inhabitants either ignorant or suspicious of his mission. Many settlers were 'greatly astonished at my being unarmed' in the wilderness. He continued to the north-eastern tip of Tasmania, spending several months on Bass Strait islands helping to free Aboriginal women from virtual slavery to sealers: 'miscreants who ought to be forthwith removed,' Robinson described them. 'The black women said that the sealers beat them very much – flogged them.' But after their liberation 'the women enjoyed some hilarity, standing on the rocks and singing: would make a good picture,' he added.

Robinson returned briefly to Hobart by boat to obtain further instructions. From October to December 1831, he penetrated inland from Great Oyster Bay on the east coast practically to the centre of the island. After protracted negotiation he managed to persuade the aggressive remnants of the Big River tribe to accompany him back to Hobart under the government's protection. 'As always', he wrote, 'my object was not to capture by force but by persuasion and argument.'

For nearly three years more Robinson continued to travel round the island, rescuing isolated groups of Aboriginals from the disinterest or persecution of white sealers and settlers, and taking them to government camps established on Bass Strait islands.

On 14 June 1834, Robinson at last wrote, 'I am wearied of this life travelling round the country.' In October 1835 he took personal charge of the largest camp, established on Flinders Island. There, despite his best efforts to educate them in European ways, the natives continued to die off. Only about eighty were still living when Robinson was appointed Chief Protector of Aborigines in the new Port Phillip district in 1838.

With all his faults, Robinson was years ahead of most of his contemporaries in practical moral belief, geographical and survival information, and tenacity of purpose. The tragedy was that his knowledge and aspirations were not widely shared by other white Australians: even the better-organised Port Phillip protectorate collapsed after a few years under the pressure of squatting expansion. It was widely forecast that the native population would soon be only a memory of the early days. □

Woureddy *from the Bruny Island tribe, painted by Thomas Bock. Robinson took Woureddy and his wife Truganini on his journeys. They guided him, helped him communicate with tribes and showed him how to survive in the wilderness*

Dense rainforest *such as this on the Jane River frequently made Robinson's progress a misery. The trees are myrtle and Huon pine*

LADY (JANE) FRANKLIN
PIONEER AND NATURALIST

The enlightened and courageous John Franklin

Fortunately for Tasmania's development, a man keenly interested in discovering new areas was appointed lieutenant-governor in 1836. He was Sir John Franklin, whose career began as a humble midshipman under Matthew Flinders on the *Investigator*'s famous voyage round Australia.

Franklin did everything he could to encourage settlement and obtain more humane treatment for convicts. In 1841, when he was fifty-five, he began planning exploration 'of those Districts in the interior which are as yet almost unknown'.

Discovery of an easier route from Hobart across the mountains to Macquarie Harbour seemed a worthy challenge. His wife, the adventurous Lady Franklin, insisted on accompanying the governor. Why not? If a lady and her maid could conquer the mountains, the wilderness would lose most of the fear it inspired in ordinary settlers.

Franklin, the trail-blazer

The governor sent a surveyor, James Erskine Calder, ahead to cut a rough track as far as Lake St Clair and Frenchmans Cap. 'I stuck at nothing but went straight ahead like a rhinoceros,' Calder later wrote. So dense was the forest that his party 'never on an average cut more than a third of a mile a day.'

In March 1842 the governor and his retinue were able to set out on horseback. They admired the beauty of Lake St Clair, then struck camp to walk the rest of the way.

Slipping and sliding through heavy rain, they penetrated dense forests of antarctic beech and cabbage palm, to emerge at the junction of the Surprise and Franklin rivers. In the Loddon valley, they were trapped for a week by rain that had become torrential, causing every watercourse to flood. Franklin

SIR JOHN FRANKLIN
GOVERNOR OF TASMANIA

named their sanctuary on a piece of high ground Detention Corner.

As the rain eased, the travellers continued through the 'thick, slimy scrub' of the Acheron valley. Arriving at the Franklin river on 15 April 1842, they found it swirling with flood waters but falling. Two convicts managed to cross on a raft to delay the schooner *Breeze* awaiting their overdue arrival on the Gordon river. Other men built a large canoe of Huon pine, and ferried the whole party across the Franklin. A week later they were safely on board the *Breeze* after blazing a trail where no Europeans had been before.

Franklin died five years later, when his naval expedition attempting to find a north-west passage from the Atlantic to Pacific oceans was trapped in Arctic pack ice off King William Island. But the encouragement he had given to Tasmanian exploration had lasting effects.

In 1841 a contract surveyor, Nathaniel Kentish, discovered Kentish Plains in north-west Tasmania. In 1843-45 he surveyed the line of road from Deloraine to Emu Bay still

used today by travellers on the Bass Highway.

James Sprent, a government surveyor, erected more than two hundred mountaintop stations in order to complete the long-delayed trigonometrical survey and by 1859 was able to present the first authentic complete map of Tasmania, just three years after responsible self-government was introduced.

Even late in the century, new discoveries were still being made in wilderness areas. In 1878 Thomas Bather Moore, searching for new mineral deposits, discovered Lakes Margaret and Mary on Mount Sedgwick in north-west Tasmania. Five years later the government commissioned him to complete Sir John Franklin's old track from Lake St Clair to Macquarie Harbour, roughly along the route today known as the Lyell Highway.

The Franklin, *as untamed now as it was in 1842. The river was to sweep the name of the governor who sponsored natural science in the Colony into modern news headlines during the battle for its preservation in the early eighties*

Phillip Parker King takes up the challenge from Flinders

*T*he Royal Navy provided a great life for young adventurers. Phillip Parker King, born on Norfolk Island in 1791, was raised on stories of naval heroism. His father, the third Governor of New South Wales, gladly entered the boy for Portsmouth Naval Academy. More importantly, he introduced him to Matthew Flinders, seventeen years older, but still possessed by youthful enthusiasm to discover unknown Australia.

Flinders in turn introduced King to the Admiralty hydrographer, who trained the lad carefully in marine surveying techniques. By 1817, after promotion to lieutenant, King was ready to carry on the work left undone when Flinders was imprisoned by the French.

After Napoleon's final defeat, the British Government decided that 'circumstances consequent upon the restoration of Peace…rendered it most important to explore, with as little delay as possible, that part of the coast of New Holland…not surveyed or examined by the late Captain Flinders.' King, still only twenty-six years old, was instructed to examine all gulfs and openings 'likely to lead to an interior navigation into this great continent', and to report on natural resources, topography, botany, climate and native inhabitants.

King's first voyage left Sydney on 22 December 1817 in the near-new cutter *Mermaid*. Among its complement of nineteen were the young Allan Cunningham and John Roe, both destined to become notable land explorers, and the Aboriginal Bungaree, who had sailed with Flinders in the *Investigator*.

Since the monsoon season was well advanced, King decided to sail south via Twofold Bay and King George Sound to reach the northern coasts. Arriving at North West Cape on 10 February 1818, his men were 'assailed by an incredible number of flies', while 'the sea swarmed with turtles, sea-snakes, and fish of various sorts'. Flood tides on this coast frayed their ship's cables and broke most of their anchors.

The botanists landed in forty-eight degree heat, to report country of 'most desert-like appearance', covered with immense ant-hills and stunted vegetation. King named his landing point Exmouth Gulf, after 'the noble and gallant Viscount', Edward Pellew Exmouth, hero of the Napoleonic wars.

King noted frequent hot winds from the interior, leading him to conclude that 'the interior of this immense island is occupied by vast sandy deserts' — not an inland sea.

Late in February the explorers saw a one hundred and eighty-two centimetre tall Aboriginal sitting on a mangrove log, paddling furiously with his hands through the water towards an island. They captured him, calmed him down, and gave him a red cap, a bag of biscuits, an axe and a fishing line to take back to shore. The white men then landed, but could not entice the terrified tribesmen closer until Bungaree appeared. 'On his taking off his shirt they shouted loudly, and were delighted,' wrote King. But little information of value to the Euro-

An encounter between King's Mermaid and Malay proas allowed him to report that the northern coast was still visited for trepang fishing

peans could be gained from the encounter with the group.

On 4 March 1818, King sailed through Dampier's Archipelago to enter and name Nickol Bay, beyond today's town of Dampier. They anchored three kilometres from land, but so severe were the storms that 'sand was blown over us from the shore'.

Late that month they sailed between Goulburn Island and today's Arnhem Land Aboriginal Reserve, naming the passage Macquarie Strait. On land, wrote King, 'every thing bore the most luxuriant appearance; the grass was more than six feet high', and wild flowers bloomed everywhere. But natives crept through the tall grass and began removing several flagstaffs erected as a base-line for surveying operations. 'Two musquets were fired', wrote King. On 30 March a group of Aboriginals appeared above the cliffs where seamen were filling water casks. They hurled several large stones, injuring three whites.

On 16 April 1818 King sailed past Croker Island into a sheltered inlet which he named Raffles Bay, after Sir Stamford Raffles, prominent colonial administrator. A few days later, King named Port Essington after his 'late lamented friend', Vice-Admiral Sir William Essington. The explorer thought it was equal to any harbour he had ever seen, and destined to become 'a place of great trade'. But official settlements made there a few years later proved unsuccessful.

Entering Van Diemen Gulf on 25 April 1818, King named Popham Bay after Rear-Admiral Sir Home Popham, and Mounts Roe and Bedwell after the *Mermaid*'s midshipmen. The men explored the South Alligator and East Alligator rivers for some kilometres but had difficulty in landing through mud and mangroves.

On 21 May King thought he had discovered a huge navigable river. Further investigation showed it to be a strait. He named Apsley Strait that separates Melville and Bathurst islands. Shortage of bread and faulty water casks (which had foolishly been made in Sydney from old salt casks) forced King to return via Timor and Tasmania.

A narrow escape for the *Mermaid*
After surveying Macquarie Harbour and refitting the *Mermaid* in Sydney, King took John Oxley in May 1819 back to his recently discovered Port Macquarie. Together they explored the Hastings river, discovering fine 'open forest land, abundantly clothed with luxuriant grass and moderate-sized timber'. As a result of their report, the Governor established a penal settlement there in 1821 under Captain Francis Allman. Two years later, Australia's first sugar-cane was grown along the Hastings river.

Oxley returned to Sydney in the *Lady Nelson*, but King continued north in the *Mermaid*. On 23 May, he deduced there was a large river flowing to the sea from Mount Warning. Oxley later confirmed this to be the Tweed river.

Sailing carefully along the inner passage between the Barrier Reef and the mainland, King added so much to information gathered by Cook and Flinders that his directions became known as King's Route on the charts.

Late in June 1819 the *Mermaid* dropped anchor at the same spot in the Endeavour river where Cook had repaired his vessel nearly half a century before. King's men burned the grass all about to prevent a repetition of the method by

Cobourg Peninsula, *at the northernmost tip of the Northern Territory. King sailed past nearby Croker Island on April 14, 1818 naming it for the First Secretary of the Admiralty*

Four years of adventurous sailing and careful charting produce results

Captain Phillip Parker King wore out one ship in his tireless efforts to fill in the gaps on the charts of the Australian coast. He succeeded in everything *but the Admiralty's most cherished hope — that he would find 'an interior navigation into this great continent'. His charts were used for a century*

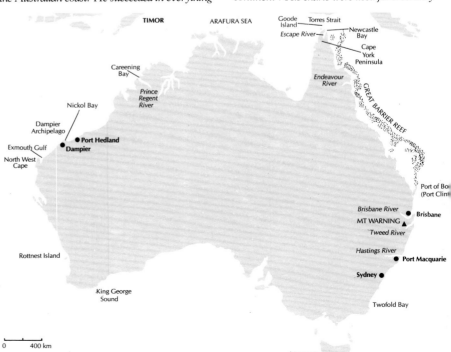

On March 27 1818, King came upon the Goulburn Islands. Three days later, angry Aboriginals confronted a watering party

which Aboriginals had attempted to drive Cook away. King sailed upriver and round the bay in a small boat, discovering the wreck of the *Frederick*, which had disappeared the previous year. There was no trace of survivors.

King himself was nearly wrecked when he sailed into Newcastle Bay on the eastern tip of Cape York Peninsula on 24 July 1819. Near an inlet the water shoaled rapidly to three fathoms. The *Mermaid* ran aground, then 'struck the ground rapidly every time that the swell

FLINDERS AND MACQUARIE NAME *AUSTRALIA*

Although Matthew Flinders proposed use of the name 'Australia' in 1814, the Admiralty instructed Lieutenant Phillip Parker King to explore the unknown coasts of 'New Holland'.

Governor Lachlan Macquarie, reporting his purchase of the 83-tonne cutter *Mermaid* for King's use, requested the British Government to adopt the name 'Australia'. On 21 December 1817, he wrote:
Lieut. King expects to be absent from Port Jackson between Eight and Nine Months, and I trust in that time will be able to make very important additions to the Geographical knowledge already acquired of the Coasts of the Continent of Australia, which I hope will be the Name given to this Country in future, instead of the very erroneous and misapplied name, hitherto given it, of 'New Holland'...

Within a few years, use of Australia became general practice.

passed by.' Had the cutter remained there all night, wrote King, 'the sea was so heavy that there would not have been the least vestige of her the following morning.' Eventually the crew managed to gybe the main sail and jerk the *Mermaid* out of the shoals. To commemorate his narrow escape, King named the entrance Escape river.

Mosquitoes, rats and cockroaches
Next day, anchoring near Goode Island, the *Mermaid's* second Sydney-made anchor broke, leaving only the bower anchor for completing the survey.

King resumed charting the northern coastline near Cape Wessel, the tip of a long chain of islands reaching from Arnhem Land into the Arafura Sea. He sailed into Boucaut Bay and discovered the mouth of the Liverpool river, later to be recommended as a site for the capital of the Northern Territory.

Here, wrote King, it was impossible to obtain any sleep, 'in consequence of the immense swarms of mosquitoes, which buzzing about in incredible numbers were not to be kept from stinging us by any measures we could devise. The tent was very soon deserted, and many other places were tried in vain; the only method at all successful, by which some relief was obtained, was by lying upon the ground within two feet of the blaze of the fire; the heat and smoke of which, with the danger of our clothes catching fire, were insignificant inconveniences com-

King's **Mermaid** *sprang a leak while surveying York Sound and was laid up on a steep beach at the height of a big spring tide for repairs. The sketch of the encampment set up at Careening Bay was made by King himself*

pared with the mosquitoes' stings'. In September 1819 King discovered the large opening of Cambridge Gulf on the north-west coast, naming it after the Duke of Cambridge. Near the entrance King sketched 'a most remarkable quadrangular-shaped mass of hills', which he named Mount Cockburn after Vice-Admiral Sir George Cockburn.

Although King could only guess at the existence of adjacent river systems, it was later discovered that the Ord, Forrest, Durack, King and Pentecost all flow into Cambridge Gulf. During the 1880s the port of Wyndham was established on the Gulf's West Arm to give access to the

Bungaree, *said to be a tribal chief, who had sailed with Flinders in the Investigator, also took part in King's first expedition to help complete Flinders's surveying work round the coast*

Kimberley goldfields and cattle stations.

With provisions again short and the cyclone season approaching, King ran for Timor and thence to Sydney by the familiar southern route. He purposely submerged the *Mermaid* on the east side of Sydney Cove in an attempt to destroy thousands of rats and cockroaches with which she was infested. This was to no avail, as a few days later the infestation was as bad as ever. The rats even ate into casks of musket ball cartridges.

King left Sydney on his third voyage of discovery on 13 June 1820. The following month the *Mermaid* ran aground off Port Clinton and was severely damaged in a storm. The cutter limped to the north-west coast to continue the survey, but could achieve little.

On 22 September 1820, the *Mermaid* was beached at an inlet of today's Prince Regent River Reserve, which King named Careening Bay. He discovered that the keel and stern-post had become almost separated from the main frame. But the spike nails which fastened the planks were 'so entirely decomposed by oxidation, that a straw was easily thrust through the vacant holes'. The only solution was to run again for Sydney.

An extraordinary collection of wildlife
For his fourth and final voyage, King was supplied with the 170-tonne teak-built brig *Bathurst*. This was large enough to carry a long-boat, which in an emergency could take anchors and warp the larger

A sound appraisal of the north-west coast

On the northern coast King investigated almost every opening for twelve hundred kilometres. At Port Essington he found a harbour 'equal, if not superior to any I ever saw', but reported that Arnhem Land was 'dreary, uninterrupted flat country'

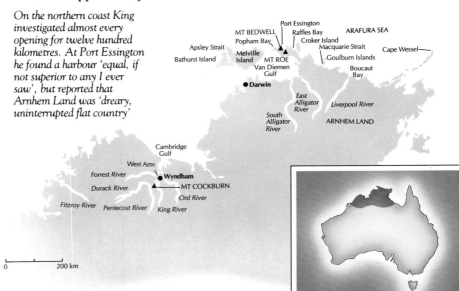

vessel off any shoals she might strike.

By 26 July 1821, King was back in Prince Regent river. Using the long-boat, he was able to discover a beautiful cascade which drops into the salt river near a fresh-water rivulet where the ship's casks could be refilled.

After charting many islands in the area, King made a swift trip to Mauritius for more provisions. On his return he sailed first to King George Sound. By January 1822 he was surveying Rottnest

Island, and from there continued northwards to join up his earlier charts as far as North West Cape.

Rats again destroyed most of the stores. *Bathurst* arrived back at Sydney on 25 April 1822 after a voyage lasting three hundred and forty-four days.

Altogether, in more than four years of adventurous sailing, King had delineated the Queensland coastline for eleven hundred kilometres south of Cape York. He had laid down a safe and convenient

track for vessels through Torres Strait. On the northern and north-western coasts from Cape Wessel westwards, he had explored practically every opening for more than twelve hundred kilometres. He had surveyed the south-western coast from Rottnest Island almost to today's Port Hedland. In addition, botanist Allan Cunningham had gathered an 'extensive and valuable collection'.

King's main regret was that there had not been sufficient time or space to collect more specimens of birds and animals. 'No country has ever produced a more extraordinary assemblage of indigenous productions', he wrote. 'No country has proved richer than Australia in every branch of natural history'.

Nearly twenty charts based on King's careful surveys were published in 1825, and remained in use for more than a century. This notable Australian-born explorer spent several years charting South American coasts before returning to his Sydney estates. For ten years from 1834 he was resident commissioner for the Australian Agricultural Company. In 1855 he was promoted rear-admiral, and died the following year, a renowned patriot who disliked the rough democracy brought by the gold rushes. □

King's own sketch, below, *of the impressive cascades on Prince Regent River in the Kimberleys, and the falls, left, as they are today. He was obviously impressed — but possibly more by the crucial fresh water than their scenic charm*

JOHN OXLEY DISCOVERS THE BRISBANE RIVER

Despite opposition *from the British Government, the settlement of Brisbane began as a penal colony. By 1846, when this sketch was drawn, it had thrown off its chains and become a base for the development of the north-east*

Charting of the Queensland coast by Cook, Flinders and King led to the closer exploration of Port Curtis and Moreton Bay by John Oxley in 1823.

Oxley sailed from Sydney in the *Mermaid* on 23 October. He soon rejected Port Curtis as a suitable harbour for sailing ships because of its numerous shoals and mangrove swamps — although in 1846 it became the site of a penal colony.

Returning southward, the *Mermaid* entered Moreton Bay and anchored off Pumicestone Channel on 29 November 1823. Oxley decided to trace the bay's little-known western shore in a small boat. On 2 December, he wrote, 'we had the Satisfaction to find the tide Sweeping us up a considerable Inlet'. Oxley had discovered the Brisbane river, naming it after the New South Wales Governor, Sir Thomas Brisbane.

The surveyor traced the river for about eighty kilometres, enthusing over the 'peculiarly beautiful' scenery and 'soil of the finest description'. He forecast that the river would allow water communication with 'a Vast extent of Country, a great portion of which appeared to me Capable of Supporting the Cultivation of the richest production of the Tropics'. Even the natives 'appeared to possess a most friendly disposition'.

A penal settlement was formed at Moreton Bay in 1826 under the fierce discipline of Captain Patrick Logan. This Scottish-born soldier conducted his own explorations, discovering the Logan river in 1826, the Albert river in 1827, and climbing the 1700-metre Mount Barney in 1828. Two years later Logan was killed in the bush, probably by Aboriginals, while exploring the upper Brisbane river.

The penal settlement was closed in 1842 and Brisbane arose on the site.

Abandoned fortresses of the north

The British Government supported Phillip Parker King's views on the importance of controlling Australia's northern sea approaches. It decided to establish a settlement at Port Essington on the Cobourg Peninsula in today's Northern Territory.

Captain James John Gordon Bremer, RN, a thirty-eight-year-old veteran of the Napoleonic Wars, was despatched on HMS *Tamar* in 1824 with a strong party of soldiers and convicts. Bremer's first act was to proclaim formal British possession of a further huge strip of Australia, from longitude 135 degrees, westwards to today's Western Australian border (129 degrees east).

Privately Bremer must have been horrified by King's choice of location, for no fresh water could be found at Port Essington. Within a week the party moved to Melville Island near by, and established Fort Dundas where a small stream entered Apsley Strait.

One of the group, Lieutenant John Roe, RN, surveyed St Asaph Bay and Port Cockburn between Melville and Bathurst islands. Roe soon reported to his old friend King that Fort Dundas had taken on 'the appearance of a fortified village'. Officers' quarters were erected within the walls of the fort, and a deep well sunk near by. Outside, about thirty huts with roofs of thatched rushes were thrown up for soldiers and convicts. A

wharf and store were built, and a large vegetable garden established.

The good times were not to last. Most of the sheep they had brought died after eating poison weed. The natives, at first shy, became aggressive. Tropical diseases ravaged the military's strength. As a crowning insult to British naval prestige, Malay pirates captured both the *Lady Nelson* and the brig *Stedcombe* which were bringing fresh provisions.

While Fort Dundas sank into tropical torpor, a further attempt to settle the north was made at Raffles Bay, at the north-eastern end of the Cobourg Peninsula. James Stirling, a thirty-six-year-old Scottish-born naval captain who had fought against the French, Spanish and Americans raised the British flag there in June 1827.

Similar problems arose as at Fort Dundas. In 1829 the government decided to abandon both settlements and concentrate for the time being on the promising south-westerly regions where Perth and Albany now stand.

'A useless hole'

By 1838, Britain was about to get involved through its traders in the Chinese opium wars which would result in the seizure of Hong Kong island. The government in London decided to make another attempt to establish a combined military and naval base at Port Essington.

A substantial force was sent under Captain Bremer on HMS *Alligator*. With him in command of the naval brig *Britomart* was Lieutenant Owen Stanley, twenty-seven-year-old son of the Bishop of Norwich. Stanley had already trained with P. P. King and John Franklin. Three store ships carried ample provisions.

This time a sufficient water supply was found at Barrow Bay, a southerly inlet of Port

Owen Stanley, a proficient draughtsman, was a lieutenant with Bremer's expedition to form a settlement at Port Essington at the northern tip of Arnhem Land. He made this sketch of the fortress built in a subsequent attempt at settlement when he returned as captain of the Rattlesnake, *some ten years later in 1847. Stanley died in 1850*

Victoria Square, near Port Essington, as it was when Captain Francis Price Blackwood, who was undertaking hydrographic surveys of the Coral Sea area in 1842, visited in the Fly

Essington. Here a new fortified settlement was built and given the name Victoria.

A single-storey government house was built within the fort. When Dumont d'Urville's scientific expedition put into the harbour a few months later, Captain Bremer entertained the French officers at a dinner which included 'good buffalo meat, a superb turkey, and excellent fowls obtained from Timor — the whole washed down with vintage Sauterne and Bordeaux wines.'

D'Urville wrote that he admired the white-haired Bremer, 'who had left his country, his family, to come to this inhospitable land.' Not one of the Frenchmen 'had the heart to destroy his illusions' about its chances of survival.

Without trade, private settlement, or other everyday function, Victoria too faded into oblivion after several years. The young biologist Thomas Huxley, visiting in 1848, called it 'the most useless, miserable, ill-managed hole in Her Majesty's dominions.' Yet perhaps it had kept other nations from settling in Australia's north.

The settlement of Victoria today — fragments of a fortress that was to have protected the nation's north. At left, the remains of walls and a fireplace from the married quarters

Ruins of the hospital kitchen stand sentinel where Captain James Bremer's brave settlers tackled the overwhelming difficulties of establishing an outpost of white civilisation

British bastions crumble into neglect and oblivion

Port Essington and nearby sites of northern settlement had some use in the continuing exploration of the north. Leichhardt was glad to see 'white houses and thatched cottages' at the end of his 1845 trek from Moreton Bay

St Asaph Bay
Port Cockburn
●Fort Dundas
Bathurst Island
Melville Island
Apsley Strait
Popham Bay
Cobourg Peninsula
Port Essington   Raffles Bay
●
Victoria
—Barrow Bay
Van Diemen Gulf
●Darwin

Britain settles in the west and claims all Australia

Once Britain appreciated the possibilities of its Australian settlements, it became determined to explore and colonise key points round the vast coastline.
In 1826 Secretary for the Colonies, Earl Bathurst ordered the occupation of Dampier's Shark Bay. This large inlet on the west Australian coast where Carnarvon now stands had just been closely examined by the French. Almost as an afterthought, Bathurst ordered that King George Sound, discovered by Captain George Vancouver in 1791, should be settled first — but that Britain should press its claim to sovereignty over the entire continent.

Governor Darling sent Major Edmund Lockyer, a forty-two-year-old Devon-born soldier already noted for his discovery of the Lockyer and Stanley rivers in Queensland, to claim and occupy King George Sound.

Lockyer's expedition of twenty soldiers and twenty-four convicts reached the site of Albany on Christmas Day 1826. After raising the flag and establishing a military camp, Lockyer set out on the first lengthy inland exploration to be undertaken in Western Australia. His aim was to reach the Swan river, but after tracing the Kalgan river to its source, shortage of provisions forced him back.

Even this sixty-four kilometre essay promised great things. 'The Country became better as I proceeded inland,' Lockyer reported. 'With a Spy glass I could plainly discern that the trees were covered with most luxuriant green foliage, from which I am confident the land there must be good.'

SIR JAMES STIRLING
GOVERNOR OF THE NEW COLONY

The foundation of Perth. *On August 12, 1829, a party of men and one woman declared a townsite 22 kilometres upstream from Fremantle on the Swan. With no stone handy, Mrs Dance, wife of the captain of the* Sulphur, *instead struck a ceremonial blow at a convenient gum tree with a hatchet*

King George Sound *was settled by Edmund Lockyer and a party of convicts and soldiers on Christmas Day 1826. By January 10, he reported buildings had been erected and a garden dug. Lieutenant Richard Dale, of the Sixty-Third Regiment, drew this panorama of the sound in 1834. By 1832, the name Albany was being used for the town on Princess Royal Harbour*

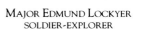

MAJOR EDMUND LOCKYER
SOLDIER-EXPLORER

CHARLES HOWE FREMANTLE
PAINTING BY A. ROBERTSON

In March 1827 Captain James Stirling arrived in HMS *Success* to explore the Swan river from its sea approaches. Using small boats, he and his men sailed beyond today's Herne Hill to trace the river to its source. His enthusiasm for the adjacent land was overwhelming:

I represent it as the Land which, of all that I have seen in various quarters of the World, possesses the greatest natural attractions… I beg leave to state briefly That the Climate is equally healthy as that of the Cape and New South Wales; that it permits Europeans to labour throughout the day and in every Season of the Year; That according to the Testimony of an experienced Person who accompanied me, the Soil is admirably calculated for every Species of Cultivation; That the Territory is abundantly supplied with fresh Water; and finally that, in the Neighbourhood of Swan River, there is Safe Anchorage, which may be easily converted into one of the finest Harbours in the World.

Greatly encouraged by Stirling's report, the British Government agreed that a colony of free settlers should be estab-lished as soon as possible with Stirling as first Lieutenant-Governor.

Captain Charles Fremantle was sent in HMS *Challenger* to take formal possession for Britain 'of all that part of New Holland which is not included in the territory of New South Wales'.

On 2 May 1829, Captain Fremantle hoisted the Union Jack on the south head of the Swan river where Fremantle now stands. Stirling's party arrived on 18 June. On 12 August 1829, the foundation of Perth was proclaimed at a vigorous ceremony in which Mrs Dance, wife of the captain of HMS *Sulphur*, blazed a gum tree with an axe.

Settlers quickly occupied all the best land on the banks of the Swan. On 2 November 1829, Stirling declared open the country eighty kilometres southwards from Perth. Settlers of 'adventurous and laudable spirit' swarmed into it. Many severe pioneering difficulties were experienced, but a foundation was laid for the heroic western exploring expeditions of the later nineteenth century. □

The celebrated Beagle adds an Australian chapter to her log of achievements

JOHN LORT STOKES
IN 1877, AS ADMIRAL

Of all ships used in the history of human exploration, HMS Beagle *should be counted among the most famous. She was only a despised ten-gun brig or 'coffin ship', but her shallow draught made her all the more suitable for the work she was to do over the next five years exploring Australian coastal waters. And on her first trip to Australia in 1836 she carried the little-known naturalist Charles Darwin, then only twenty-seven years old.*

While in South America, Darwin first noticed similarities — and yet significant differences — between fossil remains and living flora and fauna. Continuing to Australia, and taking the coach road to Bathurst, Darwin found himself 'reflecting on the strange character of the animals of this country.' Was it likely

Derby's King Sound, *where Stokes took the Beagle's yawl and a whaleboat in March 1838. The Beagle also sailed round Cape Upstart south-east of Townsville in June 1839 and into Upstart Bay. Four years later, HMS Fly and Bramber anchored there while surveying the coast. This sketch of the encampment, below, is by Harden Melville, draftsman to the expedition*

that 'Two distinct Creators must have been at work'? Or that the biblical tale of creation was merely a legend? That all living things had started as simpler forms? That they had evolved to their present state through a long process of competition for space and food? That Australia was different because it was so isolated from the rest of the world? These revolutionary notions fermented in Darwin's mind, resulting in the publication twenty-three years later of his epochal work *The Origin of the Species by Means of Natural Selection.*

More immediate concerns occupied the minds of his naval friends. The *Beagle* was sent back to Australia in 1837 under

Commander John Clements Wickham, thirty-nine, and Lieutenant John Lort Stokes, twenty-five. Their instructions were to finalise the survey of both Bass Strait and Torres Strait and complete the examination of inlets in north-western Australia that might lead to a navigable inland waterway. For more than five years the *Beagle's* crew persevered with these lonely, dangerous tasks.

Dense mangrove forests *along northern coasts often made inland penetration difficult for Stokes who was always keen to leave the Beagle and go exploring on land. He hoped that one of these northern rivers would turn out to be a navigable route to the heart of the continent*

Many discoveries were made as the little *Beagle* edged her way around the coastline. Starting at Disaster Bay in King Sound, where Phillip Parker King had been forced to abandon his north-western exploration, Lieutenant Stokes eagerly took up the challenge. 'With what delight, all minor annoyances forgotten, I prepared to enter upon the exciting task of exploring waters unfurrowed by any preceding keel,' he wrote.

Early in March 1838, Stokes took a yawl and whaleboat into a promising opening south of today's Derby. As the tide fell, he found the water became almost fresh, a sure sign of a major river. When they anchored that night, Stokes made special preparations for the huge tidal inflow he knew was coming. He was awakened by 'a loud roaring...the voice of thunder'. Then the boats were struck by the full force of the tide, 'like a wall, several feet high'. The yawl was thrown upon her side: 'had it not been for the shores lashed to each mast, she must inevitably have capsized'.

Stokes named the vigorous river after Robert FitzRoy, captain of the *Beagle*

during her voyage with Charles Darwin. Was this the long-sought access river to the interior? Stokes managed to trace it for thirty-five kilometres, but reflected that 'we were still distant 600 miles' (nine hundred and sixty kilometres) from the centre of Australia.

Stokes's crew aids Grey's expedition

During April 1838 the *Beagle*'s men surveyed several offshore islands and examined Brecknock Harbour. Despite the tidal rise here of nearly nine metres, they discovered so much 'luxuriant well-watered country' inland that Stokes considered it 'a great addition to our discoveries'. Today it is part of Kunmunya Aboriginal Reserve.

At a nearby northern inlet called Hanover Bay, the *Beagle* was able to succour an inland expedition led by the army lieutenant George Grey. Grey had started as a light-hearted twenty-six year-old explorer: when he returned wrote Stokes, 'gaunt misery had worn him to the bone'.

For the remainder of 1838 the *Beagle* surveyed the sea entrances to the Swan

Surveys by the Beagle crew take five dangerous and difficult years

Commander Wickham's instructions were to complete the surveying of Bass Strait and of Torres Strait; as well, the surveyors were to examine promising inlets on the north-west coast for a river leading to the centre. The Beagle ended her work in Fremantle in 1843

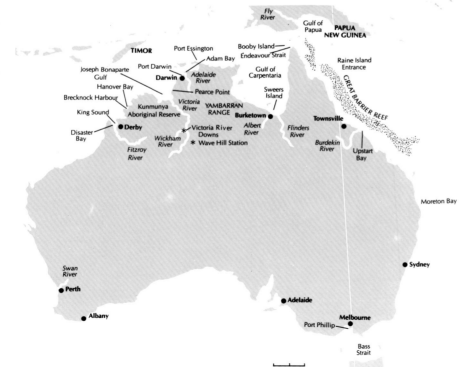

river, Port Adelaide and Port Phillip, compiling charts that remained in use for many years.

On 22 May 1839, the *Beagle* left Sydney for northern waters, re-surveying sections of the Queensland coast to assist naval and commercial shipping.

The joys of discovery
During June 1839 Wickham sailed into Upstart Bay, south-east of today's Townsville. The inlet had been discovered in 1819 by King, who believed that a substantial river must rise in mountains he could see to the south and west. After much searching, Wickham discovered its hidden entrance and named it after himself. Six years later Ludwig Leichhardt crossed the same river further inland. Not realising it was the Wickham he named it the Burdekin after a prominent Sydney benefactor, Mrs Thomas Burdekin, and it keeps that name today.

The *Beagle* left Port Essington in July 1839 to continue charting the northwest coast. On the twenty-seventh, a junior officer, L. R. Fitzmaurice, who had been sent out with a boat's crew, returned with the 'very gratifying intelligence' that he had discovered a large river at the head of Adam Bay (named after Vice-Admiral Sir Charles Adam).

Was this, at last, the way to the promised land? Stokes wrote: 'The joy a

discovery of this nature imparts to the explorer, when examining a country so proverbially destitute of rivers as Australia, is much more easily imagined than described.'

Commander Wickham named this latest discovery the Adelaide river, after the dowager Queen Adelaide. He set off in a small boat to explore its branches, but soon encountered what the mate, Ben Helpman, summed up as 'one continued mass of mangroves, mosquitoes, mud and misery'. The crew could find nowhere to land. Helpman described how their daily cooking of rations was performed without setting the boat on fire:

The anchor is laid across the bow of the boat, on this a large tin dish is laid in which

Surveyors from the Beagle *'dance for their lives' to appease and distract threatening Aboriginals who had interrupted their work*

An exploring party *travelling up the Flinders River in July 1841. This spot was called Burial Reach — a native burial platform can be seen in a tree on the right of the sketch. The Flinders too failed to reveal the promised land although today it is the heart of good cattle country*

After the *Beagle* returned to England, several British ships equipped with the most up-to-date instruments continued to survey difficult parts of the Australian coastline. They concentrated on Torres Strait and the Queensland coast, which before the gold rush was thought to be the best route to Sydney.

In 1842 Captain Francis Blackwood, thirty-three, brought the new hydrographic corvette HMS *Fly* to Australian waters, accompanied by the cutter *Bramble*. For three years they charted more than sixteen hundred kilometres of the Barrier Reef, Endeavour Strait and dangerous sections of Torres Strait.

Messages collected from the 'post office' on Booby Island showed that nearly every ship penetrated the Barrier Reef at Raine's Inlet, now called Raine Island Entrance, guided by a beacon erected there by Blackwood's men in June 1844.

Turning to the almost unknown south-eastern coast of Papua New Guinea, Blackwood sighted the Fly River, largest river in the island, flowing into the Gulf of Papua. This discovery was an essential preliminary to land exploration.

Also on board the *Fly* were two young scientists: John MacGillivray, a twenty-one-year-old zoologist, and Joseph Jukes, a thirty-one-year-old geologist.

MacGillivray collected specimens of birds, plants and shells, still housed in British and Australian museums.

Jukes concentrated on the first detailed examination of the Barrier Reef, all his conclusions supporting Charles Darwin's theory of the growth of coral reefs.

The *Fly*'s work was continued from 1853 by Captain Henry Denham in HMS *Herald*. For nine years Denham cruised Australian waters, preparing two hundred revised charts which helped to guide the vastly increased shipping of gold-rush years safely to its destination.

Raine Island's tower *was built in 1844 to guide ships to the Barrier Reef's entrance*

---

the fire is placed; the pot on top of this. The whole securely lashed down; the pulling (rowing) *makes this precaution necessary.*

Lieutenant Stokes, attempting to take bearings among the dense mangroves, cut level stumps on which to rest his artificial horizon. But the mangroves were so connected by 'a perfect network of roots' that the mercury would not settle. Stokes heartily wished he had brought one of the new pendulum horizons invented by Captain Becher, RN.

In the main branch, the boat was able to navigate forty-eight kilometres upstream in the 'deep unbroken silence'. However, the work of fully tracing its one hundred and seventy-six-kilometre course, past its crossing point with today's highway south of Darwin, had to be left to later generations.

The *Beagle* left Port Essington again on 4 September 1839 to continue the survey westwards. On the ninth the explorers discovered 'a wide bay appearing between two white cliffy heads.' The whiteness came from deposits of talc slate: Wickham named one point Talc Head.

Other rocks nearby were of fine-grained sandstone, 'a new feature in the geology of this part of the continent,' wrote Stokes, 'which afforded us an appropriate opportunity of convincing an old shipmate and friend that he still lived in our memory; and we accordingly named this sheet of water Port Darwin.'

The natives at Darwin were astounded when one of the *Beagle*'s officers used a flint and steel to light his cigar. They screamed 'irru, irru' and 'darted off most unceremoniously, clambering up the face of a precipitous cliff.'

Northern Territory's largest river

On 9 October 1839, the *Beagle* sighted Pearce Point, and entered Joseph Bonaparte Gulf. Previous explorers had been forced out of this huge bay by navigational hazards. The *Beagle* however was able to feel its way quite close to the high rocky hills. By moonlight on 17 October it anchored where a huge body of fresh water poured into the gulf. According to Stokes, several officers exclaimed at once, 'This is indeed a noble river!' Captain Wickham immedi-

Victoria River Downs *has been grazing beef cattle on its 12 000 square kilometres for over a hundred years. The Wickham River, a tributary of the Victoria, and named after the* Beagle's *commander, flows past the homestead. Katherine, 376 kilometres away, is the nearest town*

ately named it the Victoria, after the Queen of England.

Next morning the ship's boats pulled twenty-five kilometres up the 'splendid sheet of water', then suddenly found its direction changing towards the Yambarran Range, and thus 'likely to disappoint our expectation that the Victoria would prove a high road to the interior of the continent'. Just the same, the explorers had discovered the Northern Territory's largest river, and future site of the huge Victoria Downs and Wave Hill cattle stations. One of its tributaries was to be named Wickham River after the *Beagle*'s captain.

On 7 December 1839, exploring the shore around Pearce Point, Lieutenant Stokes was 'suddenly staggered by a violent and piercing blow about the left shoulder'. Looking up, he saw the cliffs 'swarming with dusky forms'. Stokes managed to pull the spear from his chest and stagger back to his boat.

For most of 1840 the *Beagle* cruised to Timor, Swan River, Albany, Adelaide and Sydney. In June 1841 it began a close examination of the Gulf of Carpentaria. By this time Stokes had replaced Wickham as captain.

On Sweers Island the explorers dis-covered an old well dug by Matthew Flinders's men. Nearby, still legible after forty years, they found the name *Investigator* cut into a tree. On the opposite side they cut the word *Beagle*. 'All the adventures and sufferings of the intrepid Flinders vividly recurred to our memory', wrote Stokes. He resolved that the first river discovered in the Gulf should be named after their predecessor.

Beagle's final Australian discoveries

On 29 July 1841, Captain Stokes discovered the outlet of Queensland's longest river where it flows into the Gulf, and kept his promise to name it after Flinders. Battling their way past shoals and mangroves in a four-oared gig, ignoring the 'huge flock of screeching vampyres' (fruit bats) and whistling ducks overhead, the men emerged to 'an indefinite expanse of limpid water reposing between two vast plains'. The area would become valuable cattle country.

In August 1841 the *Beagle* made its final major discovery in Australia. Sighting a favourable opening along the Gulf's wide southern curve, Stokes took the gig and whaleboat into the mangroves to find an encouraging freshwater stream to the north-east of today's Burketown. He

Stokes was speared *when he came ashore at Pearce Point, just to the north of the Victoria River. He had been planning to take observations of latitude and longitude. His chronometer and other instruments are shown in this reconstruction painted by Richard Bridges Beechey*

named it the Albert river.

Still thinking he might sail to the centre of the continent, Stokes named one attractive straight stretch Hope Reach. After eighty kilometres of rowing, wrote Stokes, 'a view burst upon me'. It was 'a vast boundless plain', with excellent soil of such depth that he called the view 'the Plains of Promise'.

Shortage of provisions forced a return to the ship, but not before Stokes had given 'one long lingering look to the southward'. There, he thought, on these deserted plains he could discover 'the rudiments of future prosperity' — 'the now level horizon would be broken by a succession of tapering spires rising from the many christian hamlets that must ultimately stud this country'. In fact, for many years only Leichhardt would traverse this country from east to west, while the equally doomed Burke and Wills would come tramping up from the south like men possessed. ☐

121

A ford on the Ovens River, by J.B. Henderson

CHAPTER FOUR

Explorers of the golden eastern crescent

Squatters surge south to find unknown fertile regions

During the eighteen-twenties Mexico threw off the rule of Spain, Brazil became independent of Portugal, military conspirators attempted a revolution in Russia, US President James Monroe warned European powers not to intervene in the Americas and Greece won its freedom from the Turks. The newly-discovered power of steam was applied to railways and small vessels, and men began tinkering with electricity.

In remote Australia only two settlements of any size existed — the slab of nineteen counties clustered round Sydney, and the scattering of hamlets and farms throughout Tasmania. The rapidly changing world of Europe and America meant only one thing to Australians: that good markets existed for two items that could be transported right across the globe and still be sold at a profit. The first product was whale oil and the second was wool.

Whaling in Australian waters reached a peak in the eighteen-twenties and eighteen-thirties. Dozens of noisome boiling-down stations were established on the south-eastern coast from Sydney to Portland and in Tasmania. Even in 1830 sperm oil and whalebone remained the largest items of export from Australia. Whalers and sealers explored many wild parts of the coast, showing which inlets and islands were suitable for settlement.

As oil lamps gave way to the new gas

ALEXANDER BERRY
SHOALHAVEN PIONEER

lighting, whaling gradually diminished. Fortunately the rapidly expanding wool-processing industries of Britain and Europe began to demand large quantities of raw material. Australia, with untouched grasslands and cheap convict labour, was ideally placed to fill the need. Within twenty years from 1830, wool exports grew from £2 million to £42 million. And that was largely achieved by the discovery of new lands north, south and west of Sydney.

As squatters established themselves and flocks began to multiply, the outward pressure became irresistible. One Governor wrote later that you might as well try to 'confine the Arabs of the desert within a circle' as to restrict the surge of squatters into unknown regions.

New grasslands for the merino

The first result of this process was that the great fertile arc of south-eastern Australia, running past Brisbane in the north and Adelaide in the south-east, was converted into a settled and highly productive area that is still the backbone of the economy.

A handful of explorers made the basic discoveries. Among them was a twenty-one-year-old Australian-born bushman named Hamilton Hume, who had accompanied James Meehan's party when it discovered the Goulburn Plains in 1818. Through the succeeding four years Hume continued exploring west of today's

Goulburn, along the route we now call the Hume Highway.

In 1822 Hume guided a group wishing to establish a sheep station at Gunning. In doing so he discovered the Yass river and extensive grasslands of Yass Plains, named after the Aboriginal word *yarrh* meaning running water (from which the variation yarra comes). Yass developed into a thriving centre for itinerant shearers, mounted troopers and postal services: a hard-drinking, brawling frontier town looking out on lands still little known to west and south.

Hume followed this discovery late in 1822 with an expedition guiding the prominent Sydney merchant Alexander Berry to the upper reaches of the Clyde river, inland from Ulladulla. They penetrated the mountainous region to reach almost the site of today's Braidwood, settled in 1826 by former surgeon Thomas Braidwood Wilson. In recognition of his discoveries, Hume received a one hundred and twenty-one hectare grant near other family properties at Appin, south of Campbelltown.

Meanwhile Commander Mark John Currie, RN, set out in May 1823 with his friend Brigade-Major John Ovens to look for new pastoral land south of Lake George. They took as their guide Joseph Wild, an ex-convict constable of Argyle County, who had discovered Lake George in 1820 and had ascended Gibraltar Peak to sight 'Snowy Mountains to the S.W.'.

Currie pushes south to the Monaro

Currie's party left Charles Throsby's farm at Bong Bong on 22 May. Four days later they rode past the last stock station to the south. Near Lake George they killed three emus, 'which afforded excellent coursing, equal if not surpassing the same sport with the hare in England.'

On 31 May they crossed what Currie called the South Fish river. On the following day they passed over Limestone Plains, part of today's Australian Capital Territory. Next they traversed 'a fine forest country to a beautiful small plain, which we named Isabella's Plain, after Miss Brisbane' (the Governor's daughter). A few kilometres' riding brought them to the Murrumbidgee river, second longest river in New South Wales, discovered further downstream by Charles Throsby and Joseph Wild in 1821.

Currie continued due south through 'fine forest country intersected by stony ranges'. He was blazing almost precisely the path of the present Monaro Highway from Canberra.

On 4 June 1823, in 'downy country' around today's Michelago, the white men attracted Aboriginals with an offer of biscuits. 'From these natives,' wrote Currie, 'we learned that the clear country before us was called Monaroo, which they described as very extensive: this country we named Brisbane Downs' (today Monaro Downs).

On 6 June the party crossed the icy upper waters of the Murrumbidgee, probably near today's Colinton, to discover more fine grazing land. On their right hand they could see 'a lofty range of hills extending to the south covered with snow', which they called the Morumbidgee Mountains. These were part of today's Clear Range.

Well satisfied with their discoveries, and running short of provisions, the men returned to Lake George by 10 June. Within a few years more than one hundred squatters were producing fine merino wool in the Monaro area, with the town of Cooma as their trading centre. Currie became Fremantle's first harbour master in 1829. □

The squatter's life *in the 1820s was not as idyllic as Joseph Lycett's view of Lake George near Yass suggests. Conditions soon improved and the squatters grew wealthy and powerful.*

Hume and Hovell discover a paradise for pastoralists

What kind of country lay between the Murrumbidgee river and the southern ocean? Surely it was not all snow-covered mountains of the kind that had halted further progress in the Monaro region? Or sandy waterless soil, which had caused Colonel Collins to abandon the first Port Phillip settlement in 1804? A particular group of citizens provided the answer.

The squatters' lust for new land was insatiable. After Sir Thomas Brisbane arrived in 1821 to replace Governor Macquarie, he complained that 'Not a cow calves in the colony but her owner applies for an additional grant.'

By imposing stricter rules over land grants, Brisbane attempted to consolidate settlement in coastal areas where control would be easier to maintain. Although the Governor was curious about the unknown inland, instructions from London prevented him from giving anything but token help to the new breed of squatter-explorers.

Sydney merchant Alexander Berry arranged a meeting between his young friend Hamilton Hume and a thirty-eight-year-old former sea captain named William Hilton Hovell. The resulting partnership was to bring them success, though it was marred by disagreement.

Hovell had settled on a land grant at Narellan, near Camden, and had made some exploration of the area surrounding Cumberland Plain, discovering the Burragorang valley in 1823.

Hume was an experienced explorer and a skilled bushman. Hovell's bushcraft was recently acquired, but he claimed the navigational skills necessary to calculate position and chart their progress. They decided that if the government would not explore beyond the Murrumbidgee, they would. Their scheme was to take a south-westerly course further inland, to skirt the Alps and — they hoped — come out at the sea where Western Port was shown on marine charts.

The mystery beyond the Murrumbidgee

The two men assembled their expedition at Hume's house at Appin on 2 October 1824. Each brought a bullock cart, three horses, three convict servants (one pushing a measuring perambulator), muskets and supplies for four months: 290 kilos of flour, 91 kilos of salted pork, 45 kilos of sugar, 6 kilos of tea, 5 kilos of soap and 4 kilos of tobacco.

The first part of the trip was uneventful as the little party trekked through the known regions of Mittagong and Goulburn. On 17 October they regrouped at Hume's station at Gunning, furthest point of settlement at that date.

Hovell had been taking observations, but already these were inaccurate. He

Cooma Cottage, *Hamilton Hume's third and last homestead. He retired from exploration at the age of 31 and became a prosperous pastoralist. In this photograph, Hume is on the left, holding a horse, his wife is in the centre by the chair*

HAMILTON HUME
PAINTING BY EDWARD A'BECKETT

WILLIAM HILTON HOVELL
SEAMAN-TURNED-EXPLORER

used a sextant and artificial horizon to observe the noon altitude of the sun. For longitudes, he needed an accurate chronometer, but he did not possess one.

Hovell therefore deduced the party's longitudes by dead reckoning, based on compass bearings and distances measured by an odometer counting the revolutions of a perambulator wheel. Thus his longitudes became steadily more unreliable. Hovell was aware of the problem, writing that his astronomical instruments were 'unworthy of confidence'.

The explorers spent several days in 'broken and irregular' country trying to find a way across the Murrumbidgee river. As a last resort, on 22 October they converted a bullock cart into a boat by securing a tarpaulin around its bottom and towed their goods across the swollen river. Next day they discovered 'fine Meddows' of luxuriant grass around today's Burrinjuck.

For some days more, Hume and Hovell were caught in mountainous country round Wee Jasper and the Goodradigbee river. By 31 October they had fought their way through valleys and swamps to sight 'an immence Mountain' — the 1388-metre Mount Hovell.

Reaching a grassy patch on 1 November 1824, the party halted to rest the 'much fatagued' bullocks. They shot a large kangaroo and ate it along with a thirty-centimetre freshwater crayfish taken from a stream.

The weather was now very hot: each night the men were 'tormanted by

The Murrumbidgee in an 1884 painting. *It took Hume and Hovell days to find a way across the wide deep river bordered by 'broken and irregular' country. Eventually, they converted a cart into a makeshift boat to make the crossing*

Swarms of little Flyes, not larger than a Flea, but wherever they alight they draw blood'. Hovell complained that his legs were 'one Complete sore to within a few Inches of the Knees'. He named the tormentors 'devil flies'.

Hume's mighty river

All this time the trend of the mountains was forcing the explorers further to the west. By 6 November they arrived at the site of Tumbarumba, describing the tall timber as 'moderately thick but of the very best quality'. Two days later a western view of the Snowy Mountains burst upon the travellers. Wrote Hovell: 'a prospect came in View the most Magnificeant, this was an immence highe Mountain Covered nearly one fourth of the way down with Snow, and the Sun shining upon it gave it a most brilliant appearance.'

Ragged foothills and gorges now forced the explorers to proceed due west. By 12 November they encountered 'flat, open Forest thinly timbered' near today's Table Top. Now they were making faster progress. The country, thought Hovell, 'may be compared with the best of the Cow pastures'.

The travellers were now able to turn almost due south. On 16 November, at the site of today's Albury, they suddenly arrived at the bank of 'a very fine river — at least sixty metres wide...with grass up to our middle'. Hovell cut his name 'in the solid wood of a healthy tree', and noted in his journal: 'This, I named Humes River, he being the first that saw it.' Six years later the name was changed to the Murray river, after Sir George Murray, Secretary for the Colonies.

The explorers travelled upstream in search of an easier crossing place. On 19

BULLOCKS PULL THROUGH ON MOUNTAINS AND IN BOGS

Hume and Hovell found bullock teams superior to horses when exploring difficult terrain, especially the western fringes of the Snowy Mountains in 1824.

Horses were not as sturdy as bullocks and always had to be unloaded and led carefully through uphill stretches. Bullocks simply followed their leader steadily. If one slipped, or found a slope too steep, wrote Hovell, 'the animal kneels down, and scrambles up in this posture'.

In boggy ground, horses tended to panic and work themselves deeper into the mire. The shape and strength of bullocks enabled them to cross swamps and bogs where horses could not go.

A bullock team,
painted by William Strutt.
Bullocks were both tough and reliable

November they found a spot 'where the Current is not so strong', just above today's Hume Weir.

Hovell here made use of experience gained when shipwrecked in the *Brothers* in Bass Strait eight years earlier. He showed the men how to build a framework of bush timber in the shape of a boat and to fix tarpaulin over its bottom and sides. Within five hours all stock and provisions had been taken safely across the wide stream.

The south-westerly journey continued, with the same method being used on 21 November to cross the Mitta Mitta river near Tallangatta. The next day the Kiewa river was crossed on foot at a point where 'an immense tree' had dropped from one bank to the other. The bullocks, roped together lengthwise, passed 'without either reluctance or difficulty'.

Rough mountain country

On 23 November the explorers traversed nine kilometres south-east of today's Beechworth, where much gold would later be found. The following day they crossed the Ovens river without difficulty, naming it after Major John Ovens. They were nearly five kilometres downstream of today's Myrtleford, in 'as pretty a spot, and as valuable,' wrote Hovell, 'as any I have seen since Leaveing Home.'

Where did these westward flowing rivers run? 'My Friend [Hume] has just ventured an opinion,' noted Hovell in his journal, 'that he is sure all these rivers empty themselves into the Sea.' Hovell was inclined to agree, although the exact position of this outlet remained 'a Mystery, and a problem to solve'.

On 25 November, with the great mountains still in view, the explorers named a 'Singular looking' hump to the south-east Mount Buffalo. They easily forded the King river, and on 28 November the Broken river.

By this time all were on short rations. Much of the pork, carried in bags instead of casks, had spoiled. The kangaroo dogs had not been able to catch any game and were being kept alive on a mixture of flour and water. Even when kangaroos were sighted, the dogs were in no condition to catch them.

On 1 December the party descended from the Strathbogie Ranges to find easier going past today's Merton and Yarck. Aboriginals en route remained hidden, but constantly set fires in the bush and grass around the explorers. Hovell did not seem to bear them any ill will.

Two days later the travellers discovered a fine river which they named the Goulburn, after Frederick Goulburn, Colonial Secretary of New South Wales. 'We have not seen a more agreable, and interesting Country, since leaving home,' Hovell enthused. They crossed easily on a fallen tree, shot a kangaroo, and dined happily by the banks where native willows grew in profusion.

The men passed the site of today's Yea. Still bearing south-westerly, which was now quite the wrong direction for their goal of Western Port, they wasted rations and days in climbing Mount Disappointment and trying to hack their way through impenetrable valleys round it. The horses' hooves became 'very much broken by the stones,' while 'the feet of the Bullocks are very much sweled.'

Sometimes the men had to scramble on their knees through 'Cutting Grass with edges 'as sharp as a Butchers Knife'. Hume's face was 'neatly Carved with the brambles and bryers.' One of the convicts tumbled into a thicket of this sword grass, 'which not only took away every part of his trowsers,' wrote Hovell, 'but the front flap of his Shirt also, thereby leaving him in that state, that had there been any doubt of his Manhood before, these doubts were now removed.'

The exhausted explorers retraced their steps to an easier route westwards, taking them even further away from their planned destination. On 11 December they caught two fish in King Parrot creek and killed a kangaroo for dinner. Delayed by a bushfire, they sighted Mount Piper near today's Broadford on 12 December, and 'got fresh hopes of being able to get some distance farther to the S.W. diraction.'

On 14 December 1824, the men climbed Bland's Mount near today's Beveridge, to see the 'very gratifying sight' of 'a Very extensive plain' to the south-east. They named it after the flamboyant but dedicated Dr William Bland of Sydney.

That day the measuring perambulator, much the worse for wear, fell to pieces and all hope of accurate mapping was lost. The explorers were not too concerned, for ahead of them, past today's Craigieburn, they could see the plains

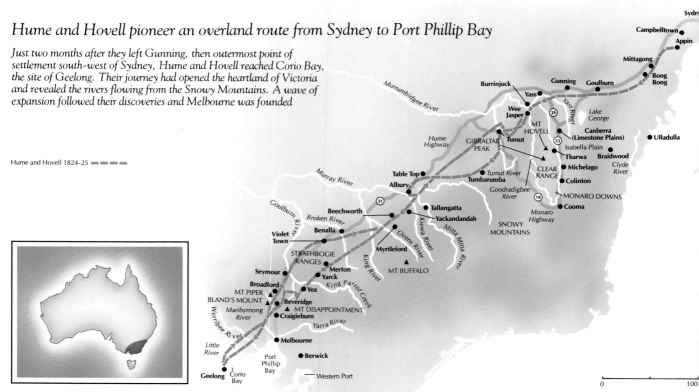

Hume and Hovell pioneer an overland route from Sydney to Port Phillip Bay

Just two months after they left Gunning, then outermost point of settlement south-west of Sydney, Hume and Hovell reached Corio Bay, the site of Geelong. Their journey had opened the heartland of Victoria and revealed the rivers flowing from the Snowy Mountains. A wave of expansion followed their discoveries and Melbourne was founded

Hume and Hovell 1824-25

An early view of the Australian Alps, *much as Hume and Hovell must have seen them. Rugged foothills forced the explorers to veer west*

and occasional forests of the Port Phillip sunkland. 'Never did I behold a more charming & gratifying sight,' wrote Hovell thankfully.

On 15 December the men crossed branches of the Maribyrnong river, supplemented their diet with two eels, and continued on to camp at the Wearyby (Werribee) river. Next day they walked through grassy plains to end their journey on the shores of Corio Bay, near the site of today's Geelong.

Hovell could scarcely contain his joy at the great discovery. The endless pastures, he wrote, would soon 'Surpass us, in the County of Cumberland, both for Sheep, or Cattle.' Squatters would receive shipping from India or England even before Hobart, and the dangers of Torres Strait could be avoided.

Hovell calculated the latitude of Corio Bay correctly as thirty-eight degrees, six minutes south, but gave the longitude as one hundred and forty-five degrees, twenty-five minutes east, which is near today's Berwick, more than eighty kilometres east of where the explorer stood. This gross error led Hovell to insist that he had arrived at Western Port, as originally planned.

Hume and Hovell began their return journey on 18 December 1824, with only enough flour to last five weeks and no meat. They crossed the Little river, naming it Dickson's creek after John Dickson, who brought the first steam engine to Australia in 1814.

The following day, the explorers were forced to kill their lead bullock, 'Poor old Captain'. They gorged themselves on his meat, and made moccasins from his hide to cover their party's bare feet.

By 21 December the men were back at the Maribyrnong river. Hovell recommended future settlers to make first choice of what he named 'Duke of Yorks Downs', which included all the present location of Melbourne as far as the Yarra river. The following day they arrived back at Mount Piper. Here they decided to strike into the flatter country inland, roughly following the route that would become part of the Hume Highway.

On 23 December the men were near today's Seymour on the Goulburn river. By the end of the month they had passed today's Violet Town and Benalla to arrive back at Whorouly.

On 8 January 1825, south-west of today's Tumut and still some two hundred and forty kilometres from the nearest sheep station, the last three kilos of flour and a handful of tea were served out to each man. Stumbling, half-starved and barefoot again, they managed to catch some fish in the Tumut river and shoot a kangaroo. This kept them going until they found an emergency cache of provisions buried on the outward journey.

On 18 January the weary travellers arrived safely at Hume's main station near Lake George, which they had left sixteen eventful weeks before.

Six days later Hume was able to report to the Governor that 'we have discovered, adjoining to that extensive Harbour [Western Port], one of the finest parts or tracts of Country yet known in Australia.' Not only had they found rich grazing lands and laid open the heartland of the future State of Victoria: they had clarified the complex river systems flowing from the Snowy Mountains.

Since these streams tended northerly and westerly, settlers revived the possibility of a great river system entering the ocean somewhere along the southern coastline. Five years later, Charles Sturt's voyage down the Murray river to the sea would confirm that idea.□

HOVELL'S MISTAKE LEADS TO AN EXPENSIVE FAILURE

Hume's and Hovell's mistake in believing they emerged at Western Port, not Corio Bay, had far-reaching consequences.

The explorers became involved in a tedious and demeaning controversy that almost obscured their achievement. After all, they had survived grave perils to open a land route to the south and discover one of the richest areas in Australia.

Their enthusiasm for the new land persuaded the government to establish a settlement at Western Port (on Hovell's faulty calculation of longitude) in 1826.

Unfortunate settlers found themselves dumped in sandy, swampy country. After a few months the expensive experiment had to be abandoned. As a result of this disappointment the whole of the Port Phillip district was left unsettled by Europeans for another decade.

A frail botanist shows a way through the inland to Queensland

In the days when Australia lay wide open for discovery, an explorer did not have to be particularly robust to go on the trail. The generally temperate climate and the assistance of loyal servants made it possible even for a tubercular weakling like Allan Cunningham to achieve greatness. His blend of discovery and botany was uniquely valuable.

ALLAN CUNNINGHAM
HE COMBINED DISCOVERY
WITH BOTANY

The Darling Downs *were regarded by Cunningham as his major discovery. Covering almost 12 000 square kilometres, the area now produces wheat, barley, sorghum, sunflower and cotton in a mosaic of crops and black soil*

Cunningham was a twenty-five-year-old botanist from England's Kew Gardens when he arrived in the raw convict settlement of Sydney in 1816. Lean, hesitant and pale, he attracted Lachlan Macquarie's sympathy. The Governor arranged for him to accompany John Oxley's expedition to the Lachlan river and P. P. King's voyage to north-west Australia in 1817. The shy young man learned to accept hardship without complaint, and fell in love with the natural wonders of his adopted country.

In 1822 Governor Sir Thomas Brisbane supported a plan outlined by Cunningham to seek an easier overland route northwards from the settled area of Bathurst to the Liverpool Plains, discovered by John Oxley in 1818. Cunningham made his first attempt in November 1822, but lost his packhorses when camping on the Cudgegong river.

Humiliated, he was forced to cover the one hundred and ten kilometres or so back to Bathurst on foot.

Conflicts with rivers and ravines

Cunningham again left Bathurst on 15 April 1823 with five packhorses, five servants and rations for ten weeks.

His party traversed the 'lofty forest hills' around the Turon river, where gold was later discovered. They continued without much difficulty over flatter, lightly forested land east of today's Mudgee until 30 April . For a time they were halted by 'perpendicular ridges and overhanging ravines' in country of 'frightful irregularity' — part of the Great Dividing Range.

Near today's Ulan, Cunningham and his men crossed a small reedy stream flowing through a bed forty-five metres wide. Cunningham recognised it as the

Goulburn river discovered by Lieutenant Lawson. By 9 May they had passed through today's Cassilis, skirting the southern face of the Liverpool Range, naming Oxley's peak after the explorer.

From this height Cunningham could see the Liverpool Plains extending northwards to the horizon. His problem was to find a way through the 'deep precipitous ravines' confronting him at every step.

For several days he explored easterly as far as today's Murrurundi. He discovered nineteen streams, all flowing towards the Hunter river, but could find no passage.

Men and animals were becoming exhausted in the constant conflict with hills, valleys and rivers. Cunningham decided to return to Bathurst by sweeping to the west and south through the foothills. This route took him through today's Scone and Merriwa to join up with his earlier camp at Cassilis.

In sight of the promised land

After resting, Cunningham thought to make one more attempt to break through the northern mountain barrier. On 5 June he climbed north-west from Cassilis, crossed Turee creek, and a few kilometres further on, near today's Coolah, achieved his goal. Cunningham wrote:

To my utmost gratification, upon tracing the line of mountain ranges, which continued very far to the N.W., a very considerable depression in the back of the main ridge...afforded me a clear, although limited, view of a part of the open plains north of this extensive barrier.

A little further on, Cunningham enjoyed 'a most beautiful and extensive view of the country before me'.

The explorer had discovered the junction of the Warrumbungle and Liverpool Ranges, at the only point where they could be crossed by stock. In the hope that it would become 'the great route of communication' to the north, Cunningham named it Pandora Pass.

It is touching to think of that frail Englishman isolated in the wilderness, his men no doubt grumbling over the shortage of food — making a final desperate effort when everything was gone except hope, struggling on just a few more kilometres to come into view at last of his promised land.

Lack of provisions forced the party to return southwards, through today's Gulgong and Mudgee to Bathurst. Within twelve months cattlemen were following Cunningham's trail to the Liverpool Plains, and the wealthy district called New England was open to European development.

Infected by the thrill of discovery, Cunningham became ambitious to link up New England with the settlement at Moreton Bay, which he visited by ship with John Oxley in 1824.

SIR THOMAS BRISBANE
GOVERNOR OF NEW SOUTH WALES
FROM 1821 TO 1825

After a number of minor explorations and a visit to New Zealand, Cunningham set forth with the support of a new Governor, Sir Ralph Darling, 'determined to explore the entire unknown country' north of New England.

FEW REWARDS FOR SOME EXPLORERS

Allan Cunningham's wonderful discovery of the Darling Downs added grazing and agricultural lands worth billions of dollars to Australia's national wealth.

Each of the convict servants who accompanied him received a gratuity of £10. For his dedication and inspiration Cunningham himself received — nothing.

The explorer returned to England in 1831 to classify thousands of botanical specimens he had gathered on his journeys through New South Wales.

His brother Richard Cunningham was appointed Colonial Botanist in 1832, but was killed by Aboriginals three years later.

Allan Cunningham accepted the same position, returning to Sydney early in 1837. He found that he was expected to use his staff to grow vegetables for government officials, and to lay gravel footpaths round Government House.

Cunningham, by this time suffering seriously from a diseased liver and advanced tuberculosis, lost patience with those who would deflect him from further exploration and botanical work.

In May 1839 he wrote to fellow-botanist Robert Brown that he was now 'a poor, decrepit, prematurely old traveller'. Six weeks later he was dead.

Cunningham finds an inland route to the north

New England's splendid grazing lands and the lush Darling Downs were settled as an immediate result of Cunningham's arduous journeys, sponsored by governors Brisbane and Darling. Consolidation and cautious expansion were the chief aims of government during this period

Cunningham 1823
Cunningham 1827
Cunningham 1828

0   100 km

On 30 April 1827 Cunningham left Segenhoe, a station on the upper Hunter river, with six convict servants, eleven horses, rations, a sextant, compass, pocket chronometer, artificial horizon and measuring perambulator.

They climbed the Liverpool Range near Murrurundi, and continued along the eastern side of the Liverpool Plains. On 11 May the party crossed Oxley's track of 1818 (today the Oxley Highway). They trekked on northerly, climbing timbered hills near today's Somerton. 'Through these gloomy woods,' wrote Cunningham, 'with scarcely a trace of either Indian or kangaroo, we patiently pursued our way.'

On 19 May they descended from stony hills into 'a beautiful well-watered valley' where the Peel river flowed west on its route to Lake Keepit.

Continuing northerly, the party followed roughly today's rail route from Manilla to Barraba into the eastern fringe of the Nandewar Range. Barren, brushy tracts alternated with patches of good soil and grass, but all areas were suffering from a severe drought. The Aboriginal population had vanished.

Good progress was made to latitude twenty-nine degrees, ten minutes. On 25 May, wrote Cunningham, 'a level, open interior, of vast expanse, bounded on the north and north-west by a distant horizon, broke suddenly on our view!' They had arrived 'in the immediate neighbourhood of a river of the larger magnitude' — which Cunningham named after Peter Macintyre, manager of Segenhoe station.

Today the area raises much fine wool, beef and crops.

The following day the party continued on to 'a handsome piece of water, evidently very deep', which Cunningham named the Dumaresq river after a prominent Sydney family. Both the Macintyre and Dumaresq rivers today form part of the border between New South Wales and Queensland.

Discovery of the Darling Downs

Drought conditions now forced Cunningham to change his course to north-easterly, following Macintyre brook past today's Inglewood. At last, on 5 June 1827, wrote the explorer:

We reached the confines of a superior country. It was exceedingly cheering to my people, after they had traversed a waste often times of the most forbidding arid character…and had borne, with no ordinary patience, a degree of privation to which I had well-nigh sacrificed the weaker of my horses — to observe, from a ridge which lay in our course, that they were within a day's march of open downs of unknown extent.

The explorers had discovered the richest part of southern Queensland. Even during the drought it was covered with 'an extraordinary luxuriance of growth'. Cunningham proudly named it the Darling Downs, after the Governor.

Cunningham's Gap in 1871. *This watercolour by H.G. Lloyd shows a road linking the Downs to Moreton Bay just 30 years after first settlement of the district in 1840. After a slow start with many setbacks, the Darling Downs flourished*

On 6 June they crossed the Condamine river near today's Warwick naming the river after Thomas de la Condamine, the Governor's aide-de-camp. Warwick later became the centre of a district renowned for its wool, wheat, dairying and timber production.

Exploring hills near his camp, Cunningham sighted the Brisbane river and 'a remarkably excavated part of the main range'. This he thought might 'prove a very practicable pass through these mountains from the eastward'.

Horses and men were so exhausted that Cunningham decided to defer the search for a route. Today another pass near by is known as Cunningham's Gap, and the road through it as the Cunningham Highway.

On 16 June, after all had rested, the party headed southward along the route

of today's New England Highway. They were steadily forced south-westerly by 'a most wild and frightful region' of mountains, until they forded the Dumaresq river again near Mount Bowman.

On 9 July Cunningham recrossed his northward path to discover the Gwydir river, naming it after Lord Gwydir. Finding its junction with the Horton river, he was able to follow the valley of the Horton southwards for many kilometres. That brought him to the central part of the Nandewar Range, not far from Barraba. The party was repeatedly stopped by rocky ravines several hundred feet in depth'.

Further hard travelling brought them back in a state of collapse on 28 July to their starting point at Segenhoe station. Their twelve hundred and eighty-seven-kilometre journey took only three

months, but had been an epic of endurance and triumphant discovery.

A route to Moreton Bay

Cunningham sailed to Moreton Bay in 1828 to try to connect his inland discoveries with the Brisbane river. He joined an expedition led by the settlement's commandant, the diligent Captain Patrick Logan.

In July 1828 they crossed the Logan river, which flows into the southern end of Moreton Bay, and sighted the forbidding McPherson Range, named by Cunningham after Major Duncan McPherson of the Thirty-Ninth Regiment.

Early in August the party turned west to search for Cunningham's Gap into the Darling Downs. They found that the Teviot Range lay in their path, and were forced northwards along Teviot brook.

Cunningham's Gap today. *This is not the gap the explorer referred to in his 1827 journal. What he saw is the pass now known as Spicer's Gap. However, Cunningham did come through here on his return from Moreton Bay in 1828*

Logan returned to his duties at Brisbane. Cunningham rested at Ipswich, then pushed south-west again with three men and two bullocks. After several days of arduous travel, on 25 August 1828 a worn-out Cunningham struggled to the top of Mount Mitchell to sight his famous pass and 'the extensive country lying west of the main range'.

He had found a practical route by which pastoral products of the Darling Downs could be taken to markets and coastal shipping. That meant fortunes for many of the squatting families who followed in the slight explorer's footsteps.□

133

An agricultural company quietly takes up huge pastures

HENRY DANGAR
SURVEYOR AND PASTORALIST

While Allan Cunningham hacked his way through totally unknown inland country seeking land that could profitably sustain a settlement, more cautious explorers were examining the rivers and countryside on the north coast of New South Wales in the hope of discovering fertile land that could be settled easily and quickly.

In 1824, squatting had been encouraged to expand by the formation in London of a £1-million enterprise named the Australian Agricultural Company.

The British Government granted the company over four hundred thousand hectares of land, to be selected in northern New South Wales, on condition that it employed fourteen hundred transported convicts.

The company appointed as its Australian controller Robert Dawson, forty-two-year-old manager of Viscount Barrington's estates in Berkshire, England. Dawson bought six hundred European breeding sheep which proved unsuitable for Australian conditions.

In Sydney, Surveyor-General John Oxley suggested that an excellent area for the company's operations would be between the Manning river and Port Stephens, discovered by James Cook in 1770.

Dawson explored some of the land, and pronounced it suitable. Stock numbers were built up by local purchases, but many sheep became diseased and died.

After some years of unsatisfactory management, Dawson was dismissed, and control given to Sir William Edward Parry, prominent naval officer and explorer.

Parry engaged a Cornish-born surveyor, Henry Dangar, to discover better land for the company's sheep. Dangar had already established a reputation as the official planner of Newcastle, surveyor of the road from there to Maitland, and explorer in the Muswellbrook and Hunter river districts.

The company needed huge pasturage. Dangar recommended the Liverpool Plains district which had already been traversed by John Oxley and Allan Cunningham. Two stations totalling close to two hundred and fifty thousand hectares, known as Warrah and Goonoo Goonoo, near today's Quirindi and Tamworth, were taken up. More than twenty illegal squatters were already grazing sheep on this choice land. They were evicted, some of them driving their flocks with heavy losses over the Moonbi Range to discover still untouched areas south of today's Armidale.

The Australian Agricultural Company finally became profitable, assisted by coal sales from Newcastle and the discovery of gold on its Peel river holdings.

Expansion northwards along the coast of New South Wales

As inland New South Wales was being opened up, the coast became more intensively settled in gentle parallel with the harsher challenges of the interior. Newcastle, Port Stephens and Port Macquarie soon were important bases

0   100 km

Sturt tackles the mystery of the inland waterways

Early exploration of the main rivers of western New South Wales had simply ended in bafflement. To the south-west of Sydney, the Macquarie river appeared to dissipate in the Macquarie Marshes. To the west, the Lachlan river also seemed to lose itself in impenetrable swamps. Did these rivers reach the ocean or flow into the fabled inland sea?

CHARLES STURT
PAINTING BY CHARLES WHEELER

The man who would solve these mysteries and lay down the true shape of Australia's major inland river system appeared in Sydney in 1827. He was Charles Sturt, thirty-two-year-old son of an English legal family in Bengal. Sturt had fought in the British Army in Spain and Canada, and in 1825 had been promoted to captain when on duty in Ireland.

This cultured young man arrived in Sydney in the *Mariner* in charge of a shipment of transported convicts. Although in a position to enter into colonial politics his interests lay in another area. While acting as military secretary to Sir Ralph Darling, he persuaded the Governor to give him command of his first expedition. The aim: to continue tracing the course of the Macquarie river

Macquarie Marshes *and their seemingly impenetrable reed beds. Sturt discovered a way round the marshes that had halted Oxley, by travelling north-west to reach the Darling*

into the continent's boundless interior.

Sturt, ignorant of Australian conditions, wisely selected the expert bushman Hamilton Hume to organise the details. They established a base camp at today's Wellington, where several rivers meet. On 7 December 1828 they moved along the north bank of the Macquarie river past today's Dubbo and Narromine.

By 20 December the party had reached Mount Harris, discovered by John Oxley in 1818. Like Oxley, Sturt needed a boat to attempt to follow the course of the Macquarie. Like Oxley, Sturt was defeated by the seemingly endless reed beds. But where Oxley had turned east to reach the coast on foot, Sturt decided to turn westwards towards the interior.

This decision led the party to the discovery on 1 January 1829 of the lower reaches of the Bogan river, named after an Aboriginal word meaning 'birthplace of a king'. In a season of severe drought, it was little more than a chain of

waterholes. Nevertheless they followed the Bogan downstream, then veered south of today's Bourke to arrive suddenly on 2 February at 'a noble river'. Sturt named it the Darling.

Yet how noble was this parched watercourse? 'The men eagerly descended to quench their thirst,' wrote Sturt. 'Nor shall I ever forget the cry of amazement that followed their doing so, or the looks

The Darling near Menindee. *Sturt called it a 'noble river', but found it salt and guessed from its wide banks that it had a tendency to flood*

The Darling near Menindee. *Sturt called it a 'noble river', but found it salt and guessed from its wide banks that it had a tendency to flood*

Hovell had crossed various parts of the Murrumbidgee river and other streams. All seemed to flow in a general westerly direction. What was the final destination of all these little-known waterways?

To the chagrin of Surveyor-General Thomas Mitchell, Governor Darling again selected Sturt, an amateur to Mitchell's mind, to look for the answers.

Important discoveries in the far west

Accompanied by George Macleay, son of the Colonial Secretary, Sturt's party left Sydney on 3 November 1829. They took a collapsible eight-metre whale boat on one of their bullock drays. Travelling south-west through sparsely-settled country, they reached the Murrumbidgee on 25 November near today's Jugiong. 'The scenery around us was wild, romantic, and beautiful,' Sturt enthused.

Here the river was twenty-four metres wide, roaring and foaming. The party continued for many days with their bullock drays, past the furthest sheep stations of legal and illegal squatters, past the sites of Gundagai, Wagga Wagga, Narrandera, Darlington Point and Hay.

Even this twenty-six-day stage of the journey was filled with important discoveries. On 3 December 1829, near a plain which natives called Pondebadgery (today Wantabadgery), Sturt wrote that the 'richness of soil and appearance cannot be surpassed'.

As the party proceeded west of today's Narrandera, Sturt noted that the soil was

of terror and disappointment with which they called out to inform me that the water was so salt as to be unfit to drink!'

In some trepidation, the party continued down the Darling. Near East Toorale, almost to the junction with the Warrego river, Sturt and Hume agreed that it would be dangerous to continue in the face of appalling heat, swarms of flies and a shortage of good water.

They returned to Mount Harris, and during March explored the length of the Castlereagh river, through today's Coonamble to the junction with a lower section of the Macquarie (about seventy-five kilometres west of today's Walgett). On 30 March they crossed the Macquarie but could find 'not a drop of water or a blade of grass'. By 21 April, after four and a half months, the party was back at

Wellington, weary and dispirited.

Sturt and Hume had failed to discover much new grazing land. But they had added a major drainage channel, the Darling, to the known map of Australia.

They had also added a new puzzle. It was obvious from its wide banks that the Darling carried a vast volume of water to the west or south-west when in flood. What happened to all that water? Did it go to the inland sea of popular legend?

Sturt did not think the interior a place 'likely to become the haunt of civilised man' and his unfavourable report diverted the government's attention to another puzzle of half-finished exploration.

In 1817 John Oxley had traced much of the route of the Lachlan river. From 1821 to 1824 Charles Throsby, Mark Currie, Hamilton Hume and William

Sturt and Hume follow the Macquarie and find the Darling

In 1828, the colony was languishing from a terrible drought. Governor Darling thought this was a good time to try to get through the Macquarie marshlands while rivers were very low. After splitting into smaller parties and trying various routes, Hume and Sturt reached the Bogan in January 1829 and discovered the Darling in February

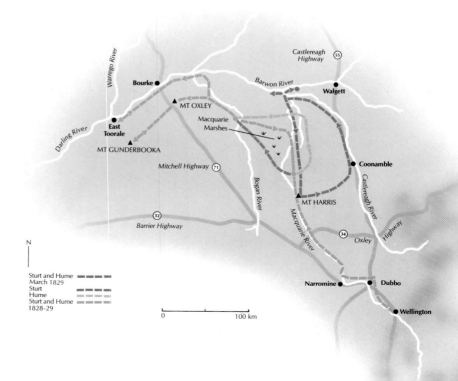

Sturt and Hume
March 1829
Sturt
Hume
Sturt and Hume
1828-29

0   100 km

becoming more sandy, the vegetation thinner, and saltbush more common. 'We are now on a boundless flat,' he wrote on 16 December.

On Christmas Day 1829 Sturt rode north to sight the Lachlan river swamps which had baffled John Oxley. Then he continued along the Murrumbidgee, to discover that this route too was 'covered with reeds as far as the eye could reach'. But the river was still so large and the main channel so deep that Sturt could not believe it too would terminate in a swamp.

On 26 December, Sturt ordered the whale boat to be put together, and a sawpit dug so that a skiff could be built from native timber to take additional provisions. By 6 January 1830 both boats had been constructed, painted and launched just below today's town of Maude. Sturt selected seven of his best men to accompany him 'on the desperate adventure for which I was preparing'. The remainder of the party were to wait at the camp for a week in case the river party was forced back, and then return to the Goulburn Plains.

As Sturt had hoped, the strength of

William Rowell *painted this scene of Sturt's party preparing to confront hostile Aboriginals near the junction of the Murray and Darling. Sturt, like some other early explorers, tried to avoid fighting and harming Aboriginals*

the current took them through the whole reedy area, past today's Balranald. Then the channel narrowed: 'In some places huge trees lay athwart the stream, under whose arched branches we were obliged to pass.' The whaleboat's awning was torn away and their skiff holed, while 'We were carried at a fearful rate down its gloomy and contracted banks.'

Hume's river becomes the Murray
But on 14 January 1830, 'we were hurried into a broad and noble river.' Sturt continued that 'Such was the force with which we had been shot out of the Morumbidgee, that we were carried nearly to the bank opposite its embouchure, whilst we continued to gaze in silent astonishment on the capacious channel we had entered.'

Although Sturt could not know it, this was the Hume river discovered by Hume and Hovell in 1824. Sturt named it after Sir George Murray, Secretary of State for the Colonies, and that name was unfairly allowed to supersede Hume's.

Sturt wrote that he 'could not doubt its being the great channel of the streams from the S.E. angle.' The explorers floated easily down this 'high road', which 'raised our hopes to the highest pitch', and were soon past the sites of Mildura and Merbein.

On 23 January, near Wentworth, the party narrowly escaped disaster. They were confronted with 'a vast concourse of natives', painted in an alarming fashion and armed for battle. As the whale boat approached sandbanks on which several hundred natives stood screaming and

A distillation plant, *a dismantled whale boat and sheep were included in the supplies Sturt took on his Murray expedition in 1830*

The Murray River near Albury, painted by James Willis. Its bends virtually doubled the straight-line distance between ports, and it could be used only eight months of the year, but river transport opened up the inland

Work-horses of the river wait patiently at the South Australian ports of Murray Bridge (1894) above, and Morgan (c. 1905)

Paddle boats follow Sturt's trail

Exploration and settlement of the inland river basin were greatly accelerated when Mississippi-style paddle steamers came into service along the Murray.

In 1848 John McKinlay, then a squatter on the Murray near Robinvale, urged the South Australian government to establish a system of river boat transport.

A new governor, Sir Henry Young, supported the idea. In 1851 rich prizes were offered to the first steamboats to navigate the Murray from the port of Goolwa in South Australia to the Darling river.

Francis Cadell, a thirty-one-year-old Scottish-born shipbuilder, won first prize with ease. He launched the iron paddle-steamer *Lady Augusta* at Goolwa on 23 August 1853, steamed twenty-two hundred kilometres to Swan Hill by 17 September,

and returned with a large cargo of wool, sheepskins and tallow.

Meanwhile, William Randell, a twenty-nine-year-old Devon-born steam-mill operator, built a boat called the *Mary Ann* from red gum, and began trading up the Murray with squatters who were desperate for supplies and outside communication.

Paddle steamer services made new settlers more confident about proceeding into unknown districts. The river trade reached its peak in the eighteen-seventies, but by the time of the First World War had been superseded by the railways.

Echuca's 500 metre-long wharf, built high to allow for the annual 'rise' of the river, made the town Victoria's second largest port. Tied alongside is the restored wool-carrier Pevensey

FRANCIS CADELL
SHIPBUILDER, RIVER-BOAT CAPTAIN

shouting, the white men loaded their guns and prepared for the worst.

Suddenly a tall Aboriginal whom Sturt had befriended further upstream emerged from the bush. Apparently he had been silently following the explorers. This Aboriginal threw himself on the tribal leader, and pushed him back 'with a vehemence and an agitation that were exceedingly striking.' The diversion en-

abled. the whale boat to pass by safely.

Almost immediately Sturt found himself at the junction of 'a new and beautiful stream' which he felt 'could be no other than the Darling.' At this point its water was fresh and its banks green and lightly timbered: Sturt's men exclaimed 'that we had got into an English river'.

'I directed the Union Jack to be

Lake Alexandrina, *at the mouth of the Murray, was painted in 1847 by William Cawthorne, in a collection titled* Views of South Australia. *A schoolteacher as well as painter, Cawthorne was closely interested in Aboriginal welfare*

hoisted', Sturt wrote, 'and giving way to our satisfaction, we all stood up in the boat, and gave three distinct cheers.'

Ten days of easy sailing down the Murray past today's Renmark, Loxton and Waikerie brought the explorers to Morgan, where the great river turns southward for its final descent to the sea.

New problems arose. The country deteriorated into 'barren and sandy' wastes where no birds or animals could be shot for food. Much of the salt meat had been ruined when the skiff hit a concealed log and sank. The men had eaten so much Murray cod that they could stomach it no longer. They began to complain of sore eyes and physical weaknesses: precursors to scurvy. 'It might well be doubted whether their strength would hold out,' wrote Sturt.

He calculated that they were probably less than two hundred kilometres from the southern coast — so close to a triumphant conclusion. Over-riding his fears, Sturt decided to press on. On 9 February 1830 the whale boat glided into 'a beautiful lake...a fitting reservoir for the noble stream that had led us to it.' Sturt could see Mount Lofty to the north-west, while to the south-west 'there was a clear and open sea visible.'

They had arrived at the huge fresh-

EUROPEAN DISEASES DECIMATE RIVER TRIBES

The gentlemanly Sturt was perplexed and horrified to find that 'the most loathsome of diseases' prevailed among the Aboriginals along his route. Smallpox and venereal disease were rampant.

In the Murrumbidgee section, Sturt thought, the native population had been severely affected and seemed reduced to less than one hundred. 'I am persuaded that disease and accidents consign many of them to a premature grave,' he wrote.

In the Murray section, between today's Mildura and Renmark, Sturt described on 26 January 1830 how 'Syphilis raged amongst them with fearful violence; many had lost their noses, and all the glandular parts were considerably affected.'

Even little children suffered. 'So young were some, whose condition was truly disgusting,' wrote Sturt, 'that I cannot but suppose they must have been born in a state of disease.'

Suspicion that white men had introduced these awful diseases probably turned many tribes against invaders.

Yet others remained friendly, and even offered women to Sturt's party. 'Like all savages, they consider their women as secondary objects, oblige them to procure their own food, or throw to them over their shoulders the bones they have already picked, with a nonchalance that is extremely amusing,' the explorer added.

It is hard to say why European diseases had spread so far down the rivers by the time of Sturt's discoveries. Possibly someone on Oxley's or Hume and Hovell's expeditions infected one or more native women. Possibly the first squatters, who had reached as far as Gundagai by 1830, did the same. Possibly sealers, who discovered Sturt's Lake Alexandrina a year before his arrival, were responsible.

All of these points are hundreds of kilometres from where Sturt was so horrified by the effects. It seems likely that the polygamous nature of Aboriginal intercourse, their semi-nomadic lifestyle and their low resistance to introduced diseases, made them especially vulnerable.

water Lake Alexandrina, which Sturt named after the princess who later became Queen Victoria. On 11 February the party camped at Encounter Bay, and walked along a sandspit to find that entry to the lake from the sea seemed almost impossible except in calm weather.

With supplies running low, on 13 February the men turned for home. Existing on only thirty-four grams of flour and a little salt meat per day, they faced an exhausting row against the current. 'The slightest accident,' wrote Sturt, 'would inevitably be attended with calamity.' Yet he could not resist halting on 17 February, near today's Blanchetown, to collect samples of selenite (crystallised gypsum), 'although they added very considerably to the weight of our cargo.'

Surviving heat, floods and hunger

Rowing in shifts from dawn until seven or even nine at night, with only an hour at noon to eat their bread and water, the hungry men repassed Morgan on 21 February and turned east. One evening they were able to shoot nearly a dozen black-tailed parrots and eat them, but other birds were scarce. Now the weather became oppressive. 'We perspired to an astonishing degree,' wrote Sturt, who took his turn at the oars. Some men after rowing 'poured a considerable quantity of perspiration from their shoes'.

By 6 March 1830 the explorers were nearly back to the junction with the Darling river, where rapids crossed the Murray. This time their boat 'spun round like a top' and had to be hauled by hand through the slippery rocks.

Arriving back at the junction with the Murrumbidgee river on 17 March, the men found that flood waters made rowing even more difficult. Alarming symptoms sapped their strength: 'Their arms appeared to be nerveless; their faces became haggard, their persons emaciated, their spirits wholly sunk.' One man began raving like a maniac; others fell unconscious at the oars.

When all hope seemed lost, they managed to kill several swans. The flesh revived them a little. By 11 April 1830, after an epic journey 'during which we could not have pulled less than 2000 miles' (over three thousand kilometres), the explorers were back at their depot near today's Narrandera. 'The men were completely sunk,' wrote Sturt.

They were still about one hundred and thirty kilometres from the nearest station at Wantabadgery. Sturt sent his two strongest men ahead on foot, calculating it would take them eight days to reach the station and return. On 18 April 'the last ounce of flour' was served out to the remainder. The following morning, when total starvation loomed, the two

A crested pigeon, Geophaps lophotes, *shown here in an engraving from a sketch by Sturt for his journals. Today, these birds are widespread*

Lake Alexandrina. *This shallow freshwater lake is fed by the Murray, which enters it on its northern edge, some 77 kilometres from the sea. Sturt crossed the lake to reach the ocean*

Although not an expert surveyor, Charles Sturt did his best to chart the course of the Murray river.

'For this purpose I had a large compass always before me, and a sheet of foolscap paper,' he wrote.

'As soon as we passed an angle of the river, I took the bearings of the reach before us, and as we proceeded down it, marked off the description of country, and any remarkable feature.

'This chart, was, of course, erroneous in many particulars, since I had to judge the length of the reaches of the river, and the extent of its angles, but I corrected it on the scale of the miles of latitude we made during the day…'

Sturt probably meant to write 'miles of longitude'. Latitude would not help him much on a river running east and west.

Sturt continued that his chart was 'of inconceivable value and comfort to us on our return, for, by a reference to it, we discovered our place upon the river, and our distance from our several encampments. And we should often have stopped short of them had not the chart shown us that a few reaches more would bring us to the desired spots.'

men stumbled back into camp with a few supplies. 'Their knees and ancles were dreadfully swollen,' wrote Sturt, 'but they met us with smiling countenances.'

Travelling in easy stages, the whole party succeeded in reaching Wantabadgery by 28 April, although one of the rescuers, a soldier named Hopkinson, 'had so much over-exerted himself that it was with difficulty he crawled along.' Sturt returned to Sydney on 25 May to resounding acclaim. The *Sydney Gazette*

wrote that 'Captain Sturt has inscribed his name in indelible characters upon the records of our history.' His friend Governor Darling reported that Sturt had added 'in a highly important degree' to knowledge of the interior.

Later analysts have thrown doubts on the nature of Sturt's achievement, accusing him of exaggerating hardships, concealing some events, 'puffing' his own importance, and not doing much for the almost anonymous convicts and soldiers who nearly gave their lives so that his ambitions could be satisfied.

Yet it remains true that Sturt redrew the map of the south-east, showing how the biggest rivers joined to form a waterway comparable to the Mississippi. Even if he was not the original discoverer of

Both Flinders and Baudin *sailed past the mouth of the Murray and failed to see it. This painting by George French Angas shows the lake entrance viewed from the South Australian side*

the Murray river, it seemed fair enough for him to write in later years that 'the very river which had appeared to have been so misplaced, was made the high road to connect the eastern and southern shores of a mighty continent.'

Squatters with their stock were not slow to follow up Sturt's discoveries, to extend the settlement of southern New South Wales and push across the Murray river into Victoria. And the account of his explorations, published in London in 1833, considerably influenced proposals for a new colony in South Australia.□

Sturt's journey down the Murray proves both a triumph and a disappointment

Solving the puzzle of the inland rivers proved that Sturt was not only a great explorer, but that he was one of those who could endure terrible hardships to achieve his goals. The journey back along the Murray all but killed most of his party and ruined his health. However, his success was tinged with a sense of disappointment that the lands contained within the Murray-Darling drainage system were not more fertile. Before long, the 'surrounding desolation', as he described it, was to be transformed by twentieth century technology into the intensive food production region that we know today as the Murrumbidgee Irrigation Area

Collet Barker discovers site of Adelaide

When Sturt returned to Sydney, he suggested that the country west of Lake Alexandrina was worth examining as a site for settlement and for a port.

While Sturt was recovering from his ordeal, Governor Darling appointed Captain Collet Barker of the Thirty-Ninth Regiment to lead a new expedition. Barker, forty-five, had an excellent record of friendship with Aboriginal tribes at Raffles Bay and King George Sound.

During April 1831, Barker explored the eastern shores of Gulf St Vincent, climbed Mount Lofty, and discovered a port for the future Adelaide.

Barker found a south-easterly route over the Central Highlands to arrive on 30 April on the sandspit where the Murray river flows into the sea. He decided to swim across the channel, with his precious compass strapped on top of his head. He disappeared into sandhills on the east side.

A native woman later told a rescue party that three Aboriginals had speared Barker to death and thrown him into the sea. His body was never found.

Three years later, after the writings of Edward Gibbon Wakefield on systematic col-

COLONEL WILLIAM LIGHT
A SELF-PORTRAIT

onisation had provoked the interest of British investors, a South Australian Colonization Commission was formed in London.

In 1836, Malayan-born Colonel William Light, fifty, was appointed Surveyor-General of the proposed colony. He examined Encounter Bay for several weeks cruised throughout Gulf St Vincent before finding Barker's river (Port Adelaide) on 21 November.

Light chose the site of Adelaide *and painted this view of the surveyors' camp near the Torrens. His choice met strong opposition from Governor Hindmarsh who wanted the settlement moved to the coast. Light resigned in protest and Hindmarsh was promptly recalled to London*

Meanwhile Light's deputy, George Kingston, discovered a short river flowing from the Mount Lofty Ranges into marshes on the coastal plains. He named it after Colonel Robert Torrens, chairman of the colonization commissioners.

Bitter controversy followed, but Light approved the river as a site for Adelaide. On 24 December 1836, he wrote in his journal:
Walked over the plain to that part of the river where Mr Kingston had pitched his tent, with a small party of the surveying labourers. My first opinions with regard to this place became still more confirmed by this trip, having traversed over nearly six miles of a beautiful flat...affording an immense plain of level and advantageous ground for occupation...I was delighted with the appearance of the country...
The reasons that led me to fix Adelaide where it is I do not expect to be generally understood or calmly judged of at present. My enemies, however, by disputing their validity in every particular, have done me the good service of fixing the whole of the responsibility upon me. I am perfectly willing to bear it; and I leave it to posterity, and not to them, to decide whether I am entitled to praise or to blame.

It was less than seven years since Sturt's great river voyage, but settlers were already laying the foundations of a capital city.

Major Thomas Mitchell grasps at opportunities for greatness

*T*homas Livingstone Mitchell, *the irascible Surveyor-General who was overlooked as leader for two important inland expeditions, could not believe that an inexperienced explorer like Charles Sturt had discovered the true nature of the inland waterways. 'Geographical research cannot be entrusted with advantage to amateur travellers,' Mitchell wrote tersely.*

SIR THOMAS MITCHELL
A CONTROVERSIAL EXPLORER

The surveyor had been born of poor parents in Scotland, but managed to gain sufficient education to serve as a topographical officer in the 1809-1814 Peninsular War against Spain and France. In 1828, thirty-eight-year-old Major Mitchell succeeded John Oxley as Surveyor-General. He immediately began compiling a general trigonometrical survey of the known areas of New South Wales — a huge task which Oxley had sworn could never be achieved.

In 1831, after his enemy Governor Darling left the colony in disgrace, Mitchell was permitted to organise his first expedition into unknown country. The aim was to investigate rumours about a vast river alleged to flow northerly from northern New South Wales.

Mitchell himself was inclined to favour the story on scientific grounds. The 'extensive arc' of the Great Dividing Range, he wrote, must concentrate the inland rivers into a basin similar to the watershed of the Amazon. 'We must believe its estuary to be amongst those unexplored inlets of the Sea, which Captain King saw on the North Western Coast,' said Mitchell. But the Australian inland had some surprises yet in store.

Mitchell's party left the Hunter river on 30 November 1831. As befitted professionals, they measured each day's march with surveyors' chains, undertook careful trigonometrical readings from prominent landmarks, checked their position by stars and moon on clear nights and entered the results in field books.

Approaching the steep Liverpool Range, thirteen bullocks had to be attached to the carts to drag them up one at a time. Despite these delays, by 11 December the party had reached the furthest-out stock station near the Peel river at Tamworth.

Mitchell's hopes short-lived

Five days later, guided by a friendly native named 'Mr Brown', Mitchell came to the Namoi river. Here he discovered a rough stockyard where convict George Clarke had hidden stolen cattle during his life as a bushranger.

Two canvas boats brought by Mitchell were assembled and painted over Christmas in thirty-seven degree heat. On 29 December 1831 most of the party embarked, but submerged logs ripped the fabric and the plan for a river voyage was abandoned.

Returning to their bullock carts, the men followed the north bank of the Namoi nearly as far as today's Narrabri. With the river now tending westerly, Mitchell headed north into the 'majestic but exhausting mountains of the Nandewar Range.

On 9 January 1832 the surveyor discovered a broad river bed. Debris high in the trees beside the river showed 'the astonishing height and extent of its floods'. At first he thought this must be the fabled Kindur river. But further investigation showed it to be part of the Gwydir river already discovered by Allan Cunningham in 1827.

The Loddon River, *which Mitchell called the Yarrayne, sketched by the major himself. Once across, Mitchell, whose previous two expeditions had been seemingly futile, realised he had at last discovered something of great value to the colony*

More subdued, on 21 January Mitchell wrote, 'I began to consider the matter very hopeless of finding a northern river.' He pressed on with a small party, mapping the Gwydir downstream, then going north to reach Cunningham's Macintyre river (later known here as the Barwon) near today's Mungindi on 23 January.

By then Mitchell had 'lost all confidence' in the Kindur legend. On 6 February 1832 he learned that two men left behind at Gurley creek depot had been waddied to death by Aboriginals.

A heavy-hearted Mitchell decided to abandon the quest and return to civilisation. Five of the thirteen surviving convict assistants were granted tickets-of-leave for their uncomplaining loyalty, although the expedition itself could be regarded only as a failure.

Brushes with Aboriginals

Mitchell spent the next three years supervising the detailed survey of the nineteen counties round Sydney within which settlement was legally permitted.

By March 1835 he was ready to lead a second expedition into western New South Wales. Sturt's discoveries still rankled. 'The ostensible object,' wrote Mitchell, 'is the further course of the Darling discovered by Sturt, but I expect this will lead, not southward as he thought...but northward'. By June he would know how wrong he was.

Mitchell's large and well-equipped party left Boree station on 7 April 1835. Heading north-west they made good progress to Sturt's Bogan river.

Here, somewhere to the south-west of today's Dandaloo, the forty-two-year-old botanist Richard Cunningham (younger brother of Allan Cunningham) wandered away from the party on 17 April to gather plant specimens. He was missing all night. Shots were fired and the bugle sounded at dawn, but still he did not appear. In three groups Mitchell's men scoured the countryside for nearly two weeks without success. Mounted police later arrested three Aboriginals who confessed to killing Cunningham with nulla-nulla and spears.

During May the expedition resumed its trek northwards along the Bogan river, now almost a dry bed. The weather was 'beautifully serene and clear' and the Aboriginals mostly friendly.

Unfortunately, near a waterhole on 14 May the convict overseer Alexander Burnett startled a native, who threw a hunting boomerang. Burnett wounded him with a musket shot: both men had to

Mitchell Plateau in the Mount William Ranges. Determined to survey his 'Australia Felix', Mitchell endured a freezing night on Mount William, which he named for William IV

be given medical attention. Wrote Mitchell: 'I determined in future to sound my bugle where I meant to encamp, that any natives might not be surprised by our too sudden approach.'

Failures along the Darling

On 25 May 1835 Mitchell arrived at the Darling river. A slight current still flowed in the Darling, and the water was fresh. A few kilometres further on, the party felled trees at a lagoon to build a stout stockade which Mitchell named Fort Bourke after the Governor, Sir Richard Bourke. The stockade was about twelve kilometres west-south-west of today's town of Bourke.

Mitchell contradicts Sturt over the Darling

After his 1831-32 journey in search of a river flowing through the north-west of New South Wales somewhere beyond the Gwydir, he set out in March 1835 to travel down the Darling, convinced he would prove that it did not join the Murray as Sturt had claimed

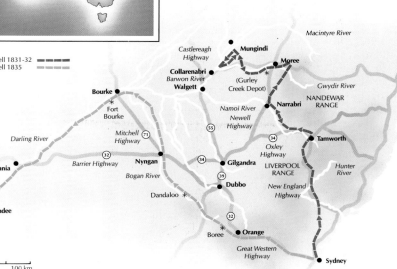

Mitchell 1831-32
Mitchell 1835

100 km

A CONVICT'S TALE INSPIRES MITCHELL

Early in November 1831 the rumour ran quickly through Sydney. A runaway convict claimed he had found an immense river flowing north of the Liverpool Plains into the Gulf of Carpentaria, where sandalwood and bêche-de-mer abounded.

The convict was 'George the Barber' — twenty-five-year-old George Clarke, transported for armed robbery. He had escaped from a chain gang near Bathurst, found the fabled river which Aboriginals called the Kindur, seen many 'Hippopotamuses and Ourang Outangs', and been recaptured by mounted police.

Surveyor-General Mitchell persuaded the Acting Governor, Colonel Sir Patrick Lindesay (himself a keen naturalist) to allow him to test Clarke's amazing tale.

After Mitchell's expedition left, Clarke escaped from gaol, was re-transported to Norfolk Island then to Van Diemen's Land, escaped again, and eventually he was executed for burglary in 1835.

Mitchell's party then attempted to sail down the Darling in two portable boats. So low was the stream, and so blocked with debris, that they soon resumed horse and bullock transport.

Most Aboriginals along the river remained friendly, although Mitchell was 'disgusted with their greediness' in stealing his handkerchief and pocket compass.

On 29 June the party arrived at the site of today's Wilcannia, and on 10 July at today's Menindee. Here seven convicts sent to fetch water were attacked by a tribe of Aboriginals with their women. One man fired his musket into the mob and, wrote Mitchell, 'most unfortunately wounded the gin already mentioned; who, with a child fastened to her back, also slid down the bank and lay apparently dying, with her legs in the water.'

Mitchell wrote bitterly: 'I was indeed paying dearly for geographical discovery.' Yet 'it seemed impossible in any manner to conciliate these people.'

Still no glory for Mitchell
By now the party had travelled nearly five hundred kilometres down the Darling. Mitchell weighed up the risks of proceeding further into hostile territory with his weary team and sparse provisions, and wisely decided to return. Besides, he had gone far enough south to be fairly sure that Sturt was right and he was wrong — and that the Darling probably did maintain its southerly course and flow after all into the Murray.

With the best of intentions, Mitchell had failed again to achieve any historic feat of exploration.

In 1836 Mitchell made yet another attempt to prove — or disprove — the course of the Darling. He set out to reach his furthest point at Menindee, but again was forced back by severe drought.

His only alternative was to continue following the Lachlan and Murrumbidgee rivers to the Murray, find the point where Sturt alleged the Darling entered the Murray, and then follow the Darling upstream to Menindee.

Even this plan failed. Mitchell did indeed find the river junction on 31 May 1836, and followed the Darling upstream as far as today's Hazeldell station. The appalling heat and lack of grass along 'this hopeless river' made him decide to return and explore the fertile country round the Murray. Yet the drought was a blessing in disguise for the luckless

vallies' around today's Wedderburn, later a gold-mining centre. A group of Aboriginals, gesturing south-east towards today's Melbourne, said that 'a station of white-fellows was there.' This was Batman's and Fawkner's illegal pioneering settlement on the Yarra river.

On 10 July 1836 Mitchell crossed the Avoca river, and passed near the present sites of St Arnaud and Stawell. The surveyor was in ecstasies. 'We had at length discovered a country ready for the immediate reception of civilized man, and fit to become eventually one of the great nations of the earth,' he wrote.

A hunting party killed two emus, extracting the female's eggs, which 'afforded us a light and palatable breakfast for several days.'

On 13 July Mitchell with six men climbed Mount William. They spent two uncomfortable days without food in sub-zero temperatures taking angles by theodolite 'for the construction of an accurate map of the whole country.'

Two of the convicts collapsed, but the party pressed on beyond today's Horsham to reach, on 18 July, a stream flowing swiftly towards the south coast. Mitchell adopted the native name Wimmera for it. All round, he wrote joyfully, the richness of the soil 'could scarcely be surpassed in any country.' Today it is one of Australia's great wheat granaries.

The view from Mount Arapiles, *looking towards Mitre Lake, as first seen and painted by Mitchell in July 1836. Below,* the same view today. *Western Victoria's Wimmera district now grows wheat, fine wool and fat lambs*

Mitchell: it led to his discovery of some of Australia's best pastoral country.

Reaching Swan Hill on 20 June 1836, Mitchell named the locality after 'the number of these birds whose beautiful notes were incessantly heard during the night'. He climbed Mount Hope on 28 June, to decide that the country ahead 'was too inviting to be left unexplored.'

Worthwhile discoveries at last

On 1 July Mitchell discovered the Loddon river, giving it the native name Yarrayne. The party engineered their way across its steep banks by building a bridge of sleepers across a fallen tree, and entered luxuriant country where 'kangaroos were to be seen on all sides'.

During the next few days Mitchell crossed 'well-watered, grassy flats or

Still trekking westerly, on 23 July 1836 Mitchell climbed an isolated 275-metre sandstone peak, which he named Mount Arapiles after a rocky eminence in Spain. From the summit he could see twenty-seven circular lakes on the level plains all round — a view that might have belonged to 'the moon as seen through a telescope'.

The homeward journey

Mitchell decided to veer south-westerly, to discover what streams fell from the mountainous Grampians to the coast. On 31 July he came to 'a fine river', some thirty-five metres wide, and named it after Lord Glenelg, Secretary of State for the Colonies. Often wallowing in mud, the party traced the Glenelg downstream past today's Casterton and Dartmoor, discovering several other fine streams such as the Wando and Wannon en route. The land was 'everywhere alike good; alike beautiful', wrote the surveyor.

Mitchell then took to the boat, to sail to the mouth of the Glenelg on 20 August 1836. Here he was disappointed: a sand-bar near today's Nelson prevented access to the sea. Returning to his depot upstream, Mitchell decided to strike eastwards across country. The homeward journey had begun.

Late in August the party crossed today's Heywood, where they rested while Mitchell and a few men rode south. He forded and named the Fitzroy river, to emerge near Portland Bay on 29 August.

On the beach Mitchell was astonished to see fresh cattle tracks and shoe prints. Following them around the bay, he found

several wooden sheds and 'a considerable farming establishment'. This was the secret squatting enterprise of the Henty family, who were 'importing sheep and cattle as fast as vessels could be found'. But the Hentys received their official visitors courteously, giving them as much flour and vegetables as they could load on their horses and some gin.

Mitchell's present to the Exchequer
By 12 September the expedition, now hurrying six hundred kilometres homewards before provisions ran out, reached today's Hamilton. Mitchell abandoned one of the portable boats, but still insisted on climbing prominent hills to continue his running survey.

Following a roughly parallel but more southerly route to Lake Repose, past today's Dunkeld, Mitchell decided on 20 September to split the party and make a quick dash on horseback to the nearest known settlement on the Murrumbidgee. The slow, exhausted bullocks and most of the convicts were left behind with two months' rations, to be doled out by the vituperous second-in-command, thirty-six-year-old Granville Stapylton.

Yet help was only a few kilometres away, at the new settlement of Melbourne. On 29 September Mitchell's party rode past today's Castlemaine, delighted by land 'resembling an English park'.

Two days later they veered south-east past today's Kyneton to climb the 5349-metre Mount Macedon, named after the Greek hero Philip of Macedon. From here Mitchell was able to view Port Phillip, and 'a mass of white objects which might have been either tents or vessels'. But he could see no signs of life — 'no stockyards, cattle, nor even smoke' — and decided to return to his north-easterly route.

During October the party crossed the Victorian rivers discovered by Hume and Hovell, which flow northerly into the

Edward Henty *welcomes a surprised Mitchell to Portland Bay. The Henty brothers took up their lands without official permission and few people knew the remote settlement even existed*

Murray. To these Mitchell added discovery of the Campaspe and Coliban rivers.

Crossing the Broken river on 13 October, one convict named James Taylor fell off his horse into a deep hole and drowned — the only white casualty of the whole expedition. Eleven days later Mitchell reached an out-station on the Murrumbidgee and was able to send

THE CLOUD OVER MITCHELL'S CAREER

Major Mitchell, much to the advantage of his enemies, seemed unable to avoid deadly clashes with Aboriginal tribes during his expeditions.

While travelling along the Murray in 1836, near today's Robinvale, Mitchell's party was followed by a large tribe which he claimed to recognise as enemies from his previous expedition to the Darling river. At night the natives set fire to the bush all round the explorers' camp.

Convinced they would attack again, Mitchell set an ambush on 27 May 1836. As the Aboriginals advanced 'with prodigious shouting and war cries', a section of Mitchell's party outflanked them and immediately began firing.

The natives fled. 'Numbers were shot in swimming across the Murray', Mitchell stated in his report. 'Amongst those shot in the water, was the chief.' At least six others were killed.

At first Governor Bourke suppressed this section of Mitchell's report. The story leaked out and after newspaper agitation an official inquiry was ordered and it cleared the Surveyor-General.

Mitchell persistently lobbied for a knighthood in recognition of his services to surveying and exploration. Lingering doubts in London about his attitude and behaviour towards the Aboriginals delayed the honour until 1839, when he was practically bankrupt.

supplies to the beleaguered party in the rear.

On the map completed after his return, Mitchell named today's Victoria 'Australia Felix', for it was the most felicitous land for settlement he had ever seen. 'Flocks might be turned out upon its hills, or the plough at once set a-going on the plains,' he reported. According to his assistant Stapylton, Mitchell valued the discovery 'as a present worth 60 millions to the Exchequer of England'.

Despite this valuable achievement, Mitchell even now could not win the esteem of his contemporaries or quieten his detractors. First he had to face the suspicions of Governor Bourke over the killing of the Darling river Aboriginals. Even when Sir George Gipps succeeded Bourke, the new Governor could only report disdainfully to London:

The long and expensive journies of Sir Thomas Mitchell in the years 1835 and 1836, though highly interesting, led to no discoveries which could be turned to profit, with the exception perhaps of the fertile land of Australia Felix, which would surely have been reached by the ordinary advance of our graziers, even though he had never visited it.

Scores of squatters had already rushed into the rich country, driving their flocks along the deep ruts cut by Mitchell's drays into soil which the explorer described as resembling 'Pease Soup or Hasty Pudding'.

Pastoral families subsequently made millions from these discoveries. Mitchell spent all his assets working on his books and maps in London. He narrowly escaped being imprisoned for debt, and fled back to his official work in Sydney where many of his contemporaries continued to dislike and avoid him.□

The Glenelg River, *which Mitchell named after the Secretary of State for the Colonies. After charting its course to Discovery Bay, the party faced a gruelling return to Sydney*

Mitchell proves that the Murray and Darling join, then discovers his 'Australia Felix'

In 1836, he left Orange, followed the Lachlan and Murrumbidgee to the Murray, and the Murray to where it joined the Darling. Now knowing that Sturt was right and he was wrong, the explorer turned south and south-east to reach the gentle pastures of Victoria's Western District. Mitchell was so impressed with this country he called it 'Australia Felix'

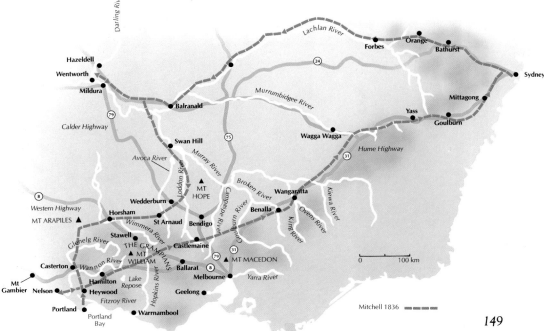

Conquest of the Australian Alps

Everyone who saw the great southern mountains was amazed that a sunburnt country could also offer extensive snowfields as found in the most northern parts of Europe. The mountains, though not particularly high, could be equally dangerous and beautiful.

Johann Lhotsky, an effervescent Czech immigrant who was first to explore the Australian Alps systematically, described in 1834 the 'sublime and extensive view' of the 'panorama of mountains' and 'luxuriant Alpine meadows' which surpassed his 'most sanguine expectations'.

Lhotsky, a trained botanist and physician, decided at the age of thirty-four that he wanted to penetrate 'the very heart of the Australian Alps', which were unknown apart from Hume and Hovell's distant observations and descriptions in a few squatters' letters.

The amateur explorer left Sydney early in January 1834 accompanied by four servants. He possessed only one long-suffering horse, which pulled a cart containing piles of special paper for drying specimens, ten thousand insect needles and a dozen books. Coming back, the space was filled up with animal skins, dried plants, insects and mineral specimens for exhibition in Sydney.

Knowing little of rural conditions, Lhotsky did not bother to take much food or water, assuming there would be plenty of English-style inns along the way. He found to his dismay that the so-called Great South Road of Mitchell's maps petered out at Liverpool. There was no public house between the Pack Inn near Marulan and the last inn at Goulburn.

Fortunately, wrote Lhotsky, 'I was always welcomed in the houses and huts of the humble and lower classes', who sold him salted provisions. 'As to the high and wealthy,' continued Lhotsky, 'I received from them no civility whatever.'

On 29 January 1834 the curious little party reached Limestone Cottage, the homestead on Robert Campbell's station, Duntroon, near today's Canberra. Here Lhotsky was able to present letters of introduction, prepare for his mountain journey, renew his supplies, and relieve himself from the terrible heat by frequent 'aerial baths' (presumably cold showers).

Lotsky reaches the Snowy

On 4 February Lhotsky headed south into the Monaro Plains. Beyond that was practically unknown territory. From 9 to 12 February the men rested at a remote stockman's hut on the Murrumbidgee river near today's Bredbo. Then they

Limestone Cottage *at Duntroon belonged to Robert Campbell, one of the first settlers in the Canberra district. When Lhotsky stopped there in 1834, Campbell had only just been given an official grant to his 2000 hectares*

climbed steadily to pass the site of today's Cooma on 16 February.

Here Lhotsky detoured south-east to investigate mineral waters at a spot he named Richard Bourke's Spring, near today's Rock Flat. The waters would, he judged, be efficacious in treating the syphilis he found 'rather common' among the convict shepherds of the Monaro.

Returning to Cooma and heading south-west, Lhotsky reached today's Delegate on 24 February 1834. The following day he discovered the swiftly-flowing icy waters of the Snowy river, rushing southwards to the sea. Although his statements were later disputed, Lhotsky continued to 'solemnly claim the priority' of his discovery.

Lhotsky reached his furthest point west near today's Thredbo Village on 4 March. 'The waterpots were covered with ice an inch thick,' wrote the explorer. 'It was impossible to go farther.' But from his highest point, he could see to the south-south-west 'a very extensive plain, called by the natives Omeo.'

In a vain attempt to reach the plain, Lhotsky retraced his steps to cross the Snowy river on 9 March. Three days later he veered west to encounter Mount Deddick. But here the Snowy was more than sixty metres wide, and impassable. 'Almost dead from fatigue', Lhotsky was forced to give up and return to Sydney.

These important discoveries were ignored by Major Mitchell and other officials. Lhotsky, almost bankrupt, was forced to sell firewood and vegetables to earn a living. After failing to gain a government scientific post or any remuneration for his expedition, he left for Hobart Town in 1836.

Rich lands of the Omeo district

The year after Lhotsky's forgotten expedition, a Monaro squatter named George Mackillop attempted to find a passage from Monaro Plains to the southern coast.

By taking a more easterly route than Lhotsky, Mackillop managed to cross the Snowy river near its head, at Jacob's Ladder, continuing to where the river cuts today's Victorian border.

A westerly trek took him past today's Suggan Buggan and the headwaters of the Buchan and Tambo rivers to Lake Omeo, to reach the rich Omeo tableland previously sighted by Lhotsky. Here in 1836 Mackillop established his historic station Strathdownie, containing '60,000 acres of as fine land as I have seen anywhere in the Colonies.'

The honour of finding a route through the rugged ramparts of Gippsland to the southern coastline fell to Angus McMillan, a twenty-nine-year-old Scot from the Isle of Skye.

McMillan was employed by Captain Lachlan Macalister and James McFarlane as manager of Currawong station on the Monaro Plains. He persuaded his employers to allow him to search for new pastures further south.

McMillan left in May 1839, accompanied only by an Aboriginal guide, who tried to murder him while he slept. His only other navigational aid was a

Mount Kosciusko, *painted by Viennese Eugène von Guérard in 1867. He arrived in Australia in 1852, travelled and sketched in the Victorian goldfields, and painted many landscapes especially concentrating on mountains and waterfalls*

pocket compass and an old chart by Matthew Flinders. Nevertheless he was able to find good land and establish a cattle station for Macalister at Ensay on the Tambo river.

In January 1840 McMillan formed a stronger party with four other white men and two native guides. After riding through 'some of the worst description of country I ever saw', he succeeded in penetrating south-westerly past today's Bairnsdale (originally Bernisdale, after a village on Skye) and Bruthen.

Aboriginals along the route were not aggressive; most fled yelling from the white men. 'I fancied they took both man and horse to constitute one animal,' wrote McMillan. Later he managed to speak to one old man, who wore several dried human hands round his neck. 'After

having shaken hands with us all, he thought it necessary to go through the same form with the horses, and shook the bridles very heartily.'

On 16 January 1840 McMillan discovered and named Lake Victoria, part of a large system of brackish lakes running parallel to the coast. 'The grass was up to our stirrup-irons as we rode along, and was absolutely swarming with kangaroos and emus,' wrote McMillan. Wild ducks made 'an excellent supper'.

Further to the west McMillan discovered the Nicholson, Mitchell, Perry, Avon, Macalister, and Thomson rivers, naming them after friends and notables. The explorers rode their horses across these streams, floating their provisions alongside in hollowed logs.

Climbing a low hill on 18 January, McMillan decided that 'it put me more in mind of the scenery of Scotland than any other country I had seen,' and named it Caledonia Australis. 'Here was a country capable of supporting all my starving countrymen,' he added thoughtfully.

First to climb Mount Kosciusko
After arrival at the La Trobe river near today's Sale on 23 January 1840, lack of provisions forced a return, even though the explorers had nearly reached a usable sea outlet at Corner Inlet. The complete track was finally opened by McMillan in 1841 and W. A. Brodribb in 1842.

An inland route from McMillan's track to Western Port was discovered in 1840 by Paul Edmund de Strzelecki, a world-wandering forty-three-year-old Polish self-taught geologist.

In Sydney, Strzelecki, interested in doing geological surveys, persuaded the wealthy grazier James Macarthur, who was on the lookout for new grazing lands, to finance and accompany him on an expedition through the Alps to the

Snowy River National Park *preserves a largely unspoiled area of the mountain scenery that so impressed Lhotsky, Strzelecki and McMillan*

Angus McMillan *and the two native guides from his 1840 expedition, one of four journeys he led into the Gippsland district between 1839 and 1841. Cattlemen soon followed his trails*

STRZELECKI THE ERRATIC SCIENTIST

Paul de Strzelecki's discovery of areas bearing silver, china clay and coal were valuable to the growing colonies, and helped to win him a knighthood. His name appears on maps in several states.

His other scientific work was sometimes erratic. After his instruments were sold to the government, they were found to be inaccurate and useless for surveying. Settlers complained that his map of Gippsland gave 'a very incorrect idea of the courses of the rivers'. These matters were not sorted out until government surveyor Thomas Townsend plotted careful maps of Gippsland and the mountains later in the eighteen-forties.

Anthropologists reacted with hilarity to Strzelecki's theory that after Aboriginal women mated with Europeans it became

His 1845 book, *describing the mineralogy and geology of the country, proved to be a valuable reference for more than 40 years*

biologically impossible for them to procreate with native males. 'Utterly inconsistent with all the known facts,' snorted the *Ethnological Society Journal* in London.

---

southern ocean. There a harbour could be built to export pastoral products.

On 12 March 1840 the two men climbed Mount Townsend, believing it to be the highest peak in the Alps. From the top they could see several other crests. With an instrument called a clinometer, which Strzelecki used instead of a theodolite, he could tell that one peak was about fifteen metres higher.

Anxious for fame, Strzelecki determined to climb Australia's highest mountain and name it after a Polish patriot, Tadeusz Kosciuszko. Alone, late on the afternoon of 15 March, he struggled through snow to the 2227-metre peak.

The explorer described his triumph in a letter home:

The highest peak of the Australian Alps — it towers over the entire continent which, before my coming had not been surmounted by anyone, with its everlasting snows, the silence and dignity with which it is surrounded — I have reserved and consecrated as a reminder for future generations upon this continent of a name dear and hallowed by every Pole, to every human, to every friend of freedom and honour — Kosciuszko.

No one can deny Strzelecki his moment of glory. But after he reached Ensay station late in March, he was not entirely frank about events.

During Angus McMillan's absence, young Matthew Macalister replenished Strzelecki's provisions, and led the expedition part of the way along the southwesterly route pioneered by McMillan. Macalister described the nature of the rivers ahead and the best crossing places.

In his published accounts, Strzelecki implied priority in his discovering 'country hitherto untrodden by white man'. He omitted all mention of McMillan's expeditions, and even tried to rename the Scot's major landmarks and rivers. (Although Strzelecki's name of Gippsland, after the then Governor, has remained, in the end, McMillan's names were officially adopted on all maps.)

Strzelecki's party left McMillan's track after crossing the Avon river. They used up most of their food in struggling through dense bush near Lake Glenmaggie. Rations were reduced to one biscuit and one slice of bacon a day. By the time they reached the Thomson river in mid-April, wrote James Macarthur:

The expedition was in a deplorable condition...everyone was so exhausted that they could not cope with the difficulties. Strzelecki, who was the only one accustomed to this kind of hardship, kept his strength up and even though he was carrying a heavy load of instruments and paper weighing 45 lbs, he led his companions day after day through the heavily entangled and almost impossible to cross bush. They watched him as he made his way through using his bare

---

Across the Alps and into Gippsland — and a new rich region opens up

From the Monaro plains to Gippsland is not a great distance by Australian standards, but the first settlers had to cross the rugged Snowy Mountains to find the land between the ranges and the coast. Great stands of timber and well-watered grasslands were their rewards. Then gold was discovered at Omeo in 1852, with even richer finds at Walhalla a decade later

Lhotsky 1834
Mackillop 1835
McMillan 1839
McMillan 1840
Strzelecki 1840

Canberra (Limestone Plains)

SNOWY MOUNTAINS

Murrumbidgee River

Snowy Mountains Highway

Indi River

Bredbo

MONARO PLAINS

▲ MT TOWNSEND
▲ MT KOSCIUSKO

Cooma

Rock Flat

Thredbo Village

Dalgety

Snowy River

Jacob's Ladder

OMEO PLAINS

Monaro Highway

Lake Omeo

Suggan Buggan

Currawong

▲ MT DEDDICK

Cann Valley Highway

Princes Highway

Tambo River

Ensay

Buchan River

Mitchell River

Nicholson River

Macalister River

Avon River

Orbost

Thomson River

Perry River

Bruthen

Melbourne

La Trobe River

Lake Glenmaggie

Bairnsdale

Lake Victoria

Western Port

Sale

Loy Yang

Lake Wellington

Korumburra

Tarra River

Corinella

Leongatha

South Gippsland Highway

Corner Inlet

Port Albert

0   50km

A valley in the Monaro Range, *south-west of Cooma, painted sometime between 1838 and 1847. Colonial painters were just beginning to be aware that history was being made; many of them combined landscape with historical detail in their work and followed trailblazers into new regions in search of scenery that would inspire them*

food they had, and even pointed the way to the nearest squatting station.

The explorers' arrival in the four-year-old settlement of Melbourne on 28 May 1840 caused a sensation, turning men's eyes to the prospect of establishing timber mills and cattle runs in the well-watered areas of Gippsland. Strzelecki himself continued his career as a geologist-explorer in Tasmania under the patronage of Sir John Franklin.

William Adams Brodribb, one of the early overlanders to Melbourne, formed an expedition in 1842 to discover a place where stock could be landed from the sea into Gippsland. After several false leads he discovered the outlet of the Tarra river, and near it, a landing place which he named Port Albert after the Prince.

While their chartered vessel returned to Melbourne, Brodribb and his partners travelled on horseback to make a comparatively trouble-free trip north-easterly over the La Trobe river, to a large lake which they named Wellington after the famous Duke.

Turning westerly, they avoided most of the difficulties that had nearly killed Strzelecki, and arrived safely at Melbourne. Here the government allowed them to purchase a 'special survey' of 5140 acres (two thousand and eighty hectares) near Port Albert at a cost of £1 an acre. This enterprise failed in the depression of the eighteen-forties, and the settlement of Gippsland was left mainly to less ambitious smallholders.□

hands and knees, or as he threw himself into the thicket to open the way for those who shared the difficult conditions with him.

The explorers came to the La Trobe river at the end of April 1840. They were forty-eight kilometres upstream from McMillan's furthest point, and here it was possible for them to cross. With only enough flour left to make three dampers, a decision was imperative. Should they hasten back to Ensay and throw themselves on Angus McMillan's mercy?

No, said Strzelecki. He blithely calculated Western Port to be forty kilometres away. His longitudes were well astray — in fact the distance was one hundred and twelve kilometres in a straight line.

Abandoning their horses and belongings, the starving men walked on southwards past today's Loy Yang, then westwards through 'dense scrub, interwoven with grasses and encumbered with gigantic trees', past today's Leongatha and Korumburra, roughly along the route of the South Gippsland Highway. They existed on wombats and koalas caught by their Aboriginal guide, Charlie Tarra, sometimes tearing them to pieces and eating them raw.

On 12 May the emaciated men stumbled on the derelict 1826 settlement of Corinella, on Western Port Bay. Convict shepherds were in possession. In friendly fashion they shared the little

HOW THE SNOWYS BECAME THE MULTICULTURED MOUNTAINS

A Czech, two Scots and a Pole between them discovered the secrets of the Australian Alps and their wild river systems during the eighteen-thirties.

This international triumph was magnified one hundred and twenty years later, when the gigantic Snowy Mountains hydro-electric and irrigation scheme was begun in the nineteen-fifties.

Thousands of immigrants from many nations, contributing a variety of skills, helped to carve tunnels through the mountains, divert rivers, and build vast reservoirs to utilise the melting snows.

Constructed in stages over twenty-five years, it was the biggest single public project Australia had undertaken up to that time and is one of the largest schemes of the kind in the world.

In Cooma, *workers from the Snowy Mountains scheme tackle the English language*

A construction camp *near Jindabyne in 1955. Workers faced conditions not unlike those met by explorers*

Empire-builders move stock into the empty lands of the south

John Batman meets chiefs *from the local tribes of Port Phillip. His treaties by which he claimed thousands of hectares in return for a miscellany of cheap goods and a promise of rent parallel the purchase of Manhattan from American Indians*

While explorers and settlers descended on Port Phillip from the north, illegal squatters from Van Diemen's Land were planning to take up lands across Bass Strait.

The year was 1835. In Britain the great parliamentary Reform Act was in operation, the first Factory Act to regulate working conditions had been passed, and slavery had been banned throughout the British Empire. In the United States, Samuel Morse exhibited his first crude electrical instrument for transmitting messages along a wire.

None of this seemed to have much relevance in the wilderness that was Victoria. All that mattered was the promise of rich new grazing lands, and the fortunes to be made from the rough work of growing and shipping wool.

The first squatter to enter Port Phillip Bay was John Batman, thirty-four-year-old son of a transported convict. Batman had settled at Kingston in Tasmania, married a convict girl, and become friendly with a government surveyor named John Helder Wedge.

The two men frequently discussed Hume and Hovell's discoveries of 1824, and the failure of the Western Port settlement of 1826. In 1834 they invited several other ambitious graziers to join them in an enterprise called the Port Phillip Association.

On behalf of this group, Batman with three white employees and seven Sydney Aboriginals sailed for Port Phillip on 28 May 1835 in the cutter *Rebecca*. They anchored first off Indented Head on the Bellarine Peninsula, then sailed on to Corio Bay, site of Geelong. Batman walked about fifty kilometres over the virgin countryside, exclaiming in his diary, 'I could never have imagined it possible that so fine a country existed on the face of the globe.'

Batman gets a bargain

On 2 June the explorers sailed to the head of Port Phillip Bay, tracing the course of the Salt Water (Maribyrnong) river by boat and on foot. On 5 June they came to a solitary hill which Batman named Mount Iramoo. This was possibly today's Mount Kororoit, but according to a recent analysis more likely to be Redstone Hill near Sunbury. After

climbing to its peak he could see '40 miles or more each way of Beautifull Plains of the best description.'

Changing direction easterly, the party came on 6 June to a stream running south — possibly today's Merri creek or Plenty river. Here Batman encountered eight chiefs among the Aboriginals who, he claimed, 'possessed the whole of the country near Port Phillip.' The intrigued natives were simply agreeing to any proposition put to them — and in the same spirit they agreed to Batman's terms to 'sell' to the Association two hundred and forty-five thousand hectares in return for a number of 'Blankets, knives, looking Glasses, Tomahawks, Beads, scissors, flour &c. &c.'

On the return journey to their ship on 7 June, Batman's party became entangled in the West Melbourne swamp, and had to force their way through dense tea-tree scrub. 'To our great surprise,' wrote Batman, 'when we got through the scrubb we found ourselves on a much larger River than the one we went up.'

The party had accidentally rediscovered the Yarra river, first seen by surveyor Charles Grimes in 1803, then forgotten. At the bottom of today's Queen Street, Batman came to a rocky outcrop running right across the river, creating a miniature waterfall. Above this outcrop, the water was fresh, clear and bountiful. 'This will be the place for a village,' Batman wrote in his diary on 8 June 1835. Today the city of Melbourne covers the north bank.

The government takes control
Immediately they heard the news of Batman's discoveries, his partners in the Port Phillip Association prepared to occupy the new land. 'You can have no idea of the sensation this Port Phillip Scheme has created,' Batman's friend John Wedge wrote to his father.

Wedge had conducted much exploration for the Survey Department in Tasmania since 1824. Refused leave of absence, he promptly resigned and sailed to Port Phillip in July 1835 to make a professional survey of the vast holdings the Association thought it owned. All the best land round Melbourne, between the Yarra and Werribee rivers, was allotted to the seventeen partners. Small ships began transferring their stock to Port Phillip, which in a short time was transformed into a busy, well-known and highly productive area.

Alarmed by the extempore nature of these events, the Sydney government declared the Port Phillip settlement illegal. The so-called agreement with the Aboriginals, with its far-reaching implications was cancelled, although the Port Phillip Association was finally paid

JOHN BATMAN
ONE OF MELBOURNE'S FOUNDERS

£7000 compensation for its unauthorised entry into pioneering work.

Captain William Lonsdale of the Fourth Regiment was sent with a few soldiers and convicts in September 1836 to take control of the infant settlement. Hard on his heels came government surveyors, who began the work of laying out Melbourne and measuring the surrounding countryside.

But it was too late to stop the eager

spread of squatters into all fertile parts of Victoria. By 1838 they had explored much of the central and western districts, pushing aside the wandering Aboriginal tribes. By 1847 Melbourne was large enough to be declared a city. Never had a new colony grown so rapidly.

Faced with a *fait accompli*, all the government could do was to charge the squatters £10 a year for the lease of each run, and appoint roving commissioners and Aboriginal Protectors to supervise their activities as best they could.

None of these attempts at official control had much effect on the yearning of sheepmen for access to limitless lands. 'We here see a British Population spread over an immense territory beyond the influence of Civilization, and almost beyond the restraints of Law,' Governor Gipps complained to London.

Much new pastoral land was found in Victoria's Western District as a result of the disappearance of two Hobart lawyers, Joseph Tice Gellibrand and George Brooks Hesse.

The men left Geelong in February 1837 on a trip along the Barwon river. Intending to visit Captain Charles Swanston's station, they rode further west into unexplored country past today's Birregurra. On a date unknown, they were killed by Aboriginals and their bodies apparently thrown into the shallow fresh-water Lake Colac.

Several search parties failed to find their remains, but discovered instead large areas of grazing land. As a result, Hugh Murray, the Lloyd brothers and

Squatters fan out from Port Phillip to settle Victoria's centre and west

During the late eighteen-thirties, while Melbourne was fast growing, men looking for good grazing land investigated the gaps between the routes of explorers such as Hume, Hovell and Mitchell. Expansion in Victoria took place much more rapidly than it had done in New South Wales, where the Blue Mountains had delayed the westwards spread for over 20 years

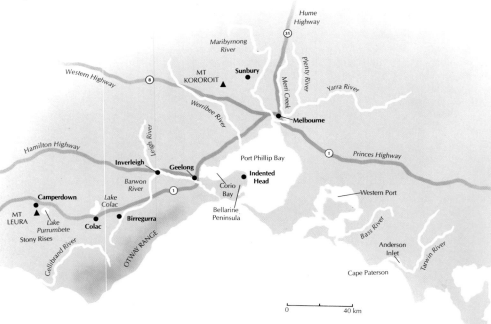

Melbourne in 1839. *This painting was made from memory in 1875, but Fawkner's Hotel with its turret is correctly shown facing the Yarra*

William Carter 'joined together for mutual protection' and moved their flocks to the Colac area in September 1837. These settlements were in turn leap-frogged by the Manifold brothers, John and Peter, who had emigrated from Cheshire via Van Diemen's Land. In December 1838 the Manifolds pushed their flocks north of the marshy Stony Rises to discover the beautiful fresh-water Lake Purrumbete and vantage point of Mount Leura near today's Camperdown. Magnificent bluestone mansions finally arose over the wool-rich plains all round.

George Russell, pioneer of Golf Hill near today's Inverleigh, left a graphic picture of how the first settlers took their land, often with little more to their names than determination and optimism.

Clutching Wedge's map in one hand and a pocket compass in the other, the twenty-four-year-old squatter left Melbourne on foot with a friend in March 1836. They had one borrowed pack-horse to carry their provisions.

In the winding valley of the Leigh river, where the land was 'thickly covered with a close sward of grass and herbs', Russell, with great satisfaction, selected the site for his future homestead.

Altogether the men walked three hundred and twenty-two kilometres through almost deserted countryside. The long rough kangaroo grass cut through their boots and socks: 'When I reached Melbourne my toes were bleeding from the constant irritation,' wrote Russell.

Overlanders, a new breed of explorer

Meanwhile, on the better-known land around Western Port, Scottish-born Samuel Anderson and Robert Massie had established a cattle run, wheat farm, flour mill and salt-works on the Bass river. They found the Tarwin river, Anderson Inlet and coal deposits at Cape Paterson.

At the same time, a special breed of

JOSEPH HAWDON
OVERLANDER 1836 AND 1838

CHARLES BONNEY
OVERLANDER 1838

KOALAS FOR BREAKFAST

Like Aboriginals and explorers before them, the first settlers in south-eastern forests sometimes had to rely for sustenance on that unique marsupial, the koala (named after the Aboriginal word *colo*).

White settlers often called the slow-moving marsupials 'monkeys' or 'sloths'. W. A. Brodribb wrote: 'The flesh is far from being nice, and very tough, still we were glad to eat it.' By comparison, possums were considered a delicacy.

W. Odell Raymond, son of the New South Wales Postmaster-General, lived for eight days on koalas and lyre birds for breakfast while struggling through the dense Gippsland bush in 1842. 'In the evening, by way of change,' he wrote, 'we had the monkey, and tea without sugar.'

Koalas were once common in the bush, but were almost exterminated for their fur before the Second World War. In one year alone, 1924, two million pelts were exported. The animal is now totally protected and with careful restocking, is again widely distributed. Few today would dare harm our best-loved mammal.

157

HAPPY DAYS WITH THE OVERLANDERS

Instead of the perils encountered by explorers only a few years earlier, overlanders, certain of their destinations, often seemed to enjoy their leisurely treks, with ample food available on the hoof.

Joseph Hawdon, camping on the Goulburn river with Charles Bonney en route to Adelaide in 1838, wrote:

At a distance of thirty yards the men had formed a circle round a large blazing fire, and were amicably discussing the chances of our rather hazardous expedition. The cook, to contribute to the general amusement, had mounted a box by way of stage, and was dancing a hornpipe in capital style, to the music of a fife played by another of the party. At the conclusion of each dance he was warmly cheered by his companions, whose plaudits causing a rush among the sheep, the bells of the flock tinkled in romantic concord. Within five yards of the merry group was the fold, enclosing twelve hundred sheep, and a little to the left was a herd of between 300 and 400 cattle, gazing in mute astonishment at the jocund performance round the fire.

Overlanders in a bush camp. *Exploring parties scouted ahead looking for good grazing.*

Their contribution to knowledge about the countryside helped the settlers who followed

overlanders had emerged. These men made large profits by blazing trails through unknown territory, and driving stock along them to sell at high prices at their journey's end.

George Grey, the explorer, wrote with obvious admiration: 'Urged on by the hope of profit, they have overcome difficulties of no ordinary kind, which have made the more timid and weak-hearted quail ... Almost every Overlander you meet is a remarkable man.'

The first overlander to take stock across the Murray river was probably William Wyse, acting on behalf of his employer Charles Ebden. Late in 1835, Wyse formed Mungabareena run on the present site of Albury, then crossed the river to form Bonegilla run on the Victorian side. He also planted the first wheat grown along the Murray.

Ebden himself followed a year later with his manager, Charles Bonney, son of an English clergyman. Bonney and Ebden were both only about twenty-four years old at the time. Together they commanded a team of convict servants who drove a huge mob of ten thousand sheep from Goulburn to Melbourne — the first stock to complete such a journey.

Droving by Samuel Thomas Gill. Overlanders frequently feature in traditional outback paintings by artists such as Gill, and in stories by writers such as Henry Lawson, who portrayed bush characters with dignity and affection

A romanticised aspect of overlanding, illustrated in the Picturesque Atlas of Australasia during the 1880s, demonstrates the bushmen's popular appeal

AN APPARITION FROM THE VICTORIAN BUSH

When John Wedge and his survey party landed at Indented Head near Geelong in 1835, they were startled to encounter an enormous suntanned white man dressed in animal skins, with the initials W. B. tattooed on his arm.

The man had forgotten how to speak English. Words slowly came back to him. Wedge then discovered that he was William Buckley, a former soldier transported for theft, who had been brought to the Sorrento settlement in Port Phillip thirty-two years earlier.

Escaping into the bush, Buckley was adopted by an Aboriginal tribe and given a new identity.

Wedge arranged for the 'wild white man' to be pardoned. Buckley was taken into the government service, where he performed valuable work as an Aboriginal interpreter. He died in Hobart in 1856, aged a venerable seventy-six.

The story of William Buckley *captured the imagination of the rumour-ridden colony*

The first overlanders to cover the complete distance from Sydney to Melbourne were three British immigrant friends, Joseph Hawdon, John Gardiner and John Hepburn. They travelled during the second half of 1836, followed Major Mitchell's tracks much of the way, and arrived in Melbourne just before Christmas, enabling them to sell their cattle at the high price of £10 a head.

In 1838 Hawdon pioneered the fortnightly 'pony express' mail route between Melbourne and Yass. The same year he and Charles Bonney drove the first stock from Howlong to Adelaide along the Murray river, losing only four head of cattle and adding new information to the map as they went.

Lake Bonney and Lake Victoria were named en route. At the latter, wrote Hawdon, 'Each individual of my party testified his loyal respect for the august personage whose name I had selected, by drinking Her Majesty's health in a glass of brandy, following the toast with loud and hearty huzzas.' □

Stock and mail routes link settlements

All at once, it seemed, South Australia was opened to settlement, the Port Phillip land rush was on and there was a pony express mail service between Melbourne and Yass. This was the fastest growing period of occupation in British colonial history and Melbourne's rich hinterland was the main reason growth came so quickly and so easily

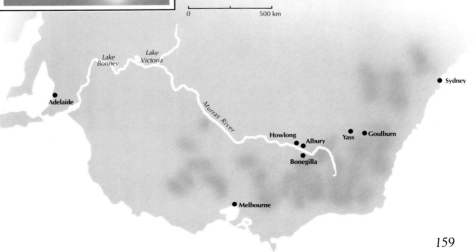

A route through swamp and plain to Portland

THOMAS HENTY
A FOUNDER OF PORTLAND

A southerly overland route to Portland Bay was pioneered by Captain Foster Fyans, police magistrate at Geelong. Although Fyans took an experienced surveyor, H. W. H. Smythe, no detailed maps or directions of the journey seem to have survived.

Ordered to Portland to investigate allegations that Henty shepherds had murdered Aboriginals, Fyans and Smythe with two mounted troopers left Geelong on horseback late in May 1839, steering by compass.

At first they headed south-west along the Barwon river through 'fine and beautiful country'. Then, wrote Fyans, 'we fell in with innumerable difficulties' — probably in the steep foothills of the Otway Range.

A more westerly course across easier country brought them to 'a fine river with a rapid stream of fresh water' — probably the previously unknown Gellibrand river.

They crossed upstream, and headed through marshy country (today's Swan Marsh?). Suddenly they were surrounded by hundreds of Aboriginals brandishing spears. Ordering the troopers to draw their sabres, the explorers charged through the mob to safety.

Their route over flatter country past today's Cobden and Warrnambool was uneventful. Arriving probably at the Moyne river near today's Port Fairy, they emptied a native fish trap: 'We broke a long fast,

enjoyed an excellent breakfast,' wrote Fyans.

More large swamps delayed their progress, but on 10 June 1839 Smythe climbed a tall tree and announced that Portland Bay was in sight. The men were worn out: food totally exhausted, 'and barely a shoe to our feet'.

Fyans found that the Henty settlement had increased to nearly three hundred Europeans. Although most of the inhabitants seemed 'a sad set of ruffians', from all the evidence Fyans could gather, allegations of racial war had been exaggerated. 'No doubt numerous bad and improper acts have been committed and hid from us,' he added.

A properly measured survey of the inland route from Melbourne to Portland and to the South Australian border was carried out by surveyor Charles James Tyers in 1839-40.

Australian produce had to be exported if the *nation* were to grow independent; and explorer-*settlers* such as the Hentys of Portland Bay soon *became* vigorous merchants as well as wealthy *pastoralists*. The brothers owned this 573-tonne *clipper*-built ship, the Frances Henty, *which* *carried* agricultural exports to Britain

CHARLES TYERS
SURVEYOR OF PORTLAND BAY

Tyers's main assignment was to determine the exact position of the border line between today's Victoria and South Australia at longitude one hundred and forty-one degrees east.

With Thomas Townsend as his assistant, and seven convict servants, Tyers left Melbourne on 8 October 1839. The party slowly worked its way south-west to Geelong, then north-westerly over the flat Western District plains past today's Lismore to the ancient volcano Mount Elephant.

Hemmed in by extensive swamps south of today's Hamilton, Tyers eventually found a way round Lake Linlithgow, to discover the Hentys' track blazed from their Wannon river property to Portland.

Tyers settles an argument
The party surveyed Portland Bay from 14 November to 11 December, preparing the way for today's town to be built.

After a five-day journey further west along the coast, Tyers arrived at the mouth of the Glenelg river. His observations settled an old argument: the Glenelg mostly fell within the Victorian border.

The effect of these expeditions was to open many more areas of the Western District to pastoral and agricultural settlement. With reliable maps, the rough days of squatting were coming to an end. Systematic land tenure and the era of squatters' mansion-building were in sight.

The spread from Melbourne to South Australia

Portland Bay, 362 kilometres west of Melbourne, was home to sealer William Dutton in 1829, but the first permanent European settlers were the Henty family who moved there from Tasmania in 1834 and set up a pastoral empire long before the colonial government in London had decided how to divide the land taken up by the Port Phillip Association

Landing Kennedy's horse from the Tam O'Shanter, *by Owen Stanley*

CHAPTER FIVE

The conquest
of Queensland

New outposts of civilisation are established to the north

Major events reshaped British expansion during the early eighteen-forties. New Zealand was separated from New South Wales and made into a colony with its own governor. Convict transportation from Britain almost ceased. The penal settlement at Moreton Bay closed down, and free immigration into Queensland began.

After Allan Cunningham's discoveries in southern Queensland, the first squatters trekked along his route with mobs of sheep and cattle. In the lead was Patrick Leslie, a twenty-five-year-old Scot who had learned the wool trade under the Macarthurs of Camden.

Early in 1840, accompanied by one convict servant, Leslie thoroughly explored the Darling Downs. With his brother, he then settled on the historic property near today's Warwick known as Canning Downs, named after Sir George Canning, British Foreign Secretary.

The Leslies were quickly followed by other pioneers including Henry Stuart Russell, twenty-two-year-old son of an East India Company official. In 1841 Russell established Cecil Plains station on the Condamine river, about eighty kilometres west of today's Toowoomba.

Early in May 1842, with another settler named Andrew Petrie, Russell sailed up the Queensland coast in a light ship's boat to search for even more grazing land. On 10 May the men discovered the Mary river, later named in honour of Lady FitzRoy, wife of the New South Wales Governor. Today it is the site of Maryborough.

Russell and Petrie sailed about eighty kilometres upstream, to encounter two naked white men, with 'eyes wild and unable to rest for a moment on any one object'. They were escaped convicts, who had been living with Aboriginals for years and could now speak only 'black gibberish'. The explorers took them back to the settlement at Brisbane.

On his return to Cecil Plains, Russell decided to explore unknown hilly country north of the Darling Downs.

Ambitious squatters open up south-east Queensland

Much of the exploration of Australia was carried out, not by explorers playing a professional role, but by the settlers who followed in their tracks. The pattern was common to many regions. Explorers blazed their way through new countryside, marking trees, mapping the route. But the path was narrow and knowledge was limited to the area traversed and what could be seen from hills and treetops. Men who were seeking their own land to settle made equally daring journeys, adding more information to the initial discoveries

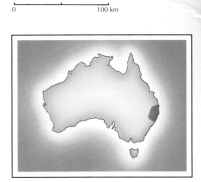

PATRICK LESLIE
QUEENSLAND'S FIRST SQUATTER

164

This trip brought him in November 1842 to discover the head of the Burnett river, which empties into Bundaberg Harbour. However, official credit was given to James Charles Burnett, a surveyor who discovered the outlet five years later.

Closer to the northern limits of Russell's property at Cecil Plains, a Scottish settler named Richard Todd Scougall claimed a vast area of about one hundred and twenty-two thousand hectares, running from today's Bunya Mountains National Park, down Jimbour creek, to the Condamine river. Here Scougall grazed eleven thousand sheep and seven hundred cattle which he had overlanded from the Hunter river.

Homes on the edge of the unknown

In 1842-3 a severe pastoral depression bankrupted many pioneer squatters. Scougall lost Jimbour. Thomas Bell, a wealthy Irish immigrant, was able to take

Cecil Plains was one of the first properties established on the Darling Downs. Henry Stuart Russell founded the station on the banks of the Condamine in 1841. Conrad Martens painted many properties in New England and on the Downs, usually with the patronage of landowners

the property over for only £3200, and put his sons in charge.

At that time the slab homestead on Jimbour formed the western and northern outpost of European civilisation in Queensland. No sooner had the Bell sons moved in than a strange party of ten wayfarers, led by the lean and absent-minded German 'Doctor' Ludwig Leichhardt, arrived at the property and asked for food and shelter.

At the time it must have seemed ludicrous, but these inexperienced explorers were about to revolutionise European knowledge of all the lands to the north and north-west. □

Leichhardt gambles with fortune and finally loses

Atall, vague, hungry-looking man. One who was always pondering, whose eyes seemed to look through you to distant horizons. Silent, sometimes depressive, then optimistic without cause. Dogged, insistent on his own aims. Selfish, indifferent to his companions' welfare. A navigator whose skills were disputable, but who succeeded in the greatest overland expedition in Australian history. Lucky for just that one time: then pushed his luck so far that he perished with all his companions. That was Friedrich Wilhelm Ludwig Leichhardt, discoverer of central Queensland and a route to northern Australia.

Leichhardt was the son of a Prussian farmer. Scholarly by nature, he pursued many branches of learning but never completed a university degree. Aged twenty-eight, he sailed to Australia in 1841, partly to evade compulsory military service, partly to study natural sciences in a barely-touched field. For more than two years he wandered alone through northern New South Wales examining its botany, geology and agriculture.

On visits to Sydney, Leichhardt was accepted as a learned 'doctor'. When Governor Gipps delayed in authorising official exploration through the unknown lands from Queensland to north-western Australia, Leichhardt and several friends decided to raise a private expedition.

The party of ten enthusiastic young men left Jimbour station on the Darling Downs on 1 October 1844, singing 'a full chorus of God Save the Queen', as they went. They were guided mainly by John Arrowsmith's latest map of Australia, which in this locality showed very little detail beyond an outline of the coast and a few rivers.

To transport the party's five hundred and forty-four kilos of flour and other articles, Leichhardt had exchanged some of his horses for bullocks. 'Neither my companions nor myself knew much about bullocks,' he remarked cheerfully — but they quickly learned. The amateur explorer was also proud of outfitting the expedition with ponchos. They were made of light calico saturated with oil to help keep out tropical downpours.

In leisurely fashion members of the party followed the boggy banks of the Condamine river, botanising to their hearts' content, and sometimes getting lost so that their Aboriginal guides, Harry Brown and Charley Fisher, were kept busy tracking them.

After five weeks the men were still only about one hundred and sixty kilometres north-west of Jimbour. Already one of the bullocks had to be killed and dried to eke out their rations. The camp was named Dried Beef Creek.

Living off the land

On 6 November 1844, Leichhardt discovered the Dawson river, naming it after one of several squatters who had assisted the expedition. Here the men caught many crayfish, jewfish and eels to vary their diet. By cautious experiment, Leichhardt found that several plants growing near waterholes could be cooked and eaten to ward off scurvy, although severe diarrhoea was often a side-effect.

By late November, goannas, possums, emus, kangaroos and birds of all kinds were 'gladly consigned to our stewing-pot'. 'It is remarkable how soon man becomes indifferent to the niceties of food,' Leichhardt added.

One bullock tore a flour bag, scattering seven kilos of flour on the ground. The men scraped it up, well mixed with leaves and dust, and made a dark porridge: 'a mass which every one of us enjoyed highly,' wrote Leichhardt. After that incident, kangaroo skins were used to cover the flour-bags.

Oil that dripped from emus during cooking was used to lubricate the muskets. Leichhardt occasionally drank a mugful as 'a good anti-rheumatic'.

On 27 November 1844, the party discovered Expedition Range, naming its highest peak Mount Nicholson after Dr Charles Nicholson, who had tried to persuade the New South Wales Governor to back the expedition.

Through all of December and into January 1845 the explorers slowly penetrated hilly country along the Comet river, where the brightness of shooting stars filled Leichhardt with ecstasy.

'Our daily allowance of flour was now reduced to three pounds,' the explorer wrote on 5 January. Yet no sense of urgency could be detected in his journal. As needs increased, he added, 'our desires become more easily satisfied'.

On 12 January 1845, Leichhardt came to the junction of the Comet river with a chain of lakes: 'the finest succession of large sheets of water we had seen since leaving the Brisbane.' In wet seasons this was obviously a major watercourse: Leich-

A novice explorer in Gulf country

Leichhardt's first journey covering nearly 5000 kilometres, opened up vast areas of grazing land in central Queensland, but his later even more ambitious expeditions, in 1846 and 1848, failed

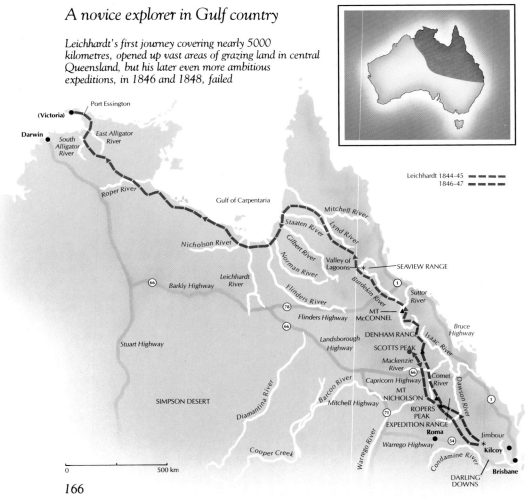

Leichhardt 1844-45 ▬▬▬
1846-47 ▬▬▬

166

hardt named it the Mackenzie river after Sir Evan Mackenzie, first man to take up land at Kilcoy near Brisbane.

A talent for getting lost

Leichhardt lost himself for several days in the surrounding ridges. His only companion, the Aboriginal Harry Brown, managed to shoot two pigeons which made dinner. The following day, wrote Leichhardt, 'I swallowed the bones and the feet of the pigeon, to allay the cravings of my stomach.'

Finding the main party again, they drank litres of tea and later feasted on nests of the native bee, 'full of the sweetest and most aromatic honey we had ever tasted'. Wild marjoram found growing all about was added to give extra strength to their tea and soup. 'A dish of cockatoos for supper' was also thoroughly enjoyed by the explorers.

On 27 January 1845 Leichhardt discovered the source of the Isaac river in what he called Peak Range. He named the river after Frederick Isaac, a Darling Downs squatter; the south-eastern height Roper's Peak after John Roper, who climbed it; and the north-western point Scott's Peak, after Helenus Scott, a settler on the Hunter river.

Much of February and March 1845 was spent travelling northward and resting along the Isaac river. One day Leichhardt threatened to withhold rations from Charley Fisher for disobedience of orders. In reply, the Aboriginal hit Leichhardt in the face, loosening two of his teeth. After banishment from the camp, Charley came back humbly enough and was forgiven. Then, for several days Leichhardt was laid low with severe lumbago.

LUDWIG LEICHHARDT
A REMOTE, STUBBORN LEADER

Yet there was satisfaction in the discoveries of this period — much fine pastoral land, and on 7 March, a new river which Leichhardt named after William Henry Suttor, who had donated four bullocks to the expedition.

On 2 April 1845, Leichhardt rode east of Mount McConnel to find a much larger river joining the Suttor. He named it the Burdekin after Mary Ann Burdekin, wealthy widow of Sydney merchant Thomas Burdekin, who had helped Leichhardt financially. It was the same river whose outlet had been discovered by

Great walls of rock reminded Leichhardt of the ancient fortresses of his native Germany as he battled his way through the eastern fringe of the Carnarvon Range in Queensland in 1844. He named one area Ruined Castle Valley

Commander J.C. Wickham in 1839; Wickham had named it after himself, but Leichhardt's naming prevailed. The Suttor-Burdekin junction is today the site of the Burdekin Dam, Australia's biggest water conservation project since the Snowy Mountains Scheme.

Leichhardt traced the Burdekin north-westerly upstream to its source in the Perry Range, which he named after Samuel Augustus Perry, New South Wales Deputy Surveyor-General. Unfortunately this name was later changed to what was considered the more commercially attractive Seaview Range.

Early in May 1845 Leichhardt left the Burdekin river, which turned to the north-east, and struck out to the north-west, towards the Gulf of Carpentaria. On 4 May he came to a well-watered spot which he called the Valley of Lagoons, partly covered with 'a very pleasing poplar-gum forest'. This later became the site of a notable squatting enterprise.

By 23 May the expedition, still pushing north-westerly, arrived at the Lynd river. Leichhardt named it after Sydney philanthropist Robert Lynd, whose support had enabled him to devote his early days in Australia to natural science.

Next day the expedition halted to celebrate Queen Victoria's twenty-sixth birthday with a fat cake. The rare treat of sugar with their marjoram tea was also allowed. After that there was 'nothing left but the saturated rags of our sugar bags...which we boiled up with our tea'.

On 16 June 1845, Leichhardt discovered a new and broader river joining the Lynd, which he named the Mitchell, after the New South Wales Surveyor-General. 'Much more tortuous in its course,' Leichhardt noted in his journal, perhaps sardonically.

Death in the night

By the last week in June the half-starved party was near the east coast of Carpentaria. The smoke of native fires could be seen all around. On the night of 28 June Leichhardt was aroused by loud shouts. Aboriginals had thrown a shower of spears at the tents, hitting three men.

The remaining explorers fired their guns. At the frightening noise the attackers fled. John Roper suffered a barbed spear through his arm: the shaft had to be broken off and the head pulled right through. Another spear had passed through his cheek into the optic nerve. Altogether, six spears had struck him, five had found Calvert. Nineteen-year-old James Calvert had spears in his groin and knee: these had to be cut out with a sharp knife. John Gilbert, thirty-five, bird collector for the famous John Gould and an experienced bushman, dropped dead with a spear through his neck. He was buried where he fell, the grave site remaining undiscovered until 1983.

After two days' rest the wounded men said they were able to proceed. On 5 July 1845 the party came to 'a fine salt water

river' — the Staaten river, originally discovered by the Dutch.

The first sight of the Gulf of Carpentaria was hailed by all with loud hurrahs. 'We had now discovered a line of communication by land, between the eastern coast of Australia and the Gulf of Carpentaria,' Leichhardt enthused. 'We had travelled along never failing, and, for the greater part, running waters: and over an excellent country, available, almost in its whole extent, for pastoral purposes.'

But the hardy explorer was still not content. Instead of heading for home, he took his party south-west round the great curve of the Gulf.

Progress was faster now. The explorers were fortunate to be travelling during an unusually dry season when rivers were low but waterholes still full.

On 12 July they crossed the 'broad sandy bed' of a river running through 'most beautiful country'. This was named the Gilbert after their dead companion. Plenty of food was now available, in the form of fish, teal, geese, emus and kangaroos, which could be seasoned with salt from dried-up pools near the sea.

In quick succession the party crossed the Norman, Flinders, Leichhardt, Nicholson and other rivers flowing through the Gulf country. Moving through knee-deep kangaroo grass, horses and bullocks regained excellent condition. Leichhardt discovered how to eat the hard, woody pandanus fruit by boiling

The Gilbert River, *which flows into the Gulf of Carpentaria, probably looked much as it does in this photograph when Leichhardt's party crossed it during the dry season of 1845*

A regular item of diet *among Aboriginals encountered by Leichhardt was the fruit of the pandanus palm. He found that they neutralised its noxious characteristics by roasting it, or by soaking the wedge-shaped segments in water*

THE DAILY ROUTINE IN LEICHHARDT'S CAMP

Leichhardt tried to keep his camp running to a regular procedure.

On the first expedition he recorded that his own task was to light the camp fire each evening. The Aboriginal Harry Brown fetched water to make tea. James Calvert weighed out a bare kilo of meat per man to be stewed for a late dinner, and about six hundred grams of flour for a 'fat cake' (made with suet or animal fat).

While the meat was cooking, Leichhardt wrote up his log or collected plants. At sunset a loud cooee from the camp summoned all to dinner.

'Many circumstances have conspired to make me strangely taciturn,' wrote Leichhardt, but his companions were usually 'full of jokes and stories'.

Harry Brown sometimes sang the group to sleep with 'corroborri songs' rendered in his 'melodious plaintive voice'.

Each morning, wrote Leichhardt, he was awakened early by the settlers' clock — 'the merry laugh of the laughing-jackass' (kookaburra).

With a cooee Leichhardt roused his companions. Harry Brown stirred the fire

Meat from a bullock *killed to supplement the expedition's rations was preserved for future use*

and made a litre of tea for each man. James Calvert added salt and marjoram to stew that had been cooking slowly all night, and served each about a kilo.

'I naturally had a great antipathy against comfort-hunting and gourmandizing,' Leichhardt wrote, but he was delighted

by hanging strips in the sun to cure. The camp site was named Dried Beef Creek

with the abundance of food along most parts of the route.

At about 7 a.m., sixteen-year-old John Murphy and the Aboriginal Charley Fisher brought in horses and bullocks from their grazing, and the new day's four-hour march began.

---

the pulp until it lost the noxious elements which had previously blistered his lips and tongue.

On 19 October 1845, the explorers came to an immense freshwater river, more than four hundred and sixty metres broad. Leichhardt named it after John Roper, who had seen it two days earlier when scouting ahead for the best route. The country all round was lush with grass, lagoons and wildlife.

Unfortunately three of the best horses drowned after stumbling down steep banks. Unable to increase the loads on

his bullocks, Leichhardt was forced to throw much of his hard-won botanical collection into the campfire. 'Tears were in my eyes,' he wrote.

In this area fruit bats were plentiful and easily caught. Leichhardt tossed them into the stew-pot. 'A little strong,' he mused, 'but in messes made at night, it was always difficult to find out the cause of any particular taste.'

By 17 December 1845 the party had trekked down the South and East Alligator rivers, through today's vast national parks and nature reserves, to reach the

military establishment at Port Essington, where Commandant John McArthur had long ceased to expect them. Instead of the six months planned, their incredible four thousand eight hundred and twenty-seven-kilometre journey had taken more than fourteen months.

'I was deeply affected in finding myself again in civilized society, and could scarcely speak,' wrote Leichhardt.

Welcomed as heroes

The explorers were taken back to Sydney on the schooner *Heroine*. After their arrival on 29 March 1845, an extraordinary welcome was given by colonists excited by the prospect of endless pastoral expansion.

'I thought the whole town would go mad with joy,' Leichhardt wrote in a private letter. 'Even the family of Sir Thomas Mitchell are treating me with justice.' A substantial public subscription was raised, and a memorial to John Gilbert, a talented naturalist, was erected in St James Church, Sydney.

Most important of all, the trail had been blazed for the settlement of practically all of eastern and central Queensland, and ultimately the 'north end' of the Australian continent.

Peculiar Leichhardt might have been, but no other man since James Cook had opened such a vast extent of territory to European-style development.

Fruit bats *provided Leichhardt and his men with sustaining, if unpalatable, meals. The hopes of many explorers to live at least in part off the land were repeatedly dashed, as Leichhardt found*

Leichhardt's second expedition, however, was a complete fiasco. He left Jimbour on 7 December 1846 with eight men, this time intending to cross the entire continent somewhere south of his earlier route, then work his way down the west coast to Perth.

The expedition traversed only eight hundred and five kilometres to the northwest in seven months. After crossing the Dawson river the men had to force their way through nearly one hundred and sixty kilometres of 'the most horrible country the foot of a white man ever trod', wrote Henry Turnbull.

James Calvert, *left, John Murphy and John Roper survived Leichhardt's first expedition. Both Calvert and Roper suffered spear wounds*

This time the party experienced the full rigour of the wet season. For three weeks it rained heavily with scarcely a minute's break. Horses, mules, forty bullocks, one hundred and eight sheep and the two hundred and seventy Tibetan goats taken for milk and meat frequently sank up to their bellies in mud: 'we had to unload them and by sheer strength drag them on to firm ground.'

The tents, made of lightweight oiled calico instead of tough, hard-wearing duck, tore to ribbons, and the men were soaked through night and day. Fiercely aggressive paper-nest wasps (*Polistes tasmaniensis*) attacked them, leaving immense swellings 'more painful than the bite of a snake'.

Battling through to the Mackenzie river, the entire party was stricken with fever and ague. For four weeks, they lay in camp 'utterly helpless with disease'. Often they had only cold muddy water to drink because no one was strong enough to light a fire and make tea.

A thirty-three-year-old nurseryman from St. Kilda named Daniel Bunce, severely criticised Leichhardt's behaviour as leader during this period.

Since the sick men were unable to eat meat, Bunce had planted mustard and cress seeds near the Mackenzie river camp. Returning to harvest the crop, he found it had all disappeared. Leichhardt's boot prints were in the mud near by. On being challenged, the leader 'at once admitted that he had cut and eaten it', without offering any to the starving men who could not move from their blankets.

Next day Bunce boiled a sheep's head to make soup. Unfortunately the pot spilled on the ground. Leichhardt, 'deaf to the remonstrances of the patients very quickly and quietly swallowed the whole, bones excepted'.

With most of the stock scattered, it seemed pointless to proceed. As the men slowly recovered, Leichhardt insisted on one more push into the Peak Range. Here, in the aftermath of tropical rain, the sky was 'almost darkened' with sandflies: 'their sting was frightful'.

In humid forty-two-degree heat, the men rode completely covered up, but their horses' legs and bellies were frequently 'streaming with blood from the bites'. It was impossible to eat without swallowing 'about twenty flies' with every spoonful of food.

Again the nine men were stricken with fever: most could not even crawl to a creek for water. Leichhardt in addition suffered torments from rotting teeth. In June 1847 he finally gave up and decided to return to Jimbour station, having achieved almost nothing.

After resting for two weeks, the dogged explorer spent part of August 1847 tracing the course of the Condamine river and its tributaries. He then returned to Sydney to organise a new attempt to reach Western Australia from Queensland. Daniel Bunce was invited to accompany him but refused.

The secret of Leichhardt's death
Leichhardt's final expedition of seven men left Allan MacPherson's station Cogoon, north-west of today's Roma, on 4 April 1848. The straggling line of fifty bullocks, twenty mules and seven horses was last seen heading north-westerly towards the Warrego river. Then it disappeared entirely into the immensity of the inland. No conclusive evidence of its fate has ever been found.

During following years, several

earches were made for Leichhardt's remains. In 1852 an official party under Hovenden Hely reported that the explorers had apparently been killed by Aboriginals in western Queensland.

A. C. Gregory searched large areas in the late 1850s, and found trees on the Barcoo river blazed with the letter L. During the eighteen-sixties parties searching for survivors of the Burke and Wills expedition found similar blazed trees much further north near the Flinders river in the Gulf country.

In 1865 Melbourne women raised £4000 for a 'Ladies' Leichhardt Search Expedition', but this collapsed in dissension before it reached the search area.

Six years later a party of Queensland mounted police under James Gilmour found skeletons, pieces of European clothing and other relics on the Diamantina river, suggesting that Leichhardt had turned back from the Simpson Desert and had died with all of his men on the return journey.

In 1873 a horse thief named Andrew Hume claimed to have spoken to a 'wild white man' who was living happily with a native tribe in western Queensland. The survivor, said to be August or Adolf Classen from Leichhardt's party, told him that the men had mutinied and killed

their leader. All except himself had then been murdered by Aboriginals.

Sixty-five years went by. In 1938 the South Australian government sponsored an expedition under Dr A. Grenfell Price to search for several skeletons sighted on the edge of the Simpson Desert. Bones, teeth, pieces of ancient leather and iron, and two coins old enough to have been

AUGUSTUS GREGORY
FOUND TREES BLAZED WITH AN L

Flood plains in the Channel Country. *During periods of heavy rain in western Queensland, rivers in this region spill their banks and water stretches over the vast plains. In 1848, the Diamantina, above, and Cooper Creek flooded, possibly trapping Leichhardt's party*

carried by Leichhardt were found. Other investigators believe Leichhardt's party perished after floods swept down the Diamantina river and Cooper creek in 1848. The explorer Ernest Giles thought that 'Everybody and everything must have been swallowed up in a cataclysm and buried deep and sure in the mud and slime of a flood.'

These stories are not necessarily incompatible: simply no conclusive proof exists. Although the full truth will probably never be discovered, even today some people hope to find additional evidence to solve the mystery.

Perhaps the last word should remain with one of Leichhardt's admirers, the bushman Henry Turnbull. 'It does not seem to me a matter of much consequence that his bones should be collected to be deposited in holy ground,' Turnbull wrote. 'He rests in a holier spot than any consecrated by man...the sad wind sighs over him, and the warm sun shines upon him...It is just such a resting place as any lover of nature would choose.' □

171

Mitchell's dream evaporates on the banks of the Barcoo

Ludwig Leichhardt's successful journey across northern Australia in 1845-46 robbed Sir Thomas Mitchell of glory he felt was rightfully his. The Surveyor-General had arranged for Leichhardt to be employed as naturalist on an official expedition to the north. As we have seen, Leichhardt wearied of government delays and set off with his own party.

Mitchell was left fuming in his Sydney office, convinced that a great river flowed from southern Queensland to the Gulf of Carpentaria. When approval for the search finally arrived from London, and Mitchell's expedition left today's Orange on 16 December 1845, Leichhardt was already in sight of Port Essington.

Mitchell, now fifty-four, had prepared carefully for what he imagined would be the crowning point of his career. As his second-in-command he took twenty-seven-year-old Edmund Besley Kennedy, Guernsey-born professional surveyor, who had assisted C. J. Tyers to lay out Portland. With them were thirty trusted convicts and black trackers, eleven wheeled vehicles full of provisions, one hundred and twelve bullocks, seventeen horses, two hundred and fifty sheep, and two boats that were used mainly as water troughs for the stock.

For many weeks the huge caravan trekked northerly along known sections of the almost-dry Bogan and Macquarie rivers, painfully picking its way from one water-hole to another. A flash flood along the Macquarie bogged the expedition and slowed it down even more.

Temperatures were appalling: up to fifty-three degrees in the shade. Three of the best kangaroo dogs expired in the heat. Mitchell and several others went temporarily blind from ophthalmia: leeches were attached to their eyelids in an endeavour to find a cure.

The explorers' fortunes improved early in March 1846 when they discovered lakes, abundant fresh water, and 'rich natural pasturage' along the Narran river. Although temperatures stayed above thirty-seven degrees, Mitchell's northerly course took him across today's Queensland border to discover on 24 April the Maranoa river, which he named after an Aboriginal word meaning 'human hand'.

In late summer the river bed was practically dry. Mitchell veered northeast to travel along water-holes of the Cogoon river. On 8 May 1846 he came to fine country, 'a champaign region', which he named FitzRoy Downs after Henry FitzRoy, Duke of Grafton.

On 17 May Mitchell again encountered the Maranoa river, camping there until Kennedy's measuring party caught up. The Surveyor-General decided to take a small party on a dash towards the

Gulf of Carpentaria, fully expecting to find his great river and solve 'the hidden mystery of the division between the northern and southern waters'.

Leaving Kennedy in charge at the depot, Mitchell spent much of June 1846 exploring and naming peaks in the Great Dividing Range where the Maranoa, Warrego and other rivers rise.

Continuing northwards, on 21 July Mitchell's hopes were raised anew by discovery of the Belyando river. But this stream soon dissipated into pools, channels and long reaches.

By 10 August Mitchell had reluctantly come to the conclusion that the Belyando could not lead him to his goal. He returned southwards towards Mount Salvator, on 1 September crossing 'an almost boundless extent of the richest surface in a latitude corresponding to that of China, yet still uncultivated and unoccupied by man.'

From his depot near Mount Playfair, Mitchell decided to try the country further inland in his determined search to find his dream river.

Severe difficulties were encountered in rough country to the west, although the explorers 'cut off all the roundabouts and steep pulls, where this could be done, by laying logs across such gullies as we were obliged to cross.'

On 11 September the party scrambled through 'a scrub of matted vines, which hung down like ropes, and pulled some of us off our horses.' Next day they forced their way through brigalow and mulga scrub bearing 'hard spiky dry branches, which project like fixed bayonets, to

Mitchell *was at the Condamine River on the Darling Downs when he was overtaken by a courier with the news that Leichhardt had completed his epic journey to Port Essington. The boats Mitchell took were never to float on the waters of the Gulf of Carpentaria, but they were useful for crossing rivers. A number of the early explorers hauled boats great distances hoping to discover an inland sea: they were used to store supplies and as water troughs for the stock*

In 1845 Mitchell crossed the Darling *on his way north. A great publicist, he wrote widely on military, engineering and agricultural subjects, as well as about his four journeys of exploration*

receive the charge of ourselves, horses and flour-bags.'

Suddenly, on 15 September 1846, climbing through a gap in the Warrego Range, Mitchell was overjoyed to discover a new river running north-easterly 'to the remotest verge of the horizon'. He was certain that this discovery would prove to be 'the realization of my long cherished hopes…a reward direct from Heaven for perseverance.'

The party now rode easily over 'the finest and most extensive pastoral regions I had ever seen', to come to what is now called the Barcoo river, near today's Blackall. The stream was 'as large as the Murray'; without doubt the 'El Dorado of Australia', Mitchell enthused. And it headed more or less in the right direction for the Gulf. In brief, it was 'a river leading to India'.

Alas, the dogged explorer was once again to be cheated out of his ambition. Short of provisions now, he hurried his men back with the great news. Later explorers had to discover that the Barcoo soon changed course to the south-west, to become the same river as Sturt's Cooper creek, flowing finally into Lake Eyre. Mitchell's dream was simply a chimera, one of many that taunted explorers of the unknown. □

His fourth expedition ends on a false triumphant note

On his last expedition, Major Mitchell believed he had at last discovered the great river that so many believed flowed north to the Gulf. He named it the Victoria and confidently returned to Sydney. He was wrong. The river swung south to join Cooper Creek: it was re-named the Barcoo. However, Mitchell had discovered valuable grazing land, including the Maranoa region

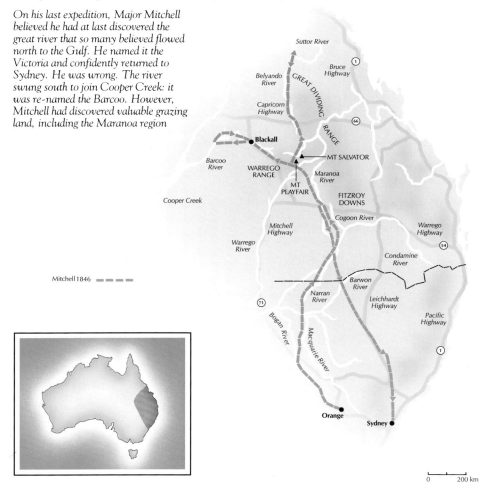

Mitchell 1846 ━ ━ ━

0   200 km

Kennedy's lonely death ends a tragic expedition

*O*bsessed by his need for recognition at home, Sir Thomas Mitchell arranged to take a year's leave to supervise publication of his Journal of an Expedition into the Interior of Tropical Australia *in London. Before leaving Sydney, he sent his young assistant Edmund Kennedy to trace the Barcoo river to its imagined outlet in the Gulf of Carpentaria.*

Kennedy left Parramatta on 13 March 1847 with a small party, reaching Mitchell's furthest point on the Barcoo five months later. He soon discovered that his chief's great theory about 'a river to India' was wrong. On 15 August Kennedy wrote, 'The fall was most provokingly evident to the southward...I am convinced that we are now upon Cooper's Creek.'

The young surveyor persevered with his south-westerly trek, and was rewarded on 20 August 1847 by discovery of an important tributary, which he named the Thomson river after E. Deas Thomson, Colonial Secretary. This stream came from the north — perhaps Mitchell's theory of river communication with the Gulf could be proved after all?

Intending to head directly for the Gulf, Kennedy returned in high hopes to

his depot on 16 September 1847. There he found that Aboriginals had dug up the expedition's one hundred and eighty-one kilos of carefully concealed flour and mixed it thoroughly with clay. There was no possibility now of continuing a northwards push through unknown drought-stricken country.

Living mainly on fish, birds and a little flour saved from the dirt, Kennedy's party managed to reach the furthest-out cattle station on the Barwon river just before Christmas 1847. Here the settlers sold them sufficient flour and tea to continue their journey.

The news that Kennedy brought back severely embarrassed Sir Thomas Mitchell in London and delighted his many enemies. The Governor, Sir Charles FitzRoy, reported to the Secretary of State that it was important to

establish the nature of the territory to th[e] north of Mitchell's explorations of 184[6] and that he had decided to place Edmun[d] Kennedy in charge of a fresh expedition.

One of the government's chief aim[s] was to find a harbour on Cape Yor[k] Peninsula where steamships could coal o[n] the run between Singapore and Sydne[y.] Settlement of the hinterland would fol[-]low as a matter of course.

For this expedition, Kennedy decided the exhausting trek northwards from Syd[-]ney should be avoided by landing th[e] party at a suitable point on the Queens[-]land coast. The men would begin the tre[k] into unknown regions while still fresh[,] ambitious and well-provisioned.

A confident leader

By coincidence, HMS *Rattlesnake* unde[r] Captain Owen Stanley was about t[o] leave Sydney to continue its survey o[f] Queensland and Papua New Guine[a] waters. Stanley convoyed the barque *Tam[?]* O'Shanter *with Kennedy's party t[o] Rockingham Bay, between Townsvill[e] and Cairns, on 21 May 1848. Th[e] explorer seemed 'in high spirits an[d] confident of success,' wrote Joh[n] MacGillivray, the ship's naturalist.

Kennedy proceeded inland throug[h] swampy ground before turning in a north[-] north-westerly direction parallel with th[e]

Queensland coast. But the reality of north Queensland's mountains and jungles was quite different to the favourable views seen by travellers on passing ships. After a hellish trip lasting nearly five months, it was not until 9 November 1848 that Kennedy and his starving party tumbled down the northern foothills of the Great Dividing Range to Weymouth Bay, north of today's Scrubby Creek mining area.

In desperation, Kennedy left eight sick men, two horses and a little flour at Weymouth Bay. He took the remaining three white men, a Muswellbrook Aboriginal named Jackey Jackey, horses and provisions on a dash to Port Albany at the tip of Cape York, where the schooner *Ariel* was awaiting their arrival.

Near the Shelburne river, one of the three whites accidentally shot himself in the shoulder. Kennedy decided to leave the other two to care for him, and pushed on with Jackey Jackey.

Tragic waste and suffering

Early in December 1848 these last two travellers arrived at the mangrove swamps of the Escape river, almost within sight of their destination.

One evening, probably 11 December, they were surrounded by Aboriginals. According to Jackey Jackey's later statement about the event, the attackers 'threw plenty of spears, and hit Mr Kennedy in the back first.'

Jackey Jackey kept the Aboriginals at bay with gunfire while he cut the barb out of his employer's back. Then more spears hit Kennedy in the leg and right side, finally killing him. Jackey Jackey himself was wounded over one eye, but caught Kennedy as he fell back and died. 'I was crying a good while until I got well,' the black man said later.

Jackey Jackey escaped by wading along creek with only his head above water. After struggling for nearly a fortnight he managed to reach the supply ship and give news of Kennedy's fate.

The *Ariel* hastened down the coast to rescue the two groups which Kennedy had left behind. Now the full nature of the tragedy became apparent.

The three men left on the Shelburne river had completely disappeared, and were never found. The eight men left at Weymouth Bay had tried to survive in forty-degree temperatures by boiling down their horses into soup. William Carron, the expedition's twenty-five-year-old botanist, described how the

weakened, fever-ridden men died one after another. The survivors, too weak to dig graves, weighted the bodies with stones and rolled them into the water.

Occasionally Carron was able to shoot a pigeon and once a wallaby. Friendly Aboriginals gave the survivors 'a little vegetable paste, and some pieces of turtle's entrails, with some shark's liver'. Given a fat blue-tongued lizard, Carron opened it 'and took out eleven young ones, which we roasted and ate'.

By 30 December 1848, Carron's arm and hip bones had worked their way through his wasted flesh. As he lay almost insensible on the ground, Jackey Jackey led a party from the *Ariel* to his rescue. Only one other man, a labourer named William Goddard, was still alive.

Jackey Jackey becomes a hero

Carron more or less recovered in Sydney, and worked on the Botanic Gardens staff until a year before his death in 1876. Jackey Jackey was idolised by the public for his attempt to save Kennedy: so many people bought him congratulatory drinks that he became an alcoholic, and was burned to death in 1854 when he drunkenly rolled into a fire.

Altogether ten men including Kennedy perished on the expedition. Sir Thomas Mitchell, back from London, took gloomy pleasure in denouncing the enterprise as a waste of lives and money.

Mitchell himself made no more important explorations. Controversial to the last, he fought a duel with a man he considered had impugned his honour. He invented a steamship propeller that used the principle of Aboriginal boomerangs. In 1855 he died of pneumonia in the middle of an inquiry into the unsatisfactory state of his department. □

A well-planned expedition disintegrates into a journey of horror

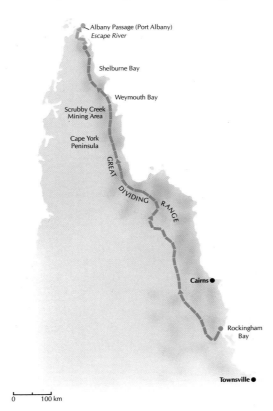

Albany Passage (Port Albany)
Escape River

Shelburne Bay

Weymouth Bay

Scrubby Creek
Mining Area

Cape York
Peninsula

GREAT DIVIDING RANGE

Cairns ●

Rockingham
Bay

Townsville ●

0   100 km

It seemed extremely logical to land Kennedy's party on the coast at the southernmost point of the country to be explored and for it to progress northwards. Three factors turned the plan into a débâcle: the terrain, the weather and aggressive Aboriginals. Dense jungle ran from the coast to the Great Divide, swamps and mangroves confused the river mouths, the wet season was severe, the Aboriginals attacked mercilessly. Ten men, including Kennedy, were to die

Jackey Jackey's
route to the *Ariel*
Kennedy 1848

175

Land-takers find a bonanza beyond the Tropic of Capricorn

Five of the Archer brothers (*bearded*) who *pioneered settlement in north Queensland. In all, seven brothers were in Australia at various times. In 1855, the Archers established Gracemere Station on the Fitzroy River, which they had discovered. The homestead,* right, *still stands near the city of Rockhampton*

*E*dmund Kennedy's doomed expedition of 1848 proved one thing. The most sensible method of conquering the tropics was not to attempt full-scale overland exploration. A better approach was to land coastal parties, who could work their way inland along suitable watercourses. Ambitious squatters in search of new pastures could be relied upon to infiltrate gradually past the worst obstacles and make overland discoveries.

Far away from these scenes, Europe during the eighteen-fifties and eighteen-sixties was expending its energies in the Crimean War, while the United States of America tore itself to pieces in a bitter Civil War over slavery. The revolutionary ideas of Karl Marx and Charles Darwin were beginning to undermine old certainties about economics, evolution and religious belief. But in Australia, philosophical ideas seemed of little consequence. Men thrilled to more material ambitions. Huge gold deposits had been found in New South Wales and Victoria — and when most of the gold had been dug up, new land lay almost for the taking in the north.

One of the first major squatting enterprises north of Brisbane was launched by the Archer brothers. Three of these brawny young men, born in Scotland but raised in Norway, had already taken up the most northerly run in the Moreton district during the eighteen-forties.

In 1848 David and Thomas Archer followed the tracks of J. C. Burnett along the Burnett river, past today's Bundaberg, and established two sheep runs.

Five years later Charles and William Archer discovered the Fitzroy river, which runs into Keppel Bay, naming it after Governor Sir Charles FitzRoy. Colin Archer sailed the first boat up the river in 1855. On the site of Rockhampton they established their famous sheep and cattle station Gracemere, part of which still exists with its original ironbark homestead.

In 1859 another Scottish settler, George Elphinstone Dalrymple, thirty-three, led a private expedition from Rockhampton to the Burdekin river district. This region was already known from the explorations of Wickham, Leichhardt, and A. C. Gregory, but remained unsettled until Dalrymple returned in 1860 to report discovery of the Bowen and Bogie rivers, and 'one of the finest and largest pastoral and agricultural regions of Australia'.

Queensland meanwhile had won separation from New South Wales. The new government promptly authorised formation of the first settlement in north Queensland, naming it Bowen, after the first Governor, Sir George Bowen.

A long jetty to take cattle exports was built in the shelter of North Head and stockmen moved rapidly into the hinterland. 'There is something almost sublime in the steady, silent flow of pastoral occupation over north-eastern Australia,' said Governor Bowen.

Appointed to government service, George Dalrymple went north to establish the port of Cardwell in Rockingham Bay in 1864. Near by he discovered the naturalists' paradise of the Herbert river, naming it after Sir Robert Herbert, first Premier of Queensland. His next expedition took him across the Rockingham Range and opened up a dray road from Cardwell to pastoral land in the interior.

In 1865 Dalrymple was elected to the Queensland Legislative Assembly as the first member for Kennedy, then for a brief period he was Colonial Secretary. He quit politics in 1867. In 1869 he took up Oxford Downs on the upper Burdekin, but his pastoral ventures failed.

For two years he was an assistant gold commissioner, then in 1873 he was given

Settlers brave the unknown to carve out pastoral kingdoms

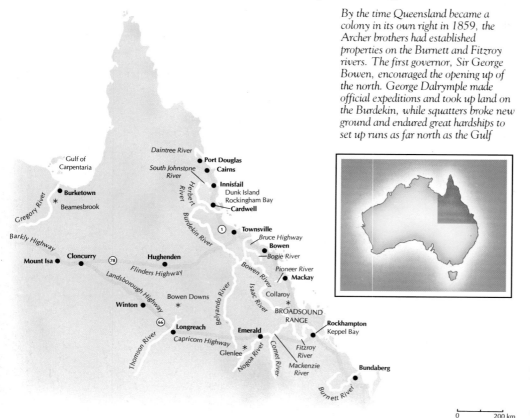

By the time Queensland became a colony in its own right in 1859, the Archer brothers had established properties on the Burnett and Fitzroy rivers. The first governor, Sir George Bowen, encouraged the opening up of the north. George Dalrymple made official expeditions and took up land on the Burdekin, while squatters broke new ground and endured great hardships to set up runs as far north as the Gulf

eadership of an official expedition to xplore the rivers round today's Innisfail nd Cairns. Always alert to the economic ossibilities of new discoveries, he con-idered Dunk Island suitable for growing offee, sugar and cotton.

On the mainland, travelling up the outh Johnstone river, Dalrymple was nthralled by the panorama of 'a vast and itherto hidden region' — most of it overed by tropical jungle, but with at east one hundred and twenty thousand ectares suitable for sugar production.

North of today's Port Douglas, along he Daintree river (named after the rominent geologist who later became a istinguished photographer, Richard Daintree), Dalrymple discovered 'soils so ch and of so vast extent' that they must orm 'a lasting heritage in the hands of an dustrious and provident people.'

tock route to Bowen

Meanwhile other explorers and settlers ad been busy opening up fresh areas of Queensland. In 1860 a thirty-four-year-ld Scot named William Landsborough oined forces with a thirty-three-year-old rish drover, Nathaniel Buchanan. They eft Rockhampton to search for new land o the north. Along the Thomson river heir supplies ran out and they were orced to exist on stewed greenhide. But hey discovered over thirty-eight hundred quare kilometres of pastures which be-ame Bowen Downs station. Buchanan lazed the first stock route four hundred nd eighty kilometres to Bowen.

Buchanan's wife Katherine, whom he arried in 1863, was for some time the nly white woman in the district, guard-ing the adobe homestead while her hus-band pursued new ambitions.

In 1864 Buchanan established Beamesbrook, near today's Burketown — the first station in the Gulf country.

John Mackay, a twenty-one-year-old droving friend of Nathaniel Buchanan, joined the northern land rush in 1860. With four other whites and an Aborigi-nal named Duke, Mackay rode from Armidale to Rockhampton, then north into unknown country between the Burdekin and Isaac rivers.

For weeks they attempted to follow Leichhardt's map, battling through dense brigalow scrub over the Broadsound Range to the Isaac. Then they had to hack their way through almost impene-trable rainforest, to reach eventually 'a bold deep river' flowing towards the coast, which they named the Mackay (later changed to the Pioneer) river.

Short of food, the settlers attempted to drink the sap from milkwood trees, which poisoned them. Tropical fever, probably malaria, struck most of the party. Duke died, and the remainder were near death by the end of June 1860. They were living off stewed goanna. In that vast area never previously seen by Euro-peans, three more land-seekers came across their camp and assisted them back to the nearest station. Today the district they pioneered is one of Australia's biggest sugar and dairy producers.

Another Scot named John Graham MacDonald rode even longer distances in 1860 to claim his share of northern lands. Aged twenty-six, MacDonald left Geelong in southern Victoria to ride two thousand kilometres to Rockhampton.

Joined there by his brother Peter, the two young men explored the wilds of the Nogoa and Belyando rivers before secur-ing the extensive run known as Glenlee.

After assisting in the foundation of Bowen, John MacDonald established several stations, including Carpentaria Downs, in a huge area of hitherto unex-plored land stretching from the upper reaches of the Burdekin, west to the Gregory river in the Gulf country. □

Members of George Dalrymple's *1859 expedition, which was privately funded to examine the watershed of the Burdekin River. The following year, Dalrymple founded north Queensland's first town, Bowen*

Unsung work of government surveyors

After the better-known discoverers made their mark on history, an enormous amount of detailed exploration remained to be carried out by official surveyors who had the task of plotting maps and planning roads.

These men underwent experiences every bit as arduous as the long-range explorers'. Surveying the Shoalhaven river area in 1824, Robert Hoddle wrote: 'I have travelled as wretched a wilderness as ever man trod upon.'

In the mountainous Colo river area northwest of Sydney, convicts working for surveyor Frederick D'Arcy in the winter of 1831 had no shelter at night and only what food they could carry on their backs. One man begged to be returned to the comparative luxury of life on a chain gang breaking rocks.

Surveying the Snowy Mountains in 1846, Thomas Townsend found he could no longer sleep out at night with impunity, 'the days being generally excessively hot, the nights severely cold'. The men, he reported, were liable to be seized with fever and ague under such harsh conditions. Many who had been raised in the closely settled British Isles felt

Ever on the move, *surveyors hacked tracks through the bush that became rough roads for following travellers*

Makeshift camps *with crude canvas lean-tos were the lot of T.H. Jensen's survey party in the Gympie district, Queensland, in 1908. Often in the field for long periods, surveyors led lonely lives and enjoyed few of civilisation's comforts*

oppressed by the sheer immensity of the Australian bush.

Some surveyors sacrificed their health, even their life to the labours of mapping new territory. Granville Stapylton, sent to survey the coast south from Brisbane in 1840, was speared to death by Aboriginals, along with his assistant William Tuck.

Two chainmen *wait patiently while a surveyor takes a bearing and a labourer blazes a tree. The hard slog of surveying new territory on foot was done with remarkable speed and thoroughness*

Official expeditions reach the wild frontier of Cape York

Somerset. The name evokes visions of rolling downs, cool streams and cider apples. But the Australian Somerset is an almost abandoned steamy tropical settlement near the tip of Cape York Peninsula. It was established in 1863 when British and colonial governments agreed that a coaling station was needed to supply the increasing number of steamships threading through the maze of islands within the Barrier Reef.

FRANK AND ALEXANDER JARDINE
GALLANT BROTHERS WHO FOUGHT
THEIR WAY UP THE CAPE

The Queensland government sent John Jardine, fifty-six-year-old Scottish-born magistrate at Rockhampton, to supervise the remote settlement. Artisans taken there by boat built a government residence, police station, customs house, barracks for marines, and a hospital, whose ruins are barely visible today.

The government agreed that two of Jardine's sons should drive two hundred and fifty store cattle overland, about fourteen hundred and fifty kilometres up Cape York to Somerset. A surveyor, Archibald Richardson, would accompany them to map unknown country. So began one of the most difficult feats of overlanding and exploration ever achieved.

The group under twenty-three-year-old Frank Jardine and his twenty-one-year-old brother Alexander left the coast at Bowen in May 1864. With the lessons of Edmund Kennedy's disaster well in mind, they decided to avoid the east coast. Travelling north-westerly along the Burdekin river, they arrived safely at the furthest station, J. G. MacDonald's Carpentaria Downs, on 30 May.

While Frank Jardine selected cattle and horses for the expedition, Alexander spent several months exploring the little-known country to the north. He became convinced that Leichhardt's map of the area was faulty, particularly his depiction of the all-important rivers.

The northwards cattle drive finally began on 11 October 1864, just as Queensland's first railway was being built in the south. Accompanying the brothers were three white drovers and four black trackers. The stony beds of dry creeks cut their freshly-shod horses' hooves badly.

Leaving the cattle to rest, the brothers rode north-east searching for Leichhardt's Lynd river. They found a stream but could identify none of Leichhardt's landmarks for the Lynd. They named it Byerley creek; it is now called Red river.

On 5 November a grass fire destroyed half of their provisions and nearly all their equipment. On 14 November the party reached what they thought to be Leichhardt's Mitchell river, but later found it to be the Staaten discovered by Carstensz in 1623.

A fortnight later Aboriginals attacked, scattering the stock. One hurled a spear at Frank Jardine. 'The fellow who threw it never threw another,' he wrote grimly.

On 3 December 1864 the men caught a large shovel-nosed shark in a salt river, and jerked (dried) its flesh in the same way as for beef. Two weeks later, near the junction of the Alice and Mitchell rivers, they were surrounded by a large tribe of aggressive natives. Quick work with the carbines dropped 'eight or nine', and the remainder fled.

Arriving at the long-desired Mitchell river, two days were spent taking the cattle across its broad stream and several branches. Aboriginals again attacked, this time 'about thirty being killed' before the remainder retreated.

Heavy rain began on 21 December. By early January 1865 the men found they were driving the cattle through almost endless bogs and over numerous creeks which had begun to flow.

On 5 January they discovered the Archer river, passing through 'a valley of great richness and beauty', covered after the rain with gorgeous wildflowers. They

An epic cattle drive and a gold rush briefly open doors to the north

The pointing finger of land that is Cape York is still thinly populated today. In 1864-65, the Jardine brothers proved the harshness of the western region when they struggled for months to drive a mob of cattle to the tip of the cape. In the early seventies, William Hann found alluvial gold in the Palmer River, but the rush that followed was short-lived

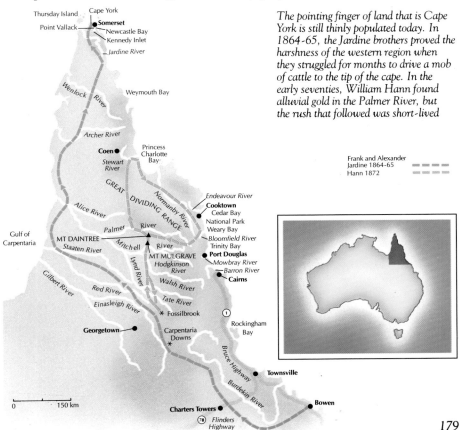

Frank and Alexander
Jardine 1864-65
Hann 1872

179

named the river after their friends the Archer brothers of Gracemere Station.

Approaching the Wenlock river on 11 January 1865, the cattle sank into 'execrable country, so boggy as to be barely possible to traverse', and infested with crocodiles. Five beasts could not be pulled out even with ropes: they were hastily slaughtered where they sank and converted into jerked beef.

During the next few days, the horses began eating plants which none of the men realised were poisonous. By 17 January, only fifteen of their original forty-two horses were still living. For some days after that, the men, now almost naked, had to cut their way with axes through tangled trees and vines, hacking a lane for the cattle to follow.

During late January and early February 1865 the Jardine brothers set off ahead of the main party to find a track to Somerset, which they believed was near. To their astonishment, they encountered instead an unknown large river flowing north-westerly into the Gulf. The Governor afterwards named it the Jardine to commemorate their trip. For some weeks the brothers traced the river in search of a crossing place, enduring continuous tropical rain, and living off scrub turkey eggs, shellfish and a goanna.

On 23 February they found enough dry nonda wood — the only suitable timber in the area — to build a raft. Once across the Jardine, they encountered a friendly tribe near Kennedy Inlet, who guided them to their father's door in Somerset.

During March the sons returned for their cattle, rafting them across the Jardine and establishing a station at Point Vallack, a few kilometres from Somerset on Newcastle Bay.

In 1873 Frank Jardine married Sana Solia, seventeen-year-old niece of the King of Samoa. Behind their homestead

RICHARD DAINTREE
GEOLOGIST AND PHOTOGRAPHER

they established a huge coconut plantation which still stands. After Jardine's father retired, Frank acted as semi-official administrator, until the settlement was transferred to a better harbour on Thursday Island. Frank Jardine died of leprosy in 1919, leaving among his relics a carbine with forty-seven notches carved on the stock. Each notch represented a man he had killed.

Hann's search for gold

The next major expedition to Cape York was led by William Hann, thirty-five-year-old son of a settler on the Upper Burdekin river.

In 1872 Hann was commissioned by the Queensland government to explore Cape York as far as latitude fourteen degrees south (today's Coen), and report on its pastoral and mineral possibilities. The Suez Canal had now been open for three years, and the prospect of increased exports to Europe loomed large.

Hann first attempted to trace some of the many rivers that run easterly into Princess Charlotte Bay. Long inland detours were necessary where he was unable to return to the coast.

Later the same year Hann was ready for a fresh assault on the difficult peninsula. Assembling a party with a geologist, botanist, surveyor, two bushmen, an Aboriginal named Jerry, and an unnamed 'black gin', Hann left Ezra Firth's northernmost station Fossilbrook on 26 June 1872.

Traversing the upper reaches of the Lynd and Mitchell rivers during July, the party discovered the Tate river (named after Thomas Tate, Hann's botanist), and the Walsh river (named

Starving explorer William Hann, *exhausted from battling the coastal belt of jungle, had believed his party doomed when he turned inland and found grassland along the Palmer River*

Sluicing for gold *in a Cape York stream. The Palmer River was Queensland's richest alluvial goldfield. In the peak year of 1878, more than seven million grams were recovered*

after W. H. Walsh, the Queensland Minister for Mines, who had promoted the expedition).

On 2 August 1872, Hann discovered and named Mount Mulgrave, which presented 'a grand and magnificent appearance' as it rose abruptly to three hundred and ninety-six metres above the surrounding country.

Further into the Great Dividing Range the explorers discovered Mount Daintree, naming it after the geologist Richard Daintree, who was Hann's partner in Maryvale station. A few kilometres to the north lay 'a noble river', which Hann named after the Queensland Premier, Sir Arthur Palmer. The search for minerals now began in earnest. Hann offered a reward of two hundred and fifty grams of tobacco to the first man who found gold. On 6 August the surveyor Frederick Warner was successful and 'excitement was consequently high'. The explorers rode further along the Palmer valley, finding high-grade alluvial gold in almost every bar and bend of the river.

By September 1872 the party had penetrated to the eastern side of the Great Dividing Range and discovered good grazing land along the Stewart river, named after Thomas Stewart, one of Hann's bushmen.

They followed the Stewart easterly almost to its outlet in Princess Charlotte Bay, then turned south through fine stringybark country.

On 12 September the party discovered a 'large and remarkable river' which they named after the Marquess of Normanby, Governor of Queensland. Here they saw 'numerous alligator heads' impaled on a tree, no doubt left by Aboriginals.

JAMES VENTURE MULLIGAN
EXPLORER AND PROSPECTOR

Riding south-easterly, Hann tried to find Cook's Endeavour river, but missed it because his sextant was out of order.

Continuing south through today's Cedar Bay National Park, the party fought through dense scrub and precipitous country to discover early in October 1872 the Bloomfield river, which flows into Weary Bay.

It seemed impossible to penetrate further south along the coast. 'We have jumped into the thick of our difficulties,' wrote Hann. Horses and explorers were exhausted, provisions nearly gone. Hann shot a python on 10 October. It measured nearly five metres: 'the largest snake I ever saw.' Rather than waste such good food, Jerry looped it round his neck and carried it for days.

On 12 October a desperate Hann decided he would have to turn inland and attempt to find the Palmer river again. At one stage he wrote, 'Our doom is sealed'. Picking their way over jungle-clad mountains, the visibly wasting explorers and horses finally found the grasslands of the Mitchell and Palmer rivers and were able to recoup their strength. By mid-November 1872 they were safely back at Fossilbrook.

Gold rush on the Palmer

Immediately the Hann expedition's discovery of gold on the Palmer river was announced, a restless thirty-six-year-old Irish prospector named James Venture Mulligan set off to pursue it.

On 5 June 1873 he left Georgetown with a party of six men, following Hann's tracks to Mount Mulgrave. Although constantly attacked by Aboriginals, the venturesome miners won nearly three thousand grams of gold from the Palmer and its tributaries in a few days.

A rush began: by the end of the year five hundred miners had found their way to the remote area. One shipment of gold alone weighed some one hundred and forty-three thousand grams.

Mulligan meanwhile blazed a trail from the Palmer to today's Cooktown, enabling thousands more gold-seekers (including many Chinese) to participate in the rush. Mulligan continued to find gold, silver and tin. His gold discoveries at Hodgkinson river led to the development of Cairns and Port Douglas.

After a life filled with adventure, Mulligan died in 1907 following a fist fight at Mount Molloy, north of Cairns. Aged 70, he had tried to protect a woman against the advances of a drunk.

These and other explorers and gold-seekers brought a veneer of European civilisation to north Queensland. But it remained wild frontier territory for many years, and even today is sparsely settled in most areas. □

John Horrocks's expedition, north of the Flinders Ranges in 1846, by S. T. Gill

CHAPTER SIX

The lure of the unknown west and centre

The first tentative steps beyond Albany and Perth

While the eastern colonies swung eagerly into the pastoral boom of the eighteen-thirties, the west remained a backwater, forgotten and neglected. The early settlers did their best to discover and develop new land, but even by 1850 the population of the entire colony of Western Australia was less than six thousand Europeans.

Enthusiasm for western settlement was still high when Captain John Wakefield left the site of Albany in 1828 to see what lay to the north. He penetrated about fifty kilometres into the Porongorup Range from where he could see the Stirling Range further north over the Kalgan river.

The following year Thomas Braidwood Wilson, a thirty-seven-year-old surgeon who had worked his passage on convict ships, made the first overland expedition westwards along the coast from Albany. He went fifty kilometres as far as Wilson Inlet, turned northerly to pass Mount Lindsay and reached today's Kendenup, before shortage of provisions forced him to turn back.

Naval and military officers continued to make expeditions into unknown territory. During 1829 Ensign Robert Dale of the Sixty-Third Regiment led successful breakouts from Perth to explore the upper reaches of the Helena river to the east and the Avon river to the north-east. These expeditions provided some of the best land yet found in the new colony, and led to the foundation of the important rural centre of Northam.

During the same year, Lieutenant William Preston, RN, and Dr Alexander Collie, RN, traced the Canning river to its source in the hills now traversed by the Albany Highway. They also explored the Darling Range inland from Cape Leschenault, about one hundred kilometres north of Perth. In November 1829 they sailed to Géographe Bay about two hundred kilometres south of Perth where Baudin had anchored in 1801, discovering the important Preston and Collie rivers named after them.

By 1830 the good pastures within easy reach of Perth had all been taken up. Governor Sir James Stirling decided to investigate reports of suitable land near the coastline one hundred and forty kilometres south of Perth. On a southerly point of Koombana Bay he established a military post at what was then called Port Leschenault. Today this is the busy port of Bunbury, handling exports of timber, wheat and other products.

Bunbury was named after twenty-four-year-old Lieutenant Henry William Bunbury of the Twenty-First Regiment, who in 1836 made an exploratory trip south of Perth from Pinjarra to Busselton. On the way he discovered valuable mineral sands and pasture lands.

Traverses of the south-west corner

An overland route between Perth and Albany was opened in 1831 by Captain Thomas Bannister. He took a generally southerly course from Perth to strike the southern ocean near today's Cliffy Head, then followed the route of what is now the South-Western Highway to arrive safely at King George Sound.

Government surveyors and botanists played their usual pioneering role. Surveyor-General of the new colony from its foundation in 1829 was thirty-two-year-old John Septimus Roe. As a youth Roe had accompanied P. P. King's voyages round the continent, and J. G. Bremer's abortive settlement at Port Essington in northern Australia.

At the beginning of West Australian

GEORGE FLETCHER MOORE
HE BELIEVED IN AN INLAND SEA

Albany, on Princess Royal Harbour in King George Sound, had such natural advantages of deep safe waters and a rich hinterland that it was the principal port on the west coast until 1900

settlement, Roe was kept busy with the charting of harbours and surveying of town allotments. By 1835 he was able to take the Governor on a trip to lay down the main route from Perth to Albany. During this expedition the Stirling Range was named after the Governor. Christmas Day 1835 was celebrated 'at a most sumptuous board' on the Hotham river, including soup, roast cockatoo and kangaroo, and plum pudding.

Roe made many other short exploratory surveys around Perth and Albany. His great testing time in the desert, an almost-fatal trip made in 1848 when he was more than fifty years old, is described on page 207.

Pioneer families lead the way

During 1831-2, the assistant surveyor Raphael Clint, thirty-four-year-old son of an English artist, mapped much of the Swan, Canning and Kalgan rivers. He also explored the district between the Porongorup and Stirling ranges.

James Drummond, a forty-five-year-old pioneer from the foundation days of 1829, acted as unpaid government botanist for the first three years. He helped to explore the Helena, Avon and Toodyay valleys, living off profits from his own grazing stock while developing botanical gardens in Perth.

In 1836 Drummond settled at Hawthornden in the Toodyay valley, north-east of Perth, naming the property after his Scottish birthplace. From here he continued to make botanical investigations for the government.

During the eighteen-fifties James Drummond's sons took the first stock to the Murchison River district in the north. Mary, wife of John Drummond, was the first white woman to live there.

Reports of good land and rivers round Géographe Bay attracted John Garrett Bussell, twenty-nine-year-old son of a Hampshire clergyman. Bussell had settled near a military post at Cape Leeuwin, but found the dense karri forest too difficult to clear. At one stage he and his family were reduced to eating boiled grass.

In 1832 Bussell explored the Vasse river area of Géographe Bay and formed the first settlement. The track which he and his brothers cut through the bush became the main street of today's Busselton. Their first butter, cheese, potatoes and wheat were soon being exported to Perth.

Up to 1840, all these explorations had been a matter of pecking away at likely-looking spots round the south-western

corner of Western Australia. Curiosity about the vast inland, a total blank on the map, was provoked by George Fletcher Moore, a thirty-two-year-old Irish barrister who emigrated in 1830 and established the first merino stud at York, ninety kilometres east of Perth.

Intrigued by the unknown country behind the Darling Range, Moore journeyed northwards in 1836. His lively mind reasoned that 'As no river of any magnitude flows from the north into the Swan throughout all its course, it appeared fair to presume that some drain for the waters of that district would be found at no great distance.'

He was right. The result was the discovery of the Moore river, which flows through good grazing country and swampland before reaching the Indian Ocean near today's Guilderton.

Later in 1836, Moore took Colonial Secretary Peter Brown and Perth merchant George Leake on an expedition east and north of the Avon and Mortlock rivers. They found extensive tracts of fertile agricultural and grazing land.

In 1839 Moore led an expedition to the coast around Champion Bay. He reported favourably, but the town of Geraldton was not surveyed until 1850.

During his journeys Moore paid close attention to Aboriginal folklore. One group told him of a remarkable river running far away to the north-east, and 'out the other side'. Other natives told him of 'a great water ten days' journey to the east; that it was salt: you could not drink it'. Standing on the hills near that water, 'you would look down upon the sun rising out of the water beyond them'.

Even more strange, 'the inhabitants were of large stature...the women had fair hair, as long as white women's hair'. Moore's informants 'seem all to be aware that they are living on an island'. They appeared, he said, 'to be speaking of the other side of the island'.

Moore concluded that 'there must exist, at no very great distance, a body of water so broad, that they could not see across it'. He felt that it probably emerged at North West Cape, practically cutting the continent in two.

So convinced was Moore by these legends that in 1837 he published a book entitled *Evidences of an Inland Sea*. The great dream of a fertile well-watered land in the centre of Australia had begun again and would continue to lure adventure-seekers into the most pitiless deserts on the face of the earth.□

Early journeys concentrate on the south-west corner

The need for more good pasture and the convenience of having an overland link with the port at Albany drew a number of early explorers east and south from Perth. George Fletcher Moore was among the first to look inland. In 1836 he investigated east of the Darling Range

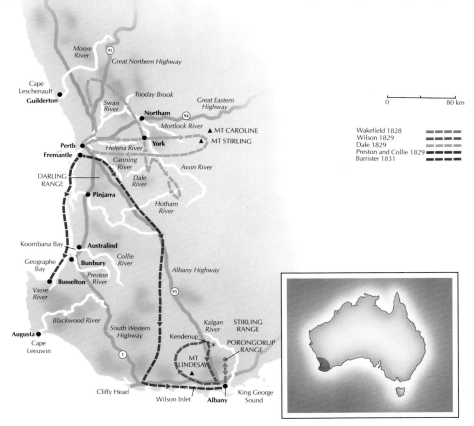

Wakefield 1828
Wilson 1829
Dale 1829
Preston and Collie 1829
Barrister 1831

0   80 km

George Grey blunders bravely up and down the west coast

Towards the end of 1837, an explorer of unusual sensitivity landed with a party of five men on the remote shores of Hanover Bay in north-west Australia. He was twenty-five-year-old George Grey, only son of a British officer killed in the Peninsular War. Grey ran away from a harsh boarding school, and had to be privately tutored at the expense of his mother's new husband, Baronet of Wivenhoe.

Service as an army lieutenant in Ireland convinced the compassionate young Grey that the peasants' fearful poverty could be alleviated only by emigration to fertile new lands. Why not northern Australia?

Grey won support for his idea from the Colonial Office and Royal Geographical Society. With a party of a dozen men, and assistance from his friend Lieutenant Franklin Lushington, Grey chartered the one hundred and forty-tonne schooner *Lynher* in Cape Town, filling her with provisions, thirty-one sheep, nineteen goats and six dogs. Only one man in the party had seen northern Australia before, and that was from the deck of a ship.

The expedition soon developed into a tragi-comedy. After sailing through Brunswick Bay and landing at Hanover Bay on 2 December 1837, with only one water-bottle apiece, Grey and five men lost themselves in deep ravines. They could find no fresh water. Two of their dogs died in the intense heat. The party barely managed to get back to the coast. There Grey was caught by a huge rush of tidal waters and nearly drowned while swimming across an estuary.

This desolate coastline had been scorned by early Dutch and British mariners. Perhaps, thought Grey, if he pushed inland he would find great rivers rushing to a fertile interior instead of wasting themselves in the ocean. The image of a delightful inland sea was now rampant in the minds of many settlers.

A satisfactory camp was finally established near the mouth of P. P. King's Prince Regent river. Lushington sailed for Timor to buy twenty-six ponies to use as packhorses, while Grey made several short trips into today's Kunmunya Aboriginal Reserve to acclimatise his men.

Problems plague the party

Along streams swollen by the wet season, he found multitudinous bird life almost begging to be shot for the cooking pot. Grey began to glow again with enthusiasm. 'No country in the world is better watered than this portion of Australia,' claimed the newcomer.

At last, on 29 January 1838, the would-be explorers were ready to begin their task of blazing the first overland trail southwards to Perth.

SIR GEORGE GREY
EXPLORER, GOVERNOR, POLITICIAN

By this time the wet season was fully upon them. Rivers burst their banks and flooded low areas. Forced to high ground, Grey's men encountered precipitous hills and ravines. The heavily-laden ponies stumbled and injured themselves: seven died. The men had to carry essential stores on their own backs. It took ten days to accomplish what Grey had imagined would be one day's march. On 11 February, Grey foolishly split the party and went ahead with two men to find a better route. Suddenly, he wrote, 'each tree, each rock, seemed to give forth its black denizen, as if by enchantment.'

Surrounded by yelling Aboriginals, Grey held his fire until a spear whistled past his head. He shot one man in the arm, but was immediately speared in the hip. He wrenched out the spear, advanced towards the nearest native and shot him dead.

'The effect was electrical,' wrote Grey. 'The tumult of the combat ceased: not another spear was thrown, not another yell uttered. Native after native dropped away, and noiselessly disappeared.'

Grey spent the next two weeks recovering from his wound in a tent where temperatures reached over fifty-seven degrees and humidity was stifling.

Although the flesh was still suppurating, Grey insisted on continuing. The party traversed the Macdonald Range by 27 February 1838, on which day 'a magnificent view' thrilled every man. From the summit they could see stretching for many kilometres 'a low luxuriant country, broken by conical peaks and rounded hills, which were richly grassed to their very summits.'

This was surely the spot for mass emigration from Britain. 'I painted in

Images of a fertile land lure Grey towards the interior

George Grey had no reason for it, but he believed that the country inland from Hanover Bay would be better than along the barren coast. It is ironic that he attempted to penetrate it during the 1837-38 wet season. Flooded rivers forced him to turn back, deceived by ephemeral conditions

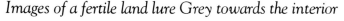

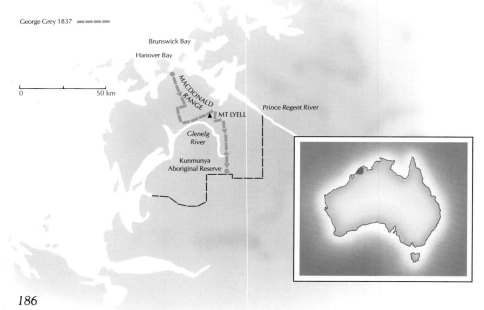

George Grey 1837

Brunswick Bay
Hanover Bay

0   50 km

MACDONALD RANGE
MT LYELL
Prince Regent River
Glenelg River
Kunmunya Aboriginal Reserve

fancy the rapid progress that this country would ere long make in commerce and civilization,' wrote Grey, 'and my weakness and fatigues were all forgotten.'

Fervent optimism leads Grey on

After crossing several marshes and streams, on 2 March the explorers climbed a low hill and stood still in amazement. Grey wrote: 'There burst upon the sight a noble river, running through a beautiful country, and where we saw it, at least three or four miles across, and studded with numerous verdant islands'.

This was the Glenelg river in full flood. Grey named it after Lord Glenelg, Colonial Secretary of State.

The explorers traced the course of the river westwards as best they could, often wading through extensive marshes. On 13 March 1838 they discovered and climbed Mount Lyell, naming it after a geologist, Charles Lyell.

From its peak they could see the Prince Regent river to the north and the Glenelg river to the south, 'meandering through as verdant and fertile a district as the eye of man ever rested on'.

Grey was exhibiting all the innocence of an explorer new to Australian conditions, over-anxious to announce tremendous discoveries without seeing the land under different seasonal conditions.

Near the head of the Glenelg river, on 26 March Grey discovered the first of the extraordinary cave paintings that inspired many theories about their inspiration (see page 21). Three days later Grey discovered another cave whose roof showed a man's figure over three metres long, clothed from the chin downwards in a flowing red garment.

Grey's party returned to Hanover Bay on 17 April 1838, and sailed to Mauritius to recover from their ordeals. 'I do not

This red-robed figure among Aboriginal paintings on the roof of a cave mystified Grey. It seemed to suggest that he was not the first European to explore the north-west hinterland

Rushing tidal waters near Brunswick Bay almost drowned Grey as he attempted to swim across an estuary. Waterfalls between these two rocky headlands are created by the tide's passage

think that since the days of Robinson Crusoe, any one has been through so much personal adventure as I have lately undergone,' wrote Grey.

But a sense of partial failure remained in the young man's mind. After all, he had not found an overland route to Perth. He persuaded the West Australian Governor, Sir James Stirling, to allow him to make another attempt.

This time Grey proposed to land far to the south-west of his previous exploration, at Shark Bay. From there he planned to explore to the north as far as North-West Cape. Then he would turn south for the overland trip to Perth.

Again Grey misread Australian conditions. Apologists have often claimed that Grey was plagued with bad luck. In fact his own miscalculations got him and his men into terrible scrapes. It was only through remarkably good luck that most of them survived.

The new tale of woe began in February 1839 when Grey landed three whaleboats and stores from an American whaler on Bernier Island in Shark Bay. Grey cheerily farewelled the whaler before checking to see whether the island contained fresh water. It did not.

An immediate move was essential, but strong gales began, destroying one whale-

boat and some provisions. The men buried the remaining food, and set out in heavy seas on 1 March to find water. Nearby Dorre Island also proved waterless. They rowed desperately for the mainland, 'ammunition damaged; the chronometers down; and both boats so stoved and strained, as to be quite beyond our powers of repairing them effectually'.

After penetrating thick mangrove swamps, on 5 March 1839 Grey was delighted to find channels of what he believed was 'a stream of magnitude'. But about five kilometres inland the water suddenly vanished. 'This huge river bed was perfectly dry, and looked the most mournful, deserted spot imaginable,' wrote the puzzled explorer.

Nevertheless it obviously flowed at some seasons, so Grey named it the Gascoyne river after 'my friend, Captain Gascoyne'. It turned out to be the longest river in Western Australia, stretching eight hundred kilometres from the Carnarvon Range to the sea. Its delta was covered with 'gently sloping grassy rises', and many lagoons. Grey fancied that soon a teeming British population would follow his steps, 'and be eagerly and anxiously examining my charts'.

A desperate dash for Perth

Meanwhile the main problem was one of survival. Grey and his men were forced to exist on 'disgusting damper and a small piece of pork'. Aboriginals stole their fishing lines, insects bit them savagely, and Grey sometimes gave way to 'a gloomy foreboding'.

Rowing back to Bernier Island on 20 March 1839, the men found the ocean had swept over their food reserves, leaving only a cask of salted meat and a little

Rich land between the Murchison and Greenough rivers was at its wet season greenest when Grey was in the region. Near the mouth of the Murchison his whaleboats were wrecked in the surf and his long walk to Perth began

flour still edible. 'I sat down and read a few chapters of the Bible,' wrote Grey.

Grey resolved to sail back to Perth in the leaking whaleboats. The exhausted men rowed as far as Gantheaume Bay, about four hundred kilometres to the south. Here both boats were wrecked in the thundering surf. Grey recorded: 'No resource was now left to us but to endeavour to reach Perth by walking; yet when I looked at the sickly faces of some of the party, and saw their wasted frames, I much doubted if they retained the strength to execute such a task.'

Yet Grey's amazing luck was still holding. They had been wrecked at the very point where the large Murchison river flows into the sea. Grey named it after British scientist Sir Roderick Murchison. Here the men could drink as much as they wanted before setting off down the coast. Each carried four hundred and fifty grams of salt meat and nine kilos of fermenting flour to see him through nearly five hundred kilometres of unknown territory.

Near today's Geraldton, Grey crossed and named several rivers in a lush area which he called the Victoria District after the new Queen. Despite his fatigue, Grey kept it in mind as another ideal place for immigrants to settle.

Some of the men were now so weak that the group could travel only about sixteen kilometres a day. Food was almost exhausted. On 10 April 1839 Grey decided to make a desperate dash for Perth with the five strongest men, and send back a relief party.

By 14 April, Grey's selected men had eaten their last food and swallowed their last water. Three terrible days followed with nothing at all to eat or drink. The

men were all too weak to complain: as they staggered on, the silence was 'only broken by groans and exclamations'.

On 17 April the dying men came across a pool of liquid mud and wallowed in it. Next day they found a little fresh water and some mussels, and managed to shoot a cockatoo. Even so, Grey felt a desire to sink into the sleep of death'.

But his luck held. On 20 April friendly Aboriginals found and fed them. Sustained by belief and willpower, Grey left his men and walked alone the last few kilometres into Perth. No one recognised the emaciated explorer: the Governor was stunned by 'the miserable object that stood before him'.

A rescue party set off immediately, but reported that one of Grey's men, Frederick Smith, died before they arrived.

Grey had now had his fill of exploration. In June 1839 he was promoted to captain and appointed resident magistrate at King George Sound. In 1841 he was named Governor of South Australia, where he did his best to relieve the prevailing depression and assist Aboriginals. Grey, still favoured by fortune, was appointed Governor of New Zealand in 1845, knighted in 1848, sent to govern Cape Colony in 1854, returned to a stormy political career in New Zealand and died in 1898 aged eighty-six.□

GRAND PLANS FOR SETTLEMENT COLLAPSE IN RUINS

Leschenault Inlet had only a whaling station and a depot for shipping horses to India when the Western Australian Company acquired land there for Australind. The site is now a suburb of Bunbury

Two disastrous large-scale attempts at colonisation followed the early exploration of Western Australia.

One of these was organised by Thomas Peel, thirty-six-year-old cousin of the British Home Secretary, Sir Robert Peel.

The government allotted more than two hundred thousand hectares south and east of Perth to a private syndicate led by Thomas Peel, provided sufficient immigrants and capital were introduced.

Settlers faced a succession of disasters, including starvation and attacks by Aboriginals. Peel was ruined financially.

A second enterprise, called the Western Australian Company, was floated in 1840 to promote settlement on lines suggested by Edward Gibbon Wakefield.

A large area of land on the Leschenault Inlet, north of Bunbury, was bought.

The promoters planned a major port named Australind as the colony's chief communication with India. Within a few weeks, more than three thousand town allotments and four hundred forty-hectare farmlets had been sold to British investors.

The explorer George Grey caused a panic by claiming that the port should be established much nearer to India, at today's Geraldton. The Australind scheme collapsed, most settlers abandoning their blocks and moving to Bunbury or Perth.

Grey barely survives a journey from the Gascoyne to Perth

Soon after landing at Shark Bay in 1839, misadventures forced Grey to give up his plan to explore to the north before blazing a trail to Perth.

The return journey became a retreat, then, with the wrecking of his whaleboats, a grim forced march for survival across 500 harsh kilometres

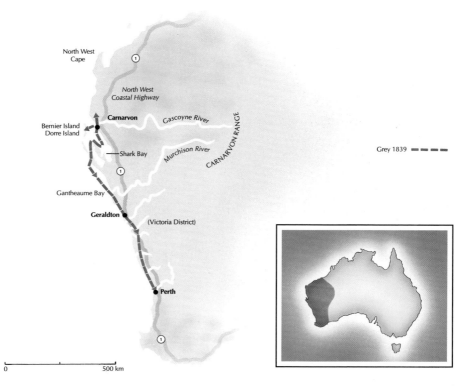

Eyre, the roving hero, comes riding out of the east

By the late eighteen-thirties the main focus of Australian exploration had moved to South Australia. Here, a few years earlier, the first free settlers had arrived under the aegis of the South Australian Company, determined to prove that a colony could be successfully developed in wilderness without a supply of convict labour.

Despite early problems, the population soon far exceeded that of Western Australia. Before long, new agricultural and grazing lands were needed to absorb its rapid growth.

The man determined to lead South Australians into the promised land rode out of the east early in 1839. He was Edward John Eyre, tall and handsome, twenty-three years old, the son of a Bedfordshire clergyman. Eyre had emigrated to Sydney while still a youth, and learned the overlanding trade by droving stock to the Liverpool Plains, Molonglo and Port Phillip.

After making about £700 profit in 1837 by selling sheep and cattle in booming Melbourne, Eyre decided on a fresh overlanding venture. 'I was most anxious to be the first to arrive in South Australia overland from Sydney — as yet no one had made the attempt', he wrote.

Eyre set off from Limestone Plains (today's Canberra) on 21 December 1837 with a fresh mob of one thousand sheep and six hundred cattle supplied by Robert Campbell from his Duntroon station. A month later the overlander replenished his supplies in Melbourne. Rather than trek back to the Murray river and take the known route to Adelaide, he decided to strike west across country from the Campaspe river. In theory this would greatly shorten the distance to Adelaide.

Eyre's decision nearly led to disaster. Only short sections of his proposed route were known from Major Mitchell's maps, and even the maps confused some of the rivers flowing north and south.

The first warning signs came on 19 February 1838, when Eyre found that the delightful lakes described by Mitchell near the Grampians had dried up. Summer storms provided a little water and persuaded Eyre to drive the stock northwest through sandy wastes covered with stunted mallee scrub.

After 'a horrifying march' in humid weather, with men and stock distressed from thirst and the dogs choking and panting, Eyre decided on 1 March that 'there was now nothing for it but to retrace our steps'. The animals were turned back to face the last watering place and released. 'They all set off pell mell together as fast as they could,' wrote Eyre, 'sheep and cattle and horses mixed up together heterogeneously in the race.'

Tracking back to the almost-dry Wimmera river, on 27 March 1838 Eyre was guided by friendly Aboriginals to an unknown freshwater lake, covered with innumerable water fowl. He named it after Sir John Hindmarsh, first Governor of South Australia.

While stock and men rested, Eyre and two companions spent the first week of April reconnoitring to the north. Eyre's feet swelled and he had to ride barefoot through endless waterless scrub. On 9 April his best horse died of thirst. Eyre set the remainder free to find their way back, while he hobbled along with gun over shoulder and a little bread in his pack.

On 10 April 1838 the party's last drop of water was gone. 'We felt very weak and as if with scarcely strength enough to do anything,' Eyre wrote. 'I was very restless all night long, with violent pains in my limbs and joints.'

The following day and night they managed to crawl back to Lake Hindmarsh, but the four horses they abandoned were never found.

By 21 April Eyre was sufficiently

Eyre hoped the Flinders Ranges would help him reach the centre. He knew he could find grass and water among these rugged gorges, but soon saw the ring of salt lakes that lay beyond the hills.

ecovered to attempt a westerly route from the lake. But here the country was even worse, covered with spiky spinifex. Aboriginals told him that to survive they had to collect dew at night from the grass. 'With a heavy heart I turned back to rejoin my party,' wrote Eyre.

There was nothing for it but to drive the stock all the way back to Major Mitchell's Yarrayne (Loddon) river, north to the Murray, then to Adelaide.

Arriving at the Loddon river on 8 May 1838, Eyre was horrified to find it practically dry, reduced to only a few waterholes. With great difficulty his men worked their way up to the Murray and along its reedy backwaters. Fortunately the Aboriginals were friendly and willing to barter: 'they seemed especially surprised that we did not require wives,' Eyre noted wryly. Huge Murray cod, pigeons and duck eked out the men's rations.

On 10 June the party arrived at the Darling junction, and on 12 July 1838 in Adelaide, after a journey totalling two and a half thousand kilometres. Because of the delays encountered when he tried to penetrate the mallee country, Eyre had been beaten by Joseph Hawdon and Charles Bonney, who arrived with the first cattle three months earlier.

His remaining cattle were sold to the hungry colonists for a profit of £1300.

By October 1838 Eyre was back at Limestone Plains preparing to drive a mob of one thousand sheep to Adelaide. This time he followed a much safer route along the Murrumbidgee and Murray rivers, covering the twelve hundred kilometres in only fourteen weeks.

On 12 March 1839 Eyre was able to say that he had overlanded the first sheep to South Australia, had opened 'the high road by which the countless thousands would soon follow' — and had made a clear profit of £4000.

The idealistic young man decided to spend this money not on accumulating further wealth, but on the 'useful and honorable career' of exploring unknown parts of Australia.

Magnificent runs discovered

At this time the only expedition to the north in South Australia had been conducted by John Hill, who discovered the head of the Hutt river one hundred kilometres north of Adelaide, naming it after Sir William Hutt, a British politician who had supported the South Australian Company. The course of this river and the country around it were 'utterly unknown and untraversed'.

Eyre decided to investigate. On 1 May 1839 he lifted his drunken overseer John Baxter on his horse, and with two other whites and two blacks left Adelaide. Next day they passed the last settlement on the Gawler river and struck out due north, discovering 'magnificent runs' and 'very fine blue limestone' waiting to be exploited by squatters.

On 7 May the party came to the Hutt river. At this time of year Eyre saw it as 'a fine chain of large deep pools', surrounded by 'thousands of acres of the richest alluvial land'.

On 10 May Eyre altered his course to north-westerly to approach Spencer Gulf. He named a distant peak Mount Remarkable, then was suddenly halted by a precipitous gorge filled with 'a hundred little hills and glens'. Picking his way carefully down, Eyre wrote that it 'seemed so wild and fantastic that I named it the Devil's Glen, and the stream which flowed thro' it the Rocky River.'

From here the country steadily deteriorated, becoming scrubby, stony and almost waterless. By 15 May 1839 the party had arrived at the head of Spencer Gulf. Raging with thirst, they followed a native track to discover water at Depot creek, one of several streams in the area.

Individual members of the party explored in all directions before returning to Depot creek. Eyre himself went north through 'very rough and stony' country to discover today's Mount Eyre. Ahead of him were the red-tinted 'very high barren ranges' later named the Flinders Ranges.

To the west stretched the apparently endless salt mud-flats of Lake Torrens, named after the chairman of the Colonization Commissioners.

John Baxter meanwhile went eighty kilometres south-west to discover the Baxter Hills, but could find no grass or water. North, all that could be seen was 'the whole country gradually declining to the level sandy region of the interior'.

Eyre, the successful drover, decides to explore northern South Australia

Although his 1838 attempt to find an overland route to Adelaide across the mallee district of Victoria failed, Eyre successfully managed two enormous and difficult overlanding expeditions to Melbourne and Adelaide. He felt he was well suited to the task of exploring totally unknown country north and west of Adelaide

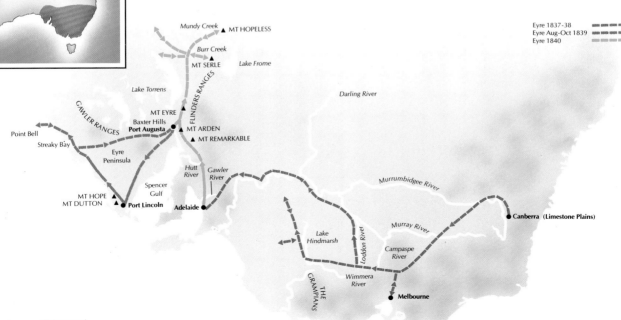

Eyre 1837-38
Eyre Aug-Oct 1839
Eyre 1840

Lake Torrens is a salt mudflat for most of the time, but in a wet season, it spills its banks and can overflow as far as Spencer Gulf. It is the second largest of South Australia's lakes

While the horses were rested, Eyre and Baxter walked nearly fifty kilometres down the west side of Spencer Gulf, without sighting any better country.

With only a month's provisions left, Eyre returned by an easterly route, which took the group via part of the Murray river before their safe arrival in Adelaide on 29 June 1839. Eyre sat down to write his careful reports; Baxter 'inevitably got drunk and was not sober again for fully a week afterwards.'

Could a breakout be made somehow to the west? In August 1839 Eyre took Baxter and two Aboriginals by ship from Adelaide to Port Lincoln, near the point of Eyre Peninsula, later named after him by Governor Sir George Gawler.

The party left Port Lincoln on 5 August 1839 — Eyre's twenty-fourth birthday. They rode along the coastline past Mount Dutton and Mount Hope to arrive at Streaky Bay, named by Matthew Flinders in 1802 after discoloured streaks in the water.

From here Eyre struck out to the east, discovering and naming the 152-metre Gawler Ranges. He continued easterly to familiar ground in the Baxter Hills.

But the one-thousand-kilometre ride through largely unexplored country ended in another disappointment. 'We never crossed a single creek, river, or chain of ponds,' wrote Eyre, 'nor did we meet with permanent water anywhere, with the exception of three solitary springs on the coast.'

Early in 1840 he tried again to break through the harsh lands of the north. Starting from Adelaide on 18 June 1840 with a Union Jack sewn by the adoring women of Adelaide, and forty sheep to provide food for his eight men, Eyre headed for Port Augusta to pick up extra stores that had been taken there by boat.

His plan was to skirt Lake Torrens, and use the 'broken and picturesque' Flinders Ranges as stepping-stones to the centre of Australia. 'In its continuation were centered all my hopes of success,' Eyre recorded in his journal, 'because in its recesses alone could I hope to obtain water and grass for my party.'

Hemmed in by salt lakes

Eyre's idea was soon shattered. At first he was encouraged on 25 August 1840 by discovery of Mundy creek, named after his friend Alfred Mundy, South Australian Colonial Secretary; and the brackish Burr creek, named after Thomas Burr, deputy Surveyor-General.

But after climbing Mount Serle on 27 August, Eyre saw 'the realization of my worst forebodings'. On every side he appeared to be hemmed in by a vast circle of salt lakes. Even to the east he could see the 'broad, glittering belt' of Lake Frome, named later after Edward Charles Frome, Surveyor-General.

Tasting the water in nearby streams, Eyre found it 'as salt as the sea'. He did not suspect that here, millions of years ago when the area was cool and fertile prehistoric monsters had grazed.

Making one further attempt on 2 September 1840, Eyre climbed a peak which he named Mount Hopeless. Here he found 'a new and still more dis heartening feature' — brine springs which poisoned pools at their source.

This, coupled with additional views of the surrounding salt lakes, wrote Eyre 'closed all my dreams as to the ex pedition'. He returned despondently to try the country on the other side of Spencer Gulf.

Another eighteen years would pass before later explorers broke the 'horseshoe hoodoo' of the northern salt lakes, and found a way past the expanse of Lake Eyre to the interior of the continent. □

Surveyor-General Frome titled his Sketch A first view of the salt desert — called Lake Torrens: he was looking at what is now known as Lake Frome. Eyre had reported that Lake Torrens extended in an arc north of the Flinders Ranges

Eyre's miserable march across the waterless Nullarbor Plain

Proud young Edward Eyre, who had always triumphed over difficulties in the past, refused to admit defeat. If the great horseshoe of salt lakes stopped him from going north — very well, he would see what sort of country lay past Streaky Bay to the west. So began one of the greatest sagas of human physical endurance in Australian history.

Towards the end of 1840, Eyre gathered a party of experienced men at Port Lincoln. They followed their previous coastal route to Streaky Bay and established a depot. Then they continued overland through dense waterless scrub, past today's Ceduna and Cactus Beach, to reach Fowlers Bay on 17 November. Although the bay was surrounded by salt swamps, Eyre was able to replenish his water and provisions from the government cutter *Waterwitch*.

Now the moment of decision was upon the young explorer. Everyone expected him to head north into the unknown interior. Citizens of Adelaide had helped the expedition financially, expecting that Eyre would solve the mystery of what lay behind the ring of salt lakes.

This scheme was almost foolproof, for in any emergency, Eyre could return to Fowlers Bay and the certainty of rescue by boat. Sir George Gawler had written begging, practically ordering, Eyre not to attempt a crossing of the Nullarbor. The people of Adelaide were interested in the exploration of South Australia, not Western Australia.

There were serious practical reasons why Eyre should not attempt the Nullarbor. Fowlers Bay was the last known port for hundreds of kilometres where a ship could safely anchor. And while waiting for supplies, Eyre had already made two attempts to break through harsh country to the head of the Bight, losing three of his best horses.

EDWARD JOHN EYRE
IN 1845, WHEN HE WAS 29

For motives which he never made quite clear, Eyre threw all caution away, plunging for the westerly course. Perhaps he suspected that inland was simply useless desert; perhaps he was attracted by Matthew Flinders's dream of 1802 that hidden waterways lay behind the Nullarbor cliffs.

Whatever his reasoning, Eyre cautiously reduced the exploring party to five men — himself, John Baxter, and three Aboriginals — sending the remainder back to Adelaide. This made it possible for the party to proceed with only one dray loaded with water and food, six sheep, and ten horses which could be alternately ridden, put in harness, or allowed to rest.

Eyre judged the horses fit enough to leave on 25 February 1841. Farewelling the men sent back to Adelaide, he reflected that 'the bridge was broken down behind us, and we must succeed in reaching King George's Sound, or perish.'

The first stage of the journey, through today's Yalata Aboriginal Reserve, was strenuous but practicable. Despite hot north winds — which again made Eyre doubt the presence of any large inland sea — by 2 March the little group with their sheep and horses had reached the head of the Bight. Here they watered at native wells named on Eyre's map as Yeer-cumban-kauwe, at one hundred and thirty-one degrees longitude.

In the grip of thirst and hunger

On 7 March 1841, Eyre decided to ride ahead with one of the Aboriginals to look for water. On and on they rode, about two hundred and seventeen kilometres. By 11 March, wrote Eyre, 'we had been four whole days and nights without a drop for our horses, and almost without food also (for parched as they were they could not feed upon the dry and withered grass we found).'

On the fifth morning, when hope of survival was gone, Eyre spotted a break in the cliffs, and a low sandy shore. Near it they found 'a well beaten native pathway' leading to sandhills and a series of small wells filled with fresh water. By a miracle they had arrived at Eucla, just west of the South Australian border. (A telegraph station, now in ruins, was built there in the eighteen-seventies.) Eyre waited for the other men and sheep to catch up and recover. On 18 March 1841 they began following native tracks to the west, but could find no more water. After sixty-four kilometres Eyre was forced to send the men and horses back to Eucla for

Eyre achieves the impossible by crossing the Nullarbor

On 25 February 1841, Eyre confidently set out on what was thought to be an impossible journey – the crossing of the dry Nullarbor Plain. He reached Albany on 7 July after suffering shocking privations with the Aboriginal Wylie, the other triumphant survivor of this dangerous expedition

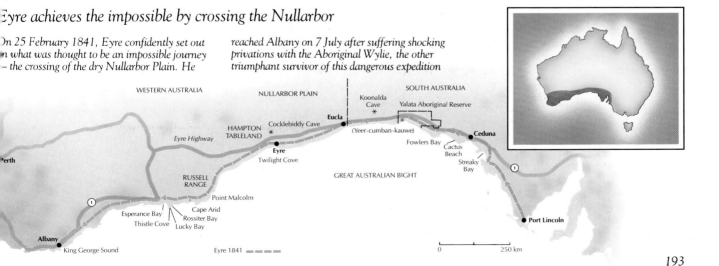

193

water, while he watched over the three remaining sheep. Apart from these, and berries gathered from bushes along the route, the only food left was sixty-four kilos of flour.

Left alone with half a litre of water per day, Eyre wondered how he could possibly cover the remaining nine hundred and sixty-six kilometres to King George Sound. When his men returned with the dray six days later, Eyre lightened it by throwing out most of their clothes, horse-shoes and firearms — and a prized copy of Sturt's *Expeditions*.

The party continued through thick scrub as soon as the moon rose on 26 March 1841. The horses lost condition so fast that the men had to walk. Forced sometimes on to the beach, 'utmost vigilance' was needed to stop the animals drinking sea water. After one hundred and eighty kilometres without water, it was, wrote Eyre, 'a fearful and heart-rending scene to behold the noble animals which had served us so long and so faithfully, suffering the extremity of thirst and hunger.'

On 29 March the explorers found 'immense numbers of fish' in the shallows, cooked them, and washed them down with the last drop of water. Before sunrise Eyre took a sponge, and the natives took handfuls of fine seagrass, to gather dew to make tea. At breakfast they ate their last crust of bread. 'Never was a meal more truly relished,' wrote Eyre.

They were now at about one hundred and twenty-six degrees, fifty minutes longitude. As the morning sea mist cleared, Eyre saw sandhills ahead of them to the south-west. Dunes near the shore changed to 'a pure white sand'. After travelling about sixteen kilometres in increasing heat along the beach, Eyre decided to dig between two white ridges. On reaching one hundred and eighty centimetres, came the 'joyous news' of fresh water. 'In this last extremity we had been relieved,' wrote Eyre.

The spot where the men dug is still known as Eyre. In later years a telegraph relay station, now abandoned, was built near the well which saved Eyre's party. Today the Eyre Highway runs about

thirty kilometres to the north, across the Hampton Tableland.

When all were fully rested, on 10 April 1841 Eyre took one Aboriginal back over their tracks to a point almost thirty-seven kilometres eastwards where some of their stores had been buried. The two men lived on stingrays which they managed to spear in the surf, and drank from water kegs carried on the back of the strongest horse.

Returning with supplies to the well, Eyre had difficulty in persuading John Baxter to continue westwards. Baxter thought they should give up and return to the large cache of supplies buried at Fowlers Bay. He claimed he could go no further on a diet of fish and water.

On 16 April Eyre decided to kill the weakest 'thin and emaciated' horse for food. 'I could not bring myself to eat any to-day, so horrible and revolting did it appear to me,' wrote Eyre — but Baxter and the Aboriginals gorged themselves.

'They looked like ravenous wolves,' Eyre observed — but by 18 April he forced himself to eat some of the dried flesh before blowflies infested it. Even so, the two white men were crippled with dysentery for some days.

Murder in the night

As they recovered, Eyre faced the reality of what lay before them. To the west he could see more cliffs, ninety to one hundred and twenty metres high. That meant another long waterless stage — just how long, Eyre could not know. They were still more than eight hundred kilometres from King George Sound, and the country between was unknown.

On 26 April, one of the Aboriginals shot a wallaby. With this, and a little fish, flour and water packed on the remaining horses' backs, the party set out again the following morning. Baxter was still unwilling, but started off with the 'obedience and fidelity with which he had ever served me,' wrote Eyre.

On 29 April, tragedy struck. That night, at a spot past today's Twilight Cove above the cliffs which are now called Baxter Cliffs, Eyre took first watch over the horses, which were grazing some distance from the camp.

At about 10.30 pm, wrote Eyre, 'I was startled by a sudden flash, followed by the report of a gun.' Eyre ran towards the camp, where he found the Albany Aboriginal Wylie, crying out in alarm 'Oh Massa, oh massa, come here'. Upon reaching the camp, Eyre was 'horror struck to find my poor overseer lying on he ground, weltering in his blood, and in the last agonies of death.'

The other two Aboriginals, Joey and Yarry, had apparently become frightened by Baxter's unwillingness to proceed further into waterless country. They had already absconded once before, but had been forced to return when they could not find food. Now they were past breaking-point. Stealing the only two serviceable guns from beneath an oilskin, and much of the provisions, they probably murdered Baxter when he tried to stop them. All that remained was eighteen kilos of flour, a little tea and sugar, and eighteen litres of water.

'The frightful, the appalling truth now burst upon me, that I was alone in the desert,' wrote Eyre. 'The horrors of my situation glared upon me with such starting reality, as for an instant almost to paralyse the mind...Ages can never efface the horrors of this single night.'

Eyre was not quite alone. Wylie had remained loyal, but even though they were friends, Eyre was not sure how far he could rely on his fidelity. They rounded up the horses, 'knowing that if they got away now, no chance whatever would remain of saving our lives'.

Eyre's habitual optimism soon returned. After continuing to about longitude one hundred and twenty-five degrees, twenty minutes, on 1 May 1841 he was heartened by the appearance of banksia shrubs, which he knew abounded towards Albany. But fatigue came easily now. 'I would gladly have laid down and slept for ever,' wrote Eyre. Nothing but 'a strong sense of duty' kept him urging himself and Wylie to continue.

On 3 May, after crossing one hundred and twenty-nine kilometres of 'sandy, scrubby and rocky ridges', the eternal limestone cliffs at last petered out. This is now Point Culver. The escarpment to the south-west is called Wylie Scarp. The two men found a track to the beach, and there, 'to our great joy and relief', a native well.

Horse meat causes dysentery

Eyre found more wells further along the beach, but nothing for the horses to eat except coarse grass. On 8 May the weakest horse was killed. Wylie built a camp oven and during the night roasted about nine kilos of meat to chew. The remainder was hung over trees to dry.

Again this diet caused painful dysentery. To compensate, wrote Eyre, 'we indulged in a piece of bread, and a spoonful of flour boiled into a paste' with brackish water. Constantly beset by weakness and an awful languor, men and horses were 'scarcely able to put one foot before the other'.

On 17 May 1841 the porous limestone country gave way to granite, and a little fresh water was found trickling down a rock. 'This was the only approximation to *running* water which we had found since leaving Streaky Bay,' Eyre wrote excitedly. Now there was green grass for the horses to graze upon, and the first kangaroos to be shot for the pot.

Wylie surpassed himself in gluttony. 'He commenced by eating a pound and a half of horse-flesh, and a little bread, he then ate the entrails, paunch, liver, lights, tail, and two hind legs of the young kangaroo, next followed a penguin, that he found dead upon the beach, upon this he forced down the whole of the hide of the kangaroo after singeing the hair off, and wound up this meal by swallowing the tough skin of the penguin; he then made a little fire, and laid down to sleep, and dream of the pleasures of eating,' Eyre noted in wonderment.

Men and horses rested and feasted at Point Malcolm from 19 May for seven days. Wylie hunted more kangaroos, while Eyre managed to catch dozens of rock-fish and crabs on the shoreline. He named the Russell Range a few kilometres inland after Lord John Russell, Colonial Secretary of State.

The horses fattened so quickly that Eyre thought it safe to ride them again. The men headed for the well-grassed

Desert sands are swallowing the old telegraph station built at Eucla on the site where Eyre had found native tracks leading to wells

ridges of Cape Arid, then made good time over high sandy downs towards Lucky Bay, named by Matthew Flinders for its abundant fresh water and wood.

Supplies of flour were now almost exhausted. They dug up gum tree roots, roasted them and crushed them between stones into a semblance of flour. 'It is of an agreeable flavour, wholesome, and satisfying to the appetite,' wrote Eyre.

Travelling along the shore near Thistle Cove on 2 June, Eyre thought he saw a sail. 'Having hastily made a fire upon one of the sand-hills, we fired shots, shouted, waved handkerchiefs, and made every signal we could to attract attention, but in vain,' wrote Eyre.

Behind a rocky island about ten kilometres distant, they saw the masts of a barque. Eyre mounted his best horse and rode along the beach as fast as he dared. He arrived at an inlet which he later named Rossiter Bay after the barque's captain (today called Mississippi Point).

Eyre lit a small fire and hailed the ship. A boat instantly put off, 'and in a few moments,' wrote Eyre, 'I had the inexpressible pleasure of being again among civilized beings' of the French whaler *Mississippi*.

Eyre and Wylie were treated with great kindness by captain and crew. Their horses were even shod by the ship's blacksmith. But the more Eyre rested, the more determined he became to complete his journey overland.

On 14 June the two explorers were landed with ample supplies of flour, ship's biscuit, rice, beef, pork, sugar, tea, wine, cheese, butter, brandy and tobacco — as much as their horses could carry.

A hero's reception in Adelaide
Although King George Sound lay less than four hundred and eighty kilometres west, severe hardship still had to be endured. After passing good country at Esperance Bay, Eyre and Wylie began to suffer from cold and rain — particularly when most of their new clothing was destroyed on 24 June by a spark from the campfire. 'The showers came down in perfect torrents,' wrote Eyre. 'We were literally walking in water.'

Two weeks' miserable march over ironstone and sandstone country brought them at last to Albany on 7 July 1841. Wylie was greeted by his tribe as one who had returned from the dead. The government awarded him £2, a medal and rations for life.

Eyre rested for a week at the government residency, then sailed back to Adelaide on 13 July. He had no discoveries of any economic importance to report — no rich pastures, no bountiful rivers.

Yet he was welcomed by many as a hero who had shown what really lay between South Australia and Western Australia.

With this first deep penetration of desert regions, a subtle change came over the nature of Australian exploration. Pastoral lands might still be the avowed objective, but achievement would no longer be judged on its practical results. Acclaim would come from hurling oneself against impossible odds, without caring too much whether the result was life or death. The lure of the desert gripped the imagination of Australians and would continue its hold to this day.

Eyre himself retired from exploration to take up controversial appointments in New Zealand and Jamaica. He left behind a warning for others who would try to solve the puzzles of the inland, 'I have never met with the slightest circumstance to lead me to imagine that there should be an inland sea, still less a deep navigable one...I do so believe, that a considerable portion of the interior consists of the beds or basins of salt lakes or swamps...I think, also, that these alternate with sandy deserts'.□

The whaler Mississippi *was sailing among the islands of the Recherche Archipelago when Eyre sighted her. He rode 10 kilometres along the beach to hail the ship and was soon taken aboard*

Koonalda Cave was occupied by Aboriginals 18 000 years ago, according to fossil evidence. Most caves have small openings on the surface and are difficult to find in the featureless plain

Awesome cliffs and caves of the Nullarbor

Edward Eyre was the first European to stand on the great limestone cliffs where the Nullarbor Plain begins on the eastern side of the Great Australian Bight.

In his report to the South Australian government, Eyre described the cliffs as 'the precipitous banks of an almost level country of moderate elevation (three or four hundred feet) which the violent lash of the whole of the Southern Ocean was always acting upon and undermining.'

After riding for many kilometres along the cliffs, Eyre wrote:

I was in no instance able to descend; their brinks were perfectly steep and overhanging, and in many places enormous masses appeared severed by deep cracks from the main land, and requiring but a slight touch to plunge them into the abyss below.

These massive layers of limestone were deposited millions of years ago when the area was submerged by the sea. After the Miocene period, the sea-bed rose to form a vast exposed flat surface.

Rain eventually soaked through the porous limestone to create extensive underground lakes and rivers. One of the best-known is Koonalda Cave, one hundred and thirteen kilometres east of Eucla, with its hidden lake ninety-one metres long and twenty-seven metres deep. Another, Cocklebiddy Cave, is about sixty-four kilometres from where Eyre's overseer Baxter was murdered.

Alfred Delisser explored the treeless inland area in 1865-66, naming it Nullarbor by combining the two Latin words, *nulla* and *arbor* — no tree.

Eyre Highway follows the coastline close to the route of the explorer for hundreds of kilometres

The awesome limestone cliffs of the Great Australian Bight are constantly being eroded by pounding waves

Sturt is defeated by the horrors of travel in the centre's deserts

Charles Sturt disagreed heartily with his young friend Edward Eyre. Discussions raged back and forth after Eyre's return to Adelaide from his epic journey across the Bight. No, there is nothing to the north except arid plains, salt lakes and claypans, said Eyre. But there could be an inland sea further north, replied Sturt.
There was only one way to settle the question, and that was for Sturt to organise an expedition and see for himself. He was convinced that if he could travel far enough into the centre, 'sooner or later I should be stopped by a large body of inland waters'.

Poor Sturt had been deeply disappointed after his historic voyage down the Murray river in 1830. Grateful South Australian colonists named him Surveyor-General in 1838, but he was superseded by the appointment of Edward Frome direct from London. Sturt was now sitting in the boring post of Registrar-General at a much lower salary.

His health was not good. Vitamin deficiencies and perpetual sun-glare on the Murray voyage had sent him almost blind: ten years later he had still not fully recovered. Inside buildings he sometimes was forced to walk with arms outstretched to find his way.

In 1844 Sturt was forty-nine: an old man for those days. But he felt he must undertake this last great adventure, and pestered the government until it gave permission. At the Colonial Office in London, Lord Stanley agreed that Sturt could explore as far north as latitude twenty-eight degrees, in an attempt to solve the puzzle of rivers which flowed inland but did not emerge at any known point on the coast.

Sturt cheerfully left Adelaide in mid-August 1844 with a substantial expedition of fifteen men, six drays, thirty bullocks, eleven horses, two hundred sheep, and a boat in which he proposed to sail the waters of his inland sea.

Seven tonnes of stores were carried in the drays. Yet another Union Jack had been embroidered by Adelaide women to be planted in the centre of the continent.

Sturt's plan was to avoid the hideous ring of salt lakes north of Adelaide by trekking eastwards along the Murray River and northwards along the Darling, before striking inland from Menindee. 'It will be a joyous day for us to launch on an unknown sea, and run away towards the tropics,' Sturt wrote blithely to Governor George Grey.

The expedition took a leisurely and uneventful two months to reach Lake Cawndilla near Menindee in New South Wales on 10 October 1844. From there it struck out north-west, but made slow progress past today's Broken Hill and across the Barrier Range. This land would later be used for grazing, which in turn would lead to a boundary rider's discovery of the mineral wealth of Broken Hill.

Sturt departed Adelaide with a cavalcade of well-wishers. His plan to explore north to 28 degrees latitude was a compromise. His original, grander proposal to explore and survey the entire interior over a two-year period was turned down

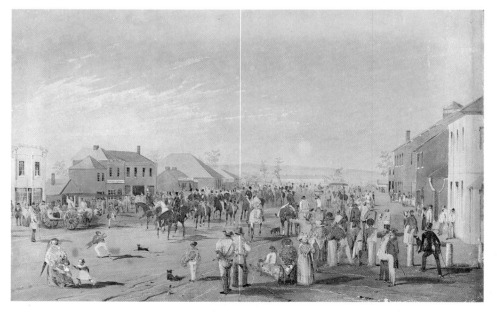

Sturt sent two of his men as far west [as] Yandama creek, near Eyre's Lake From[e] and Mount Hopeless. They reported su[ch] forbidding terrain that Sturt decided on [a] northerly course instead.

This fortunate choice brought th[e] party to fresh water at Flood creek on [?] December 1844, and Depot Glen und[er] Mount Poole (named after the secon[d] in-command, James Poole) on 27 Janua[ry] 1845. Here there seemed to be enou[gh] water to meet the expedition's needs [—] four and a half thousand litres a day.

Sturt's slow progress in nearly s[ix] months of travelling landed him in t[he] worst of an inland summer. Every day t[he] temperature reached forty degrees. 'T[he] lead dropped out of our pencils, our sign[al] rockets were entirely spoiled; our hair, [as] well as the wool on the sheep, ceased [to] grow, and our nails had become as britt[le] as glass,' the explorer wrote.

While most of his men rested, Sturt made short trips on horseback north and east. On one of them, during February 1845, he wrote: 'We were then in one of the most gloomy regions that man ever traversed. The stillness of death reigned around us, no living creature was to be heard...It was marvellous to me that such a country should extend to so great a distance without any change.'

Trapped in an underground chamber
There was no hope of the entire party moving further inland until rain fell. They were trapped at the permanent water of Depot Glen for more than five months, living in an underground chamber which they dug into the earth. 'We were locked up,' wrote Sturt, 'as effectually as if we had wintered at the Pole.'

Each day the sun beat down mercilessly, and the men grimly chewed their mutton and damper. No vegetable food could be found anywhere. Seeds planted were 'burnt to cinders the moment they appeared above the ground'.

On about his fiftieth birthday, Sturt began to develop 'violent headaches, unusual pains in my joints, and a coppery taste in my mouth.' Then 'my mouth became sore, and my gums spongy'. The medical officer, John Harris Browne, told him that these were the dreaded symptoms of scurvy. Others in the party were beginning to be afflicted as well.

Sturt attributed the disease to too much bacon, and returned to a diet of fresh mutton, which by now was 'perfectly tasteless'. This did not prevent his assistant James Poole from dying after great suffering. He was buried under a grevillea not far from the mountain bearing his name.

At last, on 12 July 1845, rain began to

The Simpson Desert's seemingly endless parallel sand dunes and its dry claypans repelled Sturt's party. He twice crossed part of the southeastern corner now called Sturt's Stony Desert

fall. Sturt sent the weakest men back to Adelaide. Had he followed the Governor's instructions, he should have returned with them, but, as he wrote, 'I would rather that my bones had been left to bleach in that desert than have yielded an inch of the ground I had gained at so much expense and trouble.'

As the rain continued, flash floods poured down dry creek beds, 'foaming and eddying amongst the rocks'. Suddenly Depot Glen was filled to the brim. Sturt pondered on the treacherous nature of Australian rivers. 'I would not trust the largest farther than the range of vision; they are deceptive all of them,' he wrote.

On 18 July 1845, Sturt's remaining

nine men urged their bullock teams north-west through boggy land around the glen. Within a few days they came to sandy country where the rain and heat resulted in 'grass and thousands of young plants already springing up'.

By 28 July the party was able to establish another depot on Lake Pinaroo, at a spot Sturt called Fort Grey. Here they built a blockhouse and stockyard, and planted pumpkins and melons.

Sturt spent two weeks on short reconnaissances west to the salty Lake Blanche, north to Stokes Range, and north-east towards Grey Range. Everywhere was sand, clay and salt, with the surface water fast disappearing. If the country continued like this to the north-west, Sturt reflected, 'it would be highly imprudent to venture into it with the whole party.'

For the northwards dash, Sturt chose only three men, and took fifteen weeks' provisions packed on four of the strongest horses. The little group left Fort Grey on 14 August 1845, at first heading north-westerly. 'Spinifex generally covered the sand ridges, which looked like ocean swells rising before us,' wrote Sturt.

On 18 August the party came to 'a beautiful sheet of water', about fifty-five metres broad, where 'many flights of parrots and pigeons' came at sundown. Sturt named it Strzelecki creek after the Polish explorer. The horses grazed happily all around.

Continuing north-west, on 24 August Sturt found that 'A wall of sand suddenly rose before us'. For thirty-two kilometres the men and horses toiled on, each succeeding sand ridge assuming 'a steeper and more rugged character'.

Discovery of Sturt's Stony Desert
Even worse lay ahead. From the top of one of the ridges, Sturt viewed 'an immense gloomy plain', dark purple, completely covered in iron-coated stones, with no vegetation at all to be seen. Today the hellish area is still known as Sturt's Stony Desert. The explorer theorised that the stones, as well as the sand ridges, once had been swept together by 'the mighty current' of a vanished ocean.

The party stumbled across this dreadful plain by 27 August 1845, 'as lonely as a ship at sea', steered only by a wildly fluctuating compass. There was little water, 'not a blade of anything for our horses', which gnawed all night on the bark of the only three trees found.

Next day, after crossing Goyder lagoon, 'sandy ridges once more rose up in terrible array against us'. Vanquishing these, and following a north-north-west course along the dry valley of Eyre creek, they found an open box-tree forest and a large well. Near by was a deserted Aboriginal village containing nineteen huts and water troughs and grinding stones.

Further north Sturt could find only greasy black muddy holes in the creek bed. High sandy ridges still hemmed them in. 'Unless I used great precaution our retreat would be infallibly cut off,' he wrote on 31 August.

On 4 September his hopes flared anew, when a section of Eyre creek was found 'full both of water and grass'. Continuing northwards and north-easterly, on 6 September Sturt was thrown into despair when the ground water turned salty.

The scene all round was 'the most forbidding that our eyes had wandered over'. To the west and north-west could be seen only steep and rugged sand dunes — the eastern ramparts of the unconquered Simpson Desert. To the north and north-east were the sparkling white beds of salt lagoons.

The men were all sick from existing on two kilos of flour each per week, and an occasional wild bird. Dr Browne showed renewed symptoms of scurvy.

James Poole, Sturt's second-in-command, found Depot Glen, which assured the survival of the expedition, but Poole himself was to die there

Evelyn Creek flows from a low range of hills above Depot Glen. Its water lasted throughout the heat of an appalling summer, during which the party sheltered in an underground room. In July, heavy rain caused the creek to flood

The horses were gaunt and weak. 'We had penetrated to a point at which water and feed had both failed,' wrote Sturt. On 8 September 1845 he wisely decided to retrace his steps across the Stony Desert to Fort Grey.

Sturt wrote to his wife, 'We had ridden from first to last a distance of 963 miles, and had generally been on horseback from the earliest dawn to 3 or 4 often to 6 o'clock, having no shelter of any kind from the tremendous heat of the fiery deserts in which we had been wandering, subsisting on an insufficient supply of food, and drinking water that your pigs would have refused.'

One final effort was possible. In explanation, Sturt wrote to his wife: 'What hope is there for me if I return to Adelaide now having literally done nothing, and with the means still in my power of doing more?'

From 9 October to 17 November Sturt again went north to Strzelecki creek, tracing it upstream to its junction with Cooper creek near today's Innamincka.

Continuing north by west towards today's Birdsville, Sturt was once again forced back by the intractable country and increasing heat. At fifty-two degrees in the shade their thermometer burst. Two horses died. They had travelled fourteen hundred and seventy-six kilometres through appalling conditions in five and a half weeks.

Back at Fort Grey the men found the formerly reliable waterhole fast drying up. Sturt feebly proposed a last desperate dash to the centre of the continent, but was firmly over-ruled by Dr Browne.

Sturt almost immediately collapsed with scurvy, his leg muscles seizing up in constant spasms. Prostrate, he was taken back in a cart to today's Blanchetown, arriving 15 January 1846, while Browne fed him nourishing saltbush berries.

Although Sturt had been stricken by the apparent failure of his final expedition, South Australians welcomed him back warmly. He received governmental promotions, until forced to retire because of the further deterioration of his sight in 1851. The heroic explorer died in 1869 just before a knighthood was approved, but his widow was allowed to use the title Lady Sturt.□

CHARLES STURT
COURAGEOUS IN ADVERSITY

Sturt was fascinated by a colony of stick-nest rats (Leporillus conditor), which had built a nest one metre high. The rodents weave small sticks together to form a cone like a beehive, with passages leading to separate nests

The dream of an inland sea evaporates in fierce summer heat

Hoping to outflank the salt lakes that had proved a barrier to Eyre, Sturt headed east along the Murray River then turned north to follow the Darling, before veering north-west towards the centre of the continent. But during his long journey he was repeatedly blocked by the very conditions he had planned to avoid by this roundabout route

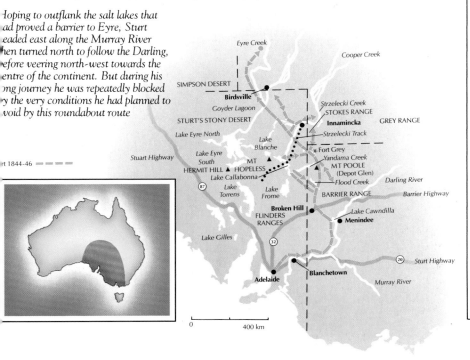

WATER BAGS OUT OF BULLOCK HIDES

When daily temperatures of thirty-seven degrees and more began to dry up the water at Depot Glen, Sturt decided to kill several of his bullocks and convert their skins into water containers.

Daniel Brock, the expedition's rather puritanical collector, described the process in his journal:

A bullock was shot and drawn up by its neck, and carefully skinned from the neck downwards, the skin being drawn back over the carcass, leaving the hairy side inwards. It is lashed in a dray, the water poured into the neck, and the huge bottle filled when safe. The orifice was carefully sewed up. In drawing off the water, a string is unfastened at the tail which acts as a spout.

Each skin held about nine hundred and fifty litres. After a few days, wrote Brock, the skins 'began to smell, and consequently tainted the water'. The explorers had no alternative but to drink it.

Wildlife and blossoms of the desert fringes

Charles Sturt was one of the first Europeans to see and describe some of the wildlife that congregates on and about waterways in central Australia.

North of Cooper creek in 1845, Sturt collected the beautifully tinted little spinifex pigeon (Geophaps plumifera), notable for its long vertical orange crest. Evidently, wrote Sturt, it took pleasure in 'basking in the tremendous heat'.

Near Fort Grey, Sturt found hundreds of the now rare dusky hopping-mouse (Notomys fuscus). Like kangaroos, they 'hopped on their hind legs', Sturt observed, 'and held the tail perfectly straight and horizontal.'

At Depot Glen, Sturt described large flights of parrots, parakeets, corellas, and spotted black bitterns. All suddenly departed one day as the water began to dry up.

Passing near today's Broken Hill, Sturt collected a short-lived vivid scarlet bloom, Clianthus formosus, which later became popular as Sturt's desert pea.

The seeds of many species lie dormant for long periods in the sandy soil, until enough rain falls to dissolve their protective coating. Then the desert suddenly springs into gorgeous life, which just as suddenly seems to disappear until the next rain, but not before dropping new seeds to await their turn in the cycle.

In arid country, the dingo needs to keep within easy reach of drinking water. If it can catch plenty of mammals, it can survive without a daily drink during winter months

The dusky hopping-mouse, like other hopping-mice, finds enough water in its diet of seeds, green plants and insects to survive without drinking. By day it stays in its burrow deep below the dunes, emerging only in the cool of night

Sturt's desert pea, a low trailing annual with silky grey-green leaves, flowers in the desert from July to January

Massed displays of ephemeral plants, most of them, like these everlasting daisies (Helipterum floribundum) of the papery-flowered Compositae family, are responsible for the total transformation of the desert landscape after rain. Their flowering season is from July to September.

The goanna, Varanus giganteus, or perentie, which grows to two and a half metres, is at home in the desert. Australia's largest lizard lives in deep crevices, coming out to hunt birds, mammals, insects or carrion

The spinifex pigeon lives permanently in arid grasslands, unlike a lot of birds that come and go. It lives on the ground and walks long distances. Flight is fast and low over the ground in short bursts. Flocks of up to 15 birds keep close to springs and soaks during drought

John Horrocks is shot by his camel

The bad-tempered Harry was the first camel used in inland Australia

In 1846, electric telegrams were being sent regularly over Samuel Morse's first permanent wire between the American cities of Washington and Baltimore. In Ireland, a mysterious black blight continued to ravage the potato crop and thousands of people were dying of starvation in that unhappy land. With no alternative source of food, two million planned to emigrate. In Adelaide, Charles Sturt rested, slowly recovered from scurvy and brooded over his failure to discover new fertile lands somewhere in the vast interior.

Younger men came to the fore, and optimism returned. John Ainsworth Horrocks, an enterprising twenty-eight-year-old Lancashire-born grazier on the Hutt river north of Adelaide, had been experimenting with the use of dromedaries — one-humped camels — to replace horses in the exploration of arid areas.

Nine of the beasts were imported from the Canary Islands. By 1846 only one remained, a bad-tempered animal named Harry. Horrocks decided to take Harry and five horses on a trip to the north in search of new pastures. 'I have great hopes of finding a country,' he wrote to his sister. 'It suits my temper, as I want a more stirring life.'

Five other men joined the expedition, including an up-and-coming young watercolourist named Samuel Thomas Gill. He wished to make the first professional paintings of the strangely-tinted inland as described by Eyre and Sturt.

Horrocks's expedition left Penwortham (named after his home in England) on 29 July 1846. After a few kilometres the axletree of their cart broke, but a blacksmith at Clare, further north on the Hutt river, quickly repaired it.

Next morning they purchased thirteen goats from a local settler, and drove them ahead as a reserve food supply.

JOHN AINSWORTH HORROCKS
AN UNLUCKY ADVENTURER

On 1 August, travelling through 'very soft and sticky' soil on Gulnare Plains (named after Horrocks's favourite greyhound), Harry the camel began to show its real nature. It seized one of the goats in its mouth, and 'would have broken its back,' wrote Horrocks, if a man had not quickly rescued it.

Later that day Harry bit the cook, a man named Garlick, on the head — inflicting 'two wounds of great length above his temples.'

The following day the expedition passed the last sheep station to the north, at today's Gladstone, where the Messrs Hughes donated a leg of mutton.

The party rested for several days at Samuel White's cattle station, near today's Wirrabara. The owner selected a fine calf for them from his eleven thousand head of stock.

By 7 August the explorers reached Colin Campbell's homestead near Melrose, at that time the most northerly cattle station. Here the settler gave them the rare treat of a large lump of butter.

Traversing the well-grassed plains of today's Mount Remarkable National Park, Horrocks discovered on 10 August a steep pass between Mount Remarkable and Mount Brown. Several uncomfortable days and bitterly cold nights on rocky ground sent most of the goats lame. 'They amused themselves by leaping on our tent and tearing it in several places,' Horrocks wrote in his journal.

On 17 August the men managed to load close to one hundred and sixty kilos of provisions on the camel's back, and led it down 'a nasty narrow valley'. It galloped off, scattering the load all down the pass. Loaded again, it became enraged and bit into two bags of flour, 'making in each a large hole'.

Through stony and desolate country
By 21 August 1846, the expedition had reached Eyre's old camp at Depot creek. The parched horses drank for hours, and the worst-behaved goat was killed for a celebratory dinner.

On a short trip west-north-west, Horrocks and Gill found only stony and desolate country, the plains covered with stunted trees, deteriorating into innumerable sandhills. Aboriginals threatened them with spears when they drank from a pool of muddy water.

From 28 August Horrocks and Gill explored in a north-westerly direction, the artist sometimes riding Harry the camel. On 1 September they penetrated as far as a salt lake which Horrocks named Lake Gill. Unfortunately this was later renamed Lake Dutton.

By the lakeside, Horrocks decided to shoot 'a beautiful bird' to add to their collection. Gill stopped the camel and began unfastening the shot belt. Meanwhile Horrocks, standing alongside, was screwing the ramrod into his gun.

'At this moment,' wrote Horrocks in his last letter, 'the camel gave a lurch to one side, and caught his pack in the cock of my gun, which discharged the barrel I was unloading, the contents of which first took off the middle fingers of my right hand between the second and third joints, and entered my left cheek by my lower jaw, knocking out a row of teeth from my upper jaw.'

Gill stayed at the spot to nurse the wounded man. Their assistant, Bernard Kilroy, walked one hundred and thirteen kilometres through the night back to

A wounded Horrocks shelters in his tent, while Gill waits for help. This scene shows the furthest point reached by the expedition

An ill-fated expedition is recorded by artist Samuel Gill

Horrocks's trek northwards in the steps of Eyre added little to knowledge of South Australia beyond the last lonely cattle station near Melrose. His hopes of finding new pastures were cut short by a tragic accident that took his life. But with him was a young artist, S. T. Gill, whose watercolours of the 1846 expedition provide a lasting record

Horrocks 1846 ━ ━ ━ ━

Depot creek to fetch the men and horses.

The cortege made its way back to Horrocks's station. A doctor summoned from Adelaide could not heal the infected wounds: Horrocks died 'without a struggle' on 23 September 1846.

Upon his death, the station hands dragged Harry the camel into a stockyard and shot it. The first bullet only wounded the beast: enraged, it lunged out and bit the head of an Aboriginal stockman. A second shot completed the execution.

Horrocks's tragic expedition may not have discovered much that was new. But by taking S. T. Gill with him, Horrocks unconsciously bequeathed to posterity some of the first and finest paintings of explorers in Australia's arid regions.□

A way is found round the dreaded barrier of salt lakes

The apparently unbroken horseshoe of salt lakes blocking South Australians from getting into Central Australia defeated even experienced explorers like Eyre and Sturt.

In 1843 the Surveyor-General, Edward Frome, made his attempt to break the hoodoo. He tried to penetrate to the north-east, but found his progress prevented by the crusted salt bed of Lake Frome, which was later named after him.

'All our dreams of discovery of a large fresh-water lake now vanished,' wrote Frome. 'We turned with disgust from this dreary spot.'

The mystery of what lay on the other side of the horseshoe barrier continued to tantalise the pioneer South Australians.

In 1856, a forty-year-old London-born geologist, Benjamin Herschel Babbage, searching in the Flinders Ranges for gold, discovered instead the MacDonald creek; then a large brackish lake which he called Blanchewater (now Lake Blanche); and grazing land to the north of Mount Hopeless.

Even more important, Aboriginals told Babbage of a land gap to the north-east between Lake Blanche and Lake Callabonna, today called the Strzelecki Track.

Investigating Lake Blanche in 1857, the current Surveyor-General, Arthur Henry Freeling, wrote that 'Neither boat nor folding punt could be floated. After tremendous exertions of walking in mud to our knees,

a few inches of water was all that was found.'

After this discouraging report, the government in 1858 sent Benjamin Babbage to attempt penetration of the horseshoe lakes from Eyre's route to the north-west.

Babbage discovered Hermit Hill south of Lake Eyre, and from its height was able to see clear country to the west.

He also discovered the first of many artesian mound springs, which finally enabled the dreaded salt lakes to be circumvented, and country lying to the north-west of the horseshoe to be settled by pastoralists.

Lake Eyre South is the smaller of the two salt lakes that together make Lake Eyre; they are connected by a narrow channel. The area has an evaporation rate twenty times higher than its rainfall, which averages 127 millimetres a year

Lake Eyre is usually seen as a vast stretch of saline mud, much of which is covered with a dazzling crust of salt several metres deep; the lake is filled with water only rarely

John Roe leads the way to great mineral discoveries

Seven years after Eyre's tortuous walk across the Bight, the West Australian government decided to authorise exploration east from the coast in the hope of finding better country. To conduct its expedition, it appointed John Septimus Roe, the colony's Surveyor-General since 1829. Now, in 1848, Roe was fifty-one — too old for the unknown trials which lay ahead, he admitted later. But he was an experienced, enthusiastic explorer who was tough enough to survive his ordeals and live to the remarkable age of eighty-one.

Roe's party left Perth on 8 September 1848, advancing in easy stages until it reached the easternmost sheep station called Nalyaring, near today's Nalya, by 17 September.

Following a general easterly direction, they soon left the good grassy areas and entered 'scrubby sand-plains and eucalyptus thickets'. Fortunately the Aboriginals were friendly, showing them locations of wells and springs.

In freezing weather the small party passed extensive chains of salt lakes, then went through today's Karlgarin until longitude one hundred and nineteen degrees was reached.

Roe felt this land was 'apparently unfit for any useful purpose', although later it was used for wheat and sheep growing. Despondent, he turned to proceed in a southerly direction and reached the coast at Cape Riche early in October 1848.

With new supplies, Roe headed up the Pallinup river, and then north-east towards the interior once again. On 22 October he was delighted to find a large tract of fertile country around today's Gairdner river. Known to the natives as Jerramungup, it became the homestead of the pioneering Hassell family.

Further to the north-east the country again became poor and scrubby, interspersed with brackish lakes. On 29 October Roe discovered Mount Madden, naming it after the new Colonial Secretary, Dr Richard Madden.

From its red granite height Roe could see another peak to the south-east, which he named Mount Short after Augustus Short, first Anglican bishop of South Australia and Western Australia. But the overall look of the surrounding country remained totally discouraging.

Misery for the horses

By 3 November, past salty Lake Hope and Bremer Range, the horses had been without water for two days, while each man had only half a litre left. When small pools were found, the parched horses rushed into the water fully laden and were extricated with difficulty.

For a couple more days Roe headed south to find grassy patches to revive the horses. Had he continued to travel north he might well have discovered the rich goldfields of Kalgoorlie and Coolgardie and altered the pattern of Western Australia's growth to prosperity.

Instead, on 9 November 1848 Roe headed easterly once more into 'the frowning sea of scrub'. Again the party became entangled in extensive salt marshes. Two horses collapsed and were abandoned. The rest were saved only by a providential shower: the men collected water in tin plates and fed it to the parched animals.

Following a south-easterly course to skirt the worst salt lakes, on 13 November Roe discovered Mount Ridley, naming it after one of his party. From its bare granite peak could only be seen 'a distant horizon as unbroken as that of the sea itself'.

After another rest, the party pushed eastward again on 15 November, finding at last a copious fresh spring and good grass at Mount Ney. Touchingly, Roe named it after his favourite horse, which was too weak to go any further. On the night of 17 November, alone in the clear vastness, the explorers enjoyed a dazzling red-tinted display of Aurora Australis in the southern sky.

About eighty kilometres to the east, Roe could make out the outlines of Russell Range, discovered seven years earlier by Edward Eyre.

To reach it, the weakened explorers had to hack their way with axes through several kilometres of dense scrub. They came to hastily-abandoned Aboriginal

JOHN SEPTIMUS ROE
SURVEYOR ON SEA AND LAND

An aging surveyor's fruitless search for minerals and new pastures

John Roe's 1848-49 expedition to investigate the inland east of Albany for pastures and minerals was his sixteenth journey of exploration. It was also the toughest. His party struggled through salt marshes and hacked its way through dense scrub. Sadly for him, gold-rich Coolgardie and Kalgoorlie were north of his path. He found only a little coal

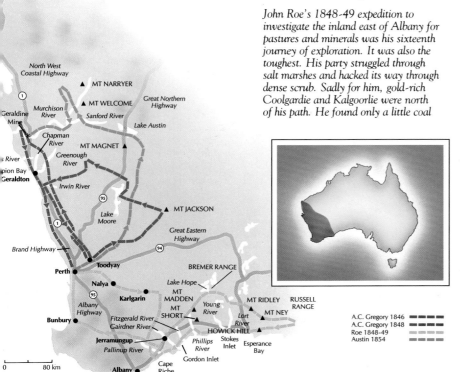

A.C. Gregory 1846	▬▬▬
A.C. Gregory 1848	▬▬▬
Roe 1848-49	▬ ▬ ▬
Austin 1854	▬ ▬ ▬

Roe vainly searched Stokes Inlet, and the Lort and Young rivers that enter it, for signs of coal. The hope was to establish a coaling station for use by shipping on the continent's south-west coast

campfires, and left gifts of biscuit in the baskets. But nothing would induce the natives to come out of hiding.

After a slight improvement in grass and water, by 20 November travel again became difficult. Each morning, Roe recorded in his journal, 'The poor horses staggered up to their saddles with a despondency and aspect which seemed to upbraid us with their treatment.' By 22 November the animals were 'streaming out in those profuse cold sweats which are always the forerunner of a complete and fatal break up'.

On the lookout for coal seams

With only a few kilometres to his objective, Roe abandoned most of the equipment and urged the dying animals onwards. But at the foot of the 'bare naked' Russell Range, not a blade of grass or any water could be found.

Next morning, at the north-eastern extremity of the range, their Aboriginal guide Bob found 'a splendid run of excellent water' and grass, saving the lives of the whole party.

After resting for four days, Roe decided that the expedition was doomed if it penetrated further into 'so fearful and impracticable a country'. They began to return south-west on 28 November.

On 2 December 1848 Roe reached the 'lofty and remarkable' 265-metre Howick Hill, which he named after Lord Howick, Secretary for the Colonies.

Waterholes were now drying up, leaving 'half a bushel of tadpoles' in the bottom of each, and causing intense diarrhoea when drunk.

By 7 December the party was abreast of Esperance Bay, discovering the first watercourses seen in over six hundred kilometres, and many circular holes leading to underground lakes. Grass, ducks and swans were now easier to find. Kangaroos were also plentiful. But the paws of the expedition's footsore dog had been wrapped up in leather, and it was able to catch only one young kangaroo.

Roe spent several days carefull examining the short rivers which flow into Stokes Inlet. His main objective wa to discover coal, which might make the establishment of a coaling port feasible but none could be found.

The easternmost stream he named th Lort river, after Captain J. Lort Stokes o HMS *Beagle*. The other main strean flowing into Stokes Inlet he named th Young river, after Sir Henry Young Governor of South Australia.

Arriving at the Phillips river on 2 December 1848, Roe resumed his search for coal, but to his disappointment, foun only slate and shale.

On Christmas Day the party rested to enjoy roast kangaroo, a pudding made o soaked biscuit and sugar, and an allow ance from their medicinal brandy.

Two days later, on the Fitzgerald river Roe excitedly reported the discovery o extensive beds of coal and bitumen which burned in a 'most satisfactory manner. He named the river after th new Governor, Charles Fitzgerald.

At the end of December Roe explore southwards, naming Gordon Inlet afte Gordon Gairdner, who long helped to decide the destiny of Australian colonie from his desk in the Colonial Office.

By early January 1849 the part covered the remaining few kilometres to George Cheyne's property at Cape Riche which they had left three months before After resting, they rode easily throug great forests of red gum, mahogany an jarrah on the track to Bunbury, arrivin safely in Perth on 2 February.

Roe's expedition had travelled abou three thousand kilometres in fiv months. Few discoveries of importanc had been made, and he overstated the significance of finding coal, but at leas the nature of much of the interior had been described for those pastoralists will ing to move into marginal country. Grea mineral discoveries would follow almos automatically. □

AUGUSTUS GREGORY EXPLORES NORTH OF PERTH

While John Roe was struggling to penetrate arid country to the east of Perth, his assistant surveyor, Augustus Charles Gregory, twenty-nine, was opening up new stretches of pastoral and mining country to the north.

Already Gregory had been acclaimed for his discovery in 1846 of coal seams on the Irwin river, about sixty kilometres south of today's Geraldton.

Gregory mined it with a tomahawk, and soon 'had the satisfaction of seeing the first fire of Western Australian coal burning cheerfully in front of the camp'.

Now, late in 1848, Gregory set out to push further north, but was baffled by an 'immense sea of dense thicket of acacia and cypress'.

The party could not penetrate it, 'the saddle-bags being almost torn to pieces, and the horses quite worn out with continual exertions in dragging their packs through the thickets'.

Forced westerly then northerly through waterless country, they were finally saved by emerging at the Murchison river near today's Geraldine Mine. Indications of lead and other minerals were found.

Rugged escarpments soar above the Murchison in today's Kalbarri National Park

Camping by a tributary of the Bowes river, north of Geraldton, the explorers were invited by a friendly Aboriginal tribe to share their women. On refusal, the women 'commenced pelting the party, with stones', Gregory reported.

In this area, and along the Greenough and Chapman rivers, the explorers found tens of thousands of hectares of excellent pastoral land, leading to the settlement of the Geraldton area.

Robert Austin is misled by mirages

Assistant Surveyor Robert Austin and eleven companions nearly perished in 1854 when they tried to penetrate desert country inland from Champion Bay in Western Australia.

More than half their horses died after eating the bright orange flowering bush, gastrolobium. 'Their heads were swollen, their eyes protruded and were dull, the hollow over the eye was puffed out with air, the nostrils were swollen up and dry, the upper and lower lips were dreadfully swelled,' Austin wrote sadly.

On 25 August 1854 the surveyor watched his compass needles swinging wildly. This led him to the discovery of Mount Magnet, which is to the east of the Greenough river and south of Lake Austin.

Austin described the area as 'probably one of the finest gold fields in the world'. But it was overshadowed by gold discoveries in eastern Australia. Because of its remoteness and danger, Mount Magnet could not be developed until the eighteen-nineties.

Forced to abandon most of his food and equipment, Austin pushed on towards the Murchison river. He took two Aboriginal guides ahead of the main party to search for water. For some days they existed 'without any other food than half a rat each'.

On 11 September 1854 they headed for a large lake on the horizon. But the only water in it, wrote Austin, was 'the delusive effect of refraction on the dry bed.' The Aboriginal guide Narryer called the mirage 'walkaway and tell lie water', since it kept receding and 'deceitfully luring us on'.

One of the main party, Charles Farmer, caught his rifle on a branch and shot himself in the arm. The wound became infected: he died in agony on 27 September.

On 2 October 1854 Austin discovered a little water in the Sanford river, which he named after W. H. Sanford, Western Australia's Colonial Secretary.

Eight days later the party arrived at the Murchison river, but were dismayed to find it dry. Even by digging holes in the river bed they could obtain only salt water.

On 14 October they moved on to find a little grass and water at Mount Welcome. Even here they could not rest, for clouds of small black flies threatened to choke anyone who opened his mouth.

The now-desperate men continued towards Shark Bay. They marched in the cool of the night, 'stripped to our boots and trowsers, to get the benefit of the dew'. The horses died one by one. Austin turned back.

Sustained only by moisture from a few

Islands seem to float above the shimmering surface of the water. But there is no water: the effect is an optical illusion. In a desert, the hot air near the ground is less dense than the layers of air above, and rays of light are refracted towards an observer, creating an impression of water

soaks, and reduced to the last of their flour rations, the emaciated survivors staggered into the Geraldine Mine on the lower Murchison on 20 November, where miners fed them until help arrived from Perth.

Despite his sufferings, Austin could still report his belief that four large tributaries whose dry beds he found connecting with the Murchison must be indications of 'a fertile country to the eastward'.

Eastward was even worse desert, but Austin could not bring himself to admit it. The mirage still filled his mind.

Many a traveller in the Australian outback has been deceived by a sight such as this. The appearance of a mirage is so realistic it takes a disciplined mind to reject it

Border of the mud desert near Desolation Camp, by Ludwig Becker

CHAPTER SEVEN

Courageous invaders of the hostile deserts

The Gregory brothers confine their efforts to following the northern fringes of the deserts

Suddenly interest in central Australia faded for a time. The attention of the whole world focused on New South Wales and Victoria, where huge deposits of gold were discovered. In the other Australian colonies, exploration practically came to an end. Tens of thousands of gold-hungry emigrants poured into south-eastern ports, especially in Victoria. South Australia and Tasmania lost a large proportion of their workforce as townsmen and rural workers flocked to the diggings. In Western Australia the labour shortage finally became so serious that settlers asked for, and received, a resumption of convict transportation from Britain.

AUGUSTUS CHARLES GREGORY
A METHODICAL, CAUTIOUS LEADER

Not until the mid-eighteen-fifties, when easily-won gold had vanished from the diggings, did men's thoughts turn again to the still-unknown areas of Australia. Thousands of failed gold-seekers were now crying out for land on which they could establish farms in their adopted country. This revival of land hunger set the scene for future exploration.

European empire-building was also at work. In 1854 Japan and Thailand were opened to Western traders. Soon France occupied Indo-China (Vietnam), while Britain decided to take over the entire governance of India. The *Great Eastern*, largest steamship of the decade, was launched on the Thames to transport large numbers of emigrants and troops across the world with unprecedented speed. The first ocean telegraphic cables were laid on the sea bed, transforming communication between nations.

Australia was now seen as a vital link in Britain's world network. No other nation, London decided, should have a share of the southern continent.

In 1855 the British government decided to spend £5000 on a scientific expedition across northern Australia, to assess accurately the best areas for new settlement. Stokes and Sturt were consulted, and the thirty-six-year-old West Australian surveyor Augustus Gregory was chosen to organise and lead the biggest professional inland expedition so far mounted.

Gregory's first move was to ask the elderly Sir Thomas Mitchell for practical advice. Irascible to the last, Mitchell 'refused in a most discourteous manner', Gregory wrote to Sturt.

Gregory gathered his forces at Moreton Bay during July and August 1855. They consisted of eighteen men, including botanists, geologist and artist; fifty horses; two hundred sheep; and provisions for eighteen months. Gregory made sure of including plenty of lime-juice to prevent scurvy.

This well-equipped party was shipped to Victoria river in the Northern Territory in the barque *Monarch* and schooner *Tom Tough*, landing at Treachery Bay (Pearce Point) on 18 September 1855.

Here abundant grass and water had been reported, but the horses had to swim more than three kilometres through mangrove swamps to get to the shore. 'Three were drowned, one lost in the mud and mangroves, and one went mad and rushed into the bush,' Gregory reported.

The explorers spent most of October 1855 examining country across the Fitzmaurice and Victoria rivers to the south. Although much of it was well grassed, the sun had dried out most of its value as feed. Two horses died, and three were mauled by crocodiles.

The men shot turkeys, hawks and cockatoos for the pot. Large bats were also taken: 'the flesh was white and was eaten, but it had an unpleasant flavour,' Gregory remarked.

Difficulties with boats

During this brief expedition, further troubles struck at home base. Under the frequently-drunk Captain Gourlay, *Tom Tough* ran aground, taking in a metre of water before tarred blankets stopped the leak. A large quantity of bread, peas and rice was destroyed.

On shore, fresh water ran short, and 'a great number' of the sheep died. On 29 October, one of the party's kangaroo dogs was taken by a crocodile. Two days later Gregory found that intense heat had melted the indiarubber composition covering their inflatable boat.

By mid-November 1855 the boat had been patched up by Thomas Baines, the expedition's artist. Baines and Gregory began an expedition up the Victoria river on 15 November. Again severe heat destroyed the waterproofing, and they returned after only two days.

A week later, Gregory decided to leave on horseback with four men and

twenty days' provisions. This time he managed to penetrate beyond the steep valley of the Victoria river to the grassy flood plains inland. To his amazement, he could see from driftwood lodged high in the trees that floods sometimes reached over fifteen metres — an enormous volume of water to be borne into Joseph Bonaparte Gulf.

On 13 December Baines and the farrier R. Bowman, were searching for missing horses when they were threatened by Aboriginals on the banks of a freshwater tributary to the south. The expedition's geologist, J. S. Wilson, demanded that the stream be named after Norton Shaw, the secretary of the Royal Geographical Society. But Gregory decided to call it the Baines river, and that name is still used today.

When his next expedition set off for the south, Gregory left Wilson angrily seething at the base camp. The geologist later refused to work unless guaranteed a place in the main expedition to Moreton Bay. Gregory promptly suspended him,

replacing him with Dr Ferdinand von Mueller, who had been seconded from his duties as Victorian government botanist to accompany the expedition.

The southward-bound party of nine men left camp on 3 January 1856 with thirty-six horses and provisions for five months. The weight of two and a half tonnes, carried on thirty packhorses, meant that at the beginning each horse had to carry eighty-two kilos.

The expedition continued south-westerly along the Wickham river until 23 January. Two horses perished in deep rocky ravines and others had shoes 'torn from their feet'.

Proceeding south on 28 January, Gregory formed another base camp at Depot Pile, then selected a smaller party to continue south on 30 January.

By 9 February 1856 Gregory had left behind all running water, to arrive at the red sands of a desert, stretching across the horizon from east to south-west.

The only practical route seemed to be westerly, away from the interior. Follow-

ing the almost dry beds of creeks, Gregory penetrated low sandstone ranges to discover on 22 February good grass round a creek which he named after Sturt. South was 'a mass of hilly country', which Gregory named Mount Wittenoom after the prominent West Australian family.

Gregory continued to trace Sturt creek to the south-west. Although much of it was dry, he was delighted by pools containing 'great numbers of ducks, cockatoos, cranes and crows', surrounded by extensive grazing plains.

But by 1 March 1856 the party again entered desert fringes marked by 'low ridges of drifted sand'. Gregory named the highest of a range of low sandstone hills to the south-east after the botanist Mueller and a smaller hill Mount Wilson, after the geologist.

Now the water pools gradually turned

These scrubby grass plains in the Northern Territory today are pastoral holdings feeding vast cattle herds. In 1855, Gregory was able to cross them fairly easily on his west-east trek

salty. Nothing more was visible to the south-east but an 'unbounded waste'. On 10 March, having followed Sturt creek for nearly five hundred kilometres, Gregory gave up the trek into what he called 'the Great Australian Desert'. Much of the land he traversed later became cattle stations, but at the moment there seemed no place for pastoralists or immigrants here.

Back at Depot creek on 28 March 1856, Gregory learned from Thomas Baines that Aboriginals had frequently tried to destroy the camp by setting fire to dry grass. Intense heat had reduced the store of salted pork to one-fifth of its original weight. Rats and white ants had consumed other reserves.

Provisions from Timor

Gregory did not delay in organising another expedition. This time he decided on a fifteen-day reconnaissance to the east, in preparation for his major push to the Gulf of Carpentaria.

Four men left on horseback in humid weather on 2 April 1856. They rode across richly-grassed basalt plains, intersected with flowing tributaries of the Victoria and Wickham rivers. On 16 April Gregory named Mount Sanford, before returning to Depot creek in a much happier state of mind.

Several weeks were spent organising the main expedition. *Tom Tough* left for Timor to purchase fresh provisions, which it was to take to the Gulf to meet the overland party at the Albert river.

The camp cook mixed the remaining preserved beef with flour and baked it to make 'meat biscuits', weighing one-third less than the ingredients. Saddlery was repaired and horses reshod.

By 21 June 1856 Gregory was ready to leave on the first push across northern Australia from west to east. Although it duplicated much of Leichhardt's east to west expedition of 1844-45, Gregory's was felt to be a more scientific effort, commanded by men who could survey and analyse landforms more accurately.

Gregory selected six men to accompany him. They were his younger brother Henry, Dr Mueller, Dr J. R. Elsey as surgeon, and three stockmen. With them were seven saddlehorses, and twenty-seven packhorses carrying six months' provisions.

By the second week in July 1856 the party had traversed the grassy tableland which divides watercourses flowing to the north-west coast from those which fall into the Gulf.

At this stage of the journey the Aboriginals seemed peaceful: 'On our approach,' wrote Gregory, 'most of the women decamped with their bags and nets containing their valuables, while the men stood spear in hand gazing on the strange sight, as we passed them.'

On 12 July the party passed the site o today's Mataranka. Two days late Gregory named the swampy Elsey cree after the expedition's surgeon. Her springs rose in the limestone and on th banks 'large quantities of mussel-shell showed the frequent camps of the blacks.

All of this would become good pas toral and buffalo-hunting country ir future years. Gregory's men felled hug fan palms, up to twenty-four metres high and extracted the pulp for vegetables.

By 15 July 1856 Gregory reache Leichhardt's Roper river, surrounded b lagoons in which *Nymphaea caerulea*, th gigantic water-lily, thrived. Bowma killed a young emu for dinner.

On 21 July the expedition's trouble began, when two of the best saddle horses dropped dead after eating poison ous plants. South-east of the Roper rive the country suddenly deteriorated int rocky arid regions. Dr Mueller ofte became separated from the party whil collecting plant specimens, riding muc greater distances. On 29 July Gregor noted with exasperation that the botanis had knocked up four horses since January

With some difficulty the party trav ersed dry creek beds to arrive at th McArthur river on 4 August. South-eas was only 'miserable sandy country'. Littl grass could be found for the horses unt the Robinson river was reached. Her Gregory observed that disruption of th

Gregory brings a professional approach to inland exploration

On his 1855-56 expedition from the Victoria River to Moreton Bay, A.C. Gregory passed through country already travelled by Leichhardt who had crossed the north in the opposite direction. But Gregory's professionals contrasted strongly with Leichhardt's party of amateurs. Gregory had explored the Victoria River area before his long trek began. In 1858 he found a way through S.A.'s salt lakes maze

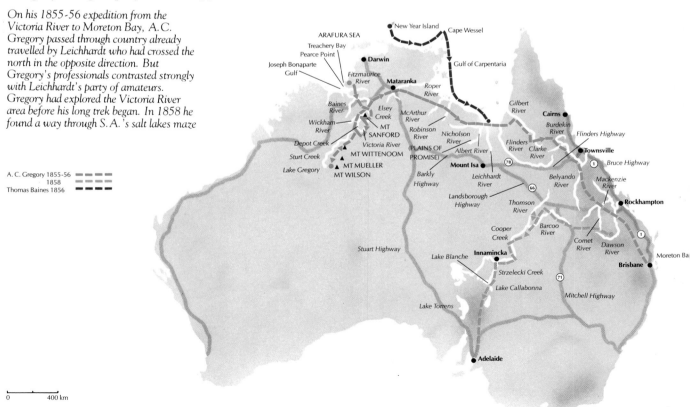

A. C. Gregory 1855-56
1858
Thomas Baines 1856

0   400 km

rocky strata had 'caused fertile patches', enabling the explorers to cross country otherwise barren and inhospitable.'

Gregory had now begun to appreciate the extent of the continent's arid interior. 'To the south there is little to expect besides a barren sandy desert,' he wrote on 14 August 1856.

Later that month, hindered by country consisting of steep sandstone ridges covered with spinifex, the party struck major problems. The starving horses by now barely had strength to move, and had to be rested frequently. Bowman was attacked by scurvy, suffering leg pains and swelling gums.

They were now following the dry bed of the Nicholson river towards the Gulf. At length, on 31 August 1856, they arrived at the Albert river. Here they blazed a tree and buried a metal powder canister to tell Baines of their movements when he arrived by boat.

Since there was no way of knowing what had happened to the *Tom Tough*, Gregory determined to complete the journey overland to Moreton Bay. Later he was severely criticised for not proceeding south to examine more closely the so-called Plains of Promise which John Stokes of the *Beagle* had discovered fifteen years earlier. But Gregory knew that Gulf rivers were short, the harbours poor, the grass quite sparse, and the hinterland forbidding. He decided to play safe.

After resting, the party saddled up again on 3 September 1856. The following day, arriving at an unnamed freshwater stream which Leichhardt had wrongly supposed to be the Albert river, Gregory named it the Leichhardt after his renowned predecessor.

On 9 September the explorers reached the Flinders river, and on 21 September the Gilbert river. Their weakest horse was slaughtered and cut into strips to dry, 'the liver and heart furnishing the party with an excellent dinner.'

Gregory followed the waterholes of the Gilbert River almost to its source, then turned due east to strike the head waters of the Burdekin. Excellent grass and timber were found on 20 October between the Clarke and Burdekin rivers.

The worst of the journey was now over. On 30 October 1856 Gregory was able to write happily that 'the extent of country suited for squatting purposes is very considerable — water forming a never-failing stream throughout the whole distance [of the Burdekin].'

On 4 November Gregory passed the latitude of Thomas Mitchell's last camp on the Belyando river, enabling him to connect Mitchell's 1846 route on the map with Leichhardt's 1844-45 trip.

By 15 November the party reached the Mackenzie river, and two days later the

Comet river, where they found a tree blazed with Leichhardt's initial.

On 21 November 1856 they came to the Dawson river, and thus to the northernmost stations, where they met with 'a most hospitable reception'.

After all the expense and careful preparation, after three thousand kilometres by sea and eight thousand kilometres by land, Gregory's main achievement had been to identify untouched pastoral lands in the Northern Territory and Queensland. He had gone slightly closer to the interior than Leichhardt's first expedition had done. But his forebodings on the dangers of central Australia did not penetrate the minds of less cautious explorers.

Search for Leichhardt

In 1858 Gregory was commissioned by the New South Wales government to search for traces of Leichhardt's last tragic expedition across the north.

Gregory took his brother Charles and six other men on horseback for the attempt. Travelling westerly from Juanda Station on the Dawson river on 24 March 1858, they made good time to the Barcoo river, but ran into appalling drought. Plains which Thomas Mitchell had described twelve years earlier as 'covered with the finest grass' were now bare of vegetation and almost waterless.

*Artist **Thomas Baines,** who accompanied Gregory's expedition (see page 218), painted this scene from the Aboriginal viewpoint. Baines and the farrier had gone in search of stray horses*

On 21 April 1858, Gregory discovered by a pool on the Barcoo a Moreton Bay ash blazed with the letter L. Careful searches all about disclosed no remains.

The sight of desert to the west again urged the cautious Gregory away from central Australia. After a brief attempt northwards up the Thomson river, he turned south-westerly, tracing the dry Barcoo bed down to its junction with Cooper creek, then veered a little west to Strzelecki creek.

By continuing southwards, Gregory was able to cross dry land between Lake Blanche and Lake Callabonna, confirming that Lake Torrens was not a continuous horseshoe shape.

On hearing Gregory's reports, Charles Sturt, retired to Cheltenham in England, at last abandoned his lifelong dream of an inland sea. 'I believe the desert extends with unvarying sameness to the south coast,' he wrote in 1858, 'and that any anticipation of good from an exploration of it would end in disappointment.'

Still no European had ever seen the centre of Australia. The challenge remained, provoking to those who would dare to defy the obvious.□

Francis Gregory explores the north-west for pastoralists

While his older brother Augustus Gregory cautiously picked his way across northern Australia, Francis Thomas Gregory discovered a considerable spread of grazing land along the upper Murchison river, running from today's Pia Aboriginal Reserve north towards Mount Murchison.

Using a pocket sextant and artificial horizon with treacle instead of mercury, Francis Gregory roughly surveyed the area so that squatters could find their way to it.

In gratitude, settlers raised money for the thirty-seven-year-old explorer to buy horses and provisions. His brief was to examine the Gascoyne river area about one hundred and eighty kilometres further north.

Gregory spent from 14 April to 23 June 1858 on the assignment. He found ample fresh water between the Murchison and Gascoyne rivers, and many edible roots, wild melons and fig-like fruit.

Crested quail, dark brown pigeons, doves and 'the elegant *Geophaps plumifera*' (red-bellied spinifex pigeon) were also abundant.

En route to the Gascoyne, Gregory named Mounts Matthew, Hale, Gould, James, Samuel, and Phillips and the Kennedy Range; and the Lyons river.

Attempting to penetrate to the north-east, the explorer soon encountered 'dry barren scrubs', and was forced back to the Gascoyne and Lyons rivers.

Near Mount Augustus, which he named after his brother, Gregory found on 2 June 1858 what he called 'strong evidences of the cannibalism of the natives'. Near a camp fire lay 'bones of a full-grown native that had been cooked', with teeth marks on the edges.

FRANCIS THOMAS GREGORY
A CAPABLE YOUNGER BROTHER

Some of the ribs that were lying by huts had part of the cooked flesh still attached.

Although about four hundred thousand hectares of apparently fertile land was discovered during his three-thousand-kilometre trip, the prudent Gregory warned that 'it would be very hazardous to risk flocks and herds' until the country had been visited during different seasons — good and bad.

In 1861 the British and West Australian governments subscribed £3350 to an expedition organised by Francis Gregory and English cotton manufacturers, to explore land around Nickol Bay, near today's Dampier in north-west Australia.

The motive was to import 'a large body of Asiatic labourers' who would grow cotton in the area, replacing supplies lost from the southern states of America during the upheaval caused by the Civil War.

Gregory and his party of eight men sailed to Nickol Bay in April 1861, landing near the mouth of the Nickol river. Here they sowed cotton plants to test the soil, but the experiment was cut short when sailors accidentally burnt the crop during Gregory's absence.

Using twenty horses that had been donated by would-be settlers, Gregory explored the coastal regions, then on 27 May moved south-west to encounter the 'beautiful grassy banks' of the Maitland river.

Gregory continued south-westerly, looking for larger rivers from the interior which might enable him to penetrate the rocky foothills of the Hamersley Range. He named these extensive horizontal sandstone cliffs after Edward Hamersley, one of the expedition's main promoters, little dreaming of the enormous mineral wealth they contained and the role they would play in the future.

On 29 May 1861 Gregory discovered the Fortescue river and named it after C. S. P. Fortescue, Colonial Under-Secretary. Its pools were full of fish, its banks lined with flowering trees and tall fan palms.

Gregory had no doubt that its black peat soil would soon support 'a rich and thriving settlement'. He traced it easterly nearly to the site of today's Millstream, then turned south to discover the Hardey river. Two days more brought him to another river which he named the Asburton. From a point a little beyond it he could see Mount Augustus, which he had named on his earlier trip to the Gascoyne. Satisfied, Gregory returned by a slightly more easterly route to Nickol Bay, discovering more streams and pastures on the way.

On 29 July 1861 Gregory and his men left to explore the country eastward. They discovered more pastoral country near today's Roebourne and the Sherlock river, which Gregory thought 'would in itself support a larger population than is at present contained in the whole of the colony.'

On 27 August Gregory named another river to the east after Lord De Grey, one of his backers. To the south-east he encountered the Oakover river, not realising until later that it connected with the De Grey.

Although water was plentiful, the horses were becoming distressed by continuous travel over rocky ground where feed was scarce. In thirty-eight degrees heat the explorers attempted to penetrate inland through what is now called the Gregory Range.

By 9 September 1861 the horses' eyes were 'absolutely sunk into their heads', while the heads themselves had also shrunk, producing 'a very unpleasant and ghastly expression.'

Ahead of them the explorers could see only dry sandy country. Gregory wrote wistfully that they were within 'a very few miles' of the spot where 'from various geographical data, there are just grounds for believing that a large river may be found to exist, draining Central Australia.'

He was quite wrong. Fortunately for his party's survival, the horses were too exhausted

A prudent warning follows discoveries of seemingly fertile land

Backed by hard-nosed businessmen, Francis Gregory found thousands of hectares of fertile land, but urged his patrons to wait the passing of a few seasons before putting in livestock

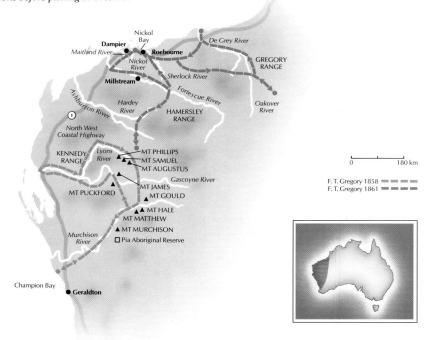

o penetrate further. Gregory followed his
-lder brother's cautious example and on 11
September began the retreat to Nickol Bay,
rriving safely on 17 October.

On his return to Perth, Gregory urged
olonisation of the million or so hectares of
astoral and arable land he had found. He
lso pointed out that beds of pearl shells in
Nickol Bay could be of 'immediate import-
nce' to the colony's economy.

The government assisted by offering set-
lers leaseholds of forty thousand hectares free
or four years. The first man to take up the
and was forty-three-year-old Walter
Padbury, uneducated son of an Oxfordshire
armer, who had risen from being a humble
hepherd near Perth to become a leading
tockholder and miller.

Early in 1863 Padbury took two small
essels filled with the first breeding stock to
he De Grey river. His success soon attracted
ther pastoralists to the area.

Pioneers who tried to settle at Roebuck
Bay in 1864 were less fortunate: they were
lubbed to death by Aboriginals as they slept.

Melbourne-financed groups, which began
perations further north at Camden Harbour
nd the Victoria river in 1864-65, were also
nlucky, most of their sheep dying from
ating unidentified poison weeds.

Yet by 1866, when Edward Hooley opened
he first stock route from Champion Bay to
Nickol Bay, successful settlers were grazing
ixteen thousand sheep and three hundred
attle on one million, two hundred thousand
ectares of the land discovered by Francis
Gregory five years earlier.

*Porcupine grass, often wrongly called spinifex,
rows where little else will on these rocky slopes
olling towards the Hamersley Range. The grass
as little nutritional value for stock*

An artist's adventurous life in the company of explorers

Augustus Gregory was so impressed by the leadership qualities of his expedition's artist, the thirty-four-year-old Norfolk-born Thomas Baines, that he gave him command of a party sent in the *Tom Tough* to buy fresh provisions in the East Indies.

The schooner arrived in Timor on 28 July 1856 in such unseaworthy condition that Baines decided it would be prudent to leave it there for major repairs.

At the end of August 1856 he managed to acquire another schooner, the *Messenger*, and hastily set sail to try to keep his rendezvous with Gregory at the Albert river.

But the weather was against him. Contrary winds and strong currents in the Arafura Sea prevented the schooner's progress. Baines anchored off New Year Island, and prepared the longboat to complete the journey to the Gulf with oars and sail.

The boat was fitted along each side with inflatable tubes, made of canvas and waterproof calico. These were blown up with a pair of bellows connected by a screw valve. According to Baines, the tubes were successful in preventing 'a great deal of the ripple of the sea washing into the boat.'

Baines and two volunteers rowed away from the schooner on 23 October 1856, not knowing that Gregory had already continued his trek into Queensland.

Battling strong gales, the strange little craft clawed its way round the northern Australian coastline. Off Cape Wessel on 7 November the men were attacked by natives in canoes pretending to offer turtles, and had to shoot one man before they fled.

After a journey of more than twelve hundred kilometres, Baines arrived at the Albert river on 17 November 1856 — the day when Gregory's overland party reached the Comet river far to the east.

Fortunately the *Messenger* had been able to make headway, and picked up the men from the longboat at the Albert river.

With a renewal of adverse winds, Baines decided to return to Timor, then sailed round the western and southern coastline to reach Sydney safely on 30 March 1857.

Before coming to Australia, Baines had spent most of his life in Africa, where he served as a war artist during the Kaffir War.

Baines continued his colourful adventures in Africa. In 1858 the famous missionary Dr David Livingstone appointed him artist to the Zambesi expedition. Baines later led an expedition to develop the first Rhodesian gold mines. He died in 1875 while in the middle of plans for further exploration.

Pack horses had to be loaded each day with saddlebags containing the expedition's equipment. The bags hooked onto the saddle and they could be detached easily in an emergency

A classic Australian tragedy: the story of Burke and Wills

Out of the blue, the compact little colony of Victoria decided to solve the mystery of the continent's interior. By the end of the eighteen-fifties, Victoria was the most prosperous corner of Australia. Effects of its huge gold discoveries flowed into every aspect of society. Wealthy squatters grazed flocks and built mansions on fertile lands that only twenty years earlier had been occupied by native tribes. Substantial cities like Melbourne, Geelong and Ballarat arose at strategic points. Culture and science were promoted as the means of developing a superior civilisation. The Age of Optimism was in full swing.

In Melbourne, a branch of the Royal Society met to discuss intellectual questions of the day. Among its members was Ferdinand von Mueller, who had accompanied Augustus Gregory's expedition across northern Australia.

On his return to Melbourne Dr Mueller persuaded the Royal Society to organise an expedition to penetrate central Australia and fill in that great blank region on the map. The Society launched a public appeal. By 1859 a total of £9000 had been subscribed; planning began.

Even before selecting a leader, the Society sent to India for a camel team to transport equipment. Although John Horrocks had pioneered the use of camels in 1846, this was to be the first full-scale test in Australia.

An Englishman named George James Landells was commissioned to bring twenty-five camels from Karachi. To handle them, he engaged three sepoys and a young Irish soldier John King.

This exotic group landed at Station Pier in Melbourne on 15 June 1860. With whites and sepoys dressed in oriental costume, the camels were paraded through enthusiastic crowds to stables behind Parliament House. Here they were joined by several more dromedaries purchased from a vaudeville company.

Meanwhile the Royal Society was trying to find a leader for the expedition. Gregory was approached, but at the age of forty he preferred to take up his appointment as first Surveyor-General of the new colony of Queensland.

The Society advertised for candidates. Finally it selected a thirty-nine-year-old Irish-born police superintendent named Robert O'Hara Burke. The appointment seemed extraordinary to some. Despite an excellent police record, Burke was renowned for emotionalism and impulsiveness. He had no experience at all of exploration or navigation. Yet his undoubted courage and dashing nature must have appealed to the selection committee. Landells was appointed second-in-command.

Burke rapidly got together his equipment. More than twenty tonnes of baggage was accumulated, including guns, rockets, saddlery, one hundred and twenty mirrors for the Aboriginals, tents, camp beds, a library of exploration books, four hundred and fifty-four litres of lime juice and rum to prevent scurvy, and vast quantities of preserved food. Never had such a well-equipped expedition been seen in Australia.

Some later writers claimed that Victoria's real motive in sending the expedition was to lay claim to any pastoral land found in western Queensland. This notion conflicts with the instructions given to Burke. They allowed him remarkable freedom to change course whenever conditions required.

Burke's flexible instructions

On 18 August 1860 the exploration committee instructed Burke in writing to establish a base at Sturt's Cooper creek. From there he should preferably proceed north, and attempt to reach Leichhardt's track near the Gulf of Carpentaria.

Should this route prove impossible, Burke was instructed to turn westwards, and try to connect John McDouall Stuart's recent discoveries with Augustus Gregory's path of 1856.

If this attempt also were to fail, Burke was instructed to link his explorations with those of Francis Gregory near Mount Gould, from there travelling down the Murchison river to the Western Australian coast. It might then be possible to return 'by a more direct route through South Australia to Melbourne'.

The major motive for this wide-ranging expedition appears to be pure curiosity about the unknown inland. It was best expressed at a public dinner before departure, when the Rev. John Storie said to Burke:

If there really exists within our great continent a Sahara — a desert of sands, parent of hot winds, we should like to know the fact. If great lakes on whose verdant banks thousands of cattle might feed, tempt men to build new cities, let us know the character and the promise of the land by the true report of a true man.

On 20 August 1860, a crowd of fifteen thousand loyal Victorians gathered at Royal Park to cheer away their first and last major expedition. 'All classes of society hastened to take a farewell of these pioneers of civilisation and progress, some of whom perchance may never return,' said the *Age* newspaper with mordant accuracy.

In the late afternoon Burke led out the caravan on his handsome dappled grey horse Billy, followed by packhorses, twenty-seven laden camels, and two wagons that were convertible into punts.

As soon as the open plains north of Melbourne were reached, the party split into two lines, with camels on the right, for the horses could not stand their stench. One of the sepoys deserted and fled back to Melbourne when told that dinner would consist of salt pork.

Crowds of settlers and miners came out to farewell the explorers as they

ROBERT O'HARA BURKE
AN IMPROBABLE LEADER

WILLIAM JOHN WILLS
BURKE'S SECOND CHOICE

passed Heathcote, Bendigo and Swan Hill. But already the impetuous Burke was dissatisfied with his progress. Arriving at Balranald on 15 September 1860, he decided to dump half of their tents, sugar and lime juice. Several quarrelsome men were dismissed.

On the Darling river, Burke questioned George Landells's policy of giving rum to the camels and drivers to prevent scurvy. A shouting match developed, Landells resigned, and Burke smashed every bottle of rum.

As his new second-in-command, Burke promoted William John Wills, a twenty-six-year-old Devon-born surveyor and astronomer with no experience of desert conditions.

Despite these problems, Burke safely reached the furthest settlement, the tiny town of Menindee, early in October 1860. He established a depot eleven kilometres up the Darling river, leaving it in charge of Dr Herman Beckler, a German-born surgeon. Beckler resigned after a dispute with Burke about the safety of proceeding further into the interior at that late time of year.

With a more compact party of eight whites and one sepoy, Burke pushed on northwards on 19 October. Each evening they blazed a tree with the letter B and the number of the camp, so that the remainder of the expedition could follow easily with bulk supplies.

On 29 October the advance party reached Torowoto Swamp, sighting Sturt's old track of 1845. They penetrated canegrass swamps to cross today's Queensland border, reaching Bulloo Lake just east of Grey Range. Here were plenty of fish and birds for the pot.

An impulsive decision

On 20 November they camped on Cooper creek. At the time it was not flowing, but consisted of a series of fine waterholes hundreds of metres long, surrounded by reeds, grass, eucalyptus and mulga trees.

Burke and Wills each made quick dashes to the north, but encountered only waterless country and searing temperatures, forcing them back each time. Beside a large coolibah tree, which still stands, they established Depot LXV.

The crucial moment of decision now arrived. If they stayed put during summer, they were reasonably safe. At worst they could fall back on Menindee.

But Burke wanted quick results, a dashing victory. He was aware that far to the west, John McDouall Stuart was probably continuing his heroic efforts to cross the continent from South Australia to the north coast. Burke's committee in Melbourne urged him on, writing 'The honour of Victoria is in your hands.'

A cautious explorer like Gregory would have jibbed. But Burke's impulsive nature was in favour of challenging the unknown — even at the worst time of year. Sudden thunderstorms and the appearance of more rain clouds to the north set his feelings into action.

On 16 December 1860, Burke divided his party yet again. Four men were left behind at Depot LXV to await the main party and build a timber stockade called Fort Wills. In charge was William Brahe, a German-born stockman. Burke left him no written instructions, simply telling him (claimed Brahe) that if the party did not return in three months, Brahe was to take his group back to Menindee.

To accompany him on the eleven-hundred-kilometre dash to the Gulf, Burke chose Wills, a middle-aged former seaman named Charles Gray and the young ex-soldier John King.

They selected the six best camels to carry provisions for three months, and took Burke's horse Billy.

This bold little party headed south-west down Cooper creek on 16 December 1860. Their intention was to find Sturt's northward track of 1845, follow his waterholes, then penetrate further northwards if they could. Wills kept a journal of events in consultation with Burke, who occasionally scribbled random notes in a tattered notebook.

Burke rode his dappled grey horse Billy between the two columns to keep camels and horses apart. The scent and appearance of camels was known to disturb both horses and cattle

Along Cooper creek the men were pestered by Aboriginals, who alternately wanted to steal their belongings or join them in a corroboree. Shots were fired to frighten them away. 'They appear to be mean-spirited and contemptible in every aspect,' wrote Wills, little dreaming what the future held.

On 19 December 1860, Burke left Cooper creek and steered north of west across sand ridges covered with saltbush. At sunset they found several waterholes filled with 'good milky water', so calm that Wills was able to use them as a horizon for his observations.

Wills's misplaced enthusiasm

Next day they came to a large lagoon, swarming with 'wildfowl of every description'. Aboriginals camped on its banks gave them fish in exchange for beads and matches. The whites rejected an offer of native women for the night.

On 21 December the party found yet another 'splendid waterhole' for their camp site. Wills enthused that the country so far was 'of the finest description for pastoral purposes', with plenty of apparently permanent waterholes and feed.

But as they proceeded north-westerly, the high sand ridges became bare and 'exceedingly abrupt'. Lagoons began to dry up and turn salty.

On 23 December the men skirted the edge of Sturt's forbidding Stony Desert. 'About sunset,' wrote Wills, 'three flocks of pigeons passed over us, all going in the same direction, due north.' In fading light the men pressed on, to reach 'a delightful oasis in the desert' which they named Gray's creek after their seaman companion who sighted it first. Here they rested to celebrate Christmas Day twenty-four hours early.

Loading their animals with four hundred and fifty-four litres of fresh water, the party proceeded northerly on 25 December. After a few kilometres, Wills wrote, 'we were agreeably pulled up by a

LUDWIG BECKER
NATURALIST AND ARTIST

magnificent creek', filled with deep fresh water and too wide to cross. Wills thought it might be Eyre creek, but in fact it was the Diamantina river.

The men followed it past today's Birdsville for six days until it turned easterly, where they were able to cross its almost-dry bed. On 30 December they refilled with ten days' supply of water and struck out northerly direct for the Gulf.

On New Year's Day the explorers arrived at King creek, one hundred and twelve kilometres from today's Bedourie. Burke named it after John King. Here there is a gap in Wills's record. All we have is a notation on his map: 'Natives inclined to be troublesome.'

Nothing else is known until 5 January, when the party arrived at today's Burke river, downstream from its junction with Wills creek. Both were of course named after the explorers. Here they found a 'mud paddock' designed for catching fish, and 'heaps of shells' where natives had feasted.

Upstream they sighted two brolgas, further inland than known before. Burke was now feeling the strain of the long trek. 'I am satisfied that the frame of man never was more sorely taxed,' he wrote in a rare mood of complaint.

Burke and Wills *found adequate water, feed for their animals and game for their pot in the expedition's first months. Birds, such as these little corellas (Cacatua pastinator) near the Diamantina River, are still plentiful*

Excellent equipment was one of the expedition's chief assets. Large quantities of preserved food remained with the base groups while Burke's little party starved

The explorers crossed the Tropic of Capricorn. They refilled with water near today's Boulia, and proceeded over grassy plains with 'everything green and luxuriant'. Ducks and pigeons rose from every small creek they passed, while bustards fled from their approach.

By 12 January the party was ascending the De Little Range, crossing several flowing creeks and noting numerous anthills up to one metre high. By 14 January they were in the Standish Ranges a few kilometres east of today's Dajarra.

Another gap now appears in the journals. On 20 January 1861, about forty-eight kilometres from today's Mount Isa, the men passed over stony ground covered with quartz pebbles, and crossed 'very rugged quartz ranges of an auriferous character'. Iron ore was scattered everywhere.

A further week's gap appeared in Wills's journal, while Burke had suspended his notes altogether. On 21 and 22 January they must have passed close to Mary Kathleen uranium mine, with today's Cloncurry a few kilometres further east. On 26 January Wills noted on his map, 'Ants very troublesome.'

His next journal entry, for 27 January 1861, has the party travelling north-easterly by moonlight, and searching for water from springs in the sand. 'Palm trees are numerous, and some bear an abundance of small round dates [nuts], just ripening,' he wrote. A camel named Golah refused to continue.

They were now following the dry sandy bed of the Cloncurry river to its junction with the Flinders river, and thus heading directly for the Gulf. Provokingly, Wills's journal ceased entirely for this final section of the odyssey.

It resumed again on 9 February 1861, when the explorers had somehow reached Camp 119 on the brackish Bynoe river, a tributary of the Flinders. Here heavy rain had fallen and the camels bogged.

Now only about fifty kilometres from the Gulf itself, Burke and Wills decided to leave the rest of the party in camp and make a final dash on foot to the sea. Loading the horse Billy with three days' provisions, the two men floundered through 'soft and rotten' country.

Mangroves bar the way

Near the sea they ate yams abandoned by the Aboriginals, and found 'one of the prettiest' native camps they had seen. On 11 February 1861 they crossed extensive marshes and came to a salt tidal channel surrounded by mangrove swamps.

Even now the two men were to be cheated from their goal. The sea was just beyond, but without a boat they had no way of reaching it or even seeing it. Without making any triumphant note in the journal, they turned back to find their companions at Camp 119 and prepare for the return journey.

The problem now was to get back to Cooper creek before their supplies ran out, and before the time limit of three months expired, when William Brahe was due to return to Menindee.

The journey from Cooper creek to the Gulf had taken nearly two months. More than two-thirds of their provisions were gone. They had only thirty-eight kilos of flour, thirteen kilos of preserved meat, and eleven kilos of biscuit and rice. Burke reduced the daily rations to one hundred and twenty-five grams of flour and a little meat for each man.

New difficulties struck almost immedi-

ately. They had made only a few kilometres south when Wills recorded severe storms on 21 and 22 February 1861. The ground near the Flinders became so boggy the camels could not walk over it.

The storms were followed by days of such humidity, wrote Wills, 'that the slightest exertion made one feel as if he were in a state of suffocation…gave one a helpless feeling of lassitude.'

With constant effort the despondent explorers pushed southwards to the junction of the Flinders and Cloncurry rivers. On firmer ground, the tropical rains left better effects: 'everything is so very fresh and green,' wrote Wills on 25 February. Portulaca could be boiled as vegetables, and there was ample feed for the animals — including the abandoned camel Golah, found on 2 March.

The following evening, at what Wills called Eureka Camp, Charley Gray rode over a huge black and yellow snake, more than two and a half metres long and eighteen centimetres round the belly. The ex-seaman killed it with his stirrup iron. The party ate it at what Wills called 'Feasting Camp', causing Burke to suffer severe giddiness and dysentery.

They rested on 5 March 1861 at the part of the Cloncurry river where Wills had noted 'date palms' on the outward trip. The men feasted on the ripe nuts. Again Golah had to be abandoned, after it refused to go any further.

For several days more, water and feed were plentiful, and the dry desert air began to replace the awful humidity of the Gulf country. The party made fair

On 5 January, 1861, Burke's party sighted two brolgas further inland than they had seen these birds before. Although feeling the strain of his trek, Burke decided to push on for the Gulf, finally reaching his goal in February

progress across grassy plains until 13 March, when torrential rain recommenced. Again the ground turned boggy, impeding the camels' progress.

On 20 March, with rain continuing, Burke decided to lighten the party's load by twenty-seven kilos, leaving various items hanging in a pack from branches. Little progress was made over 'slippery slimy mud' for the next two days, but at least an 'abundance of fine rich portulaca was just bursting into flower along all these channels'.

In what he called Native Dog Camp on 25 March, Wills found Charley Gray hiding behind a tree eating a floury gruel called skilligolee. Gray admitted he had taken the flour without permission.

Burke exploded in rage and gave Gray what John King described as 'six or seven slaps on the ear.' Wills called it 'a good thrashing' and added, 'There is no knowing to what extent he has been robbing us. Many things have been found to run unaccountably short.'

Supplies were now almost exhausted, and they were still only near latitude twenty-four degrees south, about five

The route to the Gulf; and the search expeditions that followed

Sheer determination took Burke and Wills to the Gulf and back to Cooper Creek. They discovered nothing of value, but expeditions in search of them found grazing land and minerals

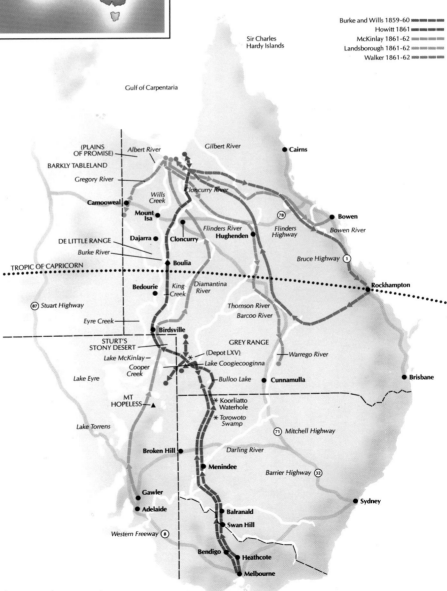

undred kilometres from Cooper creek. On 30 March 1861, at a camp that Wills ardonically named Boocha's Rest, they not the camel Boocha, cut him up, ate s much as their shrunken stomachs could old, and jerked the remaining meat.

By 7 April they were back at the lmost-dry Diamantina river. Its pools ow had 'a slightly brackish taste of a eculiar kind', and most of the green feed or the animals had dried up.

On 8 April, wrote Wills, the party alted fifteen minutes to send back for iray, who gammoned [pretended] he ould not walk.'

Two days later it was time to sacrifice urke's faithful horse Billy, 'who was so educed and knocked up for want of food, hat there appeared little chance of his eaching the other side of the desert.' The eat was 'healthy and tender, but with-ut the slightest trace of fat.' However, it rengthened them sufficiently to traverse turt's Stony Desert again by 15 April.

The ordeal proved too much for harley Gray. He constantly fell behind, nd had to be tied across his camel's addle under the blazing sun. On 16 April e became delirious and died in his edroll before dawn the next day. His eakened companions spent all day cratching out a shallow grave, buried im and placed most of their remaining ossessions in a tree overhead.

udwig Becker, the sensitive talented naturalist ith the expedition, recorded this campsite on the arling, which he shared with the doctor, erman Beckler. Becker, who was in his fifties, ed at Bulloo from dysentery and scurvy

Cooper Creek full of water is an unusual sight. The stream runs through arid country and can remain dry for long periods between rains

The three survivors were now only about one hundred and ten kilometres from Fort Wills. On they crept, carrying rifles, bedding and spades to dig holes in the creek bed. But when they tried, no water could be found.

A huge final effort was made on the weekend of 20 and 21 April 1861. The three men found a waterhole at last, ate all their provisions except a few grams of dried meat, and took turns to ride the two remaining camels.

At last, at 7.30 pm on 21 April, they arrived at Fort Wills, with 'legs almost paralyzed,' wrote Wills, 'so that each of us found it a most trying task only to walk a few yards.'

At the depot all was ominously quiet. Loud coo-ees failed to raise response. Then Wills saw lettering freshly blazed into the coolibah tree — the most famous tree in Australian history. It read:

DIG
3 FT. N.W.
APR. 21 1861

About a metre to the north-west they saw freshly-turned earth. Digging hastily, they found twenty-three kilos of flour, twenty-seven kilos of oatmeal, twenty-seven kilos of sugar, ten kilos of rice, seven kilos of dried meat, and smaller items. 'We were not long in getting out the grub that Brahe had left,' wrote Wills, 'and we made a good supper of some oatmeal porridge and sugar.'

Brahe had also left a note. It communicated 'the pleasing information', Wills wrote ironically, that he had left that very morning for Menindee.

Brahe was entitled to make that decision. He had waited through the long dreary summer more than four months — not the three months he said Burke had requested. He and his men were showing

WILLIAM BRAHE
EXPEDITION FOREMAN

severe symptoms of scurvy. He faced a lengthy almost waterless ride of close to six hundred and fifty kilometres back to Menindee. No messages at all had reached him from the outside world. Any sensible man would have retreated before his own party became endangered.

Burke's dilemma

Now, sitting underneath the Dig tree, Burke was faced with a final crucial decision. The great dash to the Gulf had succeeded, but how could his little party's lives be saved?

The first alternative was to chase along Brahe's tracks. But Burke's men and camels were exhausted, whereas Brahe's were undoubtedly rested and fresh. If they failed to catch up with Brahe, they would surely perish in the long arid stretches to Menindee.

There was an apparently sensible alternative. For the time being they had ample food and water. If they followed Cooper creek west then south, they would come to a police outpost that had been established at Mount Hopeless, two hundred and forty kilometres away.

After resting for two days, the explorers buried a message beneath the Dig tree telling of their adventures and intentions. They neglected to add a new blaze advising any rescuers to dig for it. The oversight sealed their fate.

On 23 April 1861, the still-weak men moved slowly down the south bank of Cooper creek. Although they covered only eight kilometres on the first day, Wills wrote: 'We find the change of diet already making a great improvement in our spirits and strength.' He again began keeping a full journal.

The following day a group of Aboriginals gave them the 'great treat' of five kilos of fish traded in exchange for matches and leather straps.

Through 'splendid saltbush country' with frequent waterholes, camels and

The coolibah tree carved by Brahe with the instruction DIG still stands beside Cooper Creek. Had Burke also marked the tree, or had Brahe checked the cache on his return, the lives of both Burke and Wills might have been saved

men kept on improving. 'The leg-tied feeling is now entirely gone,' Wills wrote on 26 April. 'In less than a week we shall be fit to undergo any fatigue whatever.'

Their misfortunes began again on 28 April. Linda the camel got itself bogged in 'bottomless quicksand'. For two days the men struggled in vain to extricate it, finally shooting it and cutting off whatever flesh they could reach.

The last camel, Rajah, was loaded with all the jerked meat and other goods. On 2 May it began 'trembling greatly' — the warning sign of exhaustion. The men threw away tin plates, sugar, ginger, tea and cocoa to lighten the animal's load.

Collapse of the last camel

Continuing down Cooper creek, the party came to the last waterhole on 4 May. Wills reconnoitred south, but found only cracked soil and sand ridges. On 7 May the camel refused to rise, even without a load. Apparently it soon died, for on 10 May Wills noted that Burke and King were jerking its flesh.

Meanwhile the whites had been befriended by a tribe of blacks. In exchange for pieces of mackintosh, the Aboriginals gave them large quantities of fish, 'a couple of nice fat rats', and 'bread, which they call nardoo.' This was followed with a narcotic of dried leaves known as bedgery, pedgery, or pitchery. 'It has a highly intoxicating effect, even when chewed in small quantities,' Wills noted.

With no water to be found on their intended route, the men realised they would have to live like the Aboriginals for a few months, until the season changed or help came.

On 10 May Wills searched the neighbourhood for nardoo seed, but could find none. However, he gathered and boiled large beans called padlu, which were quite sweet, 'like French chestnuts.'

While Wills tried to devise a way of trapping birds and rats, Burke and King walked along the creek bed looking for their Aboriginal friends. All had disappeared. The three men were now alone.

While all this was happening, William Brahe continued to trek back to Menindee. At Bulloo Lake he met the main body of the expedition, which had lazed at Menindee for several months awaiting further orders, but had at last stirred themselves to travel north.

This part of the expedition, commanded by stockman William Wright, fell into complete chaos. Horses died in the extreme heat, rats and Aboriginals plundered the stores, and five men fell seriously ill with scurvy and dysentery. During February 1861 two of them died. On 28 April the expedition's artist, Dr Ludwig Becker, also succumbed.

The caravan retreated to Koorliatto waterhole so that the other sick men might recover. Brahe meanwhile was having second thoughts about his departure from Cooper creek. What if, against all the odds, Burke had turned up?

On 3 May 1861, Brahe and Wright made a dramatic one hundred and twenty-nine-kilometre dash on horseback to Cooper creek. They examined the Dig tree on 8 May. Nothing new had been carved into it. The ground round about had been raked smooth by King and seemed undisturbed to the rescuers. Fresh campfires on the site were 'undoubtedly' those of Aboriginals.

Satisfied, Brahe and Wright mounted and rode away. Yet on that day, Burke and his companions were only about forty-eight kilometres down the creek

NARDOO'S LIMITED VALUE AS SURVIVAL FOOD

The nardoo plant (*Marsilea drummondii* or *Marsilea hirsuta*) helped Burke and his companions survive for many weeks. This fern grows in swampy land near seasonally flooding inland rivers.

When the swamps dry up, the spore cases fall to the earth and are harvested. The starch-rich spores inside the hard, woody cases are ground between two stones into a yellow flour. The husks must be blown or sifted out before cooking.

On 24 May 1861, Wills wrote in his journal that nardoo cakes had become the party's 'staff of life'.

Collecting the seed was sometimes troublesome, but on 27 May the explorers found a flat expanse covered with an abundant crop. 'The ground in some parts was quite black with it,' Wills wrote.

Unfortunately the nardoo was not nutritious enough to keep Burke and Wills alive the eleven weeks until a rescue party

When the water recedes, the plants wither, leaving their seedpods lying on the ground

arrived. Nardoo was eaten also by John McKinlay's expedition, which attempted to rescue Burke.

'When cooked it is not very nice, leaving a nasty sensation in the throat,' McKinlay wrote in his journal, 'but it will sustain life for a long time.'

Wills exclaiming over the 'nice fat rats' they had been given.

On 16 May 1861, Burke decided to make a last desperate attempt to reach the police post at Mount Hopeless. On the following day, trekking slowly south-west then south-south-west, their confidence increased when they found a flat area covered with nardoo plants. Now, at the worst, 'we were in a position to support ourselves,' Wills wrote.

His journal entries ceased for some days. After seventy-two kilometres through waterless country they were forced to fall back to the Cooper.

On 27 May Wills returned alone towards the depot to deposit his journals. He again encountered the friendly tribe, sharing their gunyah and eating 'abundance of nardoo and fish.'

Next day constipation and 'extremely painful' stools slowed him down. He finally reached the depot on 30 May. 'No traces of any one except blacks having been here since we left,' he wrote on the spot where Brahe and Wright had searched three weeks earlier.

Wills dug up the cache. No, nothing new here. No fresh blaze on the Dig tree. He buried his latest journals and a letter giving their location down the creek — and again left no new sign on the tree.

Feeling 'very weak and tired', Wills gathered and boiled some portulaca on 31 May. By 2 June he was back at the tribe's camp. They had moved on: Wills could find only 'a few fish bones' to grind with

his teeth. Later he saw a large fish trying to swallow a small one: he grabbed them and ate them both.

Next day Wills found the Aboriginals five kilometres downstream. They plied him with fish and nardoo cakes. For three days he stayed 'to see what I could learn as to their ways and manners.'

Returning to Burke and King on 6 June, Wills learned they too had been 'well supplied' by the Aboriginals for a time. But Burke had fired his revolver at a native trying to steal some oilcloth from their gunyah. The whole tribe vanished, leaving the weakening whites to gather nardoo as best they could. On 10 June they shot a crow, but three days later felt so weak they could scarcely drag themselves to the waterhole.

Death by starvation

For a fortnight the men continued to exist mainly on nardoo. On 16 June they finished the last of the camel meat.

Wills found himself 'completely reduced' by the diet, which gave him 'enormous stools' but little nourishment. Burke too began to fail; while King 'holds out by far the best.'

By 22 June Wills was unable to stand up. His legs and arms were 'nearly skin and bone.' Even King was now 'terribly cut up' and could no longer gather enough seed for all three men.

At the end of June 1861 Burke decided their only hope was to go in search of the Aboriginals. He and King left

three and a half kilos of nardoo cakes with the helpless Wills and began to walk back along the creek.

Burke collapsed on the second day, probably 29 June. In a despairing note to the exploration committee he wrote: *I hope we shall be done justice to. We fulfilled our task, but were [*here Burke began to write abandoned, but crossed it out*] not followed up as I expected. The depot party abandoned their post. R. O'Hara Burke.*

That night Burke asked King to put his pistol in his right hand and told him to continue alone. Next morning Burke could not speak: he died at about 8 am.

King wandered on for some days, existing on nardoo, then was lucky enough to shoot four birds. Three he took back to Wills, but when he got there, Wills too was dead.

King returned up the creek and finally found the tribe. 'They appeared to feel great compassion for me,' he said later, 'and gave me plenty to eat.' He shot several crows for them, and cured one woman's ulcerated arm with silver nitrate. After that she fed him nardoo morning and evening.

For two months King lived a nomadic life with the tribe until the first relief party arrived to rescue him and take the tragic tale to the outside world. □

Burke, Wills and King *read the note telling them that the base party had left only hours before. Gill's painting shows their dejection but not the horrors of their physical condition*

Howitt finds King and retrieves the bodies of Burke and Wills

Concern over the vanished explorers began to spread in Melbourne even while Burke, Wills and King were fighting their way back from the Gulf to Cooper creek. Urged on by Wills's father, Victorian newspapers began campaigning for the expedition committee to send a search party.

A party of four rescuers finally left Melbourne on 26 June 1861 — a few days before Burke died of starvation on Cooper creek.

In command was Alfred William Howitt, an experienced thirty-one-year-old anthropologist and bushman. At Swan Hill they met William Brahe, who gave them the first intimations of disaster. Howitt strengthened his party, taking some of the original men and camels back to Menindee, site of Burke and Wills's first depot.

On 13 September 1861, he arrived at the Dig tree on Cooper creek. Brahe assured him that nothing there had changed. There were no fresh blazes on the tree.

Howitt took Brahe's word, leaving the cache undisturbed. The party continued downstream, and on 15 September found

camel and horse tracks running everywhere.

Edwin Welch, a surveyor with the rescue party, rode off to examine a branch of the creek. His horse bolted towards a group of Aboriginals, scattering them and leaving behind a 'solitary figure, apparently covered with some scarecrow rags.' The sun-blackened derelict, wrote Howitt, 'tottered, threw up its hands in the attitude of prayer, and fell on the ground.'

It was John King, the sole survivor. Fed on rice, butter and sugar, King slowly recovered and told Howitt his appalling story.

Two days later King was able to lead the party to Wills's shallow grave. Dingoes had dug up the body and savaged it, but his journals were recovered — and that is why we know most of the tragic story of Burke and Wills today.

On 21 September 1861, Burke's partly-eaten body was also found. The rescue party placed it in a Union Jack and buried it in a deep grave under a box tree. 'It is impossible to describe the feelings of sadness and awe,' wrote a solemn Howitt, 'that filled our minds

ALFRED HOWITT
EXPLORER AND
ACCOMPLISHED BUSHMAN

This massive monument eventually marked the Melbourne graves of Burke and Wills. The 36 tonne block of raw granite was hauled 100 kilometres from quarries in Harcourt. Monuments and memorial stones sprang up in Victorian provincial cities and along the explorers' route into the interior, as well as in Totnes, Wills's birthplace in Devon, England

s we gazed on the spectacle — the remains of brave Burke.'

Howitt tried to send the news back to Melbourne by carrier pigeons, but kites swooped out of the sky and destroyed them. He distributed presents to the Aboriginals who had helped Burke's party, including twenty-three kilos of what they called 'white fellow nardoo' — milled flour.

On 28 September 1861, the cache under the Dig tree was at last exhumed: Howitt now knew the full horror that had befallen the expedition, with all its missed chances.

They caused an extraordinary sensation when released in Melbourne. A Royal Commission set up to investigate causes of the débâcle blamed Burke for setting off for the Gulf without waiting for the main party, William Wright for not hastening north from Menindee and opening the cache, and the exploration committee for not stirring itself to action sooner.

Alfred Howitt returned to the Cooper to dig up the explorers' bones for Victoria's first state funeral, held on 21 January 1863.

Melbourne had never known such a day. About forty thousand people lined the streets to watch the massive funeral carriage, drawn by six black horses, escorted by dragoons and a military band. The Governor himself took part in the long procession to the cemetery.

A thirty-six tonne monolith of raw Harcourt stone was later lowered over the grave, on a pedestal extolling Burke and Wills as 'comrades in a great achievement, companions in death, and associates in renown.'

The two men were also the subject of the first bronze statue ever made in Victoria, which today stands in the City Square. All told, the government spent nearly £60 000 on the original expedition, rescue parties, inquiries and memorials — equivalent to several million dollars today.

A public subscription raised £3135 for King, the survivor. He never fully recovered, and died in St Kilda of tuberculosis nine years later, aged thirty-three.

The Victorian Government voted £2090 to Wills's mother in Devon and £500 each to his two sisters.

Burke left seven shillings and eight pence in his bank account, and a debt of £18 5s 3d to the Melbourne Club. It was finally settled by the discredited exploration committee.

Yet Burke scarcely deserves the opprobrium which has clung to his name ever since the disaster. After achieving the expedition's aim, he seemed to be pursued by a malignant fate determined to destroy him.

Faced with the same circumstances at each crucial turning point, most experienced explorers would probably have made the same decisions. All that Burke needed was a little more luck, and that was denied him.

JOHN KING
SOLE SURVIVOR

A funeral carriage *that was a replica of the one which bore the Duke of Wellington to his grave in St Paul's Cathedral, London, carried Burke and Wills to their resting place*

Deserts like this *defeated Burke and Wills: 'extensive flats, sandy plains, covered with herbs dried like hay', Wills wrote to his sister*

Search and rescue parties go looking for Burke and Wills

'The entire company of explorers has been dissipated out of being, like dewdrops before the sun,' the Melbourne *Age* said angrily in June 1861.

While supporting Howitt's expedition to find Burke, the newspaper urged the committee to send a second party by ship to the Gulf, in case Burke and his companions were trapped there.

The Victorian government agreed to dispatch its pride and joy, Her Majesty's colonial ship *Victoria*. The five hundred and eighty tonne steam sloop was the first warship built for any British colony and was the keystone of Victoria's defences.

HMCS *Victoria* left Melbourne on 4 August 1861, accompanied by the brig *Firefly*, considered more suitable for sailing shallow waters near the coast.

The Queensland government cooperated by supplying a party of eight men (including four black trackers) under William Landsborough, a thirty-six-year-old Scot.

HMCS Victoria, carrying 158 crew and under the command of Captain W.H. Norman, was dispatched to spend six months as a search base

They left Brisbane on the *Firefly* on 24 August 1861. Eleven days later the brig struck a reef off the Sir Charles Hardy Islands, and the party's horses had to be swum ashore.

The *Victoria* managed to pull *Firefly* off the reef and tow her to the Albert river in the Gulf by 1 October 1861. By this time Howitt had already found the bodies of Burke and Wills, but there was no quick way of sending this news to the north.

On 15 November 1861, Landsborough was ready to leave the Gulf. South-south-west of the Albert river he discovered another large stream, which he named the Gregory river after the Queensland Surveyor-General.

Early in December the party found themselves on 'a finely undulating, park-like plateau...richly clothed with the best grasses.' They named it the Barkly Tableland after Sir Henry Barkly, Governor of Victoria.

John McKinlay (centre) poses with members of his search party: (from left) John Davis, Bobby Poole, J.P. Kirby and P. Wylde. They spent nine days marooned by floodwaters on a hilltop not far from where Burke and Wills died of thirst

On 20 December 1861, Landsborough came to another large but almost dry water-course on an extensive blacksoil plain. He named it the Herbert river, but this was later changed to the Georgina, after the Queensland Governor's wife.

Returning past today's Camooweal to the Albert river, Landsborough learned that another bushman, Frederick Walker, had found Burke's tracks on the Flinders river.

Landsborough decided to set out for the Flinders with a dual purpose: to discover further traces of the missing explorers, or if

that failed, to report on pastoral country.

Late in February 1862, Landsborough came to the extensive Plains of Promise seen years before by John Lort Stokes of the *Beagle.* Fortunately it was a dry season, and Landsborough rode across the plains.

From the Flinders river Landsborough turned west past today's Richmond and Hughenden, then south to the Barcoo and Warrego rivers.

This route yielded him no further trace of Burke's path, but it did lead to the discovery of a great deal of new pastoral country. Only then he reached a station near today's Cunnamulla did Landsborough hear the result of Howitt's expedition.

In October 1862 Landsborough at last reached Melbourne. He was acclaimed as the first explorer to cross all Australia from north to south and his glowing reports caused a rush of settlers to the Gulf country.

The explorer later became a controversial police magistrate at Burketown. Towards the end of his life he was awarded £2000 for his Gulf country discoveries.

McKinlay too finds a grave in the desert

A further Burke rescue effort was mounted by the South Australian government. It appointed a tall, shy, forty-two-year-old Scottish-born bushman named John McKinlay to lead a horse and camel party of ten men to the north.

McKinlay set out from Gawler on 14 August 1861, on the same day that Landsborough's sea-borne expedition left Brisbane for the Gulf. By 22 September McKinlay arrived at the northernmost squatting station, Blanchewater, and five days later passed Lake Torrens.

On 28 September 1861, the men in charge of the four camels lost themselves in what was then called the Fifty Miles Desert. Roaming without water for two days, 'death seemed inevitable.' Under the blazing sun, they tied themselves on the camels' backs and gave them their heads. The animals immediately turned south, and after travelling all night, arrived at 'a beautiful sheet of water' which saved their lives.

McKinlay established a base at Lake Buchanan, now Lake Coogiecooginna, near Cooper creek for several weeks. Following Howitt, he found many traces of Burke's party, and dug up Charley Gray's grave.

On the night of 28 October 1861, a savage storm 'rent to atoms' their tents and blew many of their possessions into the desert.

But McKinlay still had plenty of provisions. On 17 December 1861 he decided to leave the Cooper and press on regardless — a decision which nearly involved his party in tragedy similar to Burke's.

On 20 December 1861, the explorers arrived at a deep freshwater lake which they named Lake McKinlay. Here they enjoyed 'splendid bathing' and shooting.

Heavy rain commenced early in February 1862. On 14 February the expedition crossed Burke's track and came across the skeleton of his horse Billy, which had been killed and eaten ten months before.

The ground everywhere was now turning into bog. McKinlay found that he was being forced steadily to the east of Burke's track. By 2 April 1862, the party's flour was almost finished. 'We are all as hungry as hunters,' wrote one of his party, John Davis.

There was no way for McKinlay to return via the western shores of Lake Eyre to Adelaide, as instructed. The only course was to plod on to the Gulf and hope to catch HMCS *Victoria* before it left.

By early May 1862 the party had followed the Leichhardt and Albert rivers to the Gulf, where a shark was caught to eke out their rations. There was no sign of a ship.

Diet of boiled crow and bullock hide

After having travelled more than thirty-two hundred kilometres, the weakened men were now faced with a trek of close to one thousand kilometres to Queensland.

The party continued to the Gilbert river by 16 June 1862, when all their provisions were gone. Here John Davis wrote: 'The old camel is to be killed! Old and worn out, with sores all over him, he will be a nice morsel, without the slightest bit of fat to be seen.'

On 5 July 1862, the explorers arrived at the Burdekin river and followed its north bank downstream, eating boiled crow and bullock hide.

Near the coast they loaded their belongings on a hastily-built raft on 27 July and crossed with crocodiles (misnamed alligators) swimming close by. 'I never expected to get across,' wrote Davis. 'I thought that one of us must go, as the alligators were close to us.'

The last camel was killed and eaten on 30 July. Suddenly, after riding on for sixteen kilometres, the party spied cattle tracks and then two white men. The expedition had arrived at the furthest station on the Bowen river, and was safe. Back in Adelaide by October 1862, McKinlay was awarded £1000 and his men six months' pay each.

The final Burke rescue expedition was led by Frederick Walker, forty-one-year-old commandant of native police who had been dismissed for drunkenness.

Walker led a party of eleven men on horseback from Rockhampton on 7 September 1861. Quickly he had them across the Barcoo and Thomson to the Flinders river, where he found Burke's last camp, and reported the fact to HMCS *Victoria.*

Walker then followed Burke's tracks southwards for some distance. Running short of food, he and his men returned during March 1862, where they heard of Howitt's success.

None of these relief expeditions could have done anything to succour Burke and Wills. Their main value was in discovering new grazing and mining areas, and showing that determined men, well equipped, could survive in many parts of the inland.

John McDouall Stuart blazes a trail through the centre of the continent

JOHN McDOUALL STUART
SURVEYOR AND EXPLORER

While Burke and Wills were undergoing their agony, an experienced explorer of a different kind was persistently pressing northwards, on a roughly parallel route some hundreds of kilometres further to the west.

John McDouall Stuart, born in Scotland in 1815, had been a member of Charles Sturt's expedition of 1844, which tried to penetrate to the continent's geographical centre.

After that failure, Stuart worked as a surveyor and real estate agent for many years. But when the South Australian government in 1859 offered a reward of £2000 to the first person to cross Australia from south to north, Stuart took up the challenge.

In 1858 and 1859 Stuart had led minor but strenuous expeditions west of Lake Eyre, searching for new grazing lands. His discoveries during these explorations, named after prominent South Australians, included Davenport creek (George Davenport), Hawker creek (G. C. Hawker), Blyth creek (Arthur Blyth), Hanson Rise (R. D. Hanson), Mount Kingston (G. S. Kingston), Peake creek (C. J. Peake), Neales river (J. B. Neale), Mount Harvey (J. Harvey), Mount Dutton (F. T. Dutton), and Mount O'Halloran (T. S. O'Halloran).

Stuart became fascinated all over again by 'the mysterious interior of Australia'. He felt drawn ever northwards, fanatical in his ambition to solve its mysteries. On 2 March 1860, he left Chambers creek with a small party, hoping for a quick dash to the Gulf. Heavy rain started a few days later, and one horse was lost crossing the Peake creek. By late March, Stuart came to good soil along Frew (now Hamilton) creek: 'the best for grass that I have ever gone through'.

On 1 April 1860, Stuart realised that his right eye, damaged by many years of taking solar observations, had become useless. 'I now see two suns instead of one, which has led me into an error of a few miles,' he wrote despondently.

But he pressed on, across today's South Australian border, then slightly west of today's town of Finke, naming Mount Beddome, Mount Daniel and Mount Humphries. On 4 April Stuart discovered a fine stream flowing south, surrounded by 'beautiful red soil' and

The northward view from the peak showed sandy and apparently waterless country. On 25 April Stuart headed northwesterly to discover Mount Denison, with its abundant freshwater springs and luxuriant feed, naming it after the New South Wales Governor.

Two days later he climbed the nearby 1139-metre Mount Leichhardt, naming it after the explorer. Further to the northwest, Stuart also climbed Mount Barkly, naming it after the Victorian Governor. But the country now seemed waterless once again.

By 13 May 1860, feeling very stiff and ill after being thrown from his horse, Stuart was forced to retreat to Central Mount Stuart for water and rest.

Provisions were running short. 'Scurvy has taken a very serious hold of me,' wrote Stuart. 'My hands are a complete mass of sores that will not heal...My mouth and gums are now so bad that I am obliged to eat flour and water boiled.'

Stuart remained determined. 'I must now do everything that is in my power to break this barrier that prevents me from getting to the north,' he wrote on 16 May. Next day he observed that 'the muscles of my limbs are changing from yellow-green to black.' Yet — 'I am determined not to give in.'

When one of his men found a small supply of water to the north, Stuart decided to push on, although writing, 'I could hardly sit in my saddle.' They were now close to today's Stuart Highway.

In succession the tired party passed and named Mount Gwynne (after South Australian Justice E. C. Gwynne), the Forster Range (after Anthony Forster, MLC), and Mount Strzelecki. Although in considerable pain, the men climbed prominent points to build stone cairns as surveying points. 'It is killing work,' wrote Stuart.

On 29 May 1860, the explorer named

large gum trees. He named it the Finke river after William Finke of Adelaide, who had financed much of Stuart's previous exploration.

To the north Stuart could see a range of flat-topped hills, with one pillar sticking up like 'a locomotive engine with its funnel.' Reaching this remarkable sandstone feature on 6 April 1860, he named it Chambers Pillar after wealthy landowner James Chambers, who had helped to finance the current expedition.

Other hills nearby resembled 'old castles in ruins', standing in the midst of sandhills and thickets. After examining them with great difficulty — 'hands torn by the scrub, and the flies a perfect torment' — Stuart named the area the MacDonnell Ranges after Sir Richard MacDonnell, Governor of South Australia. At his nearest point, Brinkley Bluff, Stuart was about fifty kilometres west of today's Alice Springs.

On 22 April 1860, Stuart wrote: 'Today I find from my observations of the sun [with his left eye] that I am now camped in the centre of Australia.' Next day the men climbed the nearest red sandstone peak, Central Mount Stuart, and planted the Union Jack on a pole supported by large stones.

'We then gave three hearty cheers for the flag, the emblem of civil and religious liberty,' wrote Stuart.

The unstoppable Stuart pushes through the centre to the north

John Stuart, an unlikely hero who was orphaned by the age of 13 and was labelled 'delicate' when he arrived in Australia, went on to become the first white man to stand in the country's geographical centre and the first to press on from there to the northern sea. The breakthrough to the centre came after Stuart discovered Chambers Creek while on an expedition to find grazing land west of Lake Torrens. He used the passage to take subsequent expeditions through to the north, but was forced back twice before achieving his goal, reaching Chambers Bay in July 1862

Stuart 1860-62 ▬▬▬

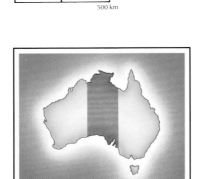

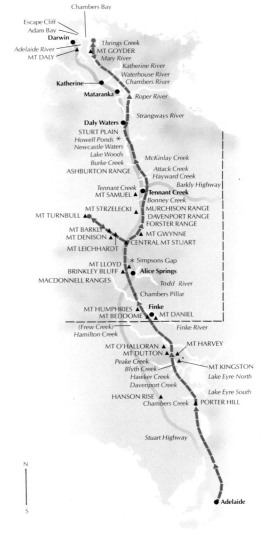

500 km

the sandstone and quartz Davenport Range after Samuel Davenport, MLC, and on 1 June the Bonney creek after Charles Bonney, Commissioner of Crown Lands. Discovery of water and fish in the creek revitalised the party.

On the north bank, they began ascending granite hills which Stuart named the Murchison Range, after Sir Roderick Murchison. On 5 June he climbed the 436-metre ironstone Mount Samuel, naming it after his brother. Today's town of Tennant Creek lies five kilometres to the north-north-east.

A few kilometres further on, Stuart discovered a watercourse lush with 'excellent feed', which he named Tennant creek after John Tennant of Port Lincoln.

With renewed energy, the party pushed another fifty kilometres north to discover Hayward creek, named after Frederick Hayward, and after that a sheet of water abounding in birds and fish.

Strategic retreat at Attack Creek

About ten kilometres further north, at what Stuart called Attack creek, his expedition came to a sudden end.

On 26 June 1860, a group of 'tall powerful fellows' sprang fully armed out of the scrub. They seemed 'in a great fury', bawling and 'performing some sort of a dance.' Stuart made signs of peace, but in reply was showered with boomerangs. His little party was pursued back to Hayward creek.

Stuart reluctantly decided it would mean destruction to continue. Prudently, he realised that 'all the information of the interior that I have already obtained would be lost' unless he retreated.

On the return trip the party found that native cucumber and other vegetables

had shot up. They ate copious quantities boiled in sugar, relieving the symptoms of scurvy by the time they returned to Chambers creek in September 1860.

When Stuart got back to Adelaide the following month, the Victorian expedition under Burke had already reached its main base at Menindee. The competitive spirit spread to South Australians. Their government promptly voted £2500 to enable Stuart to equip himself more thoroughly for the race to be first to reach the north coast.

Late in November 1860 Stuart's party of twelve men and forty-nine horses (but no camels) set off. Problems with 'town bred' horses kept them at Chambers creek until 1 January 1861. After that they made good time back to the MacDonnell Range by March. Here the rain 'came down in torrents', delaying their progress but assuring sufficient feed and water.

This time they passed their previous furthest point at Attack creek without trouble, and kept on northwards during April and May 1861.

Early in June Stuart discovered Newcastle Waters, a stream running into Lake Woods from the north.

On 6 April 1860, *Stuart and his party of four came upon a huge pillar of standstone, rising more than 30 metres out of the desert. This sketch is by G. F. Angas, for Stuart's journals*

Chambers Pillar *still stands out above the sandy plain, a natural monument to John Stuart, one of the nation's grittiest explorers. Many explorers were to use it as a landmark*

On his left hand, to the west, all he could see was the practically featureless Sturt Plain, with 'a few sand rises having scrub on them.' This seemed to form 'a complete barrier between me and the Victoria River.' Several attempts to cross it simply exhausted the party and used up provisions. The horses, wrote Stuart on 12 June, 'look as if they had done a month's excessive work.'

Stuart retreated to the Ashburton Range, planning to circumvent the vast waterless plain by travelling north-east to the Gulf. On 1 July he discovered McKinlay creek, naming it after John McKinlay, and followed it north-east through stony country to a low hill. From here he looked out over 'a complete sea of white grassy plains.' But again there was 'No appearance of water' and it seemed 'hopeless to proceed further.'

On 10 July Stuart returned to his base camp at Burke creek, named after the explorer who had died only a few days earlier on Cooper creek, although Stuart could not know this. At Burke creek the Aboriginals had attacked with boomerangs and scattered the spare horses.

By this time the men's boots had

disintegrated and, wrote Stuart, 'We are all nearly naked.' They were ten weeks' ride from the nearest station, but only four weeks' provisions were left. On 12 July 1861, Stuart once again confessed failure and turned the party homewards.

With everything he had learned about the northern country, Stuart was convinced that just one further push would see him through to the coast.

Indomitably, he returned to Newcastle Waters with another party of ten men in April 1862. He established a depot at Howell Ponds (named after John Howell of Adelaide), a few kilometres west of today's Stuart Highway.

On 23 May 1862, riding almost due north, Stuart found a small creek which soon began 'improving wonderfully'. It broadened, deepened, became 'splendidly grassed' and was surrounded by gum and mulga forest with crimson-blossomed bean trees. Stuart named the area Daly

Waters, after Sir Dominick Daly, newly appointed Governor of South Australia.

Stuart's intention was still to try for the Gulf. He headed north-north-east, to find on 14 June 1862 the Strangways river, named after H. B. Strangways, South Australian Crown Lands Commissioner. But there was no water, and the grass was 'quite dry and withered.'

Persevering, on 25 June Stuart arrived at 'a large sheet of deep clear water', the junction of the Strangways and Roper rivers. The party traced the Roper upstream, followed by Aboriginals who set fire to the grass. 'They are not to be trusted', wrote Stuart. 'They will pretend the greatest friendship one moment and spear you the next.'

On 27 June the party succeeded in crossing the broad Roper, in an area which Stuart thought was 'certainly the finest country I have seen in Australia' with excellent soil and tall waving grass.

Water draws Stuart northwards

'I must go where the water leads me,' Stuart had written earlier that month. Following this principle, the Roper took them back westwards, where on 30 June Stuart named a tributary the Chambers river, after his friend James Chambers.

Still tracing the Roper, on 5 July 1862 Stuart passed over today's Mataranka Station. Here he found a large river branch coming from the north, which he named the Waterhouse after H. W. Waterhouse, the expedition's naturalist.

Once again, on 8 July 1862 Stuart discovered the Katherine river, naming it after a daughter of Chambers.

Success was at last within Stuart's grasp. Disregarding renewed symptoms of scurvy, on 10 July he arrived at an upper reach of the Mary river. He was delighted by beautiful views of gorges and tableland, its valleys filled with tall fan palms which the explorers saw for the first time.

Further north Stuart named Mount Daly after the Governor, and Mount Goyder after the Surveyor-General.

A surprise for weary men: the sea

After crossing swampy ground where 'clouds of mosquitoes gave them no rest night and day', the party arrived at the northward-flowing Thrings creek, named by Stuart after one of his men.

The explorer knew by his observations that they were now near the sea, but kept it from his men as a surprise. At last, on 24 July 1862, after crossing a broad valley and penetrating a line of dense bushes, Stuart 'advanced a few yards on to the beach, and was gratified and delighted to behold the water.' His startled men 'gave three long and hearty cheers.'

The happy group made camp by Chambers Bay, named in honour of a

DARWIN IS CHOSEN FOR A TOWNSHIP

Three British tries at colonising the exposed northern coastline had failed by 1838. In 1863 South Australia annexed the territory and in 1868 made its seat of government the new town at Port Darwin, named Palmerston by the Surveyor-General, George Goyder

After Stuart's success, the South Australian government sent explorer John McKinlay by sea in 1865 to select a base for permanent settlement of the north.

Others favoured Adam Bay, outlet of the Adelaide river. McKinlay insisted that Port Darwin, discovered by HMS *Beagle* in 1839, was far superior because of its port and hinterland.

McKinlay continued overland to the east, and was trapped in June 1866 by the flooded Adelaide river system.

The expedition's horses were shot, their flesh jerked for food, and their hides stretched over the framework of a large boat made from bush timber. In this crude craft, all fifteen men managed to cross the rippling floodwaters and land safely at Escape Cliff after a risky six-day voyage.

On their return to Adelaide, McKinlay's advice on Darwin was accepted. The South Australian Surveyor-General, G. W. Goyder (already famous for his rainfall line showing the safe limits of agricultural expansion), was sent to Darwin in 1869 to survey town and country allotments.

Hundreds of settlers soon began arriving, completing British-Australian domination of the whole continent.

daughter of James Chambers who had made Stuart a Union Jack with his name embroidered in the centre. This flag was raised at the mouth of the Mary river, which Stuart had thought was the Adelaide, on 25 July. The future port-city of Darwin lay about one hundred kilometres to the south-west.

Stuart felt he had now achieved all his objects. The party had travelled through 'one of the finest countries men could wish to behold.' From Newcastle Waters to the sea, 'the main body of horses have been only one night without water,' Stuart wrote enthusiastically. 'If this country is settled, it will be one of the finest Colonies under the Crown.'

The return journey nearly ended in tragedy. Back on the Strangways river by August 1862, Stuart became almost blind with glare and scurvy. 'I am now quite incapable of taking observations at night,' he wrote on 21 August.

By mid-October his legs had gone. 'I was then enduring the greatest pain and agony that it is possible for a man to suffer,' Stuart wrote. Each morning he had to be lifted into the saddle. On 20 October his ankles turned 'quite black'. On the twenty-sixth his men constructed a stretcher between two horses and carried him that way, until one of the horses kicked it to pieces.

After riding again, Stuart was 'seized with a violent fit of vomiting blood and mucus.' By 28 October he could give no more orders: 'the power of speech has completely left me.' He was now 'reduced to a perfect skeleton.' The younger men shot a horse and feasted, but Stuart could swallow only tea and boiled flour.

Rebuilding the stretcher, the men managed to get Stuart back to Porter Hill on 7 December 1862. Here he slowly recovered, although so affected that he lived less than four years more.

Significant political results follow

After a huge public welcome in Adelaide on 21 January 1863, Stuart was awarded the life income on a fund of £3000: his companions shared £1500.

All told, the explorer had ridden more than sixteen thousand kilometres in his dogged search for an overland route. His success had significant political results: in July 1863 control of the Northern Territory was transferred from New South Wales to South Australia, which became responsible for it until 1910.

South Australia also became prime mover in the gigantic task of building an overland telegraph line, which followed Stuart's path most of the way. Eventually, road and rail links followed the same route through the continent's heart.□

A triumph of construction: the Overland Telegraph Line

Telegraph station at The Peake in 1890. During construction each station was sent 'two years' supply of rations and . . . seeds . . . everything that will conduce to the health and comfort of persons living in the distant interior'

Only seven years after Stuart's return from the north, work began on the mighty Overland Telegraph project, which would give an isolated Australia instantaneous communication with the rest of the world.

In 1870 the British-Australian Telegraph Company accepted South Australia's proposal to connect an underwater cable extending

Builders of the Telegraph: *From left, Darwin's postmaster J.A.G. Little, engineer Robert Patterson, Todd, and surveyor A.J. Mitchell*

from Java to Darwin with a twenty-nine hundred-kilometre overland wire built between Darwin and Adelaide. The Australian end of this vast project was controlled by Charles Todd, Postmaster-General.

Todd immediately sent John Ross, a fifty-three-year-old Scottish-born bushman, to mark a trail from Adelaide to Katherine. This had to have enough water and good timber to supply the labouring parties who would be raising thirty-six thousand poles. Ross followed Stuart's route practically all the way,

except in the MacDonnell Ranges where he deviated to discover the Todd river. Another party under W. W. Mills discovered the site of today's Alice Springs (named after Mrs Alice Todd), and Simpsons Gap between Mount Lloyd and the MacDonnell Ranges.

Completion of the Telegraph Line in the tropical north was a trial of endurance. By 22 August 1872 the first overseas cables were being received in Adelaide, and Australia's isolation from the western world had been ended for all time.

CHARLES AND ALICE TODD
HE WAS POSTMASTER-GENERAL

John Forrest finds new routes between Perth and Adelaide

In 1867 the Canadian colonies federated into one British Dominion. Two years later the Suez Canal opened, bringing Britain's empire ever closer together. Most of the Australian continent east of the projected Overland Telegraph Line had now been explored and mapped. But west of the line, vast unknown areas still teased many minds.

A young Western Australian surveyor named John Forrest, born in 1847 of poor Scottish immigrants, set out to solve these mysteries.

In 1869 Forrest was appointed to lead a six-man expedition from Perth north-east into unknown arid areas, where Aboriginals had reported sighting the bones of murdered white men. Perhaps they were the remains of Leichhardt's party lost some twenty years before?

During his one hundred and thirteen-day search, Forrest came to the large brackish Lake Barlee, naming it after West Australian Colonial Secretary Frederick Barlee.

Other landmarks discovered included Mounts Ida, Leonora, Malcolm and Margaret. Forrest recommended that a geologist should be sent to examine these thoroughly: one day they would yield huge mineral wealth.

But there was no trace of Leichhardt's party or of the fine lands claimed by Aboriginal informants. Forrest wrote disgustedly: 'What a native calls good country is where he can get a drink of water and a wurrong [desert rat]; and if there is an acre of grassy land they describe it as a very extensive grassy country.'

Early in 1870 Governor Sir Frederick Weld commissioned John Forrest to make a careful examination of the pastoral possibilities of the unseen country inland from the Great Australian Bight.

Since Eyre's epic trip thirty years before, no one had succeeded in getting to Western Australia except by sea. Prospects of federation made it desirable to find a land route and establish settlements if possible.

Forrest planned the venture as carefully as he could. The schooner *Adur* was sent to the safe harbours of Israelite Bay and Eucla, and instructed to wait at each place with reserve supplies until the overland party arrived.

Forrest's six-man group, including his young brother Alexander as second-in-command, left Esperance on 9 May 1870. They traversed poorly-grassed plains to Israelite Bay, re-provisioned, and celebrated Queen Victoria's birthday on 24 May with a twenty-one gun salute fired from their rifles.

The explorers set out on the dangerous trip to Eucla over five hundred kilometres away, on 30 May 1870, carrying three months' provisions on horseback.

While most of the party stayed near the coast with the packhorses, Forrest made 'flying trips' inland. He discovered considerable areas of grassy country, but each time was forced to keep searching for rock holes containing fresh water.

Even fifty to sixty kilometres inland, none of the hoped-for fresh streams or lakes could be found. 'Since leaving Cape Arid I have not seen a gully or water-course of any description — a distance of 400 miles,' Forrest wrote on his arrival at Eucla on 2 July 1870. Ample supplies could be found there by digging wells.

Vast grasslands — but no water

A gap of two hundred and twenty-five kilometres still remained to the nearest South Australian settlement at Fowlers Bay. On 8 July the explorers farewelled the *Adur* and pushed out over 'vast grassy plains', that seemed almost waterless.

With only one hundred and thirty-six litres of water carried on horseback, the party barely managed to reach the head of the Bight late on 17 July 1870. 'Many of the horses could scarcely walk, and a few were delirious,' Forrest wrote. Yet by digging less than a metre into the sand an 'abundance of water' was found. 'We all felt very tired,' Forrest added languidly.

On 23 July the travellers reached Colona, westernmost station of Degraves

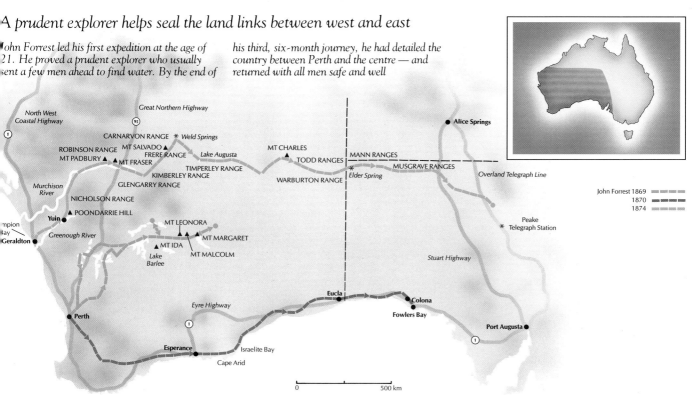

A prudent explorer helps seal the land links between west and east

John Forrest led his first expedition at the age of 21. He proved a prudent explorer who usually sent a few men ahead to find water. By the end of his third, six-month journey, he had detailed the country between Perth and the centre — and returned with all men safe and well

John Forrest 1869
1870
1874

and Company. Here they were met by a police trooper sent to escort them to Fowlers Bay. By 25 August 1870 they reached Adelaide, and were greeted with 'hearty cheers' along their route.

The expedition had apparently achieved little more than Eyre's. 'We passed over many millions of acres of grassy country,' Forrest reported, 'but I am sorry to say I believe entirely destitute of permanent water.'

However, the political results were important. By 1877 a telegraph line was completed, largely along Forrest's track, putting Western Australia in touch with the eastern colonies and the world.

Sea communication remained of greatest importance to the west, but during the twentieth century modern road and rail systems were built near the explorers' southern routes.

Forrest turns to the centre

Meanwhile, John Forrest turned his attention to the central areas of Western Australia. Perhaps here he could find a route to the east supplied with water and stock feed. 'It would be the finishing stroke of Australian discovery,' he wrote with new confidence.

On 1 April 1874, Forrest left the small settlement of Geraldton on Champion Bay with his brother, three other white men, two black trackers, twenty-one horses and eight months' provisions.

The party headed north-east towards the Nicholson Range, watershed of several of the western rivers.

In his application for government funds, Forrest had claimed that in the opinion of geographers, 'the existence of a large river running inland from the watershed of the Murchison is nearly certain.' He was soon to be disillusioned.

The party left Burges's station Yuin on the Greenough river on 13 April 1874. Alexander Forrest went on ahead to Poondarrie, but here it was necessary to dig waterholes for the horses.

John Forrest already wished he had brought camels. 'The necessity of obtaining water for the horses entailed upon us many wearying deviations from the main route,' he wrote.

On 24 April Forrest was relieved to reach the 'splendidly grassed country' of the Murchison river. For several days the horses had ample feed and water, while the men dined on duck and cockatoo.

As the party proceeded upstream, the river began to break into many channels, and the water turned brackish. On 5 May 1874, friendly Aboriginals warned them there was no water on the branch they were following and led them to a pool.

The following day Forrest named the Robinson Range after Governor Sir William Robinson, and Mounts Fraser and Padbury after supporters of the expedition. All were in ironstone country, which made Forrest's compass useless: instead he took bearings from hilltops with a circumferentor.

Forrest continued along the bed of the Murchison for several days more, over 'splendid feeding country' with plenty of

Their horses were weak, but Forrest's party were in good spirits as they crossed this desert country: their tracks were criss-crossing those of another explorer, Giles, and they knew that they were nearing their goal of the Telegraph

'This is a great day in my journal and m journey', wrote Forrest on 17 July 1870. H reached the head of the Bight, rode along th beach, then turned north for settled district

fresh water pools. To the south-east he named the Glengarry Range in honour of his friend Maitland Brown, settler at Glengarry near Champion Bay: and the Kimberley Range after a Colonial Secretary of State.

By the end of May 1874, Forrest arrived at a series of fresh springs which later formed part of the Canning Stock Route. 'There is a most magnificent supply of water and feed — almost unlimited and permanent,' he enthused.

Forrest named the nearby Carnarvon Range after a Colonial Secretary of State; Mount Salvado after Bishop Rudesindus Salvado of New Norcia monastery north of Perth; and the Frere Range after Sir Bartle Frere, president of the Royal Geographical Society.

On 2 June 1874, Forrest was delighted to discover an abundance of clear fresh water: 'one of the best springs in the colony.' He named it Weld Springs after Governor Weld. The men rested for two weeks, eating pigeon, emu and kangaroo.

On 13 June the party was attacked twice by a large group of Aboriginals, who only retreated when two were badly wounded by rifle fire.

During the remainder of June, Forrest cautiously penetrated dry spinifex country south-east of Weld Springs, riding ahead of the main party to find water and to advance in short stages. On 22 June he named the 'remarkable red-faced' Timperley Range after W. H. Timperley, police inspector at Champion Bay.

Forrest seems to have found fresh water and feed near Lake Augusta, but then encountered 'the most wretched country I have ever seen.' On 2 July the horses 'completely gave in.' Climbing a hill, Forrest saw a horizon 'as level and uniform as that of the sea...very cheerless and disheartening.'

He persevered through the whole month, finding just enough water in rock pools to support the party. By 2 August 1874 he confessed: 'I now began to be much troubled by our position... We were over one thousand miles from the settled districts of Western Australia. The next water was sixty miles back, and there seemed no probability of getting eastward.' He made preparations for 'a last desperate struggle.'

On 6 August, still relying on rock pools, the party camped 'not far from Mount Charles' in the Todd Ranges. Next day they entered the granite Warburton Range and found grass for the horses, but all the gullies were dry.

Through the desert at last

On 8 August the horses almost collapsed — 'scarcely moving, and ourselves parched with thirst.' At noon the men scratched out a hole and found salty water. They drank about a litre each, but the horses would not touch it. Later that day the black-trackers found 'little drops in the granite rocks'.

With the continuing discoveries of occasional water pools and patches of grass, by 13 August Forrest considered they were at last through 'that awful, desolate spinifex desert.'

Another bad moment passed on 22 August when no water could be found. The Aboriginal Windich shot a wurrung, and after examining its stomach, announced that it had just drunk water. Within eight hundred metres the men found 'a most splendid spring', which Forrest named Elder Spring after his supporter Thomas Elder of Adelaide.

During early September the party passed the Mann and Musgrave ranges in South Australia. Most provisions were gone, and the horses 'all weak and knocked-up', but on 27 September 1874 they finally reached the Overland Telegraph line. 'Long and continued cheers came from our little band,' wrote Forrest.

Soon they were at Peake telegraph station, and on their way to a triumphant welcome in Adelaide.

Although Forrest was the first explorer to cross the central regions from west to east, he did not overstate the significance of his discoveries. Most of the country, he wrote, 'I do not think will ever be settled.' There were many grassy patches, 'but they are so isolated . . . that it would never pay to stock them.'

Like other desert explorers, Forrest's main achievement was to replace the old illusions with knowledge of the reality of the Australian inland.

Back in Perth, Forrest was promoted to Deputy Surveyor-General. In 1890 he was elected Premier. He entered the first Federal Parliament in 1901, and became the first native-born baron before his death in 1918.□

John Forrest's party for his third expedition in 1874 consisted of his brother Alexander, guides Tommy Windich and Tommy Pierre, James Sweeney, and policeman James Kennedy

Alexander Forrest opens up the wealth of the Kimberley

While John Forrest was beginning a long political career, his younger brother Alexander continued to work as an explorer and surveyor.

In the eighteen-seventies the vast Kimberley area of Western Australia was known only from George Grey's fumbling expedition of 1837-8 and a few other forays touching its edges.

Alexander Forrest led an eight-man party from Beagle Bay into this unknown area on 22 April 1879.

After travelling through fertile country abounding with game, they arrived at the 'magnificent Fitzroy River' on 8 May.

For three weeks the men travelled easterly along the river's grassy flats, past Mount Anderson, and the future sites of Liveringa, Noonkanbah and Quanbun stations. Within a few years these areas would support hundreds of thousands of sheep.

At the end of May 1879 Forrest reached Fitzroy Crossing, near the junction of the Fitzroy and Margaret rivers. He crossed and headed north to discover the Oscar and King Leopold ranges. Following government instructions, he tried to cross the mountains by a north-westerly route.

After a desperate fortnight of precipitous heights and gorges, Forrest managed to sight the ocean at Collier Bay, but was forced back to the Fitzroy river. 'I have never exerted myself so much in my life', he wrote.

Forrest's twenty-two-year-old brother Matthew was 'continually wandering in his mind' from severe sunstroke, and the other men were suffering from exhaustion.

From Fitzroy Crossing, Forrest continued

Alexander Forrest's party of eight. Members were Forrest's young brother Matthew, geologist Fenton Hill, Arthur Hicks, John Campbell, James Carey, Tommy Dower, and Tommy Pierre, who had served with John Forrest

Lilmaloora Station was founded in 1887 on the banks of the Lennard River, less than 10 years after Alexander Forrest's journey through the Kimberley travelling along the Fitzroy to Geikie Gorge, Oscar and King Leopold Ranges

o the east Kimberley area. Near the upper reaches of the Margaret river and today's Halls Creek he discovered the 692-metre Mount Barrett, naming it after his fiancée.

Here was 'the most splendid grassy plain' of nearly half a million hectares, capable of supporting large numbers of stock. What was more, thought Forrest, certain areas seemed likely to yield gold. His opinion was later published and led to the first successful gold rush in Western Australia.

Continuing eastwards, Forrest came to a magnificent river which he named after Sir Harry Ord, Governor of Western Australia.

Shortage of rations prevented Forrest from carrying out his plan to trace the Ord to its outlet in Cambridge Gulf.

By 24 August 1879, only twenty-seven kilos of flour remained. Most of the horses had been killed for food. The only solution was a forced march of one hundred and sixty kilometres through dry country to the Overland Telegraph Line.

Forrest and one companion went ahead, eating on the way a large snake and drinking the blood of a hawk they managed to shoot. After three days they reached the telegraph, found an iron tank full of water, and by September 4 were able to take help back to the rest of the party.

After Forrest's return via Darwin to Perth, the government moved quickly to allow settlers into the fertile areas he had discovered. Long pastoral leases were offered, at an annual rent of just ten shillings per one thousand acres (four hundred hectares). Freeholds could be bought outright for just ten shillings (one dollar) an acre.

The pioneer leaseholder, the Murray Squatting Company, took up more than forty-eight thousand hectares near Beagle Bay in 1881, and was shearing the first sheep on its Yeeda station by the following year.

In north-eastern Kimberley, the first settler was Nathaniel Buchanan, who in 1883

A pastoral Ophir was what W.A. Surveyor-General Malcolm Fraser wanted, and in the grasslands of the Kimberley Alexander Forrest found it. Soon 20,000 sheep would graze here

The Ord River. *Forrest followed it for a week until he reached its junction with the Negri River, then struck out for the Telegraph Line*

stocked Ord River station with four thousand cattle, then went on to found Wave Hill.

He was followed closely by the Durack family, who left Queensland in 1883 to drive a huge mob of cattle over the explorers' routes and establish Argyle Downs station (since inundated by the Ord Dam).

King Leopold Range remained a barrier to settlement until 1898, when an aging stockman named Frank Hann (younger brother of Queensland explorer William Hann) found routes along the Charnley and Isdell rivers.

The discovery was expanded in 1901 by Frederick Drake-Brockman, government surveyor, who mapped some two and a half million hectares of good grazing land.

Forrest brothers find fame and fortune for the west

Western Australian-born brothers John and Alexander Forrest added important knowledge to the maps of their home state with their expeditions into the north-west. While John was the trail-blazer, it fell to the younger Alexander to find sought-after grazing land

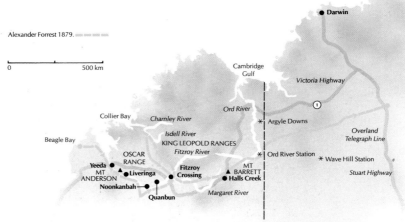

Alexander Forrest 1879.

0   500 km

Darwin

Cambridge Gulf

Victoria Highway

Ord River

Collier Bay

Charnley River

Argyle Downs

Overland Telegraph Line

Beagle Bay

Isdell River

KING LEOPOLD RANGES

Fitzroy River

Ord River Station

Wave Hill Station

OSCAR RANGE

Yeeda

Fitzroy Crossing

MT BARRETT

Stuart Highway

MT ANDERSON

Liveringa

Halls Creek

Noonkanbah

Margaret River

Quanbun

Warburton competes with Gosse to cross the desert

While John Forrest was planning his trip from west to east, controversy broke out in Adelaide on the best means of crossing in the opposite direction.
One of the contenders was Major Peter Egerton Warburton, son of a Cheshire clergyman, who had played a notable part in early exploration around Lake Eyre. Warburton creek, running almost parallel to the Birdsville Track, was named after him.

RICHARD WARBURTON, PETER WARBURTON AND J.W. LEWIS

Late in life, Warburton's remaining ambition was to complete the first crossing of the central continent from east to west. Even though he was supported by Thomas Elder, the South Australian government refused to provide aid.

Officials claimed that being nearly sixty, the hardbitten Warburton was too old to go on a long expedition through unknown arid regions. Instead they selected William Christie Gosse, a thirty-year-old government surveyor, to lead an expedition to the west.

In a fine fury, old soldier Warburton went back to his friend Thomas Elder. This wealthy fifty-four-year-old Adelaide merchant had already imported one hundred and twenty-four dromedaries for breeding on his Beltana property north of Parachilna. They had proved invaluable in carrying materials for the telegraph.

Major Warburton put forward a scheme which took Elder's fancy. Together they would organise the first Australian expedition to use camels only. They would rush them to Alice Springs and set off quickly for the west. Not all the facilities of government would beat them in this private enterprise.

Warburton, with his son Richard, two white bushmen, a black-tracker and two Afghan camel drivers, left Alice Springs at the head of a team of seventeen camels on 15 April 1873. They were eight days ahead of Gosse.

Caught in the waterless wastes

At first Warburton travelled nearly sixty kilometres north along the Telegraph Line (today the Stuart Highway) to known water at Burt creek. From here he tried to strike south-west direct for Perth, but was caught in almost waterless areas of the Mereeni Valley.

Warburton was forced north along the Derwent river until he could try north-westerly, then west again, over spinifex and mulga country. Intervals of tall casuarina forest gave 'a melancholy beauty to the scenery'.

All round Central Mount Wedge on 6 May 1873, there was 'not a scrap of feed nor a drop of water.' By now horses would have died, and even for the camels 'things were not looking well.' Fortu-

nately a soakage spring and rock pools were found next day.

From the vicinity of Mount Hardy, during May and early June, Warburton was able to make about eighty kilometres west and even some distance south towards Mount Stanley. But here the country was covered with claypans, salt lakes, sandhills and spinifex.

Turning back, Warburton investigated the north and north-west. Again waterless sandstone ridges and spinifex forced him back. On 18 June the men on their camels rode down an Aboriginal boy, caught him, and learned that a native well lay to the west. Its ample water kept them going for some time.

Last will and testament in Hindustani

Sahleh, one of the camel drivers, was now 'very ill' with scurvy. He dictated his will to Warburton in Hindustani. During early July 1873, while father and son nursed Sahleh, one of the bushmen members of the expedition, John Lewis, rode one hundred and sixty kilometres north-west to discover another native well. Three camels were lost.

'I had hoped to have been close to Perth by this time,' Warburton wrote disconsolately on 29 July. 'How greatly have my expectations been disappointed!' Already they had ridden twenty-seven hundred and thirty-five kilometres to make only about six hundred kilometres in a straight line from Alice Springs.

By 5 August Warburton was in sight of Mount Russell, just over the Western Australian border. About nineteen kilometres north-east of the mount, Warburton came to Mary Springs, with abundant fresh water, although surrounded by salt lakes.

During August, saltpans and sand ridges continued to force the party north-west. On 30 August they discovered the freshwater Lake Lucas, and enjoyed the 'rare treat' of many birds to eat.

On the same day, they captured and tied up a young native woman, 'intending that she should point out native wells to us.' Unfortunately, wrote Warburton, 'the creature escaped from us by gnawing through a thick hair-rope, with which she was fastened to a tree.'

On 4 September they succeeded in capturing a 'hideous old hag'. Warned by the previous escape, 'we secured this old witch by tying her thumbs behind her back, and haltering her by the neck to a tree.' Warburton added peevishly: 'She kept up a frightful howling all night.' Two days later they let her go, after finding she was leading them in the opposite direction to native wells.

By mid-September, in the vicinity of Mount Hughes, the party was again desperate for water. On 14 September 1873, Warburton's riding camel broke down. 'We could only get her on her legs again by lighting some spinifex under her tail,' he reported.

Next day the master bull camel ate some poisonous plants, and was abandoned near a well. The young bull camels began to fight for position.

Tents, heavy baggage jettisoned

On 18 September three more camels fell ill and refused to move. One was shot for meat: 'very poor food; the animal was old and quite worn out.'

All the camels were now so weak that on 20 September Warburton jettisoned tents and other heavy items, keeping only guns, food and a little clothing. On 26 September eight camels were left.

For several days the explorers vainly tried to track down native wells to the north. 'Trudging over these hills of loose burning sand is enough to kill a strong well-fed man,' Warburton complained.

To make matters worse, the 'improvident Afghans' had eaten all their rations of flour and meat. 'They, who profess to be able to do with less than any one else, have now none at all,' wrote Warburton. They were given a little from the reserves to keep them alive.

At last, on 4 October 1873, one of the white stockmen found a well to the south-west. This led to the discovery of a succession of good wells in a westerly direction. 'I am determined,' wrote Warburton, 'to risk everything, and make a final push for the river Oakover. Some of us might reach it, if all could not.'

With only seven camels left, the great westerly trek began on 8 October. Separated at one stage from the party, Warburton was befriended by a number of Aboriginals, who stroked his grey beard. They gave him wallaby meat, 'without which I should not have reached our camp that night, for I was utterly exhausted by heat, hunger and fatigue.'

Following native wells and the smoke of their campfires, by 20 October 1873 the party thought it had passed through the worst of the Great Sandy Desert. They were now reduced to a spoonful of flour and water for breakfast, a 'hard, sinewy bit' of camel meat for lunch, and roasted acacia seed for dinner.

Still following a line of wells, they continued southwards on 31 October. On 4 November they turned west-south-west 'to commence our flight to the Oakover.' To lessen weight even more, they kept only a few bottles of medicine 'and ate up all the rest.' By this time Warburton was 'reduced to a skeleton. I could scarcely rise from the ground.'

Travelling in the cool of the night, and steering by the stars, the party managed to cover about thirty kilometres in each stage. By 11 November 1873, all flour, tea and sugar was gone: they were existing solely on camel meat.

Warburton hoped that the younger men would survive: 'As for myself,' he wrote, 'I can see no hope.' On 12 November: 'Unless it please God to save us, we cannot live more than twenty-four hours...the smallest bit of dried meat chokes me.' Later the same day: 'The country is terrible. I do not believe men ever traversed so vast an extent of continuous desert.'

His son managed to shoot a small bird. 'It was only about the size of a sparrow,' wrote Warburton, 'but it did me good.'

The explorer managed to hold out until 14 November. Then John Lewis appeared with a bag of water found at a well nineteen kilometres away. The following day they shot a camel which had gone blind, and managed to eat some of it with the aid of more water from the well. Now five camels remained.

Feeling stronger, Warburton made two 'rushes' for the headwaters of the Oakover, but was forced to fall back on the well each time. On 19 November 1873, he sent most of the party ahead with the best camels to make a final desperate search for the river.

Father and son, left behind, tried to survive on small fruit picked from bushes. By this time Richard Warburton too could scarcely drag himself along.

Lewis returned on 25 November with the news that he had reached the Oakover. To celebrate, wrote Warburton, 'we killed a camel at sunset, and supped largely off heart and liver,' saving the kidneys and tongue for a hearty breakfast.

As soon as the moon rose on 1 December, the men set off on a four-day walk to the river. They tried to sleep in the shade of bushes during the day, but tormenting ants continually woke them up. By the second day Warburton could 'scarcely crawl'; by the fourth day he had to be tied full-length on a camel's back.

They covered the last thirty-two kilometres in seven hours, to arrive at last at permanent water on a tributary of the Oakover river.

Supplies arrive from De Grey station

On 6 December 1873, another camel was killed and eaten. Five days later the Oakover river itself was reached. Cockatoos and stewed camel's foot provided a good dinner.

A few days later Warburton sent John Lewis downstream with the last two active camels to search for help. On 19 December the last broken-down camel left in camp was killed, but had little meat left on it. The hide, head, feet and tail still seemed to contain nourishment, so these were boiled down into soup.

By Christmas Day none of the men could walk, and all were suffering from scurvy and diarrhoea. 'We are daily dropping down a peg or two lower,' Warburton wrote listlessly.

At last, on 29 December 1873, John Lewis returned. He had found the De Grey station managed by Charles Harper, who had given him ample supplies and six horses for a speedy return upstream.

Within a few days the party gained enough strength to move downstream, and eventually boarded ship for Fremantle and Adelaide.

All told, they had travelled about six and a half thousand kilometres, to make the first east-west crossing. Warburton lost the sight of one eye, but lived until the age of seventy-six, receiving honours and £1000 from the government which had previously spurned him. □

The first east-west crossing of the central continent

Starting from the Overland Telegraph, Peter Warburton set off on the longest of three desert expeditions that began in 1873. He pushed westwards, but failed to observe the country thoroughly, as he travelled a great deal by night

Warburton 1873 ▬ ▬ ▬ ▬
Gosse 1873 ▬ ▬ ▬ ▬

MT HUGHES
* De Grey
GREAT SANDY DESERT
Roebourne
De Grey River
Oakover River
Lake Lucas
Mary Springs
*
Lander River
MT HARDY
GILES RANGE
CENTRAL MT WEDGE
REYNOLDS RANGE
MT RUSSELL
MT STANLEY
Derwent River
MT LIEBIG
MT PALMER
MEREENI VALLEY
Alice Springs
MACDONNELL RANGES
MANN RANGES
MT OLGA
Lake Amadeus
AYERS ROCK
CAVENAGH RANGE
ALLANAH HILL
Wall Creek
MT SQUIRES
TOMKINSON RANGES
MT CHARLES
MUSGRAVE RANGES
Hamilton Crossing
Alberga Creek
Overland Telegraph Line
Stuart Highway

0 ——————— 500 km

Gosse becomes the first European to see Ayers Rock

Williams Gosse left Alice Springs with his official exploring party — 'four white men, three Affghans, and a black boy' — eight days after Warburton's private expedition. He was under strict instructions to avoid the opposition during the race to Perth. On 23 April 1873, Gosse first headed north-west, thus avoiding the difficulties of the MacDonnell Ranges. After that the hazards of the desert ruled his movements.

Reaching the Reynolds Range on 3 May, Gosse continued to travel north-west as far as Giles Range, naming it after Ernest Giles. He established a depot on the dry Lander river, where water could be found by digging holes in its bed.

Each attempt to change to a southerly course was frustrated, because no water could be found anywhere. 'This is the driest country I have ever been in,' he wrote. The horses suffered dreadfully: 'The poor brutes were fifty-one hours without water.' One ridden by Gosse's brother Henry, the party's botanical collector, dropped dead underneath him.

Not until 21 May 1873, when Gosse found 'a fine long waterhole' on the dry Warburton creek, could the party begin to travel southerly.

Heavy rain began on 28 May and continued for several days, filling rock pools and waterholes, but making the ground boggy. On 6 June Gosse crossed Warburton's westerly track, but decided to keep going south-westerly, through the foothills of the MacDonnell Ranges.

Climbing the 1524-metre Mount Liebig on 14 June 1873, Gosse could see sandhills extending far to east and west: 'They have the appearance of an immense ploughed field, and are far better to look at than to travel over.'

For several days Gosse and his brother searched around Mount Liebig for grass and water. On 30 June they shifted camp to Glen Edith, a waterhole to the south near Mount Palmer. Here they gleefully captured three bullocks in 'splendid con-

WILLIAM GOSSE
SURVEYOR AND EXPLORER

dition', which had escaped from Alice Springs a few months earlier. 'I think it would be a pity to disappoint them after they have shown such a decided taste for exploring,' Gosse wrote drily.

By cautious stages, always making sure

Near by, Gosse saw a spur of rock low enough to make it possible to climb the steep face: 'After walking and scrambling two miles barefooted, over sharp rocks, succeeded in reaching the summit.'

To the south-east Gosse could see a line of hills which he named Musgrave Range after the new Governor of South Australia, Sir Anthony Musgrave.

Today the whole area of Ayers Rock and Mount Olga is known as Uluru National Park, and is closely supervised by Aboriginal rangers with Federal Government support. Regarded as one of the world's wonders, it attracts many thousands of tourists.

On 21 July 1873, Gosse returned northwards to Lake Amadeus, crossing its salt pans safely to make Winnall Ridge. He found a native well, and was able to bring the remainder of his party down Kings creek to Ayers Rock on 27 July.

A few days later Gosse set out again to the south-south-west, heading for a feature which he named Allanah Hill. Here was only a dry native well. Returning to Ayers Rock, on 3 August Gosse met its male Aboriginals for the first time. 'They were all fine looking young men,' he wrote, 'about 5ft. 8in. high, wearing their hair in the shape of a chignon.'

Ranges, which straddle the border of Western Australia. Traversing alternately 'beautiful country' and mulga forests, Gosse arrived on 3 September 1873 at the edge of a spinifex desert. 'I obtained anything but a cheerful outlook — sandhills as far as I could see,' he wrote.

Pressing on, he noted on 7 September: 'no sign of water...the most wretched lookout I have had.' A little moisture was found by digging in gullies.

By 16 September Gosse had crossed the Cavenagh Range and arrived at Mount Squires. 'The poor horses seem to suffer terribly for want of water,' he wrote. 'The weather is so hot, the sweat has been pouring off them ever since we started this morning.' Their legs were 'raw and fly-blown' from injuries caused by the spinifex spikes.

On 17 September 1873, having penetrated nearly to longitude one hundred and twenty-seven degrees east, Gosse was compelled to write: 'The safety of my party obliges me to give up all hope of advancing further.' The dream of winning the race to Perth was over.

Gosse returned on a more southerly route through Musgrave Range, charting new water sources as he went. Aboriginals helped them on occasion: 'We gave them some damper and lucifers' [matches], wrote Gosse on 28 October. 'They seemed greatly pleased, especially with the lucifers, which they stuck through holes in their noses.'

of water ahead before moving the main party, Gosse now made steady progress to south and west. Early in July 1873 he approached Lake Amadeus, and on the twelfth day sighted Mount Olga, already discovered by Ernest Giles.

Gosse was now riding camels instead of horses, impressed by their long endurance without water. But 'camel travelling is very tiring,' he complained. 'It is more like riding a knocked-up cart colt.'

Even camels needed a drink now and then. Lack of water forced Gosse to take a more southerly course. For this reason, on 18 July he sighted to the south-west a large sandstone hill. The following morning, Gosse reported, 'When I got clear of the sandhills, and was only two miles distant, and the hill . . . coming fairly into view, what was my astonishment to find it was one immense rock rising abruptly from the plain.'

He named it Ayers Rock, after Sir Henry Ayers, former Premier of South Australia. 'This rock is certainly the most wonderful natural feature I have ever seen,' wrote Gosse.

Next day the explorer rode round the base of the monolith. He found a strong spring pouring down steep gullies into a deep hole and named it Mággie Springs.

From 8 August 1873 Gosse camped at Mount Olga, trying to climb it with some trepidation, feeling 'not so sure about being able to get down again.'

For several days he searched for feed and water to the south-west, around Stevenson's Peak and the Mann Ranges. Recent heavy rain encouraged quick growth of grass and herbs, and on 21 August the main camp moved forward to Mount Charles.

En route they were able to collect what Gosse called wild peaches (quandong). 'They make very nice jam when boiled, and have kept the party in good health,' he wrote.

Riding ahead to the west, Gosse discovered and named the Tomkinson

The sweet quandong (Santalum acuminatum) *is in fact rather acid. It can be eaten raw, but is more often made into jams or jellies. It grows to six metres in all the mainland states*

But great care now had to be taken in drinking surface water, as certain tribes added 'some preparation to stupify the emu', making it easy to spear them.

By early December, following Alberga creek, Gosse was close to the Telegraph Line. Aboriginals here called it 'whitefellow wheelbarrow curteyabba'.

At last, on 13 December 1873, Gosse struck the telegraph at Hamilton Crossing, and followed it north to the nearest relay station at Charlotte Waters.

Gosse's best efforts to reach the western coast had failed: practically all he would be remembered for was his discovery of Ayers Rock. He was promoted to Deputy Surveyor-General but died in 1881, aged only thirty-eight. □

An unlucky Giles takes on the continent's forbidding centre

*I*n Asia, France occupied Hanoi, capital of North Vietnam. In the Pacific, Britain took control of Fiji. In the USA, Alexander Graham Bell was tinkering with something called a tele-phone, meaning 'hearing at a distance'. In Africa, H. M. Stanley found Dr. Livingstone at Ujiji. And in Australia, a British-born explorer named Ernest Giles was determined to prove that the terrifying central deserts of the continent could be crossed by Europeans.

ERNEST GILES
EXPLORER AND BUSHMAN

During the remarkable burst of desert exploration that took place in the early eighteen-seventies, Giles was first in the field. For some years he achieved less success than others, but he persevered longer and finally won through.

Giles's first expedition began in 1872 when a Melbourne friend, Dr Ferdinand von Mueller, asked him if he would try to break through from east to west, collecting specimens of new plants on the way. Although von Mueller was Victorian government botanist, he offered to finance the expedition privately.

Giles was thirty-seven years old, and had led a rather aimless life as a gold-digger and stockman. He gladly accepted von Mueller's offer.

Giles was seized by glowing visions. Ahead he saw 'room for snowy mountains, for races of new kinds of men…for fields of gold and golcondas of gems, for a new flora and a new fauna.'

Surprising discovery of Palm Valley
On his first modest expedition Giles was accompanied by two white bushmen. The little party rode from Chambers Pillar on 22 August 1872 then followed the Finke river to the north-west.

At the end of August they discovered the Glen of Palms (now Palm Valley), where the river bed was lined with eighteen-metre-tall palm trees. In the soft earth Giles planted cucumber, melon and vegetable seeds given to him by von Mueller.

Giles turned west along Rudalls creek at its junction with the Finke. Early in September 1872 he named Gosse's Range (Gosse Bluff today) after Henry Gosse, William Gosse's youngest brother.

In mid-September Giles and his men were forcing their way through dense mulga and mallee scrub. By September 21 they reached Mount Udor, named for water pools found here (Latin *udus* means moist or wet). Further westwards lay only waterless impenetrable scrub.

On 1 October 1872, Giles turned south into tussock country, finding occasional trees covered with ripe quandong: 'the most palatable and sweetest I have ever eaten.' After two days without water, the party came to caves painted with 'strange devices of snakes, principally in white', and near by found a rock pool. Giles named it the Tarn of Auber, after an Edgar Allan Poe poem.

Arduous searching to the south-west failed to find more water, but to the east Giles discovered a pool surrounded by fig trees, which he named Glen Edith after one of his nieces.

On 11 October 1872, Giles headed south. After about eighty kilometres he came to a creek bed bordered by 'magnificent' grass. Giles enthused over its beauty and named it the Vale of Tempe.

Further travel to the south and south-west brought Giles to more barren country. Leaving a tiny waterhole which he named Glen Thirsty, he ventured towards a great shimmering lake, but found it covered with a crust into which the packhorses' legs began to sink. 'We were powerless to help them,' he wrote, 'and we sank up over our knees, where the crust was broken, in hot salt mud.'

The Glen of Palms, today's Palm Valley, was named for its rare palms, remnants of an era 5 000 000 years ago when a large part of the centre was covered in rainforest

The horses at last got themselves out of the quagmire, their mouths filled with blue salt mud.

Giles named this frightful region Lake Amadeus, after the King of Spain, a patron of science. From its shores he could see about seventy kilometres to the south the extraordinary outline of Mount Olga, named after the king's wife.

With the temperature exceeding thirty-seven degrees every day, Giles made a last dash westerly towards Mount Unapproachable, but again one of the horses became bogged in a vast salt lake. 'I had no choice but to retreat, baffled,' wrote Giles.

He returned by a more southerly route, discovering fresh water in creeks flowing from George Gill Range, named after his brother-in-law. Here the country was full of ferns and wildflowers to 'charm the eyes and hearts of toil-worn men'. Further on, at Middleton's Pass, the men were able to catch dozens of large fish resembling Murray cod.

By 1 December 1872 the party was safely back at Charlotte Waters telegraph station, having crossed sixteen hundred kilometres of country previously unknown to Europeans.

Giles had now been bitten hard by the discovery bug. He wrote: 'The wild charm and exciting desire that induce an individual to undertake the arduous tasks that lie before an explorer, and the pleasure and delight of visiting new and totally unknown places, are only whetted by his first attempt.'

In response to the explorer's pleas, von Mueller managed to raise several hundred pounds for a fresh venture, and the South Australian government was persuaded to give £250.

Giles's second expedition to the west left Ross Waterhole on Alberga creek on 4 August 1873.

Second-in-command was William Harry Tietkins, who had attended the same school as Giles in London before emigrating to work in the bush.

When the expedition arrived at good water near today's Sentinel Hill on 30 August 1873, his lieutenant's twenty-ninth birthday, Giles named the spot Tietkins Birthday creek. They celebrated with 'an excellent supper of parrot soup'.

Early in September 1873, while the party was exploring Officer creek south of the Musgrave Ranges, Aboriginals rushed them with 'horrible yells' and 'spears advanced'. Volleys of rifle fire scared them off, but Giles reflected later: 'The white man is a trespasser in the first instance;' he feared 'eternal obloquy'.

Such midnight fears did not prevent Giles from pressing on. His new route round the Musgrave Ranges brought him to Mount Olga from the south. On 14 September 1873 he at last had the thrill of riding round and attempting to climb these 'vast and solid, huge, and rounded blocks of bare red conglomerate stones'.

The men collected beautiful black and gold swallowtail butterflies (*Papilio demoleus*), then enjoyed 'a most luxurious bath in the rocky basins'.

From Mount Olga, Giles veered south-west along Gosse's track through the Mann and Tomkinson ranges. Here he turned west and established a depot at Fort Mueller.

For several frustrating weeks during October and November 1873, Giles tried to penetrate westwards. His desert camps proved 'simple agony', waterless, tormented by 'a continual cloud of sand and dust', with sleep made impossible by swarms of 'numerous and annoying' ants which 'bit us to the verge of madness'.

Northwards trek after recuperation

On 9 November Giles made a last attempt. Leaving a waterbag in a tree, he rode on alone, due west, with the thermometer at thirty-nine degrees. The only water he could find was a putrid abandoned native well: one bucket-full made his horse sick and it later died. At longitude one hundred and twenty-five degrees, thirty-seven minutes, Giles was forced to return, at death's door himself.

The party spent two months recuperating at Fort Mueller, then trekked north on 16 January 1874 towards the Rawlinson Range.

Along the way Giles reflected on the difficulties of walking when their horses were too weak to carry them. 'The greatest walker that ever stepped would find more than his match here,' he wrote. 'In the first place the feet sink in the loose and sandy soil, in the second it is densely covered with the hideous porcupine [*Triodia*]; to avoid the constant prickings from this the walker is compelled to raise his feet to an unnatural height... Again, the ground being hot enough to burn the soles off one's boots, with the thermometer at something like one hundred and eighty degrees in the sun, and the choking from thirst at every movement of the body, is enough to make any one pause before he foolishly gets himself into such a predicament'.

For three months Giles again tried doggedly to break through to the west, south-west and north-east from their permanent base at Circus Water in the Rawlinson Range.

On these waterless forays, four horses died in the extreme heat. On 18 February 1874, Giles narrowly escaped death when he was thrown by an old black mare named Diaway and dragged along.

During March, Giles explored the Petermann Ranges, naming them after German geographer Dr Augustus Petermann. Their steep serrated ridges made the explorer feel he might be walking on the moon. Watering their

Lake Amadeus, the 'infernal lake of mud and brine'. In his valiant attempts to go round it, Giles had missed the land bridge between this lake and another, now known as Lake Neale

horses at a brook, he and Tietkins were again attacked by natives, and drove them off with revolver fire.

On 19 April 1874, Giles decided to make a last dash of one hundred and sixty kilometres to the west. Alf Gibson, a young stockman, volunteered to go with him. They took two riding-horses and two packhorses laden with provisions.

By 21 April they crossed Lake Christopher and soon were enclosed in sandhills covered with enormous clumps of porcupine grass. Fortunately the hills ran east and west, enabling the two men to travel west in the hollows.

Next day, with waterbags emptying rapidly, Giles released the packhorses to find their own way back to the depot. Two full twenty-two-litre kegs were hung in a tree.

Giles makes a disastrous decision

On 23 April 1874, when more than one hundred and forty kilometres from Circus Water, Gibson's horse knocked up and refused to go any further. The men had to turn back, taking turns to ride Giles's mare which soon became distressed.

Giles instructed Gibson to leave him alone in the desert, ride back to the water kegs, then hasten to the depot for help.

That night Giles followed the tracks on foot by the light of the moon. He arrived at the kegs by noon next day, to find nine litres of water left for him. Drinking a little, and hoisting a sixteen-kilo keg on his shoulder, he staggered on

eastwards, covering only about eight kilometres a day, his head swimming.

On 29 April, still thirty kilometres from the depot, Giles drank the last drop from the keg. By moonlight he made a final frenzied burst, and fell on the Circus Water at dawn.

For a day he drank and rested. Next morning he heard a faint squeak, and saw a dying baby wallaby. 'I pounced upon it and ate it, living, raw, dying — fur, skin, bones, skull, and all,' he wrote.

On 1 May, Giles reached the depot at Fort McKellar, where he was welcomed as 'one new risen from the dead'. No sign of Gibson or the horses had been seen. The men retraced westwards, and found that Gibson had left the track in a southerly direction long before reaching Circus Water. 'Who can tell his place of rest?' asked Giles sombrely.

Giles and Tietkins continued the search for Gibson until they too nearly perished. 'I well remember lying down and begging Giles to push on and leave me, for I was so weak, I did not wish to live,' Tietkins wrote in later years. 'I managed to get back to camp somehow, and to recover after some time, but Giles was delirious and in a high state of fever for many days'.

Gibson's fate preyed on Giles's mind for years. He named the area Gibson Desert after the lost man. 'Many trials and many bitter hours must the explorer of such a region experience,' Giles wrote.

Giles's disappearance sealed the fail-

MALLEE-FOWL PROVIDE A BUSH LUXURY

The mallee fowl: *able to exist almost without water, it was valuable to a bush diet*

Ernest Giles was one of the first explorers to describe the mallee-fowl (*Leipoa ocellata*), once common in dry scrub.

The adult birds, which rarely fly, are about six hundred millimetres long, with a handsome mottled plumage of rufous, brown and white.

Giles saw their nests on his second expedition near Fort Mueller in October 1873. He wrote:

These birds, which somewhat resemble guinea-fowl in appearance, build extraordinarily large nests of sand, in which they deposit small sticks and leaves; here the female lays about a dozen eggs, the decomposition of the vegetable matter providing the warmth necessary to hatch them. These nests are found only in thick scrubs. I have known them five to six feet high, of a circular conical shape, and a hundred feet round the base. The first, though of enormous size, produced only two eggs; the second, four, and the third, six. We thanked Providence for supplying us with such luxuries in such a wilderness.

Ernest Giles makes a romance of desert exploration

Giles lost a companion in the Gibson Desert during his second expedition and was forced back to the Overland Telegraph Line. After his successful east-west crossing in 1875, he set out again, from west to east, more or less retracing the route of his second expedition over the final stages. He sub-titled his travel book The Romance of Exploration . . .

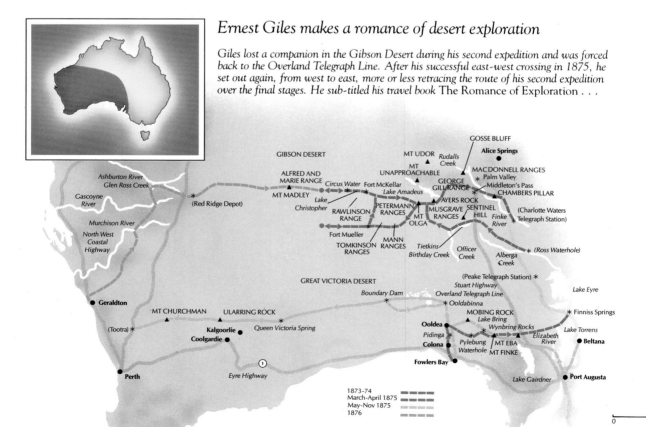

1873-74
March-April 1875
May-Nov 1875
1876

0   400 km

re of Giles's second expedition. The survivors retreated to Mount Olga and Ayers Rock in June, then followed their old track via George Gill Range to arrive at Charlotte Waters by 13 July 1874.

Within a few months Giles learned to his chagrin that both John Forrest and Major Warburton had succeeded in crossing the central desert regions.

But Giles was still determined to write his name into Australian exploration. Plenty of opportunity was left: the whole vast area south of Forrest's and Warburton's central lines to the Great Australian Bight remained unknown.

This time Giles was assisted by Thomas Elder, who gave him fresh horses, provisions, and the first two camels Giles had used. The aim was to search for new pastoral country by travelling from Fowlers Bay northerly to a known waterhole, then turning east to reach Elder's northernmost station at Finniss Springs.

Giles's third expedition left Fowlers Bay on 13 March 1875. In searing temperatures they passed the outermost sheep station at Colona, then after a salt lagoon came to 'a pretty little place' called Pidinga. Here were rock holes containing thousands of litres of water. The country was covered with broom, cypress pines, casuarina and acacia.

About one hundred and forty kilometres north of Colona, their Aboriginal guides led them to a shallow native well called Youldeh (today Ooldea). After digging out the well and slabbing its sides to keep back the sand, some water was found. 'The whole region was glowing with intense heat,' wrote Giles.

The party's native guides led them easterly from one small waterhole to the next. Some were 'almost putrid from the number of dead and decaying birds, rats, lizards, and rotten leaves' in them, and contained only 'a filthy black fluid'.

Far from being good pastoral land, the country consisted mostly of 'very high and scrubby red sandhills,' with patches of mallee or mulga scrub.

On 26 March 1875, the party arrived at Pylebung waterhole. Giles was astonished to find it dammed. Aboriginals had used small wooden shovels to build a one and a half metre-high white clay wall: the first time he had ever heard of a native attempt at water conservation.

Five days later, when the party was 'choking with thirst and sleepless with anxiety', their guides led them to a large rock pool called Wynbring.

The horses begin to die of thirst

From Wynbring Rock, Giles could see Mount Finke to the south-east. But when they reached it early in April, with men and animals in 'a perfect lather of sweat,' Giles found it waterless: 'the most desolate heap on the face of the earth'.

Next day the oldest horse lay down in the sand and 'stretched out his limbs in the agony of thirst and exhaustion'. It had to be abandoned.

Giles continued east-north-east across waterless rises and past dry salt lagoons to Mount Eba. Their situation was desperate. The last water at Wynbring was more than one hundred and ninety kilometres back; the next known water at Finniss Springs was two hundred and forty kilometres ahead.

Mount Olga — '*it displayed to our astonished eyes rounded minarets, giant cupolas, and monstrous domes*'. *At its base, Giles found the two-month-old tracks of Gosse's party, and freshwater springs which still flow today*

At two hundred and forty kilometres from Wynbring, Giles's own horse Chester lay down to die. 'We were all in the last stage of thirst and wretchedness,' he wrote, after putting a bullet through the creature's forehead.

A few kilometres further on, the eyes of the last horse, Formby, sank right back into its head. Giles shot it too.

The men's lives now depended on their two camels, carrying the tiny remaining stock of food and water.

On about 10 April 1875 (Giles's dates are vague), the party stumbled on a claypan containing a small supply of discoloured water. Men and camels sank into the yellow mud and drank until they could hold no more.

Trekking on through better country, the party even found a waterhole where they were able to shoot a small teal for dinner. The last few kilometres to Finniss Springs were like a holiday after the dangers they had endured.

This perilous expedition brought back information about the kind of country lying west of Finniss Springs, and located permanent waterholes. Giles used this knowledge for his fourth and most important expedition.

Thomas Elder again provided most of the finance and twenty-two camels. To manage them, Giles took Sahleh, the Afghan camel driver who had accompanied Major Warburton. Second-in-command was William Tietkins.

Three other whites and the Aboriginal guide Tommy Oldham went along.

The expedition left Elder's camel-breeding station at Beltana on 6 May 1875. First they travelled southerly to Port Augusta to top up the stores. At the start, each of the fifteen pack camels carried huge leather bags filled with about two hundred and fifty kilos of provisions.

By 23 May the party was ready to leave. They had an easy journey to the Elizabeth river, west of Lake Torrens, shooting wild duck along the way. A well-sinker named Moseley told them where to find fresh water near the salt Lake Gairdner. Here on 6 June the explorers found 'whitish but good water' which curdled when made into tea.

Rain at last fills water holes

They continued north-west to skirt Lake Gairdner, then resumed a westerly course. On 15 June Giles was back on his former track leading to the 'fertile little gem' of Wynbring Rock.

En route two camels were poisoned by eating a fennel-like plant, probably of the *Euphorbiaceae* family. The driver gave them hot butter as an emetic and thus saved their lives.

Heavy rain fell at Wynbring on 22 June 1875, coming down 'so fast that the camels could drink the water right at their feet'. After four days' rest the party pushed on north-westerly past Lake Bring to Mobing Rock, where large native wells were found brimming with water.

Here Giles changed direction to west-erly, to arrive safely at his old Youldeh depot on 5 July ahead of his party.

Giles occupied the next few days with a quick dash south to send letters from Fowlers Bay, while two of his men reconnoitred northwards, to find a small native well at Ooldabinna.

After Giles's return at the end of July, he again pushed westwards into the Great Victoria Desert. He passed across a region of great salt lakes between longitudes one hundred and thirty and one hundred and thirty-one degrees where 'the weird, hideous, and demoniacal beauty of absolute sterility' reigned supreme.

The men pushed with difficulty through porcupine grass, then through a desolate region of thick scrub: 'The silence and the solitude of this mighty waste were appalling to the mind,' wrote the ever-sensitive Giles.

Crossing the border into Western Australia, at two hundred and fifty kilometres from Ooldabinna Giles found a small native dam where bronze-wing pigeons were shot for dinner. He named it Boundary Dam. Further west was more dense scrub interspersed with salt lakes, but no fresh water at all.

Giles was forced to return to Ooldabinna, taking a parallel route about sixty-five kilometres to the south in the hope of discovering a better path. At this time of year there was ample feed but no surface water — the camels suffered a three hundred and fifteen kilometre-long waterless stage before reaching Ooldabinna on 23 August 1875.

Next day, 'having filled up everything that could hold a drop of water', the party set out for the west. Giles led on foot with his compass, or on a 'beautiful white' gelded camel which he called Pearl Beyond all Price.

By 3 September 1875, they were back at Boundary Dam. After resting for a week, Giles set off on his final plunge into the unknown. The nearest charted landmark to the west, Augustus Gregory's Mount Churchman, lay nine hundred and sixty-five kilometres away. Giles offered to provide camels and provisions for anyone who wanted to turn back to safety, but 'One and all declared that they would live or die with me.'

Oldham follows emu tracks to water

From 10 to 25 September, the party pushed across the Great Victoria Desert. For five hundred kilometres from Boundary Dam it was waterless — covered with mallee scrub, porcupine grass, and occasional grassy plains with saltbush.

On 22 September, more than three hundred and eighty kilometres from the last known water, Giles shared out most of the remainder from the casks among the camels: 'like parting with our blood'. Four days later, when all the men expected to perish within a few days, the Aboriginal Tommy Oldham came rushing back from the lead, screaming 'Water! water! plenty water here!'

He had followed the tracks of the first emu seen, and discovered 'a small funnel-shaped hollow' filled with fresh water,

Giles's camel team was a sensation when it arrived in Perth in October 1875. As they entered Fremantle, his own beast 'fairly jibbed and I had to walk and lead her so that I was hidden in the crowd and Mr Tietkens . . . appeared to be the leader as his camel went all right', he wrote. A local newspaper took this photograph of the party with some admirers and surrounded by green feed. Giles 'ventured to dedicate' the spring and the entire desert 'to our most gracious Queen', Victoria.

With plenty to drink, even enough water to bathe, the party lingered at the oasis until 6 October 1875. Refilling water casks, they again set off hopefully. Their route lay only eighty to one hundred kilometres north of the golden riches of Kalgoorlie and Coolgardie.

About three hundred weary kilometres of waterless scrub and spinifex were traversed before Oldham again found a large native well at Ularring Rock on 13 October 1875.

The local Aboriginals all seemed friendly, yet, Giles wrote later, 'war was in their hearts'. Probably they were worried by the enormous quantity of water drunk by the camels.

Late on 16 October the Europeans were attacked by more than one hundred shouting natives. Giles and his men felt they had no alternative but to fire into their midst, wounding several. They retreated as suddenly as they had appeared and gave no further trouble.

A feast of mutton, butter, eggs . . .

Eleven days later, after battling through more dense scrub, the party arrived at the bare granite peak of Mount Churchman. By this time all were suffering from scurvy and eye trouble.

On 4 November 1875 they arrived at the farthest out-station of a sheep property named Tootra, owned by the Clunes brothers. After feasting on mutton, butter, sugar and eggs, they quickly regained good health, and were able to follow the trail of settlement towards Perth.

John Forrest organised welcomes in the larger towns, insisting that the explorers wear their ragged garments to show people what they had been through.

Yet Giles was conscious that his efforts had apparently been in vain. He had covered four thousand kilometres in this expedition, 'but unfortunately found no new areas of country suitable for settlement'. However, added Giles, 'the explorer does not make the country, he must take it as he finds it'.

The only value seemed a negative one: 'it points out to the future emigrant or settler, those portions of our continent which he should rigorously avoid'.

One great puzzle remained in the centre of Australia, which the routes of other explorers had not solved. How far to the west did the desert that had claimed Alf Gibson extend?

As the celebrations in Perth palled, Giles determined to return to the area, but this time to penetrate it from the west. With Thomas Elder's permission, he led the camel team from Perth on 13

In the Great Victoria Desert Giles's party came across porcupine grass, mallee, pine and the occasional quandong tree — but no water

January 1876 northwards through the settled country of Geraldton and the Murchison and Gascoyne rivers.

By 10 May 1876 the party arrived at the almost dry bed of the Ashburton river, about four hundred and eighty kilometres inland from the western coast. After heavy rain, they discovered permanent water in a tributary, called Glen Ross creek after Alec Ross, a young member of the party. A depot was formed a few kilometres further on.

Already Giles was suffering a recurrence of sandy blight, and was forced to abandon a short trip to the northeast. 'I was in such pain,' he wrote, 'that I ordered an instant retreat, my only desire being to get back to the depot and repose in the shade'.

Following the easterly line of the Ashburton river, by 30 May 1876 the last small water-hole was passed. The country ahead was unknown, but Giles felt sure the Gibson Desert began here. 'So far as I knew,' he wrote, 'the next water was in the Rawlinson Range of my former horse expedition, a distance of over 450 miles'.

Facing the 'dreaded sandhills' again

The party carefully filled their water casks and left Red Ridge depot on 2 June. Soon 'the first waves of the dreaded sandhills were in view'. Next day 'the solitary caravan was now launched into the desert, like a ship upon the ocean'.

On the evening of 4 June the camels were turned loose to forage. Next morning the men discovered that several had eaten poison plants during the night, and were unable to move. 'We made them sick with hot water, butter, and mustard,' wrote Giles, 'and gave them injections with the clyster pipe' (used for administering rectal enemas).

Within a day the camels had recovered from the worst, and Giles decided to push on. The party now entered an area 'so desolate that it is horrifying

even to describe'. The only living object in this 'vast sandy region' seemed to be the slow-moving caravan itself.

After ten days without finding water, the expedition saw a few gum trees near a low hill, Mount Madley. They dug near the roots and found enough water to supply the camels. Here Buzoe, Alec Ross's riding camel, died from its privations. Almost immediately the apparently empty desert sprang to life: 'a swarm of eagles, crows, hawks, vultures, and at night wild dogs' descended to tear at the camel's carcass.

On 25 June 1876, Giles reached the Alfred and Marie Range, furthest point sighted on his 1874 expedition. The range itself seemed waterless: only a shallow rocky pan at the northern end yielded a little water for the camels.

Giles spent several days searching for Gibson's remains but found no trace. The party followed the old route to the Rawlinson and Musgrave ranges, finding their old watering places brimming. By 23 August 1876 they were back at Peake telegraph station.

In many respects Giles was the most unlucky of Australian explorers. The vast distances he covered, together with his tenacity, should have yielded some good pastoral or mining country. Instead, there was almost nothing. Even Giles was driven to complain that he expended 'five of the best years of my life'. An Italian knighthood and a gold medal from the Royal Geographical Society did not seem much recompense for his efforts.

Late in life Giles joined the gold rush to Coolgardie, but even then had little luck. To survive, he was forced to take a clerk's job in the mine warden's office. He died of bronchial pneumonia in 1897, aged sixty-two. □

The vast extent of arid lands proves a bitter disappointment

Even by the eighteen-forties, people could not bring themselves to believe that vast areas of inland Australia were almost uninhabitable. They preferred to dream of endless rich pastoral lands.

Many explorers risked their lives, and even sacrificed them, to bring back the truth. As a result of their reports, people finally realised that Australia was the driest inhabited continent. Only the 'golden eastern crescent', some tropical areas of the north, and part of the south-western corner were suitable for continuous agriculture.

By far the greatest part of Australia still consists of arid country where rainfall is slight and erratic, evaporation high, and usable run-off low.

As a result, vast deserts spread over the western and central regions of the continent. Sturt discovered the barren eastern edge of the Simpson Desert in 1845. He described it as 'a sandy sea; ridge after ridge succeeding each other as far as the eye could stretch'.

The main plant in such areas is the horrible spiky hummock grass Triodia, wrongly called spinifex. Its drought-resistant roots and needle-like leaves can survive the most extreme conditions. It provides enough shelter and food for a few forms of desert wildlife.

The Gibson Desert, far to the east of the Simpson, was discovered by Ernest Giles in 1873. Although its main features have now been mapped, and tracks connect its scattered wells, settlement is practically impossible.

Immediately to the north-west, the Great Sandy Desert was crossed by P. E. Warburton in 1873 and the Canning Stock route was pushed through in 1906; it is now little used except by mining prospectors.

To the south, the Great Victoria Desert, which merges into the Nullarbor Plain, was crossed by Ernest Giles in 1875. This vast area too is almost uninhabitable.

The Simpson Desert *is perhaps the most forbidding of the large sandy wastes. On 6 September 1845, Sturt stood on a sandhill at Eyre Creek and looked over what seemed to be an impassable succession of high, parallel sand ridges*

In the Great Victoria Desert, below, named by Giles, his men found its silence and sameness so remorselessly oppressive, they themselves fell silent, communicating only in whispers until they found water on the seventeenth day

'I called this terrible region that lies between the Rawlinson Range and the next permanent water . . . to the west, Gibson's Desert, after this first white victim to its horrors', wrote Giles after the loss of the young Alfred Gibson

Dry and harsh almost beyond European endurance, the deserts gave explorers their toughest challenge

Australia's worst deserts — the Simpson and Tanami, the Great Sandy Desert, the Great Victoria, and the Gibson — all merge imperceptibly to make what used to be known as the 'dead heart', a huge slab of country hostile to even the most cautious and sensible explorers. This arid expanse touches all of the mainland states, making up most of Western Australia, South Australia and the Northern Territory. Semi-arid fringes reach out to the coast in places

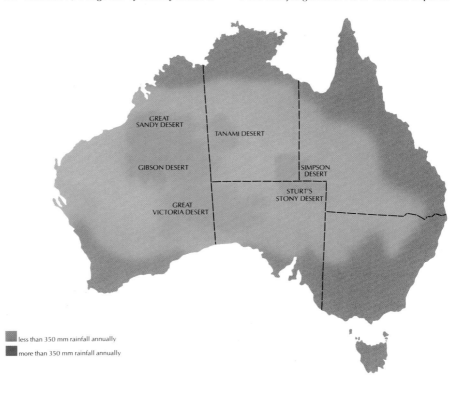

GREAT SANDY DESERT

TANAMI DESERT

GIBSON DESERT

SIMPSON DESERT

STURT'S STONY DESERT

GREAT VICTORIA DESERT

▪ less than 350 mm rainfall annually
▪ more than 350 mm rainfall annually

The MacDonnell Ranges near Alice Springs, starting point for many expeditions

CHAPTER EIGHT

The age of scientific expeditions

Lindsay and Wells find the desert a hard test of all their expertise and planning

During the eighteen-eighties, Western science and technology seemed likely to conquer the world. Rapid-fire armaments and steel battleships poured forth. In 1885 Britain took over Burma and Kenya. In 1889 France completed the world's tallest steel structure, the Eiffel Tower, and continued its colonial conquests.
Burgeoning cities extended upwards with lifts and outwards with tramways. Electric power began to supplant gas and steam. In America, George Eastman produced an easy-to-use camera, which he called a Kodak. Even for desert exploration, a new era began, in which expeditions had to be called 'scientific' to win public interest and financial support.

That grand old South Australian promoter of exploration successes and failures, Sir Thomas Elder, had been knighted for his efforts in 1878. Even in 1890, at the age of seventy-two, he offered to help finance a voyage to Antarctica. There was little other support and the project lapsed.

The following year Elder agreed to equip what would be called The Elder Scientific Exploring Expedition. Organised by the South Australian branch of the Royal Geographical Society, its purpose was to fill gaps between tracks of the heroic desert explorers of the eighteen-seventies, and devote closer attention to the nature and people of arid lands.

As leader, the Society chose thirty-five-year-old David Lindsay, a surveyor who had explored parts of Arnhem Land and laid out Alice Springs. Second-in-command was Lawrence Allen Wells, thirty-one, also an experienced surveyor. With two such experts, how could anything go wrong?

Their splendidly-equipped expedition left the Everard Ranges in northern South Australia on 6 June 1891, heading west with forty-four camels carrying a variety of instruments and provisions.

Nature was ready for the scientists. At first the going was easy, but around Blyth Range on the West Australian border there had been no rain for years. Even the spinifex and mulga were dying or dead. There were no interesting desert plants for the party's botanists to examine.

Lindsay pressed on to Fort Mueller, and found the well there 'absolutely dry'. A little water was left in Forrest's rockhole further west, but most other watering places discovered by Forrest and Giles west of the Warburton Range were empty. Aboriginals were chewing the roots of kurrajong trees for moisture.

When the camels had gone three weeks without a drink, and were on the point of failing, Lindsay saw a procession of natives heading towards Mount Squires. He followed them and found an 'abundance' of life-saving water.

To the west lay Giles's Great Victoria Desert. Six hundred and forty kilometres of it had to be crossed to reach known water at Queen Victoria's Spring. Well, if Giles with his puny forces had done it, a

scientific expedition should have no trouble. From 31 August 1891, the camels went twenty-four days without water across the dreadful sandhills.

When the men got to the spring, they were horrified to find it dry. Several litres of water were obtained only by digging. Unable to return to Mount Squires, Lindsay was forced to admit that 'Our position was now somewhat critical.'

The only certain water lay over two hundred kilometres south-west in the Fraser Range. Lindsay doubted whether the camels could make it — and when they died, men would perish too.

Halfway, the party's first stroke of luck occurred when they noticed their dog'

LIFE-SAVING HERBS

Portulaca, known also as purslane in Europe, exists in nearly 200 species round the world

Unlike maritime explorers, land-based expeditions usually could not carry large enough amounts of lime or lemon juice to prevent the awful disease of scurvy.

Australian explorers were forced to rely on whatever edible native vegetation they could find to remedy the deficiency.

The most common was portulaca, or pigweed, a low-growing succulent herb whose leaves and seeds could be eaten raw, or boiled into a broth suitable for scurvy patients who could not chew.

Portulaca and other native foods saved the lives of many noted inland explorers.

The Elder Scientific Expedition's caravan ...ets out from Mount Cootanoorina. The ...xplorers had taken the train to nearby Warrina

...aws were damp. Near by they found a ...ell, and carefully collected enough ...nuddy water to give the camels eleven ...tres each. This carried them through to ...raser Range station on 3 October 1891. ...ere they rested four weeks to recover.

From this point, Lindsay made a quick ...lash south to report progress through the ...elegraph station at Esperance Bay. The ...vire clicked back his instructions: to ...ravel direct towards the headwaters of ...he Murchison river and examine the ...lmost unknown country en route.

On 4 November 1891, the party ...tarted north-westerly through country ...rowing ever drier. Native wells with ...nly enough water to support a few ...Aboriginals were quickly sucked dry by ...ne thirsty camels.

After one waterless stretch of seven ...ays, the camels looked worse than ever. ...o obey instructions, thought Lindsay, ...ould mean 'certain destruction and loss ...f the whole party.'

He decided to veer westerly towards ...ne town of Southern Cross, centre of the ...ilgarn diggings. This brought the party ...ery close to the future site of Coolgardie, ...n country which Lindsay noted on his ...ap as 'auriferous'.

Lindsay was able to get some water at ...outhern Cross and save his camels. ...hen he returned to a north-westerly ...oute as instructed. Soon he struck an- ...her waterless stage, during which the

camels took seven days to cover one hundred and forty-four kilometres.

Eventually on 2 January 1892 the weary party reached Lake Annean near the upper Murchison. Here they formed a depot and stopped to recover. But ill-feeling that had been welling during their ordeal erupted and all the scientists bar Wells resigned their posts.

Lindsay made a five hundred and thirty-kilometre dash to the telegraph office at Geraldton, where he discovered that he had been relieved of command and instructed to return to Adelaide.

Lawrence Wells, who had criticised Lindsay's decisions in his own reports to Adelaide, took charge. On 17 February 1892 Wells led the newly-fattened camels eastwards from Annean Station across the Montague Range. After four days he reached the edge of settlement, and struck out across auriferous ground to discover Lake Way, south of Wiluna.

The first heavy rains in three years enabled the party to cross barren country and reach the large salty Lake Wells. The men used empty water kegs to build punts and float their provisions across. Near the lake, Wells claimed to have discovered 'splendid pastoral country', but it was largely reliant on occasional storms.

After travelling to the western edge of the Great Victoria Desert, Wells wisely turned south, then took a parallel path

The 'scientific expeditions' begin to fill in the last gaps

Lindsay and Wells were sent to investigate an area in Western Australia called 'Block A', between Forrest's 1874 and Giles's 1875 routes, 'for the purpose of completing the exploration of Australia'. Their findings were disappointing

Lindsay's complement of scientists: *naturalist R. Helms, medical officer F. J. Elliot, surveyor Lawrence Wells, geologist Victor Streich and F. W. Leech, pictured here with their assistants*

back westwards, enabling him to discover Lake Darlot and Mount von Mueller before returning to Annean Station. Here he learned that the expedition was to be broken up.

All told, the Lindsay-Wells explorations covered over seven thousand kilometres, more than half of them through new country, and mapped about twenty million hectares.

An inquiry in Adelaide later exonerated Lindsay from blame over the scientists' defections.

Both Lindsay and Wells put the best face on their results, claiming that some of the new country might soon support 'a fairly large population'.

In fact, their thousands of kilometres of back-breaking travel had discovered almost nothing of value. That was not their fault: it was the cruel, adamantine nature of the country itself which broke people's hearts and lives. □

Elder expedition, Lindsay
and Wells 1891-92

WARBURTON RANGE

MONTAGUE RANGE

Fort Mueller

North West
Coastal Highway

Lake Way

Annean
Station

Lake Wells

MT
SQUIRES

BLYTH RANGE

EVERARD RANGES

Lake Annean

Lake Darlot

MT VON MUELLER
Great Northern Highway

Murchison River

GREAT VICTORIA DESERT

Geraldton

Stuart Highway

Queen Victoria Spring

Coolgardie

Eyre Highway

Southern Cross

FRASER RANGE

Perth

Great Eastern
Highway

Fraser Range Station

Esperance Bay

0   500 km

Horn and Winnecke take a team of academics and naturalists to observe the centre

Probably the most successful 'scientific' expedition of the late nineteenth century was financed by William Austin Horn, a former South Australian stockman who had made a fortune from copper and silver mines.

Partly self-educated, and fascinated by the pre-history of Australia, Horn agreed in 1894 to organise and equip the Horn Scientific Expedition to carry out scholarly research in central Australia.

To organise his expedition, Horn selected thirty-seven-year-old Charles Winnecke, an Adelaide-born surveyor and bushman who had already proven himself with camel expeditions north of Lake Eyre in 1881 and 1883. On those trips Winnecke added to geographical knowledge by discovering patches of good land around Mounts Winnecke, Cornish and Central Mount Hawker, besides collecting eighty-five new plant varieties to be classified by Ferdinand von Mueller, former director of Melbourne's botanical gardens and a founder of the National Herbarium.

Scientific members of the 1894 expedition included Ralph Tate, professor of natural science at Adelaide University; Baldwin Spencer, professor of biology at Melbourne University; Edward Stirling, leading Adelaide anthropologist; J. A. Watt, geologist; F. W. Belt, naturalist; and George Keartland, a Victorian compositor turned ornithologist. Sir Charles Todd and Sir Thomas Elder lent modern instruments for testing magnetic variation and dip in the centre.

Horn accompanied his expedition with its twenty-three camels from Oodnadatta on 5 May 1894, returning to Adelaide when they reached Idracowra Station on the Finke river.

On this section of the journey, Horn named Mount Peterswald after W. J. Peterswald,

South Australian Police Commissioner; Mount Falconer after the Earl of Kintore, Governor; and the Newland Ranges after Simpson Newland, president of the Royal Geographical Society of South Australia.

Winnecke led the caravan during the rugged journey north-west through today's Haasts Bluff Aboriginal Reserve. On 16 June 1894 he named Mount Stirling after the expedition's anthropologist. Further north he named Belt

Philanthropist and mining magnate William Horn financed an expedition of scientists, pictured here resting at Alice Springs mid-1894. In research of natural history, they explored many unknown areas, finding six mountain passes

This cairn, right, *was erected by members of the Horn expedition to mark what they believed was the site of Gosse's camp on Kings Creek*

A FROG THAT HAS ITS OWN WATER STORE

A water-logged chamber and full bladder keep the frog moist through dry periods

The most remarkable creature found by the Horn expedition was the burrowing or waterholding frog (*Cyclorana platycephalus*).

As waterholes begin to dry up, the frog fills itself with water, swelling it out 'until it looks like a small orange'.

It then burrows into the clay, and hibernates until the next rain.

Desert Aboriginals learned how to find the frogs' hiding places, and when water was in desperately short supply, they would squeeze out the moisture.

A new breed of explorer moves into the outback

Charles Winnecke put aside his private surveying work to lead an expedition that was to carry out scholarly research and bring back wildlife collections, photographs and scientific observations

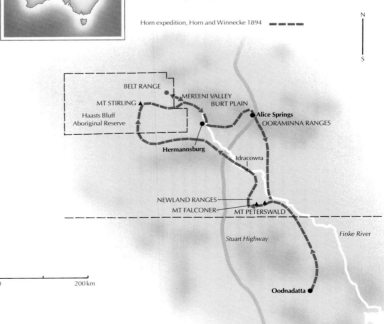

Horn expedition, Horn and Winnecke 1894 ▬ ▬ ▬

N
S

BELT RANGE
MT STIRLING
MEREENI VALLEY
BURT PLAIN
Haasts Bluff Aboriginal Reserve
Alice Springs
OORAMINNA RANGES
Hermannsburg
Idracowra
NEWLAND RANGES
MT FALCONER
MT PETERSWALD
Stuart Highway
Finke River
Oodnadatta

0   200km

range after another member, F. W. Belt, an
Adelaide solicitor and amateur naturalist who
was Horn's brother-in-law.

A great deal of fossil country was investigated in the Mereeni Valley and escarpment,
named after a local Aboriginal word.

After visiting Burt Plain to the north, the
expedition replenished its supplies at Alice
Springs then moved south-east to the Ooraminna Ranges. Here F. W. Belt found 'numerous new and rare plants'.

The scientists travelled westerly through
Inke Gorge and established a base at
Hermannsburg Mission from where they could
closely examine areas first described in
explorer Ernest Giles's detailed journals.

They returned to Oodnadatta on 5 August
1894, having travelled thirty-five hundred
kilometres without serious incident, mapped
seven million hectares, and identified more
than half of it as 'good pastoral country.'

EARLY STUDIES OF BIRDS IN ARID REGIONS

The zebra finch is the smallest but most widespread of Australia's finches. It lives close to pools and drinks by immersing its face in water and sucking. Flocks may number 100 or more

George Arthur Keartland, the *Age* compositor turned ornithologist, was thrilled
by new species of birds he collected during
the Horn Scientific Expedition of 1894.

In mid-June, near the MacDonnell
Ranges, he shot and stuffed 'fifteen
specimens of that most rare bird the
Princess Alexandra parakeet' (*Polytelis*
Alexandrae), a brilliantly-plumed parrot
about which little is known even today.

Later the scientists followed flights of
the more common zebra finch (*Taeniopygia*
guttata) to water sources.

Keartland claimed that the finches
could actually smell water far off, but
scientists are still not sure if this is true.

Large collections were made in several
departments of science. More than one hundred and seventy new species of beetles,
spiders, reptiles and molluscs were added to the
record, along with many plants previously
unknown in the centre. Hundreds of photographs were taken of striking natural features.

In 1896 the *Journal of the Horn Scientific
Exploring Expedition* was published. It contains
delightful lithographic plates made from drawings of specimens collected by the expedition's
specialists. The scientists felt they were just in
time to photograph Aboriginals living near
pastoral stations before they lost all their
traditions and faced extinction. Charles
Winnecke took a sombre view of their future.
'The doom of these has already been sealed,'
he wrote. 'Their indescribably filthy habits
and vices are fast hurrying them out of
existence.' Even the biologist Baldwin Spencer felt that 'In contact with the white man
the aborigine is doomed to disappear.'

Alexandra's parrot, also known as princess parrot, was sketched for the expedition's journals

Another page from the expedition journal shows the water-holding frog (top), the ornate burrowing frog and the meeowing frog

Lizards encountered by the Horn expedition included the fast-moving painted dragon

The Calvert expedition: disaster in the name of science

All kinds of people were attracted to Australia by tales of vast mineral wealth still to be exploited. Among them was an adventurous eighteen-year-old named Albert Frederick Calvert, son of a Middlesex mining engineer.

Calvert led three expeditions between Lake Gairdner in South Australia and the upper Murchison River in Western Australia between 1890 and 1892.

One writer drily remarked that Calvert's 'most important discovery was the rare spinifex parakeet' (the night parrot, *Pezoporus occidentalis*, now thought to be extinct).

However, south-east of today's Marble Bar, he claimed also to have found 'many thousand tons of conglomerate... saturated with native gold'. This was sufficient for the youth to float a company, attract the Earl of Caledon to its board, and name the area Mount Caledon.

Calvert returned home to marry and promote his company. He landed again at Albany in 1895 with a considerable entourage, including a younger brother who died of typhoid within a few weeks.

ALBERT F. CALVERT
EXPLORER AND BUSINESSMAN

In January 1896 the Royal Geographical Society of South Australia accepted Calvert's offer to finance a 'scientific expedition' which would open a stock route from the north-western goldfield to the Northern Territory, and search for Leichhardt's remains on the way.

As expedition leader, Calvert appointed the thirty-six-year-old surveyor Lawrence Wells, who had taken over command of the Elder Scientific Expedition of 1891 from David Lindsay.

In June 1896 Wells's party shipped to Geraldton, then went by rail to Mullewa where twenty-five camels were bought for £20 each. Heading north-easterly, the party made good time along known tracks to Lake Way, near Wiluna. By August a depot was formed at Lake Augusta.

While most of the party rested after their nine hundred and sixty-kilometre trek, Wells planned a flying trip northwards to look for new water sources in the Great Sandy Desert. He took only two men: a tall Adelaide youth named George Lindsay Jones, nephew of David Lindsay.

Lake Disappointment was so named because it was vast but contained only salt water. Wells skirted it, after naming Sir Fowell headland after Sir Thomas Fowell Buxton. He was searching for water in the Great Sandy Desert

d a Beluchistan camel driver named
ejah Belooch, to manage seven camels
den with food and water.

Wells's small group continued north-
asterly. He named the salt Lake
arnegie after a contemporary explorer,
avid Carnegie; Keartland Hills after the
nithologist; and salt Lake Buchanan
ter the explorer Nathaniel Buchanan.

A small waterhole was found at
lount Bates, then nothing for over three
indred kilometres, not even feed for the
imels. On 25 August 1896, Wells no-
ced a common bronzewing pigeon fly-
g westwards, and followed its path to
scover a brackish native well which he
imed Midway.

After drinking and bathing, Wells
turned quickly to the depot, passing
ver the Calvert Range named after the
xpedition's promoter.

ommunication plans go up in smoke

he full expedition party headed north-
sterly again on 14 September 1896,
eavily laden with water. By 8 October
ey reached Separation Well. Here
'ells decided that his cousin Charles
ederick Wells should have a chance to
ake his own discoveries. He dispatched
m with George Jones in a west-north-
st direction, giving no firm instruc-
ns but to rejoin the main party at the
lown water of Joanna Spring, three
ndred kilometres to the north. Failing
at, they should meet on the nearest
pint of the Fitzroy river.

Even the main party with all its
struments could not locate Joanna
pring. Searching continually in searing
mperatures — up to sixty degrees even
der canvas — several camels died.

Walking alone one day, Lawrence
'ells was stricken with the dazed brain
id delirium of dehydration, and was
ved only when he managed to attract
e attention of other members of the
rty by setting fire to a clump of
orcupine grass.

Wells had arranged to send up smoke
gnals to guide the smaller party, not
alising that native fires would cause this
stem to fail.

With only one hundred and sixty
res of water left, Wells decided on 31
ctober 1896 to march for the Fitzroy
ver, about one hundred and fifty kilo-
etres further north.

More camels died on the way, but on
November the party was able to plunge
to the river's cool water and save their
vn lives. They had travelled about three
ousand kilometres, nineteen hundred
them through almost waterless desert.
was courageous, but was it scientific?

At Separation Well in the previous
ctober, Charles Wells and George Jones
id taken the three best camels and two

hundred and seventy litres of water and
struck bravely into the merciless desert
towards Mount Macpherson.

Nobody knows exactly when they
died. Four search parties covered more
than five and a half thousand kilometres
but failed to find them until 27 May
1897. Their bodies had been mummified
by the intense heat: Wells's cousin lay on
the sand 'with features perfect and outstretched open hand'. The bodies were
only twenty-two kilometres from Joanna
Spring. All their belongings had been
taken by Aboriginals.

The remains of the two young men
were taken to Adelaide. They lay in state
at the Exhibition Building, surrounded
by scores of floral tributes. Thousands of
people filed past the coffins to pay tribute
to their courageous efforts.

Wells was criticised by some for splitting his expedition, but he had simply
followed well-known techniques of exploration and surveying. The Royal Geographic Society expressed 'utmost confidence' in his judgement, and he was

given other surveying and prospecting
assignments before his death in 1938.
However, not so much confidence was
expressed in Albert Calvert, the man
who had started it all.

His gold mines had petered out and he
was unable to pay the expedition's debts.
Bankrupt in 1898, he fled to Spain, wrote
thirty-six books on that country, received
a Spanish knighthood in 1924, and died
in London in 1946.

The last word on the Calvert/Wells
disaster lies with Simpson Newland,
South Australian pioneer and president
of the local Royal Geographical Society:
*The chapter of Australian exploration closed
as it began, with deeds of splendid endurance
and courage, with deeds of awful suffering,
and with the loss of heroic lives. I say 'closed'
for it can not be supposed that any other
expedition will ever be fitted out, for there is
nothing more to discover. The blanks still
untraversed might wisely be left to the
squatter, the prospector, and other hardy
adventurers to fill up when seasons and
opportunity serve.* □

Wells's expedition ends in tragedy amid the harsh red dunes of the desert

*Lawrence Wells's second contribution to the endeavours of
'scientific' exploration took him into the Great Sandy Desert
in 1896. There he found little more than a series of
hardships. Three search parties went out in his tracks
seeking two lost members of the expedition*

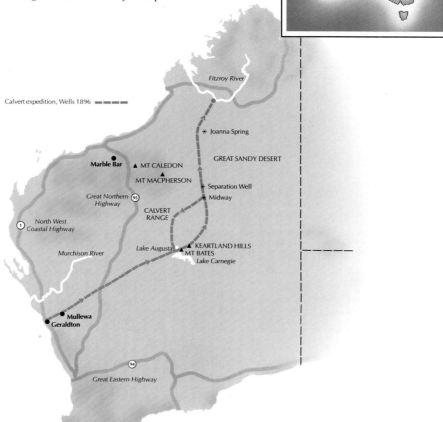

Calvert expedition, Wells 1896 ▬ ▬ ▬ ▬

Fitzroy River

✱ Joanna Spring

GREAT SANDY DESERT

● Marble Bar
▲ MT CALEDON
▲ MT MACPHERSON
✱ Separation Well
✱ Midway

Great Northern (95) Highway
CALVERT RANGE

① North West Coastal Highway

Lake Augusta ▲ KEARTLAND HILLS
▲ MT BATES
Lake Carnegie

Murchison River

● Mullewa
● Geraldton

(94)
Great Eastern Highway

0   300 km

Land of gold and adventure

Among the adventurous young men attracted to Western Australia during the last years of the nineteenth century were the Hon. David Wynford Carnegie, fourth son of the Earl of Southesk, and his friend Lord Percy Douglas.
The eager twenty-one-year-old Scots joined the gold rush to Coolgardie in September 1892. They quickly learned the bushcraft necessary to survive on the desert fringes. But they found little gold, even after joining the new rush to Kalgoorlie that followed Patrick Hannan's discovery of some nuggets in June 1893. Most of the gold lay deep in the Golden Mile.

Carnegie was commissioned by the Hampton Plains Pastoral Company to prospect the almost unknown arid area east and north-east of Coolgardie. In 1894, with remarkably little planning or equipment, Carnegie simply took 'a few camels' and enough canvas to make two large water-bags. By this time he seems to have taught himself the elements of navigating by instruments.

Accompanied only by a bushman named Gus Luck, Carnegie travelled first to Ernest Giles's 'unfailing' Queen Victoria Spring — and found it dry until dug out to a dangerous depth.

The two men left the spring on 22 April 1894, steering due north into unknown country between the routes of Giles and Lindsay. They carried only one hundred and sixty litres of water, and their home-made canvas bags already were leaking.

On 27 April Carnegie sighted and named Mount Luck and Mount Douglas on the north-western fringe of the Great Victoria Desert. Five days later they reached today's Cosmo Newberry Aboriginal Reserve, where Carnegie named Mount Fleming after the commandant of Western Australia's military forces.

To the north-west, near Mount Shenton, they found 'an excellent little soakage'. 'What a joy that water was to us!' wrote Carnegie.

Gold 'sprinkled like pepper'
During May the two men examined auriferous country between Mount Grant westerly to Mount Margaret, but could find no gold. On 30 May they moved south-west to Niagara creek, and here at last found 'a fine big reef' with 'gold sprinkled through the stone like pepper'.

They returned to Coolgardie by 22 June 1894 to file their claims, after a journey of more than thirteen hundred kilometres in ninety days.

From November 1894 to February 1895, Carnegie made a second commissioned trip from Coolgardie with a larger party, this time heading easterly towards Lake Roe.

He took a portable condenser, designed to evaporate water from salt lakes into drinkable water. The labour involved seemed scarcely worth the trouble:

DAVID WYNFORD CARNEGIE
GENTLEMAN-EXPLORER

'The boilers required constant attention day and night, the fires had to be stoked, and the water stored.' Most of each day was spent chopping and carrying firewood. But after practice the men were able to produce eighteen litres an hour.

South-west of Lake Roe, at Cowarna Rocks, Carnegie was able to find a little fresh water by delving into a narrow hole in the granite outcrop. Other than that, men and camels were entirely dependent on the condenser.

Christmas 1894 found Carnegie further again south-west at Mount Monger, where prospectors were scratching out a little gold.

Early in 1895 the party headed northerly towards Mount Ida and Lake Darlot, where new gold strikes were rumoured. The camels became hopelessly bogged in a channel of Lake Darlot. In blistering heat they had to be unloaded and dug out.

Yet the labour seemed worthwhile. On 17 February 1895 Carnegie took a walk, and 'stepped right on to an outcrop of quartz showing beautiful gold!' Alone he rode four hundred and eighty kilometres south to file the claim at Coolgardie, almost dying on the way from severe attacks of typhoid fever.

While convalescing in Perth, Carnegie sold his share in the mine and returned briefly to England in October 1895. But he could not resist the call of the desert. By July 1896 he was back in Coolgardie, arranging an expedition which would try to find a direct stock route between northern cattle stations and the southern goldfields.

Carnegie's new party of four men and nine camels left Coolgardie on 9 July 1896, heading northerly through the small settlement at Menzies.

Heavy rain turned the tracks into deep mud, but also changed much of the countryside to lush green pasture. 'Almost every bush held a nest, usually occupied by a diamond-sparrow,' Carnegie noted.

The Great Victoria Desert looms
From the vicinity of Doyle Well on 2[?] July, Carnegie changed direction to east north-east, heading for Mount Worsnop and mapping the unknown country as he went. South of Lake Darlot, the camels again became bogged in salt mud and had to be dragged out.

By 31 July 1896, the travellers reached the unmistakable edge of the Great Victoria Desert. As they continued north-easterly, their water was soon almost exhausted. Every waterhole they found was dry.

Carnegie now began to capture isolated Aboriginals and tie them up — even fed one on salt beef — until they revealed their water sources. On 1[?] August the whites forced one native to show them the entrance to Empress Spring, where there was a large underground cavern leading to an endless supply of fresh water. The camels drank more than seventy-five litres each, and the men as much as they could hold.

After several days' rest the party was able to push on to Mount Worsnop and Alexander Spring, named by John Forrest in 1874 after his brother.

Gravel wastes provide some food
On 22 August 1896, Carnegie left the 'kindly little oasis' and continued northerly, through a 'deadly monotonous' region which he thought should be called The Great Undulating Desert of Gravel. It was part of the Gibson Desert, which had caused Ernest Giles such agony on his east-west crossings. Only an occasional bounding 'spinifex rat' (probably a rufous hare-wallaby), or distant birds broke the eerie stillness.

Late in September 1896, Carnegie sighted the Browne Range, naming it after old mining acquaintances. Here were signs of native camps and a little feed, but no water, until a flock of 'diamond-sparrows' (finches) was sighted at a small hidden well. Meanwhile the camels had prospered on the fleshy desert plant parakeelya (*Calandrinia balonensis*), found amongst the spinifex bushes. Even the men fried its stalks and declared it to be 'quite good eating.'

A few days further north, water was again short. A captured native woman could show them only a stinking muddy well, into which they plunged regardless.

'None of our friends or relatives would have recognised us now!' wrote Carnegie. 'Clothed in filthy rags, with unkempt hair and beards, begrimed with mud, and burnt black by the sun, wherever its rays could penetrate our armour of dirt, we were indeed a pretty lot.'

Ahead they could see only the 'vast howling wilderness' of the Great Sandy Desert. Again they rode down native tribes, but now used gifts to persuade them to share water from their wells.

At last, after travelling six hundred and seventy kilometres including deviations, the party emerged from the desert on 16 November 1896. Nine days later they struck the bed of the Mary river, whose frequent shady pools 'made a welcome change after the awful desolation of the desert'.

Changing direction on 30 November to reach Halls Creek, Carnegie heard a

ALFRED CANNING FINDS AN OVERLAND STOCK ROUTE

Pastoralists in north-western Australia faced the perennial problem of distance from markets. David Carnegie failed in his attempts of 1896-97 to find a well-watered overland route along which stock could be driven to the southern goldfields. His track was too far inland, through deserts that still defy white settlement.

The problem was partly solved in 1906 by Alfred Canning, forty-six-year-old Victorian-born surveyor of the Western Australia Lands Department.

Using a team of eight men and twenty-three camels, Canning managed to blaze a trail over fourteen hundred kilometres from Wiluna to Halls Creek in the Kimberleys, with daily stages between waterholes not exceeding a longish twenty-four kilometres.

Canning returned over the same route in 1908 to construct permanent wells, ensuring a steady supply of water to support large mobs of stock.

Canning *(centre) in his sixties. He had blazed the trail for Australia's longest stock route*

But when sea transport improved, the route fell into disuse.

In 1929, aged nearly seventy, Canning twice walked the entire distance, showing men where to clean out the neglected wells so that droving could resume.

The last mob of cattle was driven over the route in 1958. Today it attracts many tourists seeking adventure in the desert.

---

shot in the distance and turned back. He found that one of his men, Charlie Stansmore, a bushman descended from pioneer settlers from Perth, had slipped on a rock while chasing a kangaroo and shot himself through the heart.

On 4 December 1896, Carnegie reached Halls Creek, where he learned by telegraph of the disappearance of two men from the Calvert/Wells expedition. He offered help, but it was too late.

Carnegie began the return journey on 22 March 1897, travelling to the east of his original course, across Sturt creek to the outermost Denison Downs Station, then south-easterly again through the Great Sandy Desert and today's Balwina Aboriginal Reserve. En route he named Stansmore Range in memory of their dead companion.

Again he had to cross endless sand ridges, and persuade or force scattered Aboriginals to reveal the location of wells.

On his return to Coolgardie early in August 1897, Carnegie reflected that 'It has been my fate, in all my exploration work, to find none but useless country, though when merely prospecting on the goldfields I have been more fortunate. My work has had no better result than to demonstrate to others that part of the interior that may best be avoided.

'No mountain ranges, no rivers, no lakes, no pastoral lands, nor mineral districts has it brought to light; where the country was previously unknown it has proved only its nakedness; nevertheless I do not regret one penny of the cost or one minute of the troubles and labours entailed by it.'

Soon back in England, Carnegie was awarded the Gill Medal by the Royal Geographical Society for his explorations. Taking up a government post in Nigeria, he was killed by a poisoned native arrow at the age of twenty-nine. The short romantic life of Australia's last major nineteenth-century explorer was dramatically extinguished. □

Last of the nineteenth century explorers

The aristocratic David Carnegie used the profits from his gold finds to fund his exploration. He discovered some of the least rewarding regions, but had no regrets

Halls Creek
Sturt Creek
Mary River
(Denison Downs Station)
GREAT SANDY DESERT
Balwina Aboriginal Reserve
STANSMORE RANGE
Great Northern Highway
Canning Stock Route
GIBSON DESERT
North West Coastal Highway
BROWNE RANGE
Alexander Spring
MT WORSNOP
Cosmo Newberry Aboriginal Reserve
Wiluna
MT SHENTON
MT GRANT
Lake Darlot
MT FLEMING
Doyle Well
MT DOUGLAS
MT IDA
MT LUCK
Niagara Creek
MT MARGARET
Menzies
GREAT VICTORIA DESERT
Queen Victoria Spring
Lake Roe
COWARNA ROCKS
Eyre Highway
Coolgardie
MT MONGER
Great Eastern Highway

0   500 km

Carnegie 1894 = = =
1896 = = =
Canning Stock Route = = =

Spencer and Gillen search the inland for evidence of human evolution

As Australia approached the twentieth century, explorers had managed to penetrate practically every part of the continent. And yet, many of their journeys could best be described as flying trips, designed to cross hostile environments as quickly as possible. Detailed knowledge could come only with the slow, meticulous expeditions of anthropologists, botanists, zoologists and cartographers. They would seek scientific information about the land and everything that lived on it. Their discoveries would intrigue academics throughout the world.

One of the most tenacious of these scientist-explorers was Walter Baldwin Spencer, a brilliant Lancashire-born, Oxford-educated biologist. When only twenty-seven years of age, he was appointed in 1887 as Melbourne University's first biology professor.

Spencer joined the successful Horn Scientific Expedition of 1894. This was the start of a lifelong love affair with central Australia in its natural state, before the European impact changed it too greatly.

In those days, Charles Darwin's evolutionary theories still reverberated. Spencer realised that Australia's arid areas, a practically untouched field for observation, could provide answers to questions about human evolution. Years later he was to write: 'It is difficult for students of the present day to realize the excitement of those times when everything was new and stimulating.'

Most previous travellers had seen Aboriginals as standing in the way of European progress. Few appreciated that the white man's high consumption of natural resources — especially water in arid areas — could shatter thousands of years of tribal balance with the environment. At best, friendly Aboriginals might be used as guides, and as providers of natural foods.

Only rare explorers, such as Alfred Howitt who found the remains of Burke and Wills, were interested in the systematic study of tribal lore.

During the Horn expedition, Spencer was fortunate to meet Francis James Gillen, forty-nine-year-old son of poor Irish immigrants, who had improved his prospects in life by joining the South Australian post office as an eleven-year-old messenger boy and slowly rising through the ranks of the civil service.

Gillen spent many lonely years as an operator along the Overland Telegraph Line from Darwin. Unlike most Europeans, he tried to understand and conciliate the Aboriginals. Gillen built up a remarkable collection of artefacts which he eventually sold (after heavy losses on mining speculations) to the National Museum of Victoria.

This amateur anthropologist always walked about unarmed and unafraid. He became so trusted by Aboriginals around Alice Springs that they named him Oknirrabata (great teacher), and admitted him to many of their secret ceremonies as a brother of the Arunta tribe, the largest group in the centre.

Partnership to study Aboriginal lore

In 1892 Gillen was appointed head of Alice Springs post and telegraph station. Two years later, after the Horn expedition had returned home, Baldwin Spencer stayed behind to discuss Aboriginal lore with the knowledgeable postmaster, beginning a life-long partnership.

Their friendship and harmony of ideas led Spencer to return to Alice Springs in 1896 for a joint venture with Gillen.

Baldwin Spencer with the Arunta elders near Alice Springs in 1896. Each of these men was the head of a particular totem group. Baldwin was to write a book about the Arunta in 1927, subtitling it a 'study of a stone-age people'

Their aim was to study the puzzling ceremonies of desert tribes, which obviously had traditional meanings.

Normally the scheme would have required a major expedition and years of exhausting travel through arid regions in search of individual tribes. Due to Gillen's unique reputation with the Aboriginals, he was able to persuade them to conduct a cycle of secret initiation ceremonies near Alice Springs, on a site previously abandoned because of its nearness to white settlement. There Gillen and Spencer erected a gum-tree wurley in which they lived and kept their photographic equipment for several weeks in temperatures of up to forty-six degrees.

The two men were permitted to watch and photograph the male circumcision ceremony, conducted on adolescents. Spencer described the event: a male Aboriginal assistant 'grasped the foreskin, pulled it out as far as possible and the operator cut it off.' The boy, 'in a more or less dazed condition', was supported by two men who said to him, 'You have done well, you have not cried out.' Sacred bull-roarers or churinga were pressed on the wound to help stem the bleeding, and the boy soon recovered.

About six weeks later, the more fearful operation of subincision took place. One man stretched the silent boy's penis as far as possible. The operator approached 'and quickly, with a stone knife, laid open the urethra from below', from its head right back to its junction with the scrotum.

Other men came up and tied on a tassel, telling the boy he was now a man and had no more operations to fear. He was told to squat upon a shield into which the blood flowed. It was then emptied into the fire and consumed.

For some weeks until the young man's wound healed, he lay only on his back, 'for otherwise the organ would grow crooked'. For the remainder of his life, he would micturate in a squatting position, into a hollow scraped in the soil.

Many anthropologists believed that subincision had begun as a primitive form of contraception, allowing most of the man's semen to drop to the ground instead of entering the woman's uterus. If so, its real purpose had been disguised for thousands of years by elaborate ceremonial surrounding the operation.

By the time Spencer and Gillen began their studies, they found that the Aboriginals seemed to be ignorant of any link between intercourse and pregnancy. Instead, the tribes believed that any object such as an animal or plant on which the woman's attention was fixed at a critical moment became her totem, entered her womb, and was transformed into a human child of the same totem.

Spencer doubted the contraception theory of subincision, pointing out that 'The Arunta native does not hesitate to kill a child — always directly it is born — if there be an older one still in need of nourishment from the mother.' With infanticide so common, he felt there was no need for a painful operation like subincision to control tribal numbers.

But Spencer could not suggest any other logical reason for the event.

During intervals between the ceremonies, the two anthropologists questioned Aboriginals on their family and tribal relationships, laying down wax matches with different coloured heads to establish the complex kinship lines.

A world-first in anthropology

Spencer found that the tribes were divided into clear exogamous groups. The effect was to prevent the marriage of brothers with sisters, of parents with their offspring, and of certain cousins with each other. The biological result was to prevent in some degree the birth of genetically faulty children — even though once again the reality had been overlaid by thousands of years of traditional religious prohibitions.

During January 1897 Spencer packed up his cameras and travelled by camel to Undiara, a ceremonial site east of Henbury, about one hundred and fifteen kilometres south-west of Alice Springs. Here in the past, Aboriginal artists had covered a rock shelter with totemic paintings, which Spencer photographed.

All this pioneering work was published in 1899 in a book called *The Native Tribes of Central Australia*. It showed the western world that the apparently primitive Aboriginals of the desert fringe had evolved a complex system of totems, taboos, traditions and spiritual relationships with the natural order around them.

The great British anthropologist, James Frazer, author of *The Golden Bough*, announced that the two Australians had opened a new era in the study of early humanity. 'In immortalizing the native tribes of Central Australia, Spencer and Gillen have at the same time immortalized themselves,' Frazer wrote.

One of the last living museums

Now world-famous, the two men began planning the most ambitious scientific expedition yet seen in Australia. Their aim was to establish an ethnographic record of tribal life from central through to northern Australia, before, as they assumed, it disappeared forever.

Spencer saw the outback as one of the world's last living museums of untouched native culture — of possibly the world's oldest continuous culture. By recording its authentic natural state, the progress of humanity from stone-age existence to modern civilisation might be established.

Support for the undertaking came from many quarters. James Frazer again backed Spencer in planning 'probably the finest piece of anthropological research that could be done in the world.'

Enthused by the vision of the human race's seemingly inevitable evolution to a

Journeys taken to discover a fast-disappearing way of life

The partnership between the amateur anthropologist Gillen and the Oxford-educated Spencer led to a new kind of expedition. The two men concentrated on discovering and recording a traditional Aboriginal lifestyle that was fast disappearing. But even their well-planned journeys were made difficult by the hazards of the Australian desert

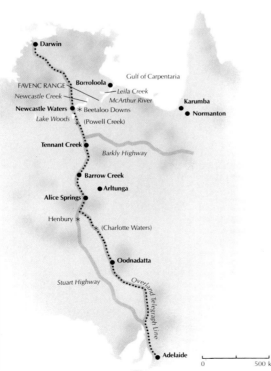

Darwin
Borroloola
Gulf of Carpentaria
FAVENC RANGE
Leila Creek
Newcastle Creek
McArthur River
Karumba
Newcastle Waters
Beetaloo Downs
Normanton
Lake Woods
(Powell Creek)
Tennant Creek
Barkly Highway
Barrow Creek
Arltunga
Alice Springs
Henbury
(Charlotte Waters)
Oodnadatta
Stuart Highway
Overland Telegraph Line
Adelaide
0   500 km

The Warramunga tribe allowed Spencer to take photographs of this burial ceremony. The men of the tribe are standing over the grave, while the women approach carrying an arm bone

higher state, David Syme, tight-fisted proprietor of the Melbourne *Age*, promised £1000 towards the cost of a new expedition — provided that reports and photographs were sent exclusively to his newspapers. Spencer's father lent another £400; and South Australia also donated £400. That government gave Spencer free use of the Overland Telegraph Line, lending him portable tapping equipment through which messages could be sent in Morse code at no cost.

In March 1901 the expedition travelled by train from Adelaide to Oodnadatta. At this small desert camel depot they were met by forty-five-year-old mounted trooper Harry Chance, who had already organised food depots for the expedition along lonely stretches of the Overland Telegraph.

At that time Australia's overseas telegraphic communication still depended on a single strand of wire running across the continent from Darwin. Interruptions frequently occurred when the wire broke or termites ate the wooden poles. The only alternative communication between Alice Springs and Oodnadatta was a fortnightly horseback mail service.

Trooper Chance took charge of the expedition's practical arrangements, leaving the experts free to concentrate on field research. He was backed up by two Charlotte Waters Aboriginals, Purunda and Erklikiliaka, who looked after the party's twenty horses.

Supplies included thirty-six hundred kilos of flour, three hundred kilos of sugar, six hundred tins of meat, one hundred and eighty kilos of tobacco, one hundred and thirty kilos of dried fruit and vegetables, and sixty-eight kilos of tea. Much of this was given to Aboriginals en route as rewards for information. Other presents came out of a store of four hundred butcher's knives, four hundred hatchets, four hundred pocket-knives, and hundreds of tobacco pipes. Unlike

traditional explorers, the party also took large quantities of collecting jars, preserving spirit and rolls of cloth to keep dust out of their delicate equipment.

As Spencer and Gillen travelled through the outback in 1901, they observed that 'the natives live on the most friendly terms with, and are most kindly treated, both by the officers of the telegraph line, the few patrol officers of the mounted police, where such are stationed, and the holders of the few scattered cattle-runs.'

A permanent record of tribal life

Only one year later, all this began to change for the worse. Discovery of gold at Arltunga, about ninety kilometres east-north-east of Alice Springs, led to a sudden influx of about four thousand white miners of varying morality. Their activities throughout the north began to shatter local tribal systems. Spencer and Gillen had arrived in time — one crucial year out of forty thousand — to record Aboriginal life in an almost pure state.

In the first year of the present century, Spencer could still write:

The aborigine is a true nomad, wandering from place to place over the country which belongs to the tribe... he has not reached the agricultural state of civilisation and has no idea of cultivating cereals or of laying in a stock of food to maintain himself during the time when food is scarce. He lives from hand to mouth without any thought of the morrow. When food is abundant he eats in plenty and is quite happy; when it is scarce he accepts the conditions philosophically and, if hungry, merely tightens his waist belt and patiently waits till . . . he can find something to eat...

Fortunately his very lack of power to control nature, though he is firmly convinced that he can do so, has been the means of sharpening his powers of observation, and he can obtain water and food in comparative abundance in places where a civilised man would die of thirst and starvation. There are,

however, times when even the aborigine with all his bush-craft, and this is simply marvellous, is unable to contend against the fierce heat and drought . . . and perishes miserably

Spencer and Gillen used two of the latest products of western civilisation — the movie camera and sound recording apparatus — to make a permanent record of tribal life.

Movie film had been used only once before in the field, during Alfred Haddon's 1898 Cambridge Anthropological Expedition to Torres Strait. Spencer imported a primitive Warwick camera and nine hundred and fourteen metres of film from London. This was set up in front of the Aboriginals' ceremonial grounds, with Spencer directing and Gillen cranking the handle.

Although the camera would hold film that lasted only three minutes, and extreme heat shrank its wooden case, the pair managed to make some of the world's earliest scientific films. These were processed by the Salvation Army film unit in Melbourne (who at the time were making the world's first feature-length film). Spencer and Gillen's effort still survives in reprocessed form, but the Salvation Army film has long disappeared.

Spencer and Gillen also pioneered the use of sound recording in Australian field work. They used an Edison concert phonograph with five-inch (one hundred and twenty-seven millimetres) wax cylinders to record Aboriginal songs, corroborees, conversations and quarrels. Fifteen cylinders have survived.

Improvised darkrooms in the desert

During the year-long journey from Charlotte Waters Telegraph Station to Borroloola in the Gulf of Carpentaria, Spencer also shot nearly five hundred excellent glass-plate still photographs of Aboriginal life. At night he developed and enlarged them in improvised darkrooms. Often the temperature was so high 'it was difficult to keep the film from frilling completely off the plates.'

The party left Alice Springs on 25 May 1901 for the long journey northwards. They stayed for several weeks at Barrow Creek Telegraph Station (now a town on the Stuart Highway), studying rites of the Kaitish tribe. Late in July 1901 they moved two hundred and twenty-five kilometres further north to Tennant Creek, home of the Warramunga tribe.

Here, on the almost bare, arid plain, they became the first white men ever to study the entire death and burial ceremonies of a central Australian tribe.

In October 1901 the party moved further north past Lake Woods to Newcastle Waters. Here they left the Telegraph Line and headed east-north-east towards the Gulf of Carpentaria, hurrying to beat the monsoon season and its dangerous flood waters.

Along Newcastle creek they were given every assistance by settlers at Beetaloo Downs station, although the homestead at that time consisted of a tent fly and a wurley.

One evening they were surprised to see two strange Aboriginals arriving with 'paper yabber' carried in a cleft stick. These were telegrams, which had arrived at Powell creek after their departure. The two natives had followed the party's tracks for over three hundred and twenty kilometres, their safety through strange territory guaranteed by the 'paper yabber' they carried. The messengers were rewarded with food, tobacco and knives.

Later in the trip, when supplies were running short, Spencer sent a 'paper yabber' to the nearest stockman, forty-eight kilometres away — the sole white man within a radius of one hundred and sixty kilometres. The stockman promptly filled his packs with beef and rode to help them, 'just as if it were an ordinary part of the day's work.' Only a few years before, no such help was available to explorers.

Camping on Leila creek, a tributary of the McArthur river, Spencer wrote that 'None of this country has been mapped, except in the vaguest way.' Only the

innate topographical sense of Trooper Chance and his native assistants got the party and their wagon through 'decidedly rough' valleys where the Favenc Range begins the descent from tableland to coastal flood plain.

One day, when the men were skinning birds in their wurley, with the temperature at forty-six degrees, banks of dark clouds rolled across the sun. Without further warning, a 'roaring wind' swept up the valley, bringing 'rain in a perfect deluge'. Everything in the camp was blown away — even Spencer and Gillen were 'every now and then lifted off our feet by a terrific gust of wind.'

Stranded at Borroloola

After the cyclone passed, the party collected what it could find, and hastened on to Borroloola, central point of the McArthur river district. Once Borroloola had been a busy frontier town, where criminals on the run and hardbitten prospectors fought for survival. Mounted police had cleaned it up, but now it was almost a ghost town.

Spencer and Gillen arrived early in November 1901, and decided to await the quarterly visit of a coastal steamer bringing supplies from Darwin. But news came that the steamer had foundered. In December heavy rain began to fall. The stranded anthropologists settled under the floorboards of the deserted, bat-infested courthouse at Borroloola to sit out the stifling humidity and high temperatures of the monsoon season.

Christmas Day 1901 was celebrated at the local store with hot soup, roast meat and vegetables, plum pudding, warm ale and wine, coffee, cigars and whisky, all of

which Spencer thought 'horrible' and 'unnatural'. Yet the expedition itself had only a bag of flour and a tin of biscuits left in its own stores.

By January 1902 it seemed to southern newspapers that the expedition might be in danger of perishing. Flood waters had cut off the township, and no telegraphic communication was available. Was this to be another Burke and Wills saga?

Spencer's wife went to interview the Victorian Premier, Alexander Peacock. Harried by continuous press speculation, Peacock agreed to seek help from other state governments. On 31 January, Queensland ordered its pilot boat *Vigilant* to rescue the 'lost' explorers. A week later, the master of the *Vigilant* steamed up the flooded McArthur river and plucking the men from under the Borroloola court-house.

The two men returned to a warm mayoral welcome in Brisbane, and renewed interest from all newspapers and their readers about Australia's mysterious, frightening northern regions.

Spencer and Gillen cooperated in one further expedition, a quick trip north-west of Lake Eyre in 1903. A few years later Gillen's health began to fail: he died in 1912, aged fifty-seven.

Spencer went on to a busy career at Melbourne University and other institutions, but somehow found time for further expeditions in the Northern Territory. In 1912 he was appointed Commonwealth Chief Protector of Aborigines, to reconcile racial clashes.

In 1929, aged sixty-nine, Spencer died almost with his field boots on — investigating the primitive Indian inhabitants of storm-swept Tierra del Fuego. □

The members of Spencer's 1901-02 expedition, at Alice Springs. Gillen is seated on the left and Spencer on the right. Behind them are Erklikiliaka, Harry Chance and Purunda

HOW TO ESCAPE A CROCODILE

Baldwin Spencer was anxious to secure a large Northern Territory crocodile for his museum collection. The problem was that when disturbed, the reptile immediately glided into the water. Even if shot, it promptly sank to the bottom.

Aboriginals near Borroloola advised Spencer that if seized by a crocodile, he should poke his fingers into its eyes. This 'may so disconcert the beast that it lets go and you can escape.'

The natives also told Spencer that when crossing a crocodile-infested river, they placed an old woman in the rear. They believed that a crocodile always seized the last person, 'and the loss of an old woman does not matter very much.'

Using poisoned bait, the Borroloola Aboriginals killed a crocodile for Spencer. Unfortunately for Spencer's collection the crocodile's odour was so horrible after being skinned that everything had to be burned on the spot except the head.

Antarctica's icy wastes lure a new breed of explorers

After the virtual conquest of the Australian continent, explorers' eyes turned hungrily towards new fields of heroic endeavour. Directly to the south, over wild and merciless seas, lay another huge unknown continent. What did it matter that Antarctica seemed forever a frozen waste? Early adventurers felt they had to find out more about it — if only because it was there, forbidding yet compelling. So through explorers' efforts, Australia came to control nearly half of a unique area now greatly desired by other nations.

DOUGLAS MAWSON
GEOLOGIST AND EXPLORER

In some ways the conquest of Antarctica parallels the exploration of Australia itself. An English buccaneer, Lionel Wafer, made a Dampier-like approach in 1687 from Cape Horn, recording 'Hills of ice' from which came 'cold blasts of wind'. James Cook, on his second great voyage in 1773, became the first known captain to cross the Antarctic Circle. On his dangerous voyage the rigging of HMS *Resolution* froze solid: 'Our ropes were like wire, our sails like plates of metal and the sheaves froze fast in the blocks,' wrote Cook. With extreme difficulty he sailed along the edge of the pack ice as far south as seventy-one degrees latitude before fleeing to warmer seas.

The Antarctic continent itself was not sighted until nearly half a century later. In January 1820 a Russian naval captain named Thaddeus von Bellingshausen sailed the *Vostok* and *Mirnyi* along the ice floes. He reached the position sixty-nine degrees, twenty-one minutes south by two degrees, fourteen minutes west on 27 January, putting him in sight of the land mass. Apparently mistaking it for yet more icebergs, Bellingshausen sailed away without claiming rights of first discovery to the continent.

Only three days later, British naval officer Edward Bransfield, guided by a merchant captain named William Smith, sailed to latitude sixty-four degrees south, to make the first confirmed sighting of the mainland at Trinity Peninsula. Bransfield surveyed part of the coastline before sailing to the South Shetlands.

Sealers and whalers visited these harsh lands for some decades, living largely off penguin meat and salted provisions. Before long the fur seal colonies were practically obliterated, even whales became scarce, and for another fifty years adventurers turned their attention to Arctic regions instead. Antarctica slipped into the realm of hazy legend.

Australia becomes interested

During that half-century the great feats of Australian inland exploration and settlement were accomplished. In 1874 HMS *Challenger*, on a world cruise, became the first steamship to cross the Antarctic Circle. Scientists on board collected data hinting at unsuspected biological wealth in far southern regions.

Australians became intrigued. In August 1886 the Royal and Geographical societies of Victoria requested the government to finance the first-ever scientific expedition to travel over the Antarctic continent. An unimaginative Premier more interested in local land speculation rejected the proposal.

The savants persevered. In 1888 the Australasian Association for the Advancement of Science set up an Antarctic Exploration Committee, with Baldwin Spencer as one of its leading members. Two Swedish naturalists offered £5000 towards a joint Swedish-Australian expedition, provided Victoria raised a similar amount. But with the collapse of the Melbourne land boom, funds could not be found. The Victorian government again missed its chance to pioneer Antarctic land exploration.

Private entrepreneurs began to fill the gap. In 1895 Henryk Johan Bull, a Norwegian businessman, arranged a voyage in the whaler *Antarctic* to help investigate new areas. He took a friend, a Norwegian immigrant named Carsten Egeberg Borchgrevink. They found lichen growing on an offshore island within the Antarctic Circle, the first discovery of plant life so far south.

The party landed briefly on the mainland at Cape Adare on what is now the

---

Demanding though the desert had been, the icy wastes of Antarctica produced many parallels in hardship and courage, despite the obvious contrasts. But by now, technology was beginning to play a part — if at first an inefficient one — in the exploration of harsh environments. Ernest Shackleton's 1907 expedition took the first car to the Antarctic — an Arrol-Johnston, which was housed in a garage of packing-cases

Borchgrevink Coast. This was the first confirmed landing on the continent.

Other nations took renewed interest. The sixth International Geographical Congress, meeting in London in 1895, decided to make Antarctica its main subject for investigation.

Borchgrevink managed to raise enough cash from a British publisher to lead ten enthusiasts in the five hundred and twenty-tonne *Southern Cross* back to Cape Adare. It took them forty-three days to penetrate the pack ice, but on the 'boisterous, cold and gloomy' 18 February 1899, the explorers managed to land at Cape Adare. Two prefabricated huts were assembled on the beach, to make the first permanent encampment in Antarctica, and the first to survive an entire winter.

The men spent the rest of 1899 on field survey trips, taking magnetic readings, and gathering samples of quartz and mosses, birds, fish, seals and penguins.

They survived appalling conditions. During one terrifying gale the men's lives were saved only by bringing their seventy-five sledge dogs into the tent for warmth. One man later died anyway, possibly of scurvy.

In February 1900 the party moved by ship to the Ross Ice Shelf. Again they nearly perished when a mountain of glacier ice collapsed, creating a huge wave that swept them out to sea. But they managed to land, travelling southwards by sledge over part of the silent, barren ice-cap, which sent 'an indefinable sense of dread to the heart.'

Borchgrevink's success ushered in the great age of Antarctic exploration. Now that he had proven men could survive

conditions there for long periods, a famous, although rather pointless, race began to reach the geographical pole.

In the early years of this century, expeditions including British ones led by Robert Falcon Scott and by Ernest Shackleton penetrated ever deeper into the centre of Antarctica.

Shackleton's effort of 1907-1909 included a fifty-year-old Welsh-born Sydney University geologist, Professor T. W. Edgeworth David, already noted for discovering South Maitland coalfield by scientific deduction. David turned his wondering eye to the evolution of coral reefs, then to past ice ages, becoming a world expert on both subjects.

The Edgeworth David-Mawson team

Shackleton invited David to head his scientific team in Antarctica. The professor took one of his best former students. He was a twenty-five-year-old Yorkshire-born geologist named Douglas Mawson, whose parents had emigrated to Sydney soon after his birth. In 1905, the young geologist had already discovered his adopted country's first big radioactive ore body at Radium Hill, South Australia, south of today's Barrier Highway.

After disembarking from the *Nimrod* in February 1908, Shackleton and his men continued exploration towards the geographical pole. David, Mawson and a Scottish-born naval surgeon named Alistair Forbes Mackay set off separately in September 1908 to locate the magnetic pole. At first they tried a novelty, using a motor car adapted for icy conditions, but the engine overheated badly as the wheels spun, vainly trying to gain a

The icebergs and floes that threatened the sailing ships of the early Antarctic explorers also helped them survive — small bergs were fished from the sea whenever needed to replenish the supplies of fresh drinking water on board

bit of traction in the ice and snow.

The three men decided to manhandle a sledge containing food, tent and Union Jack. Restrictions on weight meant they were constantly on short rations. They survived largely on plasmon biscuits, tea leaves brewed over and over, and seal meat softened in a biscuit tin heated with burning seal blubber.

The explorers were constantly in danger of disappearing into hidden crevasses. 'The ice was simply seamed with them,' wrote David. Frostbite stripped the skin from their lips and noses, while the sun burned their exposed hands.

But by 16 January 1909, the three men were first to reach the magnetic pole, which has since moved far away due to movements in the earth's liquid core. At the spot where Mawson's compass pointed directly to the ground, they planted the flag, took possession for Britain, and gave the traditional three cheers. Altogether they trekked two thousand and thirty kilometres in horrendous conditions, returning cheerfully on board the *Nimrod* to give news of their historic achievement.

A Norwegian explorer, Roald Amundsen, reached the geographic South Pole on 14 December 1911, triumphing over Robert Scott's party which did not arrive until 18 January 1912. 'Great God!' wrote Scott, 'this is an awful place and terrible enough for us to have boured to it without the reward of riority.' On the return journey through lizzards Scott's entire party perished.

Meanwhile, after his return home, and urning down an offer by Robert Scott to nclude him in his ill-fated expedition, Douglas Mawson managed to raise funds om government and private sources to nance the first Australasian Antarctic xpedition. This was designed to conentrate on purely scientific ends instead f dramatic sledge dashes to the pole. It eveloped into the greatest exploration ffort so far undertaken by Australia utside its own shores.

To save money, Mawson chartered an ld six hundred-tonne sealing vessel, the teamship *Aurora*. His party of thirty-one olunteers sailed out of Hobart on 2 December 1911.

Mawson's terrible adventures

They went first to Macquarie Island, an olated speck thirteen hundred and eventy kilometres south-east of Tasaania. The island had been discovered in 810 by an Australian sealer who named after Governor Lachlan Macquarie, but as rarely visited after its fur seals were xterminated to make fashionable hats, oats and shoes.

Mawson established a primitive wiress station on Macquarie Island, thus ioneering the use of radio in Antarctic xploration. He left a party of five men to elay messages and conduct daily eteorological observations.

Early in January 1912, the *Aurora* ntered an inlet on the Antarctic contient, which Mawson named Commonealth Bay. Constant hurricanes kept the rea fairly free of ice. A landing was ossible on a windswept rocky arm amed Cape Denison, after Sir Hugh enison, Sydney newspaper proprietor

who helped promote the expedition. Here eighteen men set up the main base camp with buildings of Baltic pine.

A third party of eight men under another old Shackleton hand named Frank Wild was landed twenty-four hundred and ten kilometres further on at the Shackleton Ice Shelf, Queen Mary Land.

Around the main camp, violent winds — 'a black-white writhing storm' — roared twenty-four hours a day. Erection of radio masts took five months, then were smashed to the ground within a few weeks. Faint Morse code messages were received at Macquarie Island, but no replies could be picked up for a year.

Mawson also attempted the first use of aircraft in Antarctica. He had brought a Vickers REP aeroplane mounted on skis which had been damaged in an accident. Its wings were removed, and the body used as a ski tractor to pull heavy loads to a depot at Aladdin's Cave, nine kilometres to the south.

The men spent most of the fierce winter months of 1912 entertaining each other with games, concerts and reminiscences. By early August they were ready for spring exploration. Sledging parties fanned out in all directions, testing their skill in varying conditions for up to eighty kilometres.

In November 1912 the serious work began. The party split into five groups headed for various destinations. Mawson led the most dangerous of the journeys — the Far Eastern trek through George V Land. With him was Dr Xavier Mertz, twenty-eight-year-old Swiss skiing champion; and Lieutenant Belgrave Ninnis of the Royal Fusiliers. Their three sledges of supplies were pulled by eighteen Greenland huskies.

During November and early December

From left: Mackay, David and Mawson, their Union Jack firmly planted at the magnetic pole. They had to trek back to the ship on half-rations

WHY THE ANTARCTIC ATTRACTED AUSTRALIANS

More than the simple desire to be first in unknown territory took successive generations of Australian explorers deeper and deeper to Antarctica.

Douglas Mawson, greatest of the pioneers, proposed that Australia and Antarctica were once part of the same continent. It followed that mineral wealth similar to Australia's probably lay under the polar ice-cap.

Mawson's expedition of 1911-13 laid the scientific foundations for future Australian work in the region. His parties carried out six major land traverses and were able to document considerable sections of the three thousand-kilometre coastline.

At the main camp, magnetographs installed in a hut behind a high stone windbreak monitored the erratic path of the South Magnetic Pole. Other re

searchers conducted pioneering studies into geology, marine biology, meteorology and the southern aurora.

Mawson's twenty-two-volume report also warned of the danger of extinction of richly varied wildlife — whales, seals, penguins, albatrosses.

After Mawson's second major expedition of 1929-31, Australia claimed huge slices of Antarctica. Attorney-General J. G. Latham told Federal Parliament on 26 May 1933 that as well as economics and science, defence was a major motive, because: '...embarrassing circumstances would arise if any other power assumed the control and administration of the area.' Latham added that Alaska also had been regarded as useless, and was sold to the United States of America for a trifling sum. Later it became 'one of the Eldorados of the world.'

Today Antarctica's riches are thought to be immense. Its oceans swarm with krill, *Euphausia superba*, tiny shrimp-like creatures rich in protein. Krill are the most abundant animal in the world. Their potential as a renewable food source has attracted special interest from the Soviet Union and Asian nations.

The mountains of Antarctica are believed to hold the world's greatest coal reserves. Iron ore is plentiful, although uneconomic to mine at present. Many promising samples of gold, silver, chromium, manganese and other valuable minerals have been found. Most important of all, Antarctica's oil reserves have been estimated at 'tens of billions of barrels'. Half a dozen nations are trying to discover oil and natural gas reservoirs below the sea bed. Japan is particularly active.

Mawson's party traversed tortuous icy 'waves' and crevasses surrounding Mertz and Ninnis glaciers, named after the two subordinates. On 14 December Mawson and Mertz safely crossed a treacherous crevasse — one of thousands of deep cracks in the ice, often concealed by soft snow 'bridges' which could collapse at any time. Looking back, they realised that Ninnis had disappeared without a sound. Gazing down the last awful crevasse, they saw one of Ninnis's sledge dogs lying broken-backed on a ledge nearly fifty metres from the surface. Below that was a gaping chasm.

The tragedy seriously endangered the remaining pair. With Ninnis had disappeared their only tent and much of their supplies. They were more than five hundred kilometres from base camp, with only ten days' food for themselves and nothing for the remaining dogs to eat except rawhide harness.

Mawson and Mertz immediately turned for home. Each night they made a crude shelter from a canvas cover draped over skis. On 15 December they killed their first dog and devoured it whole, eating even the stewed paws. The last dog died on 25 December.

Poisoned by dogs' livers
On most days the men could cover only about ten kilometres. On 1 January 1913 Mertz complained of strange pains, blaming their diet of dog meat. Five days later he was so weak that Mawson had to haul him on the sledge. On 7 January Mertz became delirious and died.

Even the remarkably fit Mawson was now in a bad way. He cut the sledge in half with a pocket knife, but was so weak that sometimes he could pull the reduced weight only one or two kilometres a day. Sometimes he was reduced to crawling like a dog. 'I felt I might collapse at any moment...' Mawson wrote. 'Several of my toes commenced to blacken and fester.' On 11 January his soles separated from his feet, and had to be painfully strapped back on. His hair was falling out, and now his fingers began festering too. Unknown to the explorer, he was suffering not only from frostbite but also Vitamin A poisoning, the result of eating the huskies' livers.

On 17 January the exhausted Mawson fell into a crevasse, and was saved only by harness attached to the sledge. He could barely hoist himself back to fall spent on the snow. Then on 29 January, with the frozen dog meat almost gone, he sighted a cairn built by a search party a few hours earlier. They had left behind a package of food, which Mawson devoured. That thoughtfulness saved his life.

His strength partly renewed, Mawson staggered back to Cape Denison by 8 February 1913, only to see the *Aurora* disappearing on the horizon. Fortunately a small party had remained to continue the search, and they nursed Mawson back to full vigour. The men sat out a second winter on the ice, during which one unimaginable hurricane blew at an average of one hundred and seventy-two kilometres per hour for eight hours.

On 12 December 1913 the *Aurora* returned on schedule, and took the men back to a heroes' welcome in Adelaide.

Wilkins pioneers aerial exploration
The First World War prevented further Australian forays, although British efforts continued with Shackleton's adventure-filled expeditions of 1914 and 1920.

Second-in-command of the latter expedition was George Hubert Wilkins, a descendant of South Australian pioneers. Wilkins had served in the Australian Flying Corps and then took part in the England-Australia air race of 1919. From 1923 to 1925 he led an expedition for the British Museum to Arnhem Land. But his main enthusiasm was the use of aircraft for exploration.

In 1926 Wilkins won American backing for flights over northern polar regions. Two years later, when he was forty, he was given command of the Wilkins-Hearst Antarctic Expedition, sponsored by the American Geographical Society, newspaper publisher William Randolph Hearst and others.

Wilkins could now prepare for the fir Antarctic flights. He bought tw Lockheed Vega monoplanes and sailed t Deception Island in the South Shetlan in November 1928. On 16 November h made the first flight, and on 20 Decem ber carried out a reconnaissance ove Graham Land on the continent itself.

Eight years earlier, Wilkins had trie to reach the area on foot, but was turne back by unclimbable cliffs. Now, in hi aeroplane, wrote Wilkins, 'I had a tre mendous sensation of power and freedor — I felt liberated.'

In a few hours of flying, Wilkin discovered nearly one thousand kilc metres of previously untraversed land But there were limitations to the ne method. Wilkins's aerial photograph seemed to show that Graham Land wa divided by sea channels into severa islands. This was disproved in 1936 b another Australian, thirty-one-year-ol John Rymill, who led overland survey which demonstrated that Wilkins 'channels' were simply transverse lanc glaciers. The lesson for cartographers wa that aerial surveys were almost useles without ground control points.

Meanwhile the French governmen revived its interest in Antarctica. Reach ing back for support to a southern voyag made in 1840 by Dumont d'Urville, the French in 1924 claimed sovereignty over Adélie Land, directly south of Australia Norway too began to show signs o

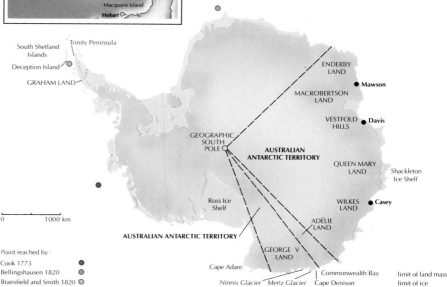

Tenacious explorers put Antarctica's features on to twentieth century maps

By 1958, after just 139 years of intensive exploration Antarctica, the world's last unknown continent, had bee investigated by some 50 major expeditions. Today tourists in cruise-liners and sightseers in planes come i comfort to see the continent once travelled across at grea peril, and world powers vie for its mineral resources

South Shetland Islands
Trinity Peninsula
Deception Island
GRAHAM LAND
GEOGRAPHIC SOUTH POLE
Ross Ice Shelf
0   1000 km
AUSTRALIAN ANTARCTIC TERRITORY
Cape Adare
Ninnis Glacier Mertz Glacier Cape Denison
Commonwealth Bay
GEORGE V LAND
ADÉLIE LAND
WILKES LAND Casey
QUEEN MARY LAND
Shackleton Ice Shelf
AUSTRALIAN ANTARCTIC TERRITORY
VESTFOLD HILLS Davis
MACROBERTSON LAND
ENDERBY LAND
Mawson
limit of land mass
limit of ice

Point reached by :
Cook 1773
Bellingshausen 1820
Bransfield and Smith 1820

Cape Horn
ANTARCTIC CIRCLE
Heard Island
Macquarie Island
Hobart

wanting to annex territory. The response in Britain and Australia was an exact parallel to the early days of exploration, when fears of foreign settlement stimulated more decisive occupation of the whole Australian continent.

A joint British, Australian and New Zealand Antarctic Research Expedition (BANZARE) was soon organised. To lead it, Douglas Mawson obtained leave from his work as Professor of Geology at Adelaide University.

From 1929-31, Mawson and a strong scientific team cruised the islands of the far south and the coast of Antarctica, using Scott's old steamship *Discovery*, which had been refitted with modern instruments. Climate, geology and marine biology were closely studied.

Mawson's geographers concentrated on accurate mapping from Enderby Land to King George V Land. Several landings were made to plant the Union Jack and formally annex large territories. A Gipsy Moth seaplane made regular survey flights, discovering a new area which was named Mac.Robertson Land after Sir Macpherson Robertson, a Melbourne chocolate manufacturer who was the expedition's main private backer.

Australian Antarctic Territory

The result was proclamation of the Australian Antarctic Territory in 1936. The area claimed was six million, ninety thousand square kilometres, and a coast

of seventy-five hundred kilometres, but again a world war interrupted Australian work in the region. In 1948, the Federal government established a permanent Antarctic Division under thirty-six-year-old scientist-explorer Dr Phillip Law. Australian National Antarctic Expeditions (ANARE) set up scientific bases on Heard and Macquarie islands, but failed to reach the Antarctic coast because of unusually heavy pack-ice.

In 1954 a specially strengthened ice-breaker, the *Kista Dan*, managed to penetrate the ice and establish Australia's first permanent base, named Mawson, in Mac.Robertson Land. Three years later a

Casey, Australia's third permanent Antarctic base, was an experiment in design. Its units were built in a line across the prevailing wind on a raised iron frame to prevent snowdrifts

second base was established six hundred and fifty kilometres to the east, near the ice-free Vestfold Hills. This was named Davis after John King Davis, captain of vessels used for Mawson's historic expeditions. A third base, Casey after Australian-born Governor-General Lord Casey, opened in Wilkes Land in 1969.

Since then, teams of scientists working under arduous conditions have investigated the geology of exposed rock areas, discovered fossils, taken extensive core samples by drilling through the ice sheet, completed much mapping, charted ice movement, observed solar activity and weather patterns, and studied ocean life. Satellites have been used for various types of information-gathering.

Prospects of utilising Antarctica's rich resources have attracted increasing attention from major powers in recent years.

After world cooperation during International Geophysical Year, the first Antarctic Treaty came into force in 1961. Its twelve signatories, including the Soviet Union and United States of America, agreed that the continent should remain demilitarised and nuclear-free, and should not be commercially exploited until safeguards against environmental damage have been established.

Today twelve nations maintain more than forty research bases. The prospect of national rivalries and spoliation of resources alarms many. Dr Phillip Law, for instance, believes that a non-competitive consortium should be established to manage the region... a kind of miniature world government. Others feel that Australia should be recompensed for its pioneering efforts when exploitation of Antarctica's wealth begins. □

A HUGE FROZEN CONTINENT

Antarctica's basic statistics are stunning. It covers about fourteen million square kilometres — nearly twice the size of neighbouring Australia.

The ice sheet that grips most of Antarctica is the largest body of ice in the world. In some areas it is several kilometres thick, locking up nearly seventy per cent of the planet's fresh water.

If the ice ever melted, ocean levels would rise nearly sixty metres throughout the world, inundating most coastal cities and causing inestimable damage.

Removal of the ice would reveal a much smaller rocky continent, about the same size as Australia. Vast mineral wealth is hidden within this land mass.

Its ice cap helps to make Antarctica the world's highest continent. Australia's average elevation above sea level is three hundred and forty metres, but Antarctica's is twenty-three hundred metres. This height increases frigidity, wind velocities, and the many difficulties of exploration and settlement.

The ocean of ice surrounding the Antarctic continent shrinks from nearly nineteen million square kilometres in winter to less than three million square kilometres in summer. Icebergs are produced where-

Paradise Bay, known for its spectacular scenery, is fringed by steep mountains and by glaciers; both were a barrier to early exploration

ever the ice sheet meets the ocean. Their average life is perhaps about four years, during which time they will travel to warmer seas. Large icebergs continually break off and float northwards to present serious danger to shipping.

Desert explorers take to the skies to complete their work

*D*ouglas Mawson's pioneering attempt in 1912 to use aircraft to explore Antarctica was a *failure. But·when planes were greatly improved during the emergencies of the First World War, other Australians realised their advantages for sweeping forays over desert regions.*

Aircraft allowed explorers to skim quickly over difficult terrain. They also led to the new field of aerial photography. Interesting features could be photographed, then mapped and studied at base before ground parties went out on more detailed surveys.

The pioneer of aerial exploration in Australia was a sixty-six-year-old Sydney hydrographer named Gerald Harnett Halligan. After Halligan's retirement from the public service, his friend Sir Edgeworth David suggested a hydrographic survey of Lake Eyre. Due to unpredictable flooding, 'most contradictory reports' on the lake came even from people living near by.

Halligan believed that an aerial survey would provide the best basis for work in the field. An imaginative defence minister, Walter Massey-Greene, authorised use of the two of the air force's best planes. They were taken by rail to Marree, where the historic first flight took off on 1 March 1922.

Halligan wanted to fly at four thousand feet, from where he could see detail of shores and islands while maintaining a general view of the lake. The pilots were conscious that they must complete a round trip of seven hundred and twenty-four kilometres without landing. If a mechanical problem were to develop while over the lake, they would need to be high enough for a long glide to firm ground. They insisted on flying at eight thousand feet.

Even so, Halligan was able to take many photographs in the clear desert air. These were used to plan a land expedition, so the lake's shores could be reached and a survey boat launched 'in the most economical and expeditious manner'. Halligan proved that endless reconnaissance journeys by horse or camel were no longer necessary.

A year after Halligan's expedition, a Melbourne-born prospector named John Campbell Miles discovered a rich outcrop of silver-lead ore on the Leichhardt river in north-west Queensland.

The Queensland government was first to carry out an aerial survey for mining interests. An area of fifteen and a half square kilometres was inspected and photographed from the air. When Mount Isa Mines was floated in 1924, the company was quickly able to select the most favourable areas for its huge complex, and the best site for a town.

The navy and air force cooperated in 1926-27 to chart unknown sections of the Barrier Reef. HMAS *Geranium* was fitted with an aircraft, a seaplane manned by RAAF officers.

A full-time RAAF Survey flight was formed in 1927 to map large land areas with the Survey Corps. Their work was based on British experiments by Lieutenant M. Hotine of the Royal Engineers, giving block photo coverage based on parallel and level flight lines.

Hotine's report, 'Simple methods of surveying from air photographs', became the bible of topographical surveyors and cartographers. Two RAAF pilots were trained in England in the new technique, so different from their normal combat training. On their return, they and the Survey Corps completed fourteen map areas in New South Wales, Victoria and Queensland by 1930.

Queensland continued to pioneer aerial photography, using chartered Qantas planes as early as 1928 to help survey Crown lands around Barcaldine for subdivision into farming blocks.

The next important aerial exploration was conducted in 1929 by Cecil Thomas Madigan, a forty-year-old South Austraan geologist who had gone to the Antarctic with Douglas Mawson.

In 1929 Madigan won Federal government support for the first systematic attempt at aerial strip-photography. The RAAF lent him two of their new Wapiti aircraft, complete with crews and photographers using a new Eagle automatic vertical camera.

The first experimental flight over known territory around Broken Hill was followed by aerial traverses across the south Australian lakes Frome, Callabonna, Blanche and Gregory.

'It was often very difficult to determine just where the shores were,' wrote Madigan; '...it was at times difficult to say whether we were over a lake or not, as the surface below was uniformly flat, barren, and pink.'

Almost asphyxiated by leaking gases and oil, the aviators continued northeasterly to Birdsville. From here Madigan made three long survey flights over a vast unnamed desert area, stretching from the south-western border of Queensland through parts of the Northern Territory and South Australia.

Madigan names the Simpson Desert

The first flight ranged from Birdsville to Alice Springs. The second went east from Alice Springs to Lake Caroline, then eighty kilometres south, and direct back to Alice Springs. The third flight went from Alice Springs down the whole length of the desert to Oodnadatta. Altogether nearly seven thousand kilometres were flown. 'Every now and again we swooped down to within a hundred feet of the ground, and felt its hot breath, escaping gladly again to the cooler air above,' wrote Madigan.

Madigan named the desert after Alfred Allen Simpson, president of the South Australian branch of the Royal Geographical Society.

The air force technicians took hundreds of vertical and oblique photographs. The series shot in the MacDonnell Ranges was extremely successful. 'In two and a half hours more of the topography was seen and recorded than had been possible to Giles, Chewings, Winnecke, or the Horn Expedition in weeks of toil,' wrote Madigan.

But, he added, there had been little of outstanding value to photograph in the desert: 'Some claypans were seen in the northern parts of the desert and some watercourses, not hitherto mapped, near

the margins, but all the rest was a uniform monotony of sandridges...'

Just the same this first aerial view of the Simpson Desert was striking: 'The whole expanse below was like a pink and gigantic circular gridiron, ribbed with close straight sandridges from horizon to horizon... their narrowness, straightness and continuity were astonishing...'

A few years later, when helicopters were first demonstrated in Australia, Madigan was asked to make landings in the Simpson Desert with the new machine. He rejected the idea as being 'too hazardous and impracticable at that stage of development'. Instead, after a phenomenally wet season in 1937-38, Madigan decided on a land crossing.

Mistakes made by ground explorers

Extensive aerial mapping of central Australia was begun in 1930 by Donald George Mackay, sixty-year-old descendant of wealthy Scottish pastoralists at Wallendbeen station near Yass in New South Wales.

In his younger days Mackay had lived adventurously. In 1899-1900 he cycled nearly eighteen thousand kilometres round Australia in two hundred and forty days to break the record. Expeditions to Papua New Guinea, the South Pacific and Northern Territory followed.

Mackay's interest in unmapped areas of outback Australia was stimulated in 1929 by the forced landing of Kingsford Smith's *Southern Cross* in a remote part of the north-west. Two other airmen lost their lives searching for the plane.

Mackay decided to finance aerial mapping of unknown sections of the outback. In 1930 he leased two locally-built

ANEC planes from Australian Aerial Services of Melbourne. He engaged two pilots, Frank Neale and H. B. Hussey and other experts.

The six-man expedition flew the two planes, named *Love Bird* and *Diamond Bird*, to Canberra, where Prime Minister James Scullin eloquently farewelled them on 23 May 1930.

After a three-day flight the party reached Hermannsberg Mission near Alice Springs, where truck-loads of petrol were waiting. About two hundred and eighty kilometres further west, at Ilbilla Soak below Ehrenberg Range, camel parties had already set up the main base. Here the expedition's surveyor, Commander Harry T. Bennett, RN, picked up radio time signals from Melbourne Observatory and used astronomical observations to fix their exact position on the earth's surface. This was essential if their aerial maps were to be of any value to those who followed.

To maintain any kind of accuracy, flights had to be made at a fixed height along known compass bearings. Distances between features on the ground were plotted by calculation of the plane's ground speed, taking account of head or tail winds. By modern standards the method was rather rough, but it was the best available at the time.

During June 1930 the party systematically triangulated an area of about five thousand square kilometres around Ilbilla. The planes flew outward for two

From the air the patterned beauty of the desert became apparent — Sturt would have given much for this view of Eyre Creek, where he once stood on a sandhill and saw only the endless Simpson

hundred kilometres, turned right for about fifty kilometres, then turned right again for home, thus cutting wedges out of a giant circle. Instrument readings and observations were constantly radioed back to base.

From the air, mistakes made by earlier ground explorers could be clearly seen. For instance, the aviators discovered that Lake Amadeus was far smaller than shown on existing maps. It was less than a hundred kilometres instead of several hundred kilometres long.

In a region about two hundred kilometres north-west of Ilbilla, blank on existing maps, the aerial explorers discovered a huge new lake ninety-six kilometres wide and a hundred and sixty kilometres long, covering more than twelve thousand square kilometres. The Federal government named it Lake Mackay in honour of the expedition's backer. Another new lake north-west of Lake Amadeus was named Neale after the chief pilot; and one north-west of Ilbilla was named after Commander Bennett.

Mackay's team maps most areas

In 1933 Donald Mackay financed another aerial expedition, this time to explore unknown country west and north-west of the Petermann Ranges.

He bought a much faster long-range plane, an English Percival Gull. A new Federal government attempting to bal-ance its Depression-hit budget refused to waive import duties on plane or petrol. This did not stop the Aviation Department from requesting Mackay to make detailed scientific tests of radio transmission variability in desert conditions.

Mackay chose a giant triangle of five hundred thousand square kilometres of Western Australia for his new venture. The first base was established at Docker River in the Petermann Ranges; the second at Roy Hill station on the Fortescue river; and the third base at Fitzroy Crossing. Supplies and petrol were taken by camel seven hundred kilometres from Alice Springs to the first base.

From 6 to 9 June 1933, the Percival Gull was used to map the mountains, salt lakes and mulga plains surrounding Docker River. On 10 June the main party moved to Roy Hill station, flying nine hundred and eighty kilometres in one day to make the first aerial crossing of the central western desert. En route they noted the smoke of native fires, showing that the region was not entirely unpopulated as previously thought.

As soon as more petrol arrived by truck from Port Hedland, the Gull made extensive survey flights of up to four hundred kilometres in radius from Roy Hill. Although pastoralists had much firsthand knowledge of the land's features, Mackay's methods made it possible for positions to be plotted on maps.

On 22 June 1933, the Gull continue to Fitzroy Crossing, seven hundred kilo metres to the north-east. During the nex few days survey flights were made i southerly directions. On 28 June th aviators completed their huge triangle b flying nine hundred kilometres back t base camp at Docker River.

Next day, Mackay's sixty-third birth day was celebrated with a camp cassero called Ostler Joss or Dutchy's Deligh consisting of stewed bully-beef, vege tables and 'hundreds of flies'.

Several further survey flights wer made early in July to complete the map On 9 July Neale tried to land the Gu near Lake Anec, hit a mulga root, tippe up, and bent the propellor. The aviato hammered it straight and attempted t take off, but sank up to the wings in boggy patch. An SOS sent by radi brought rescuers in their spare plane, a D Havilland Moth. Together the men wer able to manhandle the Gull to firme ground and take off.

Arriving back at Mascot aerodrome i Sydney on 16 July 1933, the explorer were surprised to find a large crow including leading politicians waiting t welcome them. Suddenly, with the hir of disaster, they had become heroes.

Filling in the Nullarbor's blanks

Mackay accumulated enough money t undertake yet another aerial expeditio in 1935. This time he decided to surve the blank space of the Nullarbor Plai north of the transcontinental railway.

With two chartered planes, the part assembled at Cook station on the rail way, one thousand kilometres west c Adelaide, on 19 June 1935. From 20 t 26 June the men made seven surve flights of up to three hundred kilometre radius into the Great Victoria Desert. N stunning discoveries awaited them 'Nothing ever turned up except clay-pan and lakes, surrounded by damned monot ony,' wrote Mackay.

On 27 June the explorers moved tw hundred kilometres further west to an other rail stop named Forrest. From 2 June to 5 July they made six flights, thi time discovering the Serpentine Lakes, chain of salt ponds extending for mor than eighty kilometres in a general north erly direction.

The aviators spent from 7 to 12 Jul making five survey flights from Rawlinna. This time they found man lakes to the north-east. The largest wa named Jubilee Lake in honour of Kin

George V's twenty-five years as monarch.

Next stop was Laverton gold fields, on the outer fringe of western settlement. Two surveys were made to the north-east, connecting with flights made from Docker River in 1933.

The party then returned to their earlier bases, filling in other blanks on the map as they went. They completed thirty survey flights covering seven hundred and eighty thousand square kilometres.

In June 1937 Mackay was sixty-seven years old, but planning yet another aerial expedition. With two veterans of previous adventures, Harry Bennett and Frank Neale, Mackay scanned their earlier maps. The biggest gap seemed to be in the Northern Territory, between Mount Tanami and Wave Hill.

The team chartered a twin-engine Dragonfly and a lighter Puss Moth, hiring a camel train to take tonnes of petrol and supplies to the main base at Tanami. Mackay described this isolated settlement, inhabited only by a few dusty men 'dryblowing' for gold, as 'the Abomination of Desolation'. The area was flat and featureless, with dry stony gullies fringed by stunted trees. Yet near by, Gordon Buchanan, grandson of the pastoralist-explorer Nat Buchanan, was still eking out a living grazing cattle.

From 25 to 30 July 1937, ten survey flights were made from the ironstone landing strip at Tanami, covering a full circle of two hundred and forty kilo-metres radius. The aviators discovered the extensive Lake Buck to the north-east, naming it after Bob Buck, legendary Alice Springs camel-driver who had carted essential petrol supplies long distances through the wilderness.

On 31 July 1937, the aviators flew one thousand kilometres across the western desert to Roy Hill station on the Fortescue river in Western Australia. From there they continued another three hundred and seventy kilometres to Wiluna, to complete their 1935 survey of the area beyond Lake Carnegie. On 2 August 1937 they flew to Meekatharra, then back to Roy Hill, tail winds boosting their ground speed to nearly two hundred and fifty kilometres per hour.

Altogether they flew more than seventeen thousand kilometres in eighteen days, making feature surveys all the way. Yet most of it was 'the usual salt lake and sand-ridge country,' wrote Mackay.

By mid-August 1937 the survey task was finished: the mainland's last broad areas unseen by Europeans had been charted from the air, and the map of Australia was complete. It was not Mackay's fault that there were no extensive fertile areas left to discover, for enthusiastic settlers had long ago pushed into every likely patch of country.

Aerial mapping and photography were greatly expanded during the Second World War. On the outbreak of war in 1939, Australia was unable to supply adequately detailed maps of all operational zones, especially in northern areas.

The RAAF Survey Flight was quickly expanded and commercial fliers commandeered in a joint emergency effort. Thousands of overlapping vertical air photographs were taken and used as the basis for detailed mapping.

The photographs, with their inevitable distortions, were adjusted to control points tied where possible to ground triangulation nets. In more remote areas, astronomical fixes were used. The photographs were contoured by means of stereoscopes, frequently using heights measured by ground parties.

By such methods, hasty but detailed maps were obtained of huge areas of Australia and New Guinea where armed conflict seemed likely to occur.

The aerial programme was refined after the war, so that by the late sixties Australia finally achieved its first complete map coverage on a scale of 1:250,000. Many areas were covered on a larger scale. But maps continually become out of date: cartographers are still revising and improving the work commenced by pioneer explorers. □

Donald Mackay *led three expeditions to map the centre, sweeping out systematically from bases at Docker Creek, Roy Hill station and Fitzroy Crossing. The five flights from Roy Hill, each of a radius of up to four hundred kilometres, linked up with surveys from the other two bases*

Airborne explorers cover regions inaccessible to land travellers

Exploration from the air made the hard slog of reconnaissance journeys by horse or camel redundant and provided detailed information for map-makers. Even the barrier of the Simpson Desert was overcome by aerial explorers; they too, were disappointed not to find hidden wonders

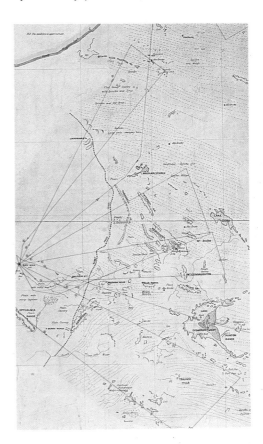

Arnhem Land: the explorers' last great untamed wilderness

Arnhem Land, named after the Dutch ship Arnhem which discovered it in 1623, occupies most of the northern hump of Australia to the east of Darwin. Its area of ninety-seven thousand square kilometres extends from the East Alligator river to the Roper river, and includes the glories of the vast, unspoiled Kakadu National Park.

Dr Herbert Basedow
GEOLOGIST

During the nineteenth century the islands and coast of Arnhem Land became well known to traders and missionaries. A few explorers, buffalo hunters and pastoralists penetrated the interior, but until quite recently most of the inland areas remained a mystery.

Most of what was known about Arnhem Land 'down south' arose from murderous clashes between the races that occurred near the coast.

In 1876 the Government Resident at Darwin reported that a gold prospecting party venturing into Arnhem Land had been attacked by Aboriginals, and two whites speared. In reprisal, forty blacks were shot.

The government boat *Woolner*, sent to investigate, was forced to defend itself against attacks by Cape Stewart Aboriginals. 'We heard that these were the worst niggers on the whole coast, surprising Malay praus, killing and eating the crews and breaking up the vessels for the iron,' reported the master.

South Australian surveyor David Lindsay attempted the first detailed inland exploration of Arnhem Land in 1883. He and three others rode northeast from Katherine to the Liverpool river. Continuing easterly towards the Goyder river, they were attacked by a large group of Aboriginals, and had to use firearms to save themselves. After further confrontations, they left their survey work incomplete.

In 1892 an Indonesian prau was wrecked near Brogden Point, the crew massacred and their belongings stolen. Darwin police arrested eight Aboriginals who admitted to the killings. The ringleader was hanged, the rest were sentenced and gaoled.

Elsewhere on the coast, increasing racial contact had the usual tragic results. In 1908 Aboriginal Protector Dr Cecil Strangman reported that the Croker Island tribe had been reduced from one hundred and fifty to forty people in only six years, by a combination of alcohol and disease. 'All the young lubras wore the gaudy dresses of the aboriginal prostitute,' he wrote.

At the mouth of the Goyder river, Aboriginals refused to allow Strangman to land until convinced he carried no firearms. They uttered pitiful cries of 'no more bang', showing how ruthless whites, Malays and Japanese had treated them. Opening one Aboriginal coffin, Strangman found the skull stuffed with pages of the Adelaide *Chronicle*.

Little was heard from Arnhem Land during the First World War. Trading and racial clashes appeared to diminish, while the remnants of coastal tribes were cared for by missions set up on Groote Eylandt and elsewhere.

Scientists bring back new knowledge of the north

The coast of Arnhem Land was well known to early explorers, but nineteenth and twentieth century scientists revealed its interior to the world.

In fully documented expeditions, they discovered a treasure-house of Aboriginal culture and a huge diversity of plants and animals

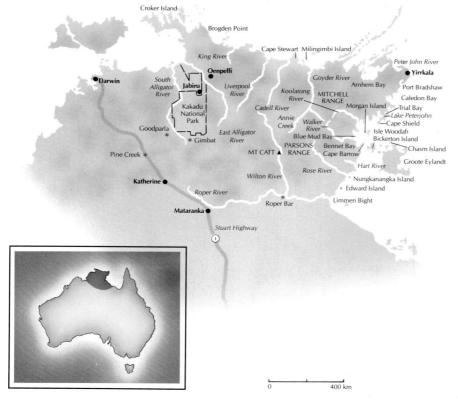

Wilkins leads a scientific party

In this quieter atmosphere, the curator of the Tasmanian Museum, Clive E. Lord, wrote in 1921 to the British Museum (Natural History), pointing out the alarming manner in which Australian wildlife was disappearing under the impact of pastoralism. Local museums could not afford to undertake large expeditions: Lord begged the British Museum to do the job before rare species disappeared.

The result was the first scientific exploration of Arnhem Land. Its leader was Captain George Hubert Wilkins,

278

Australian-born veteran of British polar expeditions. Wilkins and his collectors spent more than two years during 1923-25, ranging from the highlands of south-eastern Queensland through the Roper river area and north to Groote Eylandt. No trouble was experienced with Aboriginals, who stayed well away from the scientists.

The expedition collected more than five thousand specimens, some in almost inaccessible regions. Among the items previously unknown to science were five types of rock wallaby, a tree kangaroo, several new sub-species of ring-tailed possum, mice, water rats, freshwater prawns, gliding possums, a cuckoo-shrike, four new types of reptile, a rare slow-worm, a new snake, a new frog and many superior specimens of animals and birds already held in museums.

A second scientific expedition to Arnhem Land was organised in 1928. Donald Mackay, the wealthy grazier who helped to pioneer aerial exploration, backed a forty-seven-year-old South Australian geologist, Dr Herbert Basedow, in an ambitious programme to discover whether Arnhem Land could support a large population of farmers.

The party, complete with an expert cinematographer, left Katherine on 18 April 1928, heading east for the Roper river. A fortnight later they reached Roper Bar police station, at the head of

river navigation. Here they found waiting, as arranged, fresh supplies brought from Darwin by lugger.

On 5 May 1928, the party set off northwards along a tributary, the Wilton river, taking them into the heart of Arnhem Land. By 11 May they were camping on the slopes of Mount Catt. After passing several meteorite craters, they turned north-east along Annie creek to reach the Goyder river on 16 May. As they searched the dry land for horse fodder, Mackay realised that this country could never support a large farming population, even when huge amounts of grass grew during the wet season.

On 25 May the explorers encountered their first Aboriginal tribe, most of whom ran away shouting insults. Six days later another tribe allowed themselves to be filmed, and showed the visitors a gallery of rock carvings and paintings.

By now the party had trekked westwards across the Cadell and Liverpool rivers, through baffling sandstone valleys and dead ends, and were heading for Oenpelli mission near the East Alligator.

Here they found the most fertile areas of the whole trip. The old homestead at Oenpelli, founded by buffalo hunter Paddy Cahill in 1885, had been turned into a mission station for about two hundred Aboriginals. Their gardens were stocked with tropical fruits and vegetables, hundreds of cattle grazed in lush

paddocks, and flights of birds rose in waves from countless billabongs.

The missionaries supplied the explorers with ample food to continue their journey to Pine Creek rail station, which they reached safely on 20 June 1928 after a eleven hundred-kilometre circuit of Arnhem Land. A film of their expedition, *Mysterious Arnhem Land*, was later shown throughout the world.

Forays into tribal lands
Serious clashes with the Aboriginal population occurred early in the nineteen-thirties. Sporadic attacks on visiting Japanese trepangers culminated in the notorious Caledon Bay massacre of 17 September 1932. The Japanese had kept native women on board against their will: in revenge the Aboriginals speared five trepangers to death.

Constable A. S. McColl, sent to investigate the murders, was killed on 1 August 1933 and a party of armed police was routed. In November 1933, two white adventurers, Frank Traynor and William Fagan, who had cohabited with native women, were speared to death on nearby Isle Woodah.

On 5 May 1928, the 28 pack-horses and seven mules supporting the Mackay-Basedow expedition forded the Roper River at Roper Bar, where Leichhardt had crossed in 1845. The party headed north into little known Arnhem Land

To southern newspapers, Arnhem Land suddenly seemed in a state of armed rebellion. The Federal government appointed a young Melbourne anthropologist, Dr Donald Thomson, to investigate causes of the attacks. It was the first time administrators had tried to discover the feelings of the natives, instead of relying on white men's versions.

Thomson sets off down the Roper

Thomson's first expedition lasted from May to December 1935. He decided to approach Caledon Bay by an overland route from Darwin, so that his boat *St Nicholas*' with its ten tonnes of reserve supplies would not be endangered before he had become friendly with the tribes.

Thomson left Darwin on 29 May 1935, travelling via Mataranka to Roper Bar police station. His Aboriginal helpers loaded cameras and food into an old dinghy and three leaking dugout canoes, then set off down the Roper river.

Plenty of game was found along the route to supplement their camp rations, but whenever Thomson went to the river to drink, a native stood behind him, throwing logs into the water to frighten away crocodiles.

Thomson's party reached the mouth of the Roper on 11 June and floated into Limmen Bight, where they boarded the *St Nicholas*. A gale sprang up, forcing them northwards to Edward Island.

Thomson decided to return to the mainland with two Aboriginal companions and explore northwards beyond the Hart river to Bennet Bay and Cape

PROFESSOR DONALD THOMSON
ANTHROPOLOGIST

Barrow, just short of Isle Woodah. They travelled light: Thomson carried only a blanket and piece of canvas; a little flour, bacon, tea and sugar; a tomahawk, shotgun and cartridges; and pieces of fencing wire to make fish spears. He wore only shorts, shirt and sandshoes – without even a pair of socks.

Along the dry coastline the men were forced to drink fetid brackish water from native wells. At the mouth of the Rose river they were stranded by the rising tide on Nungkanangka Island. One Aboriginal fell ill; the other fled. When the sick man recovered, he and Thomson traversed kilometres of deep grey mud, dense prickly scrub and crocodile-infested areas

The forbidding escarpment of Kakadu National Park. Named after the vanishing Kakadu, or Gagudju, people who lived there, it has been inhabited continuously for 30 000 years

to reach their goal. Sometimes they were forced to tap swellings on melaleuca trees to win a little bitter-tasting water.

Bleeding and exhausted, feet badly blistered and legs swollen, food almost gone, the two men were saved by finding a nest of turtle eggs on the beach opposite Bickerton Island. On 19 June 1935 they buried their remaining possessions and began a forced march to Cape Barrow. Thomson had wrapped pieces of blanket round his suppurating feet: even these scraps had to be abandoned because he could not tolerate the extra weight.

At last, in the early afternoon, they encountered the Nunggubuyu tribe, who took pity on the wayfarers and guided them to the *St Nicholas* waiting for them at anchor in Bennet Bay.

Winning respect by following custom

After two days of recovery, Thomson set sail for Morgan Island, well known since the dramatic events of Matthew Flinders's visit there one hundred and thirty-two years earlier.

On 26 June Thomson sailed across Blue Mud Bay, named by Flinders after the colour of its bed, and anchored near the mouth of the Koolatong river. The natives here, who included the Isle Woodah tribe, were unfriendly and treated him with suspicion.

Thomson decided to go among them

narmed, to walk softly, follow native customs, and offer presents of tobacco. He won respect for medical magic by injecting native children with neoarsphenamine to cure awful facial and bodily lesions caused by yaws.

In July 1935 Thomson walked overland from Cape Shield to Trial Bay, where the 'aggressive' Caledon Bay natives were said to be camping.

Thomson was now living and travelling like an Aboriginal. On cold nights he shared fires lit between each pair of native guides, and sheltered behind rough windbreaks made of boughs.

On 14 July the party discovered a large lake south of Trial Bay, which Thomson named Lake Peterjohn after his twin sons.

Shortly afterwards Thomson was taken to meet Wongo, aged but still powerful elder of the Caledon Bay tribe – a 'tall, powerful man with intelligent face, deep set eyes and a heavy beard, trimmed almost in Van Dyck style.'

Thomson was able to present him with a message stick from three of his warrior sons in Darwin. They had been sentenced to death for the massacres of 1933, but their sentences had been commuted to life imprisonment.

By carefully observing native etiquette, Thomson was finally accepted by Wongo as *gaminyarr*, a kinship term meaning daughter's son. Wongo made no

THE JOYS OF EXPLORATION

Even in modern times, perils had to be endured, but many Australian explorers viewed their expeditions as the best part of their life. Major Mitchell, searching for the so-called Kindur river in 1831-32, wrote: 'even war and victory, with all their glory, were far less alluring than the pursuit of researches such as these.'

Other men were fascinated by the serenity of bush and plain. Evelyn Sturt, brother of the famous explorer, observed as he rode through the Murray district in 1837 that 'The country at this time was most beautiful: miles of it untrodden by stock, and indeed unseen by Europeans. Every creek abounded with wildfowl, and the quail sprang from the long grass which waved to the very flaps of the saddle.' He added: 'I look back to those days as to some joyous scene of schoolboy holidays.'

Even the taciturn Ludwig Leichhardt was actually seething inside with 'different states of the brightest hope and the deepest misery'. On long reconnoitring rides, he wrote in 1845, 'he who is thus occupied is in a continued state of excitement, now buoyant with hope, as he urges on his horse towards some distant range or blue mountain, or as he follows the favorable bend of a river; now all despairing and miserable, as he approaches the foot of the range without finding water'...

secret of his part in the massacres, stating he had only defended his people against intruders. He accepted the government's warning, relayed by Thomson, against any further aggression.

Thomson sailed further north to Port Bradshaw. Although not recovered from severe fever, on 24 July 1935 he set out on another overland trip, this time across the rugged neck of the peninsula towards Arnhem Bay. His fever developed into dysentery, and he began voiding large quantities of blood.

Driftwood raft to beat crocodiles

Nevertheless Thomson reached Arnhem Bay in two days, in the vicinity of Peter John river, again named after his sons. To cross its crocodile-infested waters, his guides made a crude raft of driftwood tied together with strips of green cotton-tree bark. For food, the party roasted yams and stalks of swamp fern. On 30 July they

were picked up by the *St Nicholas* and taken to Milingimbi Island, where Thomson was able to radio his report to the Federal government.

Now accustomed to living as a native, on 9 October 1935 Thomson began his longest overland expedition. This time he crossed eastern Arnhem Land, from Milingimbi back to Blue Mud Bay, then along the Walker river to Parsons Range.

First traversing the rugged hills of the Mitchell Range, Thomson encountered small groups of nomadic hunters. Their bodies were smeared with mud to prevent kangaroos from smelling them as they approached. Although they were unused to Europeans, Thomson found them always friendly. He was the first white

Arnhem Land Aboriginals *explain the symbolism of their bark paintings to Charles Mountford in 1948. A Yirrkala man uses his pipe to make a point clear*

man permitted to visit and photograph the Aboriginal flint quarry at Ngillipidji on the upper Walker river, from where the Aboriginals' sharp spear heads and cutting tools found their way to all parts of Arnhem Land.

Returning to Blue Mud Bay, Thomson was impressed to find that his tribal friends had kept the *St Nicholas* well supplied with water and firewood in his absence. On 29 October he sailed to Groote Eylandt, where he was at last able to process hundreds of superb photographs he had taken of Aboriginals.

During December 1935, Thomson studied tribal customs in the Roper river and upper Wilton river areas. Intense heat and humidity forced him to abandon a planned trip across unexplored regions of Arnhem Land to the then-unknown source of the East Alligator river.

The government instructed Thomson to return south and report fully on his expeditions. The anthropologist concluded that despite abundant food, the native population was well on the way to extinction. There were probably no more than fifteen hundred Aboriginals left in all north-eastern Arnhem Land.

Thomson recommended 'absolute segregation' of the tribes for a long period so that their ancient social structure might be preserved. Their only contact with other races should be through patrol officers trained in anthropology, and doctors who would systematically eliminate leprosy, yaws and other introduced diseases that threatened their existence.

The X-ray paintings of Oenpelli impressed the Mountford expedition, as they have art-lovers and anthropologists since, with their elaborate depictions of skeletons and internal organs — stomach, heart and alimentary canal — of animals

With the assistance of Health Minister W. M. Hughes, Thomson was able to return to the north in 1936, and secure the release of Wongo's three sons from gaol. Their return cemented Thomson's acceptance into Wongo's tribe.

Further expeditions in central and northern Arnhem Land followed. Thomson concentrated on learning tribal dialects and traditions so that he could defend in court Aboriginals charged with offences against white man's law.

During May 1937 he was authorised to fly over Arnhem Land in an RAAF Seagull amphibian. The flights gave Thomson a unified view of Arnhem Land's topography, helped to define its confusing river systems, and showed the massive invasion of Japanese fishing boats along the coastline. In some areas, up to seventy Japanese luggers could be seen at one time from the air.

War threatens the northern coasts

At King river in north-western Arnhem Land, Thomson found that unchecked prostitution of Aboriginal women — including little girls — by Japanese had destroyed local tribal structures. Such callous defiance of Australian law had reduced white prestige to zero. 'I felt I had failed utterly,' Thomson wrote bitterly in his journal.

Japanese interference in the north ceased only with the outbreak of the Pacific war in 1941. By that time Thomson was an RAAF officer. He suggested that Arnhem Land Aboriginals should be organised into a coast-watching and guerrilla strike force against possible Japanese invasion.

The idea was accepted: Thomson sailed back to Arnhem Land in charge of the armed steamship *Aroetta* and began

Reflections on an ancient art. *Centuries of paintings in reds, yellows and whites made from ground ochre and kaolin were found in rock galleries at Oenpelli. Black was from charcoal*

recruiting his old tribal friends into the Special Reconnaissance Unit, charged with guarding sixteen hundred kilometres of coastline.

Many Aboriginals were delighted to learn that they could now spear Japanese at will if they landed. They thought the white man had at last learned common

THE LEGEND OF LOST WHITE WOMEN

During the nineteen-twenties tales reached the cities about two white women who were said to have been shipwrecked and adopted by tribes in Arnhem Land.

In March 1922 the steamship *Douglas Mawson* sank during a cyclone in the Gulf of Carpentaria and all aboard were thought to have drowned. Then it was rumoured that a woman passenger and her fourteen-year-old daughter had been rescued by Caledon Bay Aboriginals.

There seems no foundation for the story. Groote Eylandt missionaries believed that some of their English-speaking half-caste women who returned to tribal life were mistaken for Europeans, and the stories spread from there.

A lengthy police investigation in 1925 was unable to find any evidence of 'lost white women' in Arnhem Land.

Mountford expedition members make camp near a lagoon at Oenpelli (Charles Mountford is third from right). The scientific team comprised an anthropologist, botanist, biochemist, dietitian and specialists in mammals, birds and fish

sense. They were 'fighting people, killers,' wrote Thomson, 'whom I would have liked to lead in action against the Japanese.' But the war receded before any invasion was attempted.

After the war Thomson began one of the first campaigns urging the Federal government to take responsibility for Aboriginal affairs and land rights. He opposed establishment of the Woomera rocket range because of its effect on nomadic desert tribes, conducting several expeditions into the Great Sandy Desert to study their way of life.

The lure of Arnhem Land's history

Back in Arnhem Land, Aboriginal history was further investigated in 1948 by the largest scientific expedition ever to take the field in Australia.

This move arose from two films, *Tjurunga* and *Walkabout*, made in 1940-42 by Adelaide anthropologist Charles P. Mountford. Information Minister Arthur Calwell was so impressed by the films that he arranged for their screening throughout the United States of America.

As a result, the United States National Geographic Society and the Australian government jointly financed an expedition, designed to investigate the origins and development of human life in Arnhem Land, collect native artefacts, and accurately record the animal, bird and plant life of the north.

In April 1948 Mountford established the first camp on Groote Eylandt, where naturalists plunged eagerly into their work. Further camps were set up at Roper river, Yirrkala and Oenpelli. The old days of tough overland trekking were gone: despite heavy rain the RAAF was able to transport the scientists and some of their equipment from place to place by Catalina flying boat, while launches took bulkier items.

All told the Mountford expedition collected thirteen thousand five hundred plant specimens, thirteen thousand fish, eight hundred and fifty birds, four hundred and sixty skins, several thousand Aboriginal implements and weapons, and many bark paintings. Specimens were distributed to museums and herbariums throughout the world.

Among the extraordinary creatures studied was a needlefish, popularly known as 'long tom', which could rise above the water and fly across the surface for nearly one hundred metres.

On Chasm Island, just north of Groote Eylandt, Mountford found the rocky art galleries made by vanished Aboriginals and described by Matthew Flinders. These and the splendid cave paintings of Oenpelli with their stunning examples of X-ray art were photographed and sketched for the world to see.

At Yirrkala, guided by the veteran bushman Bill Harney, naturalists found a scarlet-flowered mangrove unknown to science. In a cave near the Oenpelli camp, searchers found a stone adze with an intact wooden handle — the only one to have been found in this condition in the entire continent.

World publicity for this expedition again focussed attention on the need to protect remote northern areas from potentially damaging exploitation.

Official attempts to regulate commercial activities in Arnhem Land had begun in 1931, when the region was declared an Aboriginal reserve. As we have seen, this system was largely ineffective against white Australian or Asian intruders.

In 1964 the small Woolwonga Aboriginal Reserve west of Jabiru township was proclaimed a wildlife sanctuary. In 1972 the area was greatly expanded by proclamation of the Alligator Rivers Wildlife Sanctuary.

In 1979, after the Ranger Uranium Environmental Inquiry, the Federal government incorporated and extended these areas into a great Kakadu National Park of sixty-one hundred and forty-four square kilometres. This is being declared and protected in stages.

Some areas of pastoral leasehold in stage three, at Goodparla station on the South Alligator river and nearby Gimbat, have been left open for further mineral exploration until 1991. □

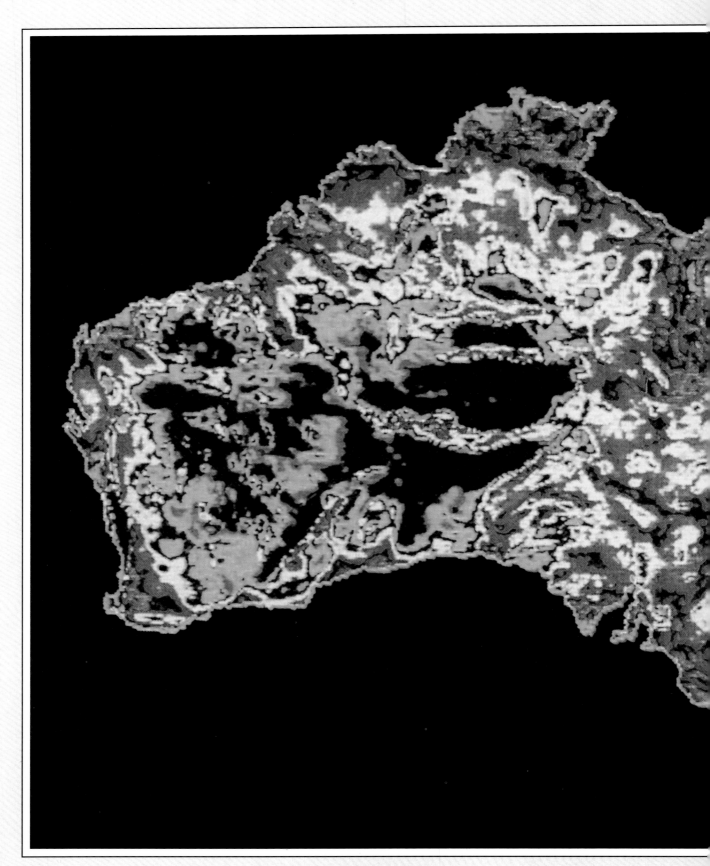

Satellite imagery provides all kinds of information, such as data on continental gravity

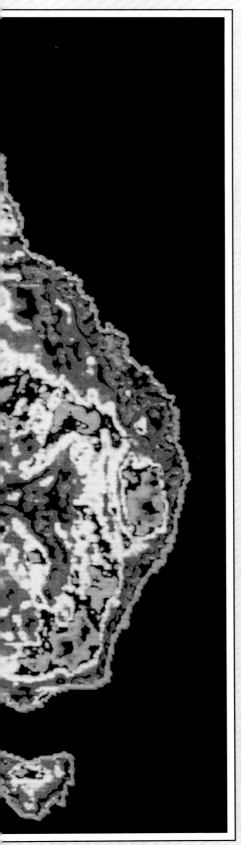

CHAPTER NINE

New technology revolutionises exploration

How modern mapping keeps pace with modern needs

From the earliest times, explorers have tried to define their position on the face of the globe, so that others may follow in their path. Until the present century, they were limited by what is now regarded as elementary technology.

Even during the Second World War, navigation relied basically on compass bearings and 'steering by the stars'. The age-old problems still existed of establishing one's position on a globe whirling through space, and accurately mapping the earth's curved surface on flat paper.

In Australia, the rather rough map-making of pioneer explorers was improved over a long period by colonial and state government surveyors. Their departments were often starved for staff and funds, and were heavily influenced by piecemeal economic development.

Early in the present century, most farming lands, ports and urban areas had been fairly well mapped. But details of vast areas of Australia were still vague. The triangulation survey of New South Wales begun by Major Mitchell, for instance, still covered less than one-third of the State. This gap in accurate knowledge of remoter areas began to be filled early this century. Defence planners knew that incomplete maps were almost useless for strategic purposes. The first Commonwealth Defence Act of 1903 provided for a Survey Section to be raised as part of the Royal Australian Engineers. In 1910, six topographers were seconded from the British Army to begin the first comprehensive triangulation survey of the whole continent.

As war appeared likely, in 1912 another six topographers and two draftsmen were enlisted locally. By the outbreak of the First World War in 1914, they had thoroughly mapped thousands of square kilometres of military training areas near Sydney, Melbourne and Adelaide.

Under the pressures of war, the section was transformed in 1915 into a separate corps — today known as the Royal Australian Survey Corps. Faced with urgent map-making tasks in preparation for battle, its surveyors made some of the first experiments with cameras held over the side of frail Australian Flying Corps aircraft traversing the deserts and oases of the Middle East.

That war was supposed to have ended all wars: the strength of the corps was slashed to only fourteen. During twenty years of peace, these few men continued to produce topographical maps of areas that seemed strategically important to Australia's defence.

In co-operation with the RAAF Survey Flight, formed in 1927, aerial photographs were used together with ground control points to map large areas of New South Wales and Victoria.

In 1936 the Survey Corps began linking up and reconciling the separate triangulation surveys which had been made by State authorities in Queensland New South Wales and Victoria.

The outbreak of the Second World War again caused hasty strengthening of the Survey Corps, and commencement of an emergency strategic mapping scheme. In 1940, thirty-seven-year-old Melbourne surveyor Lawrence FitzGerald, who had joined the corps in 1923, was named to lead the 2/1 Corps Field Survey Company to the Middle East.

FitzGerald was impressed by a technique adapted by British Army surveyors for establishing survey control for mapping in sparsely settled areas of the Libyan desert, where normal triangulation was not feasible.

This was known as position line observation, and used theodolite observations to selected stars. Computation could fix the observer's ground position to within a hundred metres.

Libyan desert technique for outback

FitzGerald saw that the same technique could be used for mapping the vast and often featureless outback. The Survey Corps adopted the method in Australia without delay, and applied it to great advantage for many years until it was superseded by satellite position-fixing. Returning to Australia in 1943, FitzGerald was appointed director of the Survey Corps. He expanded its personnel to seventeen hundred to meet United States and Australian demands for operational maps guiding Pacific battles.

Thousands of aerial pictures taken by the RAAF Photographic Squadron were combined with land surveys to produce maps at short notice. By 1945 the corps had supplied commanders with more than twenty million printed maps.

The laser ranging telescope at Orroral Geodetic Observatory in the Australian Capital Territory's Orroral Valley. This remarkable telescope bounces laser beams off the moon and satellites, which allows the observatory to define precisely its own position in the world's main reference systems. Orroral receives data on satellite navigation and positioning systems. The observatory also gives the precise time scale, known as Universal Coordinated Time Australia

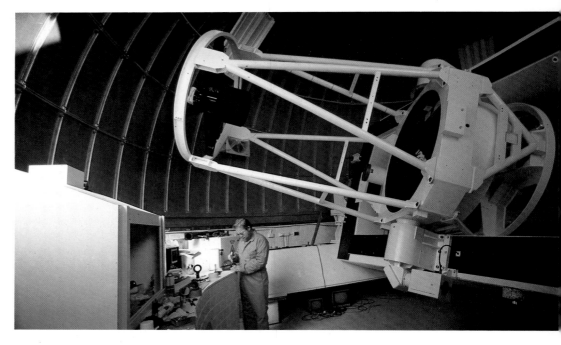

The end of this war did not mean ragmentation of the Survey Corps. More han four hundred stayed on: they began he work of mapping imaginative civil rojects, such as the Snowy Mountains ydro-electric scheme, and the damming f the Burdekin-Nogoa-Comet rivers.

In 1946 the men surveyed desert areas r establishment of the Woomera rocket nge, and in 1947 prepared administrat-e maps for the national census which aped Australian postwar planning.

Despite these advances, the national apping effort was still disorganised. In 946 the Commonwealth formed a co-dinating National Mapping Council, ith Federal and State representatives. oday's Division of National Mapping Natmap) developed from it.

Natmap was given the task of produc-g a metric series of topographic maps r the whole of Australia and to coordi-ate its work with the other mapping ganisations. This national effort con-nues today, as maps are revised and oduced at various scales to show in-easing amounts of detail. Old-time xplorers would be astonished to see how eir successors have delineated every rt of the continent over which they ace painfully stumbled.

As in the earliest days of Australian xploration, modern maps too could not e accurately connected unless the pre-se position of starting points was estab-hed. Longitudes, for instance, were nce based on astronomical calculations y pioneer observatories located near pital cities — particularly the historic dney and Melbourne observatories.

entral observatory takes over
ne of Natmap's tasks was to operate a odern observatory. Orroral in the Aus-lian Capital Territory is now the pri-ary geodetic site for co-ordinate defi-tion in the Australian area.

Faced with the task of re-surveying a rge continent carrying a small popu-tion, Australian map-makers have gerly taken up new technology.

Postwar topographical mapping was ised largely on improved aerial pho-graphy. In 1948, a Lincoln bomber was ted out with the latest cameras to begin rip photography of the whole country. he results were described as 'the first orough mapping of Australia'. A later ries tied to ground control surveys, and rrected for distortion, produced accu-e maps of most of Australia on a scale 1:100 000, where one centimetre on e map represents one kilometre.

State authorities and mining explora-n companies began their own pro-ammes of low-level aerial photography d mapping, for a multitude of end uses. Today's aerial photographers take ad-

vantage of techniques similar to those used in space flights. Infra-red photo-graphs taken from aircraft flying at me-dium levels often show superior detail to digitised images transmitted back to earth from satellites.

Another system, known as 'terrain profiling', uses a laser beam to measure the height of the ground over which the aircraft is flying. Back on the ground, science made its first major impact on land surveying methods in 1957 with introduction of the Tellurometer. This is a mobile distance-measuring unit, in-vented in South Africa, which transmits VHF radio waves to a far-off unit. The time taken for the signal to return is accurately measured, giving the distance between units to within a few centi-metres of accuracy.

Computers change land surveying
Within several years, many thousands of kilometres of Tellurometer traverses had been measured in remote areas by the Survey Corps and Natmap.

A further great change came to land surveying with the introduction of computer-assisted methods.

In the mid-nineteen-seventies, the Survey Corps installed the first Automap system, in which stereoscopic plotting equipment was integrated with computers

Doppler satellite receivers, Geoceivers, used to determine position to within one and a half metres, are the most radical change ever made in field survey techniques. The Geoceiver is operated by scientists from Orroral observatory

to store all the necessary information digitally, instead of in the visual form familiar ever since maps were first made.

As technology and operators im-proved, major advantages were found with digitisation. Many of map-making's repetitive tasks were eliminated. Obsol-ete information could be easily replaced. Separation of data for maps on special themes was greatly simplified. Editing and redrawing of maps brought up on visual display units became easier. The way was opened to incorporate other forms of digital data (such as census results) into new analytical maps.

Already Natmap offers computer-generated maps of Australian cities, showing detailed population, socio-economic and ethnic characteristics.

Information on other areas is being digitised so that users may select details of roads, railways, buildings, waterways, contours, vegetation and other features.

The process of revising maps can have no end, for as long as nature and human beings continue to change the face of the earth, new maps will be needed. □

Exploration continues below the waves

Charting of dangerous waters round Australia was maintained by the Royal Navy throughout the nineteenth century. The various colonial governments often assisted with surveys close to their own shores.

Unknown hazards abounded, sometimes causing disaster. On 28 February 1890, the passenger ship *Quetta* struck an uncharted rock in Adolphus Channel, north of Cape York. More than one hundred and thirty people drowned, causing a public outcry. The charts were hastily revised by the Queensland gunboat *Paluma*.

By the First World War, some Admiralty charts of Australian waters had been in use for more than a century, and were a mass of corrections. Despite all the work that had been done, Australia's seas were one of the world's most inadequately charted areas.

To help remedy the problem, a Royal Australian Naval Surveying Service was formed in 1920 under Captain John Robins.

HMAS *Geranium* was fitted out to begin re-surveying isolated anchorages round the coastline, and assisting commercial shipping in trouble. In 1923 *Geranium* pulled the steamer *Montoro* off Young Reef, east of Cape York Peninsula; and four years later she towed the steamer *Tasman* off Clerke Reef. Meanwhile, she continued to survey the shoal waters that make the sea approaches to Darwin so dangerous.

In 1925, naval authorities decided that sections of the Great Barrier Reef should be re-surveyed for strategic and commercial purposes. *Geranium* began systematic charting of the Cumberland Channel, which runs southeast from the Whitsunday Group. She was assisted by the first HMAS *Moresby*, transferred from the Royal Navy.

Geranium was specially fitted to carry a seaplane on her quarterdeck. Hundreds of aerial photographs provided a mosaic of the reef's outcrops to guide the detailed work of making depth soundings.

North of Whitsunday Island, triangulation from one landmark to another gave a broad reference base within which more detailed surveys could be completed.

Survey vessels on daring missions

During the Depression, such ambitious projects were abandoned. The Navy concentrated on updating harbour surveys at Melbourne, Port Macquarie and Huonville.

As international tension increased during the nineteen-thirties, it seemed essential to complete the survey of seas near Darwin. Commercial shipping could find its way through recognised channels, but the Navy might be required to fight anywhere.

HMAS *Moresby* was recommissioned 1933, and spent the remaining years up to t Second World War in northern waters. P posals to build additional survey vessels Australia were rejected by the Treasu When the Japanese conquered Singapore a advanced on Papua New Guinea and Aust lia, lack of good charts caused extraordina difficulties in defending the area.

As strengthened allied forces began rolli back the Japanese, many daring missions we performed by RAN survey vessels to cha enemy-held coastlines where seaborne lan ings were planned.

After the War, the RAN Hydrograph Office at Garden Island in Sydney w appointed charting authority for Australi waters and many offshore islands. Th survey ships were retained — the Barco Lachlan and Warrego, each named after riv prominent in Australian land exploration.

A systematic programme began to repla all old charts with up-to-date metric versio produced by new technology.

The huge increase in Australia's impo export trade after the nineteen-fifties, and t introduction of ever-larger ships, diverted tl

RAAF officers manned the seaplane, a Fair IIID. They set it up on the Geranium's quarterdeck and used a derrick rig, shown here, load and offload it. The Geranium was the first survey ship to use an aircraft for charting, and possibly the smallest to carry a plane on its deck, precarious business in rough weather

The seaplane from the Geranium *flew over the Coral Sea east of Townsville and photographed outlying reefs such as Wackett, Ross and Hewitt, named after the pilots. Other reefs they discovered were named Napier and Bugatti because the commander of the* Geranium, *Harry T. Bennett, was a passionate lover of automobiles*

hen the sloop HMAS Geranium *began surveying the Barrier ef in 1925, the Navy Board had reason to believe that Japan knew re about the reef waters than Australia did. It was known that rling fleets contained men who had served in the Japanese Navy. e reef's hazards were possibly more familiar to these sailors than to st Australian Navy Officers. Here, the 1250-tonne Geranium is n with the seaplane clinging to her quarterdeck*

ogramme. From 1960 to 1970, emphasis s placed on surveying new deep-draught ipping routes, and sea approaches to new neral export areas.

To exploit the huge iron ore deposits of the lbara region in Western Australia, for stance, HMAS *Barcoo* in 1963 re-surveyed e deep-water approaches to Mermaid und, where today's port of Dampier was er established. Two years later HMAS *oresby* surveyed a new deep-draught route to rt Hedland, enabling huge ore-carrying ips to load iron ore from Mount ldsworthy and the Ophthalmia Range.

harting the continental shelf

e work of charting the Barrier Reef and any other areas still continues, but the chnology has changed enormously. Instead using sextants and chronometers, a survey ip fixes its precise position at any particular ne by signals from shore stations and vigation satellites. Lead-lines have been placed by echo-sounders, which obtain ntinuous depth profiles; sonar is used to an the entire seabed analysing the reflection low-frequency pulses.

The Defence Science and Technology ganization (DSTO) in conjunction with dustry is developing a particularly rapid ethod of surveying shallow coastal waters, own as the Laser Airborne Depth Sounder ADS). A low-flying aircraft transmits laser ams of green and infra-red. Infra-red gives e height above the surface; green penetrates e water and sends back continuous data on ctuations in the depth of the sea floor. vised marine charts and topographic maps continually being printed at the Royal

Australian Survey Corps centre in Bendigo.

When complete, the Australian maritime area will be covered by about six hundred and fifty charts. More than half have been produced. The main gaps are on the lonely north and north-west coasts. Some of these have been given a 'defence priority' rating, and are being completed more rapidly as additional survey launches are commissioned.

Systematic surveys of the continental shelf to a depth of three hundred metres have been undertaken since 1970 by the Division of National Mapping (Natmap). While hydrographic surveys are mainly concerned with pinpointing shipping hazards, Natmap con-

centrates on the topography of the seabed. The width of the continental shelf ranges from about sixteen kilometres near Port Macquarie to more than three hundred off north-western Australia. Parts of this vast area contain new oil and natural gas reserves, but must be surveyed before sampling and exploitation can begin. When Australia ratifies the United Nations Law of the Sea Convention its area of interest will increase.

Natmap constantly produces new maps of the continental shelf, in the same format as 1:250 000 scale land topographic maps, showing contours at intervals of ten metres. Some soundings are also available in digital form.

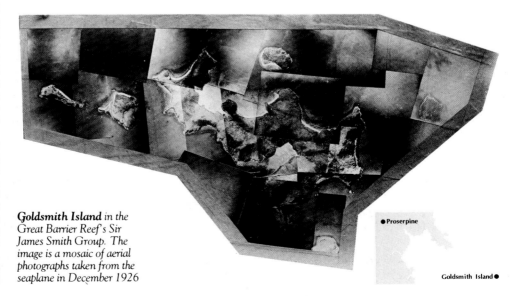

Goldsmith Island in the Great Barrier Reef's Sir James Smith Group. The image is a mosaic of aerial photographs taken from the seaplane in December 1926

● Proserpine

Goldsmith Island ●

Satellites scan the continent in a constant mission of discovery

Scientists are exploring Australia using the latest technology to probe further, deeper and wider than ever before. Their major tool is the orbiting satellite. Satellites have the ability to scan in just a few weeks a huge slice of the continent, and of its eleven million square kilometres of territorial waters, and its thirty-six thousand kilometres of shoreline. An early explorer, struggling to the top of each hill to see what lay ahead, would have been stunned by the range of information that now flows almost instantly back to base.

Scientists give the name 'remote sensing' to this new kind of exploration. The first aerial photographs could be called a type of remote sensing. But where they used only visible light, new sensing devices on satellites use other parts of the electromagnetic spectrum not visible to the eye.

Information is relayed to earth stations in the form of digitised (computer-readable) signals. The mass of data can be reproduced on screens or printed on paper, using false colour-imaging to highlight whatever detail is

needed. As with much pioneering work, the first space attempts in Australia were a partial failure. The Woomera rocket range was used in the nineteen-sixties for attempts to launch Europa satellites. Following several rocket disasters, the project was abandoned.

The world's third satellite to be successfully launched was made in Australia in just twelve months. WRESAT was carried into orbit by a United States Redstone rocket in 1967. Its instruments enabled scientists to make the first X-ray

astronomical surveys of the southern sky.

Today, the most familiar use of satellites is in weather forecasting. The United States launched its first weather observation satellites in the nineteen sixties. Improved polar orbiting satellites were then put into space by the National Oceanic and Atmospheric Administration. In 1984, Japan launched a geostationary meteorological satellite (GMS), which remains about thirty-six thousand kilometres above the equator, covering the Pacific area.

Australia continuously draws information from these sources to provide daily weather prediction services, with the now familiar pictures of cloud cover.

In scientific terms, a great leap forward came with the Landsat series of earth observation satellites, first launched by America's National Aeronautics and Space Administration (NASA), in the nineteen-seventies.

Landsat satellites, circling the earth in sixteen days at heights between seven hundred and one thousand kilometres

This infra-red photograph taken from the air, shows intensive cropping in Queensland's rich Darling Downs. Landsat images can show even greater detail, identifying crops under stress through disease, water shortage or weed infestation

use sensors to collect a broad range of information. At first Australia had to use American computer tapes to extract data. In 1979, an Australian Landsat data receiving station began to take transmissions direct from the satellites.

The site chosen was Alice Springs — not because the Alice was a traditional centre for Australian exploration, but because complete coverage of the continent and surrounding seas can be obtained from this central location.

The Landsat instrument continuously scans a swath below the spacecraft some one hundred and eighty-five kilometres wide. This strip is converted into lengths one hundred and eighty-five kilometres long, so that the imagery is ordered by scenes that are one hundred and eighty-five kilometres square. The instrument is

SATELLITE DISCOVERS NEW SHIPPING ROUTE

One of the most spectacular, and profitable, results of Landsat usage in Australia occurred in 1982.

HMAS *Flinders*, conducting hydrographic work round the Great Barrier Reef, used satellite and aerial images to help discover a new deep-water channel through the coral wall.

It was named Hydrographers Passage, to honour the normally unrecognised work of marine surveyors.

Coal ships sailing from Hay Point south-east of Mackay to Japan now cut off sixteen hundred kilometres from each trip and save millions of dollars in transport costs each year.

In this way the work of scientists and surveyors has had a major impact on Australia's export competitiveness.

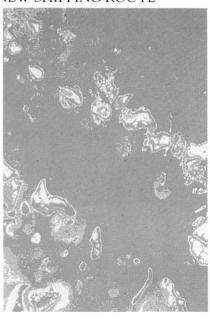

Hydrographers Passage. Yellow represents the band penetrating down to 15 metres, red from 50 centimetres to five metres, and green is areas shallower than 50 centimetres

sensitive to various wavelengths in the electromagnetic spectrum and records the amount of the sun's rays reflected by the earth's surface — from the long wavelengths of infra-red, through light visible to human eyes, to the short microwave bands.

The technique yields usable results because soil, water, crops, minerals all reflect a different amount of energy which can be measured from space. Knowing the signature (the amount of energy it reflects) of the material, the details of the terrain can be analysed.

Data gathered from Landsat transmissions enabled many different aspects of land usage in Australia to be economically studied for the first time.

Given the continent's generally arid lands and poor soils vulnerable to erosion, large-scale views provided by Landsat help agricultural scientists and landholders to avoid the unwitting destructiveness of the past, and make best permanent use of resources.

Landsat images are now used to continually monitor erosion, so that grazing patterns and crop-planting can be changed quickly when necessary. Observation shows defoliation caused by disease, clearing and fires.

The CSIRO has developed a computer programme known as Barrier Reef Image ANalysis (BRIAN) to make full use of Landsat data for reef conservation work.

BRIAN yields information on reef structure, exposure to weathering, marine life, water depth, vegetation and sediment load. The system has now been adapted to micro-computers and mar-

keted under the name Micro-BRIAN, giving every nation with coastal waters an opportunity of using satellite information at low cost.

Except in the case of the Barrier Reef, Landsat images have so far not been widely used for cartographic purposes. It is in the field of thematic mapping by broad subject that satellite exploration has yielded its best results.

Landsat receiving station at Alice Springs is run by the Australian Centre for Remote Sensing. The facility is being upgraded to take signals from the French SPOT satellite

The warm Leeuwin current flowing across the Bight is red; blue represents cold water. This is a composite from an infra-red thermal imaging device on a satellite of the US National Oceanographic Atmospheric Administration

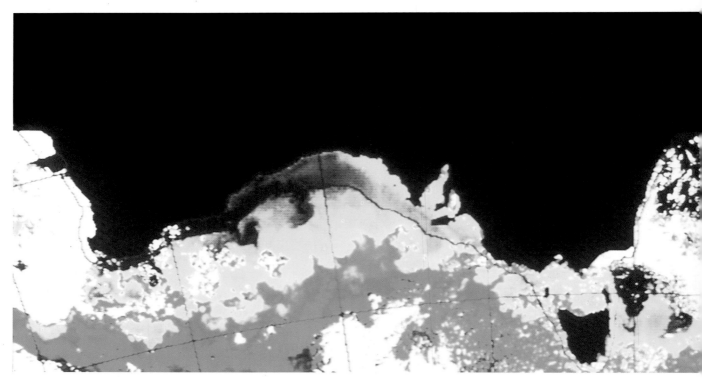

Western Australia's Canning Basin has been mapped with imagery from polar-orbiting spacecraft launched by NOAA. Ancient and intricate drainage networks have been revealed, which may contain seams of gold or diamonds

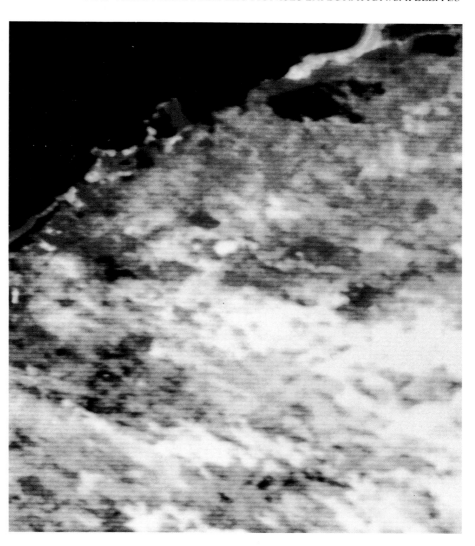

Landsat was originally designed for vegetation mapping, but the Australian mining industry soon found that Landsat images could analyse different types of surface material, giving clues to underlying geology and mining potential.

In recent years, the information contributed to two major Queensland mineral discoveries — a new gold mine at Pajingo, south of Charters Towers; and an oil strike at Tintaburra, between Grey Range and Cooper creek. The search for diamond-bearing areas in north-western Australia has also been assisted.

In central Australia, Landsat data has revealed a complex pattern of 'fossil rivers', dating back to prehistoric times when dinosaurs roamed fertile inland regions. By concentrating their research along these vanished rivers, scientists expect to discover much more about the pre-history of Australia.

Surveillance of suburban streets

A new high-resolution scanner called the Thematic Mapper was added to Landsat's range of sensors in 1982. This yields a ground resolution of thirty metres square, so that ordinary house blocks and suburban streets can be seen.

A French company, SPOT IMAGE, has introduced even more sophisticated instruments, capable of resolving any object or area larger than ten metres square. These instruments also have three-dimensional capacity, making it possible to use them for instant large-scale topographical mapping. The next revision of Australian map series will use this latest technological advance.

In a large country like Australia, remote sensing seems to offer the only economic and effective way of constantly monitoring its part of the globe.

For this reason, Australia is playing a role in development of the European Space Agency's ERS-1 satellite.

ERS-1 is one of a new generation of satellites equipped with a radar sensor and temperature analysis devices of enormous capacity. When launched, it will report on sea and land phenomena, even those obscured by weather conditions.

By the end of the century, NASA plans to operate a permanent orbiting manned space station equipped with a vast array of improved sensing devices capable of monitoring the total environment at a ground resolution of about twenty metres square. Nothing on the face of the earth will be exempt from closeup surveillance and analysis. □

HOW TODAY'S NAVIGATORS DISCOVER WHERE THEY ARE

Satellites in space have introduced a dramatic new era to exploration on land and at sea.

The first Soviet 'Sputnik' satellite was launched in 1957. American observers were able to predict its orbiting pattern by measuring frequency shifts (the 'Doppler effect') in its radio transmissions.

Scientists then realised that if they reversed the data, they could determine any receiving station's exact position on earth. The technique became known as 'Doppler position fixing'.

The final result was the launching of several US navigational satellites, the building of earth stations to receive and interpret their signals, and the development of portable receivers to utilise the information in the field.

These small receivers, which can be used anywhere on land or sea, calculate latitude and longitude to within a hundred metres almost instantly, and a few tens of metres over hours of observation. Later processing with additional information about the satellite orbits can produce results accurate within about two metres.

The successor to the Doppler system is the Global Positioning system. The prototype can almost instantly give a position of within ten metres, and if used with other receivers, can measure position differences with a precision of a few centimetres over hundreds of kilometres.

Unlike most earlier navigational instruments, satellite receivers can be used in any weather, at any time of day or night.

Australia's first receivers were introduced by Commonwealth survey and mapping authorities. Other survey organisations, shipping companies, and mineral exploration groups soon followed. Today receivers are also used to assist with surveying, mapping and investigations into the shape of the earth.

Satellite position-fixing has also been used to measure the rate at which the Australian continent is moving northwards — now recognised as about six centimetres a year. It has helped to position offshore oil rigs, and to monitor changes in Antarctic ice movements.

The technique produces detailed maps more accurate than ever before. It is so simple to use that millions of dollars in labour have already been saved.

Chronology

Year	Event

1295 — **Marco Polo**, on his return to Venice from Peking, brings back stories of a 'Great South Land' he calls *Java Maior*.

1503 — **Paulmier de Gonneville** visits the South Seas and, according to the French, lands on New Holland.

1520s — **Cristovao de Mendonca** may have touched on the Australian east coast at several points in the early 1520s, nearly two and a half centuries before Cook.

1526 — **Jorge de Meneses** accidentally discovers the north coast of New Guinea. He calls it *Os Papuas*.

1528 — **Alvaro de Saavedra** discovers more of the north coast of New Guinea giving it the name *Isla del Ora* – Isle of Gold.

1545 — **Ynigo Ortiz de Retez** sails along the New Guinea coastline and calls it *Nova Guinea*.

1606 — **Pedro Fernandez de Quiros** thinks he has found the legendary south land when he reaches Vanuatu. He names it *Tierra Australia del Espiritu Santo*.
Luis Vaez de Torres discovers Torres Strait and is probably the first European to sight the mainland of Australia.
Willem Jansz makes the first positively known landing by a European on Australian soil.

1616 — **Dirk Hartog** sights Australia's western coastline and names it *Eendrachtsland*.

1619 — **Frederik de Houtman** discovers Houtman Abrolhos and the coastline south of Perth. He names it *Dedelsland*.

1622 — **John Brooke**, in the *Tryal*, is the first Englishman to sight Australian soil. His ship is wrecked off the west coast.
The *Leeuwin*, a Dutch ship, touches on the south-west tip still known as Cape Leeuwin.

1623 — **Jan Carstensz**, in the *Arnhem*, discovers Arnhem Land and gives the first description of Aboriginals.

1627 — **Pieter Nuyts** stumbles on the south coast of WA and follows it for about 1500 km into SA, making the largest discovery so far. The true shape of Australia begins to emerge on Dutch maps.
Francois Thijssen charts part of the south-west coast between Cape Leeuwin and Nuyts Archipelago.

1628 — **Gerrit Frederikszoon de Witt**'s ship runs aground off the west coast. The area becomes known as De Witt's Land.

1629 — **Francois Pelsaert**'s ship the *Batavia* is wrecked when it strikes a reef off the west coast. While he explores the mainland for water, a mutiny takes place and the mutineers are later put to death, the first executions on Australian soil.

1636 — **Gerrit Pool and Pieter Pietersz** miss Torres Strait but sight Dundas Strait and name Van Diemen Gulf.

1642-43 — **Abel Jansz Tasman** goes in search of the Great South Land and discovers Van Diemen's Land, claiming it for Holland. He also discovers the South Island of New Zealand.

1644 — **Tasman** connects Arnhem Land to Carpentaria and charts much of the coast to the west, but fails to find Torres Strait.

1681 — **John Daniel** sights the New Holland coastline and makes a sketch survey of the Wallabi group of Houtman Abrolhos.

1688 — **William Dampier** visits the north-west coast and is the first Englishman to give a detailed account of Australia.

1696-97 — **Willem de Vlamingh** discovers Rottnest Island and the Swan river and is the last Dutch navigator of importance to Australian exploration.

1699 — **Dampier** attempts unsuccessfully to reach the east coast. He discovers Dampier Archipelago and makes the first recorded sighting of kangaroos.

1768 — **Chevalier de Bougainville** hopes to discover the east coast of New Holland and claim it for France, but he turns northwards at Bougainville Reef.

1769 — **James Cook**, in the *Endeavour*, discovers North Island and circumnavigates New Zealand.

1770 — **Cook** lands at Botany Bay claiming eastern Australia for Britain and naming it New South Wales. He also re-discovers Torres Strait, proving Australia and New Guinea are separate.

1772 — **Francois de St Allouarn** takes possession of Western Australia in the name of King Louis XVI.
Tobias Furneaux's opinion that the east coast of Van Diemen's Land is joined to New South Wales is accepted by Cook.

1772-74 — **Cook** sails to Antarctic waters proving *Terra Australia Incognita* does not exist. In 1774 he discovers Norfolk Island.

1788 — **Arthur Phillip** chooses Port Jackson for settlement and begins the land exploration of Australia with the discovery of Pitt Water and the Hawkesbury.
Jean Francois Galup de la Pérouse misses claiming New South Wales for the French by just six days. He and his men camp in the area near Botany Bay still called La Perouse.
Henry Lidgbird Ball discovers Lord Howe Island.

1789 — **William Bligh** charts much of Queensland's north-eastern coastline after being cast off by the *Bounty* mutineers.
Watkin Tench discovers the Nepean river.

1790 — **Tench and William Dawes** find the junction of the Nepean and Hawkesbury rivers but fail to cross the Blue Mountains.

1791 — **George Vancouver** discovers King George Sound but through bad weather misses discovering Bass Strait and Victoria.
William and Mary Bryant, escaped convicts, discover the site of Newcastle and a large estuary now known as Port Stephens.
James Bowen sights Jervis Bay from the convict ship *Atlantic*.

1792-93 — **Bruni d'Entrecasteaux** charts the southern coast of Van Diemen's Land discovering the Derwent river and d'Entrecasteaux Channel.

1793 — **William Paterson** is defeated in his bid to cross the Blue Mountains. He names the Grose river.
John Hayes discovers the fertile Risdon Cove, site of the first British settlement in Van Diemen's Land.

1794 — **Henry Hacking** succeeds in pushing out farther than any European has been, but fails to cross the Blue Mountains.

1795 — **George Bass and Matthew Flinders** commence their daring exploits along the east coast in the *Tom Thumb*.

1796 — **Bass and Flinders** discover Port Hacking while hoping to find a large river south of Botany Bay. Bass tries to cross the Blue Mountains.

1797 — **John Shortland** discovers coal and the Hunter river while pursuing escaped convicts.
Bass and Flinders discover the rainforest of the Illawarra Plain and report coal deposits.

1797-98 — **Bass** returns to Illawarra and finds the seams at Coalcliff. He also discovers Western Port, which is to become the base for attempts to settle the southern coast.

1798 — **John Wilson**'s party gives the first description of the southern highlands of New South Wales.

1798-9 — **Bass and Flinders** circumnavigate Van Diemen's Land proving it an island, discover the Tamar river and name Bass Strait.

1800-01 — **James Grant** surveys the Victorian coastline, naming Cape Northumberland and Seal Island and discovering Portland Bay.

1800-02 — **Nicolas Baudin** is sent by Napoleon Bonaparte to complete the mapping of Van Diemen's Land and New Holland. His crew fall victim to scurvy.

1802 — **John Murray and Charles Grimes** continue Grant's explorations, discovering Port Phillip.
Francis Louis Barrallier makes it to within 25 km of Jenolan Caves in his abortive attempt to cross the Blue Mountains.

1802-03 — **Flinders** circumnavigates Australia proving it an island.

1803 — **Charles Grimes** completes the survey of Port Phillip and discovers the Yarra.
John Bowen establishes the Risdon Cove settlement.

1804 — **David Collins** establishes a settlement at Sullivan Cove on the Derwent river, site of today's Hobart.
Robert Brown sights the Huon river from the summit of Mount Wellington and is the first white man to reach its banks.
William Paterson establishes a new outpost at Port Dalrymple.
George Caley fails to cross the Blue Mountains.
George Evans discovers the Warragamba river.

1807 — **Thomas Laycock** forges an overland route between the northern and southern settlements of Van Diemen's Land.

Grimes maps the lands around Port Dalrymple and traces the easiest route for the Midland Highway.

1810-21   **Lachlan Macquarie** makes eight exploratory tours of inspection into NSW and to Van Diemen's Land.

1812   **Evans** surveys the first practical route northwards along the coast from Jervis Bay to today's Wollongong.

1813   **Gregory Blaxland, Charles Wentworth and William Lawson** forge a route to the west across the Blue Mountains.
Evans surveys a road across the Blue Mountains, finding on the other side the Fish, Campbell and Macquarie rivers; he camps on the fertile Bathurst Plains.

1815   **Evans** discovers the Abercrombie and Lachlan rivers.

1815-16   **James Kelly** circumnavigates Van Diemen's Land in a whaleboat, discovering Macquarie Harbour and the Pieman river. He also claims discovering Port Davey but fellow merchant **Thomas Birch** says the discovery is his.

1817   **John Beamont** explores the Ouse river and the Great Lake country in Van Diemen's Land.

1817-18   **John Oxley** traces the courses of the Lachlan and Macquarie rivers in search of the legendary inland sea. Among his discoveries are the Liverpool Plains and Port Macquarie.

1817-22   **Phillip Parker King** conducts four successful expeditions, delineating the Queensland coastline and laying down a safe passage through Torres Strait.

1818   **Louis Claude de Freycinet** is sent by the King of France to complete the scientific work begun by Nicolas Baudin.
James Meehan stumbles on Lake Bathurst and the Goulburn Plains while seeking a land route to Jervis Bay.

1819   **John Howe** succeeds in finding an overland route to the Hunter river and Newcastle.
King and Oxley explore the Hastings river where a penal settlement is later established.

1821   **Charles Throsby** and ex-convict **Joseph Wild** discover New South Wales's second longest river — the Murrumbidgee.

1822   **William Lawson** finds the Goulburn river.
Hamilton Hume discovers the Yass river and Yass Plains.

1823   **Oxley** discovers the Brisbane.
Allan Cunningham finds a gap in the Liverpool Ranges which he calls Pandora's Pass.
Mark John Currie and John Ovens go in search of new pastoral land south of Lake George and discover Monaro Downs.

1824   **Hume and William Hilton Hovell** cross from the east to the south coast, sighting the Australian Alps and the Murray river and opening up the rich grazing lands of Victoria.
James Hobbs's surveys of remote harbours and their hinterlands in Van Diemen's Land enable settlement to extend.

1825   **Edmund Lockyer** explores the Brisbane river, discovering good soil and coal and the important Lockyer and Stanley rivers.

1826   **Dumont d'Urville** visits the site of Albany and is surprised the British have not occupied 'such a fine place'.
Lockyer raises the British flag at the site of Albany.
Joseph Fossey and Alexander Goldie find good country between Circular Head and Cape Grim for the Van Diemen's Land Company.

1826-27   **Patrick Logan** establishes a penal settlement at Moreton Bay and discovers the Logan and Albert rivers.
Jorgen Jorgenson fails to find an overland mountain route to Hobart, but discovers good land.

1826-8   **Henry Hellyer** discovers the Hellyer and Arthur rivers and valuable pasture lands for the Van Diemen's Land Company.

1827   **James Stirling** traces the Swan river to its source. It is decided a colony of free settlers will be established.
Cunningham discovers the richest part of southern Queensland — the Darling Downs.
Stirling raises the British flag at Raffles Bay in the Cobourg Peninsula. The settlement is soon abandoned.

1828   **John Wakefield** explores the north of Albany, sighting the Stirling Range and the Kalgan river.
Cunningham connects the Moreton Bay settlement with the Darling Downs by way of Spicer's Gap and Cunningham's Gap.

1828-29   **Charles Sturt and Hamilton Hume** trace the Macquarie river and discover the Darling.

1829   **George Frankland** plots the first true maps of inland Van Diemen's Land, correcting many errors of previous explorers.
Charles Fremantle takes formal possession for Britain of the entire continent and the city of Perth is proclaimed.
Thomas Braidwood Wilson makes the first overland expedition westwards along the coast from Albany.
Robert Dale uncovers some of the best land yet found in WA, laying the foundation of the important rural centre of Northam.
William Preston and Alexander Collie trace the Canning river and discover the Preston and Collie rivers south of Perth.
Cunningham's last journey explores the source of the Brisbane river.

1829-30   **Sturt** traces the Murrumbidgee, names the Murray and discovers it joins the Darling. His discoveries hasten settlement into southern New South Wales and into Victoria.

1830-34   **George Robinson** walks around Van Diemen's Land in an attempt to befriend the Aboriginals. Of the many landmarks he names, Arthur's Range is the only one that remains unaltered.

1830-36   **John Septimus Roe** explores about 1600 km of land from Perth to Albany and east to Russell Range.

1831   **Collet Barker** discovers Port Adelaide.
Thomas Bannister forges a route between Perth and Albany.

1831-32   **Raphael Clint** maps the Swan, Canning and Kalgan rivers and explores between the Porongorup and Stirling ranges.

1831-36   **Thomas Mitchell** proves that the Darling and the Murray form the main river system of NSW. His discoveries, including 'Australia Felix', accelerate immigration into Victoria.

1832   **John Garrett Bussell** explores the Vasse river area of Geographe Bay and founds a settlement known today as Busselton.

1834   **Johann Lhotsky** is the first to explore the Australian Alps.

1835   **Edward Henty** and his family pioneer Portland Bay, becoming Victoria's first permanent settlers.
John Batman explores the Saltwater and Yarra rivers and chooses a site for the settlement of Melbourne.
Frankland explores the sources of the Derwent, Huon and Nive rivers and completes the new map of Van Diemen's Land.

1836   **George Kingston** discovers the Torrens river; the city of Adelaide is proclaimed.
Henry William Bunbury discovers valuable mineral sands and pasture lands on an exploratory trip south of Perth.
George Fletcher Moore goes beyond the Darling Range to discover good grazing land and the Moore river.

1837   **William Hobson** surveys Port Phillip and Melbourne.

1837-38   **Edward John Eyre** discovers Lake Hindmarsh while attempting to be the first to overland stock from Sydney to Adelaide.

1837-43   **John Clements Wickham and John Lort Stokes**, in the *Beagle*, discover the Adelaide, Fitzmaurice and Victoria rivers, Port Darwin and the Flinders, Fitzroy and Albert rivers.

1838   **Hawdon and Charles Bonney** drive the first stock to Adelaide along the Murray, naming Lake Bonney and Lake Victoria.
John and Peter Manifold discover Lake Purrumbete and the rich plains of Camperdown.
James Gordon Bremer settles Port Essington.

1838-39   **Eyre** overlands the first sheep to South Australia along the Murrumbidgee and Murray rivers.
George Grey fails to find an overland route from Hanover Bay to Perth, but discovers the Glenelg and Gascoyne rivers.

1839   **Moore** leads an expedition to the coast around the site of Geraldton, bringing back a favourable report.
Foster Fyans blazes a route to Portland Bay from Geelong.

1839-40   **Charles James Tyers** surveys the inland route from Melbourne to Portland and to the South Australian border.
Angus McMillan forges a route through the rugged ramparts of Gippsland opening up valuable grazing lands.
Eyre makes two unsuccessful attempts to break through the north of SA. He finds Lake Torrens an impassable barrier.

1840   **Paul Edmund de Strzelecki** finds an inland route from McMillan's Track to Western Port, names Gippsland and becomes the first European to climb Mt Kosciusko.

1841	Eyre crosses the Nullarbor Plain to Albany and is convinced there is no inland sea. John Orr takes a party to explore Gippsland and is able to confirm the glowing reports. Edward Barker, Edward Hobson and Albert Brodribb are the first to walk from Melbourne to Gippsland. Patrick Leslie follows Cunningham's lead into southern Queensland and becomes known as the father of the Darling Downs. Stuart and Sydenham Russell discover Cecil Plains.
1842	John Franklin and his wife Jane discover an easier route from Hobart across the mountains to Macquarie Harbour, their efforts stimulating further exploration. Henry Stuart Russell and Andrew Petrie discover the Mary river and Russell sights the Boyne.
1842-45	Francis Price Blackwood and Joseph Beetes Jukes continue the surveys of Wickham and Stokes, making a close examination of the Great Barrier Reef.
1843	Edward Charles Frome explores the region of Lake Torrens, attempting to break through Eyre's horseshoe of salt lakes.
1844-45	Friedrich Wilhelm Ludwig Leichhardt crosses the continent from Brisbane to Port Essington. Sturt takes his last expedition inland but finds only desert.
1845-46	Mitchell discovers the Warrego, Belyando and Barcoo rivers and opens up the rich pastoral areas of central Queensland.
1846	Augustus Charles Gregory explores inland WA, discovering Lake Moore and finding coal on the banks of the Irwin. John Ainsworth Horrocks's expedition in the steps of Eyre ends in disaster when he is accidentally shot.
1846-47	Leichhardt's second expedition — to cross the continent from east to west — fails when he is forced to turn back.
1847	Edmund Kennedy is sent by Mitchell to trace the Barcoo river and discovers the Thomson. Kennedy's second expedition, to connect with the routes of Leichhardt and Mitchell, ends in tragedy.
1848	Leichhardt attempts once more to reach WA from Queensland; he and his entire party disappear without trace. Augustus Gregory finds excellent pastoral land leading to the settlement of the Geraldton area. He also discovers indications of lead and other minerals around the Murchison.
1848-49	John Roe explores the region between Perth and Esperance Bay, discovering Lake Hope and finding coal around the Fitzgerald.
1853	Francis Cadell proves the Murray, Murrumbidgee and Darling rivers are navigable. Charles and William Archer discover Queensland's Fitzroy river, and pioneer settlement in the north.
1854	Robert Austin leads an expedition to the interior of WA, discovering good grazing lands and water near present Dowerin, and gold at Mt Magnet.
1855-56	Augustus Gregory and Ferdinand von Mueller identify untouched pastures in the Northern Territory and Queensland.
1856	Benjamin Herschel Babbage, a geologist, goes in search of gold to the north of the Flinders Ranges, discovering instead good grazing land and Lake Blanche.
1857	George Woodroffe Goyder is deceived by recent rains into thinking the inland well-watered. Arthur Freeling discovers the paradise to be a desert.
1858	Babbage discovers that Eyre's great horseshoe lake of dry salt is really a chain of salt lakes. Francis Thomas Gregory finds good agricultural land in WA at the headwaters of the Gascoyne, Lyons and Murchison rivers. Augustus Gregory establishes that Cooper Creek, the Victoria river and the Barcoo are one and the same. He also confirms that Eyre's 'horseshoe' is really made up of separate lakes.
1859-60	George Elphinstone Dalrymple leads private expeditions to the Burdekin river district, finding rich pastoral land and the Bowen and Bogie rivers. He founds Bowen, north Queensland's first town.
1860	William Landsborough and Nathaniel Buchanan find Bowen Downs Station. John Mackay discovers the Pioneer river and one of Australia's biggest sugar and dairy districts. John and Peter MacDonald explore the wilds of north Queensland, establishing stations from the Burdekin to the Gulf. Stuart discovers the MacDonnell Ranges and Tennant Creek and reaches the geographical centre of Australia.
1860-61	Robert O'Hara Burke and William John Wills forge a route from Melbourne to the Gulf of Carpentaria, but fail to return.

1861	Francis Gregory discovers the Hammersley Range and the Fortescue, Ashburton, De Grey and Oakover rivers, opening up much valuable land. Alfred Howitt finds the bodies of Burke and Wills at Cooper creek and finds John King living with Aboriginals.
1861-62	Landsborough, in searching for Burke and Wills, accelerates pastoral settlement by the discovery of the Gregory and Georgina rivers and of the Barkly Tableland. John McKinlay leads a search for Burke and Wills from Adelaide to the Gulf, discovering the Diamantina river. Frederick Walker searches for Burke and Wills from Rockhampton to the Albert river, opening up large tracts of good country.
1862	Stuart's third attempt to cross the continent from Adelaide to the north is successful. His trail-blazing makes possible the Overland Telegraph and opens up good pasture land in the NT. Charles Gould discovers the Linda Valley and traces of silver, lead and gold in the Franklin and Gordon valleys.
1863	Ernest Henry opens a direct route to the plains of western Queensland. John Jardine pioneers settlement at Somerset, Cape York.
1864	Dalrymple finds the Herbert river and establishes Port Cardwell.
1864-65	Frank and Alexander Jardine and Archibald Richardson drive cattle overland up Cape York — one of the most difficult feats of overlanding and exploration ever achieved.
1865	McKinlay explores Arnhem Land and recommends Anson Bay as a suitable site for settlement.
1866	Peter Warburton discovers Lake Howitt and the Warburton river.
1866-67	George Strong Nares surveys the east and north-east coasts of Australia and Torres Strait in HMS Salamander.
1867	Caddell leads a sea exploration of the north coast of the NT in search of suitable areas for settlement. He discovers Cadell Strait, Elcho Island, Napier Peninsula and the Roper river.
1868	George Goyder selects Port Darwin as a suitable site for a town.
1869	John Forrest investigates a reported sighting of Leichhardt's expedition. He finds no trace of it, but discovers Lake Barlee.
1870	John Ross discovers the Todd river.
1871	John Forrest discovers suitable pastoral land in WA provided water can be obtained, and blazes a trail for a telegraph line linking WA with the east. James Smith discovers tin at Mount Bischoff.
1872	Warburton crosses the Great Sandy Desert to explore country west of the Overland Telegraph Line. Ernest Giles leads his first expedition into the 'red centre' of Australia and discovers Mount Olga. William Hann and Frederick Warner explore Cape York, discovering good grazing land and the Palmer and Daintree rivers. Warner finds gold on the Palmer.
1872-73	Dalrymple finds arable land north of Rockingham Bay.
1873	James Venture Mulligan starts a gold rush on the Palmer. William Christie Gosse discovers Ayers Rock while attempting to reach the west coast. Warburton's private expedition makes the first east to west crossing of the continent.
1873-74	Giles is defeated by the Gibson Desert.
1874	John Lewis determines the course of the Diamantina river and the size of Lake Eyre. John Forrest is the first explorer to cross the central regions from west to east.
1874-75	Mulligan discovers the Hodgkinson river where he finds gold, leading to the development of Cairns and Port Douglas.
1875	Giles succeeds in crossing from Adelaide to Perth, but finds no suitable land for settlement en route.
1876	Giles explores the Gibson Desert from the west. William Oswald Hodgkinson determines the amount of pastoral country west of the Diamantina. Gilbert McMinn and A.W. Sergison trace the course of the Katherine river.
1878	Buchanan discovers Buchanan's creek and opens up a stock route to the great pastoral district lying between the Queensland border and the Overland Telegraph Line.
1878-79	Alexander Forrest opens up the Kimberley. Ernest Favenc investigates country between Blackall and Darwin.

1878-80	**Charles Winnecke and Henry Vere Barclay** determine the border lines between South Australia and Queensland.
1882-83	**Favenc** traces the heads of the rivers running into the Gulf of Carpentaria and discovers valuable land near the Macarthur.
1883	**David Lindsay** leads a government expedition to Arnhem Land and becomes one of the great promoters of the Northern Territory. **Charles Rasp** discovers a rich silver-lead-zinc deposit in the Barrier Range, site of Broken Hill.
1890-92	**Albert Frederick Calvert** makes three scientific expeditions into central and western Australia.
1891-92	**Lindsay and Laurence Wells** map about 20 million hectares of central Australia.
1893	**Patrick Hannan** discovers gold at the site of Kalgoorlie.
1894	**Charles Winnecke** leads the successful Horn Scientific Expedition to carry out scholarly research in central Australia. One of its members is **Walter Baldwin Spencer**.
1894-95	**David Carnegie** discovers gold out from Coolgardie.
1895	**J.H. Rowe** maps good pastoral country at the source of the Gascoyne and Ashburton rivers. **Henryk Johan Bull and Carsten Egeberg Borchgrevink** make the first confirmed landing on Antarctica.
1896-97	**Carnegie**'s unsuccessful efforts to open an overland stock route confirm the aridity of the inland.
1896	**Walter Spencer and Francis James Gillen** begin their study of the Aboriginal way of life in central Australia. **Laurence Wells** leads a disastrous expedition to open a stock route from the NW goldfields to the NT. Two of the party perish.
1898	**Frank Hann** discovers copper in the Warburton Ranges and opens up the King Leopold Range for settlement.
1899	**Borchgrevink** makes the first permanent encampment in Antarctica, ushering in the great age of Antarctic exploration.
1900	**Allan A. Davidson** explores the still unknown areas between Tennant Creek and the WA border and discovers gold at Tanami.
1901	**Frederic Drake-Brockman** leads an expedition into the unknown centre of the Kimberley and finds good grazing land.
1901-02	**Spencer and Gillen** establish an ethnographic record of tribal life from central through to northern Australia.
1903	**Spencer and Gillen** conduct their last expedition, this time north-west of Lake Eyre.
1905	**Douglas Mawson** discovers Australia's first big radioactive ore body at Radium Hill, SA.
1906	**Alfred Canning** blazes a stock route to the Kimberley.
1907-09	**T.W. Edgeworth David, Alistair Forbes Mackay and Douglas Mawson** are the first to reach the magnetic pole where they plant the flag and take possession of Antarctica for Britain.
1911-13	**Douglas Mawson** leads the first Australasian Antarctic Expedition.
1922	**Gerald Harnett Halligan** pioneers aerial exploration in Australia with a survey of Lake Eyre.
1923	**John Campbell Miles** discovers a rich outcrop of silver-lead ore on the Leichhardt river.
1923-25	**George Hubert Wilkins** makes the first scientific exploration of Arnhem Land.
1928	**Herbert Basedow** leads a second scientific expedition into Arnhem Land, to see whether it can support farmers. **George Wilkins** makes the first Antarctic flights.
1929	**Cecil Thomas Madigan** makes aerial surveys of South Australia and names the Simpson Desert.
1929-31	**Mawson** leads a joint British, Australian and New Zealand Antarctic Research Expedition (BANZARE).
1930	**Harold Lasseter** perishes in the Petermann Ranges while searching for a legendary gold reef.
1930	**Donald Mackay** finances aerial mapping of central Australia, revealing mistakes made by earlier ground explorers and discovering lakes Mackay, Neale and Bennett.
1933	**Mackay** finances another aerial expedition, this time to explore unknown country west and north-west of the Petermann Ranges.
1935	**Donald Thomson**, anthropologist, investigates reports of tribal unrest in Arnhem Land. He befriends the Aboriginals.
1935-37	**Mackay** finances an aerial expedition to survey the Nullarbor Plain.
1936	**Edward A. Colson** proves the Simpson Desert can be crossed. **The Australian Antarctic Territory** is proclaimed.
1937	**Thomson** flies over Arnhem Land and helps define its confusing river systems.
1939	**Madigan** leads a professional expedition across the Simpson.
1948	**Charles Mountford** investigates the origins and development of life in Arnhem Land.
1979	**Landsat** data receiving station is opened in Alice Springs.
1982	**HMAS *Flinders*** discovers Hydrographers Passage, a new shipping route through the Great Barrier Reef, with the aid of satellite and aerial images.

Books Consulted

This is not a complete bibliography of Australian exploration. Only the most important works have been included. Square brackets indicate an explanatory note. The abbreviation LBSA shows books reprinted in the important facsimile exploration series published by the Libraries Board of South Australia.

Allen, James. *Journal of an experimental trip by the Lady Augusta on the River Murray.* Adelaide, 1853; LBSA, 1976.

Andrews, A. E. J. (ed.). *The devil's wilderness. George Caley's journey to Mount Banks 1804.* Blubber Head Press, Hobart, 1984.

Andrews, A. E. J. (ed.). *Hume and Hovell 1824.* Blubber Head Press, Hobart, 1981.

Andrews, A. E. J. (ed.). *A journey from Sydney to the Australian Alps* [Johann Lhotsky]. Sydney, 1835; Blubber Head Press, Hobart, 1979.

Andrews, A. E. J. (ed.). *Stapylton with Major Mitchell's Australia Felix expedition 1836.* Blubber Head Press, Hobart, 1986.

Andrews, Arthur. *The first settlement of the Upper Murray.* D. S. Ford, Sydney, 1920; Library of Australian History, Sydney, 1979.

Antill, H. C. *Journal of an excursion over the Blue or Western Mountains.* Sydney, 1904.

Auld, W. P. *Recollections of McDouall Stuart.* Sullivan's Cove, Adelaide, 1984.

Aurosseau, Marcel (ed.). *The letters of F. W. L. Leichhardt* (3 vols). Hakluyt Society, London, 1968.

Austin, K. A. *Matthew Flinders on the Victorian coast.* Cypress Books, Melbourne, 1974.

Austin, Robert. *Journal of Assistant-Surveyor R. Austin, commanding an expedition sent by the Government to explore the interior of Western Australia.* Perth, 1855.

Barrallier, F. L., *Journal of the expedition into the interior of New South Wales 1802.* Marsh Walsh, Melbourne, 1975.

Beaglehole, J. C. (ed.). *The Endeavour Journal of Joseph Banks.* (2 vols), Angus & Robertson, Sydney, 1962.

Beaglehole, J. C. (ed.). *Journals of Captain Cook, Vol. 1. The voyage of the Endeavour 1768-1771.* Cambridge University Press, 1955.

Beale, Edgar. *Kennedy of Cape York.* Rigby, Adelaide, 1970.

Beale, Edgar. *Kennedy, the Barcoo, and Beyond 1847.* Blubber Head Press, Adelaide, 1983.

Beale, Edgar. *Sturt. The chipped idol.* Sydney University Press, 1979.

Berndt, R. M. & C. *Arnhem Land, its history and people.* Cheshire, Melbourne, 1954.

Billot, C. P. *John Batman and the founding of Melbourne.* Hyland House, Melbourne, 1979.

Blainey, Geoffrey. *Triumph of the nomads.* Macmillan, Melbourne, 1975.

Blainey, Geoffrey. *The tyranny of distance.* Sun Books, Melbourne, 1966.

Bland, William. *Journey of discovery... by Messrs W. H. Hovell and Hamilton Hume...* Sydney, 1831; LBSA, 1965.

Blaxland, Gregory. *A journal of a tour of discovery across the Blue Mountains.* London, 1823; Sydney, 1913.

Bligh, William. *A voyage to the South Sea.* London, 1792; LBSA, 1969.

Bolton, G. C. *Alexander Forrest.* Melbourne University Press, 1958.

Bolton, G. C. *A thousand miles away.* Jacaranda, Brisbane, 1963.

Bonython, C. Warren. *Walking the Simpson Desert.* Rigby, Adelaide, 1980.

Bougainville, L. A. *A voyage around the world.* London, 1772; N. Israel, Amsterdam, 1967.

Bowden, K. M. *Captain James Kelly of Hobart Town.* Melbourne University Press, 1964.

Bowden, K. M. *George Bass 1771-1803.* Oxford University Press, Melbourne, 1952.

Bowden, K. M. *Matthew Flinders' narrative of Tom Thumb's cruise to Canoe Rivulet.* South Eastern Historical Association, Melbourne, 1985.

Boyce, D. W. *Clarke of the Kindur.* Melbourne University Press, 1970.

Bride, T. F. *Letters from Victorian pioneers.* Melbourne, 1898; Heinemann, Melbourne, 1969.

Brock, D. G. (ed. K. Peake-Jones). *To the desert with Sturt: a diary of the 1844 expedition.* Royal Geographical Society, Adelaide, 1975.

Brodribb, W. A. *Recollections of an Australian squatter.* Sydney, 1883; Ferguson, Sydney, 1978.

Brown, P. L. (ed.). *The narrative of George Russell of Golf Hill.* Oxford University Press, London, 1935.

Bryan, C. P. (Cygnet). *Swan River booklets.* Paterson Brokensha, Perth, 1935.

Bunbury, W. St P. and Morrell, W. P. *Early days in Western Australia, being the letters and journal of Lieutenant H. W. Bunbury.* London, 1930.

Bunce, Daniel. *Travels with Dr. Leichhardt in Australia.* Melbourne, 1859; Oxford University Press, Melbourne, 1979.

Bunce, Daniel. *Twenty-three years' wanderings in the Australias and Tasmania.* Geelong, 1857.

Burke & Wills exploring expedition. Melbourne, 1861; LBSA, 1963.

Burn, David. *Narrative of the overland journey of Sir John and Lady Franklin.* Mackaness, Sydney, 1955.

Byerley, F. J. (ed.). *Narrative of the overland expedition of the Messrs. Jardine...* Brisbane, 1867.

Calder, J. E. *Boat expeditions round Tasmania 1815-16 and 1824.* Hobart, 1881; Sullivan's Cove, Adelaide, 1984.

Callander, John. *Terra Australis Cognita: or, voyages to the Terra Australis.* (3 vols), Edinburgh, 1766-8; N. Israel, Amsterdam, 1967.

Calvert, A. F. *The Calvert scientific exploring expedition.* London, 1905.

Calvert, A. F. *Narrative of an expedition into the interior of North-West Australia.* London, 1892.

Carnegie, D. W. *Spinifex and sand.* London, 1898; Penguin, Melbourne, 1973.

Carron, William. *Narrative of an expedition...of the late Mr Assistant Surveyor, E. B. Kennedy...* Sydney, 1849; LBSA, 1965.

Christie, E. M. (ed.). *Journals of Benjamin Francis Helpman.* Royal Geographical Society Proceedings, Adelaide, 1943-6.

Clune, Frank. *Last of the Australian explorers: the story of Donald Mackay.* Angus & Robertson, Sydney, 1942.

Collingridge, George. *The discovery of Australia.* Sydney, 1895; Golden Press, Sydney, 1983.

Collins, David. *An account of the English Colony in New South Wales.* (2 vols), London, 1798-1802; Christchurch, 1910; LBSA, 1971.

Connell, Gordon. *The mystery of Ludwig Leichhardt.* Melbourne University Press, 1980.

Cornell, Christine (trans.). *The journal of Post Captain Nicolas Baudin.* LBSA, 1974.

Cottesloe, Lord (ed.). *Diary and letters of Sir C. H. Fremantle...* London, 1928.

Coutts, P. J. F. *Corinella. A forgotten episode in Victorian history.* Victorian Archeological Survey, Melbourne, 1983.

Cox, Kenneth. *Angus McMillan: pathfinder.* Olinda Public Relations, Melbourne, 1973; K. R. Pryse, Melbourne, 1984.

Cross, Joseph. *Journals of several expeditions made in Western Australia during the years 1829, 1830, 1831 and 1832...* London, 1833; University of Western Australia Press, 1980.

Crowley, F. K. *Forrest: 1847-1918.* University of Queensland Press, Brisbane, 1971.

Cumpston, J. H. L. *Augustus Gregory and the inland sea.* Roebuck, Canberra, 1972.

Cumpston, J. S. *First visitors to Bass Strait.* Roebuck, Canberra, 1973.

Currey, J. E. B. (ed.). *Reflections on the Colony of New South Wales.* [George Caley], Lansdowne, Melbourne, 1966.

Daley, Louise. *Men and a river. Richmond River district 1828-1895.* Melbourne University Press, 1966.

Dalrymple, Alexander. *An account of the discoveries made in the South Pacifick Ocean previous to 1764.* London, 1767.

Dalrymple, G. A. F. E. *Narrative and report of the Queensland north-east coast expedition.* Brisbane, 1874.

Dalrymple, G. A. F. E. *Report of proceedings of the Spitfire in search of the mouth of the River Burdekin.* Brisbane, 1860.

Dampier, William. *New voyage round the world.* Vol. 4, London, 1697-1709.

Darke, J. C. *Journals of expeditions in Van Diemen's Land 1833.* Sullivan's Cove, Adelaide, 1985.

Davidson, A. A. *Journal of explorations in Central Australia by the Central Australian Exploration Syndicate Ltd.* Adelaide, 1905.

Davidson, Robyn. *Tracks.* Cape, London, 1980.

Davis, John. *Tracks of McKinlay and party across Australia.* London, 1863.

Durack, Mary. *Kings in Grass Castles.* Constable, London, 1959.

Dutton, Geoffrey. *Australia's last explorer — Ernest Giles.* Faber, London, 1970.

Dutton, Geoffrey. *Founder of a city...* [William Light]. Cheshire, Melbourne, 1960.

Dutton, Geoffrey. *The hero as murderer: the life of Edward John Eyre...* Cheshire, Melbourne, 1967; Penguin, Melbourne, 1977.

Eccleston, G. C. *Major Mitchell's 1836 Australia Felix expedition.* Department of Conservation, Forests and Lands, Melbourne, 1985 (i.e., 1986).

Edwards, E. and Hamilton, G. *A voyage around the world...* [HMS Pandora], London, 1793; London, 1915.

Elder, David (ed.). *William Light's brief journal and Australian diaries.* Wakefield Press, Adelaide, 1984.

Ericksen, Ray. *Ernest Giles. Explorer and Traveller 1835-1897.* Heinemann, Melbourne, 1978.

Erickson, Rica. *The Drummonds of Hawthornden.* [James Drummond], Lamb Paterson, Perth, 1969.

Eyre, E. J. *Journals of expeditions of discovery into Central Australia...* (2 vols), London, 1845; LBSA, 1964.

Farnfield, D. J. *Frontiersman. A biography of George Elphinstone Dalrymple.* Oxford University Press, Melbourne, 1968.

Field, Barron. *Geographical memoirs on New South Wales and Van Diemen's Land.* London, 1825.

FitzGerald, Lawrence. *Java la Grande: the Portuguese discovery of Australia.* The Publishers Pty Ltd, Hobart, 1984.

FitzGerald, Lawrence. *Lebanon to Labuan.* [Australian Survey Corps], J. G. Holmes, Melbourne, 1980.

Fitzpatrick, Kathleen. *Sir John Franklin in Tasmania 1837-1843.* Melbourne University Press, 1949.

Flinders, Matthew (ed. G. Mackaness). *Observations on the coasts of Van Diemen's Land...* London, 1801; Sydney, 1946.

Flinders, Matthew. *A voyage to Terra Australis...* (2 vols and atlas), London, 1814; LBSA, 1966.

Flood, Josephine. *Archaeology of the Dreamtime.* William Collins, Sydney, 1983.

Forrest, John. *Explorations in Australia 1847-1918.* London, 1875; LBSA, 1969.

Foster, W. C. *Sir Thomas Livingstone Mitchell and his world 1792-1855.* Institution of Surveyors NSW Inc., Sydney 1985.

Frankland, George. *The narrative of an expedition to the head of the Derwent... in 1835.* Sullivan's Cove, Adelaide, 1983.

Frankland, George. *Report on the transactions of the Survey Department of Van Diemen's Land, from the foundation of the colony...* Hobart, 1837.

Furneaux, Rupert. *Tobias Furneaux, circumnavigator.* Cassell, London, 1960.

Giles, Ernest. *Australia twice traversed...* (2 vols), London, 1889; LBSA, 1964.

Giles, Ernest. *A trip west of the Peake.* Sullivan's Cove, Adelaide, 1985.

Giles, Ernest. *The journal of a forgotten expedition.* Adelaide 1880; Sullivan's Cove, Adelaide, 1979.

Gillen, F. J. *Gillen's diary: the camp jottings of F. J. Gillen on the Spencer — Gillen expeditions across Australia.* LBSA, Adelaide, 1968.

Godwin, George. *Vancouver, a life.* Philip Allan, London, 1930.

Gosse, W. C. *Report and diary of Mr W. C. Gosse's Central and Western exploring expedition.* Adelaide, 1874; LBSA, 1973.

Gould, Charles. *Exploration of the Western country, Tasmania.* Hobart, 1860.

Govett, W. R. *Sketches of New South Wales.* Gaston Renard, Melbourne, 1977.

Gowlland, R. W. (ed.). *Darke of the Peaks...* n.p., 1979.

Grant, James. *The narrative of a voyage of discovery...in the Lady Nelson...* London, 1803; LBSA, 1973; Heritage, Melbourne, 1975.

Gregory, A. C. and F. T. *Journals of Australian explorations.* Brisbane, 1884; Greenwood Press, NY, 1968; LBSA, 1969; Hesperian Press, Perth, 1981.

Grey, George. *Journals of two expeditions of discovery in North-west and Western Australia during the years 1837, 38 and 39...* London, 1841; LBSA, 1964.

Hann, William. *Copy of the diary of the Northern Expedition.* Brisbane, 1873.

Hawdon, Joseph. *Journal of a journey through New South Wales to Adelaide.* Georgian House, Melbourne, 1952.

Heeres, J. E. (ed.). *Abel Janszoon Tasman's journal of his discovery of Van Diemen's Land.* Amsterdam, 1898; Kovack, Los Angeles, 1965.

Heeres, J. E. (ed.). *The part borne by the Dutch in the discovery of Australia.* London, 1899.

298

Hilder, Brett. *The voyage of Torres...in 1606.* University of Queensland Press, Brisbane, 1980.

Horton, T. and Morris, K. *The Andersons of Western Port.* Bass Valley Historical Society, Victoria, 1983.

Hume, Hamilton. *A brief statement of facts in connexion with an overland expedition from Lake George to Port Phillip, in 1824.* Sydney, 1855.

Hunter, John. *An historical journal of the transactions at Port Jackson...* London, 1793; LBSA, 1968.

Huxley, Julian (ed.). *T. H. Huxley's diary of the voyage of HMS Rattlesnake.* Chatto & Windus, London, 1935.

Ingleton, G. C. *Charting a continent.* Angus & Robertson, Sydney, 1944.

Jack, R. L. *Northmost Australia...* (2 vols), Geo. Robertson & Co., Melbourne, 1922.

Jackson, Andrew. *Robert O' Hara Burke and the Australian exploring expedition of 1860.* London, 1862.

Jukes, J. B. *Narrative of the surveying voyage of HMS Fly.* (2 vols), London, 1847.

Kelly, Celsus. *Some early maps relating to the Queiros-Torres discoveries of 1606.* Congresso Internacional de Historia dos Descobrimentos, Lisbon, 1961.

Kenihan, G. H. (ed.). *The journal of Abel Jansz Tasman 1642...* Australian Heritage Press, Adelaide, 1964.

Keynes, R. D. *The Beagle record...* Cambridge University Press, 1979.

Kiddle, Margaret. *Men of Yesterday.* Melbourne University Press, 1961.

King, P. P. *Narrative of a survey of the intertropical and western coasts of Australia...* (2 vols), London, 1826; LBSA, 1969.

Kirk, R. L. and Thorne, A. G. (eds.). *The origin of the Australians.* Humanities Press, New Jersey, 1976.

Kruta, Valdislav, et al. *Dr John Lhotsky: the turbulent Australian writer, naturalist and explorer.* Australia Felix Literary Club, Melbourne, 1977.

Labillardiere, Jacques. *Relation du voyage a la recherchede La Pérouse.* (2 vols and atlas), Paris, 1800; London, 1802.

Landsborough, William (ed. J. S. Laurie). *Exploration of Australia from Carpentaria to Melbourne.* London, 1866.

Langley, Michael. *Sturt of the Murray.* Hale, London, 1969.

La Pérouse, J. F. *The voyage of La Pérouse round the world...* [English edition]. London, 1798.

Lee, Ida. *Commodore Sir John Hayes; with account of Admiral d'Entrecasteaux's voyage of 1792-1793.* Longmans Green, London, 1912.

Lee, Ida. *Early explorers in Australia.* Methuen, London, 1925.

Lee, Ida. *The logbooks of the Lady Nelson...* London, 1915.

Leichhardt, F. W. L. *Journal of an overland expedition in Australia from Moreton Bay to Port Essington.* London, 1847; LBSA, 1964; Doubleday, Sydney, 1980.

Light, William. *A brief journal of the proceedings of William Light.* Adelaide, 1839.

Lindsay, David. *Journal of the Elder scientific exploring expedition. 1891-1892,* Adelaide, 1893.

Lubbock, Adelaide. *Owen Stanley, RN, 1811-1850, Captain of the Rattlesnake.* Heinemann, Melbourne, 1968.

Macdonald, J. G. *Journal of ..., on an expedition from Port Denison to the Gulf of Carpentaria and back.* Brisbane, 1865.

MacGillivray, John. *Narrative of the voyage of HMS Rattlesnake...* (2 vols), London, 1852.

McIntyre, K. G. *The secret discovery of Australia.* Souvenir Press, London, 1977.

Mackaness, George. *The discovery and exploration of Moreton Bay and the Brisbane River.* (2 vols), D. S. Ford, Sydney, 1956; Review Publications, Dubbo, NSW, 1979.

Mackaness, George. *Fourteen journeys over the Blue Mountains of New South Wales, 1813-1841.* D. S. Ford, Sydney, 1950; Review Publications, Dubbo, NSW, 1978.

Mackillop, George. *Discovery of Gipps Land: Journey by Mr George MacKillop...* Sydney, 1904.

McKinlay, John. *McKinlay's diary of his journey across the continent.* Melbourne, 1863.

McKnight, T. L. *The camel in Australia.* Melbourne University Press, 1969.

MacKnight, C. C. *The farthest coast.* Melbourne University Press, 1969.

McMinn, W. G. *Allan Cunningham, botanist and explorer.* Melbourne University Press, 1970.

Macquarie, Lachlan. *Journal of his tours in New South Wales and Van Diemen's Land, 1810-1822.* Public Library of New South Wales, Sydney, 1956; Library of Australian History, Sydney, 1979.

Madigan, C. T. *Central Australia.* Oxford University Press, Melbourne, 1944.

Madigan, C. T. *Crossing the dead heart.* Georgian House, Melbourne, 1946.

Major, R. H. (ed.). *Early voyages to Terra Australis...* London, 1859.

Marchant, L. R. *France Australe...* Artlook, Perth, 1982.

Marriott, Ida. see Lee, Ida.

Mercer, F. R. *Amazing career: the story of Western Australia's first Surveyor-General.* [J. S. Roe], Paterson Brokensha, Perth, 1962.

Mercer, F. R. *The life of Charles Harper.* Westralian Farmers Co-op, Perth, 1958.

Meston, A. L. *The Van Diemen's Land Company 1825-1842.* Launceston City Council, 1958.

Mitchell, T. L. *Journal of an expedition into the interior of tropical Australia...* London, 1848; Greenwood, NY, 1969.

Mitchell, T. L. *Three expeditions into the interior of Eastern Australia...* (2 vols), London, 1838; LBSA, 1965.

Mollison, A. F. (ed. J. O. Randell). *An overlanding diary.* Mast Gully Press, Melbourne, 1980.

Moore, G. F. *Evidences of an inland sea...* Dublin, 1837.

Mountford, C. P. *Records of the American-Australian scientific expedition to Arnhem Land.* [1948], (4 vols), Melbourne University Press, 1956-64.

Mudie, Ian, *Riverboats.* Rigby, Adelaide, 1961.

Mulvaney, D. J. *The prehistory of Australia.* Thames & Hudson, London, 1969.

Mulvaney, D. J. and Calaby, J. H. *So much that is new. Baldwin Spencer 1860-1929. A biography.* Melbourne University Press, 1985.

Oxley, John. *Journals of two expeditions into the interior of New South Wales.* London, 1820; LBSA, 1964.

Parkinson, Sydney. *A journal of a voyage to the South Seas in His Majesty's ship the Endeavour...* London, 1784; Caliban, London, 1984.

Pateshall, Nicholas (ed. M. Tipping). *A short account of a voyage round the globe in HMS Calcutta 1803-1804.* Queensberry Hill Press, Melbourne, 1980.

Peron, F. and De Freycinet, D. *Voyage de découvertes aux Terres Australes...* (3 vols and 2 atlases), Paris, 1807-1812.

Perry, T. M. *Australia's first frontier.* Melbourne University Press, 1963.

Petrie, Constance. *Tom Petrie's reminiscences of early Queensland.* Brisbane, 1904; Currey O'Neil, Melbourne, 1975.

[Phillip, Arthur.] *A voyage to Botany Bay.* London, 1789; LBSA, 1968.

Plomley, N. J. B. (ed.). *Friendly mission. The Tasmanian journals of G. A. Robinson.* Tasmanian Historical Research Association, Hobart, 1966.

Polo, Marco (trans. Henry Yule). *The book of Ser Marco Polo.* London, 1875.

Polo, Marco (trans. John Frampton), *Most noble and famous travels of Marco Polo.* London, 1929.

Prineas, Peter. *Wild places.* Kalianna Press, Sydney, 1983.

Proceedings of the first Australian symposium on the Mahogany Ship: relic or legend? Mahogany Ship Committee, Warrnambool, Vic., 1982.

Queiros, P. F. *Terra Australis Incognita.* Seville, 1610; London, 1617.

Rawson, Geoffrey. *The Count. A life of Sir Paul Edmund de Strzelecki...* Heinemann, London, 1953.

Richards, J. A. (ed.). *Blaxland Lawson Wentworth 1813.* Blubber Head Press, Hobart, 1979.

Rossel, M. de. *Voyage de [Bruny] d'Entrecasteaux...* (2 vols and atlas), Paris, 1808.

Roth, H. L. *The discovery and settlement of Port Mackay, Queensland.* Halifax, England, 1908.

Royal Geographical Society Journals and Proceedings: London, Adelaide, Brisbane, Melbourne, Sydney.

Schilder, Gunter. *Australia unveiled...* Theatrvm Orbis Terrarvm Ltd, Amsterdam, 1976.

Schilder, Gunter. *Voyage to the Great South Land. Willem de Vlamingh 1696-1697.* Royal Australian Historical Society, Sydney, 1985.

Scott, Ernest. *Terre Napoléon. A history of French explorations and projects in Australia.* Methuen, London, 1910.

Sharp, Andrew. *The voyages of Abel Janszoon Tasman.* Oxford University Press, 1968.

Shillinglaw, J. J. *Historical Records of Port Phillip.* Melbourne, 1879; Heinemann, Melbourne, 1972.

Spencer, W. B. and Gillen F. J. *Across Australia* (2 vols), Macmillan, London, 1912.

Spencer, W. B. and Gillen F. J. *The native tribes of Central Australia.* Macmillan, London, 1899 and 1938; Dover, New York, 1968.

Steele, J. G. *Explorers of the Moreton Bay district 1770-1830.* University of Queensland Press, Brisbane, 1972.

Steele, W. & C. *To the great Gulf. The surveys and explorations of L. A. Wells...* Lynton Publications, Blackwood, SA, n.d. [1978].

Stevens, H. S. *New light on the discovery of Australia.* Stevens, Son & Stiles, London, 1930.

Stokes, Edward. *To the inland sea. Charles Sturt's expedition 1844-45.* Hutchinson, Melbourne, 1986.

Stokes, J. L. *Discoveries in Australia.* (2 vols), London, 1846; LBSA, 1969.

Stuart, J. M. (ed. W. Hardman). *Journals of... during the years 1858-1862...* London, 1864; LBSA, 1975.

Stuart, J. M. *J. McDouall Stuart's explorations across the continent of Australia...1861-62.* Melbourne, 1863; LBSA, 1963.

Sturt, Charles. *An expedition into the northwestern interior of New South Wales 1828.* Sullivan's Cove, Adelaide, 1983.

Sturt, Charles. (ed. J. Waterhouse). *Journal of the Central Australian Expedition 1844-5.* Caliban Books, London, 1984.

Sturt, Charles. *Narrative of an expedition into Central Australia... during the years 1844, 5 and 6...* (2 vols), London, 1849; LBSA, 1964.

Sturt, Charles. *Two expeditions into the interior of Southern Australia during the years 1828, 1829 and 1831...* (2 vols), London, 1833; LBSA, 1963; Doubleday, Sydney, 1982.

Sturt, Mrs Napier. *Life of Charles Sturt.* London, 1899.

Swan, K. and Carnegie M. *In step with Sturt.* Graphic Books, Melbourne, 1979.

Thomson, Donald. (comp. Nicolas Peterson). *Donald Thomson in Arnhem Land.* Currey O'Neil, Melbourne, 1983.

Tietkins, W. H. *Diary of the exploration in South Australia of W. H. Tietkins, 1879.* Department of Supply, Adelaide, 1961.

Tietkins, W. H. *Journal of the Central Australian exploring expedition 1889.* Adelaide, 1891.

Tipping, Marjorie (ed.). *Ludwig Becker.* Melbourne University Press, 1979.

Tooley, R. V. *The mapping of Australia.* Holland Press Cartographica, Amsterdam, 1979.

Tuckey, J. H. *An account of a voyage to establish a colony at Port Phillip...* London, 1805; Marsh Taylor & Walsh, Melbourne, 1974.

Turnbull, Henry. *Leichhardt's second journey.* Ferguson, Sydney, 1983.

Tyers, C. J. *Report of an expedition to ascertain... the boundary line between New South Wales and South Australia.* Sydney, 1840.

Walker, M. H. *Come wind, come weather.* [A. W. Howitt]. Melbourne University Press, 1971.

Warburton, P. E. *Journey across the western interior of Australia.* London, 1875; LBSA, 1968.

Waterhouse, Jill (ed.). *Edward Eyre's autobiographical narrative 1832-1839.* Caliban, London, 1984.

Webster, E. M. *Whirlwinds in the plain. Ludwig Leichhardt. Friends foes and history.* Melbourne University Press, 1980.

Webster, M. S. *John McDouall Stuart.* Melbourne University Press, 1958.

Wedge, J. H. *Diaries 1824-1835.* Royal Society of Tasmania, Hobart, 1962.

Wedge, J. H. *Official report of journeys... in the early part of 1828.* Hobart, 1828.

Wells, L. A. *Journal of the Calvert scientific exploring expedition, 1896-7.* Perth, 1902.

Wharton, W. J. L. (ed.). *Captain Cook's journal during his first voyage round the world made in HM Bark Endeavour 1768-71.* London, 1893; LBSA, 1968.

Whyte, Duncan. *Sketch of explorations by the late John McKinlay... 1861-2.* Glasgow, 1881; LBSA, 1962.

Wilkins, G. H., *Undiscovered Australia....* Benn, London, 1928.

Wills, W. J. *A successful exploration through the interior of Australia...* London, 1863.

Winnecke, C. G. A. *Journal of the Horn scientific exploring expedition.* Adelaide, 1896.

Winnecke, C. G. A. *Last explorations in the Northern Territory.* London, 1884.

Illustrations

The publishers give particular thanks to the staff of the Mitchell Library, State Library of New South Wales; the National Library of Australia; and the Mortlock Library of South Australiana.

ML — Mitchell Library, State Library of New South Wales; DL - Dixson Library, State Library of New South Wales; NK — Rex Nan Kivell Collection in the National Library of Australia; NLA — National Library of Australia; MLSA — Mortlock Library of South Australiana.

An asterisk (*) indicates a book listed on pages 298-99.

Position of illustrations on the page: t — top, c — centre, b - bottom, l — left, r — right.

Cover: t, Edward Stokes; b, Nicholas Chevalier, 'Return of Burke and Wills to Cooper's Creek', NLA. **1**: Chevalier. **6/7**: from Ludwig Leichhardt, *Journal**, State Library of New South Wales. **8/9**: detail from Flemish school, 'Interior of an Art Gallery', 17th century, reproduced courtesy the Trustees, National Gallery, London. **10**: t, R. Browne, 'Natives Fishing in a Bark Canoe, New South Wales, 1819', Dixson Galleries, State Library of New South Wales; b, Thomas Baines, 'The Artist, G. Phibbs and V. Graham in the long boat of the *Messenger*..., November 7, 1856', NK/NLA. **11**: t, Augustus Earle, 'Waterfall in Australia', NK/NLA; b, from Sydney Parkinson, *Journal**, ML. **12**: William Anderson Cawthorne, 'A Fight at the Murray', ML. **13**: tl, William Anderson Cawthorne, 'Aborigines Fishing', ML; tr, from James Atkinson, *An Account of the State of Agriculture and Grazing in New South Wales*..., 1826, ML; c, William Anderson Cawthorne, 'Native knocking down parrots with waddy', ML; b, Samuel Thomas Gill, 'Native Crouching Emu', ML. **14**: tl, from Ptolemy's *Geography*, 1486, National Maritime Museum, London, photo Michael Holford; c, carving of Shou Lao, Taoist immortal, Museum of Applied Arts and Sciences, Sydney; b, brown paper drawing from Melville Bay by Mawulan, Anthropology Research Museum, University of Western Australia, photo J.E. Stanton. **15**: t, both National Maritime Museum, London, photo Michael Holford; b, both Rijksmuseum-Nederlands Scheepvaart Museum, Amsterdam. **16**: both National Maritime Museum, London, photo Michael Holford. **17**: t, National Maritime Museum, London; bl, National Maritime Museum, London, photo Michael Holford. **18**: British Museum, photo Michael Holford. **18/19**: Tony La Tona. **19**: Bibliothèque Nationale, Paris, photo Giraudon/Art Resource. **20**: DL. **21**: t and c, from George Grey, *Journals**, ML; b, Bibliothèque Nationale, Paris. **22**: t, National Maritime Museum, London, photo Michael Holford. **23**: t, Mansell Collection; br, National Maritime Museum, London, photo Michael Holford. **24**: both Rijksmuseum, Amsterdam. **26**: t, Northern Netherlandish School c. 1620, Rijksmuseum, Amsterdam; b, Joannes van Keulen, 'Black Swans on Rottnest Island', NK/NLA. **27**: t, from John Callander, *Terra Australis**, ML; br, from F. Valentijn, *Oud en Nieuw Oost-Indien*, 1724-26, NK/NLA. **28**: Jean-Paul Ferrero/Auscape. **29**: Tasmanian Museum and Art Gallery; c, ML; b, Jean-Paul Ferrero/Auscape. **30**: l, L'Armessin, NK/NLA. **30/31**: t, British Museum, photo Michael Holford; b, Flemish school, 'Interior of an Art Gallery', 17th century, reproduced courtesy the Trustees, the National Gallery, London. **31**: t, Rijksmuseum, Amsterdam; c, National Library of Australia; b, 'India Orientalis', 1660, ML. **32**: t, from Sir Francis Drake, *The World Encompassed*, 1628, ML; bl, Patrick E. Baker/Photo Index; bc and br, Patrick E. Baker, Western Australian Maritime Museum. **33**: t, Photo Index; b, NK/NLA. **34**: t, from Sydney Parkinson, *Journal**, ML; b, from William Dampier, *A Voyage to New Holland*, ML. **35**: Michael Holford. **36**: Photo Index. **36/37**: t, Richard Woldendorp; b, Photo Index. **38**: copy of painting in National Maritime Museum, London, NLA. **40**: t, from *Historical Records of New South Wales*, Vol. I, Part I, ML; b, David Hancock/Auscape. **41**: National Gallery of Victoria. **42**: C.A. Henley/Auscape. **43**: Michael Jensen/Auscape. **46**: t, C.A. Henley/Auscape; b, Robin Morrison/Reader's Digest. **46/47**: The Photo Library. **47**: t, from *Historical Records of New South Wales*, Vol. I, Part I, ML; b, ML. **48** t, The Photo Library; b, Michael Jensen/Auscape. **49**: Dixson Galleries, State Library of New South Wales. **50**: tl, from the collection in Parham Park, Pulborough, West Sussex, photo Michael Holford; tr, Genesis Publications/ML; c and **51**, tl, from Joseph Banks, *Florilegium*, courtesy British Museum (Natural History) and Alecto Historical Editions/State Library of New South Wales; b, from Sydney Parkinson, *Journal**. **51**: tr, Sydney Parkinson, British Museum of Natural History, photo Michael Holford; bl, painting by J. Graf in the rooms of the Linnean Society, NLA; br, copyright BM(NH) AHE 1986, courtesy Alecto Historical Editions, London. **52/53**: ML. **54**: t, NLA; b, and **55**: t, from William Bradley, *A Voyage to New South Wales*... *1796-92*, ML. **55**: c, unknown artist, ML; b, Southern Media Services. **56**: t, Jeff Toghill; c, unknown artist, ML, courtesy the Misses Grylls, Wimbledon, London. **57**: t, DL; c, T. Browne, 1813, ML; cl, ML; bl, from David Collins, *An Account**, ML; br, T. Browne, 1813, ML. **58**: t, P. Slaeger after John Eyre, 'View of Part of the town of Parramatta in New South Wales, 1812', NK/NLA; b, ML. **59**: William Owen, Dixson Galleries. **60**: Bob Crombie. **61**: tc, courtesy Museum of Victoria; tr, Jean-Paul Ferrero/Auscape. **62**: t, The Photo Library; b, and **63**: Robin Morrison/Reader's Digest. **64**: all ML. **64/65**: ML. **65**: t, from *Sydney Mail*, 25 December 1880, State Library of New South Wales; c, ML. **66**: t, ML; c, Southern Media Services; b, NK/NLA. **67**: t, NK/NLA; c, ML. **68**: tl and tr, ML; bl and br, Tasmanian Museum and Art Gallery. **69**: t, ML; c, G.E. Schmida; b, Department of Water Resources, NSW. **70**: Oliver Strewe/Wildlight Photo Agency. **71**: t, Southern Media Services; b, ML. **72**: The Photo Library. **73**: ML. **74/75**: from J. Dumont d'Urville, *Voyage de la corvette l'Astrolabe*, 1826-29, NK/NLA. **76**: tl, Robert Dodd, NK/NLA; tr, ML. **77**: t, from Rolf de Rietz, *The Voyage of H.M.S. Pandora 1790-92*, ML; c, ML; b, DL. **78**: from J. Eyre and Others, *Views in New South Wales*, 1813-14, ML. **79**: t, Hugh Sawrey; bl, DL; br, Historic Memorials Collection, Parliament House, Canberra. **80**: t, Bob Crombie; bl, Cassini, NLA; br, from *Illustrated London News*, Vol. 101, 1892, NLA. **81**: Dave Watts/A.N.T. **82**: t, ML; b, Southern Media Services. **83**: t, William Faden, Eastern Hemisphere, ML; b, Flindersea australis and Eucalyptus pruinosa, from *The Australian Flower Paintings of Ferdinand Bauer*, The Basilisk Press (originals held by British Museum (Natural History).) **84**: t, National Maritime Museum, London; b, Royal Commonwealth Society, London/State Library of New South Wales. **85**: NK/NLA. **87**: t, National Maritime Museum, London; b, from Alexander Sutherland, *Victoria and Its Metropolis, Past and Present*, 1888, ML. **88**: t, ML; b, from James Grant, *The Narrative**, ML. **89**: J.M. La-Roque/Auscape. **90**: t, Nicolas Monsiau, 1817, Musée de Chateau de Versailles, photo Musées nationaux; b, from Ernest Scott, *Terre Napoleon**. **91**: Art Gallery of Western Australia. **93**: William Thomas Lyttleton, 1810-14?, ML. **94**: Graham Robertson/Auscape. **95**: t, 'Offshore Whaling with the *Aladdin* and *Jane*', Tasmanian Museum and Art Gallery; b, Miss A'Beckett, 'Captain Kelly's Rock House', private collection, photo Tasmanian Museum and Art Gallery. **96**: t, National Museum of Iceland; b, The Photo Library. **97**: tl, The Photo Library; tr, Archives Office of Tasmania. **98/99**: The Photo Library. **100**: t, Robin Morrison/Reader's Digest; b, The Photo Library. **101**: instruments in the collection of Department of Lands, NSW, photos Reader's Digest. **102**: both Robin Morrison/Reader's Digest. **102/103**: t, Robin Morrison/Reader's Digest; b, Denise Kuhne. **103**: t and cl, Robin Morrison/Reader's Digest; cr, G. Dixon/Wilderness Society; b, Bob Mossel. **104**: both Tasmanian Museum and Art Gallery. **105**: l, Tasmanian Museum and Art Gallery; r, Rob Blakers/Wilderness Society. **106**: tl, Bob Mossel; tr, Queen Victoria Museum and Art Gallery, Launceston; c, ML; b, G. Rubock/Wilderness Society. **107**: t, ML; b, from Phillip Parker King, *Narrative**, ML. **108**: b, Jean-Paul Ferrero/Auscape. **108/109** from Phillip Parker King, *Narrative**, ML. **109**: t, Augustus Earle, NK/NLA; b, from Phillip Parker King, *Narrative**. **110**: Richard Woldendorp. **111**: t, DL; b, from Phillip Parker King, *Narrative**, ML. **112**: t, ML. **112/113**: from J.B. Jukes, *Narrative**, ML. **113**: both P.R. Dermoudy, Northern Territory Museum. **114**: b, ML. **114/115**: NK/NLA. **115**: t, George Pitt Morison, Art Gallery of Western Australia; c, DL; b, ML. **116**: Photo Index. **117**: t, National Library of Australia; b, from *Sketches in Australia and the Adjacent Islands*, ML. **118** Photo Index; b, ML. **119**: both from J. Lort Stokes, *Discoveries**, ML. **120**: t, David B. Carter/A.N.T.; b, The Photo Library. **121**: NK/NLA. **122/123**: ML. **124**: t, The Photo Library; b, ML. **125**: La Trobe Library. **126**: La Trobe Library; b, ML. **126/127**: James A.C. Willis, DL. **127**: t, ML; b, DL. **129**: George Edward Peacock, ML. **130**: t, National Library of Australia; b, David Hancock/Auscape. **131**: State Library of New South Wales. **132**: ML. **133**: David Hancock/Auscape. **134**: t, ML; b, from E. Digby (ed.) *Australian Men of Mark* 1889, ML. **135**: t, NLA; b, Oliver Strewe/Wildlight Photo Agency. **136**: Bob Mossel. **137** t, from Alexander Sutherland et al., *Victoria and Its Metropolis, Past and Present*, ML; b, by permission of the Corporation of the City of Melbourne. **138**: tl and tr, MLSA; c, ML; b, courtesy Port of Echuca. **139**: DL. **140**: DL. **141**: t, from Charles Sturt, *Two Expeditions**; b, Robin Morrison/Reader's Digest. **142**: ML. **143**: t, Dixson Galleries, State Library of New South Wales; b, Art Gallery of South Australia. **144**: t, ML; b, from T.L. Mitchell, *Three Expeditions**. **145**: Bob Mossel. **146**: Dixson Galleries, State Library of New South Wales. **147**: Ralph & Daphne Keller/A.N.T. **148**: J. MacFarlane, NLA. **149**: Robin Morrison/Reader's Digest. **150**: ML, courtesy the Prell and Jeffreys family. **151**: Australian National Gallery, Canberra. **152**: t, Robin Morrison/Reader's Digest; b, NLA. **153**: NLA. **154**: t, Robert Marsh Westmacott, 'View from the Maneroo Mountains', DL; bl and br, courtesy Snowy Mountains Hydro-Electric Authority. **155**: John Wesley Burtt, La Trobe Library. **156**: William Beckworth McInnes, by permission of the Corporation of the City of Melbourne. **157**: t, W.F.E. Liardet, 'The Landing Place and Market Reserve in 1839', La Trobe Library; bl and br, MLSA. **158**: t, ML; b, S.T. Gill, NK/NLA. **159**: both from *Picturesque Atlas of Australasia*, ML. **160**: t, City of Ballaarat Fine Art Gallery; b, J.W. Lindt, ML. **160/161**: NK/NLA. **161**: tl, ML; tr, T. Robertson, La Trobe Library. **162/163**: ML. **164**: b, John Oxley Library, Brisbane. **164/165** and **165**: ML. **167**: t, Photo Index; b, ML. **168**: t, Bill Green; b, Cyril Webster/A.N.T. **169**: t, from C.P. Hodgson, *Reminiscences of Australia*, ML; b, Bill Green. **170**: MLSA. **171**: t, Bob Mossel; b, Royal Western Australian Historical Society. **172**: from T.L. Mitchell, *Journal**. **173**: Kathie Atkinson. **174**: Owen Stanley, ML. **175**: self-portrait, by kind permission of Edgar Beale. **176**: t, John Oxley Library, Brisbane. **177**: t, Robin Morrison/Reader's Digest; b, Bowen Historical Society and Museum. **178**: t, Department of Mapping & Surveying, Queensland; bl, from S.T. Gill, *Australian Sketchbook*, ML; br, Department of Mapping & Surveying, Queensland. **179**: from F.J. Byerley, *Narrative**, ML. **180**: tl, ML. **180/181**: t, The Photo Library; b, Richard Daintree, John Oxley Library, Brisbane. **181**: Royal Historical Society of Queensland. **182/183**: Art Gallery of South Australia. **184**: t, P.E. Cooper, NK/NLA; b, J.S. Battye Library of West Australian History, 1090P. **186**: Auckland City Art Gallery. **187**: t, Fiona Doig/A.N.T.; b, from George Grey, *Journals**, ML. **188**: from George Grey, *Journals**, ML. **188/189**: Photo Index. **189**: Louisa Clifton, 'A View of Koombana Bay, or Port Leschenault, Australind, Western Australia', Art Gallery of Western Australia. **190**: Photo Index. **192**: t, Bob Mossel; b, Art Gallery of South Australia. **193**: H. Wilkins, by permission of the Parliament of South Australia, courtesy Art Gallery of South Australia. **194**: from Harden S. Melville, 'Sketches in Australia', ML. **195**: Jean-Paul Ferrero/Auscape. **196**: Graeme Chapman. **197**: tl, Jean-Paul Ferrero/Auscape; tr, Bob Mossel; b, Jean-Paul Ferrero/Auscape. **198**: S.T. Gill, Art Gallery of South Australia. **198/199**: M. Gillam/Auscape. **200**: Edward Stokes. **200/201**: from Charles Sturt, *Narrative**, ML. **201**: cl, MLSA; cr, from Charles Sturt, *Narrative**, ML. **202**: both Bob Mossel. **203**: t, C.A. Henley/Auscape; cl, Cliff Winfield; cr, Bob Mossel; b, M.W. Gillam/Auscape. **204**: t, S.T. Gill, 'Travelling through the Brush', Art Gallery of South Australia; c, MLSA. **205**: S.T. Gill, 'Invalid's Tent, Salt Lake 75 Miles North-West of Mount Arden', Art Gallery of South Australia. **206**: t, Photo Index; b, Bob Mossel. **207**: J.S. Battye Library of West Australian History, 66695P. **208**: t, Bob Mossel; b, G.E. Schmida. **209**: t, Photo Index; b, Kathie Atkinson. **210/211**: Ludwig Becker, 'Border of the Mud-Desert near Desolation Camp, March 9th, 1861', La Trobe Library. **212**: John Oxley Library, Brisbane. **212/213**: G.E. Schmida. **215**: 'Bowman the horse keeper and the artist threatened with spears', NK/NLA. **216**: West Australian Newspapers Ltd. **217**: t, H.C. Prinsep, 'Party returning from King Leopold Ranges', private collection; b, Cliff Winfield/Department of Conservation and Land Management, WA. **218**: t, 'Thomas Baines with Aborigines near the mouth of the Victoria River', NK/NLA; b, 'Group of Explorers with Horses', NK/NLA. **219**: both DL. **220**: t, La Trobe Library; b, Ludwig Becker, 'Burke Crossing the Terrick Plains', La Trobe Library. **221**: t, self-portrait, La Trobe Library; b, J. Burt/A.N.T. **222**: t, S.T. Gill, 'The Burke and Wills Expedition', Dixson Galleries, State Library of New South Wales. **222/223**: Graeme Chapman. **224**: La Trobe Library. **225**: t, DL; b, Kathie Atkinson. **226**: t, J. Burt/A.N.T.; b, G.E. Schmida. **227**: Dixson Galleries, State Library of New South Wales. **228**: t, Charles Nettleton, La Trobe Library; b, DL. **229**: t, DL; c, NLA; b, Graeme Chapman. **230**: NK/NLA; b, La Trobe Library. **231**: Grenville Turner/Wildlight Photo Agency. **232**: t, Otto Rogge/A.N.T.; b, NLA. **234**: t, from John McDouall Stuart, *Journals**, ML; b, G. Deichmann/Auscape. **235**: MLSA. **236**: t, MLSA; bl, Telecom Australia; br MLSA. **238**: Bob Mossel. **238/239**: G.F. Angas, from John Forrest, *Explorations**, NLA. **239**: J.S. Battye Library of West Australian History, 5837P. **240**: J.S. Battye Library of West Australian History, 66175P; b, James Burrell Smith, private collection, courtesy Art Gallery of Western Australia. **241**: t, Photo Index, b, J. Burt/A.N.T. **242**: NLA. **244**: Derek Roff; b, MLSA. **246**: t, NLA; b, Otto Rogge/A.N.T. **247**: Derek Roff. **248**: Frank Park/A.N.T. **249**: Graeme Chapman. **250**: West Australian Newspapers Ltd. **251**: from Ernest Giles, *Australia**, ML. **252/253**: t, Gunther Deichmann/Auscape; b, Kathie Atkinson. **253**: Graham Robertson/Auscape. **254/255**: Kathie Atkinson. **256**: NLA. **257**: MLSA. **258**: t, Museum of Victoria Council; b, J. Frazier/A.N.T. **259**: t, Graeme Chapman/Auscape; c, Derek Roff; b, all ML. **260**: t, MLSA; b, Cliff Winfield. **262**: NLA. **263**: J.S. Battye Library of West Australian History, 5847P. **264, 266** and **267**: Museum of Victoria Council. **268**: Jean-Paul Ferrero/Auscape. **269**: t, Mawson Institute of Antarctic Research, University of Adelaide; b, Royal Geographical Society, London. **270**: William Hodges, ML. **271**: Mawson Institute for Antarctic Research, University of Adelaide. **273**: t, Jonathan Chester; b, Jean-Paul Ferrero/Auscape. **274**: MLSA. **275**: Michael Jensen/Auscape. **276**: M.W. Gillam/Auscape; **277**: ML. **278** and **279**: National Museum of Australia. **280**: t, Michael Jensen/Auscape; b, Herald & Weekly Times Ltd. **281, 282** and **283**: t, Howell Walker/National Geographic Society. **282**: b, Eric Brandl/Australian Institute of Aboriginal Studies. **284/285**: Bureau of Mineral Resources, Geology and Geophysics. **286** and **287**: Rodney Garnett/Division of National Mapping. **288** and **289**: all courtesy Hydrographic Service, Royal Australian Navy. **290/291**: Division of National Mapping. **291**: CSIRO Office of Space Science and Applications (COSSA). **292**: t, Australian Centre for Remote Sensing, courtesy COSSA; b, COSSA. **293**: CSIRO Remote Sensing Applications Group. Map bases by Montage Advertising.

Index

This index contains references to explorers, places and selected topics. Where names of places have changed, entries are made under both names, when known. Entries are made for the names of towns and settlements that did not exist or were unnamed at the time of exploration. Present-day state boundaries are shown.

Natural features are indexed under the distinctive part of their names, for example Lake Eyre appears under Eyre, Lake. This applies to capes, lakes, mounts, points and ports. Maps of the routes taken by explorers have been indexed under the explorer's name followed by the subheading 'routes'.

Page references in **bold** type indicate principal references; those in italic type indicate portraits.

Typesetting by Keyset Phototype Pty Ltd, Sydney
Reproduction by Curman Lithographics, Sydney
Printed and bound by Dai Nippon Printing Co. (H.K.) Ltd, Hong Kong